Data Structures and Algorithms in C and Python

Chandan Banerjee
Ph.D. (Engineering)
HOD and Professor, Department of IT
Netaji Subhash Engineering College (MAKAUT-WB)
Kolkata, India

Atanu Das
Ph.D. (Engineering)
HOD, Department of MCA
Netaji Subhash Engineering College (MAKAUT-WB)
Kolkata, India

Universities Press

DATA STRUCTURES AND ALGORITHMS IN C AND PYTHON

UNIVERSITIES PRESS (INDIA) PRIVATE LIMITED

Registered office
3-6-747/1/A & 3-6-754/1, Himayatnagar, Hyderabad 500 029, Telangana, India
info@universitiespress.com; www.universitiespress.com

Distributed by
Orient Blackswan Private Limited

Registered office
3-6-752 Himayatnagar, Hyderabad 500 029, Telangana, India

Other offices
Bengaluru, Chennai, Guwahati, Hyderabad, Kolkata,
Mumbai, New Delhi, Noida, Patna, Visakhapatnam

ISBN: 978-81-954009-0-4
First published 2023

501844

Typeset in Minion Pro 10 *by*
SRS Publishing Services, Puducherry

Printed in India by
B.B. Press, Noida

Published by
Universities Press (India) Private Limited
3-6-747/1/A & 3-6-754/1, Himayatnagar, Hyderabad 500 029, Telangana, India

Contents

List of Algorithms and Pseudocodes

List of C Programs

List of Python Programs

Preface

Data structure is a special way of organizing and storing data in the computer memory so that it can be accessed efficiently. In other words, logical and mathematical organizations of data in the computer memory are called data structures. Array, linked list, stack, queue, tree, graph, etc., are examples of data structures. Data structures are the key of many computer algorithms as they allow programmers to manage the data in an efficient way. A right selection of data structures can enhance the efficiency of an algorithm and hence, the execution speed of a computer program. Efficient memory use, reusability, and data abstractions are the major benefits of the study of data structures and algorithms. With increasing complexity of computer algorithms, the amount of data usage is increasing. This can affect the performance of the application, and can create some areas of concern like processing speed, data search time, and supporting multiple users' requests. Algorithms are language-agnostic, and programmers should be able to convert algorithms into code in the programming language of their choice. However, no programmer can do such conversion to run his/her business efficiently and effectively without a working (theoretical and practical) knowledge and experience of data structures and algorithms.

C is an old classical procedural programming language. In the early days of computers, C language was the best option for problem-solving among versatile programmers. But nowadays, a lot of programming languages have evolved with a multitude of features and facilities where the programmer's job becomes much easier. Python is one of these languages, and it has become the most preferred for all kinds of programmers and system developers. In spite of the popularity of the Python language, C is still used for hardware and system-level programming as it is executed faster compared to other modern languages.

Data Structures and Algorithms is a compulsory/core course of Computer Science (CS), Computer Science and Engineering (CSE), Information Technology (IT) and other allied disciplines in almost all Indian and overseas universities, besides many online certification courses related to CSE/IT (such as NPTEL/Swayam, etc.). This course is a pre-requisite for many other core and optional courses such as Design and Analysis of Algorithms, Operating Systems, Object-Oriented Programming, Computer Graphics, Artificial Intelligence, Machine Learning, Deep Learning, DBMS, Data Mining and Data Warehousing, Parallel Computing, Distributed Computing, Computer Networks, Internet Technologies, Network Security and Cryptography, etc.

This book incorporates the contents covering the theory and practical syllabus of both C and Python languages for implementation of data structures and algorithms prescribed by almost all Indian Universities. It may be noted that no other textbook covers both C and Python languages for Data Structures and Algorithms. There are quite a few books that cover data structures and algorithm implementation using either C language or Python. This book gives equal emphasis to implementation of the algorithms for various operations in both these languages and they are demonstrated, in sequence, by using C and Python. Spread across 14 chapters, the book explains all the necessary theories using easy, simple, and comprehensive texts, figures and examples. The necessary algorithms are presented in comprehensive formats.

The implementation of Data Structures and Algorithms using the procedural C language and object-oriented, industry-adaptive Python language will provide a unique and significant flavour to the existing literature and appeal to the new-generation students. At the end of each chapter, there are three types of questions, namely, MCQs, short answer-type questions, and descriptive-type questions. These questions are further classified into 3 difficulty levels (easy, moderate and higher-order thinking skills). The answers to all MCQs are provided with explanations as required. Each chapter includes case studies and lab exercises for practicing real problems. In addition, PowerPoint slides, source codes of the book's C and Python programming exercises, and frequently asked interview questions are available as Online Resources.

We hope that our endeavour benefits the students in their pursuit to score high in the university and competitive examinations, including placement drives.

ACKNOWLEDGMENT

We thank our students who were our source of inspiration to develop this book, keeping in mind their academic requirements in the present-day educational scenario. We also thank our Director and Principal for providing us the opportunity to teach this subject. We express our sincere gratitude to all our colleagues in the academia for their exceptional help and support. We are indebted to our family members for their sacrifice to make this project successful. Their endurance of our busy schedules and steadfast cooperation go well beyond our expectations.

We gratefully acknowledge the contribution of Mrs Moumita Banerjee in drawing some of the figures, and students Aniket Kumar, Alebhia Ash, Abhishek Kumar in developing some of the C and Python programes. We are also obliged to Mrs Dipika Pramanik for her help in typing out the book's questions.

We are also thankful to the editorial team at Universities Press (India) Private Limited, especially Mr Kallol Das, for bringing out this book in time.

We hope this book will fulfill the requirements and expectations of the students and their teachers. Errors and typos in the book, if any, are purely inadvertent and we apologize for these unintentional mistakes. Suggestions for improvement of this book are welcome and will be gratefully acknowledged. They may be sent to the following e-mail addresses:

Chandan Banerjee
chandanbanerjee1@gmail.com
Atanu Das
atanudas75@gmail.com

About the Authors

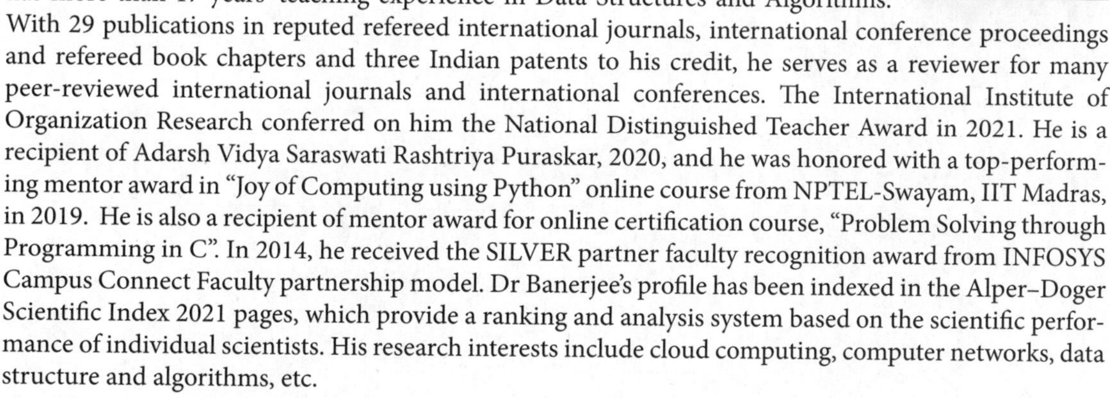

Chandan Banerjee is Professor and HOD, Department of Information Technology, Netaji Subhash Engineering College, which is under the Maulana Abul Kalam Azad University of Technology, West Bengal, India. He received his M.Sc. (Computer and Information Science) and M.Tech. (Computer Science and Engineering) degrees from University of Calcutta and was awarded a Ph.D. degree in Engineering by Jadavpur University, India.

Dr Banerjee has been teaching UG and PG courses for more than 20 years. He has more than 17 years' teaching experience in Data Structures and Algorithms. With 29 publications in reputed refereed international journals, international conference proceedings and refereed book chapters and three Indian patents to his credit, he serves as a reviewer for many peer-reviewed international journals and international conferences. The International Institute of Organization Research conferred on him the National Distinguished Teacher Award in 2021. He is a recipient of Adarsh Vidya Saraswati Rashtriya Puraskar, 2020, and he was honored with a top-performing mentor award in "Joy of Computing using Python" online course from NPTEL-Swayam, IIT Madras, in 2019. He is also a recipient of mentor award for online certification course, "Problem Solving through Programming in C". In 2014, he received the SILVER partner faculty recognition award from INFOSYS Campus Connect Faculty partnership model. Dr Banerjee's profile has been indexed in the Alper–Doger Scientific Index 2021 pages, which provide a ranking and analysis system based on the scientific performance of individual scientists. His research interests include cloud computing, computer networks, data structure and algorithms, etc.

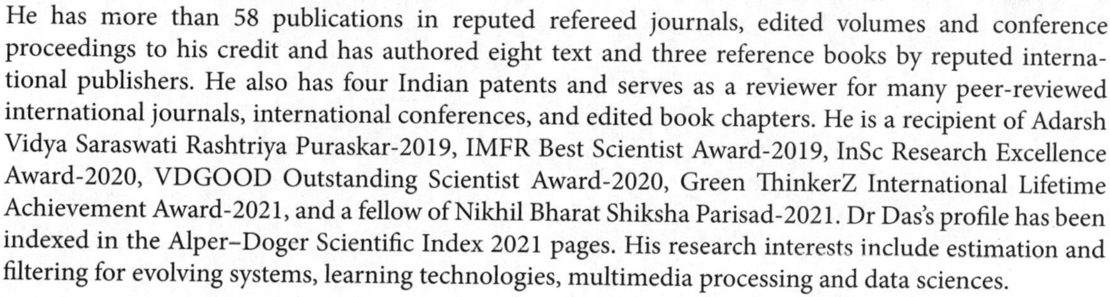

Atanu Das is HOD, Department of MCA, Netaji Subhash Engineering College, which is under the Maulana Abul Kalam Azad University of Technology, West Bengal, India. Earlier, he was HOD, Department of CSE; In-Charge, Department of IT; and Coordinator, M.Tech. (CSE) for more than six years. He received his M.Sc. (Gold Medal) degree from The University of Burdwan and M.E. and Ph.D. (Engineering) degrees from Jadavpur University, India.

Dr Das has been teaching UG and PG courses for more than 20 years and is a supervisor of a sizeable number of MCA/M.Tech. and Ph.D. research students. He has more than 58 publications in reputed refereed journals, edited volumes and conference proceedings to his credit and has authored eight text and three reference books by reputed international publishers. He also has four Indian patents and serves as a reviewer for many peer-reviewed international journals, international conferences, and edited book chapters. He is a recipient of Adarsh Vidya Saraswati Rashtriya Puraskar-2019, IMFR Best Scientist Award-2019, InSc Research Excellence Award-2020, VDGOOD Outstanding Scientist Award-2020, Green ThinkerZ International Lifetime Achievement Award-2021, and a fellow of Nikhil Bharat Shiksha Parisad-2021. Dr Das's profile has been indexed in the Alper–Doger Scientific Index 2021 pages. His research interests include estimation and filtering for evolving systems, learning technologies, multimedia processing and data sciences.

About the Authors

Chandan Banerjee is Professor and HOD, Department of Information Technology, Netaji Subhash Engineering College, which is under the Maulana Abul Kalam Azad University of Technology, West Bengal, India. He received his M.Sc. (Computer and Information Science) and M.Tech. (Computer Science and Engineering) degrees from University of Calcutta and was awarded a Ph.D. degree in Engineering by Jadavpur University, India.

Dr Banerjee has been teaching UG and PG courses for more than 20 years. He has more than 17 years' teaching experience in Data Structures and Algorithms. With 29 publications in reputed refereed international journals, international conference proceeding and refereed book chapters and three Indian patents to his credit, he serves as a reviewer for many peer-reviewed international journals and international conferences. The International Institute of Organization Research conferred on him the National Distinguished Teacher Award in 2021. He is a recipient of Adarsh Vidya Saraswati Rashtriya Puraskar, 2020, and he was honored with a top-performing mentor award in "Joy of Computing using Python" online course from NPTEL-Swayam, IIT Madras in 2019. He is also a recipient of mentor award for online certification course, "Problem solving through Programming in C". In 2014, he received the SILVER partner faculty recognition award from INFOSYS Campus Connect faculty partnership model. Dr Banerjee's profile has been indexed in the Alper-Doger Scientific Index 2021 pages, which provide a ranking and analysis system based on the scientific performance of individual scientists. His research interests include cloud computing, computer networks, data structure and algorithms etc.

Atanu Das is HOD, Department of M.C.A., Netaji Subhash Engineering College, which is under the Maulana Abul Kalam Azad University of Technology, West Bengal, India. Earlier, he was HOD, Department of CSE, In-Charge, Department of IT and Coordinator, M.Tech. (CSE) for more than six years. He received his M.Sc. (Gold Medal) degree from The University of Burdwan and M.E. and Ph.D. (Engineering) degrees from Jadavpur University, India.

Dr Das has been teaching UG and PG courses for more than 20 years and is a supervisor of a sizeable number of MCA, M.Tech. and Ph.D. research students. He has more than 58 publications in reputed refereed journals, edited volumes and conference proceedings to his credit and has authored eight text and three reference books by reputed international publishers. He also has four Indian patents and serves as a reviewer for many peer-reviewed international journals, international conferences, and edited book chapters. He is a recipient of Adarsh Vidya Saraswati Rashtriya Puraskar-2019, IMRF Best Scientist Award-2019, InSc Research Excellence Award-2020, NPDCOCD Outstanding Scientist Award-2020, Green ThinkerZ International Lifetime Achievement Award-2021, and a fellow of Nikhil Bharat Shiksha Parisad-2021. Dr Das's profile has been indexed in the Alper-Doger Scientific Index 2022 pages. His research interests include estimation and filtering for evolving systems, learning technologies, multimedia processing and data sciences.

1 Introduction to Data Structures

CONTENTS

EXPECTED OUTCOMES OF THIS CHAPTER

After going through this chapter learners will be able

- ☑ to describe the basic notions of data structures.
- ☑ to understand the categories of data types including abstract data type.
- ☑ to distinguish between linear and non-linear data structures.
- ☑ to define basic data structures such as array, stacks, queues, lists, trees and graphs.
- ☑ to know various operations used in data structure and understand the notion of dynamic memory allocations.
- ☑ to understand the importance of data structure in computer science and other allied disciplines.
- ☑ to understand and distinguish between the various properties of two most popular languages – C and Python – for problem-solving.
- ☑ to introduce and compare the different programming paradigms for data structure.

1.1 INTRODUCTION

Data and information are an integral part of the modern digital age. Data is the plural of datum but people use the term data both in singular and plural form. It is the raw facts or statistics collected together for analysis and/or reference. These distinct pieces of information make the basis for reasoning or calculation. The computer performs operations on data that may be stored, processed, or transmitted as an electronic signal. Data makes the building block of information. Information is produced by processing and revealing the meaning of the data. Accurate, timely, and relevant information is the key that helps in the decision-making process.

Without the touch of data and information technologies, we cannot nowadays survive in our professional, social, or personal life. The efficient storage of data leads to the services of information technologies that use the evolution and practices of computer science. Such implementations (storage and retrieval) have been noticed in the practices of computer science since its evolution. Not all of them were efficient, pragmatic, and trustworthy as far as data-driven application development is concerned.

Data consisting of values are stored in a digital device in a particular format. The format may be anything like integer, floating-point, Boolean, character, etc. All these formats are a data structure. Specifically, these mentioned formats are primitive data structures.

1.1.1 Definition

Definition: *Data structure is a special way of organizing and storing data in the computer memory so that data can be accessed and used efficiently. In other words, logical and mathematical organizations of data in the computer memory are called data structure. Array, linked list, stack, queue, tree, graph, etc. are examples of data structures.*

Each of these mentioned data structures has a different special way of organizing data. So, we have to choose a particular data structure based on the specific requirement(s). We will cover each of these data structures in subsequent chapters.

Organization of data is very important, especially when developers work on a large volume of data. If not done well, performing operations on these large volumes of data will be very difficult. If the data is organized effectively, then practically any operation can be performed easily on that data. Structure, on the other hand, is a cohesive whole build-up of distinct data and is also very crucial. Data organization within computer memory is the primary reporting relationship that exists within a structure that refers to the data structure. Sometimes, inbuilt data types are not sufficient to resolve a specific problem. In these cases, we require some user-defined data types which are defined using inbuilt data types. 'Structure' in C programming and 'Class' in C++ programming are examples of user-defined data type or abstract data type.

The data structure is an indispensable concept in computer science. We can define data structure in another way. A data structure (D) is a triplet. D can be defined by three tuples, i.e.,

$$D = (d, f, r)$$

where

d = set of data objects within a domain;

f = set of functions or set of operations which apply on the set of data objects;

r = set of rules which will apply during operations.

Suppose we declare a variable as integer – int a; its means a is a data object which has a domain. As we know, in C programming, 'int' variable takes 2 bytes of memory (in a 16-bit OS), which means 'int' variable has a range of values −32,768 to 32,767. This range is also known as the domain of the data object. If we add value in a variable (say, $a = 5$), it indicates that we are doing a function or operation on this data object and operations should maintain some rules. We will discuss in later chapters that there are different rules for different data structures like stack follow LIFO (last-in–first-out), queue follow FIFO (first-in–first-out), etc.

> ***Note!***
> Data structure is a special way of organizing and storing data in computer memory to access and use it efficiently.

1.1.2 Effectiveness and Advantages

Organizing or structuring data is vital for efficient program design using algorithms and implementation through codes. We may remember the effectiveness of data structure from the following statement:

"Programs = Data Structure + Algorithms"

Any problem-solving method incorporates efficient algorithms which undoubtedly fetch or retrieve appropriate data during execution of the algorithms or solution methods. The main three advantages are categorically given below:

- **Data Organization:** We need a proper way of organizing the data such that it can be accessed efficiently when we need it. Data structure offers various ways of organizing data. Thus, we have multiple options (of plan/scheme/structure) to choose for data storage according to different situations and requirements.
- **Efficiency:** The main reason for which we organize the data is to improve the problem-solving efficiency (in terms of reduced complexity and retrieval time). Often, we may wonder why we need linked lists and other structures when we can store data in arrays. The answer is, when we need to perform several operations, such as add, delete, update, and search on arrays, it takes more time in arrays than some of the other data structures. This concept will be discussed in different chapters later. So, we are interested in other data structures because of the efficiency.
- **Reusability:** Data structures can be reused, i.e., once we have implemented a particular data structure, we can use it in any other program.

1.1.3 Important Terminologies

- **Data:** Raw facts or statistics collected together for analysis and/or reference.
- **Information:** Meaningful data.
- **Data type:** A data type describes pieces of data that all share a common property. It is the form (or type) of a variable used in the program.
- **Primitive data type:** It is an elementary structure for developing sophisticated data types further.
- **Abstract data type:** It is a distinct data type outlined by some values and operations which remain hidden entirely from the users.
- **Entity:** It is something that has certain attributes to which we may assign values.
- **Memory:** It is the digital circuit where the computer stores data.
- **Primary memory:** It is the memory location from where CPU fetches and stores data.
- **Secondary memory:** It is the permanent storage location to where data is transferred after processing.
- **File management:** The process of controlling digital data to create, store, and retrieve digital data using files on a device.
- **Field:** It is a purposeful known location, usually of fixed size, for storing a unit of data like record, message, header or instructions.

- **Record:** It is a collection of fields with many different data types, typically in fixed numbers and sequences.
- **Fixed-length record:** It is one in which every field has a fixed length.
- **Variable-length record:** It is one in which every field has a variable length.
- **File:** It is a group of records related to each other.
- **File size:** It is the amount of memory or storage medium in bits or bytes, normally.
- **Key values:** A key-value store is a database that uses an array of keys where each key is associated with only one value in a collection. It is similar to a dictionary.
- **Primary key:** It is a column or combination of columns designated to uniquely identify all table records.
- **Database:** Organized collection of electronic data in the computer system for efficient storage and retrieval is known as database.
- **Array:** A collection of homogeneous (same type) data items stored in contiguous memory locations is called array.
- **List/Sequence:** It is a data type to represent a countable number of ordered values where the same value may occur multiple times
- **Linked list:** A linear collection of data elements (nodes) stored at non-contiguous memory locations is called a linked list. It consists of multiple nodes that contain a data field and an address field (or link) to the next node in the list.
- **Pointer:** It is an object that stores the location (memory address) of another value in the computer memory.
- **Stack:** It is an ordered (linear) list of a similar data type where every time an element is added, it goes on the top of the stack and the only element that can be removed is the element that is at the top of the stack.
- **Queue:** It is a collection of elements maintained in a sequence where the addition of elements takes place at one end called rear/tail and removal of elements, from the other end called front/head.
- **Tree:** It is a non-linear data structure that stores the data in the form of a hierarchy.
- **Graph:** It is a non-linear data structure with nodes (vertices) and edges (lines or arcs). An edge normally connects two nodes.
- **Heap:** It is a complete binary tree (2-tree) where the root-node key is compared with its children and arranged accordingly. Nodes are arranged based on their values here.
- **Hashing:** Hashing is the method of indexing and retrieving data to afford a faster way of finding the element using a hash key.
- **Hash table:** It is an array of that maps a key into the data structure with the help of a hash function (the hash key is generated for all the data using the function called hash function) such that insertion, deletion, and search operations are performed with constant time complexity.

1.2 DATA TYPES

A data type (basic) describes pieces of data that all share a common property. It is the kind or form of a variable that is being used throughout the program. All programming languages have their built-in data type supported by the compilers and interpreters. Most programming languages offer the use of complicated data types recursively constructed from basic types. There are four categories of data types.

These are primitive (or primary) data types, secondary data types, user-defined data types, and abstract data types. These are presented in Fig. 1.1.

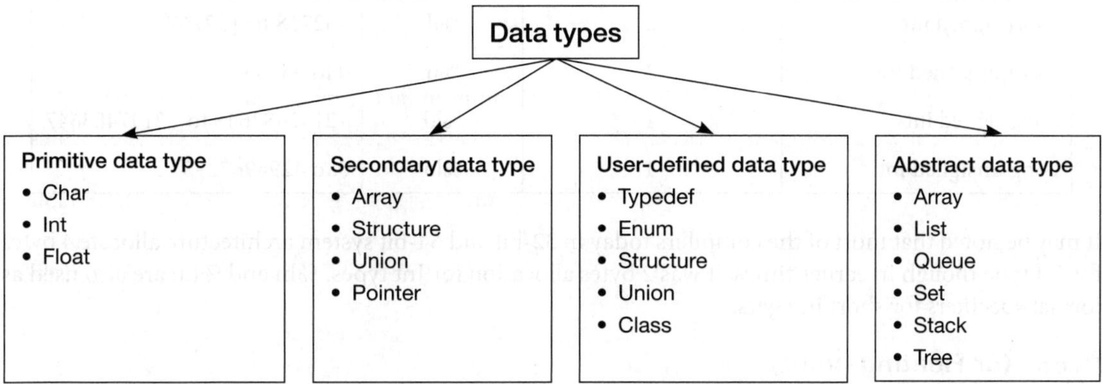

Figure 1.1 Classification of data types

1.2.1 Primitive Data Types

The primitive data type is the basic structure for building more sophisticated data types. There exists a variety of opinions on whether built-in composite types should be considered "primitive" or not. Primitive data types may not always have a one-to-one correspondence with objects in the memory. It depends on the language concerned. For example, standard C language allows 'int' data type as basic or primitive, which takes up a memory 16 bits long (16-bit architecture). Most of the programming languages of today support the following three primitive data types.

`Char` (or Character)

`Char` is a primitive data type in many languages including C. Basically, `Char` stores special characters and alphabets. C language offers the following two types of data types in `char` to perform various operations using characters.

Table 1.1 `Char` data type details

Data type	Allocated bytes	Format	Range
Unsigned `Char`	1	%c	−128 to 127
Signed `Char`	1	%c	0 to 255

As data structures guide us to the minimum utilization of memory with minimum time for program execution, the allocated computer memory of the particular data type is one of the major concerns in understanding data types.

`Int` (or Integer)

`Int` data type is used for storing integer numbers (without fraction). There are four varieties of data type `Int` in C. The details of the `Int` data type are given below with respect to the C language.

Table 1.2 `Int` data type details

Data type	Allocated bytes	Format	Range
Short signed int	2	%d	−32768 to +32767
Short unsigned int	2	%u	0 to 65535
Long signed int	4	%ld	−2147483648 to +2147483647
Long unsigned int	4	%lu	0 to 4294967295

It may be noted that most of the compilers today in 32-bit and 64-bit system architecture allocate 4 bytes for Int type though in earlier times, it was 2 bytes allocation for Int types. %hi and %hu are also used as format specifiers for short integers.

`Float` (or Floating-point)

Float is a data type used to store decimal numbers in general. Any number with a decimal point is known as a floating-point number in C language and stored using a float data type. For example, if we consider 2 as an integer (or `int`) in C, this number will be considered as 2.0 in float format. There are three varieties of `Int` data type in C. The details of the Float data type is given below with respect to the C language.

Table 1.3 `Float` data type details

Data type	Allocated bytes	Format	Range
Float	4	%f	−3.4e38 to +3.4e38
Double	8	%lf	−1.7e308 to +1.7e308
Long double	10	%Lf	−1.7e4932 to +1.7e4932

Some authors argue Boolean as a primitive data type. Boolean (or `bool`) data type is a logical data type. It can be either 'True' (or 1) or 'False' (or 0). Practically, one bit is required to accommodate the value set {'True' or 'False'}. But most of the programming languages like Java, Pascal, and Ada implement Boolean types as one or more bytes. To offer backward compatibility with an earlier version of the language, many programming languages convert Boolean to numeric types at times to provide extended semantics. A language like ANSI C and its earlier versions did not have a Boolean type. Rather, numeric value zero is taken as 'False' and any non-zero value is taken as 'True'. C++ offers `bool` as a built-in data type.

1.2.2 Secondary Data Types

These data types are derived from one or more primitive data types. In C language, the following secondary data types are offered.

Array

It is a collection of the same primitive data types. We can also refer to an array as a group of the same type of data elements that have been assigned a common name. For example, in any name, such as 'RAUNAK' or 'BIYAS', it is a collection of `char` primitive data types. The dimension of the array data type is not confined to a single one. Most of the programming languages offer multi-dimensional arrays. More on array data type and corresponding array data structure is explained in the following chapters.

Following is an example of an array declaration in C:

```
char name[10];
```

where the name is an array of size 10. A 3 × 3 matrix of integers can be stored in a 2-dimensional array given below:

```
int mat[3][3];
```

Structure

We often require data to be stored in terms of records. We cannot store the records of multiple items having different data types using an array. So, we need some other tool or data type by which we can combine the data of different types. This data type is none other than structure.

Let us think of storing the record of a student entity. Assume, we would like to store the student's Name, Roll, and Marks. We can put together all these three data items of a student using the structured data type. Consider the declaration of a student structure using C below:

```
struct student
  {
    char Name[10];
    int Roll;
    int Marks;
  };
```

Here `struct` is the keyword by which we indicate 'student' has the structure data type. Under this structure data type, three other primitive data types (`char`, `int`, and `int` here) are again declared to instruct the compiler that the student variable consists of the other three data items, Name, Roll, and Marks. The structure data type may include other non-primitive or secondary data types.

Union

The union is again a derived (secondary) data type just like structure. This is declared in the same way as structure. The difference between union and structure is that each variable in structure has separate memory allocation and all of them can be used at the same time with different values. But in the case of union, the variables use the same memory space. The space in the memory is equal to the length of the variable that has the maximum size in the case of the union.

The following is an example of the declaration of a union data type with the same example of student records storage as discussed in structure data type using C language:

```
union student
   {
     char Name[10];
     int Roll;
     int Marks;
   } std1;
```

where 'std1' is the name of the union variable declared.

Pointers

Pointers store the memory address (location) of a data type in the memory. Consider the following example of a pointer declaration in C language.

```
int *pt;
int q = 10;
pt = &q;
```

Here pt is pointer variable. '*' is used here to denote a pointer data type. q is an ordinary integer type variable. The address of q is stored in the pointer type variable pt. To indicate the memory location '&' sign is used here. So in this example, pt is a pointer of integer type. There can be a pointer to arrays and pointers to structure similarly.

The pointer data type is a very handy tool in C language. We often use pointer data type in the data structure for efficient data organization like in dynamic memory allocations.

1.2.3 User-defined Data Types

Suppose an application requires a special type of data type, which is not available as built-in data type. Then programmers can create and implement their own type data. The data types that are defined by the user are called the user-defined derived data type. Programming languages like C offer facilities of user-defined data types. Class, Structure and Union also come under the user-defined data types. In C, user-defined data types are typedef and enum and are described below.

Typedef

Typedef provides us a meaningful and short way or name to call a data type that has already been declared. Consider the student data type declaration in structure data type explanation. When we need to declare any student using the structure type declaration, we have to write the following:

```
struct student std1;
```

This completes the student type variable std1 declaration. By using the typedef, we can give a short name to any data type. An example of this is given below:

```
typedef struct student std;
```

Whenever we require student, we can declare it as just

```
std std1;
```

std is a user-defined data type that we can remember meaningfully and/or is shortly provided by the C language.

Enum (Enumerated Data Type)

The enum data type provides a scheme to create our own data type and give it the values that data type will be assigned. Consider the following enum declaration in the C language:

```
enum course
{
   BTECH, BCA, BSC, BBA, MBA, MTECH;
};
enum course std1, std2;
```

Here, according to the declaration, `std1` or `std2` can take all the valid values which are mentioned in the list 'BTECH, BCA, BSC, BBA, MBA, MTECH'. Now we can have the following valid assignment.

```
std1 = MTECH;
std2 = BTECH;
```

Consider the following assignment:

```
std1 = BA; /* Not valid */
```

The above will not be a valid assignment as per the `enum` data type definition since 'BA' is not in the list of `enum` course data types.

1.2.4 Abstract Data Types

Abstract data type (ADT) is a distinct data type outlined by some values and operations, which remain hidden entirely from the users. The keyword `abstract` is used to indicate that the operations (we perform) remain hidden from the users completely. ADT works as a mathematical model. It is a collection of data values (or information) that share similar specific behaviors or qualities. These specified behaviors or qualities are identified independently of the specific implementations. Normally, ADT is defined with primitive data types, but operation logics remain hidden while defining. Array, list, queue, set, stack, and tree are examples of ADT.

There are two components of each ADT. These are:

- **External:** It is also called public part of the ADT. It consists of the conceptual picture of the structure. It provides how the object looks like from users' point of view and organization of the data structure. The external component also provides the conceptual operations that the user can perform on the ADT.
- **Internal:** It is also called private part of the ADT. It represents how the structure is stored. It also provides the implementation of the operations (the actual code).

The primary benefits of using ADT are:

- Codes become easy to understand.
- Implementations of ADTs can be changed without requiring changes to the program.
- ADTs can be reused in future programs.

Note!

ADT is made of primitive data types, but the operation logics are hidden.

A good program uses abstraction. It helps the program to understand, modify, execute smoothly, and thus increase efficiency. The implementation of an ADT is often referred to as a data structure. Programmers provide a physical view of the data in this implementation. A collection of programming constructs and primitive data types are used here. Operations like initializing, adding data, accessing data and removing data can be applied to ADT.

1.3 DYNAMIC MEMORY ALLOCATION

An array is a collection of homogeneous elements. Once the size of an array is declared, you cannot change it in run time. Sometimes, the size of the declared array may not be sufficient, or it more than sufficient. To resolve this, we can allocate memory during program execution. This is known as dynamic memory allocation.

Library functions for dynamic memory allocation are `calloc()`, `malloc()`, `realloc()` and `free()` in C language. These functions are defined in the <stdlib.h> and <alloc.h> header file of C language. So, a programmer has to include or attach any one of these header files with the program.

malloc()

The `malloc()` is a function that stands for memory allocation in run time. It is used to allocate a block of memory dynamically. It reserves memory space of a specified size (or length) and returns the void pointer. The pointer returned is usually void type. So, we can assign the `malloc` function to any pointer. The syntax of the `malloc` function is given below.

```
ptr = (cast_type *) malloc (byte_size);
```

Here, `ptr` is a pointer of cast_type. The `malloc` function returns a pointer to the allocated memory of byte_size. Following is the example syntax with C language using `malloc`:

```
ptr = (int *) malloc (100);
```

calloc()

The `calloc()` stands for contiguous allocation. This C library function is used to allocate multiple blocks of memory. It allocates (reserves) the memory space to complex data structures such as arrays and structures. `calloc()` is used to allocate multiple blocks of memory space while the `malloc()` is used to allocate a single block of memory space. The block size is same when allocated by `calloc()`. The syntax of the calloc function is given below.

```
ptr = (cast_type *) calloc (n, size);
```

The above C syntax is used here to allocate *n* memory blocks of the same size. The pointer which is currently at the first byte of the allocated memory space is returned. The pointer returned is generally of void type. So, we can assign a `calloc()` to any pointer. If there is an error towards allocating memory space like a shortage of memory, then a null pointer is returned.

realloc()

Programmers can augment more memory to already allocated memory during program execution using the `realloc()` function. It increases the current block size while leaving the original content intact. `realloc` stands for reallocation of memory. `realloc()` is also used to reduce the size of the previously allocated memory. The syntax of the realloc() is given below.

```
ptr = realloc (ptr, newsize);
```

It allocates a new memory space with the specified new size.

> **Note!**
> We can allocate memory manually during run-time. This is known as dynamic memory allocation.

free()

`free()` library function is used to dynamically deallocate the memory in C language. Allocated memory using `malloc()` and `calloc()` functions is not deallocated automatically and leads to wastage of memory. The `free()` is used to reduce wastage of memory by deallocating or freeing it. The syntax of the free function is given below.

```
free(ptr);
```

1.4 CLASSIFICATION OF DATA STRUCTURES

Several data structures have already been mentioned in the previous discussion. Their characteristics are not similar. All the data structures can be divided into two classes, linear and non-linear. A linear data structure can again be divided into static and dynamic data structures. An array is an example of a static data structure whereas a linked list is an example of a dynamic data structure. Stack and queue are considered as static data structures if stack and queue are implemented using the array. Stack and queue can also be considered as dynamic data structures if implemented using linked lists. Generally, we prefer using a dynamic data structure because of its advantages over static data structure to implement stacks and queues in the program implementations.

Again, trees and graphs are examples of non-linear data structures. These classifications are presented below in Fig. 1.2.

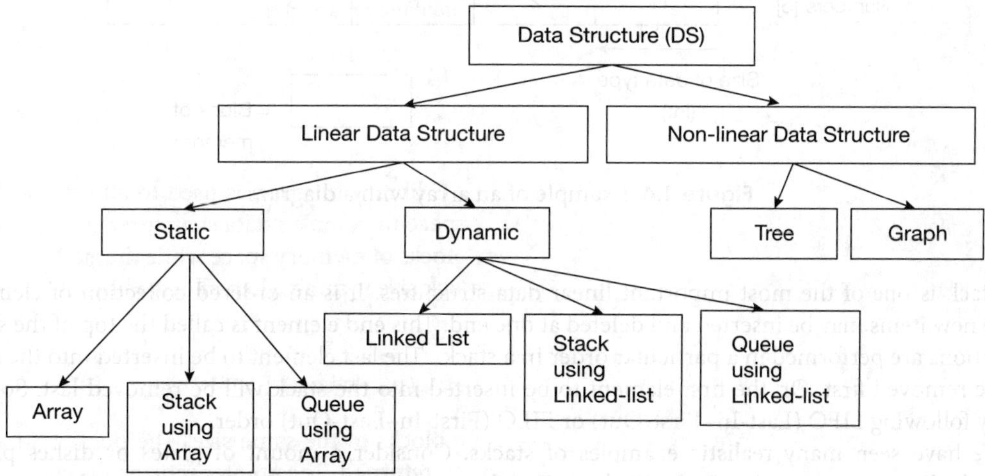

Figure 1.2 Classification of data structures with diagram

The following sections briefly present the above data structure.

1.4.1 Linear Data Structure

Elements of the linear data structure are accessed sequentially. However, the elements can be stored in these data structures in any order. Examples of linear data structure are linked list, stack, queue, and array.

Array

An array is a collection of homogeneous elements stored at contiguous memory locations. Calculating the memory location of each element is very easy here. Memory location of an element is found by simply adding an offset to a base value (or memory location of the first element). An array is a static and linear data structure.

Arrays are zero-indexed normally. This means, the index 0 is assigned to the first element, the index 1 is assigned to the second element, and so on . The index equal to "1 less than the array's size" is assigned to the last element.

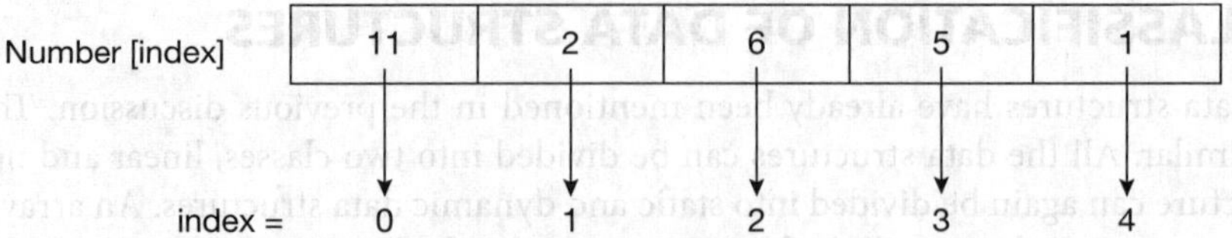

Figure 1.3 Representation of an array with a diagram

The elements are related in some way in the collection of an array. For example, an array for storing phone numbers. Arrays are the most frequently used data structure and these are directly built-in within most programming languages.

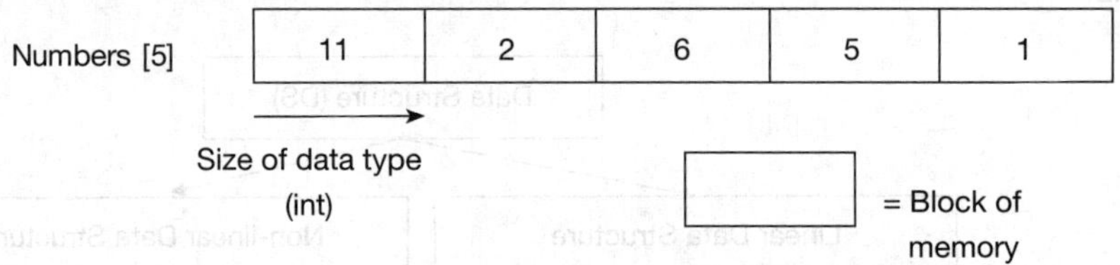

Figure 1.4 Example of an array with a diagram

Stack

The stack is one of the most important linear data structures. It is an ordered collection of elements where new items may be inserted and deleted at one end. This end element is called the top of the stack. Operations are performed in a particular order in a stack. The last element to be inserted into the stack will be removed first. Or, the first element to be inserted into the stack will be removed last. So, it is simply following LIFO (Last-In–First-Out) or FILO (First-In–Last-Out) order.

We have seen many realistic examples of stacks. Consider a mount of plates or dishes placed (or stacked) one upon another in the kitchen. The plate at the top is the first one to be used whereas the bottom-most plate remains unused for the longest time in the stack.

Arrays allow us to insert and delete elements from any position within the list. This means items can be inserted or deleted from the beginning or the end or even from the middle also. The array is not at all suitable for representing the list when insertion and deletion, both are required only at one end, either at the beginning or at the end of the list. Stack is best suitable data structure in such situations. The following Fig. 1.5 presents the push and pop operations on the stack.

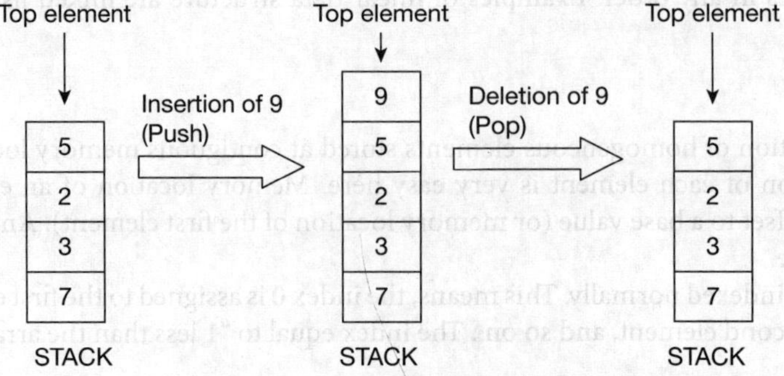

Figure 1.5 Stack operations

Queue

Queue is also a linear structure. Operations are performed in a particular order in queue. The queue is an abstract data structure like stack. The first element is to be inserted at one end, called the REAR (also called the tail). Elements are removed from the other end, called as FRONT (also called the head). The order of operation in queue is First-In–First-Out (FIFO), which means that the element inserted first will be removed first. We remove the least recently added item in a queue, unlike stack where we remove the most recently added item. A queue is open at both its ends, as opposed to stack.

We have seen many realistic examples of queues. A real-world example of the queue can be a single lane in a bank teller counter, where the customer enters first, gets the service and exits first. New customers join the line at the rear end (last). The teller serves the customer at the front of the line. Thus, the first customer in line will be served first in the queue (Fig. 1.6).

Figure 1.6 Queue example

Circular queue is a variety of queue. It is also a linear data structure and follows the FIFO (First-In–First-Out) principle. But instead of ending the queue at the last position, it again starts from the first position. Hence, the queue behaves like a circular data structure.

Linked List

Linked list is a linear and dynamic data structure. However, elements are not stored at contiguous memory locations here. It consists of multiple nodes that contain a data field and an address field (or link) to the next node in the list. Thus, it forms a chain-like structure.

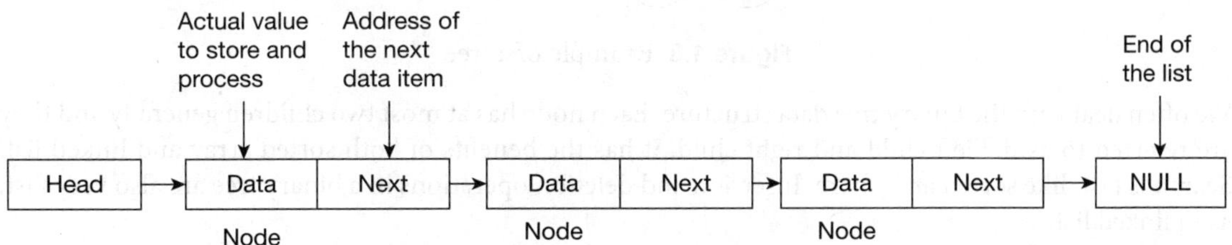

Figure 1.7 Representation of a linked list

Here, 'Head' is not a separate node but it is a reference to the first node. If the list is empty, the head is a null reference. The advantages of the linked list are:

- The linked list is dynamic in nature. Memory allocations take place in non-contiguous locations when required in linked list.
- Stack and queue data structure can be implemented easily using the linked list.

- It reduces access time.
- Insertion and deletion operations can be easily implemented in a linked list.

The disadvantages of the linked list are:

- Reverse (or inverse) traversing is difficult in a singly linked list.
- Each node of a linked list has to be accessed sequentially. Random access of elements is not allowed in the linked list.
- Memory is wasted in a linked list since the pointer requires extra memory for storage.

> **Note!**
> Elements of the linear data structure are accessed sequentially.

1.4.2 Non-linear Data Structure

Elements are stored and accessed in a distributed manner in non-linear data structure. Thus, it ensures non-linear ordering of elements in the memory organization. Tree and graph are examples of non-linear data structure.

Tree

The tree represents the nodes (or vertices) connected by edges (or link) in the form of a hierarchy style. The first node of the tree is called the root node. A tree is similar to the linked list where a chain of nodes connects through "next" pointers. Each node of a tree remains connected to multiple nodes. Hence, the tree is a non-linear type of data structure. A tree may either be empty (no nodes), or have a root and zero or more sub-trees. The sub-trees are also ordered.

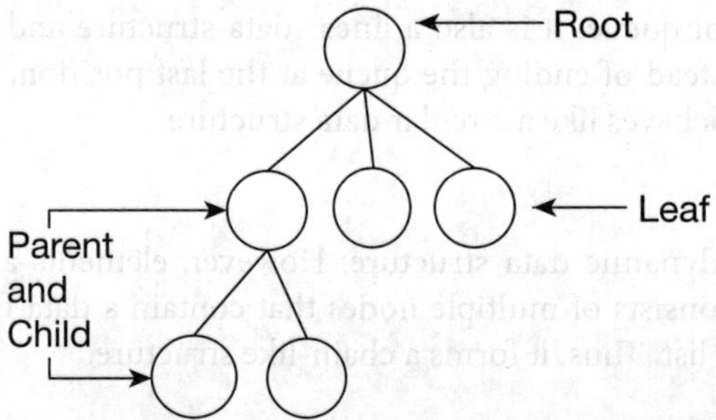

Figure 1.8 Example of a tree

We often deal with the binary tree data structure. Each node has at most two children generally and they are referred to as the left child and right child. It has the benefits of both sorted array and linked list. Search is fast, like sorted array here. Insertion and deletion operations in a binary tree are also very fast, as in linked list.

Each node of a binary tree contains three components:

- Pointer to the left sub-tree.
- Pointer to the right sub-tree.
- Data element.

An empty tree is represented by a NULL pointer. A binary tree is represented using a linked list as shown in Fig. 1.9.

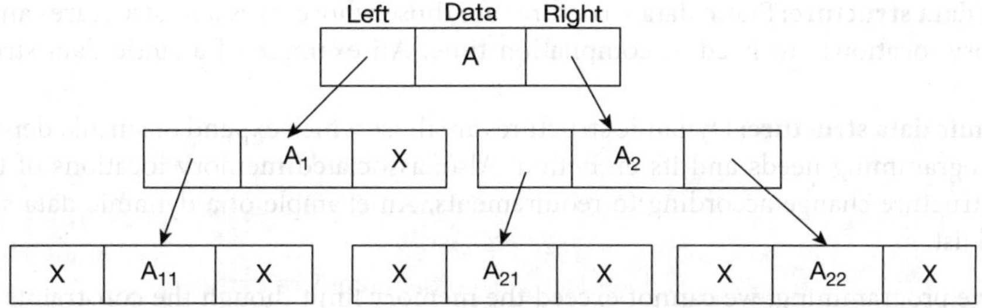

Figure 1.9 Representation of binary tree using a linked list

Graph

A graph is a non-linear data structure. It consists of nodes and are connected by edges (or links). The interconnected objects are represented by points termed as vertices, and the links that connect the vertices are called edges. The nodes are also referred as vertices and the edges are referred to as lines (or arcs) that connect any two nodes in the graph.

Formally, a graph is a pair of sets (V, E), where V is the set of vertices and E is the set of edges, connecting the pairs of vertices. It consists of a finite set of vertices (nodes V) and a set of edges (E) that connect a pair of nodes. The graph is denoted by G and G = (V, E).

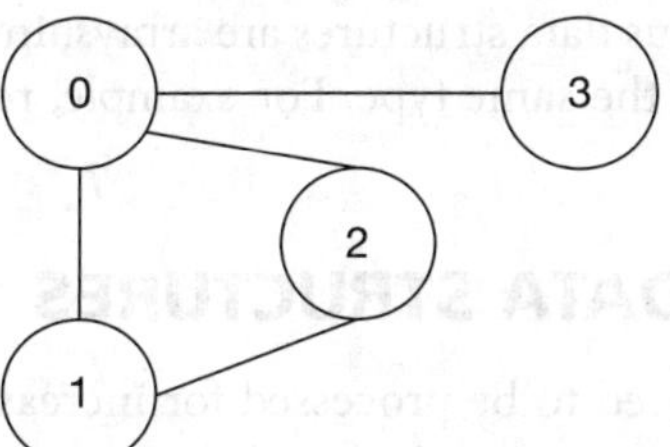

Figure 1.10 Example of a graph

In the graph as shown in Fig. 1.10,

$$V = \{0, 1, 2, 3\}$$

$$E = \{(0,1), (0,2), (0,3), (1,2)\}$$

$$G = \{V, E\}$$

> **Note!**
> Elements of non-linear data structures are stored and accessed in a distributed manner.

1.4.3 Other Classification Approaches

There are other approaches to data classification depending on how data is conceptually organized or aggregated.

Static and Dynamic Data Structure

There are two types of data, static data, and dynamic data. Static data is the data that does not change. For example, the date of birth is static data. On the other hand, dynamic data is capable of accommodating changes according to the requirements. It may change after update to the associated record. For example, the age of a person is dynamic data. To organize both these data, two data structures are given below:

- **Static data structure:** Static data structures are those whose sizes and structures and associated memory locations are fixed at compilation time. An example of a static data structure is an array.
- **Dynamic data structure:** Dynamic structures are those which expand or shrink, depending upon the programming needs and its execution. Also, associated memory locations of the dynamic data structure change according to requirements. An example of a dynamic data structure is a linked list.

In competitive programming, we cannot exceed the memory limit though the constraints on memory limit are not very high initially. Given the high value of the constraints, we cannot allocate a static data structure of large size, and hence dynamic data structures can be useful in these contexts.

Primitive and Non-primitive Data Structure

Primitive data structures are those data structures that are atomic or inseparable. An example of a primitive data structure includes integer, character, etc. The data structures that are separable and not atomic are called a non-primitive data structure. Examples of non-primitive data structures are arrays, records, etc.

Homogeneous and Non-homogeneous Data Structure

Homogeneous data structures are those data structures where all the elements of the structure are of the same type. Examples of homogeneous data structures are arrays. In a non-homogeneous data structure, the elements may or may not be of the same type. For example, records are a non-homogeneous data structure.

1.5 OPERATIONS ON DATA STRUCTURES

Data stored using data structures need to be processed for increasing the efficiency of its structure so that retrieval becomes easier. Such processing incorporates certain operations to be performed on the data set. Frequently used operations are listed below for quick understanding:

- **Search:** To search an item in a data structure.
- **Sort:** To sort items in a certain order.
- **Insert:** To insert an item in a data structure.
- **Update:** To update an existing item in a data structure.
- **Delete:** To delete an existing item from a data structure.
- **Merge:** To combine the records in two different lists or files.
- **Traverse:** To access each record exactly once.

> ***Note!***
> Array, stack, queue, and linked list are examples of linear data structure whereas tree and graph are examples of non-linear data structure.

1.6 ALGORITHMS AND DATA STRUCTURES

A program is defined by the combination of data structure and algorithms. An algorithm is a finite set of instructions or logic, written in order, to accomplish a certain predefined task. An algorithm is not the complete code or program, it is just the core logic (solution) of a problem, which can be expressed either as an informal high-level description as pseudo code or using a flowchart.

Programmers can encounter abstract data types, which are rather simple to use but involve more-or-less complicated algorithms to make them work internally. In contrast, data structures do not expose their users to algorithms. The other possibility is that the programmer has an algorithm, which he/she wants to be able to simply use, but which needs data structures internally to make it work as intended.

In general, one can say that algorithm implementation involves data structures for their internal state representation. Data structures and algorithms are closely related to each other. Ultimately, programmers choose appropriate data structures, which are very closely related to the algorithms. They change the focus of the resulting abstract data types ever so often for this purpose.

1.7 CHOOSING APPROPRIATE DATA STRUCTURES

It has been already explained (Section 1.1.2) that a program is developed by using appropriate data structure with the algorithm for effective data organization, increasing efficiency of the program, and reuse of the implemented data structure. Programmers have to identify appropriate data structures that can efficiently organize the data for a particular implementation of the algorithm. Here, we present the situations of choosing appropriate data structures:

1. **Array**
   - When storing homogeneous data.
   - When using contiguous memory locations in the computer's memory.
   - When the memory requirement (size) of data is known beforehand.
   - When static (doesn't change once allocated) nature of data structure is prescribed.
2. **Linked List**
   - When the memory allocation is dynamic, i.e., it expands or shrinks depending upon the programming needs and its execution.
   - When random access to stored data elements is not required normally.
   - When constant time requirement for insertion of data is recommended.
   - When iteration operation is required to be implemented without recursion as allowed in the doubly linked list.
   - When data insertion and retrieval are to be performed faster than array (possible in the doubly linked list).
3. **Stack**
   - When data insertion and retrieval are to be performed in LIFO order.
   - When arithmetic expressions are to be converted to other orders.
   - When arithmetic expressions are to be evaluated.
   - When parsing operations are to be performed for the syntax of instructions.
   - When using backtracking for finding the path of a related problem.
   - When implementing recursion operations.
4. **Queue**
   - When data insertion and retrieval are to be performed in FIFO order.
   - When an ordered data is required as an output.
   - When there are no restrictions on choosing either static or dynamic data structures specifically.
5. **Tree**
   - When the arrangement of data is to be done in a non-linear fashion.
   - When searching is to be performed from a huge data set.
   - When efficient memory searching is prescribed as requirement.
   - When traversing operation is to be performed on a data set in sorted order.
   - When data arrangement or organization is important, as in file organization, database operations in fields like financial data mining, handwriting recognition, image processing, and broadcasting in computer networks.

6. **Heap**
   - When an implementation of a priority queue is required.
   - When trying to access a particular element like maximum or minimum value very quickly.
   - When implementation of graph algorithms is required using traversal methods.
7. **Hashing**
   - When we need a mapping of keys to values in a tabular form.
   - When faster reading of data is required.
   - When there is a need for efficient searching of a database, as in the case of search engine implementations, routing table operations, etc.
8. **Graph**
   - When the arrangement of data is to be done in a non-linear fashion.
   - When implementation of networks and graph theory problems are to be performed.
   - When solution to the shortest path problem is required.
   - When we need to reduce the costing of different traversing problems.

> **Note!**
> Choosing an appropriate data structure is highly essential for developing efficient computer programs for problem-solving as well as in the design and implementation of algorithms.

Programmers need to be very careful while identifying a particular data structure for the implementation of a given problem and its corresponding algorithm. An inaccurate choice may cause misuse of computational time and overutilization of memory space that may adversely affect the cost of the project, as a whole.

1.8 FILE ORGANIZATION

A file could be defined as a contiguous set of words or bytes. It is a collection of data. Users can store different forms of information in a file. For example, source codes, images, text documents, etc. Files are of different types depending on the information stored in a file and therefore each file has its structure. It is the job of the operating system to map this sequence of files into physical memory. The part of an operating system that maps various files to the physical memory is called file organization and management system. Different file access methods are available, by which the information in the file can be accessed.

There are three major ways of organizing a file:

- **Sequential Access:** In this method information in the file is processed in order, one by one. This is the most common mode of access to files. For example, text editors usually access files in this fashion.
- **Direct Access:** Direct access is based on the storage characteristic of a file. In this method of record access, the file is viewed as a numbered sequence of blocks. The file allows arbitrary blocks to be read or written. There are no restrictions on the order of reading and writing for a direct access file.
- **Indexed Sequential Access:** Indexed sequential access file combines both sequential file and direct access file organization. In an indexed sequential access file, records are stored randomly on a direct access device such as an external disk by a primary key. This file has multiple keys that can be alphanumeric, in which the records are ordered. The data can either be accessed sequentially or randomly using an index. The index is stored in a file and read into the memory when the file is opened.

Six operations are normally used to organize a file. Users can perform the following file operations for the same.

- **Create:** Creates a file in the memory.
- **Read:** Reads from a file.
- **Write:** Writes within a file.
- **Execute:** Loads and executes a file.
- **Append:** Appends information at the end of a file.
- **Delete:** Makes free the space allocated to a file.

Note!
A file could be defined as a contiguous set of words or bytes for the collection of data.

1.9 DATA-RELATED OTHER SUBJECTS

Many subjects have already evolved in the field of computer science and engineering based on the acquisition, structuring, processing, management, and inference of data and information. All have their foundation lines in data structure and algorithms. These are briefly described below.

DBMS

Database Management Systems (DBMS) is a collection of computer programs (or software) for efficient storage, process, manipulation, retrieval, and maintenance, (i.e., usage and management) of data as a whole. The purpose of DBMS is to answer all the above-noted problems. Today's DBMS offers solutions for all of these. Examples of popular DBMS software include MySQL, Oracle, MS-Access, etc. Examples of database applications include library management system, enterprise resource management (ERP), banking systems, etc.

Data Mining

Data mining is the process of discovering patterns in large data sets involving methods of statistics, machine learning, and database systems.

Data Warehousing

Data warehouses (DWs) are central repositories of integrated data from one or more sources. These are used for reporting and data analysis. Business intelligence or data analytics are based on these data warehouses.

Data Science

Data science is a multidisciplinary field that uses scientific methods, processes, algorithms, and systems to extract knowledge and insights from structured and unstructured data. It is also considered as a science of decision-making. Data science is related to data mining and big data.

Big Data

Big data is a field of study that uses techniques to analyze and systematically extract information from data sets that are too large or complex to be dealt with by traditional data-processing application software.

AI and machine learning are very much dependent on the techniques or algorithms for automatic, fast, effective, and efficient decision-making. These algorithms cannot work efficiently without appropriate data structures. So, learning data structure and algorithms development is as important today as it were in the early days of computing.

1.10 C AND PYTHON FOR PROGRAM DEVELOPMENT

C is a very old classical programming language. In the earlier days of computer programming for problem-solving, C language was the best option for versatile programmers. But nowadays, a lot of programming languages have evolved with a multitude of features and facilities where programmers' jobs become much easier. Python is one of these languages and it became the most preferred language for all kinds of programmers and system developers. Despite the popularity of the Python languages, C is still used for hardware and system-level programming as it is executed faster compared to other modern languages. Chapter 2 in this book presents all necessary concepts of Python language in a nutshell. The following table presents the features of both these languages briefly in a comparative manner.

Table 1.4 Comparison of Python and C languages

Parameters	Python language	C language
Introduction	Python is a general-purpose, high-level, interpreted, object-oriented programming language.	C is also a general-purpose, compiler-based procedural computer programming language.
Implementing data structures	There is ease of implementing data structures with built-in insert and append functions.	Implementing data structures requires its functions to be explicitly implemented.
Usage	Writing code in Python is easier as the number of lines is less, comparatively.	C program syntax is harder than Python.
Speed	Interpreted programs (Python) execute slower as compared to compiled programs.	Compiled programs (C) execute faster as compared to interpreted programs.
Declaration of variables	There is no need to declare the type of variable in Python. Python is a dynamically typed language and hence there is no need for a declaration. A given variable can be stuck on values of different types at different times during the program execution.	In C, the type of a variable must be declared when it is created, and only values of that type can be assigned to it.
Function renaming mechanism	Supports function renaming mechanism, i.e., the same function can be used by two different names.	C does not support the function renaming mechanism. This means the same function cannot be used by two different names.
Built-in functions	Python has a large library of built-in functions.	C has a limited number of built-in functions.
Complexity	The syntax of Python programs is easy to learn, write, and read.	The syntax of a C program is harder than Python.
Memory-management	Python uses an automatic garbage collector for memory management.	In C, the programmer has to do memory management on his/her own.
Applications	Python is a general-purpose programming language.	C is generally used for hardware-related applications and system programming.

(*Continued*)

Table 1.4 *(Continued)*

Parameters	Python language	C language
Pointers	No pointer functionality is available in Python.	Pointers are available in C.
Error debugging	Error debugging is simple. This means it takes only one instruction at a time. The instruction is compiled and executed simultaneously. Errors are shown instantly and the execution is stopped at that instruction.	Error debugging is difficult in C as it is a compiler-dependent language. This means that it takes the entire source code, compiles it, and then shows all the errors.

1.11 PROGRAMMING PARADIGMS IN DATA STRUCTURE

The choice of a programming language is highly crucial for complex computational problem-solving. It is observed that practitioners often stir in this regard and start creating complex programs to handle their projects using the theoretical and practical knowledge of data structures. Several programming paradigms (a set of assumptions, concepts, values, and practices) are in the picture for implementation of algorithms with the data structure manipulations.

Programming paradigms also offer different ways of viewing reality for the programming along with a specific philosophy of writing programs and thinking about logic. Three major programming paradigms, viz., procedural programming, object-oriented programming, and functional programming are in practice and explained here.

1.11.1 Procedural Programming (PP)

Procedural programming is the first programming paradigm that a new developer can easily learn. Procedural programming directly instructs a device on how to complete a task in logical steps. This programming paradigm uses a direct top-down approach that treats data and procedures as two different entities. It is also known as inline programming because it follows a top-down approach. Procedural programming splits the program into procedures or functions that contain a sequence of steps to be carried out. C, Fortran, Pascal, etc. are examples of procedural programming language.

Advantages

- It is general-purpose programming.
- Codes are simple and easy to implement in compilers and interpreters.
- The program flow can be followed easily.

> **Note!**
> The procedural programming directly instructs a device on how to complete a task in logical steps called procedure.

Disadvantages

- The procedural code is often not reusable since we need to recreate the code when it needs to be used in another application.
- It is difficult to relate real-world objects.
- Importance is given to the operations rather than the data.
- Data is exposed to the whole program construction. It is not very friendly in terms of security.

1.11.2 Object-Oriented Programming (OOP)

The OOP approach is based on the collection of objects. An object encapsulates the data and methods as a primary entity to execute all necessary data storage and manipulation using the variables and functions. Objects can also be taken from one program and used to resolve another problem with small or nil alterations of code. It is a programming model that organizes software design around data or objects, rather than functions and logic. C++, Java, Python, etc. are examples of object-oriented programming languages.

Advantages

- OOP is easy to manage because of modularity and encapsulation concepts.
- Objects are the entities within themselves and they are reusable in other programs.
- OOP is easy to understand.

Disadvantages

- OOP tends to be slower and it uses a high amount of memory.
- Since programs are often found in-built, this approach may take a longer time to create objects and execute the program.
- It overemphasizes the data component of software development and does not focus on computation or algorithms.
- OOP code may be complicated to write and take a longer time to compile and hence functional programming has emerged as an alternative.

> ***Note!***
> The OOP approach is based on the collection of objects that encapsulates the data and methods as a primary entity for data storage and manipulation using the variables and functions.

1.11.3 Functional Programming (FP)

It is a programming technique that emphasizes on the functional factors required for creating and implementing the programs. This type of programming languages is specially designed to handle symbolic computations and list processing applications. This paradigm is of declarative type and everything works in pure mathematical functions style. It focuses on 'what to solve' instead of 'how to solve'. Expressions are used here instead of statements. Python supports FP relatively easily because everything is an object here though it is not a primary functional language. Some other characteristics of FP are given below.

- It is designed on the concept of mathematical functions that use conditional expressions and recursion to perform computation.
- This approach directly uses the functions and functional calls instead of flow controls like loop statements and conditional statements like `if-else` and `switch` statements.
- It supports popular concepts such as abstraction, encapsulation, inheritance, and polymorphism, like in OOP.
- Haskell, JavaScript, Erlang, Lisp are examples of functional programming languages.

Advantages

- **Efficient parallel programming:** FP languages have no mutable state and hence there are no state-change issues. One can program "Functions" to work in parallel as "instructions". Such codes support easy reusability and testability.

- **Efficiency:** Functional programs are more efficient because they consist of independent units that can run concurrently.
- **Bugs-free code:** Programmers can write error-free codes.

Disadvantages

- FP requires a large memory space. Programmers need to create new objects every time to perform actions.
- It is used in such situations where programmers have to perform lots of different operations on the same data set.

> ***Note!***
> Functional programming emphasizes the functional factors required for creating and implementing the programs specially designed to handle symbolic computations and list processing applications.

Table 1.5 Comparison of procedural, object-oriented, and functional programming

Basis for comparison	Procedural programming	Object-oriented programming	Functional programming
Definition	The program is divided into small functions.	The program is based on the concept of objects.	The program is based on the evaluation of functions.
Data	It uses immutable data.	It uses mutable data.	It uses immutable data.
Approach	It follows a top-down approach.	It follows a bottom-up approach.	It follows a bottom-up approach.
Execution	Statements are executed in a particular order.	Statements are executed in a particular order.	Statements can be executed in any order.
Support	It provides support to parallel programming.	It does not support parallel programming.	It provides support to parallel programming.
Use	It gives importance to the operation rather than the data.	It is used when there are many things with a few operations.	It is used only when there are a few things with more operations.
Element	The function is more important than data.	Data is more important than function.	Variables and functions are basic elements.

QUICK RECAP

☑ Data is the raw facts or statistics collected together for reference or analysis. Information is produced by processing and revealing the meaning of the data. The efficient storage of data leads to the services of IT using the evolutions and practices of computer science and engineering.

☑ A data type describes pieces of data that all share a common property. It is the form of a variable that is being used throughout the program. Four classes of data types are primitive, secondary, user-defined, and abstract data types.

☑ Data structure is a special way of organizing and storing data in computer memory so that it can access and use the data efficiently. Every data structure follows some specific principles.

☑ The Abstract Data Type (ADT) is made of primitive data types, but operation logics are hidden. There are external and internal components of an ADT. Operations that can be applied to an ADT are initializing, adding data, accessing data, and removing data.

- ☑ Sometimes the size of the declared array may be insufficient or could be a waste of memory. To solve this issue, we can allocate memory manually during run-time. This is known as dynamic memory allocation and implemented using `malloc()`, `calloc()`, `realloc()`, and `free()` C library functions.
- ☑ Data structure can be classified in various ways including primitive and non-primitive data structures, static and dynamic data structures, and homogeneous and non-homogeneous data structures besides the important linear and non-linear data structures.
- ☑ Elements of the linear data structure are accessed sequentially; however, the elements can be stored in these data structures in any order. Elements of non-linear data structures are stored and accessed in a distributed manner.
- ☑ Array, stack, queue, and linked list are examples of linear data structure whereas tree and graph are examples of non-linear data structure.
- ☑ The importance of data structure lies in algorithm development. Data structure and algorithms together build a strong foundation of computer science and other allied evolving and upcoming technologies like machine learning, data sciences, big data analytics, etc.
- ☑ Choosing an appropriate data structure is highly essential for developing efficient computer programs for problem-solving as well as in the design and implementation of algorithms.
- ☑ A file could be defined as a contiguous set of words or bytes for the collection of data. The major ways of organizing the file are sequential access, direct access, and indexed sequential access. The six operations of file organizations are create, read, write, execute, append, and delete.
- ☑ C languages have been observed as the most useful tool for algorithm implementations based on the strong foundations of data structures for efficient storage and retrieval of data.
- ☑ Python is the most popular (developer's choice) language for program development for modern-age computation problems.
- ☑ Three major programming paradigms, viz., procedural, object-oriented, and functional, are in practice for data structure related programming.
- ☑ Procedural programming directly instructs a device on how to complete a task in logical steps.
- ☑ An object encapsulates the data and methods as a primary entity to execute all necessary data storage and manipulation using the variables and functions in the object-oriented paradigm.
- ☑ Functional programming emphasizes the functional factors required, especially to handle symbolic computations and applications towards list processing.

REVIEW QUESTIONS

Multiple Choice Questions (MCQ): Choose the Best Alternative

Easy

1. Find out the user-defined data type in C language from the following:

   A. Array B. Char
   C. Structure D. Float

2. Which of the following is an interpreted language?

   A. C B. Python
   C. Both of them. D. None of them.

3. Which one of these is not an operation of data structure?
   A. Search B. Sort
   C. Truncation D. Traverse
4. Which of the following is a non-linear structure?
   A. Stacks B. Lists
   C. Strings D. Trees
5. Dynamic memory allocation uses:
   A. `calloc` B. `malloc`
   C. free D. All of these.
6. Example of dynamic data structure:
   A. Array B. Linked list
   C. `Int` D. None of these.

Moderate

7. Arrays representation in memory using C language is
   A. Column major. B. Row major.
   C. Layer major. D. None of these.
8. Design of efficient algorithms requires the knowledge of
   A. Data structures. B. Programming.
   C. Both A and B. D. None of these.
9. How do you initialize an array in C?
   A. `int arr[3] = (1,2,3);`
   B. `int arr(3) = {1,2,3};`
   C. `int arr[3] = {1,2,3};`
   D. `int arr(3) = (1,2,3);`
10. Arrays are the best data structures:
    A. For relatively permanent collections of data.
    B. When the size of the structure and the data in the structure are constantly changing.
    C. For both of the above situations.
    D. For none of the above situations.
11. An ADT is defined to be a ________ model of a user-defined data type.
    A. mathematical B. data
    C. statistical D. None of these.
12. Which of the following programming paradigms uses classes?
    A. Procedural B. Object-Oriented
    C. Declarative D. Functional

Higher-order Thinking Skills (HOTS)

13. `malloc()` function in C language returns __________ by default.
    A. integer pointer B. structure pointer
    C. null pointer D. void pointer
14. Find the value of function, $f(x) = 4x$, when $x = 3$.
    A. $f(3) = 4$ B. $f(3) = 2$
    C. $f(3) = 15$ D. $f(3) = 12$
15. What do you mean by a programming paradigm?
    A. A type of procedure
    B. Style of computer programming
    C. A suite of coding environments
    D. None of these.
16. Which programming paradigm uses a sequence of instructions that instructs the computer what to do next with the input to solve a particular problem?
    A. Declarative B. Object-Oriented
    C. Procedural D. Functional
17. Suppose, a function G is defined as G: X → Y where $f(a) = a^2 + 10$. The domain X is the set of all real numbers. What is the co-domain Y?
    A. The set of all natural numbers greater than 10
    B. The set of all real numbers greater than or equal to 10
    C. The set of all real numbers less than 10
    D. None of these.

Short Answer-type Questions

Easy

1. Distinguish between data and information.
2. What is data type? Give examples.
3. Define data structure. **OR** What is data structure? Give an example.
4. What are the advantages of data structures?
5. What are the disadvantages of data structure?
6. Differentiate between structure and union data type in C language.

Moderate

7. Why pointer is an important data type in C with respect to a data structure?
8. Give the analytical definition of data structure.
9. What is the difference between linear and non-linear data structure, static and dynamic data structure, primitive and non-primitive data structures?
10. What is the difference between a static and a dynamic data structure?
11. What is an abstract data type (ADT)? Why is it important in data structure?
12. Distinguish between `malloc()` and `calloc()` library functions.

13. Write the names of operations that we can perform to organize a file.

Higher-Order Thinking Skills (HOTS)

14. What are the default return data types of `malloc()` and `calloc()` function?
15. Explain the concepts of dynamic memory allocation?
16. Consider the declaration in C language:
`int array[] = {1, 2, 3, 4, 5, 6};`
How would you access the fourth element of the array?
17. Justify that Python supports procedural, object-oriented, and functional programming paradigms.
18. How is Python superior to the C language with respect to data structure?
19. How does data structure help in data science?
20. What do you understand by dynamically typed language? Give examples with syntactical advantages.

Descriptive-type Questions

Easy

1. Describe the different data types with examples with reference to the C language.
2. Describe briefly the different classifications of data structures.
3. Write down the operations required to deal with the data structures.
4. Compare and contrast the different features of C and Python programming languages.
5. What are the differences between object-oriented and functional programming?

Moderate

6. Illustrate the importance of data structure in algorithm design.
7. Justify the popularity of Python language in the present generation.
8. Describe all C library functions for dynamic memory allocations.
9. Illustrate the three major ways of organizing a file.
10. Write the importance of data structure in computer science and allied disciplines.
11. Compare data types of C language and Python language.

Higher-Order Thinking Skills (HOTS)

12. Write a C Program to perform the addition and subtraction of two integer values using pointers.
13. Writes a Python program to print the corresponding ASCII value of the character taken as user input.
14. Which data structure can we use for efficiently creating a dictionary and spell checker? Justify.
15. What will be the output of the following C program? Explain the output.

```
# include<stdio.h>
void f(int *p)
{
    *p = 10;
}
int main()
{
    int a = 50;
    f(&a);
    printf("%d", a);
    return 0;
}
```

16. Give the output of the following Python program and explain it.

```
x = True
y = False
z = False
if not x or y:
    print(10)
elif not x or not y and z:
    print(20)
elif not x or y or not y and x:
    print(30)
else:
    print(40)
```

CASE STUDIES

1. Calculate and print the sum of the elements in an array when some of those elements may be quite large, using both C and Python languages. Analyze the source codes of the developed programs using the two different languages with respect to data types and memory allocation.
2. Find the minimum and maximum values within the input set of ten positive integers taken from users using both C and Python separately. Display the difference of these two values. Analyze the source codes of these two languages with respect to data types and memory allocation.
3. Find the appropriate data structure for the following problems and justify:
   a. Reverse a string.
   b. Random access to stored data elements is not required normally.
   c. Implementation of CPU scheduling.
   d. Finding the shortest path from a source to a destination.
   e. Implementation of the index table of a search engine.

ANSWER KEYS

Multiple Choice Questions

1. C	4. D	7. B	10. B	13. C	16. C
2. B	5. D	8. A	11. A	14. D	17. B
3. C	6. B	9. C	12. B	15. B	

2 Python Digest

CONTENTS

EXPECTED OUTCOMES OF THIS CHAPTER

After going through this chapter learners will be able

- ☑ to introduce Python as modern programming language.
- ☑ to revise the concepts of Python programming.
- ☑ to apply basic syntax of Python language.
- ☑ to explain the object-oriented programming features of Python.
- ☑ to introduce the functional programming features of Python.
- ☑ to implement simple computational problems using Python.
- ☑ to introduce Numpy array and Pandas dataframe data structures.

2.1 INTRODUCTION

Python language was developed by Guido van Rossum in the late 1980s and the early 1990s at the National Research Institute for Mathematics and Computer Science in Netherlands. When Rossum was implementing Python, he was reading the published scripts from Monty Python's Flying Circus, a BBC comedy series from the 1970s. He thought he required a name that was short, unique, and slightly mysterious, so he decided to call the language Python. It is derived from many other languages, including ABC, Algol-68, C, C++, UNIX shell, SmallTalk, Modula-3, and other scripting languages like Perl.

Python is a simple, interactive, interpreted, high level, and object-oriented scripting language. It was designed to be highly readable since it uses English keywords frequently. Moreover, it has fewer syntactic constructions than other languages. Nonetheless, Python is free and open source with highly rich libraries and frameworks to facilitate most of the computational problem-solving requirements in the present time. The present industry has accepted this technology and promoted this language to such an extent that it has already become the program developer's language of choice.

> **Note!**
> Python is a simple, high-level, interactive, interpreted, and object-oriented scripting language developed by Guido van Rossum in the late 1980s.

2.2 FEATURES OF PYTHON

The following are the major features of Python language:

1. **Easy-to-learn:** Python has only a few keywords, simple structure, and a clearly defined syntax. This allows a learner to learn (or pick up) the language quickly.
2. **Easy-to-read:** Python code is clearly defined and visible to the eyes.
3. **Easy-to-maintain:** Python's source code is fairly easy to maintain.
4. **Portable:** Python can run on a wide variety of hardware platforms and has the same interface on all platforms.
5. **Extendable:** We can add low-level modules to the Python interpreter. These modules enable programmers to add or customize their tools to be more efficient.
6. **Interactive mode:** Python has support for an interactive mode, which allows interactive testing and debugging of code snippets.
7. **Scalable:** Python provides a better structure and support for large programs than shell scripting.
8. **GUI programming:** Python supports GUI applications that can be created and ported to many system calls, libraries, and windows systems, such as Windows MFC, Macintosh, and the X Window system of UNIX.
9. **Broad standard library:** Python's bulk of the library is very portable and there is a cross-platform compatible with UNIX, Windows, and Macintosh.
10. **Dynamic data type:** It provides very high-level dynamic data types and supports dynamic type checking.
11. **Databases:** Python provides interfaces to all major commercial databases.
12. **Scripting:** It can be used as a scripting language or can be compiled to byte-code for building large applications.
13. **Structured:** It supports functional and structured programming methods as well as Object-Oriented Programming (OOP).
14. **Garbage collection:** It supports automatic garbage collection.
15. **Integration with other languages:** It can be easily integrated with C, C++, COM, ActiveX, CORBA, and Java.

> **Note!**
> Python is easy to read, learn and maintain; it is portable, structured, extendable, interactive, and scalable. It offers extensive library supports, dynamic data types and database. It supports GUI applications, object oriented programming and scripting language.

2.3 ADVANTAGES OF PYTHON

Python became the first choice for the present-generation developers. The following are the prime advantages of Python language and the reasons behind its popularity.

1. **Free:** Python interpreters are freely available and can freely be associated with the applications.
2. **Open source:** The Python programs are built and made available as a reusable package to other developers and applications as an open source. These open-source packages and codes may be modified and deployed for any given purpose and again made available to others.
3. **Beginner-friendly:** The Python learning path is friendly to beginners as well as experienced developers. Switching from one version to another is easy for Python developers.
4. **Implantation easiness:** Even without much understanding of theoretical data structures, Python developers can implement them using a set, dictionary, list, etc.
5. **General purpose and adaptability:** Python is the general-purpose programming language with a constantly increasing demand for versatile development works. Python developers can switch language very easily.
6. **Structured:** The basic and well-defined structure offered by the Python frameworks, is usually appreciated by developers while figuring out the core logic of the application. Knowing Python frameworks doesn't mean that a developer has to know them all. A developer may be asked to know one or the other depending on the project. Mostly used frameworks are Django and Flask.
7. **Easy front-end collaboration:** A Python developer has to cooperate often with the front-end team to make a match between the server-side and the client-side. Basic understanding of front-end technologies (HTML5, CSS3, and JavaScript) is crucial but not compulsory for Python developers.
8. **Advance computing abilities:** Python is a perfect programming language for Artificial Intelligence, Machine Learning (along with Deep Learning), and Data Science computation projects.
9. **Easy documentation:** Python programs perfectly fit into the documentation works for product maintenance and extensions, not only in software development but also in start-up ventures.
10. **Packages:** Packages or libraries (like header files in C) make the programmer's life easier. These also make a task's execution way faster by making the team's workflow more efficient. Python has an answer to almost any possible request for libraries as a community-based programming language.
11. **Career opportunities:** Python gives programmers immense opportunities to learn more and gain new skills that are beneficial for their career path to make it challenging and interesting. Participating in additional courses and webinars, teaching others, and being active in the programming community are a few of the ways in which programmers hone their skills and become experts in their chosen fields.

> **Note!**
> Python is used for developing the popular applications like YouTube, BitTorrent and Dropbox.

Python is normally started in one of the following three ways:

1. Command Prompt (of Operating System)
2. Python Command Line
3. Integrated Development Environment (IDE).

The common syntax of this popular language is illustrated in the following sections with examples.

> **Note!**
> All Python codes in this book have been executed using Python 3. It may be executed using all popular Python interpreters and IDEs like IPython, Python IDLE, Jupyter Notebook, Jupyter Lab, Spyder, Google Collab, PyCharm etc.

2.4 STRING AND VARIABLES

Normally, Python variables are used to store values. For example, a string variable is a series of characters, surrounded by single or double quotes.

Example 2.1 Hello world string

```
print("Hello from Python world!")
```

Output

```
Hello from Python world!
```

Example 2.2 Hello world string with a Python variable

```
msg = "Hello from Python world!"
print(msg)
```

Output

```
Hello from Python world!
```

Example 2.3 Concatenation or combining strings

```
first_name = 'Raunak'
last_name = 'Das'
name = first_name + ' ' + last_name
print(name)
```

Output

```
Raunak Das
```

> ***Note!***
> Python variables are case-sensitive.

Example 2.4 Different quotations in Python

Single (‘), double (“), and triple (‘‘‘ or “““) quotes are used in Python to denote string literals, as long as the same type of quote starts and ends the string. To span the string across multiple lines, the triple quotes are used. For example, all the following are legal.

```
my_word= 'Python'
my_sentence = "Data structure with Python."
my_paragraph = """ A Textbook of Data
Structures & Algorithms with C and Python:
Theory and Practical for University and GATE
Examinations."""
```

Output

```
<No output generated since all are comments>
```

Example 2.5 Multiline Statements

Python statements typically end with a new line. Python allows the use of the line continuation character (\) to denote that the line should continue.

```
number_one = 5
number_two = 6
number_three= 9
average= (number_one + \
number_two + \
number_three)/3
print(average)
```

Output

```
6.666666666666667
```

Example 2.6 Comments in Python

The hash sign indicates the beginning of a comment in a single line.

```
# This is the first Python program to print.
```

Example 2.7 Multiline comment

For multi-line comments, 3 single quotes (''') that are not inside a string literal are used.

```
''' This first line
This second line '''
<No output since the above 2 lines are comments>
```

> ***Note!***
> Single ('), double ("), and triple (''' or """) quotes are used in Python to denote string literals.

Example 2.8 Indentation in Python

There is no concept of braces ({}) to indicate blocks of code for class and function definitions or flow control in Python. Python identifies blocks of code by line indentation, which is rigidly enforced. The number of spaces in the indentation is variable, but all statements in the block must be indented to the same extent. All continuous lines indented with the same number of spaces would form a block.

```
a = 1
if a == 1:
  print("a is 1")
else:
  print("Output")
```

> ***Note!***
> All statements within a given block must be indented with either blank spaces or tab characters, but not a mixture of the two.

Output

```
a is 1
```

Example 2.9 Python identifiers and variables

Identifiers are used to identify a variable, function, class, module, or another object. It starts with letters from A to Z or a to z or an underscore (_) followed by zero or more letters, underscores, and digits (0 to 9).

Punctuation characters such as @, $, and % within identifiers are not allowed in Python. It is a case-sensitive programming language. Thus, in Python, Name, and name are two different identifiers. The following is a list of Python's reserved words:

and	as	assert	break	class	continue	def
del	elif	else	except	finally	for	from
global	if	import	in	is	lambda	nonlocal
not	or	pass	raise	return	try	while
with	yield	False	None	True		

Normally, Python variables are used to store and manipulate values. A variable is an object in Python since every element is termed as an object in Python. An appropriate name is given to the variable to identify and use each variable easily in the program. Every variable has a type and the type of the variable is defined by the type of value it refers to. We need to provide a name to the variable and assign it a value. In Python, variables do not require a forward declaration. Python variables have three major components:

- Variable name
- Variable type
- The value assigned to a variable.

```
# Example of variable declaration and assignments
a = 10 # Integer type (forward) declaration not required
b =10 # Integer type (forward) declaration not required
```

Here variable 'a' and 'b' is assigned to the same integer object 10 since both these variables are assigned to the same value.

Example 2.10 Python data types – I

Data types are used to define the type or nature of a variable in Python. Various types of data can be stored in the memory in Python. For example, the name of a person is stored as a string, and age is stored as a numeric value. Python has five standard built-in data types. These are the numeric, string, list, tuple, and dictionary data types. The numeric and string data types can be understood from the following example. The other data types are explained in the following sections.

```
# Numeric type
x=10
print("The data type of the variable x:",type(x))
y=10.00
print("The data type of the variable y:",type(y))
z=10+12j
print("The data type of the variable z:",type(z))
```

Output

```
The data type of the variable x: <class 'int'>
The data type of the variable y: <class 'float'>
The data type of the variable z: <class 'complex'>
```

Example 2.11 **Python data types – II**

```
# String type
myStr1= "Python"
print("The data type of the variable myStr1:",type(myStr1))
myStr2= "Python latest version is 3.7.4"
print("The data type of the variable myStr2:",type(myStr2))
```

Output

```
The data type of the variable myStr1: <class 'str'>
The data type of the variable str2: <class 'str'>
```

> **Note!**
> Python supports primitive data types – integer, floating-point, Boolean, string, list, tuple, and dictionary.

2.5 USER INPUT

Your programs can prompt the user for input. All input is stored as a string.

Example 2.12 **Prompting for a value**

```
myName = input("What's your name? ")
print("Hello, " + myName + "!")
```

Output

```
What's your name? Raunak
Hello, Raunak!
```

Example 2.13 **Prompting for numerical input**

```
age = input("How old are you? ")
age = int(age)
pi = input("What's the value of pi? ")
pi = float(pi)
print('Your Age ' + age)
input('pi = ' + pi)
```

Output

```
How old are you? 54
What's the value of pi? 3.4
Your Age 54
pi = 3.4
```

> **Note!**
> `input()` is used to take input from the terminal and `print()` is used to give output at the terminal.

2.6 PYTHON OPERATORS

Operators manipulate the value of operands.

Table 2.1 Arithmetic operators

Operators		Description	Examples

+	Addition	Add values on either side of the operator.	`x = 3; y = 2`
			`x + y`
			`Output: 5`

−	Subtraction	Subtract right-hand operand from the left-hand operand.	`x - y` `Output: 1`
*	Multiplication	Multiply values on either side of the operator.	`x * y` `Output: 6`
/	Division	Divide left-hand operand by right-hand operand.	`x / y` `Output: 1.5`
%	Modulus	Returns remainder after dividing left-hand operand by right-hand operand.	`x % y` `Output: 1`
**	Exponent	Performs exponential (power) calculation on operators.	`x ** y` `Output: 9`
//	Floor Division	The division of operands where the result is the quotient in which the digits after the decimal point are removed.	`x // y` `Output: 1`

> ***Note!***
> The division operator (/) returns a floating-point value even if both operands are integers. The floor division operator (//) has to be used for integer division.

Table 2.2 Relational (Comparison) operators

Operator	Description	Examples

==	If the values of the two operands are equal, then the condition becomes True. Otherwise, it is False.	`x = 3; y = 2`
		`x == y`
		`Output: False`

!=	If the values of the two operands are not equal, then the condition becomes True.	`x! = y` `Output: True`
>	If the value of the left operand is greater than the value of the right operand, then the condition becomes True.	`x > y` `Output: True`
<	If the value of the left operand is less than the value of the right operand, then the condition becomes True.	`x < y` `Output: False`
>=	If the value of the left operand is greater than or equal to the value of the right operand, then the condition becomes True.	`x >= y` `Output: True`
<=	If the value of the left operand is less than or equal to the value of the right operand, then the condition becomes True.	`x <= y` `Output: False`

Table 2.3 Assignment operators

Assignment operators assign the value or expression to the operand.

Operator	Description	Examples

=	Assigns values from the right-side operand to the left-side operand.	`x = 3; y = 2`
		`z = x+y`
		`Output: 5`

+=	It adds the right operand to the left operand and assigns the result to the left operand.	`y += x` `Output: 5`
-=	It subtracts the right operand from the left operand and assigns the result to the left operand.	`y -= x` `Output: 1`
*=	It multiplies the right operand with the left operand and assigns the result to the left operand.	`y *= x` `Output: 6`
/=	It divides the left operand by the right operand and assigns the result to the left operand.	`y /= x` `Output: 1.5`
%=	It takes modulus using two operands and assigns the result to the left operand.	`y %= x` `Output: 1`
**=	Performs exponential (power) calculation on operators and assigns value to the left operand.	`z = 5; z **= x` `Output: 125`
//=	It performs floor division on operators and assigns value to the left operand.	`z = 26; z //= x` `Output: 8`

Table 2.4 Logical operators

Operator	Description	Examples

`and` (Logical AND)	If both the operands are true then the condition becomes True.	`x = 3; y = 2`
		`x and y`
		`Output: 2`

`or` (Logical OR)	If any of the two operands are non-zero then the condition becomes True.	`x or y` `Output: 3`
`not` (Logical NOT)	Used to reverse the logical state of its operand.	`not x` `Output: False`

Table 2.5 Bitwise operators

Operator	Description	Examples

`&`: Binary AND	It copies a bit to the result if it exists in both operands.	`x = 3; y = 2`
		`x & y`
		`Output: 2`

(Continued)

Table 2.5 *(Continued)*

<table>
<tr><th>Operator</th><th>Description</th><th>Examples</th></tr>
<tr><td>| : Binary OR</td><td>It copies a bit if it exists in either operand.</td><td><code>x | y</code>
<code>Output: 3</code></td></tr>
<tr><td>^ : Binary XOR</td><td>It copies the bit, if it is set in one operand but not both.</td><td><code>x ^ y</code>
<code>Output: 1</code></td></tr>
<tr><td>~ : Binary One's Complement</td><td>It is unary and has the effect of 'flipping' bits.</td><td><code>~x</code>
<code>Output: -4</code>
<code>~y</code>
<code>Output: -3</code></td></tr>
<tr><td><< : Binary Left Shift</td><td>The left operand's value is moved left by the number of bits specified by the right operand.</td><td><code>x << 1</code>
<code>Output: 6</code>
<code>y << 1</code>
<code>Output: 4</code></td></tr>
<tr><td>>> : Binary Right Shift</td><td>The left operand's value is moved right by the number of bits specified by the right operand.</td><td><code>x >> 1</code>
<code>Output: 1</code>
<code>y >> 1</code>
<code>Output: 1</code></td></tr>
</table>

Table 2.6 Membership operators

Operator	Description	Examples

`in`	Evaluates to True, if it finds a variable in the specified sequence and False otherwise.	`myList = [1, 2, 3, 4, 5]`
		`3 in myList`
		`Output: True`
		`7 in myList`
		`Output: False`

`not in`	Evaluates to True, if it does not find a variable in the specified sequence and False otherwise.	`myList = [1, 2, 3, 4, 5]`
		`3 not in myList`
		`Output: False`
		`7 not in myList`
		`Output: True`

Table 2.7 Identity operators

Operator	Description	Examples

`is`	Evaluates to True if the variables on either side of the operator point to the same object and False otherwise.	`x = 10`
		`y = 10`
		`x is y`
		`Output: True`
		`x is not y`
		`Output: False`

(Continued)

Table 2.7 *(Continued)*

Operator	Description	Examples

`is not`	Evaluates to False if the variables on either side of the operator point to the same object and True otherwise.	`x = 10`
		`y = 30`
		`x is y`
		`Output: False`
		`x is not y`
		`Output: True`

Table 2.8 Unary operators

Operator	Description	Examples

–: (Unary Minus)	Negates its operand value.	`x=-5`
		`y=10`
		`print(-x)`
		`Output: 5`
		`Print(-y)`
		`Output: -10`

> ***Note!***
> Python offers identity (is, is not), membership (in, not in) and logical (not, or, and) operators interestingly, besides other operators like C language.

Table 2.9 Operators' precedence

<table>
<tr><th>Operator</th><th>Description</th></tr>
<tr><td><code>**</code></td><td>Exponentiation (raise to the power)</td></tr>
<tr><td><code>~ , +, -</code></td><td>Complement, unary plus, and minus (method names for the last two are +@ and –@)</td></tr>
<tr><td><code>*, /, %, //</code></td><td>Multiply, divide, modulo, and floor division</td></tr>
<tr><td><code>+, -</code></td><td>Addition and subtraction</td></tr>
<tr><td><code>>>, <<</code></td><td>Right and left bitwise shift</td></tr>
<tr><td><code>&</code></td><td>Bitwise 'AND'</td></tr>
<tr><td><code>^, |</code></td><td>Bitwise exclusive 'OR' and regular 'OR'</td></tr>
<tr><td><code><=, <, >, >=</code></td><td>Comparison operators</td></tr>
<tr><td><code><, >, ==, !=</code></td><td>Equality operators</td></tr>
<tr><td><code>=, %=, /=, //=, -=, +=, *=, **=</code></td><td>Assignment operators</td></tr>
<tr><td><code>is, is not</code></td><td>Identity operators</td></tr>
<tr><td><code>in, not in</code></td><td>Membership operators</td></tr>
<tr><td><code>not, or, and</code></td><td>Logical operators</td></tr>
</table>

> ***Note!***
> Parentheses, if present, are applied first, even if higher priority operators exist.

2.7 LISTS

A list stores a series of items in a particular order. We access items using an index, or within a loop. Lists allow us to store sets of information in one place, whether we have just a few items or millions of items. Lists are one of Python's most powerful features readily accessible to new programmers, and we tie together many important concepts in programming.

> ***Note!***
> List is mutable (values can be changed) data type like string in Python.

Example 2.14 Create a list

```
cities = ['Kolkata', 'Delhi', 'Mumbai', 'Chennai', 'Agra']
print(cities)
```

Output

```
['Kolkata', 'Delhi', 'Mumbai', 'Chennai', 'Agra']
```

Example 2.15 Get the first item in a list

```
cities = ['Kolkata', 'Delhi', 'Mumbai', 'Chennai', 'Agra']
first_cities = cities[0]
print(first_cities)
```

Output

```
Kolkata
```

Example 2.16 Get the last item in a list

```
cities = ['Kolkata', 'Delhi', 'Mumbai', 'Chennai', 'Agra']
last_cities = cities[-1]
print(last_cities)
```

Output

```
Agra
```

> ***Programming Tips!***
> List index is positive or negative integer. TypeError is generated if non-integer if specified.

Example 2.17 Modifying list items by changing an element

Once we have define a list, we can change individual elements in the list. We do this by referring to the index of the item we want to modify.

```
cities = ['Kolkata', 'Delhi', 'Mumbai', 'Chennai', 'Agra']
cities[0] = 'Allahabad'
cities[-2] = 'Ranchi'
print(cities)
```

Output

```
['Allahabad', 'Delhi', 'Mumbai', 'Ranchi', 'Agra']
```

Example 2.18 **Starting with an empty list and appending it**

```
cities = []
cities.append('Allahabad ')
cities.append('Patna')
cities.append('Nagpur')
print(cities)
```

Output

```
['Allahabad ', 'Patna', 'Nagpur']
```

Example 2.19 **Inserting elements at a particular position**

```
cities = []
cities.insert(0, 'Kochi')
cities.insert(3, 'Bhopal')
print(cities)
```

Output

```
['Kochi', 'Bhopal']
```

> ***Programming Tips!***
> The list methods `append()` and `insert()` cannot be called on other values such as strings or integers.

> ***Note!***
> List can be updated using index or using the built-in method `append()`, `extend()` and `insert()`.

Example 2.20 **Slicing a list**

```
megaCities= ['Kolkata', 'Delhi', 'Mumbai', 'Chennai']
first_two = megaCities[:2]
middle_three = megaCities[1:4]
middle_jump = megaCities[1:4:2]
last_three = megaCities[-3:]
print(first_two)
print(middle_three)
print(middle_jump)
print(last_three)
```

> ***Note!***
> The list elements can be accessed using the concept of slice.

Output

```
['Kolkata', 'Delhi']
['Delhi', 'Mumbai', 'Chennai']
['Delhi', 'Chennai']
['Delhi', 'Mumbai', 'Chennai']
```

> ***Programming Tips!***
> Slice method generates IndexError if the index is outside the list.

Example 2.21 Copying a list

```
megaCities= ['Kolkata','Delhi','Mumbai', 'Chennai']
copy_of_megaCities = megaCities[:]
print(copy_of_megaCities)
```

Output

```
['Kolkata', 'Delhi', 'Mumbai', 'Chennai']
```

Note!
Aliasing (second name) variables are not recommended when working with mutable objects.

Example 2.22 Removing elements by deleting an element by its position

We can remove elements by their position in a list, or by the value of the item. If we remove an item by its value, Python removes only the first item that has that value.

```
cities= ['Kolkata', 'Delhi', 'Mumbai', 'Chennai']
del cities[-1]
print(cities)
```

Output

```
['Kolkata', 'Delhi', 'Mumbai']
```

Programming Tips!
`del` method generates Error if the element is not present in the list.

Example 2.23 Removing an item by its value

```
cities= ['Kolkata', 'Delhi', 'Mumbai', 'Chennai']
cities.remove('Mumbai')
print(cities)
```

Output

```
['Kolkata', 'Delhi', 'Chennai']
```

Example 2.24 Pop the last item from a list

If we want to remove an element from the list, we can "pop" the element. If we think of the list as a stack of items, `pop()` takes an item off the top of the stack. By default, `pop()` returns the last element in the list, but we can also pop elements from any position in the list.

```
cities= ['Kolkata', 'Delhi', 'Mumbai', 'Chennai']
most_recent_cities = cities.pop()
print(most_recent_cities)
```

Output

```
Chennai
```

Example 2.25 Pop the first item in a list

```
cities= ['Kolkata', 'Delhi', 'Mumbai', 'Chennai']
first_cities = cities.pop(0)
print(first_cities)
```

Output

```
Kolkata
```

> ***Note!***
> Elements can be deleted using `del` statement, `remove()` and `clear()` methods.

> ***Programming Tips!***
> `pop()` method and `del` statement performs same task but `pop()` returns the removed element.

Example 2.26 List length

The `len()` function returns the number of items in a list.

```
cities= ['Kolkata', 'Delhi', 'Mumbai', 'Chennai']
num_cities = len(cities)
print("We have " + str(num_cities) + " cities.")
```

Output

```
We have 4 cities.
```

Example 2.27 Looping through a list

Lists can contain millions of items, so Python provides an efficient way to loop through all the items in a list. When we set up a loop, Python pulls each item from the list, one at a time, and stores it in a temporary variable, which we provide a name for. This name should be the singular version of the list name. The indented block of code makes up the body of the loop, where we can work with each individual item. Any lines that are not indented run after the loop is completed.

```
cities = ['Kolkata', 'Delhi', 'Mumbai', 'Chennai', 'Agra']
for city in cities:
print(city)
```

Output

```
Kolkata
Delhi
Mumbai
Chennai
Agra
```

Example 2.28 Printing a message for each item, and a separate message afterwards

```
cities = ['Kolkata', 'Delhi', 'Mumbai', 'Chennai', 'Agra']
for city in cities:
print("Welcome to " + city + "!")
print("We're glad to see you in "+ city)
```

Output

```
Welcome to Kolkata!
We're glad to see you in Kolkata
Welcome to Delhi!
We're glad to see you in Delhi
Welcome to Mumbai!
We're glad to see you in Mumbai
Welcome to Chennai!
We're glad to see you in Chennai
Welcome to Agra!
We're glad to see you in Agra
```

Example 2.29 Making numerical lists

```
squares = []
cubes = []
for x in range(1, 11):
    squares.append(x**2)
    cubes.append(x**3)
print(squares)
print(cubes)
```

Output

```
[1, 4, 9, 16, 25, 36, 49, 64, 81, 100]
[1, 8, 27, 64, 125, 216, 343, 512, 729, 1000]
```

Example 2.30 Sorting a list permanently

The `sort()` method changes the order of a list permanently. The `sorted()` function returns a copy of the list, leaving the original list unchanged. We can sort the items in a list in alphabetical order, or reverse alphabetical order. We can also reverse the original order of the list. Keep in mind that lowercase and uppercase letters may affect the sort order.

```
cities = ['Kolkata', 'Delhi', 'Mumbai', 'Chennai', 'Agra']
cities.sort()
print(cities)
```

Output

```
['Chennai', 'Delhi', 'Agra', 'Kolkata', 'Mumbai']
```

Example 2.31 **Sorting a list permanently in reverse alphabetical order**

```
cities = ['Kolkata', 'Delhi', 'Mumbai', 'Chennai', 'Agra']
cities.sort(reverse=True)
print(cities)
```

Output

```
['Mumbai', 'Kolkata', 'Delhi', 'Chennai', 'Agra']
```

Example 2.32 **Sorting a list temporarily**

```
cities = ['Kolkata', 'Delhi', 'Mumbai', 'Chennai', 'Agra']
print(sorted(cities))
print(sorted(cities, reverse=True))
```

Output

```
['Mumbai', 'Kolkata', 'Delhi', 'Chennai', 'Agra']
```

Example 2.33 **Reversing the order of a list**

```
cities = ['Kolkata', 'Delhi', 'Mumbai', 'Chennai', 'Agra']
cities.reverse()
print(cities)
```

Output

```
['Agra', 'Chennai', 'Mumbai', 'Delhi', 'Kolkata']
```

Example 2.34 **Using a loop to generate a list of square numbers**

```
squares = []
cubes = []
for x in range(1, 11):
  square = x**2
  cube = x**3
  squares.append(square)
  cubes.append(cube)
print(squares)
print(cubes)
```

```
[1, 4, 9, 16, 25, 36, 49, 64, 81, 100]
[1, 8, 27, 64, 125, 216, 343, 512, 729, 1000]
```

Example 2.35 **List comprehensions**

It is an elegant way of writing Python codes in simple and plain English within a single line of code

```
squares = [x**2 for x in range(1, 11)]
cubes = [x**3 for x in range(1, 11)]
print(squares)
print(cubes)
```

Output

```
[1, 4, 9, 16, 25, 36, 49, 64, 81, 100]
[1, 8, 27, 64, 125, 216, 343, 512, 729, 1000]
```

Example 2.36 **Using a loop to convert a list of names to uppercase**

```
names = ['Raunak', 'Priti', 'Biyas', 'Moumita', 'Satyam']
upper_names = []
for name in names:
   upper_names.append(name.upper())
print(upper_names)
```

Output

```
['RAUNAK', 'PRITI', 'BIYAS', 'MOUMITA', 'SATYAM']
```

Example 2.37 **Using a comprehension to convert a list of names to uppercase**

```
names = ['Raunak', 'Biyas', 'Priti', 'Moumita', 'Satyam']
upper_names = [name.upper() for name in names]
```

Output

```
['RAUNAK', 'BIYAS', 'PRITI', 'MOUMITA', 'SATYAM']
```

Example 2.38 **Use of lambda function for list comprehension**

Various built-in functions and lambda functions can create and modify lists in fewer lines of code inside the list. However, list comprehensions are usually more human-readable than lambda functions. It is easier to understand what the programmer was trying to accomplish when list comprehensions are used.

> ***Note!***
> Lambda functions are required when function objects are required.

```
letters = list(map(lambda x: x, 'Python'))
print(letters)
```

Output

```
['P', 'y', 't', 'h', 'o', 'n']
```

Example 2.39 Conditionals in the list comprehension – I

List comprehensions can make use of conditional statements (and with nested conditions) to modify the existing list. We can create a list that uses mathematical operators, integers, and `range()`.

Example 2.40 Conditionals in the list comprehension – II

```
myList1 = [x for x in range(20) if x % 2 == 0]
print(myList1)
```

Output

```
[0, 2, 4, 6, 8, 10, 12, 14, 16, 18]
```

Example 2.41 Conditionals in the list comprehension – III

```
myList2 = [y for y in range(100) if y % 2 == 0 if y % 5 == 0]
print(myList2)
```

Output

```
[0, 10, 20, 30, 40, 50, 60, 70, 80, 90]
```

Example 2.42 Conditionals in the list comprehension – IV

```
myList3 = ["Even" if i%2 == 0 else "Odd" for i in range(10)]
print(myList3)
```

Output

```
['Even', 'Odd', 'Even', 'Odd', 'Even', 'Odd', 'Even', 'Odd', 'Even',
'Odd']
```

Example 2.43 Transpose of a matrix using list comprehension

```
matrix = [[15, 25], [35,45], [55, 65], [75, 85]]
transpose = [[row[i] for row in matrix] for i in range(2)]
print(transpose)
```

Output

```
[[15, 35, 55, 75], [25, 45, 65, 85]]
```

> **Note!**
> List containing another list as an element is called nested list.

A list is used for any sequence of things that need to go in order, and we only need to look them up by a numeric index. The main difference between strings and lists is that elements of the list can be any type of data, i.e., integers, float, strings, etc, while strings can only hold a set of characters. Another difference between list and string is that lists are mutable whereas strings are immutable. The list elements can be accessed by using both positive and negative indices. Lists can be traversed using the `for` and `while` loop along with `len()` and `range()` functions. Lists respond to all of the general sequence operations we use on strings, besides the general-purpose + and * operators. Built-in list functions like `max()`, `min()`, `sorted()`, and methods like `count()`, `index()`, `pop()`, `reverse()`, `sort()`, `copy()` can be used for general problem-solving.

> **Programming Tips!**
> Lambda functions are not equivalent to inline functions in C/C++.

2.8 SETS

A set is a unique collection of items that are unordered and un-indexed. Set elements are unique. Duplicate elements are not allowed in a set. Sets are written with curly brackets. The elements contained in the set must be of an immutable type. A set itself may be modified. This is why you may find that the outputs may not be matching with the outputs provided by your Python interpreter used for executing the code snips in the following set operations.

> **Note!**
> Set is unordered, un-indexed and without duplicate elements.

Table 2.10 Methods used in set operations

Method	Description
`clear()`	Removes all the elements from the set
`remove()`	Removes the specified element
`discard()`	Remove the specified item
`pop()`	Removes an element from the set
`add()`	Adds an element to the set
`copy()`	Returns a copy of the set
`difference()`	Returns a set containing the difference between two or more sets
`difference_update()`	Removes the items in a given set that are also included in another specified set
`symmetric_difference()`	Returns a set with the symmetric differences of two sets
`symmetric_difference_update()`	Inserts the symmetric differences from one set and another

(Continued)

Method	Description
intersection()	Returns a set that is the intersection of two other sets
intersection_update()	Removes the items in a set that are not present in other, specified set(s)
isdisjoint()	Returns whether two sets have an intersection or not
issubset()	Returns whether another set contains the given set or not
issuperset()	Returns whether the given set contains another set or not
union()	Returns a set containing the union of sets
update()	Updates the set with the union of a given set and others

Example 2.44 **Create a set**

```
mySet = {'Kolkata', 'Delhi', 'Mumbai', 'Chennai', 'Agra'}
print(mySet)
```

Output

```
{'Mumbai', 'Chennai', 'Kolkata', 'Delhi', 'Agra'}
```

Example 2.45 **Access items**

```
mySet = {'Kolkata', 'Delhi', 'Mumbai', 'Chennai', 'Agra'}
for x in mySet:
  print(x)
```

Output

```
Mumbai
Agra
Chennai
Kolkata
Delhi
```

Example 2.46 **Add items**

```
mySet = {'Kolkata', 'Delhi', 'Mumbai', 'Chennai', 'Agra'}
mySet.add('Nagpur')
print(mySet)
```

Output:

```
{'Kolkata', 'Agra', 'Nagpur', 'Delhi', 'Mumbai', 'Chennai'}
```

Example 2.47 **Add multiple items to a set, using the `update()` method**

```
mySet = {'Kolkata', 'Delhi', 'Mumbai', 'Chennai', 'Agra'}
mySet.update(["Nagpur", "Ranchi", "Gangtok"])
print(mySet)
```

Output

```
{'Agra', 'Nagpur', 'Kolkata', 'Chennai',
'Gangtok', 'Mumbai', 'Delhi', 'Ranchi'}
```

> ***Programming Tips!***
> If we insert same element multiple times in a set, it is removed since set cannot allow duplicate values.

Example 2.48 **Get the length of a set**

```
mySet = {'Kolkata', 'Delhi', 'Mumbai', 'Chennai', 'Agra'}
print(len(mySet))
```

Output

```
5
```

Example 2.49 **Remove item(s) using `remove()`**

```
mySet = {'Kolkata', 'Delhi', 'Mumbai', 'Chennai', 'Agra'}
mySet.remove("Mumbai")
print(mySet)
```

Output

```
{'Agra', 'Kolkata', 'Delhi', 'Chennai'}
```

Example 2.50 **Remove item(s) using `discard()`**

```
mySet = {'Kolkata', 'Delhi', 'Mumbai', 'Chennai', 'Agra'}
mySet.discard("Delhi")
print(mySet)
```

Output

```
{'Mumbai', 'Agra', 'Chennai', 'Kolkata'}
```

Example 2.51 **Remove item(s) using `pop()`**

```
mySet = {'Kolkata', 'Delhi', 'Mumbai', 'Chennai', 'Agra'}
x = mySet.pop()
print(x)
print(mySet)
```

Output

```
Chennai
{'Kolkata', 'Delhi', 'Mumbai', 'Agra'}
```

Example 2.52 Remove item(s) using `clear()`

```
mySet = {'Kolkata', 'Delhi', 'Mumbai', 'Chennai', 'Agra'}
mySet.clear()
print(mySet)
```

Output

```
set()
```

Example 2.53 Remove item(s) using `del`

```
mySet = {'Kolkata', 'Delhi', 'Mumbai', 'Chennai', 'Agra'}
del mySet
print(mySet)
```

Output

```
NameError: name 'mySet' is not defined
```

Example 2.54 Join two sets using Union

```
set1 = {"x", "y", "z"}
set2 = {1, 2, 3}
set3 = set1.union(set2)
print(set3)
```

Output

```
{1, 2, 3, 'x', 'y', 'z'}
```

Example 2.55 Join two sets using `update()`

```
set1 = {"x", "y", "z"}
set2 = {1, 2, 3}
set1.update(set2)
print(set1)
```

Output

```
{1, 2, 3, 'y', 'z', 'x'}
# Both union() and update() will exclude any duplicate items.
```

Example 2.56 Intersection operation on two sets

```
set1 = {5, 2, 6, 4, 3, 7}
set2 = {1, 2, 3}
set3 = set1.intersection(set2)
print(set3)
```

Output

```
{2, 3}
```

Example 2.57 **Intersection operation in another way**

```
set1 = {5, 2, 6, 4, 3, 7}
set2 = {1, 2, 3}
set3 = set1 & set2
print(set3)
```

Output

```
{2, 3}
```

Example 2.58 **Difference operation on two sets**

```
set1 = {5, 2, 6, 4, 3, 7}
set2 = {1, 2, 3}
set3 = set1.difference(set2)
print(set3)
```

Output

```
{4, 5, 6, 7}
```

Example 2.59 **Difference operation in another way**

```
set1 = {5, 2, 6, 4, 3, 7}
set2 = {1, 2, 3}
set3 = set1 - set2
print(set3)
```

Output

```
{4, 5, 6, 7}
```

Example 2.60 **Checking subset**

```
set1 = {5, 2, 6, 4, 3, 7}
set2 = {1, 2, 3}
set3 = set1.issubset(set2)
print(set3)
```

Output

```
False
```

Example 2.61 Subset check in another way

```
set1 = {5, 2, 6, 4, 3, 7}
set2 = {2, 3}
set3 = set2 <= set1
print(set3)
```

Output

```
True
```

Example 2.62 The `set()` constructor

```
mySet = set(('Kolkata', 'Delhi', 'Mumbai', 'Chennai', 'Agra'))
# note the double round-brackets
print(mySet)
```

Output

```
{'Delhi', 'Chennai', 'Mumbai',
'Kolkata', 'Agra'}
```

> ***Note!***
> Set is mutable like list. All mathematical set operations can be performed on set data type.

2.9 TUPLES

Tuples are similar to lists, but the items in a tuple cannot be modified (i.e., they are not mutable).

Example 2.63 Creating and looping through a tuple

```
dims = (1975, 2009)
for dim in dims:
  print(dim)
```

Output

```
1975
2009
```

Example 2.64 Overwriting a tuple

```
dims = (1000, 6000)
print(dims)
dims = (12000, 9000)
print(dims)
```

Output

```
(1000, 6000)
(12000, 9000)
```

> ***Note!***
> Tuple indices are similar to list. `max()`, `min()` and `sorted()` will not work in list, whereas `max()`, `min()` and `sorted()` will work for a tuple with numeric and string type data.

Tuple can be traversed using the `for` and `while` loops along with `len()` and `range()` functions like lists data type. Tuples respond to all of the general-sequence operations we use on strings besides the general-purpose + and * operators.

2.10 DICTIONARIES

Dictionaries store connections between pieces of information. Each item in a dictionary is a key-value pair. When we provide a key, Python returns the value associated with that key. We can loop through all the key-value pairs, all the keys, or all the values.

> **Note!**
> Each key-value pair in a dictionary is separated by a colon (:), whereas each item of the dictionary is separated by a comma, and enclosed in curly braces.

> **Note!**
> More than one entry per key is not allowed. This means no duplicate key is allowed. When duplicate keys are encountered during the assignment, the last assignment wins.

Example 2.65 Creating a simple dictionary

```
stranger_0 = {'color': 'green', 'points': 5}
```

Example 2.66 Accessing a value

```
print("The stranger's color is " + stranger_0 [ 'color'])
```

Output

```
The stranger's color is green
```

Example 2.67 Adding a new key-value pair

```
stranger_0['x_position'] = 0
```

Example 2.68 Getting the value with `get()`

```
stranger_0 = {'color': 'green'}
stranger_color = stranger_0.get('color')
stranger_points = stranger_0.get('points', 0)

print(stranger_color)
print(stranger_points)
```

Output

```
green
0
```

Example 2.69 Adding a key-value pair

```
stranger_0 = {'color': 'green', 'points': 5}
stranger_0['x'] = 0stranger_0['y'] = 25
stranger_0['speed'] = 1.5
print(stranger_0)
```

Output

```
{'color': 'green', 'points': 5, 'x': 0, 'y': 25, 'speed': 1.5}
```

Example 2.70 Adding to an empty dictionary

```
stranger_0 = {}
stranger_0['color'] = 'green'
stranger_0['points'] =5
print(stranger_0)
```

Output

```
{'color': 'green', 'points': 5}
```

Example 2.71 Modifying values in a dictionary

```
stranger_0 = {'color': 'green', 'points': 5}
print(stranger_0)

# Change the stranger's color and point value.
stranger_0['color'] = 'yellow'
stranger_0['points'] = 10
print(stranger_0)
```

Output

```
{'color': 'green', 'points': 5}
{'color': 'yellow', 'points': 10}
```

Example 2.72 Deleting a key-value pair

```
stranger_0 = {'color': 'green', 'points': 5}
print(stranger_0)
del stranger_0['points']
print(stranger_0)
```

Output

```
{'color': 'green', 'points': 5}
{'color': 'green'}
```

> **Note!**
> We can delete items of a dictionary as well as the entire dictionary using the `del` statement.

Example 2.73 Looping through all key-value pairs

```
fav_numbers = {'Raunak': 9, 'Biyas': 7}
for name, number in fav_numbers.items():
    print(name + ' loves ' + str(number))
```

Output

```
Raunak loves 9
Biyas loves 7
```

Example 2.74 Looping through all keys

```
fav_numbers = {'Raunak': 9, 'Biyas': 7}
for name in fav_numbers.keys():
   print(name + ' loves a number')
```

Output

```
Raunak loves a number
Biyas loves a number
```

Example 2.75 Looping through all the values

```
fav_numbers = {'Raunak': 9, 'Biyas': 7}
for number in fav_numbers.values():
   print(str(number) + ' is a favorite')
```

Output

```
9 is a favorite
7 is a favorite
```

> ***Note!***
> Dictionary is traversed by iterating through all keys, all values, and all key-value pairs using `for` loop.

Example 2.76 Storing dictionaries in a list

```
# Start with an empty list.
users = []

# Make a new user, and add them to the list.
new_user = {
'last': 'raunak',
'first': 'das',
'username': 'raunakdas',
}
users.append(new_user)

# Make another new user, and add them as well.
new_user = {
'last': 'biyas',
'first': 'banerjee',
'username': 'biyasbanerjee',
 }
users.append(new_user)
```

```
# Show all information about each user.
for user_dict in users:
    for k, v in user_dict.items():
        print(k + ": " + v)
```

Output

```
last: raunak
first: das
username: raunakdas
last: biyas
first: banerjee
username: biyasbanerjee
```

Example 2.77 Storing lists in a dictionary

```
# Store multiple languages for each person.
fav_languages = {
'Raunak': ['python', 'ruby'],
'Biyas': ['c'],
'Rangan': ['ruby', 'go'],
'Arka': ['python', 'haskell'],
}

# Show all responses for each person.
for name, langs in fav_languages.items():
    print(name + ": ")
    for lang in langs:
        print("- " + lang)
```

Output

```
Raunak:
- python
- ruby
Biyas:
- c
Rangan:
- ruby
- go
Arka:
- python
- haskell
```

Example 2.78 Storing dictionaries in a dictionary

```
users = {
  'RDas': {
                 'first': 'Raunak',
                 'last': 'Das',
                 'location': 'Garia',
               },
  'BBanerjee': {
                 'first': 'Biyas',
                 'last': 'Banerjee',
                 'location': 'SaltLake',
                },
  }

for username, user_dict in users.items():
      print("\nUsername: " + username)
      full_name = user_dict['first'] + " "
      full_name += user_dict['last']
      location = user_dict['location']

      print("\tFull name: " + full_name.title())
      print("\tLocation: " + location.title())
```

Output

```
Username: RDas
      Full name: Raunak Das
      Location: Garia

Username: BBanerjee
      Full name: Biyas Banerjee
      Location: Saltlake
```

Dictionary values can be any arbitrary Python object, either standard objects or user-defined objects. However, the same is not true for the keys. Dictionary variables may be accessed [using functions `get()`, `items()`, `keys()`, `values()`], updated [using functions `update()`], and deleted easily using in-built facilities. The `clear()` method will remove all the items from the dictionary and make it an empty dictionary. The built-in method `pop()` is used to delete a key and its value. The advantage of the `pop()` over using `del` is that it provides the mechanism to print the desired value. Dictionaries may be traversed by iterating through all keys, all values, and all key-value pairs using `for` loop. Several in-built functions are provided to manipulate dictionary variables. Membership operations (`in`, `not in`) and `max`, `min`, and `sum` are applicable only to the keys in a dictionary. The `setdefault()` method returns the value of a key if the key is in the dictionary. If not, it inserts a key with a None value to the dictionary.

2.11 CONDITIONAL STATEMENTS (IF, ELSE, ELIF)

`If` statements are used to test for particular conditions and respond appropriately.

Example 2.79 Conditional tests

```
# Examples of conditional operators
equals x == 42
not equal x != 42
greater than x > 42
      or equal to x>= 42
less than x < 42
   or equal to x<= 42
```

Example 2.80 Conditional test with lists using 'in' operator

```
bikes = ['activa', 'bullet', 'trek']
print('trek' in bikes)
print('surly' not in bikes)
```

Output

```
True
True
```

Example 2.81 Assigning Boolean values

```
game_active= True
can_edit = False
```

Example 2.82 A simple `if` conditional statement

```
age = int(input('enter age '))
if age >= 18:
   print("You can vote!")
```

Output

```
enter age 23
You can vote!
```

> ***Note!***
> The statement block within `if` statement is executed depending on the value of the outcomes of the Boolean expression.

Example 2.83 **`If-else` conditional statements**

```
my_marks=int(input("Enter the marks: "))
if my_marks>=90:
   print("Grade is 'O'")
   print("Marks:",my_marks)
else:
   print("Grade is not 'O'")
   print("Marks:",my_marks)
print("Bye...have a nice day!"
```

Output

```
Enter the marks: 75
Grade is not 'O'
Marks: 75

Bye...have a nice day!
```

> ***Note!***
> The `if-else` statement also contains a Boolean expression like `if` statement.

Example 2.84 **`If-elif-else` conditional statements**

```
if age < 4:
   ticket_price = 0
elif age < 18:
   ticket_price = 10
else:
   ticket_price = 15
```

Example 2.85 **Nested `if` statements**

```
myNumber = int(input("Enter a Number "))
if myNumber%3 == 0:
    if myNumber%4 == 0:
        print("Divisible by 4 and 3")
    else:
        print("Divisible by 3 not divisible by 4")
elif myNumber%4 == 0:
    print("Divisible by 4 not divisible by 3")
else:
    print("Not Divisible by 3 not divisible by 4")
```

Output

```
Enter a Number 15
Divisible by 3 not divisible by 4
```

> ***Note!***
> The `if-elif-else` statement works in the same way as `if-else` statement.

Example 2.86 **Testing if a value is in a list**

```
players = ['al', 'bea', 'cyn', 'dale']
print('al' in players)
print('hi' in players)
```

> ***Note!***
> In a nested `if` statement, we have any number of `if...elif...else` statement inside another `if...elif...else` statement.

Output

```
True
False
```

Example 2.87 **`Switch` statement using dictionary**

Python does not support `switch` statements for handling multi-condition situations like other languages. However, we can implement `switch` statements in simple cases using the dictionary variables and a function, as given below.

```
def week(i):
    switcher = {
            0: 'Sunday',
            1: 'Monday',
            2: 'Tuesday',
            3: 'Wednesday',
            4: 'Thursday',
            5: 'Friday',
            6: 'Saturday'
           }
    return switcher.get(i, "Invalid day of week")

print(week(3))
print(week(9))
```

Output

```
Wednesday
Invalid day of week
```

> ***Note!***
> In a nested `if` statement, we have any number of `if...elif...else` statement inside another `if...elif...else` statement.

2.12 ITERATION LOOPS (WHILE AND FOR)

A `while` loop repeats a block of code as long as a certain condition is true.

Example 2.88 **A simple while loop**

```
current_value = 1
while current_value<= 5:
  print(current_value)
  current_value += 1
```

Output

```
1
2
3
4
5
```

Example 2.89 Letting the user choose when to quit

```
msg = ''
while msg != 'quit':
    msg = input ("What's your message? ")
    print(msg)
```

Output

```
What's your message? hello
hello
What's your message? quit
quit
```

Example 2.90 Using a flag

```
prompt = "Tell me something, and I'll "
prompt += "repeat it back to you."
prompt += "\nEnter'quit' to end the program. "
active = True
while active:
   message = input(prompt)
   if message == 'quit':
     active = False
   else:
     print(message)
```

Output

```
Tell me something, and I'll repeat it back to you.
Enter 'quit' to end the program. hello
hello
Tell me something, and I'll repeat it back to you.
Enter 'quit' to end the program. mr das
mr das
Tell me something, and I'll repeat it back to you.
Enter 'quit' to end the program. Quit
```

Note!

If the `else` statement is used with a `while` loop, the `else` statement is executed when the expression evaluates to a zero value as False.

Example 2.91 `Do-while` loop implementation in Python

```
do {
//statement
} while (condition);
```

The following Python codes implement the `do-while` logic used in other languages.

```
i = 1
while True:
    print(i)
    i = i + 1
    if(i> 5):
        break
```

Output

```
1
2
3
4
5
```

Example 2.92 Removing all instances of a value from a list

```
pets = ['dog', 'cat', 'dog', 'fish', 'cat','rabbit', 'cat']
print(pets)

while 'cat' in pets:
    pets.remove('cat')

print(pets)
```

Output

```
['dog', 'cat', 'dog', 'fish', 'cat', 'rabbit', 'cat']
['dog', 'dog', 'fish', 'rabbit']
```

Example 2.93 Simple `for` loop

```
for my_var in range(0,10,2):
    print(my_var)
```

Output

```
0
2
4
6
8
```

> ***Note!***
>
> The `for loop` executes a sequence of statements multiple times and abbreviates the code that manages the loop variable.

Example 2.94 Nested `for` loop

```
for i in range(1,5):
    for j in range(1,5):
        k=i+j
        print(k, end=',')
    print()
```

Output

```
2,3,4,5,
3,4,5,6,
4,5,6,7,
5,6,7,8,
```

> ***Note!***
> We can use one or more loops inside another while, or for loop as nested loop.

2.13 LOOP CONTROL STATEMENTS (BREAK, CONTINUE, PASS)

Loop control statements change execution from its normal sequence. When execution leaves a scope, all automatic objects that were created in that scope are destroyed. Python supports the following loop control statements.

Example 2.95 Using `break` to exit a loop

It brings control out of the loop.

```
prompt = "\nWhat games have you played?"
prompt += "\nEnter 'quit' when you're done."
while True:
   game = input(prompt)
   if game == 'quit':
     break
   else:
     print("I was playing " + game + "!")
```

Output

```
What games have you played?
Enter 'quit' when you're done. chess
```

> ***Note!***
> The break statement terminates the loop statement and transfers execution to the statement immediately following the loop.

Example 2.96 Using `continue` in a loop

```
banned_users = ['Srinath', 'Azahar', 'Agarkar', 'Sammi']
prompt = "Add a player to your team."
prompt += "\nEnter 'quit' when you're done. "
players = []
```

```
while True:
     player = input(prompt)
     if player == 'quit':
        break
     elif player in banned_users:
        print(player + " is banned!")
        continue
     else:
        players.append(player)
print("\nYour team:")
for player in players:
      print(player)
```

Output

```
Add a player to your team.
Enter 'quit' when you're done. Sachin
Add a player to your team.
Enter 'quit' when you're done. Birat
Add a player to your team.
Enter 'quit' when you're done. Rohit
Add a player to your team.
Enter 'quit' when you're done. quit
Your team:
Sachin
Birat
Rohit
```

> ***Note!***
> The `continue` statement causes the loop to skip the remainder of its body and immediately retest its condition before reiterating.

Example 2.97 Using pass in a loop

We use `pass` statements to write empty loops. `Pass` is also used for empty control statements, functions and classes.

```
for letter in 'Data_Structure':
    pass
print('Last Letter:', letter)
```

Output

```
Last Letter: e
```

> ***Note!***
> The `pass` statement is a null operation.

Example 2.98 An infinite loop

```
while True:
    name = input ("Who are you? ")
    print("Nice to meet you, " + name + "!")
```

Output

```
Who are you? a
Nice to meet you, a!
Who are you? b
Nice to meet you, b!
<Interrupt Exception: ctrl+c to exit>
```

> **Note!**
> An infinite loop executes a block of statements infinitely if the expression of a loop never evaluates.

2.14 FUNCTIONS

Functions are named blocks of code designed to do one specific job. It allows us to write a code once and then run it whenever we need to accomplish the same task. It accepts the required information, and returns the generated/processed information. Thus, it makes our programs easier to write, read, test, and fix, when used effectively.

The first line of a function is its definition, marked by the keyword `def`. The name of the function is followed by a set of parentheses and a colon. A string, in triple quotes, describes what the function does. The body of a function is indented one level.

To call a function, give the name of the function followed by a set of parentheses.

> **Note!**
> A function is a block of statements used to perform a single, specific, and well-defined task.

Example 2.99 Making a function

```
def greet_user():
    """Display a simple greeting."""
    print("Hello from the greet function!")

greet_user()
```

Output

```
Hello from the greet function!
```

Example 2.100 Passing a single argument

Information that is passed to a function is called an argument; information that is received by a function is called a parameter. Arguments are included in parentheses after the function's name, and parameters are listed in parentheses in the function's definition.

```
def greet_user(username):
    """Display a simple greeting."""
    print("Hello, " + username + "!")

greet_user('Raunak')
greet_user('Biyas')
greet_user('Moumita')
```

Output

```
Hello, Raunak!
Hello, Biyas!
Hello, Moumita!
```

Example 2.101 Using positional arguments

```
def describe_pet(animal, name):
    """Display information about a pet."""
    print("\nI have a " + animal + ".")
    print("Its name is " + name + ".")

describe_pet('cat', 'pussy')
describe_pet('dog', 'kit')
```

Output

```
I have a cat.
Its name is pussy.

I have a dog.
Its name is kit.
```

> **Note!**
> The word before the parentheses specifies the function name. Comma-separated variables or values within the parentheses are parameters.

Example 2.102 Using keyword arguments

```
def describe_pet(animal, name):
    """Display information about a pet."""
    print("\nI have a " + animal + ".")
    print("Its name is " + name + ".")

describe_pet(animal='cat', name='pussy ')
describe_pet(name='kit', animal='dog')
```

Output

```
I have a cat.
Its name is pussy.

I have a dog.
Its name is kit.
```

> **Note!**
> For the required arguments, the number and order of the arguments should match with the number and order of the parameter used during function definition.

Example 2.103 Using a default value

We can provide a default value for a parameter. When a function call omits this argument, the default value will be used. Parameters with default values must be listed after parameters without default values in the function's definition. So, positional arguments can still work correctly.

```
def describe_pet(name, animal='dog'):
    """Display information about a pet."""
    print("\nI have a " + animal + ".")
    print("Its name is " + name + ".")
describe_pet('pussy', 'cat')
describe_pet('kit')
```

Output

```
I have a cat.
Its name is pussy.

I have a dog.
Its name is kit.
```

> ***Note!***
> We have to assign default value from the right side of the parameters. We can't assign default value to a parameter to the left side of another parameter, which is not assigned a default value.

Example 2.104 Using None to make an argument optional

```
def describe_pet(animal, name=None):
    """Display information about a pet."""
    print("\nI have a " + animal + ".")
    if name:
        print("Its name is " + name + ".")

describe_pet('cat', 'pussy')
describe_pet('snake')
```

Output

```
I have a cat.
Its name is pussy.

I have a snake.
```

Example 2.105 Returning a single value

A function can return a value or a set of values. When a function returns a value, the calling line must provide a variable in which to store the returned value. A function stops running when it reaches a `return` statement.

```
def get_full_name(first, last):
    """Return a neatly formatted full name."""
    full_name = first + ' ' + last
    return full_name.title()

musician = get_full_name('Lata', 'Mangeskar')
print(musician)
```

Output

```
Lata Mangeskar
```

Example 2.106 Returning a dictionary

```
def build_person(first, last):
    """Return a dictionary of informationabout a person."""
    person = {'first': first, 'last': last}
    return person

cricketer = build_person('Sourav', 'Ganguly')
print(cricketer)
```

Output

```
{'first': 'Sourav', 'last': 'Ganguly'}
```

Example 2.107 Returning a dictionary with optional values

```
def build_person(first, last, age=None):
    """Return a dictionary of informationabout a person."""
    person = {'first': first, 'last': last}
    if age:
       person['age'] = age
```

Output

```
{'first': 'Kishor', 'last': 'Kumar', 'age': 54}
None
```

Example 2.108 Passing a list as an argument

We can pass a list as an argument to a function, and the function can work with the values in the list. Any changes the function makes to the list will affect the original list. We can prevent a function from modifying a list by passing a copy of the list as an argument.

```
def greet_users(names):
       """Print a simple greeting to everyone."""

       for name in names:
               msg = "Hello, " + name + "!"
               print(msg)

usernames = ['Raunak', 'Biyas', 'Rangan']
greet_users(usernames)
```

Output

```
Hello, Raunak!
Hello, Biyas!
Hello, Rangan!
```

Example 2.109 Allowing a function to modify a list

The following example sends a list of models to a function for printing. The original list is emptied, and the second list is filled.

```
def print_models(unprinted, printed):
        """3d print a set of models."""
        while unprinted:
                current_model = unprinted.pop()
                print("Printing " + current_model)
                printed.append(current_model)

# Store some unprinted designs, and print each of them.
unprinted = ['nose pin', 'bracelet', 'ring']
printed = []
print_models (unprinted, printed)

print("\nUnprinted:", unprinted)
print("Printed:", printed)
```

Output

```
Printing ring
Printing bracelet
Printing nose pin

Unprinted: []
Printed: ['ring', 'bracelet', 'nose pin']
```

> ***Note!***
> It is optional to use the formal arguments along with non-key arguments in the function definition and vice-versa.

Variables defined outside a function body are accessible from any position of the program and have a global scope. This means that local variables defined inside the function can be accessed only inside the function, whereas global variables can be accessed throughout the program body by all functions. When a function is called, the variables declared inside it are brought into the scope of the program body.

2.15 MODULES

The module is used to break down large programs into small, manageable ones. It is a Python file that contains Python statements and definitions. We can group related codes into a module to make the program easier to understand and use. A module can define functions, classes, and variables. A module can also include executable codes. There are a large number of built-in modules in Python.

We can store some functions in a separate file called a module, and then import the functions we need into the file containing the main program. This allows for cleaner program files. (We have to make sure our module is stored in the same directory as our main program.)

Example 2.110 Defining module

```
# calculator.py

def addition(a,b):
    c = a + b
    return c

def subtraction(a,b):
    c = a - b
    return c

def multiplication(a,b):
    c = a * b
    return c

def division(a,b):
    c = a / b
    return c
```

Output

```
The module file calculator.py is to be stored
in the folder as the file importing it.
```

> ***Note!***
> We can use a single module for various functionalities.

Example 2.111 Importing and working with modules

```
import calculator
s = calculator.addition(14, 15)
print(s)
m = calculator.multiplication(9,5)
print(m)
```

Output

```
29
45
```

> ***Note!***
> The import statement will import all the functionalities of the module.

Example 2.112 Importing with prior knowledge

If we do not have prior knowledge of the requirement of the attributes in a program, it is better to import all the functionalities of the module. All the attributes are imported into the current namespace using the `from-import *` statement.

```
from calculator import subtraction, multiplication
st = calculator.subtraction(19,5)
print(st)
mu = calculator.multiplication(19,5)
print(mu)
```

> **Note!**
> The `from-import` statement imports the specific function from the module. If we try to use other functions of the module it will show an error message.

Output

```
14
95
```

Example 2.113 Module aliasing

```
import calculator as cal
aa = cal.addition(40,5)
print(aa)
di = cal.division(48,8)
print(di)
```

> **Note!**
> A module can also be imported to the current namespace with its alias name.

Output

```
45
6
```

Example 2.114 Member aliasing

```
from calculator import addition as add, division as div
aa = add(300,50)
print(aa)
dd = div(24,8)
print(dd)
```

> **Note!**
> Attributes of a module can also be imported to the current namespace with its alias name.

Output

```
350
3.0
```

Example 2.115 Built-in Math module

```
import math
cc = math.ceil(4.3)
ccc = math.ceil(6)
print(cc)
print(ccc)
```

Output

```
5
6
```

Example 2.116 **Storing a function in a module (user-defined)**

```
#pizza.py
def make_pizza(size, *toppings):
    """Make a pizza."""
    print("\nMaking a " + size + " pizza.")
    print("Toppings:")
    for topping in toppings:
        print("- " + topping)
```

Output

<This file is to be stored in the python root folder or the folder where the following code file is to stored>

Example 2.117 **Importing an entire user-defined module**

```
# making_pizza.py
import pizza
pizza.make_pizza('medium', 'butter')
pizza.make_pizza('small', 'choice1', 'orange')
```

Output

```
Making a medium pizza.
Toppings:
- butter

Making a small pizza.
Toppings:
- choice1
- orange
```

Example 2.118 **Importing all functions from a module**

```
from pizza import *
pizza.make_pizza('medium', 'butter')
pizza.make_pizza('small', 'choice1', 'orange')
```

Output

```
Making a medium pizza.
Toppings:
- butter

Making a small pizza.
Toppings:
- choice1
- orange
```

> ***Note!***
> Besides user-defined modules, Python offers a number of built-in modules for different functionalities like mathematical and statistical operations.

2.16 PACKAGES

A package is a hierarchical file directory structure that defines a single Python application environment consisting of modules and sub-packages etc. We can manage a project easily by placing the same types of modules in one package and different types of modules in different packages. A package can have sub-packages and modules similar to a directory having sub-directory. A directory must contain a file named _init_.py to be considered as a package. This file can be kept empty but the initialization code is normally placed.

> **Note!**
> The Python Package Index (PyPI) is a repository of software for the Python programming language. We can download Python packages from this repository in the Internet.

Package Composition

We have to create a directory with the name of the package to compose our package including different functions with different functionalities. We have to store all the functions or a single function with different functionalities, in the directory. To make all of our functions available when we are importing the package, we need to place explicit import statements in _init_.py.

Example 2.119 Storing a function in a package (user-defined)

Consider the file myfunc.py is available in 'devices' directory. The file has the following line of code.

```
# myfunc.py (save this file in the 'devices' folder/directory)
def pc():
    myList = ['8GB RAM','2TB Hard Disk']
    print('The configuration of PC')
    for model in myList:
        print('\t%s ' % model)

def laptop():
    myList = ['2GB RAM', '1TB Hard Disk']
    print('The configuration of Laptop')
    for model in myList:
        print('\t%s ' % model)

def smartphone():
    myList = ['4GB RAM','128GB Hard Disk']
    print('The configuration of Smartphone')
    for model in myList:
        print('\t%s ' % model)
```

Example 2.120 Importing an entire user-defined package

To make all of our functions available when we are importing the 'devices' package, we need to place explicit import statements in _init_.py as follows:

```
from myfunc import *
```

After adding these lines to _init_.py, we have all these functions available when we import the devices package.

```
# testPackage.py (save this file in the folder/directory
# where 'devices' is saved
from device import myfunc
myfunc.pc()
myfunc.laptop()
myfunc.smartphone()
```

Output

```
The configuration of PC
     8GB RAM
     2TB Hard Disk
The configuration of Laptop
     2GB RAM
     1TB Hard Disk
The configuration of Smart Phone
     4GB RAM
     128GB Hard Disk
```

> ***Note!***
> The `from-import` statement will import the specific modules from the package.

PIP Package Manager

PIP is a package manager for Python packages or modules. If we do not have PIP installed, we can download and install it using the following method.

Example 2.121 Installing PIP

If Python is correctly installed, we can proceed to install PIP using the following steps in Windows OS. If PIP is not installed properly during Python installation:

- Download get-pip.py to a folder on our computer from https://bootstrap.pypa.io/ get-pip.py.
- Open a command prompt and navigate to the folder containing get-pip.py.
- Run the following command:

```
python get-pip.py
```

- PIP is now installed!

We can verify that PIP was installed correctly by opening a command prompt and entering the following command:

```
pip -V
```

> ***Note!***
> We can download and install PIP from the following page: https://pypi.org/project/pip/

Output

```
pip 18.0 from c:\users\AD\appdata\local\programs\python\python37\lib\
site-packages\pip (python 3.7)
```

Example 2.122 Using PIP Package manager for installing external packages

PIP is one of the best tools to install and manage Python packages. If we want to work with database MySQL using Python, 'pymysql' is one of the packages that can help us to do so. For example, we can execute the following code to start working with MySQL with Python.

```
import pymysql
```

Output

If the following message appears, it indicates that pymysql is not installed properly:

```
Traceback (most recent call last):
  File "<pyshell#0>", line 1, in <module>
    import pymysql
ImportError: No module named 'pymysql'
```

> **Note!**
> The `from-import *` statement is used to import all modules of a library.

We have to use the following command in the command prompt to install pymysql in the machine:

```
pip install pymysql
```

Now we can work with the 'import pymysql' Python command if the pip command has installed the external package 'pymysql' using the Internet connection available to the machine.

2.17 FILES

Python programs can read information from a file, and they can write data to files. Reading from files allows us to work with a wide variety of information; writing to files allows us to pick up where we left off the next time we run the program. We can write text to files, and we can store Python structures such as lists in data files.

Exceptions are special objects that help our programs respond to errors appropriately. For example, if our program tries to open a file that does not exist, we can use exceptions to display an informative error message instead of having the program crash.

> **Note!**
> File pointer specifies the position in the file where writing or reading take place.

Example 2.123 Reading an entire file at once

```
filename = 'myFile.txt'
with open(filename) as f_obj:
     contents = f_obj.read()
print(contents)
```

Output

```
<Content of the text file myFile.txt will be printed>
```

Example 2.124 Reading line by line

```
filename = 'myFile.txt'
with open(filename) as  f_obj:
    for line in f_obj:
print(line.rstrip())
```

Output

```
<Content of the text file myFile.txt will be printed line by line>
```

Example 2.125 Storing the lines in a list

```
filename = 'myFile.txt'
with open(filename) as f_obj:
    lines = f_obj.readlines()
for line in lines:
    print(line.rstrip())
```

Output

```
<Content of the text file myFile.txt will be printed line by line>
```

Example 2.126 Writing to an empty file

Passing the 'w' argument to `open()` tells Python that we want to write something to the file. Be careful; this will erase the contents of the file if it already exists. Passing the 'a' argument tells Python we want to append to the end of an existing file.

```
filename = 'myFile.txt'
with open(filename, 'w') as f:
    f.write("I love programming!")
```

Output

```
Content of myFile.txt'>>>I love programming!
```

> ***Note!***
> Access mode is an optional parameter and the default file access mode is read.

Example 2.127 Writing multiple lines to an empty file

```
filename = 'myFile.txt'

with open(filename, 'w') as f:
    f.write("I love programming!\n")
    f.write("I love creating new games.\n")
```

Output

```
Content of myFile.txt'>>>
I love programming!
I love creating new games.
```

Example 2.128 Appending to a file

```
filename = 'programming.txt'

with open(filename, 'a') as f:
    f.write("I also love working with data.\n")
    f.write("I love making applications as well.\n")
```

Output

```
Content of myFile.txt'>>>
I love programming!
I love creating new games.
I also love working with data.
I love making applications as well.
```

Example 2.129 Opening a file from a sub-folder in Windows

```
f_path = "C:\AD\Python\books\myFile.txt"
with open(f_path) as f_obj:
    lines = f_obj.readlines()
print(lines)
```

> ***Note!***
> The `close()` method automatically flushes the data but we can use `flush()` method if we want to flush the data before closing it.

Output

```
Content (lines) of myFile.txt will be printed in the console.
```

Table 2.11 Other methods for file manipulation

Methods	Description
`fileno()`	Returns the integer file descriptor that is used by the underlying implementation to request I/O operations from the operating system.
`isatty()`	Returns True if the file is connected to a tty(-like) device, else False.
`next(file)`	Returns the next line from the file, each time it is being called.
`truncate([size])`	Truncates the file's size. If the optional size argument is present, the file is truncated to (at most) that size.
`flush()`	Flush the internal buffer, like stdio's flush. It has no return value.

2.18 EXCEPTIONS

When we think an error may occur, we can write a `try-except` block to handle the exception that might be raised. The `try` block tells Python to try running some code, and the `except` block tells Python what to do if the code results in a particular kind of error.

> ***Note!***
> The mistake that leads to unexpected result or termination of the program execution is an error or bug. Exceptions are raised when an external event changes the normal flow of a program.

Example 2.130 Handling the ZeroDivisionError exception

```
try:
    print(5/0)
except ZeroDivisionError:
   print("You can't divide by zero!")
```

> **Note!**
> Runtime errors are a problem that was not detected when the program is parsed, but is only uncovered when a particular line is executed.

Output

```
You can't divide by zero!
```

Example 2.131 Handling the FileNotFoundError exception

```
f_name = 'myFile.txt'
try:
    with open(f_name) as f_obj:
        lines = f_obj.readlines()
except FileNotFoundError:
    msg = "Can't find file {0}.".format(f_name)
    print(msg)
```

Output

If the file does not exist the following message will be displayed:

```
Can't find file myFile.txt.
```

Example 2.132 Using an `else` block

The `try` block should only contain a code that may cause an error. Any code that depends on the `try` block running successfully should be placed in the `else` block.

```
print("Enter two numbers. I'll divide them.")

x = input("First number: ")
y = input("Second number: ")

try:
    result = int(x) / int(y)
except ZeroDivisionError:
    print("You can't divide by zero!")
else:
    print(result)
```

Output

```
Enter two numbers. I'll divide them.
First number: 5
Second number: 0
You can't divide by zero!
```

> **Note!**
> All the exceptions are subclasses of the `Exception` class. It is optional to use `else` clause with `try` and `except` clause.

Example 2.133 Avoid bare except blocks

Exception-handling code should catch specific exceptions that we expect to happen during our program's execution. A `bare except` block will catch all exceptions, including keyboard interrupts and system exits we might need when forcing a program to close.

If we want to use a `try` block and we are not sure which exception to catch, use `exception`. It will catch most exceptions, but still, allow us to interrupt programs intentionally.

```
try:
    # Do something
except:
    pass
```

Example 2.134 Printing the exception

```
try:
    # Instructions to execute
except Exception as e:
    print(e, type(e))
```

Note!
The use of `else` and `finally` clauses with `try-except` block are optional.

2.19 CLASSES AND OBJECTS

Classes are the foundation of object-oriented programming (OOP). Classes represent real-world things we want to model in our programs: for example, cars, dogs, and robots. We use a class to make objects, which are specific instances of cars, dogs, and robots. A class defines the general behavior that a whole category of objects can have, and the information that can be associated with those objects. OOP has the following three essential properties.

- **Abstraction:** We can declare abstract classes in Python as OOPs properties.
- **Encapsulation:** Classes are used to encapsulate (hide) data and methods in OOP.
- **Inheritance**: Classes can inherit from each other – we can write a class that extends the functionality of an existing class. This allows us to code efficiently for a wide variety of situations.
- **Polymorphism:** We can override (using same name for different tasks) functions and operators in OOP.

Class Abstraction

Example 2.135 Abstract classes and methods

We have to import the module to declare an abstract class.

```
from myClass from BaseClass
class abstractClass(BaseClass):
    ''' abstract methods '''
```

Note!
The abstraction helps us in creating a general idea of what a problem is and how to solve it by removing all irrelevant details and patterns.

Data Encapsulation Using Class and Object

Example 2.136 Creating and using a class

Consider how we might model a car. What information would we associate with a car, and what behavior would it have? The information is stored in variables called attributes, and the behavior is represented by functions. Functions that are part of a class are called methods.

```
class Car():
    """A simple attempt to model a car."""

    def __init__(self, make, model, year):
        """Initialize car attributes."""
        self.make = make
        self.model = model
        self.year = year

        # Fuel capacity and level in gallons.
        self.fuel_capacity = 15
        self.fuel_level = 0

    def fill_tank(self):
        """Fill gas tank to capacity."""
        self.fuel_level = self.fuel_capacity
        print("Fuel tank is full.")

    def drive(self):
        """Simulate driving."""
        print("The car is moving.")
```

Output

```
<No output generated since the class is just defined here.>
```

Example 2.137 Creating an object from the class

```
myCar = Car('Suzuki', 'Swift-Dzire', 2020)
```

Output

```
<No output generated since the object is just created with 3 proper-
ties here without any display functions.>
```

Example 2.138 Accessing attribute values

```
print(myCar.make)
print(myCar.model)
print(myCar.year)
```

Output

```
Suzuki
Swift-Dzire
2020
```

Example 2.139 Calling methods

```
myCar.fill_tank()
myCar.drive()
```

Output

```
Fuel tank is full.
The car is moving.
```

Example 2.140 Creating multiple objects

```
myCar = Car('Audi', 'A4', 2019)
myOldCar = Car('Hyundai', 'City', 2020)
myTruck =Car('Toyota', 'Tacoma', 2020)
```

Output

<No output generated since the new objects are just created with 3 attributes here without any display functions.>

Example 2.141 Modifying an attribute directly

```
myNewCar = Car('Audi', 'A4', 2019)
myNewCar.fuel_level = 6
```

Output

<No output generated since a new object is just created with 3 properties and one attribute is modified here without any display function.>

Example 2.142 Writing a method to update an attribute's value

```
def update_fuel_level(self, new_level):
    """Update the fuel level."""
    if new_level<= self.fuel_capacity:
        self.fuel_level = new_level
    else:
        print("The tank can't hold that much!")
```

Output

<No output since the method is only declared but not called for execution>

Example 2.143 Writing a method to increment an attribute's value

```
def add_fuel(self, amount):
    """ Add fuel to the tank. """
    if (self.fuel_level + amount <= self.fuel_capacity):
        self.fuel_level += amount
        print("Added fuel.")
    else:
        print("The tank won't hold that much.")
```

Output

<No output since the method is only declared but not called for execution>

Class Inheritance

If the class we are writing is a specialized version of another class, we can use inheritance. When one class inherits from another, it automatically takes on all the attributes and methods of the parent class. The child class is free to introduce new attributes and methods and override the attributes and methods of the parent class. To inherit from another class, we have to include the name of the parent class in parentheses when defining the new class.

Example 2.144 The `__init__()` method for a child class

```
class eCar(Car):
      """ A simple model of an electric car. """
      def __init__(self, make, model, year):
            """ Initialize an electric car. """
            super().__init__(make, model, year )

            # Attributes specific to electric cars.
            # Battery capacity in kWh.
            self.battery_size = 90
            # Charge level in %.
            self.charge_level = 0
```

Output

<No output since only the new inherited class is created here.>

Example 2.145 Adding new methods to the child class

```
     """-- snip from 136 —"""
     """-- snip from 144 —"""
class eCar(Car):
    def charge(self):
         """Fully charge the vehicle."""
         self.charge_level = 110
         print("The vehicle is fully charged.")
```

Output

```
<No output since only the new child class is created here.>
```

Example 2.146 **Using child methods and parent methods**

```
my_eCar = eCar('BMW', 'models', 2020)
my_eCar.charge()
my_eCar.drive()
```

Output

```
The vehicle is fully charged.
The car is moving.
```

Polymorphism Using Overriding Methods

The polymorphism property of object-oriented programming allows us to override parent class methods in a derived class. If we want different functionality of a parent class method, we can override the method in the derived class.

Example 2.147 **Overriding parent methods**

```
class eCar(Car):
     """-- snipfrom 136 --"""
     def fill_tank(self):
          """Display an error message."""
          print("This car has no fuel tank!")

my_eCar = eCar('BMW', 'models', 2020)
my_eCar.fill_tank()
```

Output

```
This car has no fuel tank!
```

Example 2.148 **Overriding operators ('+' operator)**

```
class Vector():
   def __init__(self, a, b):
         self.a = a
         self.b = b
   def __str__(self):
         return 'Vector (%d, %d)' % (self.a, self.b)
   def __add__(self, other):
         return Vector(self.a + other.a, self.b + other.b)

V1 = Vector(7, 8)
V2 = Vector(9, -3)
print(V1 + V2)
```

Output

```
Vector (16, 5)
```

> **Note!**
> We can also override operators used in Python.

Example 2.149 **Instances as attributes**

A class can have objects as attributes. This allows classes to work together to model complex situations.

```
class Battery():
      """A battery for an electric car."""

      def __init__(self, size=70):
            """Initialize battery attributes."""
            # Capacity in kWh, charge level in %.
            self.size = size
            self.charge_level = 0

      def get_range(self):
            """Return the battery's range."""
            if self.size == 70:
                  return 250
            elif self.size == 85:
                  return 290
```

Output

```
<No output generated since the class Battery is just defined here.>
```

Example 2.150 **Using an instance as an attribute**

```
   """ -- snip from 136 -- """
   """ -- snip from 144 -- """
   """ -- snip from 149 -- """

class eCar(Car):
        def __init__(self, make, model, year):
            """ Initialize an electric car. """
            super().__init__(make, model, year)
            # Attribute specific to electric cars.
           self.battery = Battery() # instances as an attributes

        def charge(self):
            """Fully charge the vehicle."""
            self.battery.charge_level = 100
            print("The vehicle is fully charged.")
```

Output

```
<No output generated since the class eCar is just defined here with an
instance as an attribute.>
```

Example 2.151 **Using the instance**

```
    """-- snip from 150 --"""
my_eCar = eCar('BMW', 'Model x', 2020)
my_eCar.charge()
print(my_eCar.battery.get_range())
my_eCar.drive()
```

Output

```
The vehicle is fully charged.
250
The car is moving.
```

Example 2.152 **Storing classes in a file before importing classes**

Class files can get long as you add detailed information and functionality. To help keep your program files uncluttered, you can store your classes in modules and import the classes you need into your main program.

```
# car.py
"""Represent gas and electric cars."""
class Car():
    """A simple attempt to model a car."""
    --snip–

class Battery():
    """A battery for an electric car."""
    --snip--

class eCar(Car):
    """A simple model of an electric car."""
    --snip--
```

Example 2.153 **Importing individual classes from a module**

```
# myCars.py
from car import Car, eCar

myBeetle = Car('Volkswagen', 'Beetle', 2019)
myBeetle.fill_tank()
myBeetle.drive()

myBMW = eCar('BMW', 'Model 1',  2020)
myBMW.charge()
myBMW.drive()
```

Output

```
Fuel tank is full.
The car is moving.
The vehicle is fully charged.
The car is moving.
```

Example 2.154 Importing an entire module

```
import car

myBeetle = car.Car('Volkswagen', 'Beetle', 2019)
myBeetle.fill_tank()
myBeetle.drive()

myBMW = car.eCar('BMW', 'Model X', 2020)
myBMW.charge()
myBMW.drive()
```

Output

```
Fuel tank is full.
The car is moving.
The vehicle is fully charged.
The car is moving.
```

2.20 FUNCTIONAL PROGRAMMING IN PYTHON

A problem can be decomposed into a set of functions using functional programming, especially in Python language. The `filter()`, `map()` and `reduce()` functions are often used as tools for functional programming in Python. It may be noted that the use of list comprehensions may be recommended in many cases instead of the use of these functions.

> ***Note!***
> List comprehension, `filter()`, `map()`, and `reduce()` are used to implement functional programming in Python.

Example 2.155 `filter()` Function

This function constrains a list from those elements for which a function returns True.

```
def chk(x):
  if(x%2 ==0 or x%3 == 0):
    return 1

elements = list(filter(chk, range(2, 20)))
print(elements)
```

Output

```
[2, 3, 4, 6, 8, 9, 10, 12, 14, 15, 16, 18]
```

> ***Programming Tips!***
> Adding or removing elements during iteration should not be performed.

Example 2.156 `map()` Function

`map()` function calls the function for each item in the sequence and returns a list of values.

```
def sqr(x):
    return x*x

myList = [1, 2, 3, 4, 5]
newList = list(map(sqr, myList))
print('Original list: ' , myList)
print('Modified list: ' , newList)
```

Output

```
Original list:   [1, 2, 3, 4, 5]
Modified list:  [1, 4, 9, 16, 25]
```

> **Note!**
> We can pass more than one sequence in the `map()` function.

Example 2.157 `reduce()` Function

`reduce()` function returns a single value with the first two elements of the sequence, then returns a value with the result and the next element, and so on.

```
import functools
def multi(x, y):
    return x*y

myList = [1, 2, 3, 4, 5]
result = functools.reduce(multi, myList)
print('Original list: ' , myList)
print('Multiplied list: ' , result)
```

Output

```
Original list:  [1, 2, 3, 4, 5]
Multiplied list:  120
```

> **Programming Tips!**
> If there is a single element in the sequence, it is returned. An exception is returned if the sequence is empty.

2.21 NUMPY ARRAY IN PYTHON

The Numpy (**Numerical Python**) is an open-source Python library used for scientific computation on multi-dimensional arrays and matrices. Besides its scientific uses, numpy library can also be used as an efficient multi-dimensional container (called *n*-dimensional array or ndarray object) of data. Using numpy, we can also perform mathematical and logical operations on arrays.

We can directly install the latest version of numpy library by connecting the device to the Internet and running the following commands on the terminal:

> **Note!**
> ndarray is the main object to deal with multi-dimensional homogeneous array with predetermined (fixed) items.

```
python -m pip install numpy
```

We can import numpy library using any of the following commands:

```
import numpy
import numpy as np
from numpy import *
```

Numpy supports a much greater variety of numerical types than Python does, like bool, complex, complex128, complex64, float, float16, float32, float64, int, int16, Int32, Int64, int8, intc, intp, uint16, uInt32, uInt64, and uint8. Numpy provides different functions, which are used to create arrays. Table 2.12 shows array creation functions defined in numpy.

Note!
We can specify the version of the Numpy library to install a specific version.

Table 2.12 Numpy functions for array creation

Functions	Description
`array()`	Returns an ndarray object from any object exposing array interface, or from any method that returns an array.
`arange()`	Returns an ndarray object containing evenly spaced values within a given range using the specified step size.
`copy()`	Return an array copy of the given object.
`empty()`	Returns an uninitialized array of specified shape and type.
`eye()`	Returns a 2-D array with ones on the diagonal and zeros elsewhere.
`zeros()`	Returns a new array of specified size, filled with zeros.
`identity()`	Returns the identity array.
`linspace()`	Returns an ndarray object containing evenly spaced values within a given range using the specified number of elements in the range.
`logspace()`	Returns an ndarray object that contains the numbers that are evenly spaced on a log scale.
`ones()`	Returns an array of specified size and type, filled with ones.
`reshape()`	Returns a new array by reshaping a given array. The number of elements of the new array should be the same as the given array.

The following examples show how to deal with numpy array:

Example 2.158 Creating an array with start, end and interval

```
import numpy as np
b = np.arange(1, 20, 4)
print(b)
```

Output

```
[ 1,   5,  9,  13,  17]
```

Example 2.159 Creating an identity matrix with 2D array

```
import numpy as np
b = np.identity(3)
print(b)
```

Output

```
[ [1.,  0.,  0.],
  [0.,  1.,  0.],
  [0.,  0.,  1.] ]
```

Example 2.160 Creating an ndarray with evenly spaced values within a given range

```
import numpy as np
b1 = np.linspace(0,  20,  11)
print(b1)
b2 = np.linspace(0,  20,  11,  dtype = int)
print(b2)
```

Output

```
[ 0. 2. 4. 6. 8. 10. 12. 14. 16. 18. 20.]
[ 0,   2,   4,   6,   8,  10,  12,  14,  16,  18,  20]
```

Example 2.161 Reshaping a 1D array into a 2D array

```
import numpy as np
a = np.arange(1,  20,  2)
print(a)
print(a.reshape(2,  5))
```

Output

```
[ 1  3  5  7  9 11 13 15 17 19]
[[ 1  3  5  7  9]
 [11 13 15 17 19]]
```

Example 2.162 Reshaping a 1D array into matrix form

```
import numpy as np
a = np.arange(1,  40,  2).reshape(5,  4)
```

Output

```
[ [ 1,   3,   5,   7],
[ 9,  11,  13,  15],
[17,  19,  21,  23],
[25,  27,  29,  31],
[33,  35,  37,  39]]
```

Example 2.163 **Accessing, summing and conditioning on ndarray object**

```
# Consider the last example ndarray definition
print(a[1][2]) # Output: 13
rowsum = a.sum(-1)
print(rowsum) # Output: array([16,    48,    80,   112,   144])
print(a[rowsum>48, :])
```

Output

```
array([[17,  19,  21,  23],
       [25,  27,  29,  31],
       [33,  35,  37,  39]])
```

An ndarray, thus created, has the properties such as ndarray.data (returns the buffer containing the actual), ndarray.dtype (returns an object describing the type of the elements), ndarray.itemsize (returns the size in bytes of each element), ndarray.ndim (returns the number of axes), ndarray.shape (returns the dimensions), and ndarray.size (returns the total number of elements).

Numpy supports a large number of functions for various mathematical and other operations. Table 2.13 provides the standard functions are that are available in the Numpy library:

> ***Note!***
> Trigonometric functions return trigonometric ratios for a given angle in radians.

Table 2.13 Functions for manipulating numpy arrays

Functions Types	Functions
Trigonometric	sin(), arccos(), arcsin(), arctan(), arctan2(), cos(), deg2rad, degrees(), hypot(), rad2deg(), radians(), tan(), unwrap()
Rounding	around(), ceil(), fix(), floor(), rint(), round(), trunc()
Exponents and logarithms	exp(), exp2(), expm1(), log(), log10(), log1p(), log2(), logaddexp(), logaddexp2()
Arithmetic operations	add(), divide(), divmod(), float_power(), floor_divide(), mod(), multiply(), negative(), positive(), power(), reciprocal(), remainder(), subtract(), true_divide()
Complex numbers handling	conj(), isreal()
Special functions	cbrt(), clip(), convolve(), fabs(), heaviside(), interp(), maximum(), minimum(), nan_to_num(), real_if_close(), sign(), sqrt(), square()

2.22 SERIES AND DATAFRAMES IN PANDAS

Pandas is an open-source Python library that provides easy-to-use data structure and data analysis tools. It was developed by Wes McKinney in 2008. It uses most of the functionalities of Numpy. The name

Pandas is taken from the words 'panel data' (multi-dimensional econometric data). We can perform five steps in the processing of data: load, prepare, manipulate, model, and analyze. Pandas provides a library to analyze data in the simplest possible way with all the instruments for data processing, data extraction and data manipulation. Pandas uses two new data structures instead of the existing data structures built into Python or provided by other libraries. These pandas data structures are designed to work with SQL relational data (or level data) and Excel spreadsheets.

We can directly install the latest version of numpy library by connecting the device to Internet and running the following commands on the terminal:

> **Note!**
> The primary focus of pandas library is to provide building blocks for the data analysis world.

```
pip install pandas
```

Pandas deals with two data structures as listed in Table 2.14.

Table 2.14 Pandas data structures

Data Structure	Dimensions	Explanation
Series	1	Labelled, homogeneous array, size-immutable.
DataFrame	2	Size-mutable, tabular structure, heterogeneous typed columns, labelled rows and columns.

2.22.1 Series

Series is a 1D labelled array capable of holding data of any type (integer, string, float, python objects, etc.). The axis labels are collectively called indexes. A pandas Series can be created using the following constructor:

> **Note!**
> Series and DataFrames are two primary data structures offered by pandas.

```
pandas.Series( data, index, dtype, copy)
```

Example 2.164 Creating series

```
import pandas as pd
import numpy as np
data = np.array([25,55,75])
s = pd.Series(data)
print(s)
```

Output

```
0     25
1     55
2     75
dtype: int32
```

Example 2.165 Creating series from dictionary

```
import pandas as pd
import numpy as np
data = {'abc' : 0., 'pqr' : 1., 'mno' : 2.}
s = pd.Series(data, index = ['pqr', 'mno', 'xyz', 'abc'])
print(s)
```

Output

```
pqr     1.0
mno     2.0
xyz     NaN
abc     0.0
dtype: float64
```

Example 2.166 Creating series from scalar and accessing data

```
import pandas as pd
s = pd.Series([1,2,3,4],index = ['a','b','c','d'])
print(s) # Displaying the series
print(s[:3])# Accessing the first three elements
print s['d']
```

Output

```
a    1
b    2
c    3
d    4
dtype: int64
a    1
b    2
c    3
dtype: int64
4
```

> ***Note!***
> Series is an object in pandas. It is also a 1D data structure similar to an array with some additional features.

2.22.2 DataFrame

A DataFrame is a 2D data structure, i.e., data is aligned in a tabular fashion in rows and columns. A pandas DataFrame can be created using the following constructor:

> ***Note!***
> DataFrame is tabular data structure very similar to a spreadsheet designed to extend series to manipulate dimensions.

```
pandas.DataFrame( data, index, columns, dtype, copy)
```

Example 2.167 Creating and displaying DataFrame

```
import pandas as pd
data = {'Name':['Atanu','Chandan','Raunak','Biyas'],'Age':[45, 44,
11, 13]}
df = pd.DataFrame(data, index = ['Roll-1', 'Roll-2', 'Roll-3',
'Roll-4'])
print(df)
```

Output

```
           Name  Age
Roll-1    Atanu   45
Roll-2  Chandan   44
Roll-3   Raunak   11
Roll-4    Biyas   13
```

Example 2.168 Creating DataFrame from dictionaries

```
import pandas as pd
data = {'Col-1' :pd.Series([1, 2, 3], index = ['x1', 'x2', 'x3']),
       'Col-2' :pd.Series([1, 2, 3, 4], index = ['x1', 'x2', 'x3',
'x4'])}
df = pd.DataFrame(data)
print(df)
```

Output

```
   Col-1  Col-2
x1   1.0      1
x2   2.0      2
x3   3.0      3
x4   NaN      4
```

Example 2.169 Addition of column in a DataFrame

```
import pandas as pd
data = {'Col-1' :pd.Series([1, 2, 3], index = ['x1', 'x2', 'x3']),
         'Col-2' :pd.Series([1, 2, 3, 4], index = ['x1', 'x2',
'x3', 'x4'])}
df = pd.DataFrame(data)

# Adding a new column to an existing DataFrame object with column
label by passing new series
print("Adding a new column by passing as Series:")
df['Col-3'] = pd.Series([11, 22, 33], index = ['x1', 'x2', 'x3'])
print(df)
```

```
print("Adding a new column using the existing columns in DataFrame:")
df['Col-4'] = df['Col-1'] + df['Col-3']
print(df)
```

Output

```
Adding a new column by passing as Series:
    Col-1  Col-2  Col-3
x1    1.0      1   11.0
x2    2.0      2   22.0
x3    3.0      3   33.0
x4    NaN      4    NaN
Adding a new column using the existing columns in DataFrame:
    Col-1  Col-2  Col-3  Col-4
x1    1.0      1   11.0   12.0
x2    2.0      2   22.0   24.0
x3    3.0      3   33.0   36.0
x4    NaN      4    NaN    NaN
```

Example 2.170 Deletion of column in a DataFrame using `del`

```
# Following statements to be added in the last example program
print("Deleting the first column using del command:")
del df['Col-1']
print(df)
```

Output

```
Deleting the first column using del command:
    Col-2  Col-3  Col-4
x1      1   11.0   12.0
x2      2   22.0   24.0
x3      3   33.0   36.0
x4      4    NaN    NaN
```

Example 2.171 Addition of rows in a DataFrame

```
import pandas as pd
df1 = pd.DataFrame([[11, 22], [33, 44]], columns = ['Col-1',
'Col-2'])
df2 = pd.DataFrame([[55, 66], [77, 88]], columns = ['Col-1',
'Col-2'])
df1 = df1.append(df2)
print(df1)
```

Output

```
   Col-1  Col-2
0     11     22
1     33     44
0     55     66
1     77     88
```

Example 2.172 Deletion of rows in a DataFrame

```
# Drop rows with label 0
df1 = df1.drop(0)
print(df1)
```

Output

```
   Col-1  Col-2
1     33     44
1     77     88
```

Example 2.173 Descriptive statistics with DataFrame

```
import pandas as pd
import numpy as np

# Creating a dictionary of series
data = {'Name': pd.Series(['Rohit', 'Rahul', 'Raunak', 'Sachin',
'Sourav', 'Gourab','Atanu', 'Chandan', 'Raj', 'Satyam', 'Partha',
'Ayush']),
'Age': pd.Series([16, 18, 20, 21, 19, 22, 23, 14, 27, 25, 23, 29]),
'Marks': pd.Series([89, 78, 92, 89, 81, 56, 75, 87, 88, 95, 76, 84]) }

# Creating a DataFrame
df = pd.DataFrame(data)
print(df.describe()) # Function computes a summary of statistics
```

Output

```
             Age      Marks
count  12.000000  12.000000
mean   21.416667  82.500000
std     4.378840  10.475079
min    14.000000  56.000000
25%    18.750000  77.500000
50%    21.500000  85.500000
75%    23.500000  89.000000
max    29.000000  95.000000
```

Note!

Pandas library is very useful for statistical analysis and decision-making.

QUICK RECAP

- ☑ Python is a simple, high-level, interactive, interpreted, and object-oriented scripting language developed by Guido van Rossum in the late 1980s.
- ☑ Python offers interesting features and advantages to work as a modern programming language and has presently captured the maximum market share.
- ☑ IDEs like IPython, Python IDLE, Jupyter Notebook, Jupyter Lab, Spyder, Google Colab, PyCharm etc. are in the market for Python program developments and interpretations.
- ☑ Python has specific identifiers, input–output methods, commenting styles, and keywords like other modern high-level languages. Indentation is used to indicate a code block unlike braces of other languages.
- ☑ Python supports primitive data types – integer, floating-point, Boolean, string, list, tuple, and dictionary.
- ☑ Python has different types of operators (arithmetic, relational, assignment, logical, bitwise, membership, identity, unary) and operators' precedence rule.
- ☑ List data type stores a mutable series of items in an order, and are accessed using an index. It can store homogeneous and heterogeneous items. Lambda functions are used when function objects are required for list comprehension.
- ☑ A set data type is an immutable collection of unique elements that are unordered and un-indexed.
- ☑ Tuples are similar to lists, but the items in a tuple are immutable.
- ☑ Dictionary data type stores connections between pieces of information where each item is a key-value pair.
- ☑ There are three conditional statements in Python: `if`, `else`, `elif`. Python does not support switch statements for multi-condition situation handling like other languages.
- ☑ Python offers `while` and `for` statements for iteration loops. Both these can be nested within themselves. Loop control statements `break`, `continue`, and `pass` are also used here for the purpose.
- ☑ Function is a block of statements used to perform a single, specific, and well-defined task. For the required arguments, the number and order of the arguments should match with the number and order of the parameter used during function definition.
- ☑ Module is a Python file that contains statements and definitions to break down large programs into small, manageable ones. Python provides many built-in modules besides user-defined modules.
- ☑ The `import` statement will import all the functionalities of the module even with an alias name for the same, along with its attributes.
- ☑ Package is a hierarchical file directory structure that defines a single Python application environment consisting of modules and sub-packages etc. PyPI is a repository of software for the Python language.
- ☑ PIP is a package manager for Python packages. It is primarily used for downloading and installing packages.
- ☑ Python programs can read information from a file, and they can write data to files.
- ☑ Even if a statement or expression is syntactically correct, it may cause an error when executed. Errors detected during execution are called exceptions. The use of `else`, and `finally` clauses with `try-except` block is optional for exception handling.
- ☑ Classes are the foundation of object-oriented programming. OOP has the four essential properties: abstraction, encapsulation, inheritance and polymorphism.
- ☑ A problem can be decomposed into a set of functions using functional programming, The `filter()`, `map()`, and

`reduce()` are used as tools for functional programming.

☑ Numpy is an open-source Python library used for scientific computation on multi-dimensional arrays and matrices.

☑ Pandas is an open-source Python library that provides easy-to-use data structure and data analysis tool. Series and DataFrames are two primary data structures offered by pandas.

☑ DataFrame is a tabular data structure very similar to a spreadsheet designed to extend series and manipulate dimensions.

REVIEW QUESTIONS

Multiple Choice Questions (MCQ): Choose the Best Alternative

Easy

1. What is the value of f(2000) for the function below?

```
def f(a):
    b = 0
    while a >= 1:
    (a, b) = (a/5, b+1)
    return(b)
```

A. 5 B. 6
C. 7 D. 4

2. Find $x(18) - x(10)$, given the definition of x below.

```
def x(n):
  sum = 0
  for i in range(2, n):
    if n%i == 0:
      sum = sum+i
  return(sum)
```

A. 14 B. 13
C. 31 D. 18

Hint: x(n) adds up the factors of n from 2 to n−1. x(18) = 2 + 3 + 6 + 9 = 20 and x(10) = 2 + 5 = 7, so the difference is 13.

3. Python supports:

A. Procedural programming
B. Object-oriented programming
C. Functional programming
D. All of these.

4. Python has the facility of:

A. Static typing
B. Dynamic typing
C. Both of these.
D. None of these.

5. What will be the output of the following Python instructions?

```
l=['x', 'y', 'z']
l += pq
l += 'pq'
print(l)
```

A. [xpq, ypq, zpq] B. ['x', 'y', 'z', 'p', 'q']
C. ['xpq', 'ypq', 'zpq'] D. [x, y, z, p, q]

6. When will the `else` part of `try-except-else` be executed?

A. When an exception occurs
B. When no exception occurs
C. When an exception occurs into except block
D. Always

Hint: The `else` part is executed when no exception occurs.

Moderate

7. Consider the following Python code:

```
a = [123, 'a', 10, 'b']
b = [1:]
c = b
d = a
b = b[0:]
b[1] = 20
a[2] = 30
```

After these execute, which of the following is correct?

A. a[2] = 30, c[1] = 10, d[2] = 30, b[1] = 20
B. a[2] = 30, c[1] = 20, d[2] = 30, b[1] = 20
C. a[2] = 30, c[1] = 10, d[2] = 10, b[1] = 20
D. a[2] = 30, c[1] = 20, d[2] = 10, [1] = 20

Hint: a[2] == 30, c[1] == 10, d[2] == 30, b[1] == 20

a and d are aliased but b and c are not, after the assignment b = b[0:]. So the update to a[2] affects d[2] while the update to b[1] leaves c[1] unchanged.

8. Consider the following function *f*:

```
def abc(x):
    if x == 1:
        return(1)
    else:
        return(x + abc(x-1))
```

Which of the following is correct?

A. The function always terminates with abc(x) = factorial of x
B. The function always terminates with abc(x) = 1 + 2 + ... + x
C. The function terminates for positive n with abc(x) = 1 + 2 + ... + x
D. The function terminates for positive n with abc(x) = factorial of x

Hint: The function terminates for positive n with abc(n) = 1 + 2 + ... + x.

9. How many '$' does this program output?

```
i = 10
while i > 0:
    i -= 5
    print('$')
    if i <= 3:
        break
    else:
        print('$')
```

A. 5 B. 3
C. 10 D. 2

10. Select the correct way to access the value of a Physics subject:

```
myDict = {
    "class":{
        "student":{
            "name":"Raunak",
            "marks":{
                "Math":95,
                "Physics":93
            }
        }
    }
}
```

A. myDict['class']['student']['marks'][1]
B. myDict['class']['student']['marks']['Physics']
C. myDict['class'][0]['marks']['Physics']
D. None of these.

11. Which of the following methods begin and end with two underscore characters?

A. In-built methods
B. User-defined methods
C. Additional methods
D. Special methods

Hint: Special methods like __init__ begin and end with two underscore characters.

Higher-Order Thinking Skills (HOTS)

12. What is the value of 'a' after the following lines are executed?

```
def abc(x):
    x = x[0:5]
    return()
    a = [44,71,12,8,23,17,16]
abc(a)
```

A. [44, 71, 12, 8, 23, 17, 16]
B. [71, 41, 12, 8, 23, 17, 16]
C. [44, 71, 22, 8, 12, 17, 16]
D. [16, 71, 12, 8, 23, 17, 44]

Hint: Since x is reassigned a value within the function, it refers to a new value and the update does not affect the value of 'a' outside the function. [44, 71, 12, 8, 23, 17, 16]

13. Suppose *a* and *b* both denote sets in Python. Under what condition can we guarantee that $a - (b - a) == a$?

A. The sets *a* and *b* should be disjoint.
B. The set *a* should be a subset of the set *b*.
C. This is true for any *a* and *b*.
D. The set *b* should be a subset of the set *a*

Hint: $b - a$ has no elements from *a*, so $a - (b - a)$ removes nothing from a and is hence always equal to *a*.

14. What is the value of this expression 2**3**2**1?

A. 8 B. 164
C. 256 D. 512

15. What is the output of the following Python instructions?

```
l = [-1, 3]
m = map(lambda y:y*2, l)
print(m)
```

A. [–2, 6]
B. Address of m
C. Error
D. –8

Hint: The code returns the address of m. Had we used the statement: `print(list(m))`, the output would have been: [–2, 6].

16. Numpy stands for?
A. Numbering Python
B. Number in Python
C. Numerical Python
D. None of these.

17. The most important object defined in Numpy is an *N*-dimensional array type called?
A. narray B. ndarray
C. nd_array D. darray

18. Pandas key data structure is called?
A. Statistics B. Econometrics
C. Keyframe D. DataFrame

19. Which of the following statements is false?
A. ndarray.dataitemSize is the buffer with the actual elements of the array.
B. ndarray is also known as the axis array.
C. In Numpy, dimensions are called axes.
D. Numpy main object is the homogeneous multi-dimensional array.

Hint: ndarray is also known as the "alias array".

20. Which of the following is the correct feature of DataFrame?
A. Labeled axes (rows and columns)
B. Potentially columns are of different types
C. Can perform arithmetic operations on rows and columns
D. All of these.

Short Answer-type and Descriptive-type Questions

Easy

1. Write the features of Python programming language.
2. What are the advantages of Python language?
3. Write the names of some IDEs for Python programming.
4. Describe the role of indentation in Python.
5. Write the different ways of writing comments in Python.
6. What are primitive data types in Python?
7. Compare list and tuple in Python.
8. Distinguish between set and list data types in Python.
9. What is a dictionary datatype in Python?
10. Which built-in methods are used to update a list datatype?
11. What is variable aliasing?
12. What are the conditional statements used in Python?
13. How to define and import a module in Python?
14. How to install a Python library?
15. What is an exception? Why is it occurring?
16. What is OOP?
17. What is tabular data structure?

Moderate

18. Can Python programs be platform independent?
19. Write the use of quotation signs in the Python program. Give examples.
20. How are multiline statements written in Python?
21. Distinguish between `elif` and `else` statements.
22. Distinguish between command line programming and scripting of Python.
23. Give an example of using IS operator in Python
24. What do understand by operators' precedence?
25. Compare the different ways of removing elements from a list.
26. What is functional programming?
27. Compare the use of `while` and `for` statements as iteration loops in Python.
28. Explain the different ways of passing arguments to a Python function.
29. What is member aliasing in Python?
30. Compare abstraction and encapsulation in Python OOP.
31. Explain the use of `map()`, `reduce()` and `filter()` in Python functional programming.
32. Write the roles of Numpy library in array processing in Python.
33. What is dataframe? How to deal with dataframe data structure in Python?

Higher-Order Thinking Skills (HOTS)

34. Write the advantages of IPython? What are the benefits and drawbacks Google Collab for Python scripting?
35. Compare between terminal and file I/O with examples codes.
36. Write the use of IN membership operator in Python.
37. Write the different ways of importing a library in a Python program. Compare their relative advantages.
38. Distinguish between `remove()` and `pop()` methods in Python.
39. What do you understand by list comprehension? Give examples.
40. Write the use of lambda function for list comprehension in Python.
41. Compare object-oriented and functional programming in Python.
42. Does Python support switch statements? If yes, give an example. If not, find some alternative way.
43. Compare function, module, package and library in Python.
44. Distinguish between series and dataframe in Pandas. Explain how Pandas can be used for statistical data analysis.
45. Compare between Numpy array and Pandas series in Python.

CASE STUDIES

1. Write a comparative analysis with Python code example for procedural, OOPs and function programming:
   a. Definition
   b. Techniques used
   c. In-built supports
   d. Python code examples.
2. Write a Python program for the following arithmetic operations on vectors using OOPs in Python:
   a. Addition
   b. Subtraction
3. Write Python codes for the following:
   a. Create three Numpy arrays for storing names, heights and weights of 15 students.
   b. Create Pandas DataFrame with the above two arrays.
   c. Find the descriptive statistics of heights and weights using Pandas methods.
   d. Find the difference between standard deviations of heights and weights.

LAB EXERCISES

Write Python programs for the following.

Easy

1. Calculate the area and perimeter of a rectangle.
2. Check whether the given number is an even number or not.
3. To ask the user for a number and print only the odd numbers from that number to zero using a `while` loop.
4. To prompt the user to enter numbers. This process has to repeat until the user enters –1. Finally, the program should print the count of prime and composite numbers entered.
5. Find the maximum of a list of numbers.
6. Add the list elements.
7. Add all elements in a tuple.
8. Count the occurrences of a word in a given sentence.
9. Add two matrices.
10. Count the number of characters in a string and store them in a dictionary.

Moderate

11. Add two complex numbers.
12. Compute the GCD of two numbers.

13. Print out the decimal equivalents of 1/2, 1/3, 1/4, ..., 1/10 using for loop.
14. Find the Least Common Multiple (LCM) of two positive integers.
15. Find the sum of all primes below 2000.
16. Find the sum of the even-valued terms of the Fibonacci series up to 100.
17. Write a program to print the following pattern:

```
1
2 3
4 5 6
7 8 9 10
11 12 13 14 15
```

18. Write a program to print the following pattern:

```
*
* *
* * *
* * * *
* * * * *
```

19. Read a string and print the string in reverse order; hence check if the string is a palindrome or not.
20. Multiply two matrices.
21. Reverse all the elements in a tuple without using the tuple function.
22. Use `split` and `join` methods in the string and trace a birthday with a dictionary.
23. Create a dictionary by combining two lists name for employee name and salary for employee salary. Use the list name as the key and salary as the value of dictionary elements.
24. Input the player's name (string) and runs (int) scored for *n* number of players where *n* should be an input from a keyboard. Store the players' details in a dictionary called 'cricket'. After preparing the dictionary, input the player's name and print the runs scored by him; otherwise to return '–1' if the player's name is not found.
25. Define the function cumulative_product to compute the cumulative product of a list of numbers; hence to find out the cumulative product of a list of numbers.
26. Define a function Reverse to reverse lists without using any built-in function; hence to find the reverse of a given list.
27. Define a function Unique to find all the unique elements of a list, and hence to find the unique elements of a given list.
28. Define a class Person. Inherit a class Faculty from the class Person, which also has a class Publication.

Higher-Order Thinking Skills (HOTS)

29. Print each line of a file in the reverse order.
30. Check if a passed string is a palindrome or not. Import the module into the main program to find whether a string is a palindrome.
31. Open a file to write data. Handle exceptions that can be generated during input/output operations.
32. Generate a random number. Raise a user-defined exception if the number is below 0.1.
33. Read a number from the user and print its square. If the number is entered (Ctrl + c is pressed), then Keyboard Interrupt is generated.
34. Define a class Student to store roll number, name, and marks in five subjects of a student. Display the information stored about the student.
35. Create a derived class employee from the class's basic information (member variables are the name, emp_id, and age), and department information (member variables are dept. name, work, and time) using multiple inheritances. Create two objects of employee class and print the details of individual objects.
36. Define an abstract class Polygon. Derive two classes Rectangle and Triangle from Polygon and write methods to get the details of their dimensions and hence calculate the area.
37. Define two Numpy arrays with 10 stock prices and their volume of trades. Find the weighted average stock price where weights are the volume of trades.
38. Define three Numpy arrays for assigning marks of 20 students in Physics, Mathematics and Computer Science. Use the Pandas library for statistical comparison of the marks obtained by these students.

ANSWER KEYS

Multiple Choice Questions

1. A	5. B	9. B	13. C	17. B
2. B	6. B	10. B	14. D	18. D
3. D	7. A	11. D	15. B	19. B
4. C	8. C	12. A	16. C	20. D

3 Algorithms and Complexity Analysis

CONTENTS

EXPECTED OUTCOMES OF THIS CHAPTER

After going through this chapter learners will be able

- ☑ to think algorithmically, and get the spirit of how algorithms are designed.
- ☑ to know the characteristics of algorithms.
- ☑ to analyze the complexity of the algorithms.
- ☑ to analyze the asymptotic performance of algorithms.
- ☑ to apply complexity analysis methods on C and Python programs.
- ☑ to synthesize efficient algorithms in common engineering design situations.

3.1 INTRODUCTION

Algorithms are used to represent the solution to our problem by using step-by-step statements. These statements can be converted into programming (computer) instructions, which ultimately form a program. This program is executed by a computer to produce the solution outputs. Here, the program takes the required data as input, processes data according to the programming instructions, and finally produces the result or output as shown in the following Fig. 3.1.

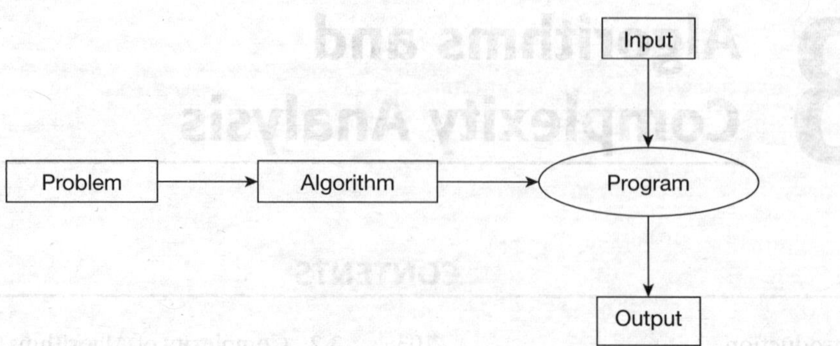

Figure 3.1 Working principle of an algorithm

3.1.1 Why do we Study Algorithms?

It is very important to study algorithms from computer programming and problem-solving perspectives. The implications of algorithms are manyfold in computer science and software development. According to the popular textbook of algorithms, namely, *Introduction to Algorithms* by Thomas H Cormen, et. al, "an algorithm is any well-defined computational procedure that takes some value, or set of values, as input and produces some value or set of values as output". Proper planning is highly essential to complete a particular task in less time and space to increase the performance of a system or application.

3.1.2 Definition

An algorithm is a step-by-step procedure to solve a particular problem. *It is defined as a sequence of statements used to perform a task.* In other words, *it is a sequence of unambiguous instructions used for solving a problem, and can be implemented as a program on a computer.* The algorithm is not the complete source code or program. It is just the core logic (solution) of a problem, which can be expressed either as an informal high-level description as pseudocode or using a flowchart. An algorithm should be understandable and unambiguous. Each of its steps (or phases) and their inputs–outputs should be clear, and must lead to one meaning only.

> ***Note!***
> An algorithm is a step-by-step procedure to solve a particular problem.

3.1.3 Characteristics of Algorithm

An algorithm must include the following characteristics:

1. **Input**: There should be internal or external inputs supplied to the algorithm.
2. **Output**: There should be at least one output obtained.
3. **Definiteness**: Every step of the algorithm should be clear and well-defined.
4. **Finiteness**: The algorithm should have a finite number of steps.
5. **Correctness**: Every step of the algorithm must generate the correct output.
6. **Effectiveness:** Execution of all operations of an algorithm requires finite time. This measures the effectiveness of the results produced by the algorithm.

3.1.4 Examples of Algorithm

Let us consider the problem of adding two numbers.

Problem Statement: Write an algorithm to add two numbers and print the result.

Algo-3.1 Algorithm for adding two numbers – 1

Step 1	Initialize the values to a and b.
Step 2	Add values of a and b and store to c (c ← a + b).
Step 3	Print c.
Step 4	End.

Algorithms describe the logic of how to solve the problem. Programmers use different programming languages like C, Python, Java for implementation of the algorithms. The above problem may also be solved using the following algorithm:

Algo-3.2 Algorithm for adding two numbers – 2

Step 1	Initialize the values to a and b.
Step 2	Print a + b as a result.
Step 3	End.

If we analyze the above algorithms, usually we find that the second method is more effective because it takes one variable less than the first algorithm. We may also note that the number of steps is less in the second case. It may also be noted that writing step numbers is optional.

Let us take another example to understand how to write an algorithm:

Problem Statement: Find the largest number from three given numbers.
Input: A list of three numbers.
Output: The largest number from the given three numbers.

Algo-3.3 Algorithm for finding the largest number from three given numbers

Step 1	Initialize three integers a, b, and c.
Step 2	Define the largest number 'max' as output.
Step 3	Compare the first number 'a' with another number 'b'; if 'a' is greater than 'b', store value of 'a' to 'max' (i.e., max ← a), otherwise, store the value of 'b' to 'max' (i.e., max←b).
Step 4	Compare 'max' with another number 'c'; if 'max' is greater than 'c' thenprint 'max' otherwise print 'c'.
Step 5	End.

3.1.5 How do we Analyze Algorithms?

The theoretical study of measuring the performance of a computer program and resource usage is the analysis of the algorithm. A problem can be solved in more than one way. So, we can say that we may have many algorithms to solve a particular problem. Figure 3.2 shows that a problem has the options to be solved by *N* number of algorithms, namely Algorithm1, Algorithm2, ..., Algorithm*N*. Hence, many solution algorithms can be derived for a given problem. The next step is to analyze the proposed solution algorithms, and to identify the best suitable algorithm for the implementation.

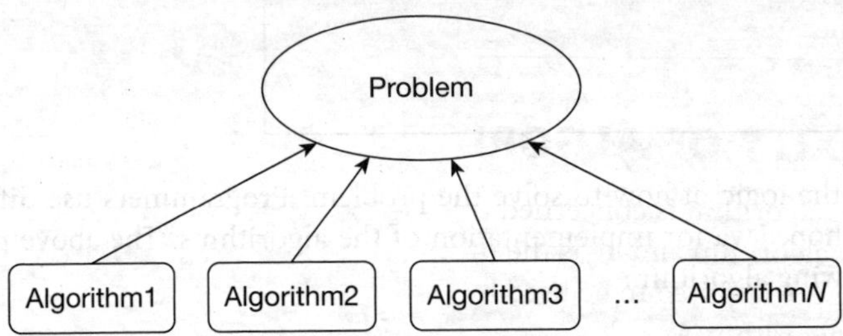

Figure 3.2 Multiple algorithms for solving a problem

Suppose, we want to go from the place "Kolkata" to "Delhi". There can be many ways to reach the destination from the source. We can go by air or by bus orby train. Depending on availability and appropriateness, we have to choose any one option that is best suited. Similarly, in computer science, there are multiple algorithms to solve a particular problem. When we have more than one algorithm to solve a problem, we need to select the best algorithm. Performance analysis helps us to select the best algorithm from many algorithms to solve a particular problem. The performance of an algorithm is a process of making an evaluative decision about the algorithms.

We compare all possible algorithms with each other and choose the best possible algorithm. To compare algorithms, we use a set of parameters or a set of elements like memory required by that algorithm, the execution speed of that algorithm, etc. Performance analysis of an algorithm is the procedure of calculating the time and space required by that algorithm. This is a theoretical analysis of an algorithm. The running time of an operation can be defined as the number of instructions executed per operation.

> ***Note!***
> A problem may have multiple algorithms to solve it.

3.1.6 Algorithm vs. Pseudocode vs. Program

An **algorithm** is a well-defined, step-by-step procedure that allows a computer to solve a problem systematically and logically.

Pseudocode is the simple version of the programming code. It is written in plain English using short phrases. This is often considered as a code between algorithms and language-specific source code for the implementation of the algorithm.

A **program** is the exact source code written for the implementation of an algorithm using all the rules of the programming language. In other words, it is a set of instructions written in a programming language to implement the algorithm to solve a problem.

The following are the differences between a program and an algorithm:

Table 3.1 Differences between algorithm and program

Algorithm	Program
Algorithms are written in pseudocode or simple English statements or written in a natural language.	Program is written in any programming language.
Algorithms are independent of programming languages.	Program is dependent on the programming language.
Algorithms are produced in the design phase of software development.	Program is produced during the implementation phase of software development.

3.2 COMPLEXITY OF ALGORITHMS

The complexity of an algorithm is concerned about how fast or slow a particular algorithm is performing. Suppose 'A' is an algorithm and 'n' is the input data size. Two major factors of interest here are how much time and space are required to be used by this algorithm 'A'. These two factors decide theoretically the efficiency of the algorithm 'A'.

Space Complexity: It is determined by the maximum memory space required by the algorithm for completing its tasks. It includes both program space and data space.

Time Complexity: It is determined by counting the number of key operations to solve the algorithm or theoretically how much time is required to complete the task of that algorithm.

There are two points which we should consider for computer programming in this context:

1. Appropriate data structures;
2. Appropriate algorithm.

The complexity of an algorithm is denoted by $f(n)$ that gives the running time and/or the storage space required by that algorithm in terms of the input data size 'n'.

> ***Note!***
> Performance analysis or complexity analysis of algorithms helps us to select the best algorithm from many algorithms to solve a particular problem.

3.2.1 Space Complexity

To calculate the space complexity, we must know the memory required to store different data types values, which in turn, depends on the compiler. For example, the C compiler (in 16-bits machine) requires the following:

- ☑ 2 bytes to store an integer value.
- ☑ 4 bytes to store a floating-point value.
- ☑ 1 byte to store a character value.

Space complexity calculation depends on data space only, and it ignores instruction space. It means, we can calculate the memory required to store variables, constants, structures, etc. only. Suppose the amount of space required by an algorithm is increasing with the increase of input dataset, then that space complexity is called *linear space complexity*.

> ***Note!***
> Space complexity can be measured by the maximum memory space required by the algorithm to complete the task.

3.2.2 Time Complexity

The time complexity of an algorithm is the total amount of time required by an algorithm to complete it sexecution. We can define complexity as a numerical function $T(n)$; i.e., the time(T) required to execute versus the input data size (n). We can say that $T(n)$ does not depend on the implementation. A given algorithm will take different amounts of time for the same input sets depending on many factors like processor speed, instruction set, disk speed, compiler, etc. The way around to estimate the efficiency of an algorithm is asymptotic. So, we can measure the efficiency of an algorithm theoretically. We will measure time $T(n)$ as the number of elementary "steps" or "statements", provided each such step takes constant time. If an algorithm requires a fixed amount of time for all input datasets, then that algorithm is said to be of *constant time complexity*.

Consider the following C code in Fig. 3.3, for example, where instructions are mapped with time units to understand the calculation of time complexity. The time required by each operation or statement to execute is considered as 1-unit time. The following example shows that the `for` loop condition will run $n + 1$ times with n successful cases and 1 failure case. The code inside the loop will run n times.

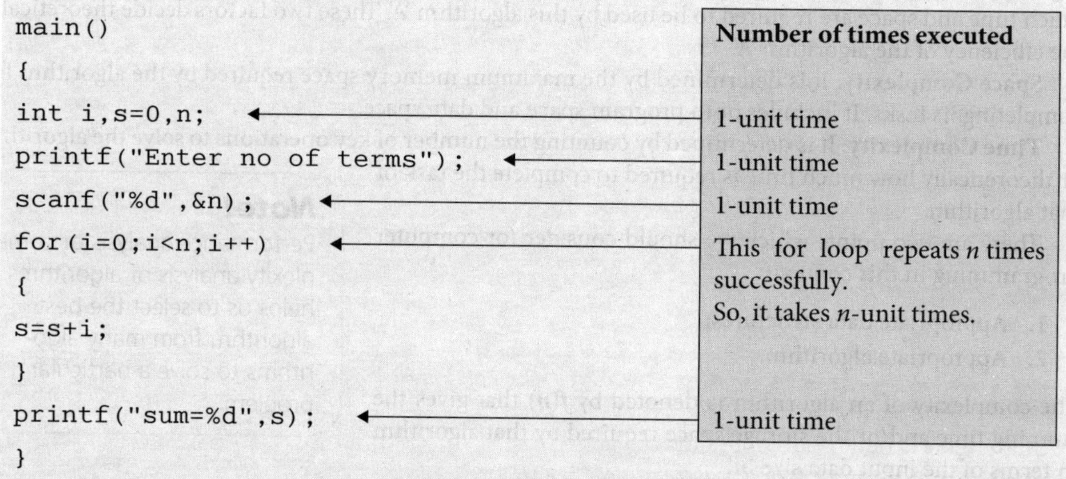

Figure 3.3 Example of time complexity calculation

The above code requires '$n + 4$' units of time to complete the tasks. Here, the exact time is not fixed, and it changes based on the n value inside the `for` loop. If we increase the value of n, then the required time also increases linearly. In most of the cases, time depends on the input size n, and we should calculate time complexity considering n as a large value. For example, we may think that the human brain may take a few seconds to sort 5 integer numbers and a few seconds more for sorting 15 integer numbers, compared to the first case. Similarly, for sorting 100 integer numbers, it may take more time (suppose in a minute or so) compared to the first and second case.

Now, suppose we want to sort 10^{10} integer numbers, then we will think of any calculating device (like a computer) because it

> **Note!**
> Time complexity can be measured by counting the number of key operations to solve the algorithm or theoretically how much time is required to complete the task.

will be a very complex and time-consuming job for the human brain. So, we will take the help of any computing device when n, the input data size, is large. Remember that, n should always be large at the time of analyzing or calculating time complexity.

3.3 ASYMPTOTIC NOTATIONS

The objective of analyzing the computational complexity is to classify algorithms according to their performances. Each algorithm is associated with a sequence ofsteps. As discussed in the Section 3.2.2, we measure the execution time of an algorithm by counting the number of steps, and therefore define an algorithmic complexity as a numerical function $T(n)$ where n is the input data size. The term 'analysis of algorithms' is used to describe the approaches to the study of the performance of the computer programs. Following are three variations of time complexities:

- *Best-case efficiency*: It is the minimum number of steps that an algorithm takes for some (specific) input datasets. The best case is possible by executing a minimum number of steps. It is denoted by the symbol big-omega (Ω). For example, if we are sorting a set of n numbers, and the input set is already sorted, then we can say that it is the best-case scenario.
- *Average-case efficiency*: It may be defined as the efficiency averaged on all possible inputs (assuming that distribution of the input is uniform, i.e., all values are equally probable). The algorithm consists of an average number of steps. It is denoted by the symbol big-theta (θ). It indicates an expected average running time of algorithms on n inputs.
- *Worst-case efficiency:* It is the maximum number of steps that an algorithm takes for some (specific) collection of input datasets. An algorithm executes the maximum number of steps in this case. It is denoted by the symbol big-oh (O) (or termed big-O interchangeably). For example, if we are sorting a set of n numbers, and the input set is in reverse (opposite) order, then we can say that it is the worst-case scenario. *Therefore, knowing worst-case time complexity assures us that the algorithm will never go beyond this time limit. This is the main reason that we always try to calculate the complexity of the algorithms in big-oh (O) notations.*

3.3.1 Definition

An asymptotic line means a line that approaches a curve but never touches it. A curve and a line that get closer but do not intersect are examples of a curve and a line that are asymptotic to each other. *Asymptotic notation is used to describe the asymptotic behavior of the complexities of an algorithm. It is a mathematical representation of its complexity.* Asymptotic notations are defined in terms of functions whose domain belongs to the natural number 'N'.

Several asymptotic notations are available but we will discuss three cases of execution of time complexities of an algorithm, namely, big-oh (O), big-omega (Ω), and big-theta (θ) for worst-case, best-case, and average-case time complexities respectively. These are very popular and efficient in terms of time complexity.

Generally, we use the most significant terms in the complexity of that algorithm, and ignore the least significant terms in the complexity of that algorithm. For example, consider the following time complexities of two algorithms.

Suppose, the time complexity of Algorithm1 is '$6n^2 + 3n + 1$',and that of Algorithm2 is '$9n^2 + 7n + 3$'. Generally, when we are analyzing an algorithm, we consider the time complexity for larger values of input data (i.e.,'n' value) as we have discussed in Section 3.2.2. The term '$3n+1$' in Algorithm1 has the least significance than the term '$6n^2$'. In Algorithm2, the term '$7n + 3$' has the least significance than the term '$9n^2$'. Here, for a larger value of n, the value of most significant terms ($6n^2$ and $9n^2$) is especially larger than the value of least significant terms ($3n + 1$ and $7n + 3$). So, we can ignore the least significant terms to represent the overall time required by an algorithm when n will be large. In asymptotic notation, we use only the most significant terms to represent the time complexity of an algorithm.

3.3.2 Big-Oh (O) Notation

The Big-Oh (O) notation is used to express the upper bound on the execution time of an algorithm. Using this notation, we denote the maximum possible amount of time that an algorithm will take to complete its tasks. A maximum possible time is taken for the execution of an algorithm in its worst-case scenario. So, big-oh (O) notation represents the worst-case time complexity of an algorithm.

Definition

Let $f(n)$ and $g(n)$ be two positive functions of 'n', where 'n' is the input data size. Then $f(n)$ is big-oh (O) of $g(n)$ if and only if there exists a positive constant C and initial integer value n_0, such that $f(n) \leq C * g(n)$ for $n \geq n_0$. So, we can say $f(n) = O(g(n))$.

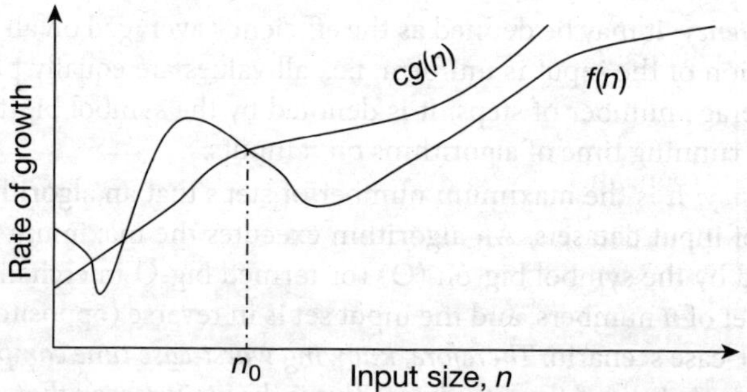

Figure 3.4 Graphical representation of big-oh (O) notation

Figure 3.4 shows a graphical representation of big-oh (O) notation, where the x-axis indicates input data size 'n' and the y-axis indicates the time $f(n)$ for the execution of the algorithm. Upper bound ($C * g(n)$ here) means the maximum time an algorithm takes to produce its outputs, expressed in terms of the size of the inputs, which is a worst-case scenario. In Fig. 3.4, the value of $f(n)$ is always smaller than its upper bound $C * g(n)$, and they never touch each other after n_0 point.

Guiding Principles

Following are some principles that are normally followed while using big-oh (O) notations:

1. The coefficients of the highest order terms should be ignored.
2. The lower order terms should be ignored.
3. The base should be changed from one constant to another constant – i.e., the base value of the logarithm should be changed by only a constant factor.
4. For example, if $T_1(n) = O(f(n))$ and $T_2(n) = O(g(n))$ then,
   (a) $T_1(n) + T_2(n) = \max(O(f(n)), O(g(n)))$
   (b) $T_1(n) * T_2(n) = O(f(n) * g(n))$

(c) $O(T_1(n)) = T_1(n)$
(d) $O(f(n).g(n)) = f(n) * O(g(n))$
(e) $O(f(n) + O(f(n))) = O(f(n))$
(f) $O(f(n)) * C = O(f(n))$ for any constant C

Nature of Curves for Asymptotic Bounds

The nature of the curve for the asymptotic bounds are given in the following Table 3.2 for the big-oh (O) functions.

Table 3.2 Nature of curve for different big-oh (O) functions

Asymptotic bound	Nature of the curve
O (1)	Constant
O (log*n*)	Logarithmic
O (*n*)	Linear
O (n^2)	Quadratic
O (n^3)	Cubic
O (2^n)	Exponential
O (*n*!)	Factorial

Analyzing Growth of Functions

The rate of growth for different asymptotic bounds are presented below in Table 3.3 for the big-oh (O) functions.

Table 3.3 Rate of growth for different asymptotic bounds

	g(*n*)					
n	$\log_2 n$	*n*	$n\log_2 n$	n^2	n^3	2^n
1	0	1	1	1	1	2
2	1	2	2	4	8	4
4	2	4	8	16	64	16
8	3	8	24	64	512	256
16	4	16	64	256	4096	65536

Relation among the complexity of the algorithms in terms of big-oh is given below:

$$O(1) < O(\log n) < O(n) < O(n*\log n) < O(n^2) < O(n^3) < O(2^n).$$

The following Fig. 3.5 presents the movements of the above seven big-oh functions, with the increase of the input data size *n* assumed to be large.

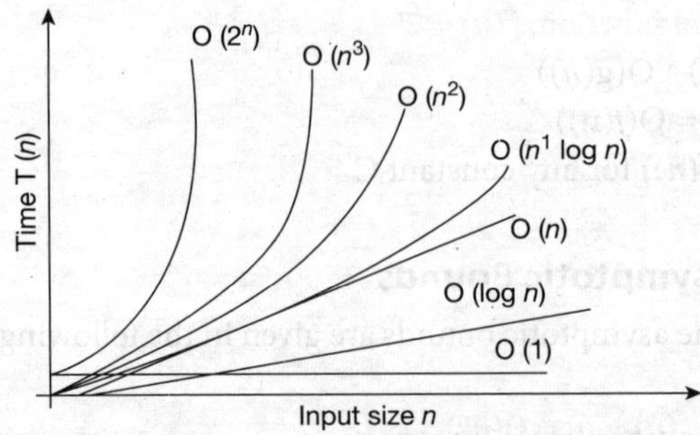

Figure 3.5 Growth of some big-oh complexity functions

Some Examples

Example 3.1 Constant function: $f(n) = 14$.

Given that $f(n) = 14 \leq 15 = 15 * 1$;
Hence, $C = 15$, $n_0 = 0$ and $g(n) = 1$,
So, $f(n) = O(1)$, [Since $f(n) \leq C * g(n)$ and $n \geq n_0$ to represent as $f(n) = O(g(n))$ by definition].

Example 3.2 Linear function: $f(n) = 3n + 2$.

Given that $f(n) = 3n + 2 \leq C * n$;
$f(n) = 3n + 2 \leq 4n$ for $n \geq 2$ and substituting $C = 4$.
Hence, $C = 4$, $n_0 = 2$ and $g(n) = n$,
So, $f(n) = O(n)$, [Since $f(n) \leq C * g(n)$ and $n \geq n_0$ to represent as $f(n) = O(g(n))$ by definition].

Example 3.3 Quadratic function: $f(n) = 6n^2 + 4n$.

Given that $f(n) = 6n^2 + 4n$;
So, $f(n) \leq 7n^2$ since $4n \leq n^2$ implies $n \geq 4$;
Hence, $C = 7$, $n_0 = 4$ and $g(n) = n^2$;
So, $f(n) = O(n^2)$, [Since $f(n) \leq C * g(n)$ and $n \geq n_0$ to represent as $f(n) = O(g(n))$ by definition].

Example 3.4 Cubic function: $f(n) = 4n^3 + n^2 + 4n$.

Given that $f(n) = 4n^3 + n^2 + 4n$
$\leq 4n^3 + 2n^2$, for $n^2 \geq 4n$ and $n \geq 4$;
$\leq 4n^3 + n^3$, for $n^3 \geq 2n^2$ and $n \geq 2$;
$\leq 5n^3$
Hence, $C = 5$, $n_0 = 4$ and $g(n) = n^3$.
So, $f(n) = O(n^3)$, [Since $f(n) \leq C * g(n)$ and $n \geq n_0$ to represent as $f(n) = O(g(n))$ by definition].

Example 3.5: Prove that $n^2 + 2n + 1 = O(n^2)$.

We must first find C and n_0 such that $n^2 + 2n + 1 \leq C * n^2$, for all $n \geq n_0$.
If $n_0 = 1$, then $1 \leq n < n^2$ for all $n \geq 1$.
So, $n^2 + 2n + 1 \leq n^2 + 2n^2 + n^2 = 4n^2$.
It follows that $C = 4$ and $f(n) = O(n^2)$.

Example 3.6: Exponential function: $f(n) = 2^n + 6n^2 + 3n$.

$f(n) = 2^n + 6n^2 + 3n$
$\leq 2^n + 6n^2 + n^2$ for $n^2 \geq 3n$
$\leq 2^n + 7n^2$ for $2^n \geq n^2$ where $n \geq 4$
$\leq 2^n + 7 * 2^n$, since $n^2 \leq 2^n$
$\leq 8 * 2^n$
Hence, $C = 8$, $n_0 = 4$,
So, $f(n) = O(2^n)$.

Example 3.7: Prove that $f(n) = n! = O(n^n)$

$f(n) = n!$
$= n * (n - 1) * (n - 2) * \ldots * 2 * 1$
$= (n^2 - n) * (n - 2) * (n - 3) * \ldots * 2 * 1$ (Multiplying the first two terms)
$= (n^3 - 3n^2 - 2n) * (n - 3) * \ldots. * 2 * 1$ (Multiplying the first three terms)
....
....
....
$\leq C * n^n$
$= O(n^n)$
So, $f(n) = O(n^n)$.

Measuring the Complexity of C and Python Programs

Example 3.1A. C program

```
#include <stdio.h>
main()
{
  int c=1, i;
for(i = 1; i <= c; i++)
{
printf("%d",i);
}
}
```

Example 3.1B. Python equivalent program

```
c=1
for i in range(1,c+1):
  print(i)
```

Answer 3.1A and 3.1B: O(1).
Explanation: The time complexity of a program is considered as O(1) if it does not contain a loop,recursion, and call to any other non-constant time function. In these examples 1A and 1B, $c = 1$ indicates that the statement inside the `for` loop will be executed just once and hence the complexity is O(1).

Example 3.2A: C program

```
#include <stdio.h>
main()
{
int i,s=0,n;                      <-- 1-unit time
printf("Enter no of terms");      <-- 1-unit time
scanf("%d",&n);                   <-- 1-unit time
for(i=0;i<n;i++)                  <-- This for loop repeats n times.
{                                     So, it takes n-unit times.
s=s+i;
}
printf("sum=%d",s);               <-- 1-unit time
}
```

Number of times executed

Example 3.2B: Python equivalent program

```
s=0
print('Enter no of terms')
n=int(input())
for i in range(n):
    s=s+i
print('sum=',s)
```

Answer: O(n).

Explanation: The time required to execute each operation/statement is considered as 1-unit time. The above code requires total $n + 4$ units of time to complete the task. Here, the exact time is not fixed, and it changes based on the value of n for the loop. If we increase the value of n, then the required time also increases linearly. In most of the cases, time depends on the input size n (used for processing) to perform the tasks, and we should calculate time complexity considering n as a large value. If n is large, then constant '4' will be negligible in '$n + 4$' expression, and we can say that the complexity of the program is O(n).

Example 3.3A: **C program**

```
#include <stdio.h>
main()
{
int i,j,n;
printf("Enter no of terms");
scanf("%d",&n);
for(i=1;i<=n;i++)
{
for(j=1;j<=n;j++)
{
printf("\nIndia");
}
}
}
```

Number of times executed

- `int i,j,n;` — 1-unit time
- `printf("Enter no of terms");` — 1-unit time
- `scanf("%d",&n);` — 1-unit time
- `for(i=1;i<=n;i++)` — This `for-i` loop repeats n times; So, it takes n-unit times
- `for(j=1;j<=n;j++)` — This `for-j` loop repeats n times for each i; So, it takes n-unit times; Total time = (n * n + 3) units.

Example 3.3B: **Python equivalent program**

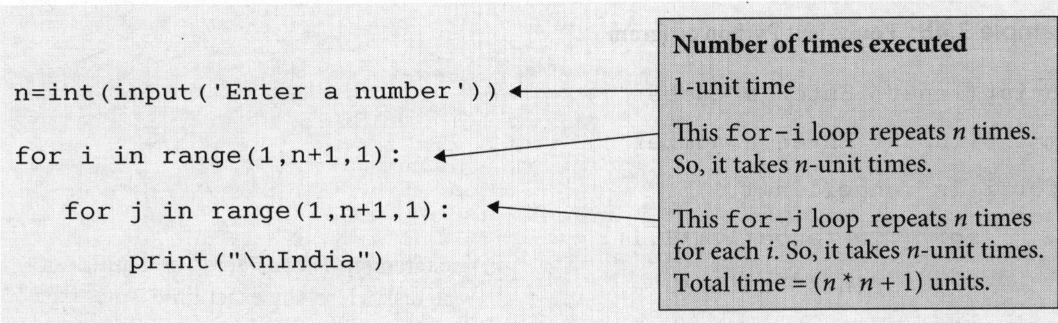

```
n=int(input('Enter a number'))

for i in range(1,n+1,1):

    for j in range(1,n+1,1):
        print("\nIndia")
```

Number of times executed

- `n=int(input('Enter a number'))` — 1-unit time
- `for i in range(1,n+1,1):` — This `for-i` loop repeats n times. So, it takes n-unit times.
- `for j in range(1,n+1,1):` — This `for-j` loop repeats n times for each i. So, it takes n-unit times. Total time = (n * n + 1) units.

Answer: O(n^2)

Explanation: The time required by each operation/statement to execute is considered as 1-unit time. In the above code,there is nested loop i and j, and each loop will be executed n times each. So, the total `for` loop will take $n * n = n^2$ unit time. If we increase the value of n then the time required also increases quadratically. We should calculate time complexity considering n is a large value. If n is large, then in constant '3' unit-time in the C program, and '1' unit-time in the Python program will be negligible, then we can say that the complexity of the code is O(n^2).

Example 3.4A: C program

```
#include <stdio.h>
main()
{
int i,j,n,m;                       <- 1-unit time.
printf("Enter no of terms");       <- 1-unit time.
scanf("%d%d",&n,&m);               <- 1-unit time.
for(i=1;i<=n;i++)                  <- This for-i loop repeats n times; So, it takes n-unit times.
{
for(j=1;j<=m;j++)                  <- This for-j loop repeats m times. So, it takes m-unit times for each i unit.
{                                     Total time = (n * m + 3) units.
printf("\nIndia");
}
}
}
```

Number of times executed

1-unit time.

1-unit time.

1-unit time.

This `for-i` loop repeats n times; So, it takes n-unit times.

This `for-j` loop repeats m times. So, it takes m-unit times for each i unit. Total time = $(n * m + 3)$ units.

Example 3.4B: Equivalent Python program

```
n=int(input('Enter a number'))
m=int(input('Enter a number'))
for i in range(1,n+1,1):
    for j in range(1,m+1,1):
        print("India")
```

Answer: O($n * m$)

Explanation: The time required by each operation/statement to execute is considered as 1-unit time. In the above code, there are nested loops i and j, and each loop will be executed n times and m times respectively. So, the total for loop will take $n * m$ unit times. If we increase the value of n and m, then the required time also increases. We should calculate time complexity considering n and m as large values and hence we can say that the complexity of the above programs is O $(n * m)$.

Example 3.5A: **C program**

```
#include <stdio.h>
main()
{
int i,j,n,k;                      <- 1-unit time.
printf("Enter no of terms");      <- 1-unit time.
scanf("%d",&n);                   <- 1-unit time.
for(i=1;i<=n;i++)                 <- This for-i loop repeats n times;
{                                    So, it takes n-unit times.
for(j=1;j<=i;j++)                 <- This for-j loop repeats i times. So,
{                                    it takes i-unit times for each j unit.
for(k=1;k<=100;k++)               <- This for-k loop repeats 100 times. So,
{                                    it takes 100-unit times for each j and
printf("\nIndia");                   i unit time respectively.
}
}
}
}
```

Number of times executed

Example 3.5B: **Equivalent Python program**

```
n=int(input('Enter a number'))
for i in range(1,n+1,1):
    for j in range(1,i+1,1):
        for k in range (1,101,1):
            print ("India")
```

Answer: $O(n^2)$

Explanation: Execution time calculation

i	*j*	*k*
1	1	1 * 100 = 100 times
2	2	2 * 100 = 200 times
…	…	…
n	*n*	*n* * 100 times

So, total execution time = 1 * 100 + 2 * 200 + 3 * 300 + … + n * 100
= 100 * (1 + 2 + 3 + … + n)
= 100 * ((n * (n – 1)/2) = O(n^2)

Example 3.6A: C program

```
#include <stdio.h>
main()
{
int i,j,n,k;
printf("Enter no of terms");
scanf("%d",&n);
for(i=1;i<=n;i++)
{
for(j=1;j<=i*i;j++)
{
for(k=1;k<=(n/2);k++)
{
printf("\nIndia");
}
}
}
}
```

Example 3.6B: Equivalent Python program

```
print('Enter no of terms')
n=int(input())
for i in range(1,n+1):
          for j in range(1,(i*i)+1):
                    for k in range(1,(n//2)+1):
                              print('India')
```

Answer: O(n^4)

Explanation: Execution time calculation

i	*j*	*k*
1	(1 * 1) = 1 time	(n/2) * 1 times
2	(2 * 2) = 4 times	(n/2) * 4 times
3	(3 * 3) = 9 times	(n/2) * 9 times
…	…	…
n	(n * n) = n^2 times	(n/2) * n^2 times

So, total number of execution steps = $(n/2) * 1 + (n/2) * 4 + (n/2) * 9 + \ldots + (n/2) * n^2$

$= (n/2) * (1 + 4 + 9 + \ldots + n^2)$

$= (n/2) * \{(n * (n + 1)(2n + 1))/6\}$

$= O(n^4)$

Example 3.7A: C program

```
#include <stdio.h>
main()
{
int i =1,s =1, n = 0;
printf("Enter no of terms");
  scanf("%d",&n);

while(s<=n)
{
i++;
s=s+i;
printf("\nIndia");
}
}
```

Example 3.7B: Equivalent Python program

```
i= 1
s= 1
n=int(input())
while s <= n:
    i += 1
    s = s + i
    print('India')
```

Answer: O($\sqrt{n}$)

Explanation: Execution time calculation

s	*i*
1	1
3	2
6	3
10	4
15	5
…	…
Up to > *n*	*k*

Total number of iterations = 1 + 2 + 3 + … + k, where k is the final (ultimate) value of i.
Therefore, $k * (k + 1)/2 > n$
Or $(k^2 + k)/2 > n = O(\sqrt{n})$.

Example 3.8A: C program

```
#include <stdio.h>
main()
{
int i =1,n;
printf("Enter no of terms");
  scanf("%d",&n);
for(i=1;i<n;i=i*2)
{
printf("\nIndia");
}
}
```

Example 3.8B: Equivalent Python program

```
n=int(input('Enter a number'))
i = 1
for i in range(1,n + 1,i*2):
    print("India")
```

Answer: O($\log_2 n$)

Explanation: Execution time calculation

i	$2^0=1$	$2^1=2$	$2^2=4$	$2^3=8$	…	2^k

$2^k = n$ where k is the final (ultimate) value of i;
Therefore, $k = \log_2 n = O(\log_2 n)$.

Example 3.9A: C program

```
#include <stdio.h>
main()
{
int i=1,n;
printf("Enter no of terms");
  scanf("%d",&n);

for(i=1;i<n;i=i*3)
{
printf("\nIndia");
}
}
```

Example 3.9B: Equivalent Python program

```
n=int(input('Enter a number'))
i = 1
for i in range(1,n+1,i*3):
    print("india")
```

Answer: O(log$_3$n).

Explanation: Execution time calculation

i	$3^0 = 1$	$3^1 = 3$	$3^2 = 9$	$3^3 = 27$	...	3^k

$3^k = n$ where k is the final (ultimate) value of i.
So $3^k = n$, therefore $k = \log_3 n = O(\log_3 n)$.

Example 3.10A: C program

```
#include <stdio.h>
main()
{
 int i, j, n,k;
  printf("Enter no of terms");
scanf("%d",&n);
  for(i = (n/2); i <= n; i++)
    {
      for(j = 1; j <= (n/2); j++)
       {
       for(k=1;k<=n;k=k*2)
         {
          printf("\nIndia");
         }
       }
    }
}
```

Example 3.10B: Equivalent Python program

```
print("Enter no of terms: ", end = " ");
n = int(input())
print()
for i in range(n//2, n+1, 1):
    for j in range(1, (n//2)+1, 1):
        k = 1
        while(k <= n):
            print("India")
            k *= 2
```

Answer: $O(n^2\log_2 n)$

Explanation: *i*-loop will execute ($n/2$)times; *j*-loop will execute ($n/2$) times; *k*-loop will execute ($\log_2 n$) times. So, $(n/2) * (n/2) * (\log_2 n) = O(n^2\log_2 n)$.

Example 3.11A: C program

```
#include <stdio.h>
main()
 {
int i, j, n,k;
printf("Enter no of terms");

scanf("%d",&n);
  for(i = (n/2); i <= n; i++)
    {
      for(j = 1; j <= n; j=j*2)
       {
         for(k=1;k<=n;k=k*2)
          {
           printf("\nIndia");
          }
       }
    }
}
```

Example 3.11B: Equivalent Python program

```
print("Enter no of terms: ",end = " ")
n = int(input())
print()
for i in range(n//2, n+1, 1):
    j = 1
    while(j <= n):
        k = 1
        while(k <= n):
            print("India")
            k*=2
        j*= 2
```

Answer: $O(n^*(\log_2 n)^2)$.

Explanation: i-loop will execute $(n/2)$ times; j-loop will execute $(\log_2 n)$times; k-loop will execute $(\log_2 n)$ times. So, $(n/2) * (\log_2 n) * (\log_2 n) = (n/2) * (\log_2 n)^2 = O(n^*(\log_2 n)^2)$.

> **Note!**
> Big-oh (O) is used to express the worst-case execution time of an algorithm.

3.3.3 Big-Omega (Ω) Notation

The big-omega (Ω) notation is just the opposite of big-oh (O) notation. It is used to express the lower bound on the running time of an algorithm. Using this notation, we can calculate the minimum possible amount of time that an algorithm will take to complete its tasks. The big-omega notation is used to represent the best-case time complexity of an algorithm.

Definition: $f(n)$ and $g(n)$ are two positive functions of n, where n is the input data size. Then, $f(n)$ is big-omega(Ω) of $g(n)$, if and only if there exists a positive constant C, and initial integer value n_0, such that $f(n) \geq C * g(n)$ and $n \geq n_0$. So,we can say $f(n) = \Omega(g(n))$.

Lower bound ($C * g(n)$ here) means the minimum time an algorithm takes to produce outputs, expressed in terms of the size of the inputs, which is a best-case scenario. In Fig. 3.6, the value of $f(n)$ is always greater than its lower bound $C * g(n)$ and they often become asymptotic but never touch each other after n_0 point.

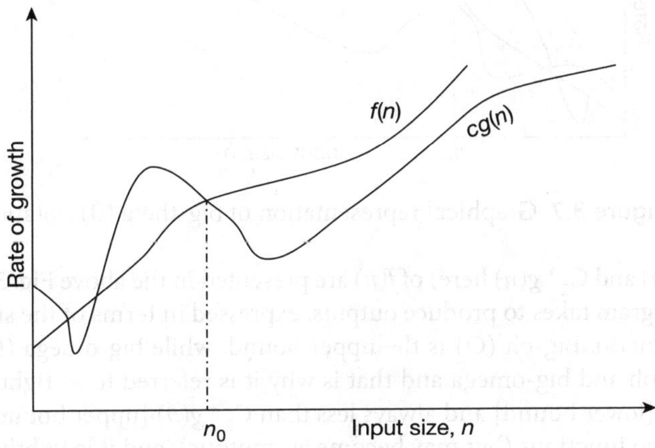

Figure 3.6 Graphical representation of big-omega (Ω) notation

Example

Suppose $f(n)$ and $g(n)$ are two functions. $f(n) = 3n + 2$ and $g(n) = n$.
If we try to represent $f(n)$ as $\Omega(g(n))$, then $f(n) \geq C * g(n)$ for all values of $C > 0$ and $n_0 \geq 1$.
$f(n) \geq C * g(n)$ must be true.
$\Rightarrow f(n) = 3n + 2 \geq C * n$, for all values of $C = 1$ and $n \geq 1$.
By using big-omega notation, we can write $3n + 2 = \Omega(n)$.

> **Note!**
> Big-omega (Ω) is used to express the best-case running time of an algorithm.

3.3.4 Big-Theta (θ) Notation

Big-theta (θ) notation is used to represent the average-case time complexity of any algorithm. In this notation, both the upper and lower bounds are denoted by big-theta (θ) for the function $f(n)$ with input size n.It is used to express the asymptotic tight bound for the functions. Using this notation, we can calculate the average possible amount of time that an algorithm will take to complete its task.

Definition: $f(n)$ and $g(n)$ are two positive functions of n, where n is the input data size. Then $f(n)$ is big-theta (θ) of $g(n)$, if and only if there exists two positive constants C_1 and C_2, such that $C_1 * g(n) \le f(n) \le C_2 * g(n)$ for all $n \ge n_0$, $C_1 > 0$, $C_2 > 0$ and $n_0 \ge 1$. So, we can say that $f(n) = \theta(g(n))$. The following Fig. 3.7 represents the big-theta function graphically along with its bounds $C_1 * g(n)$ and $C_2 * g(n)$.

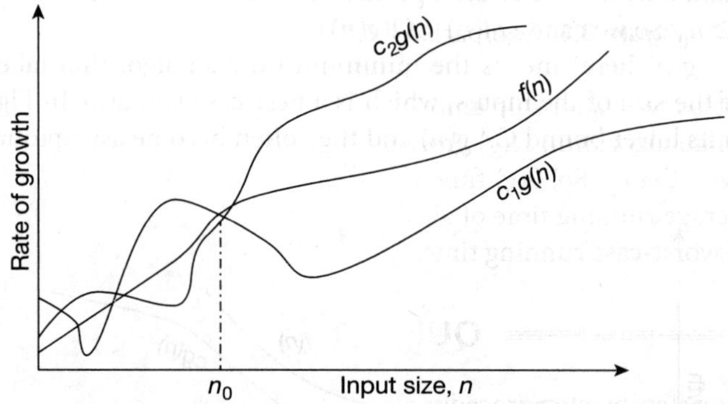

Figure 3.7 Graphical representation of big-theta (θ) notation

Tight bounds ($C_1 * g(n)$ and $C_2 * g(n)$ here) of $f(n)$ are presented in the above Fig. 3.7. Tight bounds mean the average time a program takes to produce outputs, expressed in terms of the size of the inputs, which is an average-case scenario. Big-oh (O) is the upper bound, while big-omega (Ω) is the lower bound. θ lies in between big-oh and big-omega and that is why it is referred to as tight bounds. $f(n)$ is always greater than $C_1 * g(n)$ [lower bound] and always less than $C_2 * g(n)$ [upper bound] while $n \ge n_0$. So, $f(n)$ never touches these two functions (but may become asymptotic), and it is tightly confined by these two functions.

Example

Suppose, $f(n)$ and $g(n)$ are two functions where $f(n) = 3n + 2$ and $g(n) = n$.
If we try to represent $f(n)$ as $\Theta(g(n))$, then it must satisfy
$C_1 g(n) \le f(n) \le C_2 g(n)$ for all values of $C_1 > 0$, $C_2 > 0$ and $n_0 \ge 1$.
$C_1 g(n) \le f(n) \le C_2 g(n) \Rightarrow C_1 n \le 3n + 2 \le C_2 n$ for $C_1 = 1, C_2 = 4$ and $n \ge 2$.
By using big-omega notation, we can write $3n + 2 = \Omega(n)$.
The following figure presents a comparison among the three asymptotic notations for complexity analysis.

> **Note!**
> Big-theta (θ) is used to represent the average-case time complexity or execution time of an algorithm.

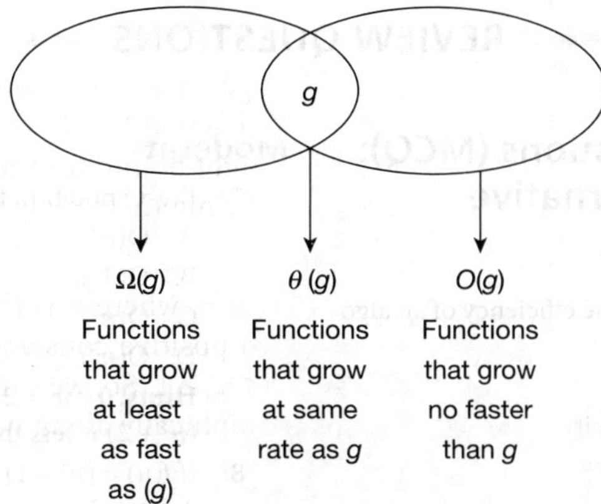

Figure 3.8 Comparison among asymptotic notations

Figure 3.8 demonstrates the relationship among the order of functions in asymptotic notations for the complexity analysis of an algorithm. $\Omega(g)$ grows at least as fast as g, i.e., $\Theta(g)$ grows at the same rate as g and $O(g)$ grows slower than g. So, $\Theta(g)$ function lies in the intersection area of $\Omega(g)$ and $O(g)$ as $\Theta(g)$ indicates expected average running time of algorithms on n inputs, or $\Theta(g)$ belongs to the intermediate zone of best-case and worst-case running times.

QUICK RECAP

- ☑ An algorithm is a step-by-step procedure to solve a particular problem. It is a sequence of statements used to perform a task.
- ☑ Algorithms must have some inputs, a well-defined procedure (definiteness), a finite number of steps (finiteness), and generate correct outputs (correctness). A problem may have multiple algorithms to solve it.
- ☑ Pseudocode is the simple version of a programming code written in plain English using short phrases. A program is the exact source code written for the implementation of an algorithm using all the rules of the programming language.
- ☑ Performance or complexity analysis of the algorithms helps us to select the best algorithm from many algorithms to solve a particular problem. This is done by calculating the time and space required by the algorithms.
- ☑ Space complexity is determined by the maximum memory space required by the algorithm to complete the task including both program space and data space.Time complexity is determined by counting the number of key operations to solve the algorithm or theoretically how much time is required to complete the task.
- ☑ Asymptotic notation is used to describe the asymptotic behavior of the complexities of an algorithm mathematically.
- ☑ Big-oh (O) notation is used to express the upper bound (or maximum possible amount or worst case) on the execution time of an algorithm.This is the most important notation since it offers an analysis of the algorithms in the worst possible situations.
- ☑ Big-omega (Ω) notation (opposite of big-oh) is used to express the lower bound (or minimum possible amount or best case) on the running time of an algorithm.
- ☑ Big-theta (θ) notation is used to represent the average-case time complexity of an algorithm offering both upper and lower bounds of the execution time.

REVIEW QUESTIONS

Multiple Choice Questions (MCQ): Choose the Best Alternative

Easy

1. Two main measures for the efficiency of an algorithm are:
   A. Time and space.
   B. Complexity and capacity.
   C. Processor and memory.
   D. Data and space.
2. An algorithm is defined as:
   A. A real-life mathematical problem.
   B. A problem.
   C. A procedure for solving a problem.
   D. None of the mentioned.
3. Which of the following cases does not exist in complexity theory?
   A. Average case   B. Worst case
   C. Best case   D. Null case.
4. Choose the appropriate outcome of the following statement "an algorithm M is asymptotically more efficient than N".
   A. M will always be a better choice for all inputs.
   B. M will always be a better choice for large inputs.
   C. N will always be a better choice for small inputs.
   D. M will always be a better choice for small inputs.
5. An algorithm can be expressed using
   A. instructions in common language.
   B. pseudocodes.
   C. flow charts.
   D. All of the mentioned.
6. Using Big-O notations, time complexity of an algorithm
   A. describes limiting behavior of the function.
   B. characterizes a function based on the growth of function.
   C. provide an upper bound on the growth rate of the function.
   D. All of the mentioned.

Moderate

7. Big-O notation for $f(n) = (n \log n + n^2)(n^3 + 2)$ is
   A. $O(n^4)$.
   B. $O(3^n)$.
   C. $O(n^2)$.
   D. $O(n^5)$.
   Hints: $0 < n^3 + 2 < n^3$, it follows that $(n \log n + n^2)(n^3 + 2)$ is less than equal to n^5.
8. If $f(n) = (n^3 - 1) / (3n + 1)$, then $f(n)$ is
   A. $O(n^2 / 3)$.
   B. $O(n)$.
   C. $O(n^2)$.
   D. $O(1)$.
9. "The algorithm is optimized" – the statement means:
   A. The algorithm is slow by time and large by space.
   B. The algorithm is fast by time and compact by space.
   C. The algorithm is fast by time and large by space.
   D. The algorithm is slow by time and compact by space.
10. There are two algorithms where Algo-A takes 1.51 milliseconds and Algo-B takes 0.8 milliseconds; which of the algorithms is better, assuming other conditions are the same?
    A. Algo-A is better than Algo-B.
    B. Algo-B is better than Algo-A.
    C. Both are equally good.
    D. None of the mentioned.
11. Suppose an algorithm's time complexity is $O(n)$, then the complexity can be defined as:
    A. Exponential
    B. Linear
    C. Constant
    D. None of the mentioned.
12. Suppose an algorithm's time complexity is $O(\log_2 n)$ then the complexity can be defined as:
    A. Exponential
    B. Polynomial
    C. Constant
    D. None of the mentioned.

13. Suppose an algorithm's time complexity is O(1) then the complexity can be defined as:
    A. Constant
    B. Polynomial
    C. Exponential
    D. None of the mentioned.

Higher-Order Thinking Skills (HOTS)

14. Find out the time complexity of the following code.

```
int a, b, k = 0, n;
for (a = n / 2; a <= n; a++)
  {
    for (b = 2; b <= n; b = b * 2)
      {
        k = k + n / 2;
      }
  }
```

    A. O(n)
    B. O(n log n)
    C. $O(n^2)$
    D. $O(n^2 \log n)$.

15. Find out the time complexity of following code.

```
int m = 0, i,j,n;
for(i = 1; i <= n; i++) {
for(j = n; j > i; j--) {
        m = m + i;
    }
}
```

    A. $O(n*\log(n))$
    B. $O(n)$
    C. $O(\log n)$
    D. $O(n*n)$

16. An array M of 15 numbers is defined by a sequence of 0's followed by a sequence of 1's. Find the smallest index i such that M[i] is 1 by probing the minimum number of locations in M. The worst-case probes by an optimal algorithm is ____.
    A. 2　　B. 4
    C. 1　　D. 5.

17. What is the complexity of multiplying two matrices of order A * B and B * C?
    A. A * B　　B. B * C
    C. A * B * C　　D. A * C

18. Suppose an algorithm has two independent time complexities, $A(n)$ and $B(n)$. The complexities of the algorithm will be the order of ____.
    A. $A(n) * B(n)$
    B. Min $(A(n),B(n))$
    C. Max $(A(n),B(n))$
    D. $\log(A(n)*B(n))$.

Short Answer-type Questions

Easy

1. Why do we study algorithms?
2. Explain the various types of asymptotic notations.
3. What are the characteristics of an algorithm?
4. What is Ω notation?
5. Define big-oh (O) notation.
6. What are the differences between the algorithm and the program?
7. Differentiate between pseudocode and algorithm.

Moderate

8. Can we write multiple algorithms for a single problem? Explain with examples.
9. What do you understand by asymptotic bounds of complexity functions?
10. How to measure the efficiency of an algorithm? Explain with a C or Python code.
11. Considering an array of N numbers, design a function that finds all positive numbers in the array that have their negative numbers in it. Find out the worst-case and average-case complexities.
12. Design an algorithm that accepts a positive integer number and displays the sum of the digits.

Higher-Order Thinking Skills (HOTS)

13. Write the nature of the curve for the following asymptotic bounds:
    $O(n^3)$, $O(1)$, $O(n^2)$, $O(n \log n)$, $O(\log n)$, $O(2^n)$.
14. Derive the asymptotic bound for the linear function $f(n) = 5n + 3$.
15. Derive the asymptotic bound for the exponential function: $f(n) = 2^n + 5n^2 + 2n$.

16. Derive the complexity of the following Python code:

```
s = 0
print('Enter no of terms')
n = int(input())
for i in range(n):
    s = s + i
print('sum = ', s)
```

17. Derive the complexity of the following C code:

```
main()
{
    int i, j, n;
printf("Enter no of terms");
scanf("%d", &n);
for(i = 1; i <= n; i++)
    {
for(j = 1; j <= n; j++)
        {
            printf("India");
        }
    }
}
```

Descriptive-type Questions

Easy

1. Write an algorithm for finding an unknown number x in a sequence and find O, θ, and Ω of the algorithm.
2. Arrange the growth rates of the following functions in the increasing order: $O(n^3)$, $O(1)$, $O(n^2)$, $O(n \log n)$, $O(\log n)$, $O(2^n)$.
3. Write the guiding principles of big-oh (O) notations.
4. Compare between big-omega (Ω) and big-theta (θ).

Moderate

5. Express the following terms in the big-oh (O) notation:

   $F(n) = (n^3 + n) / (n + 5)$

   $F(n) = 6n + 200$

6. What is the time complexity of fun() and how we can drive the complexity?

```
int fun(int n)
{
   int c = 0, i, j;
   for(i = 0; i< n; i++)
   for(j = i; j > 0; j--)
      c = c + 1;
   return c;
}
```

7. What do you understand by best-, worst-, and average-case analysis of an algorithm? Explain with examples.

Higher-Order Thinking Skills (HOTS)

8. Consider an algorithm of input size n. When $n = 4096$, the runtime is 512 mSec and when $n = 16384$ then runtime is 2048 mSec. Calculate the complexity of the algorithm.
9. Design an algorithm that finds different ways users can traverse T inches by doing jumps of 10, 20, 30, 40, or 50 inch lengths. Suppose that T is a very large number. What will be the complexity?
10. Prove: $f(n) = 100n + 5 != \Omega(n^2)$.
11. Find the complexity of the below pseudocode for $f(100)$.

```
c = 0
f(n)
{
   c = 1
   if (n < 0)
      return
   for i = 0 to n
      c= c + 1
n = n//2;
}
f(n)
print c
```

CASE STUDIES

1. Consider the following functions:
   $A(n) = 2^n$
   $B(n) = n!$
   $C(n) = n^{\log n}$
   Find out which of the following statements is true and justified.
   1. $A(n) = O(B(n))$; $B(n) = O(C(n))$
   2. $A(n) = \Omega(B(n))$; $B(n) = O(C(n))$
   3. $B(n) = O(A(n))$; $C(n) = O(A(n))$
   4. $C(n) = O(A(n))$; $B(n) = \Omega(A(n))$
2. Find out the complexity of the recurrence function given below in step-by-step order:
   $$C(n) = \begin{cases} 2C(n-1)-1, & \text{if } n > 0 \\ 1, & \text{Otherwise} \end{cases}$$
3. Find out the complexity of the recurrence function given below in step-by-step order:
   $$C(n) = \begin{cases} 3C(n-1), & \text{if } n > 0 \\ 1, & \text{Otherwise} \end{cases}$$

ANSWER KEYS

Multiple Choice Questions

1. A	4. B	7. D	10. B	13. A	16. B
2. C	5. D	8. C	11. B	14. B	17. C
3. D	6. D	9. B	12. D	15. D	18. C

4 Array

CONTENTS

EXPECTED OUTCOMES OF THIS CHAPTER

After going through this chapter learners will be able

- ☑ to explain the basic concepts of array data structures.
- ☑ to analyze the advantages and disadvantages of array.
- ☑ to understand the basic operations on array.
- ☑ to design and implement array data structure using C and Python.
- ☑ to calculate memory address in row-major and column-major order.

4.1 INTRODUCTION

In a majority of computer programs, programmers have to deal with a large number of data values. They have to use a large number of different variables to store and process these large data values. As the number of variables increases, the complexity of the program also increases, and programmers often get confused with the different variable names that need to be assigned with the numerous data values. There may be situations in which we need to work with a large number of similar data values. To make such work easier, a concept is developed that is called "array".

An array is a collection of homogeneous (similar or analogous) data items stored at contiguous memory locations. The idea is to store multiple similar items together. This makes it easier to calculate the position of each element by simply adding an offset or index to a base value. The memory location of the first element of the array is called the base address or the starting address.

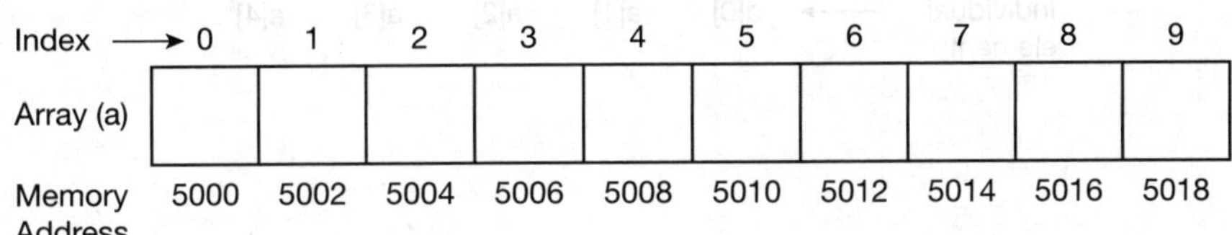

Figure 4.1 Array representation in computer memory

Figure 4.1 shows that each element can be uniquely identified by their index number in the array. For example, Fig. 4.1 represents an integer array (each location takes 2 bytes of memory) that has a maximum of 10 elements. The index of the array starts with 0. So, an array having 10 elements has indices from 0 to 9 with the base or starting address 5000 (for the above example). The C programming language offers array data type but Python does not have built-in support for arrays. Instead, the list data type in Python offers facilities to be used for the purpose.

> ***Note!***
> Array is a linear and static data structure.

4.1.1 Definition

An array is a collection of homogeneous data items stored at contiguous memory locations. This collection of homogeneous data elements is stored with a single name. The array is a linear data structure.

To understand the concept of an array, consider the following C language example,

```
int a, b, c, d, e;
```

Here, the compiler allocates 2 bytes (generally in a 16-bit processor) of memory each with name 'a', 'b', 'c', 'd', 'e'. Total $5 \times 2 = 10$ bytes of memory will be occupied. These five memory locations may or may not be in a sequence.

Instead of declaring five different values, users can declare an array. Now, consider the following declaration.

```
int a[5];
```

In the above example, the compiler allocates a total of 10 bytes of contiguous memory locations with the single name 'a'. It allows storing five different integer values (2 bytes of memory each at a time. It indicates that all five memory locations are named as 'a'.

The index of the array starts from 0. Hence, the array having 5 elements has indexed from 0 to 4. The compiler not only allocates memory but also assigns an index value to each element of the array. Figure 4.2 shows an example of an array. The individual elements of an array are recognized using a combination of the name of the array and index number.

> **Note!**
> An array is a collection of homogeneous data items stored at contiguous memory locations.

```
ArrayName [indexValue] Suppose, a[2] = 5; a[4]=10;
```

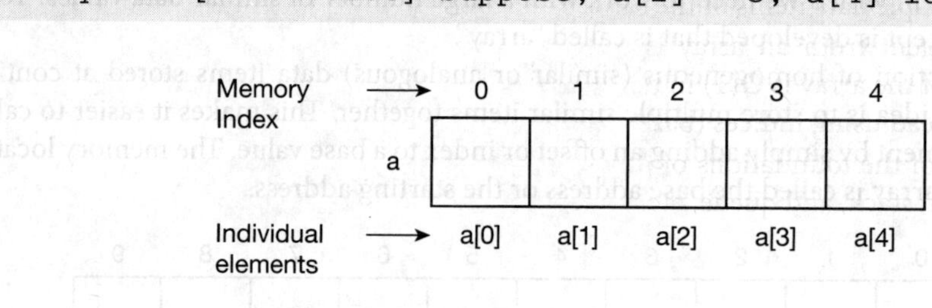

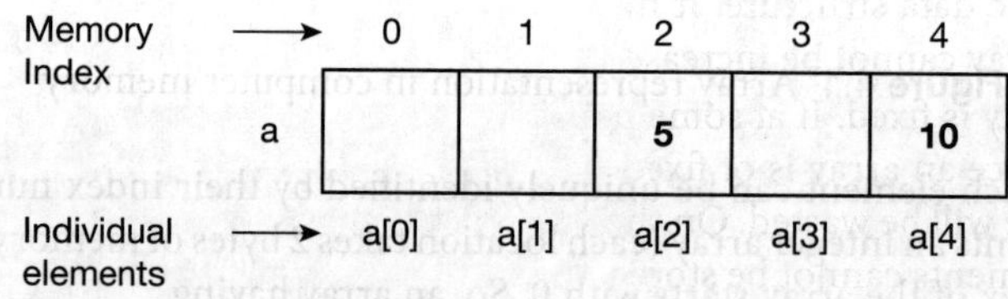

Figure 4.2 Example of an array representation with memory index and elements

4.1.2 Basic Operations

Generally, five basic operations are associated with an array. Random access is permitted within an array. Insertion and deletion take place at any index number without accessing the previous elements of that array. The following five basic operations can be performed on an array. Table 4.1 gives an indication of actions performed during these operations:

Table 4.1 Basic operations on an array

S. No.	Name of the operations	Actions in the operations
1.	Traversing	Visit or print all the array elements sequentially.
2.	Insertion	Insert an element at the given position. Insertion at random position is possible.
3.	Deletion	Delete an element from the given position/index. Deletion at random position is possible.
4.	Searching	Searches an element using the given index or by the value.
5.	Update	Updates an element at the given index.

4.1.3 Advantages and Disadvantages

Advantages

1. We can store multiple data items of the same type by using only a single name.
2. The reading element from an array is simple and efficient. Random access is possible here. The access time of the array is O(1) in both the best and worst cases. This is because any element can be instantly read using indices (base address calculation) without traversing the whole array.
3. The array is one of the foundations of other data structures. For example, other data structures such as linked list, stack, and queue, etc. are implemented using the array.

Disadvantages

1. Programmers have to declare the size of an array at the beginning of the program. So, if we are not aware of how many elements we are going to store in the array, it would make the task difficult.
2. An array is a static data structure. It means that an array is of fixed size. The memory which is allocated to an array cannot be increased or reduced during runtime.
3. The size of an array is fixed. If at some point, we need to store more elements in it then it cannot be performed. Since an array is of fixed size, if we allocate more memory than the requirement, the memory space will be wasted. On the other hand, if we allocate less memory than the requirement, then all elements cannot be stored and it will also create a problem.
4. The elements of an array are stored in consecutive memory locations. So, insertions and deletions are very difficult and time-consuming if the array size is large.

It may be noted that Python language allocates memory for the variables during runtime according to the requirements contrary to C language where memory is allocated beforehand. The data to be stored in a variable is taken care of by an object which manages the allocations of memory during the execution of the instructions to deal with the variables. So, the concept of static memory allocation using the array data type in C language is somehow not present in Python. Since all memory allocations take place during execution, this type of allocation is dynamic and need-based. When objects are no longer needed, then Python memory manager will automatically reclaim memory from them. With this notion, Python does not offer an inbuilt array data type like C language. Rather, it manages such data organization tasks with the help of an in-built list datatype.

4.1.4 Access Array Elements

The above section explained how an array is to be declared, and its various applications. This section presents how to access the elements of an array. A single operation cannot retrieve and access the elements of an array. We normally use a loop for this purpose. The value of the integer index or subscript is incremented for accessing the elements of the array while iterating the loop. The following examples present the C and Python codes for accessing the elements of an array.

> **Note!**
> Random access is possible in an array.

Example 4.1 **C source code for accessing the elements of an array**

```
#include<stdio.h>
int main()
 {
  int arr[5]; /* Array declaration */
  int i;

  for(i = 0; i < 5; i++)
   {
    /* Accessing elements of the array and assigning values
    from 1 to 5 */
    arr[i] = i+1;
   }
  /* Accessing elements of the array and displaying values */
  for(i = 0; i < 5; i++)
   {
    printf("\nElement %d: %d", i, arr[i]);
   }
  }
 /* End Program */
```

Output

```
Element 0: 1
Element 1: 2
Element 2: 3
Element 3: 4
Element 4: 5
```

> **Programming Tips!**
> In the above example, we can access the first element of the array at the 0th index (i = 0) and a value of i + 1 (i.e., 1) is assigned to the first element. Then, the index is incremented by 1 using integer increment method i++ to access the next element of the array. A value of 2 (i.e., i+1 where i = 1) is assigned to this element. Similarly, we can access the other array elements sequentially by incrementing the index until the last element located at the 4th index (i = 4) is reached. The index varies from 0 to 4 and hence the length is 5.

It may be recalled that arrays are used to store more than one value in one variable. Python does not have built-in support for arrays. List datatype of Python with homogeneous elements can be used to handle arrays.

Example 4.2 Python source code for accessing the elements of an array

```
fruits = ["Apple", "Orange", "Banana"]
print(fruits)
```

Output

```
['Apple', 'Orange', 'Banana']
```

An array element can be accessed by index number. To display the values of the first and last array elements, we can use the following statements.

```
fruits = ["Apple", "Orange", "Banana"]
first = fruits[0]
last = fruits[-1]
print(first)
print(last)
```

Output

```
Apple
Banana
```

4.1.5 Length of Array

The length of an array means the number of elements in an array. The length of an array is always one more than the maximum array index because the array index starts from zero.

Example 4.3 C source code for finding the length of an array

Built-in `sizeof()` function can be used in C programming to find the length of an array. The length is calculated using `sizeof` and then divided by the size of one element of the array.

```
#include<stdio.h>
int main()
 {
  int a[5] = {10, 20, 30, 40, 50}; int len;
  len = sizeof(a)/sizeof(a[0]);
  printf("Length of the array is %d", len);
 }
/* End Program */
```

Output

```
5
```

Example 4.4 Python source code for finding the length of an array

We can use the `len()` method to get the length of an array implemented as a homogeneous list in Python. Following example code returns the number of elements in a fruits array:

```
fruits = ["Apple", "Orange", "Banana"]
length = len(fruits)
print(length)
```

Output

3

4.1.6 Looping Array Elements

We can use the `for` or `while` or `do-while` loop to access all the elements of an array. The C source code of Section 4.1.4 has already presented looping array elements for two purposes, (1) accessing and assigning values, (2) accessing and displaying values using for a loop. The following C source code shows how to access array elements using a `while` loop.

Example 4.5 C source code for looping of array elements

```
#include<stdio.h>
int main()
 {
  int arr[5]= {10, 20, 30, 40, 50}; /* Array declaration */
  int i = 0;
  while(i < 5)
  {
   /* Accessing elements of the array and displaying values */
   printf("\nElement %d: %d", i, arr[i]);
   i++;
  }
 }
/* End Program */
```

Output

```
Element 0: 10
Element 1: 20
Element 2: 30
Element 3: 40
Element 4: 50
```

Example 4.6 Python source code for looping of array elements

The following source code can be used to access all the elements of an array defined by the Python list of homogeneous items:

```
fruits = ["Apple", "Orange", "Banana"]
# Using for loop for accessing and displaying all the array
elements
for fruit in fruits:
    print(fruit)
```

Output

```
Apple
Orange
Banana
```

4.1.7 Array Methods

We need various methods for executing different operations on arrays. Procedural programming languages like C offer facilities to define functions for conducting the said operations (in Section 4.1.2) manually. Once the functions are defined along with memory allocated for the purpose, we can repeatedly use the functions for these linear data structure operations.

On the other hand, Python offers a set of built-in functions for the purpose of manipulating list datatype that are used for linear lists or arrays. The following Table 4.2 presents the list of those built-in functions already exemplified in Chapter 2, Python Digest.

Table 4.2 Built-in Python methods for array (or linear list) manipulation

Method	Description
`count()`	Returns the number of elements
`copy()`	Returns a copy of the list
`clear()`	Removes all elements from the list
`pop()`	Removes the element at the specified position
`remove()`	Removes the first item with the specified value
`index()`	Returns the index of the first element with the specified value
`append()`	Adds an element at the end of the list
`extend()`	Add the elements of a list (or any iterable), to the end of the current list
`insert()`	Adds an element at the specified position
`reverse()`	Reverses the order of the list
`sort()`	Sorts the list

Numpy library of Python also offers numerous methods for dealing with array data structure, briefly explained in Chapter 2.

4.1.8 Array vs. List

There are many similarities and differences between array and list. Both are significant data structures for storing data in any programming language. The composition is very simple and primitive in both cases. Both can be indexed and iterated through. Programming languages offer methods to slice data elements from both array and list. The following Table 4.3 presents the differences between array and list.

Table 4.3 Difference between array and list

Array	List
Array is a linear data structure where contiguous memory allocations take place.	List is a dynamic data structure where non-contiguous memory allocation takes place.
Arrays are used to store homogeneous data elements.	Lists allow storage of heterogeneous or non-homogeneous data elements.
Array memory is static and continuous.	List memory allocations are dynamic and non-continuous.
We don't need to keep track of next memory locations with arrays.	We have to keep track of the next location with lists.

Treatments of arrays and lists vary from one programming language to another. For example, ['Atanu', 'Chandan'] is considered a list in Python whereas it is taken as an array in C, Java and JavaScript. C programming language offers in-built array data structure for dealing with homogeneous data elements. Many literatures consider arrays as linear lists, especially in the case of Python programming language. Python offers in-built list datatype for dealing with both homogeneous and non-homogeneous data elements. Numpy library of Python also offers various methods and attributes to take care of array data structure. Theoretically, lists are of two types, linear list and linked list. Chapter 5 deals with linked list data structure in detail.

4.2 ARRAY OPERATIONS USING STATIC MEMORY ALLOCATION

The insertion and deletion operations on the array are presented here using static memory allocation. These two operations are the fundamental operations that are required to deal with arrays.

4.2.1 Insertion of an Element in an Array

Insertion operation is used to insert a new element at a specific position into a one-dimensional array. To insert a new element into the one-dimensional array, we have to create space for the new element. Suppose there are *N* elements in an array, and we want to insert a new element between the first and second elements. We have to move the last *N* – 1 elements down to create space for the new element.

Algo-4.1 Algorithm of insertion operation in an array

Step 1	`TEMP = N-1, POSITION = POSITION - 1.`
Step 2	`Repeat Step 3 While TEMP ≥ POSITION.`
Step 3	`Array [TEMP + 1] = Array [TEMP].` `TEMP = TEMP - 1.`
Step 4	`Array [POSITION] = Data.`
Step 5	`N = N + 1.`
Step 6	`Exit.`

4.2.2 Insertion of an Element in an Array with C

CProg-4.1 Inserting an element into an array using static memory allocation

```
#include<stdio.h>
#include<stdlib.h>
/* Driver function */
int main()
 {
  int i, j, n_value, save, insertion, insert_element, position,
  elements, array[30];
  /* Here array named array of size 30 is used to overcome
  the overflow but input
  size should be less than 30 */
  printf("Enter number of elements of array: ");
  scanf("%d", & elements);
  for(i = 0; i < elements; i++)
   {
    scanf("%d", &array[i]);
   }
  printf("Enter insertion position: ");
  scanf("%d", &insertion);
  save = array[insertion - 1];
  printf("Enter insertion element: ");
  scanf("%d", &insert_element);
  /* Starts dumping value of insertion index to their next
  index until array doesn't completed. */
  array[insertion - 1] = insert_element;
  for(i = insertion - 1; i < elements; i++)
   {
    n_value = array[i+1];
    array[i+1] = save;
    save = n_value;
   }
  array[i+1] = save;
  /* Array with inserted elements */
  printf("Updated array is: ");
  for(j = 0; j <= elements; j++)
   {
    printf("%d", array[j]);
   }
 }
/* End of program */
```

Output

```
Enter number of elements of array: 10
2 5 15 58 98 74 15 26 69 61
```

```
Enter insertion position: 3
Enter insertion element: 120
Updated array is: 2 5 120 15 58 98 74 15 26 69 61
```

> ***Programming Tips!***
> Array of size 30 is used to overcome the overflow though the input size should be less than 30. The program will then start dumping the value of insertion index to the next index until the array is completed.

4.2.3 Deletion of an Element from an Array

Deletion operation is used to delete an element from a specific position from the one-dimensional array. To delete an element from the one-dimensional array, first we have to delete an element from the specified position, and then shift the remaining elements upwards to take the vacant space of the deleted element.

Algo-4.2 Algorithm of deletion operation in an array

Step 1	`POSITION = POSITION - 1, TEMP = POSITION.`
Step 2	`Return ARRAY [POSITION].`
Step 3	`Repeat Step 4 while TEMP ≤ N-1.`
Step 4	`TEMP = TEMP + 1.`
Step 5	`N = N - 1.`
Step 6	`Exit.`

4.2.4 Deletion of an Element from an Array with C

CProg-4.2 Deleting an element from an array using static memory allocation

```
#include<stdio.h>
#include<stdlib.h>
/* Driver function */
int main()
 {
   int i, j, deletion, position, elements, array[30];
   /* Here array named array of size 30 is used to overcome
   the overflow but input size should be less than 30 */
   printf("Enter number of elements of array: ");
   scanf("%d", &elements);
   for(i = 0; i < elements; i++)
    {
     scanf("%d", &array[i]);
    }
  printf("Enter deletion position: ");
  scanf("%d", &deletion);
```

```
    /* Starts dumping value of deletion index to their previous
    index until array doesn't completed.*/
    for(i = deletion - 1; i < elements - 1; i++)
       {
        array[i] = array[i + 1];
       }
    /* Array with deleted elements */
    printf("Updated array is: ");
    for(j = 0; j < elements - 1; j++)
      {
       printf("%d", array[j]);
      }
  }
/* End of program */
```

Output

```
Enter number of elements of array: 5
10 12 13 14 15
Enter deletion position: 3
Updated array is: 10 12 14 15
```

Note!
Insertions and deletions, both are very difficult and time-consuming operations when the array size is large.

Programming Tips!
An array of size 30 is used to overcome the overflow though the input size should be less than 30. The program will then start dumping the value of deletion index to the previous index until the array is completed.

4.3 ARRAY OPERATIONS USING DYNAMIC MEMORY ALLOCATION

When we create an array, we must specify the size at the time of the declaration itself, and it cannot be changed during the program execution time (or run time). This is a major problem when programmers do not know the number of values to be stored in an array beforehand. To solve this, the programmer can use the concept of dynamic memory allocation. *The allocation of memory during the program execution time is called dynamic memory allocation.*

In C programming, the programmer can use predefined or standard library functions to allocate memory dynamically. There are four standard library functions (which was described in Chapter 1) that are defined in the header file known as "stdlib.h". These dynamic memory functions are:

1. `malloc()`
2. `calloc()`
3. `realloc()`
4. `free()`

Note!
The allocation of memory during the program execution is called dynamic memory allocation.

4.3.1 Insertion of an Element in an Array with C

CProg-4.3 Inserting an element into an array using dynamic memory allocation

```
#include<stdio.h>
#include<stdlib.h>
/* Driver function */
int main()
 {
   int  i,  j,  n_value,  save,  insertion,  insert_element,
   position, elements, *array;
   printf("Enter number of elements of array: ");
   scanf("%d", &elements);
   array = malloc(sizeof(int) * elements + 1);
   /* Here malloc will generate no of blocks as we required
   to save memory using dynamic allocation */
   for(i = 0; i < elements; i++)
    {
     scanf("%d", &array[i]);
    }
   printf("Enter insertion position: ");
   scanf("%d", &insertion);
   save = array[insertion - 1];
   printf("Enter insertion element: ");
   scanf("%d", &insert_element);
   /* Starts dumping value of insertion index to their next
   index until array doesn't completed */
   array[insertion - 1] = insert_element;
   for(i = insertion - 1; i < elements; i++)
    {
     n_value = array[i + 1];
     array[i + 1] = save;
     save = n_value;
    }
   array[i + 1] = save;
   /* Display array with deleted elements */
   printf("Updated Array Is: ");
   for(j = 0; j <= elements; j++)
    {
     printf("%d", array[j]);
    }
 }
/* End of program */
```

Output

```
Enter number of elements of array: 10
2 5 15 58 98 74 15 26 69 61
Enter insertion position: 3
Enter insertion element: 120
Updated array is: 2 5 120 15 58 98 74 15 26 69 61
```

> ***Programming Tips!***
> malloc generates a number of blocks as we are required to save memory using dynamic allocation. The program then starts dumping the value of insertion index to their next index until the array is completed.

4.3.2 Insertion of an Element in an Array with Python

PyProg-4.1 Inserting an element into an array

```
# Taking the array input
print("Enter the number of elements of the array", end = " ")
input()
print("Enter the elements of the array ")
lists = list(map(int, input().split()))
print("Enter the insertion position:", end = " ")
n = int(input())
print("Enter the insertion element:", end = " ")
element = int(input())

# Using python insert function to insert element in the list
named lists
lists.insert(n-1, element)

# Display the updated array after deletion of an element
print("Updated array is: ", end = " ")
for i in range(len(lists)):
    print(lists[i], end = " ")
## End program
```

Output

```
Enter the number of elements of the array 10
Enter the elements of the array
2 5 15 58 98 74 15 26 69 61
Enter the insertion position: 3
Enter the insertion element: 120
Updated array is: 2, 5, 120, 15, 58, 98, 74,
15, 26, 69, 61
```

> ***Programming Tips!***
> `insert()` is used to insert elements in the list.

4.3.3 Deletion of an Element from an Array with C

CProg-4.4 Deleting an element from an array using dynamic memory allocation

```
#include<stdio.h>
#include<stdlib.h>
/* Driver function*/
int main()
 {
   int i, j, deletion, position, elements, *array;
   printf("Enter number of elements of array: ");
   scanf("%d", & elements);
   array = malloc(sizeof(int) * elements + 1);
   /* Here malloc function will generate memory blocks as we
   required in run time */
   for(i = 0; i < elements; i++)
    {
     scanf("%d", &array[i]);
    }
   printf("Enter deletion position: ");
   scanf("%d", &deletion);
   /* Starts dumping value of deletion index to their next
   index until array doesn't completed */
   for(i = deletion - 1; i < elements - 1; i++)
    {
     array[i] = array[i + 1];
    }
   /* Display the array with deleted elements*/
   printf("Updated array is: ");
   for(j = 0; j < elements - 1; j++)
    {
     printf("%d", array[j]);
    }
 }
/* End of program */
```

Output

```
Enter number of elements of array: 5
56 45 78 25 15
Enter deletion position: 3
Updated array is: 56 45 25 15
```

Programming Tips!

`malloc()` is used to generate as many memory blocks as we may require during program execution. The program then starts dumping the value of deletion index to the next index until the array is completed.

4.3.4 Deletion of Element from an Array with Python

PyProg-4.2 Deleting an element from an array

```
# Taking the array input
print("Enter the number of elements of the array:", end = " ")
input()
print("Enter the elements of the array ")
lists = list(map(int, input().split()))
print("Enter the deletion position:", end = " ")
n = int(input())

# Using python delete function to delete element in the list
named lists
del(lists[n-1])

# Display the updated array after deletion of an element
print("Updated array")
for i in range(len(lists)):
    print(lists[i], end = " ")
## End program
```

Output

```
Enter the number of elements of the array: 5
Enter the elements of the array
10 12 13 14 15
Enter the deletion position: 2
Updated array is: 10, 13, 14, 15
```

> ***Programming Tips!***
> `delete()` is used to delete elements from the list.

4.4 SLICING, SEARCHING AND UPDATING ARRAY ELEMENTS

4.4.1 Slicing Array Elements

Slicing an array means taking elements from a particular index to another given index. This section presents slicing of array elements using both C and Python.

Example 4.7 Slicing of an array

```
#include<stdio.h>
/* Driver function */
int main()
 {
  int arr[8] = {10, 20, 30, 40, 50, 60, 70, 80};
  /* Array declaration */
  int p, q, i = 0, j = 0;
  int sliced_arr[8];
  printf("\nEnter the indices between which the array to be
  sliced:");
```

```
  scanf("%d %d", &p, &q);
  i = p;
  printf("\nSliced Array Elements:");

  while(i < q+1)
  {
   /* Displaying sliced array values */
   sliced_arr[j]= arr[i];
   printf("\nElement %d: %d", j, sliced_arr[j]);
   i++; j++;
  }
 }
/* End Program */
```

Output

```
Enter the indices between which the array to be sliced: 1 3
Sliced Array Elements:
Element 0: 20
Element 1: 30
Element 2: 40
```

We can deal with arrays by using Numpy arrays besides homogeneous list datatypes in Python already discussed in Chapter 2. To pull out a slice of an array, the : operator is used when we are declaring the index. The Syntax is:

```
<array slice> = <array>[start:stop]
```

where <array slice> means the slice or segment of the array. Python counting starts at 0 by default and ends at $n - 1$.

Example 4.8 Python source code of slicing array between index 1 and index 4

```
import numpy as np
a = np.array([10, 20, 30, 40, 50, 60, 70])
print(a[1:4])
```

Output

```
[20 30 40]
```

Example 4.9 Python source code of slicing array elements from index 4 to the end

```
import numpy as np
a = np.array([10, 20, 30, 40, 50, 60, 70])
print(a[4:])
```

Output

```
[50 60 70]
```

Example 4.10 **Python source code of slicing array elements from the beginning to index 3** (where index 4 is not included)

```
import numpy as np
a = np.array([10, 20, 30, 40, 50, 60, 70])
print(a[:4])
```

Output

```
[10 20 30 40]
```

Example 4.11 **Python source code of slicing 2-D Arrays - I**

From the second segment of the array, the 2nd element, slice elements from index 1 to index 4 where index 4 is not included. The second element has index 1 because index starts from 0.

```
import numpy as np
a = np.array([[10, 20, 30, 40, 50], [60, 70, 80, 90, 100]])
print(a[1, 1:4])
```

Output

```
[70 80 90]
```

Example 4.12 **Python source code of slicing 2-D Arrays - II**

```
import numpy as np
a = np.array([[10, 20, 30, 40, 50], [60, 70, 80, 90, 100]])
print(a[0:2, 1:4])
```

Output

```
[[20 30 40]
[70 80 90]]
```

4.4.2 Searching Array Elements

Suppose we are trying to search for an element within an array. We have to give an input element which is to be searched for. For example, if the element to be searched is 30 in the array [0, 20, 30, 40, 50, 60], then the output will be displayed as the index of the searched element, which is 3 because the index starts from zero. Chapter 12 later will present a detailed discussion of all major searching methods of an element within an array using both C and Python. Here, one easy approach is presented using Python to give an idea of the method using `index()` built-in function for list analysis.

Example 4.13 **Python source code to search for an element in an array**

```
x = ["Kolkata", "India", "Mumbai"]
print(x.index("India"))
```

Output

```
1
```

4.4.3 Updating Array Elements

We can update and make changes to an array in different ways. A few examples are as follows:

Example 4.14 C source code for updating an array using assignment operator

```
int a = {10, 20, 30};
a[1] = 50;
```

Now, value 50 will replace 20 in the array at index 1 position.

Example 4.15 Python source code for updating an array with assignment operator and array module

```
from array import *
a = array('i', range(1, 9))
print("Array before update: {}".format(a))
# Update the elements at index 3
index = 3
num_array = a
num_array[index] = 20
print("array after update: {}".format(num_array))
```

Output

```
Array before update: array('i', [1, 2, 3, 4])
Array after update: array('i', [1, 2, 3, 20, 5, 6, 7, 8, 9])
```

Example 4.16 Python source code for updating an array using append() method

```
arr = [10, 20, 30]
arr.append(40)
print(arr)
```

Output

```
[10, 20, 30, 40]
```

Example 4.17 Python source code for updating an array using extend() method to add multiple items

```
fruits = ["Apple", "Orange", "Banana"]
country = ['India', 'USA', 'Australia']
fruits.extend(country)
print(fruits)
```

Output

```
['Apple', 'Orange', 'Banana', 'India', 'USA', 'Australia']
```

4.5 APPLICATIONS OF ARRAY USING STATIC MEMORY ALLOCATIONS

Following are some of the applications of arrays:

1. **To store a list of values:** Single-dimensional arrays are used to store a list of values of the same datatype. In other words, single-dimensional arrays are used to store a row of values in a linear form.
2. **To perform matrix operations:** Programmers can use two-dimensional arrays to create a matrix of similar data types. We can perform various operations on matrices using two-dimensional arrays such as matrix addition, matrix multiplication, etc.
3. **To implement search algorithms:** We use single-dimensional arrays to implement search algorithms, such as linear search, binary search, etc. (which will be discussed in a later chapter).
4. **To implement sorting algorithms:** We use single-dimensional arrays to implement sorting algorithms, such as insertion sort, bubble sort, selection sort, quick sort, merge sort, etc. These will also be discussed in a later chapter.
5. **To implement data structures:** Programmers can use single-dimensional arrays to implement data structures such as stack and queue using arrays.
6. Arrays are also used to implement CPU scheduling algorithms.

> ***Note!***
> Applications of arrays include storing a list of values, performing matrix operations, implementing, searching and sorting algorithms, etc.

4.5.1 Addition of Two Matrices Using Array with C

CProg-4.5 Adding two matrices using static memory allocation

```
#include<stdio.h>
#include<stdlib.h>
/* Driver function */
int main()
 {
   int i, j, rows, columns, array1[30], array2[30];
   /* Here 2 arrays named array1 and array2 of size 30 are
   used just to overcome overflow but input size will be
   less than 30*/
   printf("Enter number of rows of matrix: ");
   scanf("%d", &rows);
   printf("Enter number of columns of matrix: ");
   scanf("%d", &columns);
   /* Input first array */
   printf("Enter elements of first matrix: \n");
   for(i = 0; i < rows; i++)
   {
     for(j = 0; j < columns; j++)
     {
```

```
        scanf("%d", & *(array1 + i * columns + j));
      }
    }
    /* Input second array */
    printf("Enter elements of second matrix: \n");
    for(i = 0; i < rows; i++)
    {
      for(j = 0; j < columns; j++)
      {
        scanf("%d", & * (array2 + i * columns + j));
      }
    }
    /* Calculate and display result of addition */
    printf("Resultant array is: \n");
    for(i = 0; i < rows; i++)
    {
      for(j = 0; j < columns; j++)
      {
        printf("%d", *(array1 + i * columns + j) + * (array2
        + i * columns + j));
      }
      printf("\n");
    }
  }
/* End of program */
```

Output

```
Enter number of rows of matrix: 4
Enter number of columns of matrix: 4
Enter elements of first matrix:
1 2 3 4 5 6 7 8 9 10 11 12 13 14 15 16
Enter elements of second matrix:
1 2 3 4 5 6 7 8 9 10 11 12 13 14 15 16
Resultant array is
2 4 6 8
10 12 14 16
18 20 22 24
26 28 30 32
```

Programming Tips!

Two arrays named array1 and array2 of size 30 are used just to overcome overflow, but input size will be less than 30. The program calculates *(array1 + i * columns + j) + * (array2 + i * columns + j) to find the resultant elements after adding two matrices.

4.5.2 Multiplication of Two Matrices Using Array with C

CProg-4.6 Multiplying two matrices using static memory allocation

```
#include<stdio.h>
#include<stdlib.h>
/* Driver function */
int main()
 {
   int  array1[30][30],  array2[30][30],  array3[30][30],
   rows, columns, i, j, k;

   /* Here two array named array1 and array2 of size 30
   are used just to overcome overflow but input size will
   be less than 30 */
   printf("Enter number of rows of matrix: ");
   scanf("%d", &rows);
   printf("Enter number of columns of matrix: ");
   scanf("%d", &columns);

   /* Input first matrix */
   printf("Enter elements of first matrix: ");
   for(i = 0; i < rows; i++)
    {
     for(j = 0; j < columns; j++)
      {
       scanf("%d", &array1[i][j]);
      }
    }
   /* Input first matrix */
   printf("Enter elements of second matrix: ");
   for(i = 0; i < rows; i++)
    {
     for(j = 0; j < columns; j++)
      {
       scanf("%d", &array2[i][j]);
      }
    }
   /* Multiplying elements of first matrix row by column
   method */
   for(i = 0; i < rows; i++)
    {
     for(j = 0; j < columns; j++)
      {
       array3[i][j] = 0;
```

```
        for(k = 0; k < columns; k++)
         {
          array3[i][j] += array1[i][k] * array2[k][j];
         }
       }
     }

    /* Display result */
    printf("Resultant array is: \n");
    for(i = 0; i < rows; i++)
     {
      for(j = 0; j < columns; j++)
       {
        printf("%d", array3[i][j]);
       }
      printf("\n");
     }
    return 0;
  }
/* End of program*/
```

Output

```
Enter number of rows of matrix: 2
Enter number of columns of matrix: 2
Enter elements of first matrix: 2 5 4 8
Enter elements of second matrix: 4 8 6 2
Resultant array is:
38 26
64 48
```

Programming Tips!

Two arrays named array1 and array2 of size 30 each are used to overcome overflow, but input size will be less than 30. The program multiplies elements of the matrices using row-by-column method to find the resultant elements.

4.6 APPLICATIONS OF ARRAY USING DYNAMIC MEMORY ALLOCATIONS

Here, we shall use dynamic memory functions like `malloc()`, `calloc()`, `realloc()` and `free()` for the addition and multiplication of matrices in C programming.

4.6.1 Addition of Two Matrices Using Array with C

CProg-4.7 Adding two matrices using dynamic memory allocation

```
#include<stdio.h>
#include<stdlib.h>
/* Driver function */
int main()
 {
   int i, j, rows, columns, *array1, *array2;
   printf("Enter number of rows of matrix: ");
   scanf("%d", & rows);
   printf("Enter number of columns of matrix: ");
   scanf("%d", & columns);
   /* Here dynamic array is used and will generate no of
   blocks in runtime */
  array1 = (int * ) malloc(sizeof(int) * (rows * columns));
  array2 = (int * ) malloc(sizeof(int) * (rows * columns));
   printf("Enter elements of first matrix: \n");
   for(i = 0; i < rows; i++)
    {
     for(j = 0; j < columns; j++)
      {
       scanf("%d", & * (array1 + i * columns + j));
      }
    }
   printf("Enter elements of second matrix: \n");
   for(i = 0; i < rows; i++)
    {
     for(j = 0; j < columns; j++)
      {
       scanf("%d", & * (array2 + i * columns + j));
      }
    }
   /* Display the result of addition */
   printf("Resultant array is:\n");
   for(i = 0; i < rows; i++)
    {
     for(j = 0; j < columns; j++)
      {
       printf("%d", *(array1 + i*columns + j)+ * (array2
       + i * columns + j));
      }
     printf("\n");
    }
 }
/* End of program */
```

Output

```
Enter number of rows of matrix: 4
Enter number of columns of matrix: 4
Enter elements of first matrix:
1 2 3 4 5 6 7 8 9 10 11 12 13 14 15 16
Enter elements of second matrix:
1 2 3 4 5 6 7 8 9 10 11 12 13 14 15 16
Resultant array is:
 2 4 6 8
 10 12 14 16
 18 20 22 24
 26 28 30 32
```

> ***Programming Tips!***
> Here, dynamic memory allocation is used to generate a number of blocks during execution. The program calculates *(array1 + i * columns + j) + * (array2 + i * columns + j) to find the resultant elements.

4.6.2 Addition of Two Matrices with Python

PyProg-4.3 Adding two matrices

```
# Array dimension input
print("Enter the Number of Rows of the Matrix: ")
row = int(input())
print("Enter the Number of Columns of the Matrix: ")
column = int(input())

# Input 1st matrix
print("Enter the Elements of First Matrix: ")
lists = []
for i in range(row):
  a = []
  for j in range(column):
    a.append(int(input()))
  lists.append(a)

# Input 2nd matrix
print("Enter the Elements of Second Matrix: ")
lists2 = []
for i in range(row):
  a = []
  for j in range(column):
    a.append(int(input()))
  lists2.append(a)
```

```
# Display results
print("The Resultant Array Is: ")
for i in range(row):
  for j in range(column):
    print(lists2[i][j]+lists[i][j], end =" ")
  print()
## End program
```

Output

```
Enter the Number of Rows of the Matrix: 2
Enter the Number of Columns of the Matrix: 2
Enter the Elements of the First Matrix:
1 2 3 4
Enter the Elements of the Second Matrix:
2 3 4 5
The Resultant Array Is:
3 5
7 9
```

> ***Programming Tips!***
> List is used to store elements after calculating the resultant elements.

4.6.3 Multiplication of Two Matrices Using Array with C

CProg-4.8 Multiplying two matrices using dynamic memory allocation

```
#include <stdio.h>
void enterData(int firstMatrix[][10], int secondMatrix[]
[10], int rowFirst, int columnFirst, int rowSecond, int
columnSecond);
void multiplyMatrices(int firstMatrix[][10], int second-
Matrix[][10], int multResult[][10], int rowFirst, int
columnFirst, int rowSecond, int columnSecond);
void  display(int  mult[][10],  int  rowFirst,  int
columnSecond);

/* Driver function */
int main()
 {
   int firstMatrix[10][10], secondMatrix[10][10], mult[10]
   [10], rowFirst, columnFirst, rowSecond, columnSecond,
   i, j, k;
   printf("Enter rows and column for first matrix: ");
   scanf("%d %d", &rowFirst, &columnFirst);
   printf("Enter rows and column for second matrix: ");
   scanf("%d %d", &rowSecond, &columnSecond);
   /* If the column of the first matrix is not equal to the
   row of the second matrix, asking the user to enter the
   size of the matrix again.*/
```

```
   while(columnFirst != rowSecond)
   {
     printf("Error! column of first matrix not equal to row
     of second\n");
     printf("Enter rows and column for first matrix: ");
     scanf("%d %d", &rowFirst, &columnFirst);
     printf("Enter rows and column for second matrix: ");
     scanf("%d %d", &rowSecond, &columnSecond);
   }

   /* Function to take matrices data */
   enterData(firstMatrix, secondMatrix, rowFirst,
   columnFirst, rowSecond, columnSecond);

   /* Function to multiply two matrices */
   multiplyMatrices(firstMatrix, secondMatrix, mult,
   rowFirst, columnFirst, rowSecond, columnSecond);

   /* Function to display resultant matrix after
   multiplication */
   display(mult, rowFirst, columnSecond);
     return 0;
 }

void enterData(int firstMatrix[][10], int secondMatrix[]
[10], int rowFirst, int columnFirst, int rowSecond, int
columnSecond)
 {
   int i, j;
   printf("\nEnter elements of matrix 1:\n");
   for(i = 0; i < rowFirst; ++i)
    {
     for(j = 0; j < columnFirst; ++j)
      {
       printf("Enter elements a%d%d: ", i + 1, j + 1);
       scanf("%d", &firstMatrix[i][j]);
      }
    }

   printf("\nEnter elements of matrix 2:\n");
   for(i = 0; i < rowSecond; ++i)
    {
     for(j = 0; j < columnSecond; ++j)
      {
       printf("Enter elements b%d%d: ", i + 1, j + 1);
       scanf("%d", &secondMatrix[i][j]);
      }
```

```
    }
  }

void multiplyMatrices(int firstMatrix[][10], int second-
Matrix[][10], int mult[][10], int rowFirst, int column-
First, int rowSecond, int columnSecond)
  {
    int i, j, k;
    /* Initializing elements of matrix mult to 0 */
    for(i = 0; i < rowFirst; ++i)
     {
      for(j = 0; j < columnSecond; ++j)
       {
         mult[i][j] = 0;
       }
     }

    /* Multiplying matrix firstMatrix and secondMatrix and
    storing in array mult */
    for(i = 0; i < rowFirst; ++i)
     {
      for(j = 0; j < columnSecond; ++j)
       {
        for(k =0; k<columnFirst; ++k)
         {
          mult[i][j] += firstMatrix[i][k] * secondMatrix
          [k][j];
         }
       }
     }
  }

void display(int mult[][10], int rowFirst, int columnSecond)
  {
    int i, j;
    printf("\nOutput Matrix:\n");
    for(i = 0; i < rowFirst; ++i)
     {
      for(j = 0; j < columnSecond; ++j)
       {
        printf("%d ", mult[i][j]);
        if(j == columnSecond - 1)
        printf("\n");
       }
     }
  }
/* End of program */
```

Output

```
Enter rows and column for first matrix: 2 2
Enter rows and column for second matrix: 2 2
Enter elements of matrix 1:
Enter elements a11: 5
Enter elements a12: 6
Enter elements a21: 4
Enter elements a22: 8
Enter elements of matrix 2:
Enter elements b11: 6
Enter elements b12: 4
Enter elements b21: 7
Enter elements b22: 2
```

Output Matrix:

```
72 32
80 32
```

Programming Tips!
For multiplying two matrices, we have to multiply the elements using row-by-column method to find the resultant elements.

4.6.4 Multiplication of Two Matrices with Python

PyProg-4.4 Multiplying two matrices

```
# Taking matrix input from user
def input_matrix(m, n):
 # m, n -> size of Matrix (m*n)
 mat = []
 for i in range(m):
   # Enter space separated input for elements of matrix
   # Enter 'n' no. of elements row wise and press enter
   for next row elements
   temp = map(int, input('Elements Row ' +
                     str(i+1)+' : ').strip().split(' '))
   mat.append(list(temp))
 return mat

# Function for matrix multiplication
def multipy_matrices(M1, M2, m, n, o):
 # parameters:
 # M1 -> Matrix 1
 # M2 -> Matrix 2
 # m, n -> size of Matrix1 (m*n)
 # n, o -> size of Matrix2 (n*o)
 mat = []

 for i in range(m):
   tmp = []
   for j in range(o):
     tmp.append(0)
```

```
    mat.append(tmp)
  for i in range(m):
    for j in range(o):
      for k in range(n):
        mat[i][j] += M1[i][k] * M2[k][j]
  return mat

if __name__ == "__main__":
  # Input Matrix of size m*n
  print(«\n-- Matrix-1 Size m*n Matrix-2 Size n*o --»)
  m = int(input("Enter m: "))
  n = int(input("Enter n: "))
  o = int(input("Enter o: "))

  # Input Matrix 1
  print("\nInput Elements for Matrix-1 :")
  M1 = input_matrix(m, n)
  print(«Matrix 1:», M1)

  # Input Matrix 2
  print("\nInput Elements for Matrix-2 :")
  M2 = input_matrix(n, o)
  print("Matrix 2:", M2)

  M3 = multipy_matrices(M1, M2, m, n, o)
  print("\nMatrix 1 * Matrix 2:", M3)
```

Output

```
 -- Matrix1 Size m*n Matrix2 Size n*o --
 Enter m: 3
 Enter n: 3
 Enter o: 4
 Input Elements for Matrix1 :
 Elements Row 1: 12 7 3
 Elements Row 2: 4 5 6
 Elements Row 3: 7 8 9
 Matrix 1: [[12, 7, 3], [4, 5, 6], [7, 8, 9]]
 Input Elements for Matrix2 :
 Elements Row 1: 5 8 1 2
 Elements Row 2: 6 7 3 0
 Elements Row 3: 4 5 9 1
 Matrix 2: [[5, 8, 1, 2], [6, 7, 3, 0],
[4, 5, 9, 1]]
 Matrix 1 * Matrix 2: [[114, 160, 60, 27],
[74, 97, 73, 14], [119, 157, 112, 23]]
```

Programming Tips!

The program takes matrix input from the user and stores the elements. It then calculates the matrix multiplication value and displays the resultant elements.

4.7 REPRESENTATION OF 2D ARRAYS IN COMPUTER MEMORY

Continuous memory locations are also used to store-two dimensional (2D) arrays similar to a 1D array. The computer's memory stores 2D arrays as rows, one following another. The first byte's memory address is considered as the memory location of the entire 2D array. The compiler can easily identify the memory location of any element in the 2D array if the first byte's memory location and the number of columns are known. This will be discussed in Sections 4.7.1 and 4.7.2.

A 2D array is treated as an array of arrays instead of just an array with two indexes. If A is a 2D $M \times N$ array, it is a collection of $m \times n$ data elements. The pair of lengths $(M \times N)$ is called the size of the array. Each element is identified by a pair of integers (J, K) called subscripts, where $1 \leq J \leq M$, $1 \leq K \leq N$. The pair of lengths $(M \times N)$ is called the size of the array.

The length of a given dimension can be calculated from the formula, Length = UB – LB + 1, where UB and LB are the lower bound and upper bound of the array.

We can find the length of the array by the following procedure for a 2D array:

1. First, we will find the length of the 1D row array by the formula, $L_1 = UB_1 - LB_1 + 1$.
2. Then, we find the length of the 1D column array: $L_2 = UB_2 - LB_2 + 1$.
3. The length of the array (number of elements in the 2D array): $L = L_1 \times L_2$.

> **Note!**
> We can calculate the position of each array element by simply adding an offset/index to a base value since the array is linear and static.

Example

Given an array, int A (1 : 5, 1 : 4)

1. The length of the row of the 1D array, 5 – 1 + 1 = 5.
2. The length of the column of the 1D array, 4 – 1 + 1 = 4.
3. The length of the given array = $5 \times 4 = 20$.

So, there are 20 elements stored in the given 2D array, A.

2D arrays can be represented in the computer's memory using two ways. The two most common memory layouts are row-major and column-major for multi-dimensional arrays. The row-major layout of a matrix puts the first row in contiguous memory, then the second row right after it, then the third, and so on. The column-major layout puts the first column in contiguous memory, then the second, etc. When working with 2D arrays (matrices), row-major and column-major are easy to describe and are given below.

4.7.1 Column-major Order Representation of Array

Here, the array elements are stored column-wise. This means *m* elements of the first column are stored in the first *m* locations, *m* elements of the second column are stored in the next *m* locations, and so on. Column-major order is a method similar to flattening of arrays onto linear memory. The columns are listed in a sequence.

The 2D array $\begin{bmatrix} 3 & 7 & 1 \\ 5 & 6 & 2 \end{bmatrix}$ will be flattened as 3 5 7 6 1 2 if stored in a memory linearly using column-major order. The programming languages like FORTRAN, MATLAB, and R use column-major ordering. The memory offset of the array to any given element A[row][column] using columns listed first can be calculated as:

$$\text{Offset} = \text{Row} + \text{Column} \times \text{NUMROWS},$$

where NUMROWS is the number of rows in the array. In the above example, NUMROWS is 2.

A row-major array can be treated as a column-major array by using the transpose operation. Data movements in transposition operation are often found difficult, especially in non-square matrices. Though such transposition operations are performed rarely in non-square matrices, software libraries or library functions, they are defined in programming languages for these types of data movements.

4.7.2 Row-major Order Representation of Array

Here, the array elements are stored row-wise. This means, *n* elements of the first row are stored in the first *n* locations, *n* elements of the second row are stored in the next *n* locations, and so on. Row-major order is also a method of flattening arrays onto linear memory. The rows are listed in a sequence. C and many other programming languages use this row-major order approach for dealing with multi-dimensional arrays whereas FORTRAN and MATLAB do not use this representation.

The 2D array $\begin{bmatrix} 3 & 7 & 1 \\ 5 & 6 & 2 \end{bmatrix}$ will be flattened as 3 7 1 5 6 2 if stored in a memory linearly using row-major order. The difference between the addresses of array cells in increasing rows is larger than the addresses of cells in increasing columns when using row-major order representation.

The memory offset of the array to any given element A[row][column] using rows listed first can be calculated as:

$$\text{Offset} = \text{Row} \times \text{NUMCOLS} + \text{column},$$

where NUMCOLS is the number of columns in the array. In the above example, NUMCOLS is 3.
It may be noted that the above technique is also applicable for representing higher dimensional generalized arrays. So a 2 × 2 × 2 array looks like:

```
int A[2][2][2] = {{{1, 2}, {3, 4}}, {{5, 6}, {7, 8}}};
```

and the array would be laid out in a linear memory as: 1 2 3 4 5 6 7 8.

Let A be a 2D array of size M × N. Assume that the array index starts from 1 (i.e., $a[1, 1]$ is the first location). The array will be represented in the memory by a block of M × N sequential memory locations. If M = 3 and N = 3, then A will be given by:

$$A = \begin{bmatrix} a_{11} & a_{12} & a_{13} \\ a_{21} & a_{22} & a_{23} \\ a_{31} & a_{32} & a_{33} \end{bmatrix}$$

Specifically, the array A will be stored by the programming language either as, column by column known as column-major order, or row by row known as row-major order. Figure 4.3 presents both these column-major order and row-major order representations of A.

$$\begin{bmatrix} a_{11} & a_{12} & a_{13} \\ \downarrow & \downarrow & \downarrow \\ a_{21} & a_{22} & a_{23} \\ \downarrow & \downarrow & \downarrow \\ a_{31} & a_{32} & a_{33} \end{bmatrix}$$ Column-major order

$$\begin{bmatrix} a_{11} \rightarrow a_{12} \rightarrow a_{13} \\ a_{21} \rightarrow a_{22} \rightarrow a_{23} \\ a_{31} \rightarrow a_{32} \rightarrow a_{33} \end{bmatrix}$$ Row-major order

Figure 4.3 Array 3 × 3 column-major order vs. Array 3 × 3 row-major order

It may be remembered that for a linear array, the computer does not keep track of the address LOC(LA[K]) of every element LA[K] of LA, but does keep track of Base (LA), the address of the first element of LA. To find the address of LA[K] in time, independent of K, the computer uses the formula:

LOC[LA[K]] = Base (LA) + W(K − 1), where W is the number of words per memory cell for the array LA, and 1 is the lower bound of the index set of LA.

A similar situation also holds for any 2D M × N array A. For a 2D M × N array A, the computer keeps track of base [A] and the address of the first element A[1, 1] of A. The computer computes the address LOC(A[J, KJ) of A[J, K] using the formula given below:

Column-major order:

LOC (A[J, K]) = Base(A) + W [M (K − 1) + (J − 1)]

Row-major order:

LOC (A[J, K]) = Base (A) + W[N (J − 1) + (K − 1)]

It may be noted that the formula is linear in J and K, and one can find the address LOC(A[J, K]) in time, independent of J and K.

Example 4.18

Consider a 20 × 4 matrix array A. Suppose base(A) = 2000 and W = 4 words per memory cell. Calculate the 2D array using row-major order and column-major order. Assume that the array index starts from 1 (i.e., A[1, 1] is the first location).

The address of A[12, 3] in row-major order as follows:

Using the formula: LOC(A[J, K]) = Base (A) + W [N (J − 1) + (K − 1)].

LOC(A [12, 3]) = 2000 + 4 [4(12 − 1) + (3 − 1)] = 2000 + 4 [46] = 2000 + 184 = **2184.**

The address of A[12, 3] in column-major order is as follows:

Using the formula: LOC(A[J, K]) = Base(A) + W[M (K − 1) + (J − 1)].

LOC(ARRAY [12, 3]) = 2000 + 4 [20(12 − 1) + (3 − 1)] = 2000 + 4 [222] = 2000 + 888 = **2888.**

Example 4.19

Consider a 20 × 4 matrix array A. Suppose, base(A) = 2000, and there are W = 4 words per memory cell. Calculate 2D array locations using row-major order and column-major order. Assume that the array index starts from 0 (i.e., A[0, 0] is the first location) as we found in C programming.

The address of A[12, 3] in row-major order is as follows:

Using the formula: LOC(A[J, K]) = Base (A) + W [N (J) + (K)]

LOC(A[12, 3]) = 2000 + 4 [4(12) + (3)] = 2000 + 4 [51] = 2000 + 204 = **2204.**

The address of ARRAY [12, 3] in column-major order as follows:

Using the formula: LOC(A[J, K]) = Base(A) + W(M(K) + (J)]

LOC(A[12, 3]) = 2000 + 4 [20(12) + (3)] = 2000 + 4 [243] = 2000 + 972 = **2972.**

QUICK RECAP

- ☑ An array is a collection of homogeneous data items stored at contiguous memory locations. It is a linear and static data structure.
- ☑ We can store multiple data items of the same type by using only a single name. The reading element from an array is simple and efficient. Random access is possible here.
- ☑ The memory which is allocated statically to an array cannot be increased or reduced during runtime in C.
- ☑ The elements of an array are stored in consecutive memory locations. So, insertions and deletions are very difficult and time-consuming if the array size is large.
- ☑ We can calculate the position of each array element by simply adding an offset/index to a base value since it is linear and static.
- ☑ Basic operations that can be performed on an array are traversing, insertion, deletion, searching, and updates. Among these, insertion and deletions are most important and can easily be implemented using C and Python.
- ☑ We can access array elements, find the length of the array, loop the array elements for traversing, and use various in-built array methods for the array manipulation tasks, both in C and Python.
- ☑ Array and list data types have many similarities and distinctions, and these two are handled differently in C and Python.
- ☑ Array elements can be inserted and deleted both using static and dynamic memory allocations in C.
- ☑ Python deals with arrays using homogeneous list datatype, build-in array module and Numpy library. In all these cases, memory allocations are dynamic.
- ☑ We can also slice and update array elements using built-in supports of C and Python languages besides searching for elements in the array.
- ☑ Array data structure has applications for storing a list of values, performing matrix operations, implementing searching and sorting algorithms, etc.
- ☑ Both C and Python languages can be used to implement the above applications using dynamic memory allocation.
- ☑ Multi-dimensional array data are represented using row-major order and column-major order.

REVIEW QUESTIONS

Multiple Choice Questions (MCQ): Choose the best alternative

Easy

1. Which of the following is an advantage of arrays?
   A. Elements in an array cannot be sorted.
   B. Objects of mixed data types can be stored.
   C. Easier to store elements of the same data type.
   D. Index of the first element of an array is 1.
2. Which is the correct initialization of an array in C programming?
   A. int arr(3) = {1, 2, 3};
   B. int arr[3] = (1, 2, 3);
   C. int arr(3) = (1, 2, 3);
   D. int arr[3] = {1, 2, 3};
3. Which of the following is the disadvantage of arrays?
   A. Data structures like queue or stack cannot be implemented.
   B. Elements are sequentially accessed.
   C. Memory can be misused if inserted elements are lesser than the allocated size.
   D. The index value of an array can be negative.

4. Which one of these describes an array best?
   A. It contains objects of similar types.
   B. Arrays are immutable, once initialized.
   C. Array is not a data structure.
   D. A data structure shows hierarchical behavior.
5. In general, the index of the first element in an array is ________.
   A. -1   B. 2
   C. 1   D. 0
6. Transporting a matrix performs:
   A. Conversion of columns into rows.
   B. Conversion of rows into columns.
   C. Both (A) or (B).
   D. Traversing all elements.

Moderate

7. Each element of an array[20][50] requires 4 bytes of storage. The base or starting address of the array is 1000. The location of array[10][10] when the array is stored as column-major is:
   A. 1820   B. 1048
   C. 1840   D. 1840
8. For column-major, suppose each element takes 2 bytes of memory and the base address is 1000. Then what is the address of [3, 2] – the elements of a 3×4 matrix?
   A. 1010   B. 1012
   C. 1016   D. 1018

   Hint: LOC(A[J, K]) = Base(A)+ W [M (K–1) + (J – 1)]

   LOC(A[3, 2] = 1000 + 2[3(2 – 1) + (3 – 1)] = 1000 + 2[5] = 1010.
9. The elements of an array are stored successively in memory cells because:
   A. The architecture of computer memory does not allow arrays to be stored other than serially.
   B. In this way, the computer can keep track of only the address of the first element and the addresses of other elements can be calculated.
   C. Both of the above.
   D. None of the above.
10. Assuming int is of 4-bytes, what is the size of int arr[15];?
    A. 120   B. 32
    C. 60   D. 15
11. Elements in an array are accessed ________.
    A. sequentially   B. randomly
    C. logarithmically   D. exponentially
12. Arrays are the best data structures:
    A. For the size of the structure and the data in the structure are constantly changing.
    B. For relatively permanent collections of data.
    C. For both of the above situations.
    D. For none of the above situations.

Higher-Order Thinking Skills (HOTS)

13. Which of the following expressions can access the (i, j)th entry of an $(a \times b)$ matrix stored in column-major order?
    A. $b \times (i - 1) + j$ B. $a \times (j - 1) + i$
    C. $a \times (b - j) + j$ D. $b \times (a - i) + j$
14. What does the following declaration mean? int (*ptr)[10];
    A. ptr is a pointer to array
    B. ptr is an array of 10 integers
    C. ptr is a pointer to an array of 10 integers
    D. ptr is an array of pointers to 10 integers
15. Which of the following statements are correct about an array?
    1. The array int num[26]; can store 26 elements.
    2. The expression num[1] designates the very first element in the array.
    3. It is necessary to initialize the array at the time of the declaration.
    4. The declaration num[SIZE] is allowed if SIZE is a macro.

    A. 2, 4   B. 2, 3
    C. 1, 4   D. 1
16. A multi-dimensional array A[4][8] possesses how many elements in computer memory?
    A. 12   B. 23
    C. 32   D. 100

Short Answer-type Questions

Easy

1. What do you mean by an array?
2. Write the advantages and disadvantages of an array.
3. What is a two-dimensional array?
4. Distinguish between single and multi-dimensional arrays.

5. Write the ways of updating arrays in C and Python.
6. Compare array slicing in C and Python.

Moderate

7. What is row-major order and column-major order?
8. Explain the access method of all array elements.
9. Why do we need an array?
10. Draw a comparison between array and list.
11. Distinguish the techniques for finding the length of an array in C and Python.
12. What do you understand by traversing array elements?

Higher-Order Thinking Skills (HOTS)

13. Can we change the size of an array at run time?
14. Can we declare array size as a negative number?
15. Find the address of the 9th element of a 1-D array if the base address is 5000 and the memory allocation is 4 bytes for each element.
16. In a two-dimensional array A[5][6] with base address is 5000 and word size 2, find the address of A[3][5] element in row-major and column-major order. Assume that the starting index is 0.

Descriptive-type Questions

Easy

1. Write the algorithm to insert an element into an array.
2. Write the algorithm to delete an element from an array.
3. What are dynamic memory allocation functions in C programming?
4. Briefly mention the methods for array manipulations.
5. How to access array elements in C and Python? Give examples.

Moderate

6. How we can represent 2D arrays in row-major and column-major order?
7. How to represent a matrix using an array?
8. Write an algorithm to find the transpose of a matrix.

Higher-Order Thinking Skills (HOTS)

9. How can we represent 2D arrays in row-major and column-major order.
10. How to represent a matrix using an array?
11. Write an algorithm to traverse all the elements of a matrix.

CASE STUDIES

1. Justify whether the following can be implemented using arrays:
   a. Vector
   b. Matrices
   c. Rectangular tables
   d. Records of database
   e. Lists
   f. Heaps
   g. Hash tables
   h. Queues
   i. Deques
   j. Stacks
   k. Relative subroutine numbers acted upon by SWITCH statements.
   l. Emulate in-program dynamic memory allocation or allocate "dynamic memory" portably.
2. Identify the dimension(s) of the array applications, above if feasible.
3. Justify whether we can store data using an array appropriately in the following cases:
   a. Store titles of books in the library management system.
   b. Stock prices of trade by trade transactions.
   c. Climate changes indicators data.
   d. GPS locations of a mobile device.
   e. Blood sugar and pressure levels of a patient.

LAB EXERCISES

1. Write C and Python programs to reverse an array.

   Examples:
   ```
   Input : arr[] = {10, 20, 30}
   Output : arr[] = {30, 20, 10}
   Input : arr[] = {40, 50, 10, 20}
   Output : arr[] = {20, 10, 50, 40}
   ```
2. Write C and Python programs to find the maximum number and minimum number from an array.
3. Write C and Python programs to move all zeros to the end of the array.

   Example:
   ```
   Input : arr[] = {10, 20, 0, 40,
   30, 0, 50, 0};
   Output : arr[] = {10, 20, 40, 30,
   50, 0, 0};
   Input : arr[] = {10, 20, 0, 0, 0,
   30, 60};
   Output : arr[] = {10, 20, 30, 60,
   0, 0, 0};
   ```

ANSWER KEYS

Multiple Choice Questions

1. C	5. D	9. B	13. B
2. D	6. C	10. C	14. C
3. C	7. C	11. B	15. C
4. A	8. A	12. B	16. C

5 Linked List

CONTENTS

EXPECTED OUTCOMES OF THIS CHAPTER

After going through this chapter learners will be able

- ☑ To understand the importance of linked list.
- ☑ To compare array and linked list.
- ☑ To implement the abstract data type using the nodes as a linked list.
- ☑ To understand and implement the algorithms of singly, circular and doubly linked lists for inserting, deleting, searching and reversing etc.
- ☑ To understand the concepts of dangling pointers, garbage collection, and dereferencing the NULL pointer.
- ☑ To implement the inserting, deleting, and reversing linked list along with the implementation of the sparse matrix and polynomial addition with C and Python.

5.1 INTRODUCTION

We have explained the array as a simple linear data structure in the last chapter. Besides the many advantages, there are some significant disadvantages of the array because of which we need another linear data structure called the linked list. Before moving on to the linked list, we need to remember and revisit the disadvantages of an array so that we can understand the requirements of another crucial linear data structure which overcomes many limitations of the array data structure. The following are some of these major limitations or disadvantages of an array:

- We must know, in advance, how many elements are to be stored in an array. This means the size of an array must be defined in advance.
- The array is a static structure. This means the array is of fixed size. The memory which is allocated to an array cannot be changed (increased or reduced) during runtime.
- If we allocate more memory (static or fixed size) than what is required, then the memory space will be misused or wasted. On the other hand, if we allocate less memory than required, it will be insufficient and that will create insufficient memory problems.
- The elements of an array are stored in contiguous memory locations. So, insertions and deletions will be complicated, and the program will consume more time than normal, especially when the size of the array is large.

The data structure linked list has the power to get rid of these limitations of the array data structure. Though both are used to store linear data of similar types, their memory allocation mechanisms differ. Memory allocation of linked list takes place during runtime or program executions when data is added to it in contrast to an array memory location that occurs at an array declaration. This is why a linked list is called a dynamic data structure. However, it should be noted that both are linear data structures. The following sections will demonstrate many other similarities and distinctions between these two data structures.

5.1.1 Definition

A linear collection of data elements (nodes) stored at non-contiguous memory locations is called a linked list. Physical placements of elements in the memory do not take place sequentially or in order here. The linked list consists of multiple nodes that contain a data field and an address field (or link) to the next node in the list.

The nodes in the linked list are arranged in linear order or sequence, because of which this data structure is called a linear data structure. These nodes form a chain-like structure since each node links to the next node besides holding its data. The link or address or reference, whatever it may be called, holds the address location pointing to the next node, one after another, and constructs the chain. Figure 5.1 presents the simple structure of a linked list with a block diagram.

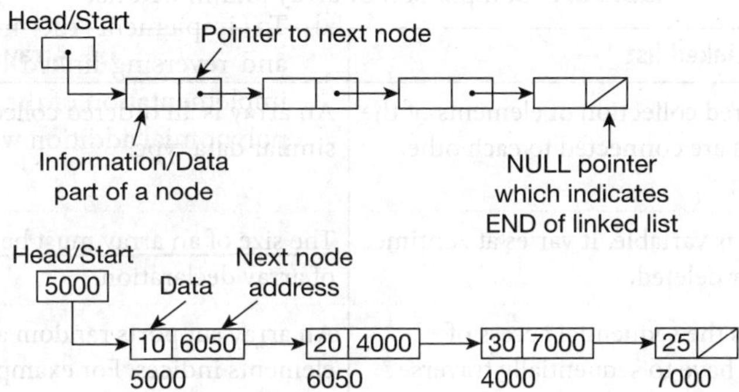

Figure 5.1 Representation of a simple linked list with an example

In Fig. 5.1, the linked list is initiated with a node called Head or Start. This Head or Start node only holds the address of the first node. It is a special node that is not counted while counting the total number of nodes in the linked list. It contains the address as a reference to the following first node as mentioned, but it holds a null reference if the linked list is empty. Other nodes of the linked list consist of two parts, namely data (or information) part and address (or reference or link part), as shown in Fig. 5.1. The first three nodes out of a total of four nodes of the linked list contain both values in the information part of the node and address data in the reference part. The last node contains a value in the data part and a null pointer in the address part. Variety may occur when the last node will refer to the first node (circular linked list). The upper diagram in Fig. 5.1 represents the structure of the linked list, and the lower diagram of Fig. 5.1 represents an example of the linked list with its values assigned. The following are the pointwise advantages and disadvantages of the linked list.

Advantages of the linked list

- The linked list is dynamic in nature, which allocates the memory when required.
- The memory allocation of the linked list is non-contiguous.
- Using the linked list, stack and queue can be implemented easily.
- Linked list reduces the memory access time.
- Data insertion and data deletion can be implemented in the linked list easily.

Disadvantages of linked list

- Each node has to be accessed sequentially in the linked list. So, no element can be accessed randomly here.
- In the linked list, the memory is wasted as pointer requires extra memory allocation for storage.
- Reverse traversing or backtracking is not possible in a singly linked list because we have only the next node address and not the previous node address.

> ***Note!***
> Linked list is a linear and a dynamic data structure.

5.1.2 Array vs. Linked List

There are some differences between the array and linked list. A few of those differences are mentioned in the introduction of this chapter. The following Table 5.1 presents the major differences between these two linear data structures in a tabular form.

Table 5.1 Comparison of array and linked list

Linked list	Array
A linked list is an ordered collection of elements of the same type but elements are connected to each other using pointers.	An array is an ordered collection of elements of a similar data type.
The size of a linked list is variable. It varies at runtime, as nodes are inserted or deleted.	The size of an array must be specified at the time of array declaration.
The linked list supports the sequential access of elements or nodes. We have to sequentially traverse the linked list up to that element.	An array supports random access directly using elements indices. For example, we can directly call an array without accessing the previous array elements.
New elements can be stored anywhere in the memory while using a linked list. The address of the memory location allocated to the newly inserted element is stored in the previous node. Thus, forming a link between the two nodes can easily be done.	Elements are stored in contiguous memory locations in a consecutive manner in an array.
Dynamic memory allocation is unique to the linked list. Memory is allocated at runtime, when a new node is added.	Static memory allocation takes place in the array, since memory is allocated as soon as the array is declared.
Insertion and deletion operations are easy to implement here. A new element is stored at the first free and available memory location, with only a single overhead step of storing the address of the memory location in the previous node of the linked list.	Insertion and deletion operation takes more time if the array size is large, as the memory locations are fixed and consecutive.
The time complexity of accessing a linked list element is $O(n)$.	The time complexity of accessing an array element is constant $O(1)$.

5.1.3 Terminologies, Operations and Applications

The basic elements of a linked list data structure are briefly presented here.

Head/Start: This is the starting node. It refers to the first node of the linked list, and hence it only contains the address of the first node. If the list is empty, the head is a null reference.

Node: Each node has the following two parts:

- **Data or information part:** Its contents are data or information. It holds the value of the linked list variable. It is also known as data or information field.
- **Link or next or address part:** Its contents are the memory address of the next or previous node. It is also known as the address field.

The following Fig. 5.2 presents the structure of a single node of the linked list.

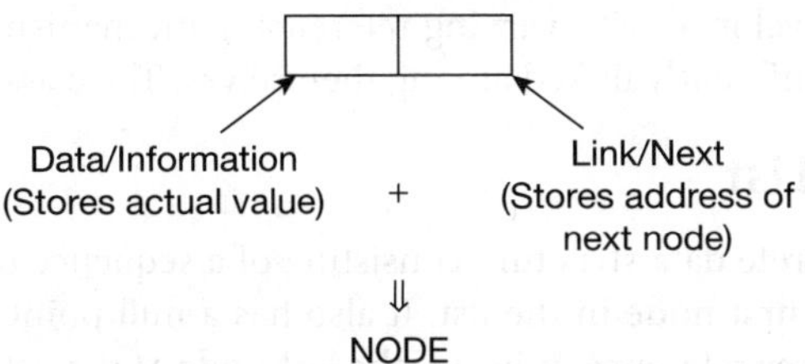

Figure 5.2 Linked list node structure

The structure of the last node is different from other nodes. The null pointer is assigned to the last node link part. This is denoted as ∅ / NULL, which indicates the end of the linked list. The following figure represents the last node structure.

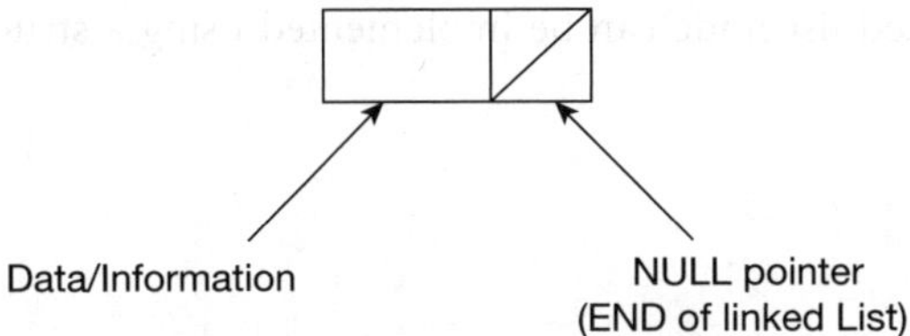

Figure 5.3 Linked list last node structure

The last node may also be structured in another way where it may refer to the first node. This happens in the case of a special data structure, called a circular linked list. This will be discussed in a next section of this chapter.

> ***Note!***
> A head/start pointer holds the address of the first node of a linked list.

Operations

The following are some basic operations that can be performed on a linked list.

Insert: Include a node at the beginning or middle (in between two nodes) or last of the list.

Delete: Removes a node from the beginning or middle (in between two nodes) or from the last of the list.

Search: Searches an element using the given key within the linked list.

Traverse: Traversing means visiting or touching the elements of the structure and doing some operation with the data.

Applications

The following are some basic applications of the linked list in data structure.

- Linked lists are used to implement stacks, queues, trees, graphs, etc.
- It is used to performing arithmetic operations on long integers.
- It is used to represent polynomials.
- It is used to represent sparse matrices.

5.2 CLASSIFICATION OF LINKED LISTS

Many linked lists may be developed with varying referencing mechanisms. There are three classes of a linked list as the nodes are differently linked among themselves. The classes are as explained below.

5.2.1 Singly Linked List

A singly linked list is a concrete data structure consisting of a sequence of nodes. It has a head or start node pointer indicating the first node in the list. It also has a null pointer reference necessarily at the last node, and that null pointer reference indicates the last node of the list. Each node stores an element (data) and a link to the next node as usual. The null object at the end is denoted by ∅. Data navigation is in the forward direction only. This means backtracking is not permitted in this singly linked list, and hence this linked list is called a singly linked list. Figure 5.1 presents the structure and an example of a singly linked list.

Declaring a node of a singly linked list

In C language, a singly linked list node can be implemented using a structure and a pointer as given below.

```
struct
  {
    int data;
    struct node *next;
  } node;
```

The above definition is used to create each node in the linked list. The data field stores the information or data and the next is a pointer to store the address of the next node. In place of a data type declaration, the next pointer (*next) is declared as a `struct` node to indicate that it is a self-referencing pointer (self-referencing pointer points to the same type [structure] of node). Here, the next pointer is a part of a node and it will point to the next node. This type of structure is called a self-referential structure.

5.2.2 Circular Linked List

In a singly linked list, each node points to its next node in the sequence, and the last node points to the null reference. In the circular linked list, every node points to its next node in the sequence, but the last node points to the first node in the list. Hence, the circular linked list is similar to the singly linked list except that the last node points to the first node in the list. The following Fig. 5.4 presents an example of a circular linked list.

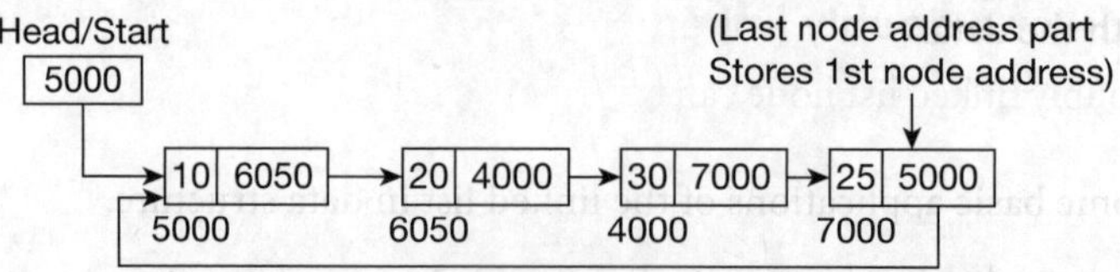

Figure 5.4 Example of a circular linked list

In a singly linked list, back traversal is not permitted but using a circular linked list, we can solve this problem. If we just replace the null pointer at the last node by the first node memory address in the singly linked list, we will get a circular linked list. This method is useful when the number of nodes in the linked list is less. If the number of nodes is large, then back traversal may take more time in the circular linked list. For example, suppose we have 1000 nodes in a linked list, and presently we are in the 988-th node. Now we are trying to access the 987-th node. In this situation, we have to traverse forward after reaching the last node. Then, we go back to the first node again, and move forward to the 987-th node. This indicates that accessing the nodes in a circular linked list is time-consuming. To overcome this problem, we have a doubly (or two-way) linked list, which is given below.

5.2.3 Doubly Linked List

In a singly linked list, every node has a link to its next node in the sequence. So, we can traverse from one node to another node only in one direction and we cannot traverse back. We can solve this kind of problem by using a doubly linked list. Doubly or two-way linked list is a sequence of elements in which every node has a data part, and two link parts to its previous element and next element in the sequence. We can traverse forward using the next address field and traverse backward using the previous address field. This linked list is also known as a two-way linked list since each node is linked in two ways. So, each node of the doubly linked list contains three fields, a data field, and two address fields. The structure of each node of the doubly linked list is given in Fig. 5.5.

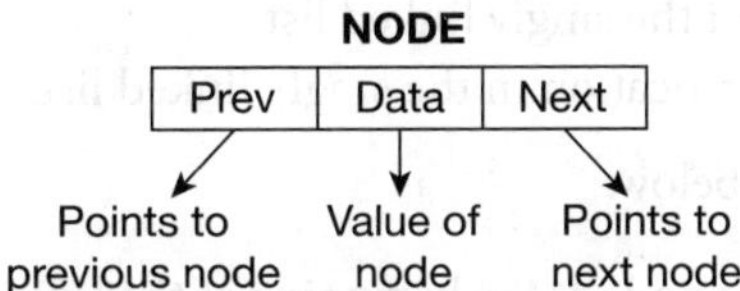

Figure 5.5 Node structure of a doubly linked list

Here, the 'Prev' field is used to store the address of the previous node of the linked list, 'Next' field is used to store the address of the next node of the linked list, and 'Data' field is used to store the actual value of that node. Elements can be navigated forward and backward. An example of a doubly linked list is given in Fig. 5.6.

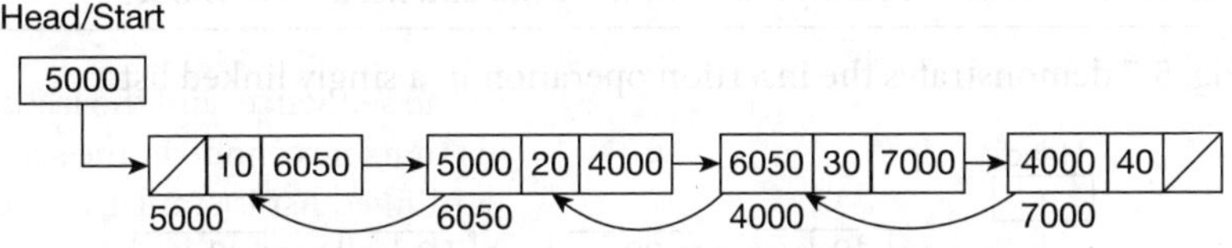

Figure 5.6 Example of a doubly linked list

Declaring a node of a doubly linked list

In C language, a doubly linked list node can be implemented using structure and pointers as given below.

```
struct
  {
    int data;
    struct node *prev;
    struct node *next;
  } node;
```

The above declaration is used to create each node in the doubly linked list. The data field stores the data. The `next` and `prev` are two pointers to store the addresses of the next node and previous node respectively.

5.3 OPERATIONS ON SINGLY LINKED LIST

Various operations can be performed on a linked list. Insertion, deletion, traversing/displaying, searching, reversing, and counting number of nodes are the major operations often used to manipulate a linked list. Among these, insertion, deletion, searching, reversing, and counting number of nodes are presented for a singly linked list in this section. Insertion and deletion of a node can take place at the beginning (or at the first node), at the end (or at the last node) and at any specific location of the singly linked list. The following sections present these operations with algorithms, C, and Python source codes.

5.3.1 Inserting Node in Singly Linked List

The insertion operation can be performed in three ways in a singly linked list as mentioned earlier. These are:

1. Inserting a node at the beginning of the singly linked list
2. Inserting a node at the end of the singly linked list
3. Inserting a node at a specific location in the singly linked list.

The algorithms for these are given below.

Algo-5.1 Algorithm for inserting a node at the beginning of the singly linked list

The following is the algorithm for the insertion of a node at the beginning or as the first node.

Step 1	Create a Newnode with a specific value.
Step 2	Check whether linked list is empty [if (head = = NULL)].
Step 3	If the linked list is empty then, set Newnode → next = NULL and head = Newnode.
Step 4	If it is not empty then, set Newnode → next = head and head = Newnode.

The following Fig. 5.7 demonstrates the insertion operation in a singly linked list.

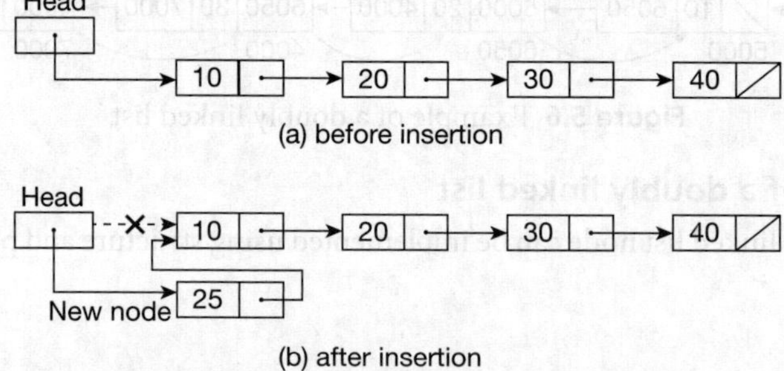

Figure 5.7 Inserting a node at the beginning of the singly linked list

The above Fig. 5.7 (a) shows that the first node was with data '10' initially. While inserting data '25' as a node at the first node of the singly linked list, the head is linked to the address of the node with data '25' and that node is linked to the second node with data '10', as shown in figure 5.7(b).

Algo-5.2 Algorithm for inserting a node at the end of the linked list

Step 1	Create a Newnode with a specific value and Newnode → next as NULL.
Step 2	Check whether list is empty [if (head = = NULL)].
Step 3	If it is empty, then set head = Newnode.
Step 4	If it is not empty, then define a node pointer temp and initialize with head.
Step 5	Keep moving the temp to its next node one by one until it reaches the last node of the list (until temp → next is equal to NULL).
Step 6	Set temp → next = Newnode.

The following Fig. 5.8 demonstrates the insertion of a node at the end of a singly linked list.

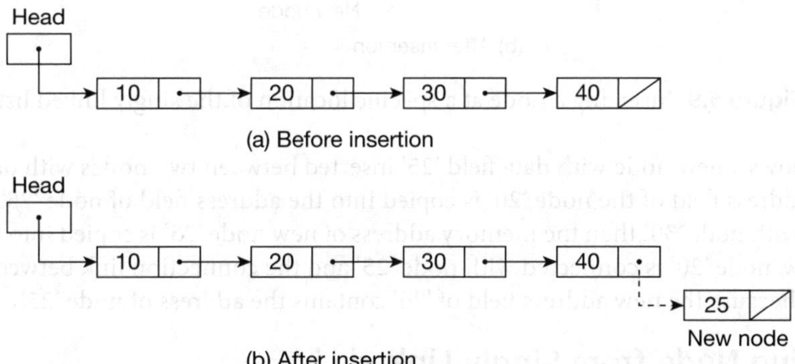

Figure 5.8 Inserting a node at the end of the singly linked list

The above Fig. 5.8 (a) shows that the last node was with data '40' initially. Figure 5.8(b) shows that the end node address field is linking to the newly inserted node with the data field '25'. The address field of the newly inserted node is NULL.

Algo-5.3 Algorithm for inserting a node at a specific location of the linked list

Step 1	Create a Newnode with a specific value.
Step 2	Check whether list is empty (head = = NULL).
Step 3	If it is empty, then set Newnode → next = NULL and head = Newnode.
Step 4	If it is not empty, then define a node pointer temp and initialize with head.
Step 5	Keep moving the temp to its next node one by one until it reaches the node after which we want to insert the Newnode (until temp → data is equal to location; here, location is the node value after which we want to insert the Newnode).
Step 6	Every time, check whether temp has reached to the last node or not. If it has reached the last node then print 'Node is not found in the list and insertion is not possible' and terminate the function. Otherwise, move the temp to the next node.
Step 7	Lastly, 'Newnode → next = temp → next' and 'temp → next = Newnode'

The following Fig. 5.9 demonstrates the insertion of a node at a specific location in a singly linked list. Figure 5.9 (a) shows before inserting data '25' as node after the node '20' and before '30' of the singly linked list,

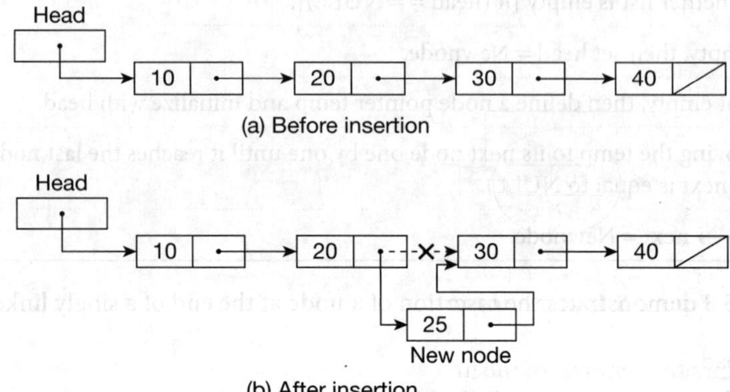

Figure 5.9 Inserting a node at a specific location of the singly linked list

Figure 5.9 (b) shows a new node with data field '25' inserted between two nodes with data fields 20 and 30. Firstly, the address field of the node '20' is copied into the address field of node '25'. So, node '25' is now connected with node '30', then the memory address of new node '25' is copied into the address field of node '20'. Now, node '20' is connected with node '25' and the connection link between node '20' and node '30' is lost because the new address field of '20' contains the address of node '25'.

5.3.2 Deleting Node from Singly Linked List

The deletion operation can also be performed in three ways in a single linked list as mentioned earlier. These are:

1. Deleting a node from the beginning of the singly linked list.
2. Deleting a node from the end of the singly linked list.
3. Deleting a node from the specific location of the singly linked list.

Algo-5.4 Algorithm for deleting a node from the beginning of the singly linked list

Step 1	Check whether list is empty (head = = NULL)
Step 2	If it is empty, then display 'Linked List is empty and deletion is not possible' and exit.
Step 3	If it is not empty, then define a node pointer 'temp' and initialize with head.
Step 4	Check whether the list is having only one node (temp → next = NULL)
Step 5	If the condition is TRUE, then set head = NULL and delete temp (Setting empty list conditions)
Step 6	If the condition is FALSE, then set head = temp → next, and delete temp.

The following Fig. 5.10(a) shows the list before the deletion of a node from the beginning of the singly linked list.

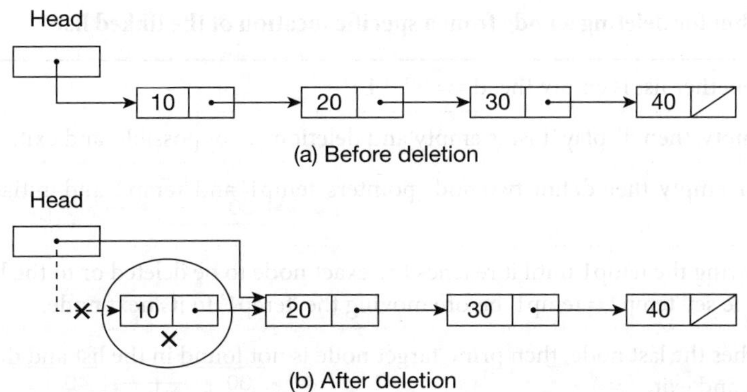

Figure 5.10 Deleting from the beginning of the singly linked list

Figure 5.10(b) shows the removal of the first node with the data field '10'. However, it requires fixing the head pointer to the second node '20' of the given list.

Algo-5.5 Algorithm for deleting a node from the end of the singly linked list

Step 1	Check whether list is empty (head = = NULL)
Step 2	If it is empty, then display 'List is empty and deletion is not possible' and exit.
Step 3	If it is not empty, then define two node pointers 'temp1' and 'temp2' and initialize 'temp1' with head.
Step 4	Check whether the list has only one node (temp1 → next == NULL)
Step 5	If the condition is TRUE, then set head = NULL and delete temp1 and terminate the function. (Setting empty list condition)
Step 6	If the condition is FALSE, then set 'temp2 = temp1 ' and move temp1 to its next node. Repeat the same process until it reaches the last node in the list. (until temp1 → next = = NULL)
Step 7	Lastly, Set temp2 → next = NULL and delete temp1.

The following Fig. 5.11(a) presents the singly linked list structure before the deletion of a node '40' from the end. Set address field of node '30' to NULL, and now connection between node '30' to node 40' is lost. So, node '40' is deleted from the singly linked list as shown in Fig. 5.11(b).

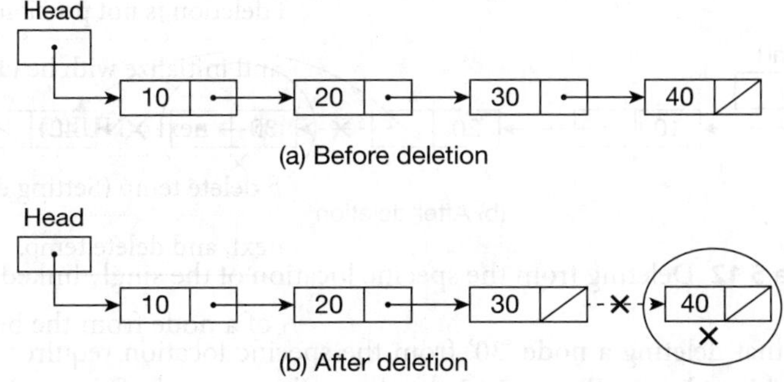

Figure 5.11 Deleting from the end of the singly linked list

Algo-5.6 Algorithm for deleting a node from a specific location of the linked list

Step 1	Check whether list is empty (head == NULL)
Step 2	If it is empty, then display 'List is empty and deletion is not possible' and exit.
Step 3	If it is not empty, then define two node pointers 'temp1' and 'temp2' and initialize 'temp1' with head.
Step 4	Keep moving the temp1 until it reaches the exact node to be deleted or to the last node. And every time set 'temp2 = temp1' before moving the 'temp1' to its next node.
Step 5	If it reaches the last node, then print 'target node is not found in the list and deletion is not possible' and exit.
Step 6	If it reaches the target node which we want to delete, then check whether the list is having only one node or not
Step 7	If the list has only one node and that is the node to be deleted, then set head = NULL and delete temp1 (free(temp1)).
Step 8	If the list contains multiple nodes, then check whether temp1 is the first node in the list (temp1 == head).
Step 9	If temp1 is the first node, then move the head to the next node (head = head → next) and delete temp1.
Step 10	If temp1 is not the first node, then check whether it is the last node in the list (temp1 → next = = NULL).
Step 11	If temp1 is the last node, then set temp2 → next = NULL and delete temp1 (free(temp1)).
Step 12	If temp1 is not the first node and not the last node, then set temp2 → next = temp1 → next and delete temp1 (free(temp1)).

The following Fig. 5.12 demonstrates the deletion of a node from the specific location of the singly linked list.

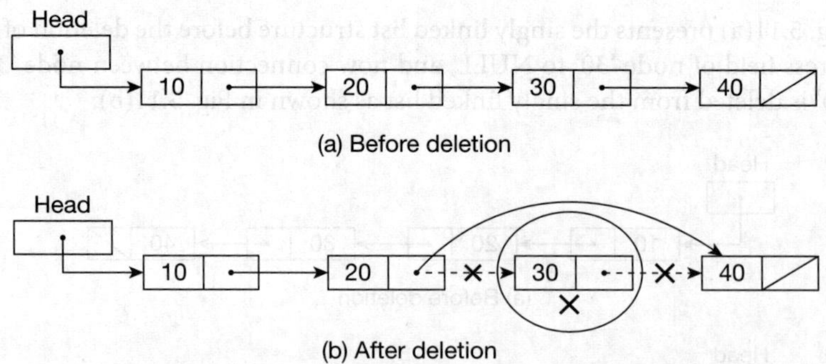

Figure 5.12 Deleting from the specific location of the singly linked list

Figure 5.12(a) shows that deleting a node '30' from the specific location requires the preceding node being removed to be skipped over. Figure 5.12 (b) shows the removal of the node with the data field

'30'. The address field part of node '30' (i.e., memory address of node '40') is copied to the address field of previous node '20'. The address field of node '20' will now point to the memory address of '40'. The connection links between node '20' to node '30' and node '30' to node '40' are lost. So, node '30' is now deleted from the list.

5.3.3 Counting the Number of Nodes in Singly Linked List

The following algorithm presents the counting of the number of nodes in a singly linked list.

Algo-5.7 Algorithm to count and display the total number of nodes in a single linked list

Step 1	Check whether list is empty (head = = NULL).
Step 2	If it is empty then, display 'List is empty' and exit.
Step 3	If it is not empty then, define a node pointer 'temp' and initialize with head.
Step 4	Initialize a counter variable with value zero.
Step 5	Keep moving temp to the next node and increment the value of the counter by 1 until temp reaches the last node of the list.
Step 6	Finally display counter variable value.

5.3.4 Operations in Singly Linked List with C

Following is the C program for implementation of the singly linked list. The operations listed below are implemented using the C source code.

1. Creation of a linked list with C.
2. Implementation of a singly linked list with C.
3. Insertion of a node in a singly linked list with C
   a) at the beginning, b) at the end, c) at a specific location.
4. Deletion of a node from a singly linked list with C
   a) from the beginning, b) at the end, c) at a specific location.
5. Searching for an element in a linked list with C.
6. Counting number of nodes in a linked list with C.

CProg-5.1 Singly linked list implementation

```
#include<stdio.h>
#include<stdlib.h>

/* Node declaration */
struct node
  {
      int data;
      struct node *next;
  };
struct node *head = NULL;
```

```
/* Function to create a singly linked list */
void create()
  {
      struct node *p, *q;
      int item; char x;
      do
      {
            q = (struct node *)malloc(sizeof(struct node));
            printf("\nEnter the data ");
            scanf("%d",&item);

            q->data = item;
            q->next = NULL;

            if(head == NULL)
              {
                  head = q;
                  p = q;
              }
            else
              {
                  p->next = q;
                  p = q;
              }
            printf("Do you want to continue?(Y/N)");
            fflush(stdin);
            scanf("%c",&x);
      }
      while(x == 'Y'|| x == 'y');
  }

/* Function to print singly linked list */
void display()
  {
      struct node *q;
      q = head;
      while(q! = NULL)
      {
            printf("%d-->", q->data);
            q = q -> next;
      }
  }

/* Function to insert a node at beginning of the singly
linked list */
void addbeg()
```

```
  {
    struct node *q;
    q = (struct node *)malloc(sizeof(struct node));
    printf("\n Enter the data ");
    scanf("%d", &q->data);
    q ->next = head;
    head = q;
  }

/* Function to delete a node from beginning of the singly
linked list */
void delbeg()
  {
    struct node *p;
    p = head;
    head = p -> next;
    free(p);
}

/* Function to insert a node at last of the singly linked
list */
void addend()
  {
    struct node *q, *p;
      q = (struct node *)malloc(sizeof(struct node));
      printf("\n Enter the data");
      scanf("%d", &q->data);
      q -> next = NULL;
      p = head;
      while(p -> next != NULL)
      p = p-> next;
      p -> next = q;
}

/* Function to delete a node from last of the singly linked
list */
void delend()
  {
    struct node *p, *prev;
    p = head;
    while(p -> next != NULL)
      {
        prev = p;
        p = p -> next;
      }
   prev -> next = NULL;
```

```
    free(p);
  }

/* Function to insert a node at a specific position of the
singly linked list */
void addafter()
  {
    int i, POS,item;
    struct node *q, *p;
    printf("Enter data");
    scanf("%d", &item);
    q = (struct node *)malloc(sizeof(struct node));
    q -> data = item;
    printf("Enter position");
    scanf("%d", &POS);
    p=head;
    for(i = 1; i < POS; i++)
     {
       p = p-> next;;
     }
    q -> next = p -> next;
    p -> next = q;
  }

/* Function to delete a node at specific position of the sin-
gly linked list */
void delpos()
  {
    int i, POS;
    struct node *p, *prev;
    printf("Enter position");
    scanf("%d",&POS);
    p=head;
    for(i=1;i<POS;i++)
    prev=p;
    p=p->next;
    if(p==head)
     {
       head=head->next;
       free(p);
       return;
     }
}

/* Function to count total number of nodes of the singly
linked list */
```

```
void count()
  {
    struct node *p; int c = 0;
    p = head;
    while(p != NULL)
      {
        c++;
        p = p -> next;
      }
    printf("\n Total number of nodes = %d",c);
  }

/* Function to search a specific node from the singly linked
list */
void search()
  {
    struct node *p;
    int f = 0, s, pos = 1;
    printf("Enter the data to be searched ");
    scanf("%d", &s);
    p = head;
    while (p != NULL)
      {
        if(p -> data == s)
         {
          f = 1;
          break;
         }
        else {
             pos++;
             p = p->next;
           }
      }

    if(f == 0)
      printf("Unsuccessful search");
    else
       printf("Successful search - data present at position
no %d",pos);
  } /* End search*/

/* Main function */
int main()
  {
    int ch;
    while(1)
```

```
    {
     printf("\n1.Create\n2.Display\n3.Insert at beg\n4.
Delete at beg\n5.Insert at end\n6.Delete at end\n7.Insert
after\n8.Delete position\n9.Count total number of nodes\n10.
Search a node\n11.Exit");
       printf("\nEnter your choice ");
       scanf("%d",&ch);
       switch(ch)
         {
            case 1: create();
                    break;
            case 2: display();
                    break;
            case 3: addbeg();
                    break;
            case 4: delbeg();
                    break;
            case 5: addend();
                    break;
            case 6: delend();
                    break;
            case 7: addafter();
                    break;
            case 8: delpos();
                    break;
            case 9: count();
                    break;
            case 10: search();
                     break;
          default: exit(0);
         }
    }
     return 0;
  }
/* End of Program */
```

Output

```
1.Create
2.Display
3.Insert at beg
4.Delete at beg
5.Insert at end
6.Delete at end
7.Insert after
8.Delete position
```

```
9.Count total number of nodes
10.Search a node
11.Exit
Enter your choice 1
Enter the data 10
Do you want to continue?(Y/N)y
Enter the data 20
Do you want to continue?(Y/N)y
Enter the data 30
Do you want to continue?(Y/N)n
Enter your choice 2
10-->20-->30-->
Enter your choice 9
 Total number of nodes=3
Enter your choice 10
Enter the data to be searched 20
Successful search - data present at position no 2
Enter your choice 3
Enter the data 5
Enter your choice 2
5-->10-->20-->30-->
Enter your choice 4
Enter your choice 2
10-->20-->30-->
```

Programming Tips!

`create()` is used to create a singly linked list. **`display()`** is used to print a singly linked list in the console. **`delbeg()`** is used to delete a node from the beginning. **`addbeg()`** function is used to insert a node at the beginning. **`addend()`** is used to insert a node at the last. **`delend()`** is used to delete a node from the last. **`addafter()`** is used to insert a node at a specific position. **`delpos()`** is used to delete a node at a specific position. **`count()`** is used to count the total number of nodes. **`search()`** is used to find a specific node.

5.3.5 Operations in Singly Linked List with Python

Following is the Python program for the implementation of the singly linked list. The operations listed below are implemented using the Python source code PyProg-5.1.

1. Creation of a linked list with Python.
2. Implementation of a singly linked list with Python.
3. Insertion of a node in a singly linked list with Python
   a) at the beginning, b) at the end, c) at a specific location.
4. Deletion of a node from a singly linked list with Python
   a) from the beginning, b) at the end, c) at a specific location.

PyProg-5.2 then presents the implementation of the following operations:

1. Find the length of a linked list
2. Search for an element in linked list
3. Remove duplicate from a sorted linked list
4. Remove duplicate from an unsorted linked list.

PyProg-5.1 Singly linked list implementation

```
'''
Creation of Linked List with Python
Implementation of a Singly Linked List with Python
Insert node in a Singly Linked List with Python
a) At beginning  b) as middle node c) at last node
Delete node from Singly Linked List with Python
a) from beginning  b) from middle node c) from last node
'''

# Class for defining node
class node:
    def __init__(self, data):
        self.data = data
        self.next = None

# Class for defining linked list
class Linked_List:
    # Constructor function
    def __init__(self):
        self.head = None

    # Function to check empty linked list
    def Is_List_Empty(self):
        if self.head == None:
            return True
        return False

    # Function to insert at beginning of linked list
    def Insert_At_Beginning(self, value):
        temp = node(value)
        temp.next = self.head
        self.head = temp

    # Function to insert at end of linked list
    def Insert_At_End(self, value):
        temp = node(value)
        temp.next = None
```

```
        if self.Is_List_Empty():
            self.head = temp
            return
        current = self.head
        while current.next != None:
            current = current.next
        current.next = temp

    # function to insert in the middle of linked list
    def Insert_After_Value(self, desired, value):
        current = self.head
        while current != None and current.data != desired:
            current = current.next
        if current == None:
            print("Element " + str(desired) + " not in list")
        else:
            temp = node(value)
            temp.next = current.next
            current.next = temp

    # Function to delete from beginning of linked list
    def Delete_At_Beginning(self):
        if self.Is_List_Empty():
            print("List is empty")
        else:
            temp = self.head
            self.head = self.head.next
            temp.next = None

    # Function to delete from end of linked list
    def Delete_At_End(self):
        if self.Is_List_Empty():
            print("List is empty")
            return
        temp = self.head
        if self.head.next == None:
            self.head = None
            temp.next = None
            return
        while temp.next != None:
            prev = temp
            temp = temp.next
        prev.next = temp.next
        temp.next = None
```

```
    # Function to delete from middle of linked list
    def Delete_With_Value(self, desired):
        if self.Is_List_Empty():
            print("List is empty")
            return
        temp = self.head
        if self.head.data == desired:
            self.head = self.head.next
            temp.next = None
            return
        while temp != None and temp.data != desired:
            prev = temp
            temp = temp.next
        if temp == None:
            print("Element " + str(desired) + " is not in list")
        else:
            prev.next = temp.next
            temp.next = None

    # Function to search within the linked list
    def Search(self, desired):
        temp = self.head
        while temp != None and temp.data != desired:
            temp = temp.next
        if temp == None:
            print("Element " + str(desired) + " not found")
        else:
          print("Element " + str(desired) + " is present in list")

    # Function to print the linked list
    def Print_Linked_List(self):
        if self.Is_List_Empty():
            print("List is Empty")
            return
        current = self.head
        while current.next != None:
            print(current.data, end = " -> ")
            current = current.next
        print(current.data)
  # Function to get length of linked list (iterative way)
    def Get_Length_Iterative(self):
       current = self.head
        length = 0
        while current != None:
           length += 1
           current = current.next
        return length
```

```
    # Function to get length of linked list (recursive way)
    def Get_Length_Recursive(self):
        def Count_Recursive(node):
            if node is None:
                return 0
            else:
                return 1 + Count_Recursive(node.next)
        return Count_Recursive(self.head)

# Execution of operations
LinkedList = Linked_List()
print("List Created!")
LinkedList.Print_Linked_List()
print("Current Length:", LinkedList.Get_Length_Iterative())

for i in range(0, 5):
    LinkedList.Insert_At_Beginning(i)

LinkedList.Print_Linked_List()
print("Current Length:", LinkedList.Get_Length_Iterative())

for i in range(5, 10):
    LinkedList.Insert_At_End(i)

LinkedList.Print_Linked_List()
print("Current Length:", LinkedList.Get_Length_Recursive())

LinkedList.Insert_After_Value(5, 9)
LinkedList.Insert_After_Value(10, 9)

LinkedList.Print_Linked_List()
print("Current Length:", LinkedList.Get_Length_Iterative())

for i in range(0, 3):
    LinkedList.Delete_At_End()

LinkedList.Print_Linked_List()
print("Current Length:", LinkedList.Get_Length_Recursive())

for i in range(0, 3):
    LinkedList.Delete_At_Beginning()

LinkedList.Print_Linked_List()
print("Current Length:", LinkedList.Get_Length_Iterative())
```

```
LinkedList.Delete_With_Value(1)
LinkedList.Delete_With_Value(5)

LinkedList.Print_Linked_List()
print("Current Length:", LinkedList.Get_Length_Recursive())

LinkedList.Search(6)
LinkedList.Search(8)
## End program
```

Output

```
List Created!
List is Empty
Current Length: 0
4 -> 3 -> 2 -> 1 -> 0
Current Length: 5
4 -> 3 -> 2 -> 1 -> 0 -> 5 -> 6 -> 7 -> 8 -> 9
Current Length: 10
Element 10 not in list
4 -> 3 -> 2 -> 1 -> 0 -> 5 -> 9 -> 6 -> 7 -> 8 -> 9
Current Length: 11
4 -> 3 -> 2 -> 1 -> 0 -> 5 -> 9 -> 6
Current Length: 8
1 -> 0 -> 5 -> 9 -> 6
Current Length: 5
0 -> 9 -> 6
Current Length: 3
Element 6 is present in list
Element 8 not found
```

Programming Tips!

`__init__()` is the constructor for initializing the object's state. `Insert_At_Beginning()` is used to insert a node at beginning. `Insert_At_End()` is used to insert a node at the end. `Insert_After_Value()` is used to insert a node in the middle. `Delete_At_Beginning()` is used to delete a node from the beginning. `Delete_With_Value()` is used to delete from the middle. `Print_Linked_List()` is used to display the nodes.

PyProg-5.2 Finding length, search, and removing duplicates from sorted and unsorted singly linked list

```
Creation of Linked List with Python for:
1) Find Length of a Linked List
2) Search an Element in Linked List
3) Remove Duplicate from a Sorted Linked List
4) Remove Duplicate from an Unsorted Linked List
```

```
# Constructor for creating node of the linked list
class Node:
    def __init__(self, data):
        self.data = data
        self.next = None

# Creating singly linked list
class SingleLinkedList:
    # Constructor for singly linked list
    def __init__(self):
        self.head = None

    # Displaying the linked list
    def print_list(self):
        cur_node = self.head
        print("Here's your list : ", end=" ")
        while cur_node:
            print(cur_node.data, end=" ")
            cur_node = cur_node.next

    # Appending an element at the end
    def append(self, data):
        new_node = Node(data)
        if self.head is None:
            self.head = new_node
            return
        last_node = self.head
        while last_node.next:
            last_node = last_node.next
        last_node.next = new_node

    # Calculating the length of the linked list
    def length(self):
        count = 0
        cur_node = self.head
        while cur_node:
            count += 1
            cur_node = cur_node.next
        return count

    # Searches for an element
    def search(self, element):
        cur_node = self.head
        index = 0
        while cur_node != None:
           if cur_node.data == element:
```

```
                return index
            index += 1
            cur_node = cur_node.next
        return False

    # Removes element from sorted list
    def remove_duplicates(self):
        cur_node = self.head
        if cur_node is None:
            return
        while cur_node.next is not None:
            if cur_node.data == cur_node.next.data:
                new = cur_node.next.next
                cur_node.next = None
                cur_node.next = new
            else:
                cur_node = cur_node.next
        return self.head

    # Sorts the list
    def sort_list(self):
        cur_node = self.head
        index = None
        if(self.head == None):
            return
        else:
            while(cur_node != None):
                index = cur_node.next

                while(index != None):
                    if(cur_node.data > index.data):
                        temp = cur_node.data
                        cur_node.data = index.data
                        index.data = temp
                    index = index.next
                cur_node = cur_node.next

# Displaying menu and executing different operations
def menu(choice):
    if choice == 1:
        data = input("\nEnter the element to be inserted : ")
        llist.append(data)
        print(f"{data} inserted successfully.\n")

    elif choice == 2:
        print(f"Length : {llist.length()}")
```

```
    elif choice == 3:
        search_element = input("Enter element to be searched : ")
        if llist.search(search_element):
          print(f"Found at index {llist.search(search_element)}")
        else:
            print("Not found")

    elif choice == 4:
        llist.remove_duplicates()
        llist.print_list()

    elif choice == 5:
        llist.sort_list()
        llist.remove_duplicates()
        llist.print_list()

    elif choice == 6:
        llist.print_list()
        print("")

# Driver code
if __name__ == "__main__":
    llist = SingleLinkedList()
    while True:
        print("""
                0. Exit
                1. Append
                2. Length
                3. Search
                4. Remove Duplicates from sorted
                5. Remove Duplicates from unsorted
                6. Display
            """)
        choice = int(input("Enter your choice : "))
        if choice == 0:
            break
        else:
            menu(choice)
# End Program
```

Output

```
Here's your list :  5 8 9 5 6 2

                0. Exit
                1. Append
                2. Length
```

```
                3. Search
                4. Remove Duplicates from sorted
                5. Remove Duplicates from unsorted
                6. Display

Enter your choice : 1

Enter the element to be inserted : 9
9 inserted successfully.

                0. Exit
                1. Append
                2. Length
                3. Search
                4. Remove Duplicates from sorted
                5. Remove Duplicates from unsorted
                6. Display

Enter your choice : 6
Here's your list :  5 8 9 5 6 2 9

                0. Exit
                1. Append
                2. Length
                3. Search
                4. Remove Duplicates from sorted
                5. Remove Duplicates from unsorted
                6. Display

Enter your choice : 5
Here's your list :  2 5 6 8 9
```

> ***Programming Tips!***
> `__init__()` is the constructor used to initialize the object's state. `print_list()` is used to display the linked list. `append()` is used to append an element at the end. `length()` is used to find the length of the linked list. `search()` is used to search for an element. `remove_duplicates()` is used to remove elements from the sorted list. `sort_list()` is used to arrange the list. `menu()` is used to display the menu options.

5.3.6 Reversing Singly Linked List with C and Python

Given a pointer to the head node of a singly linked list, the task here is to reverse the linked list. We need to reverse the list by changing the links between nodes.

Algo-5.8 Algorithm for reversing a singly linked list

Step 1	Initialize prev = NULL; current = head; next = NULL;
Step 2	Iterate through the linked list. In the loop, do the following: next = current → next (before changing next of current, save next node) current → next = prev (now change next of current; here actual reversing happens) prev = current (move prev and current one step forward). current = next.

Algo-5.9 Pseudocode for reversing a singly linked list

```
BEGIN Procedure:
   prev = NULL; current = head; save= NULL
   WHILE(current != NULL)
      save = current → next
      current → next = prev
      prev = current
      current = save
   END WHILE
   head = prev;
END Procedure
```

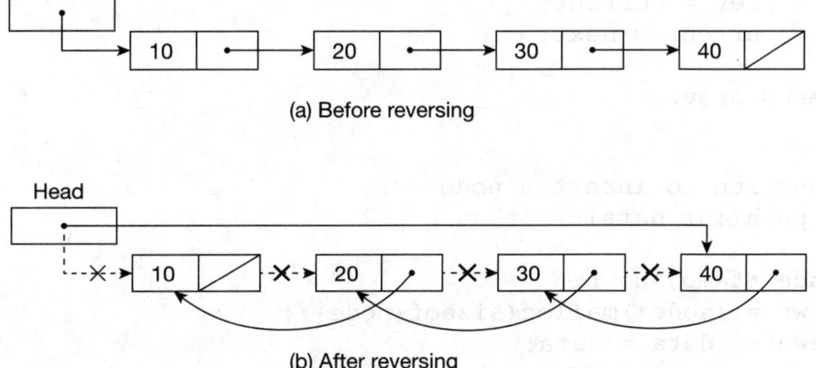

Figure 5.13 Reversing links of a singly linked list

Figure 5.13(a) shows the node structure before reversing the singly linked list and Fig. 5.13(b) shows the node structure after reversing the list. Now, the head node contains the address of the node '40', so it indicates that the last node becomes the first node of the list now. The address field of '40' holds the address of node '30' and so on. Lastly, the address field of node '10' holds NULL, which indicates that this is the last node of the list.

Following is the C program for the implementation of reversing operation in a singly linked list.

CProg-5.2 Reversing a singly linked list

```
#include<stdio.h>
#include<malloc.h>

/* Linked list node */
typedef struct node
{
   int data;
   struct node *next;
}node;

node *head = NULL;

/* Function to reverse the linked list */
static void reverse()
{
   node* prev = NULL;
   node* current = head;
   node* next;
   while (current != NULL)
   {
       next  = current -> next;
       current -> next = prev;
       prev = current;
       current = next;
   }
   head= prev;
}

/* Function to insert a node */
void push(int data)
{
   node *temp,*newn;
   newn = (node*)malloc(sizeof(node));
   newn -> data = data;
   newn -> next = NULL;
   if(head == NULL)
   {
    head = newn;
   }
   else
   {
    temp = head;
    while(temp -> next != NULL)
    temp = temp -> next;
   temp -> next = newn;
  }
}
```

```
/* Function to print linked list */
void printList()
{
   struct node *temp = head;
   while(temp != NULL)
   {
       printf("%d  ", temp -> data);
       temp = temp -> next;
   }
   printf("\n");
}

int main()
{
    push(50);
    push(40);
    push(30);
    push(20);
    push(10);
    printf("\nInitial Linked list \n");
    printList();
    reverse();
    printf("\nReversed Linked list \n");
    printList();
    getchar();
}
/* End of program */
```

Output

```
Initial Linked list
50  40  30  20  10

Reversed Linked list
10  20  30  40  50
```

Programming Tips!

`reverse()` is used to converse the list. A pointer is used to the head node to reverse the list. The concept of changing the links between nodes is used here.

Following is the Python program for the implementation of reversing operation in a singly linked list.

PyProg-5.3 Reversing a singly linked list

```
from __future__ import print_function #used for modifying how
print works

# Class for defining node
class Node(object):
  #initializing node
  def __init__(self, data = None, next_node = None):
      self.data = data
      self.next_node = next_node
```

```
    # Reversal function
    def reverse_iterative(self, n):
        last = None
        current = n
        while(current is not None):
            next_node = current.next_node
            current.next_node = last
            last = current
            current = next_node
        return last

# Chain together the node. n3 will be head while n0 the tail
n0 = Node(4, None)
n1 = Node(3, n0)
n2 = Node(2, n1)
n3 = Node(1, n2)
head = n3 # the head of the nodes
print("Before Reverse", end = " ")
while head:
    print(head.data, end = " ")
    head = head.next_node
print("\nAfter Reverse", end = " ")
head = n3  # the head of the nodes
n = Node() # will contain reverse linked_list
n = head.reverse_iterative(head)
while n:
    print(n.data, end = " ")
    n = n.next_node
## End program
```

Output

```
Before Reverse 1 2 3 4
After Reverse 4 3 2 1
```

> ***Note!***
>
> A singly linked list consists of a sequence of nodes where the last node's link part holds a null pointer to indicate the end of the list.

> ***Programming Tips!***
>
> `reverse_iterative()` is used to reverse the linked list. Changing the links between nodes concept is used to reverse the linked list here.

5.4 OPERATIONS ON CIRCULAR LINKED LIST

In line with the singly linked list, insertion and deletion are the major operations presented here with algorithms, C, and Python source codes.

5.4.1 Inserting Node in Circular Linked List

In a circular linked list, the insertion operation can be performed in three ways:

1. Inserting a node at the beginning of the circular linked list
2. Inserting a node at the end of the circular linked list
3. Inserting a node at a specific location in the circular linked list.

Algo-5.10 Algorithm for inserting a node at the beginning of the circular linked list

Step 1	Create a Newnode with a specific value.
Step 2	Check whether list is empty (head == NULL) or not.
Step 3	If it is empty, then set head = Newnode and Newnode → next = head.
Step 4	If it is not empty, then define a node pointer 'temp' and initialize with 'head'.
Step 5	Keep moving the 'temp' to its next node until it reaches the last node (until 'temp → next == head').
Step 6	Set 'Newnode → next = head', 'head = Newnode' and 'temp → next = head'.

Algo-5.11 Algorithm for inserting a node at end of the circular linked list

Step 1	Create a Newnode with a specific value.
Step 2	Check whether the list is empty (head == NULL) or not.
Step 3	If it is empty, then set head = Newnode and Newnode → next = head.
Step 4	If it is not empty, then define a node pointer temp and initialize with head.
Step 5	Keep moving the temp to its next node until it reaches the last node in the list (until temp → next == head).
Step 6	Set temp → next = Newnode and Newnode → next = head.

Algo-5.12 Algorithm for inserting a node at a specific location in the circular linked list

Step 1	Create a Newnode with a given value.
Step 2	Check whether the list is empty (head == NULL) or not.
Step 3	If it is empty, then set head = Newnode and Newnode → next = head.
Step 4	If it is not empty, then define a node pointer temp and initialize with head.
Step 5	Keep moving the temp to its next node until it reaches the node after which we want to insert the Newnode (until temp1 → data is equal to location, here location is the node value after which we want to insert the Newnode).
Step 6	Every time check whether temp is reached to the last node or not. If it is reached to the last node, then display 'target node is not found and insertion is not possible!!!' and exit; otherwise move the temp to the next node.

(Continued)

Step 7	If the temp is reached to the exact node after which we want to insert the Newnode then check whether it is the last node (temp → next == head).
Step 8	If the temp is the last node then set temp → next = Newnode and Newnode → next = head.
Step 9	If the temp is not the last node then set Newnode → next = temp → next and temp → next = Newnode.

5.4.2 Deleting Node from Circular Linked List

Algo-5.13 Algorithm for deleting a node from the beginning of the circular linked list

Step 1	Check whether the list is empty (head == NULL).
Step 2	If it is empty, then display 'List is empty and deletion is not possible' and exit.
Step 3	If it is not empty, then define two node pointers 'temp1' and 'temp2' and initialize both 'temp1' and 'temp2' with head.
Step 4	Check whether the list is having only one node (temp1 → next == head) or not.
Step 5	If it is TRUE, then set head = NULL and delete temp1 (Setting empty list conditions).
Step 6	If it is FALSE, move the temp1 until it reaches the last node. (until temp1 → next = head).
Step 7	Then set head = temp2 → next, temp1 → next = head and delete temp2.

Algo-5.14 Algorithm for deleting the end node of the circular linked list

Step 1	Check whether the list is empty (head = = NULL).
Step 2	If it is empty, then display 'List is empty and deletion is not possible' and exit.
Step 3:	If it is not empty, then define two node pointers 'temp1' and 'temp2' and initialize temp1' with head.
Step 4:	Check whether the list has only one Node (temp1 → next = = head) or not.
Step 5:	If it is TRUE, then set head = NULL and delete temp1 and exit. (Setting empty list condition).
Step 6:	If it is FALSE, then set 'temp2 = temp1 ' and move temp1 to its next node. Repeat the same until temp1 reaches the last node in the list. (until temp1 → next = head).
Step 7:	Set temp2 → next = head and delete temp1.

Algo-5.15 Algorithm for deleting a node from the specific location in the circular linked list

Step 1	Check whether list is empty (head == NULL) or not
Step 2	If it is empty, then display 'List is empty and deletion is not possible' and exit.
Step 3	If it is not empty, then define two node pointers 'temp1' and 'temp2' and initialize 'temp1' with head.
Step 4	Keep moving the temp1 until it reaches the exact node to be deleted or to the last node. And every time set 'temp2 = temp1' before moving the 'temp1' to its next node.

(*Continued*)

Step 5	If it reaches to the last node, then display 'Target node not found in the list and deletion is not possible!!!' and exit.
Step 6	If it reaches to the exact node which we want to delete, then check whether the list has only one node (temp1 → next = = head) or not.
Step 7	If the list has only one node and that is the node to be deleted, then set head = NULL and delete temp1 (free(temp1)).
Step 8	If the list contains multiple nodes, then check whether temp1 is the first node in the list (temp1 == head).
Step 9	If temp1 is the first node, then set temp2 = head and keep moving temp2 to its next node until temp2 reaches the last node. Then set head = head → next, temp2 → next = head, and delete temp1.
Step 10	If temp1 is not the first node, then check whether it is the last node in the list (temp1 → next = head).
Step 11	If temp1 is last node, then set temp2 → next = head and delete temp1 (free(temp1)).
Step 12:	If temp1 is not the first node and not the last node, then set temp2 → next = temp1 → next and delete temp1 (free(temp1)).

5.4.3 Operations in Circular Linked List with C

Following is the C program for implementation of the circular linked list. The operations listed below are implemented using the C source code.

1. Insert at the beginning.
2. Insert at the end.
3. Insert at a specific location.
4. Delete from the beginning.
5. Delete from the end.
6. Delete at a specific location.
7. Search for an element.
8. Display of elements.

CProg-5.3 Circular linked list implementation

```
#include<stdio.h>
#include<stdlib.h>

/* Linked list node definition */
struct node
{
   int data;
   struct node *next;
};

struct node *head;
```

```
/* Declaring the functions for various operations */
void beginsert ();
void lastinsert ();
void randominsert();
void begin_delete();
void last_delete();
void random_delete();
void display();
void search();

/* Driver function */
void main ()
{
   int choice = 0;
   while(choice != 7)
   {
       printf("\n\n*********Main Menu*********\n");
       printf("\nChoose one option from the following list ...\n");
      printf("\n===============================================\n");
        printf("\n1.Insert in begining\n2.Insert at last\n3.Insert
at any random location\n4.Delete from Beginning\n5.Delete from last\
n6.Delete node after specified location\n7.Search for an element\
n8.Show\n9.Exit \n");
       printf("\nEnter your choice?\n");
       scanf("\n%d",&choice);
       switch(choice)
       {
           case 1:
           beginsert();
           break;
           case 2:
           lastinsert();
           break;
           case 3:
           randominsert();
          break;
           case 4:
           begin_delete();
           break;
           case 5:
           last_delete();
           break;
           case 6:
          random_delete();
           break;
```

```
            case 7:
            search();
            break;
            case 8:
            display();
            break;
            case 9:
            exit(0);
            break;
            default:
            printf("Please enter valid choice..");
        }
    }
}

/* Function for inserting a node at the beginning */
void beginsert()
{
    struct node *ptr, *temp;
    int item;
    ptr = (struct node *)malloc(sizeof(struct node));
    if(ptr == NULL)
    {
        printf("\nOVERFLOW");
    }
    else
    {
        printf("\nEnter the node data?");
        scanf("%d", &item);
        ptr -> data = item;
        if(head == NULL)
        {
            head = ptr;
            ptr -> next = head;
        }
       else
        {
            temp = head;
            while(temp -> next != head)
                temp = temp -> next;
            ptr -> next = head;
            temp -> next = ptr;
            head = ptr;
        }
       printf("\nnode inserted\n");
    }
}
```

```
/* Function for inserting a node at the end */
void lastinsert()
{
   struct node *ptr,*temp;
   int item;
   ptr = (struct node *)malloc(sizeof(struct node));
   if(ptr == NULL)
   {
       printf("\nOVERFLOW\n");
   }
   else
   {
       printf("\nEnter Data?");
       scanf("%d", &item);
       ptr->data = item;
       if(head == NULL)
       {
           head = ptr;
           ptr -> next = head;
       }
       else
       {
           temp = head;
           while(temp -> next != head)
           {
               temp = temp -> next;
           }
           temp -> next = ptr;
           ptr -> next = head;
       }

       printf("\nnode inserted\n");
   }
 }
 /* Function for deleting a node at the beginning */
void begin_delete()
{
   struct node *ptr;
   if(head == NULL)
     {
       printf("\nUNDERFLOW");
     }
   else if(head -> next == head)
     {
       head = NULL;
       free(head);
```

```
      printf("\nnode deleted\n");
    }

  else
    { ptr = head;
      while(ptr -> next != head)
          ptr = ptr -> next;
      ptr -> next = head->next;
      free(head);
      head = ptr -> next;
      printf("\nnode deleted\n");
    }
}

/* Function for deleting a node at the end */
void last_delete()
{
  struct node *ptr, *preptr;
  if(head == NULL)
    {
      printf("\nUNDERFLOW");
    }
  else if (head -> next == head)
    {
      head = NULL;
      free(head);
      printf("\nnode deleted\n");
    }
  else
    {
      ptr = head;
      while(ptr -> next != head)
        {
          preptr = ptr;
          ptr = ptr -> next;
        }
      preptr -> next = ptr -> next;
      free(ptr);
      printf("\nnode deleted\n");
    }
}

/* Function for searching an element */
void search()
 {
  struct node *ptr;
```

```
   int item, i = 0, flag = 1;
   ptr = head;
   if(ptr == NULL)
   {
       printf("\nEmpty List\n");
   }
   else
   {
      printf("\nEnter item which you want to search for?\n");
       scanf("%d", &item);
       if(head -> data == item)
       {
       printf("Item found at location %d", i+1);
       flag = 0;
       }
       else
       {
       while (ptr -> next != head)
       {
           if(ptr -> data == item)
           {
               printf("item found at location %d ", i+1);
               flag = 0;
               break;
           }
           else
           {
               flag = 1;
           }
           i++;
           ptr = ptr -> next;
       }
       }
       if(flag != 0)
       {
           printf("Item not found\n");
       }
   }
  }

/* Function for displaying the list */
void display()
  {
   struct node *ptr;
   ptr  = head;
   if(head == NULL)
```

```
  {
     printf("\nnothing to print");
  }
  else
  {
     printf("\n printing values . . . \n");
     while(ptr -> next != head)
     {
        printf("%d\n", ptr -> data);
        ptr = ptr -> next;
     }
     printf("%d\n", ptr -> data);
  }
 }

/* Function for inserting at random position */
void randominsert()
 {
  int i, loc, item;
  struct node *ptr, *temp;
  ptr = (struct node *) malloc (sizeof(struct node));
  if(ptr == NULL)
  {
     printf("\nOVERFLOW");
  }
  else
  {
     printf("\nEnter element value");
     scanf("%d", &item);
     ptr->data = item;
     printf("\nEnter the location after which you want to insert ");
     scanf("\n%d", &loc);
     temp = head;
     for(i = 0; i<loc; i++)
     {
        temp = temp -> next;
        if(temp == NULL)
        {
           printf("\ncan't insert\n");
           return;
        }

     }
     ptr -> next = temp -> next;
     temp -> next = ptr;
     printf("\nNode inserted");
  }
 }
```

```
/* Function for deletion from random position */
void random_delete()
  {
   struct node *ptr, *ptr1;
   int loc, i;
   printf("\n Enter the location of the node after which you
want to perform deletion \n");
   scanf("%d", &loc);
   ptr = head;
   for(i = 0; i < loc; i++)
   {
       ptr1 = ptr;
       ptr = ptr -> next;

       if(ptr == NULL)
       {
           printf("\nCan't delete");
           return;
       }
   }
   ptr1 -> next = ptr -> next;
   free(ptr);
   printf("\nDeleted node %d ", loc+1);
  }
/* End of program */
```

Output

```
*********Main Menu*********

Choose one option from the following list ...
===============================================
1.Insert in beginning
2.Insert at last
3.Insert at any random location
4.Delete from beginning
5.Delete from last
6.Delete node after specified location
7.Search for an element
8.Show
9.Exit

Enter your choice?
1

Enter the node data?23
node inserted
```

```
*********Main Menu*********
Enter your choice?
2

Enter Data?56
node inserted

*********Main Menu*********
Enter your choice?
1

Enter the node data?31
node inserted

*********Main Menu*********
Enter your choice?
1

Enter the node data?65
node inserted

*********Main Menu*********
Enter your choice?
8

printing values ...
65
31
23
56

*********Main Menu*********
Enter your choice?
7

Enter item which you want to search for?
31
Item found at location 2
```

> ***Programming Tips!***
>
> It is a menu-driven C program using switch-case conditions in which different operations of the circular linked list are implemented. Here, many functions like `beginsert()`, `lastinsert()`, `randominsert()`, `begin_delete()`, `last_delete()`, `random_delete()`, `display()`, and `search()` are used for various operations.

5.4.4 Operations in Circular Linked List with Python

Following is the Python program for the implementation of the circular linked list. The operations listed below are implemented using the Python source code.

1. Insert a node at the beginning.
2. Insert a node at the end.
3. Insert of a node at a specific location.
4. Delete a node from the beginning.
5. Delete a node from the end.
6. Delete a node at a specific location.

PyProg-5.4 Circular linked list implementation (insertion, deletion)

```
'''
Insert node in circular Linked List with Python
        a) At beginning  b) as middle node c) at last node
Delete node from circular Linked List with Python
        a) from beginning  b) from middle node c) from last node
'''

# class definition of linked list node
class node:
    def __init__(self, key, next=None):
        self.key = key
        self.next = next

    def __str__(self):
        return str(self.key)

    def __repr__(self):
        return str(self.key)

# class definition of circular linked list
class circular_linked_list:
    def __init__(self, head = None):
        self.head = head
    def pretty_print(self):
        cir_list_str = ''
        current_node = self.head
        while current_node:
            cir_list_str += '-({0:1d})-'.format(current_node.key)
            current_node = current_node.next
            if current_node == self.head:
                break
        return cir_list_str
```

```
    # Insert node at the end of the circular linked list
    def append(self, key):
        new_node = node(key)
        # If there are no elements in the circular linked list
        if self.head is None:
            self.head = new_node
            new_node.next = self.head
        else:
            current_node = self.head
            # Traverse the circular linked list to find last node
            while current_node.next != self.head:
                current_node = current_node.next
            current_node.next = new_node
            new_node.next = self.head

    # Insert node at the beginning of the circular linked list
    def prepend(self, key):
        new_node = node(key)

        # This will handle an empty list too
        current_node = self.head
        new_node.next = self.head

        # If there are no elements in the circular linked list
        if self.head is None:
            new_node.next = new_node
        else:
            # If not an empty circular linked list - the last
node needs to be
            # updated with new self.head which is the new node
            while current_node.next != self.head:
                current_node = current_node.next
            current_node.next = new_node
        self.head = new_node

    # Insert after a specific node in the circular linked list
    def insert_after_node(self, afterkey, key):
        current_node = self.head
        while current_node:
            if current_node.next == self.head and current_node.
key == afterkey:
                # New node is to be appended to the list
                self.append(key)
                return
```

```
            elif current_node.key == afterkey:
                new_node = node(key)
                next_node = current_node.next

                # Update next pointers
                current_node.next = new_node
                new_node.next = next_node
                return
            else:
                if current_node.next == self.head:
                    break
            current_node = current_node.next

    def delete(self, deletekey):
        current_node = self.head
        prev_node = None
        while current_node:
            # The node to be deleted is the head node
            if current_node.key == deletekey and current_node
== self.head:
                   # Case 1 - The head is the only element in
circular linked list
                if current_node.next == self.head:
                    current_node = None
                    self.head = None
                    return
                    # Case 2 - There are more elements in the
circular linked list
                else:
                       # Traverse to end of list, update self.
head, delete head
                    while current_node.next != self.head:
                        current_node = current_node.next
                    current_node.next = self.head.next
                    self.head = self.head.next
                    current_node = None
                    return
            # Case 3 & 4 - Node to be deleted in between nodes
or last node
            elif current_node.key == deletekey:
                prev_node.next = current_node.next
                current_node = None
                return
            else:
                if current_node.next == self.head:
                    break
```

```
            prev_node = current_node
            current_node = current_node.next

if __name__ == "__main__":
    # Create circular linked list
    cir_list = circular_linked_list()
    data = [5, 8, 10, 12]
    for value in data:
        cir_list.append(value)
    print('\n----- Insert Operations ----- ')
    # Expected -(5)--(8)--(10)--(12)-
    print('\nCircular linked list elements using append --->',
          cir_list.pretty_print())
    # Prepend when the list is empty
    cir_list1 = circular_linked_list()
    cir_list1.prepend(4)
    # Expected -(4)-
    print('\nPrepend on empty list  ---> ', cir_list1.pretty_print())
    # Prepend into an existing linked list
    cir_list1.prepend(0)
    # Expected -(0)--(4)-
    print('\nPrepend on an existing list    ---> ', cir_list1.
pretty_print())
    cir_list2 = circular_linked_list()
    cir_list2.append(17)
    # Expected -(17)-
    print('\nAppend on empty list  ---> ', cir_list2.pretty_print())
    # Append operation called when inserted into a single element
list
    cir_list2.insert_after_node(17, 20)
    # Expected -(17)--(20)-
    print('\nInserting 20 after 17 - Append    ---> ', cir_list2.
pretty_print())
    # Inserting node in between nodes
    cir_list2.insert_after_node(17, 18)
    # Inserting node in between nodes
    # Expected -(17)--(18)--(19)--(20)-
    cir_list2.insert_after_node(18, 19)
    print('\nInserting 19 after 18  ---> ', cir_list2.pretty_print())
    print('\n----- Delete Operations ----- ')
    del_cir_list0 = circular_linked_list()
    del_cir_list0.append(77)
    print('\nSingle element circular linked list before deletion
--->',
          del_cir_list0.pretty_print())
```

```
    # Case 1 - Node to be deleted is head and there is only a single
element
    # in the circular linked list
    # Expected - To see nothing printed
    del_cir_list0.delete(77)
    print('\nNo linked list present after deleting only node  --->',
          del_cir_list0.pretty_print())
    del_cir_list = circular_linked_list()
    del_cir_list.append(16)
    del_cir_list.prepend(11)
    del_cir_list.insert_after_node(11, 19)
    del_cir_list.prepend(9)
    del_cir_list.append(22)
    del_cir_list.prepend(5)

    # Expected -(5)--(9)--(11)--(19)--(16)--(22)-
    print('\nCircular linked list before deletion --->',
          del_cir_list.pretty_print())
    del_cir_list.delete(5)
    # Case 2 - Node to be deleted is head and there are more elements
in list
    # Expected -(9)--(11)--(19)--(16)--(22)-
    print('\nCircular linked list after deletion of head--->',
          del_cir_list.pretty_print())
    # Case 3 - Node to be deleted is in between nodes
    # Expected -(9)--(11)--(16)--(22)-
    del_cir_list.delete(19)
    print('\nList after deletion of in between node 19 --->',
          del_cir_list.pretty_print())
    # Case 4 - Node to be deleted is the last node
    # Expected -(9)--(11)--(16)-
    del_cir_list.delete(22)
    print('\nList after deletion of last node 22 --->',
          del_cir_list.pretty_print())
    # Try to delete a non-existing node from the circular linked list
    # Expected -(9)--(11)--(16)-
    del_cir_list.delete(88)
     print('\nNo change in list when trying to delete non existing
key', del_cir_list.pretty_print())
## End program
```

Output

```
----- Insert Operations -----
Circular linked list elements using append ---> -(5)--(8)--(10)--(12)-
Prepend on empty list  --->  -(4)-
Prepend on an existing list  --->  -(0)--(4)-
```

```
Append on empty list ---> -(17)-
Inserting 20 after 17 - Append   ---> -(17)--(20)-
Inserting 19 after 18 ---> -(17)--(18)--(19)--(20)-

----- Delete Operations -----
Single element circular linked list before deletion ---> -(77)-
No linked list present after deleting only node --->
Circular linked list before deletion ---> -(5)--(9)--(11)--(19)--(16)--(22)-
Circular linked list after deletion of head--->
-(9)--(11)--(19)--(16)--(22)-
List after deletion of in between node 19 ---> -(9)--(11)--(16)--(22)-
List after deletion of last node 22 ---> -(9)--(11)--(16)-
No change in list when trying to delete non existing key -(9)--(11)--(16)-
```

Programming Tips!

`init__()` is the constructor used to initialize the object's state. `append()` is used to insert a node at the end of the circular linked list. `prepend()` is used to insert a node at the beginning of the circular linked list. `insert_after_node()` is used to insert after a specific node in the circular linked list.

Note!

A circular linked list consists of a sequence of nodes where the last node's link part holds the address of the first node.

5.5 OPERATIONS ON DOUBLY LINKED LIST

In line with singly and circular linked lists, insertion and deletion are the major operations presented here, in doubly linked list with algorithms, C, and Python source codes.

5.5.1 Inserting Node in Doubly Linked List

In a doubly linked list, the insertion operation can be performed in three ways:

1. Inserting a node at the beginning of the doubly linked list
2. Inserting a node at the end of the doubly linked list
3. Inserting a node at a specific location in the doubly linked list.

Algo-5.16 Algorithm for inserting a node at the beginning of the doubly linked list

Step 1	Create a Newnode with a specific value and Newnode → previous as NULL.
Step 2	Check whether list is empty (head = = NULL) or not.
Step 3	If it is empty, then assign NULL to Newnode → next and Newnode to head.
Step 4	If it is not empty, then assign head to Newnode → next and Newnode to head.

Algo-5.17 Algorithm for inserting a node at end of the doubly linked list

Step 1	Create a Newnode with the given value and Newnode → next as NULL.
Step 2	Check whether the list is empty (head == NULL) or not.
Step 3	If it is empty, then assign NULL to Newnode → previous and Newnode to head.
Step 4	If it is not empty, then define a node pointer temp and initialize with head.
Step 5	Keep moving the temp to its next node until it reaches the last node in the list (until temp → next is equal to NULL).
Step 6	Assign Newnode to temp → next and temp to Newnode → previous.

Algo-5.18 Algorithm for inserting a node at a specific location of the doubly linked list

Step 1	Create a Newnode with the given value.
Step 2	Check whether list is empty (head == NULL) or not.
Step 3	If it is empty, then assign NULL to both Newnode → Previous and Newnode → next and set Newnode to head.
Step 4	If it is not empty, then define two node pointers temp1 and temp2 and initialize temp1 with head.
Step 5	Keep moving the temp1 to its next node until it reaches the node after which we want to insert the Newnode (until temp1 → data is equal to location, here location is the node value after which we want to insert the Newnode).
Step 6	Every time check whether temp1 is reached to the last node. If it is reached to the last node then display 'Given node is not found in the list!!! Insertion is not possible!!!' and terminate the function. Otherwise, move the temp1 to the next node.
Step 7:	Assign temp1 → next to temp2, Newnode to temp1 → next, temp1 to Newnode → previous, temp2 to Newnode → next and Newnode to temp2 → previous.

5.5.2 Deleting Node from Doubly Linked List

In a doubly linked list, the deletion operation can be performed in three ways:

1. Deleting a node at the beginning of the doubly linked list
2. Deleting a node at the end of the doubly linked list
3. Deleting a node at a specific location in the doubly linked list.

Algo-5.19 Algorithm for deleting a node from the beginning of the doubly linked list

Step 1	Check whether the list is empty (head = = NULL) or not.
Step 2	If it is empty, then display 'List is empty and deletion is not possible' and exit.
Step 3	If it is not empty, then define a node pointer 'temp' and initialize with head.
Step 4	Check whether the list has only one node (temp → Previous is equal to temp → next) or not.
Step 5	If it is TRUE, then set head to NULL and delete temp (Setting empty list conditions)
Step 6	If it is FALSE, then assign temp → Next to head, NULL to head → Previous and delete temp.

Algo-5.20 Algorithm for deleting the end node of the doubly linked list

Step 1	Check whether list is empty (head = = NULL) or not.
Step 2	If it is empty, then display 'List is empty and deletion is not possible' and exit.
Step 3	If it is not empty, then define a node pointer 'temp' and initialize with head.
Step 4	Check whether the list has only one node (temp → previous and temp → next both are NULL) or not.
Step 5	If it is TRUE, then assign NULL to head and delete temp and exit. (Setting empty list condition).
Step 6	If it is FALSE, then keep moving temp until it reaches the last node in the list. (until temp → next is equal to NULL).
Step 7	Assign NULL to temp → previous → next and delete temp.

Algo-5.21 Algorithm for deleting a node from a specific location in the circular linked list

Step 1	Check whether list is empty (head == NULL) or not.
Step 2	If it is empty, then display 'List is empty and deletion is not possible' and exit.
Step 3	If it is not empty, then define a node pointer 'temp' and initialize with head.
Step 4	Keep moving the temp until it reaches the exact node to be deleted or to the last node.
Step 5	If it is reached to the last node, then the display 'target node is not found in the list and deletion is not possible' and exit.
Step 6	If it is reached to the exact node which we want to delete, then check whether the list has only one node or not.
Step 7	If the list has only one node and that is the node which is to be deleted then set head to NULL and delete temp (free(temp)).
Step 8	If the list contains multiple nodes, then check whether temp is the first node in the list (temp == head).
Step 9	If temp is the first node, then move the head to the next node (head = head → next), set head of previous to NULL (head → previous = NULL), and delete temp.
Step 10	If temp is not the first node, then check whether it is the last node in the list (temp → next == NULL) or not.
Step 11	If temp is the last node, then set temp of previous of next to NULL (temp → previous → next = NULL) and delete temp (free(temp)).
Step 12	If temp is not the first node and not the last node, then set temp of previous of next to the temp of next (temp → previous → next = temp → next), the temp of next of previous to the temp of previous (temp → next → previous = temp → previous) and delete temp (free(temp)).

5.5.3 Operations in Doubly Linked List with C

Following is the C program for the implementation of the doubly linked list. The operations listed below are implemented using the C source code.

1. Display the linked list
2. Inserting a node at the beginning
3. Inserting a node at the end
4. Inserting a node before a given node
5. Inserting a node after a given node
6. Deleting a node from the beginning
7. Deleting a node from the end
8. Deleting a node before a given node
9. Deleting a node after a given node
10. Deleting the entire list.

CProg-5.4 Doubly linked list implementation

```
#include<stdio.h>
#include<stdlib.h>

/* Structure for doubly linked list */
struct node
{
    struct node *next;
    int data;
    struct node *prev;
};

/* Functions declaration */
struct node *start = NULL;
struct node *create_ll(struct node *);
struct node *display(struct node *);
struct node *insert_beg(struct node *);
struct node *insert_end(struct node *);
struct node *insert_before(struct node *);
struct node *insert_after(struct node *);
struct node *delete_beg(struct node *);
struct node *delete_end(struct node *);
struct node *delete_before(struct node *);
struct node *delete_after(struct node *);
struct node *delete_list(struct node *);

/* Main function */
int main()
```

```
{
   int option;
   do
   {
      printf("\n\n*****MAIN MENU*****");
      printf("\n 1: Create a list");
      printf("\n 2: Display the list");
      printf("\n 3: Add a node at the beginning");
      printf("\n 4: Add a node at the end");
      printf("\n 5: Add a node before a given node");
      printf("\n 6: Add a node after a given node");
      printf("\n 7: Delete a node from the beginning");
      printf("\n 8: Delete a node from the end");
      printf("\n 9: Delete a node before a given node");
      printf("\n 10: Delete a node after a given node");
      printf("\n 11: Delete the entire list");
      printf("\n 12: EXIT");
      printf("\n\n Enter your option : ");
      scanf("%d", &option);
      switch (option)
      {
        case 1: start = create_ll(start);
                printf("\n DOUBLY LINKED LIST CREATED");
                break;
        case 2: start = display(start);
                break;
        case 3: start = insert_beg(start);
                break;
        case 4: start = insert_end(start);
                break;
        case 5: start = insert_before(start);
                break;
        case 6: start = insert_after(start);
                break;
        case 7: start = delete_beg(start);
                break;
        case 8: start = delete_end(start);
                break;
        case 9: start = delete_before(start);
                break;
        case 10: start = delete_after(start);
                break;
        case 11:start = delete_list(start);
                printf("\n DOUBLY LINKED LIST DELETED");
                break;
      }
   }while(option != 12);
```

```
    return 0;
}

/* Function for creating Doubly Linked List */
struct node *create_ll(struct node *start)
{
    struct node *new_node, *ptr;
    int num;
    printf("\n Enter -1 to end");
    printf("\n Enter the data: ");
    scanf("%d", &num);
    while(num != -1)
    {
        if(start == NULL)
        {
            new_node = (struct node*)malloc(sizeof(struct node));
            new_node -> prev = NULL;
            new_node -> data = num;
            new_node -> next = NULL;
            start = new_node;
        }
        else
        {
            ptr = start;
            new_node = (struct node*)malloc(sizeof(struct node));
            new_node -> data = num;
            while(ptr -> next != NULL)
            {
                ptr = ptr -> next;
            }
            ptr -> next = new_node;
            new_node -> prev = ptr;
            new_node -> next = NULL;
        }
       printf("\n Enter the data : ");
        scanf("%d", &num);
    }
    return start;
}

/* Function for printing Doubly Linked List */
struct node *display(struct node *start)
{
    struct node *ptr;
    ptr = start;
    while(ptr != NULL)
```

```
    {
        printf("\t %d", ptr -> data);
        ptr = ptr -> next;
    }
    return start;
}

/* Function for inserting node at beginning */
struct node *insert_beg(struct node *start)
{
    struct node *new_node;
    int num;
    printf("\n Enter the data : ");
    scanf("%d", &num);
    new_node = (struct node *)malloc(sizeof(struct node));
    new_node -> data = num;
    start -> prev = new_node;
    new_node -> next = start;
    new_node -> prev = NULL;
    start = new_node;
    return start;
}

/* Function for inserting node at the end */
struct node *insert_end(struct node *start)
{
    struct node *ptr, *new_node;
    int num;
    printf("\n Enter the data : ");
    scanf("%d", &num);
    new_node = (struct node *)malloc(sizeof(struct node));
    new_node -> data = num;
    ptr = start;
    while(ptr -> next != NULL)
    {
        ptr = ptr -> next;
    }
    ptr -> next = new_node;
    new_node -> prev = ptr;
    new_node -> next = NULL;
    return start;
}

/* Function for inserting node before the value */
struct node *insert_before(struct node *start)
```

```
{
    struct node *new_node, *ptr;
    int num, val;
    printf("\n Enter the data : ");
    scanf("%d", &num);
    printf("\n Enter the value before which the data has to be
inserted:");
    scanf("%d", &val);
    new_node = (struct node *)malloc(sizeof(struct node));
    new_node -> data = num;
    ptr = start;
    while(ptr -> data != val)
    {
        ptr = ptr -> next;
    }
    new_node -> next = ptr;
    new_node -> prev = ptr-> prev;
    ptr -> prev -> next = new_node;
    ptr -> prev = new_node;
    return start;
}

/* Function for inserting node after the value */
struct node *insert_after(struct node *start)
{
    struct node *new_node, *ptr;
    int num, val;
    printf("\n Enter the data : ");
    scanf("%d", &num);
    printf("\n Enter the value after which the data has to be
inserted:");
    scanf("%d", &val);
    new_node = (struct node *)malloc(sizeof(struct node));
    new_node -> data = num;
    ptr = start;
    while(ptr -> data != val)
    ptr = ptr -> next;
    new_node -> prev = ptr;
    new_node -> next = ptr -> next;
    ptr -> next -> prev = new_node;
    ptr -> next = new_node;
    return start;
}

/* Function for deleting node from beginning */
struct node *delete_beg(struct node *start)
```

```
{
    struct node *ptr;
    ptr = start;
    start = start -> next;
    start -> prev = NULL;
    free(ptr);
    return start;
}

/* Function for deleting node from end */
struct node *delete_end(struct node *start)
{
    struct node *ptr;
    ptr = start;
    while(ptr -> next != NULL)
    {
        ptr = ptr -> next;
    }
    ptr -> prev -> next = NULL;
    free(ptr);
    return start;
}

/* Function for deleting node after the value */
struct node *delete_after(struct node *start)
{
    struct node *ptr, *temp;
    int val;
     printf("\n Enter the value after which the node has to
deleted : ");
    scanf("%d", &val);
    ptr = start;
    while(ptr -> data != val)
   {
        ptr = ptr -> next;
    }
    temp = ptr -> next;
    ptr -> next = temp -> next;
    temp -> next -> prev = ptr;
    free(temp);
    return start;
}

/* Function for deleting node before the value */
struct node *delete_before(struct node *start)
```

```
{
    struct node *ptr, *temp;
    int val;
    printf("\n Enter the value before which the node has to deleted:");
    scanf("%d", &val);
    ptr = start;
    while(ptr -> data != val)
    {
        ptr = ptr -> next;
    }
    temp = ptr -> prev;
    if(temp == start)
    {
         start = delete_beg(start);
    }
    else
    {
     ptr -> prev = temp -> prev;
     temp -> prev -> next = ptr;
    }
    free(temp);
    return start;
}

/* Function for deleting Linked List */
struct node *delete_list(struct node *start)
{
    while(start != NULL)
    {
        start = delete_beg(start);
    }
    return start;
}
/* End of program */
```

Output

```
*****MAIN MENU*****
 1: Create a list
 2: Display the list
 3: Add a node at the beginning
 4: Add a node at the end
 5: Add a node before a given node
 6: Add a node after a given node
 7: Delete a node from the beginning
 8: Delete a node from the end
 9: Delete a node before a given node
```

```
 10: Delete a node after a given node
 11: Delete the entire list
 12: EXIT
 Enter your option : 1
 Enter -1 to end
 Enter the data: 23
 Enter the data : 45
 Enter the data : 85
 Enter the data : 74
 Enter the data : 62
 Enter the data : 43
 Enter the data : -1
 DOUBLY LINKED LIST CREATED

*****MAIN MENU*****
Enter your option : 2
         23        45        85        74        62        43

*****MAIN MENU*****
Enter your option : 3
 Enter the data : 15

*****MAIN MENU*****
Enter your option : 8

*****MAIN MENU*****
Enter your option : 2
         15        23        45        85        74        62

*****MAIN MENU*****
Enter your option : 12
```

Programming Tips!

It is a menu-driven C program using switch-case conditions for the implementation of the doubly linked list. Here, many functions like `create()`, `display()`, `insert_beg()`, `insert_end()`, `insert_before()`, `insert_after()`, `delete_beg()`, `delete_end()`, `delete_before()`, `delete_after()`, and `delete_list()` are used for various operations.

5.5.4 Operations in Doubly Linked List with Python

Following is the Python program for the implementation of the doubly linked list. The operations listed below are implemented using the Python source code.

1. Inserting a node at the beginning
2. Inserting a node at the end
3. Inserting a node after and before a specific node

4. Deleting a node from the beginning
5. Deleting a node from the end
6. Deleting a node between two given nodes.

PyProg-5.5 Doubly linked list implementation

```
'''
--Implementation of Doubly Linked List with Python--
    Insert node in Doubly / Two-way Linked List with Python
        a) At beginning  b) as middle node c) at last node
    Delete node from Doubly / Two-way Linked List in Python
       a) from beginning  b) from middle node c) from last node
'''

# Class definition of new node
class node:
    def __init__(self, key, next = None, prev = None):
        self.key = key
        self.next = next
        self.prev = prev

    def __str__(self):
        return str(self.key)

    def __repr__(self):
        return str(self.key)

# Class definition of linked list
class doubly_linked_list:
   def __init__(self, head = None):
        self.head = head

   def pretty_print(self):
        dbl_list_str = ''
        current_node = self.head
        while current_node:
          dbl_list_str += '-({0:1d})-'.format(current_node.key)
             current_node = current_node.next
        return dbl_list_str

   # Insert node at the end of the doubly linked list
    def append(self, key):
        new_node = node(key)
        # If there are no elements in the doubly linked list
       if self.head is None:
            self.head = new_node
        else:
```

```
        current_node = self.head
        # Traverse the doubly linked list to find last node
        while current_node.next:
            current_node = current_node.next
        new_node.prev = current_node
        current_node.next = new_node

    # Insert node at the beginning of the doubly linked list
    def prepend(self, key):
        new_node = node(key)
        # If there are no elements in the doubly linked list
        if self.head is None:
            self.head = new_node
        else:
            # Add node at the beginning of the doubly linked list
            self.head.prev = new_node
            new_node.next = self.head
            self.head = new_node

    # Insert after a specific node in the doubly linked list
    def insert_after_node(self, afterkey, key):
        current_node = self.head
        while current_node:
            if current_node.next is None and current_node.key
== afterkey:
                # New node is to be appended to the list
                self.append(key)
                return
            elif current_node.key == afterkey:
                new_node = node(key)
                next_node = current_node.next

                # Update next pointers
                current_node.next = new_node
                new_node.next = next_node

                # Update prev pointers
                new_node.prev = current_node
                next_node.prev = new_node
                return
            current_node = current_node.next
    # Insert before a specific node in the doubly linked list
    def insert_before_node(self, beforekey, key):
        current_node = self.head
        while current_node:
```

```
            if current_node.prev is None and current_node.key
== beforekey:
                # New node is to be prepended to the list
                self.prepend(key)
                return
            elif current_node.key == beforekey:
                new_node = node(key)
                prev_node = current_node.prev

                # Update next pointers
                prev_node.next = new_node
                new_node.next = current_node

                # Update prev pointers
                new_node.prev = prev_node
                current_node.prev = new_node
                return
            current_node = current_node.next

    # Delete specific key node from the doubly linked list
    def delete(self, deletekey):
        current_node = self.head
        while current_node:
            # The node to be deleted is the head node
            if current_node.key == deletekey and current_node
== self.head:
                # Case 1 - The head is the only element in doubly
linked list
                if current_node.next is None:
                    current_node = None
                    self.head = None
                    return
                # Case 2 - There are more elements in the doubly
linked list
                else:
                    next_node = current_node.next
                    current_node.next = None
                    current_node = None
                    next_node.prev = None
                    self.head = next_node
                    return
            # Node to be deleted in between nodes or last node
            elif current_node.key == deletekey:
                # Case 3 : Node to be deleted is not last node
                if current_node.next:
                    next_node = current_node.next
```

```
                prev_node = current_node.prev
                prev_node.next = next_node
                next_node.prev = prev_node
                current_node = None
                return
            # Case 4 : Node to be deleted is the last node
            else:
                prev_node = current_node.prev
                prev_node.next = None
                current_node = None
                return
        current_node = current_node.next

if __name__ == "__main__":
    # Create doubly linked list
    dbl_list = doubly_linked_list()
    data = [55, 5, 82, 61]
    for value in data:
        dbl_list.append(value)

    # Expected -(55)--(5)--(82)--(61)-
    print('\nDoubly linked list elements using append --->',
        dbl_list.pretty_print())
    # Add to the beginning of the doubly linked list
    dbl_list.prepend(85)

    # Expected -(85)--(55)--(5)--(82)--(61)-
    print('\nPrepended 85  ---> ', dbl_list.pretty_print())

    dbl_list1 = doubly_linked_list()

    # Prepend when the list is empty
    dbl_list1.prepend(0)

    # Expected -(0)
    print('\nPrepend on empty list  ---> ', dbl_list1.pretty_print())

    print('\n----- Insert After Operations ----- ')

    # Add after node 5 - key 19 - In between nodes
    # Expected -(85)--(55)--(5)--(19)--(82)--(61)-
   dbl_list.insert_after_node(5, 19)
     print('\nInsert after node 5 - key 19 ---> ', dbl_list.
pretty_print())
```

```
    # Add after node 85 - key 1 - After the beginning of list
    # Expected -(85)--(1)--(55)--(5)--(19)--(82)--(61)-
    dbl_list.insert_after_node(85, 1)
    print('\nInsert after 85 - key 1 ---> ', dbl_list.pretty_print())

    # Add after node 61 - key 44 -  Append Operation - At end of
list
    # Expected -(85)--(1)--(55)--(5)--(19)--(82)--(61)--(44)-
    dbl_list.insert_after_node(61, 44)
    print('\nInsert after 61 - key 44  --->', dbl_list.pretty_print())

    print('\n----- Insert Before Operations ----- ')
    # Add before node 82 - key 22 -  In between nodes
    # Expected -(85)--(1)--(55)--(5)--(19)--(22)--(82)--(61)--(44)-
    dbl_list.insert_before_node(82, 22)
    print('\nInsert before 82 - key 22  --->', dbl_list.pretty_print())

    # Add before node 44 - key 33 -  Before the last node
      #  Expected  -(85)--(1)--(55)--(5)--(19)--(22)--(82)--(61)--
(33)--(44)-
    dbl_list.insert_before_node(44, 33)
    print('\nInsert before 44 - key 33  --->', dbl_list.pretty_print())
    # Add before node 85 - key 66 -  At head of list - Prepend
Operation
      #  Expected  -(66)--(85)--(1)--(55)--(5)--(19)--(22)--(82)--
(61)--(33)--(44)-
    dbl_list.insert_before_node(85, 66)
    print('\nInsert before 85 - key 66  --->', dbl_list.pretty_print())

    print('\n----- Delete Operations ----- ')

    # Single element doubly linked list
    dbl_del_list = doubly_linked_list()
    dbl_del_list.append(11)
    print('\nSingle node doubly linked list -->', dbl_del_list.
pretty_print())

   # Case 1 -
    # Delete the only element in the doubly linked list which is
also the head
    # Expected - (Nothing will be printed since the list is empty)
    dbl_del_list.delete(11)
   print('\nAfter deleting the only element (also the head)  -->',
        dbl_del_list.pretty_print())
```

```
    # Case 2 - Delete the head in a doubly linked list with more
than 1 element
     # Expected -(85)--(1)--(55)--(5)--(19)--(22)--(82)--(61)--
(33)--(44)-
    dbl_list.delete(66)
    print('\nAfter deleting the head -->', dbl_list.pretty_print())

    # Case 3 - Delete a node in between other nodes in the doubly
linked list
   # Expected -(85)--(1)--(55)--(5)--(19)--(22)--(61)--(33)--(44)-
    dbl_list.delete(82)
    print('\nAfter deleting a node in between nodes -->', dbl_list.
pretty_print())

    # Case 4 - Delete the last node in a doubly linked list
    # Expected -(85)--(1)--(55)--(5)--(19)--(22)--(61)--(33)-
    dbl_list.delete(44)
       print('\nAfter deleting the last node -->', dbl_list.
pretty_print())
   # Try to delete a non-existing key from the doubly linked list -
     # Expected -(85)--(1)--(55)--(5)--(19)--(22)--(61)--(33)- No
change in list
    dbl_list.delete(99)
     print('\nNo change after trying to delete a non existing key
-->', dbl_list.pretty_print())
## End program
```

Output

```
Doubly linked list elements using append ---> -(55)--(5)--(82)--(61)-
Prepended 85 ---> -(85)--(55)--(5)--(82)--(61)-
Prepend on empty list ---> -(0)-

----- Insert After Operations -----
Insert after node 5 - key 19 ---> -(85)--(55)--(5)--(19)--(82)--(61)-
Insert after 85 - key 1 ---> -(85)--(1)--(55)--(5)--(19)--(82)--(61)-
Insert after 61 - key 44 ---> -(85)--(1)--(55)--(5)--(19)--(82)--
(61)--(44)-

----- Insert Before Operations -----
Insert before 82 - key 22 ---> -(85)--(1)--(55)--(5)--(19)--(22)--
(82)--(61)--(44)-
Insert before 44 - key 33 ---> -(85)--(1)--(55)--(5)--(19)--(22)--
(82)--(61)--(33)--(44)-
Insert before 85 - key 66 ---> -(66)--(85)--(1)--(55)--(5)--(19)--
(22)--(82)--(61)--(33)--(44)-
```

```
----- Delete Operations -----
Single node doubly linked list --> -(11)-
After deleting the only element (also the head)  -->
After deleting the head  --> -(85)--(1)--(55)--(5)--(19)--(22)--(82)-
-(61)--(33)--(44)-
After deleting a node in between nodes  --> -(85)--(1)--(55)--(5)--
(19)--(22)--(61)--(33)--(44)-
After deleting the last node  --> -(85)--(1)--(55)--(5)--(19)--(22)-
-(61)--(33)-
No change after trying to delete a non existing key -->
-(85)--(1)--(55)--(5)--(19)--(22)--(61)--(33)-
```

> ***Programming Tips!***
>
> `__init__()` is the constructor used to initialize the object's state. `append()` is used to insert a node at the end, `prepend()` is used to insert a node at the beginning and `insert_after_node()` is used to insert a node after a specific node in the doubly linked list. `delete()` is used for deleting specific key nodes from the doubly linked list.

> ***Note!***
>
> A doubly linked list is a sequence of elements in which every node has a data part and two link parts to its previous element and next element in the sequence.

5.6 TRAVERSING IN LINKED LIST

Traversing a list means visiting all the nodes in the list. Usually, when we visit a node, we would like to access (read/write/modify/display/search) the data stored in that node. Traversal through a linked list means traveling through every single node of the list and reaching the end of the list. The traversal can be in only one direction in a singly linked list, and two directions (forward and backward) in a doubly (or two-way) linked list. We can simply print (display) the value of the next data element by accessing the pointer of the next node to the current data element.

Algo-5.22 Pseudocode for traversing (visiting all nodes) a linked list

```
Traversing Procedure:
BEGIN
  Node ptr;
  ptr = head;     /* Start visiting from the first node */
  WHILE(ptr has not reached the end of the list)
     /* Write or read or modify or display or search variables
inside
        currently "visiting" ptr */
   ptr = ptr -> next;   /* ptr will point to the next node ptr */
  END WHILE
END Procedure
```

5.7 MEMORY ALLOCATION AND GARBAGE COLLECTION

During program execution, the computer memory is used for storage of variables, functions, and objects. Programmers often forget to take care of the memory locations being used. Garbage collection is a technique of memory management that automatically cleans or frees up unused memory locations. It allows the memory to be used again. All programming languages do not necessarily have a built-in garbage collection mechanism. Custom functions are required to manage unused memory.

Reference counting is a common garbage collection method. This method counts how many references are there to each object stored in memory. Objects with zero references can be deleted to free up the memory space as it is considered unnecessary. Advanced reference counting mechanisms detect objects that only refer to each other. This indicates that the objects are unused by the parent process.

Garbage collection also takes place at compile-time when a program's source code is compiled into an executable program. The compiler resolves which resources in memory will not be accessed after a certain time. It includes instructions to automatically deallocate those resources from memory. This appears as an effective way to eliminate unused objects. It must be done repeatedly to avoid deleting references required by the program.

Garbage collection may take place in two steps. First, the operating system scans through the memory and tags those cells which are currently being used by some other programs. Then in the second phase, the operating system scans the memory again to collect all untagged cells in a free pool or availability stack. These garbage collection processes remain invisible to the programmers. Garbage collection is a crucial issue in software development, since it keeps programs from using too much RAM. Besides helping programs run more efficiently, it can also prevent serious bugs, such as memory leaks, that can cause a program to crash.

> ***Note!***
> Garbage collection is a very important task of an operating system.

Dangling Pointer

A pointer pointing to a non-existing memory location is called a dangling pointer. This arises when an object is deleted or deallocated, without modifying the value of the pointer. The pointer still points to the memory location of the de-allocated memory even after deletion.

Memory Leak

When the address of a memory block is no longer known to the program, it is called a memory leak. The corresponding block cannot be freed before the end of the program execution. Functions `malloc()` and `free()` preserve limited pool (resource) of available memory for use by processes under dynamic requirements. When a program allocates memory from this pool and forgets to free up the chunk while it is no longer required, then this leads to a memory leak. This pool of memory is freed only when the program exits.

5.8 SPARSE MATRIX REPRESENTATION USING ARRAY AND LINKED LIST

In computer programming, a matrix can be defined using a 2-dimensional array. Any array with m rows and n columns represent an $m \times n$ matrix. There may be a situation in which a matrix contains a greater number of ZERO values than NON-ZERO values. Such a matrix is known as the sparse matrix. *A sparse matrix is a matrix that contains very few non-zero elements.* Approximately two-third elements of the matrix are zeros.

When a sparse matrix is represented with a 2-dimensional array, we waste a lot of space to represent that matrix. For example, consider a matrix of size 100×100 containing 10000 elements in the matrix. A maximum of 3000 non-zero elements is there approximately if it is a sparse matrix. Suppose, in this matrix, only 10 elements are non-zero values, and the remaining spaces of the matrix are filled with zero. That means, totally we allocate $100 \times 100 \times 2 = 20000$ bytes of space to store this integer matrix assuming that integers take 2 bytes each. To access these 10 non-zero elements, we have to scan 10000 times. To make it simple, we use the sparse matrix representation.

The following are the reasons why we use a sparse matrix instead of a simple matrix.

- There are lesser non-zero elements than zeros and thus lesser memory can be used to store only those elements.
- Computing time can be saved by logically designing a data structure traversing only non-zero elements.

A sparse matrix can be represented in two ways, array representation and linked list representation, as explained below.

5.8.1 Array Representation

In this representation, we consider only non-zero values along with their row and column index values. In this representation, the 0-th row stores the total number of rows, the total number of columns, and the total number of non-zero values in the sparse matrix.

- **Row:** Index of the row, where the non-zero element is located
- **Column:** Index of the column, where the non-zero element is located
- **Value:** Value of the non-zero element located at that index – (row, column)

For example, consider a matrix of size 4×5 containing 6 numbers of non-zero values. This matrix can be represented as shown in Fig. 5.14. The row and column index starts from 0.

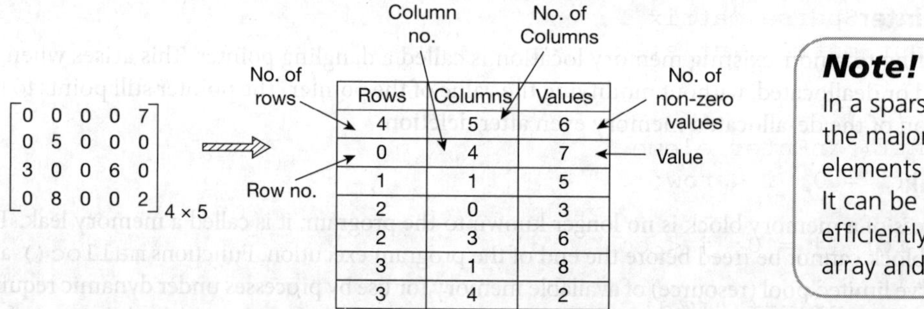

Rows	Columns	Values
4	5	6
0	4	7
1	1	5
2	0	3
2	3	6
3	1	8
3	4	2

Note!
In a sparse matrix, the majority of the elements are ZEROs. It can be represented efficiently using both array and linked list.

Figure 5.14 Sparse matrix representation

In the above example matrix, there are only 6 non-zero elements (those are 7, 5, 3, 6, 8 and 2) and the matrix size is 4×5. We represent this matrix as shown in the above Fig. 5.14. Here, the first row in the right-side table is filled with values 4, 5, and 6, which indicate that it is a sparse matrix with 4 rows, 5 columns, and 6 non-zero values. The second row is filled with 0, 4, and 7, which indicate that the non-zero value 7 is at the 0-th row and 4-th column in the sparse matrix. In the same way, the remaining non-zero values also follow a similar representation method.

In the above example, the original order of the matrix is 4×5. But when we represent as a sparse matrix, it becomes a 7×3 matrix. 7 rows because there are only 6 non-zero elements plus the first row to indicate the order of the matrix, and there are 3 columns for all cases because of row number, column number, and non-zero value. So, in final representation, the order of the matrix becomes $(n + 1) \times 3$, where n is the number of non-zero values present in the original matrix.

5.8.2 Sparse Matrix Representation Using Array with C

CProg 5.5: Sparse matrix representation using array

```
#include <stdio.h>
#define MAX 30

void input_matrix(int a[20][20], int row, int column);
void output_sparse(int b[MAX][3]);
void create_sparse(int a[20][20], int row, int column, int
b[MAX][3]);

int main()
{
    int a[20][20], b[MAX][3], row, column;
    printf("\nEnter the order of matrix (rows, columns): ");
    scanf("%d%d", &row, &column);

    input_matrix(a, row, column);
    create_sparse(a, row, column, b);
    output_sparse(b);
    return 0;
}

/* Reading Sparse matrix from user */
void input_matrix(int a[20][20], int row, int column)
{
    int i, j;
    printf("\nEnter elements of matrix\n");
    for (i = 0; i < row; i++)
    {
        for (j = 0; j < column; j++)
        {
            printf("[%d][%d]: ", i, j);
            scanf("%d", &a[i][j]);
        }
    }
}
/* Creation of Sparse matrix*/
void create_sparse(int a[20][20], int row, int column, int
b[MAX][3])
{
    int i, j, k;
    k = 1;
    b[0][0] = row;
    b[0][1] = column;
    for (i = 0; i < row; i++)
```

```
    {
        for (j = 0; j < column; j++)
        {
            if (a[i][j] != 0)
            {
                b[k][0] = i;
                b[k][1] = j;
                b[k][2] = a[i][j];
                k++;
            }
        }
        b[0][2] = k - 1;
    }
}

/* Printing Array representation of Sparse Matrix */
void output_sparse(int b[MAX][3])
{
    int i, column;
    column = b[0][2];
    printf("\nSparse Matrix representation using array \n\n");
    for (i = 0; i <= column; i++)
    {
        printf("%d\t%d\t%d\n", b[i][0], b[i][1], b[i][2]);
    }
}
/* End of Program */
```

Output

```
Enter the order of matrix (rows, columns): 3
3
Enter elements of matrix
[0][0]: 0
[0][1]: 0
[0][2]: 5
[1][0]: 0
[1][1]: 3
[1][2]: 0
[2][0]: 0
[2][1]: 0
[2][2]: 9

Sparse Matrix representation using array
3       3       3
0       2       5
1       1       3
2       2       9
```

> ***Programming Tips!***
> `input_matrix()` is used to read a sparse matrix from the user, `output_sparse()` is used to display the array representation of the sparse matrix, and `create_sparse()` is used to create the sparse matrix.

5.8.3 Sparse Matrix Representation Using Array with Python

PyProg-5.6 Sparse matrix representation using array

```
sparseMatrix = [[0,0,3,0,4], [0,0,5,7,0], [0,0,0,0,0],
[0,2,6,0,0]]

# Initialize size as 0
size = 0

for i in range(4):
    for j in range(5):
        if(sparseMatrix[i][j] != 0):
           size += 1

''' Number of columns in compactMatrix(size) should be equal to
number of non-zero elements in sparseMatrix '''
rows, cols = (3, size)

# List comprehension for creating compact matrix
compactMatrix = [[0 for i in range(cols)] for j in range(rows)]
k = 0
for i in range(4):
    for j in range(5):
        if(sparseMatrix[i][j] != 0):
          compactMatrix[0][k] = i
          compactMatrix[1][k] = j
          compactMatrix[2][k] = sparseMatrix[i][j]
          k += 1

# Printing the sparse matrix
for i in compactMatrix:
    print(i)
## End program
```

Output

```
[0, 0, 1, 1, 3, 3]
[2, 4, 2, 3, 1, 2]
[3, 4, 5, 7, 2, 6]
```

5.8.4 Linked List Representation

The linked list data structure can also be used to represent a sparse matrix. Two different nodes, namely header node and element node, are used in this linked list representation. The header node consists of three fields and the element node consists of five fields as shown in Fig. 5.15.

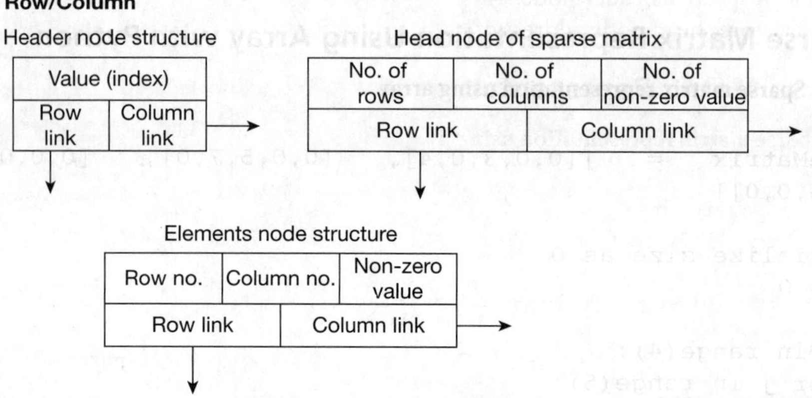

Figure 5.15 Sparse matrix – Head, header nodes and element nodes structure in the linked list

In the linked list, each node has five fields. These five fields are defined as:

1. **Row:** Index of the row, where the non-zero element is located.
2. **Column:** Index of the column, where the non-zero element is located.
3. **Value:** Value of the non-zero element located at index – (row, column).
4. **Down/up node:** Address of the next node of that column.
5. **Right:** Address of the next node of that row

Consider the Fig. 5.14 sparse matrix used in the array representation. This sparse matrix can be represented using linked representation as shown in Fig. 5.16 below.

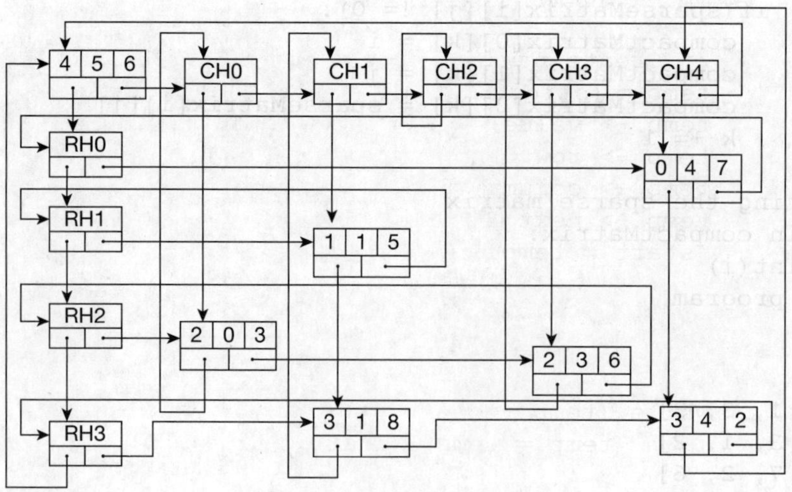

Figure 5.16 Sparse matrix representation using linked representation

In the above representation, CH0, CH1, ..., CH4 indicate the column header nodes which are used to represent indexes. RH0, RH1, ..., RH3 indicates the row header nodes which are used to represent indexes. The remaining nodes are used to represent non-zero elements in the matrix, except the very first node which is used to represent abstract information of the sparse matrix (i.e., it is a matrix of 4×5 with 6 non-zero elements). In this representation, in each row and column, the last node in the right field points to its respective header node. This always has a circular linked list nature. The last row and column link part stores head node address of row and column respectively.

5.8.5 Sparse Matrix Representation Using Linked List with C

CProg-5.6 Sparse matrix representation using linked list

```
#include<stdio.h>
#include<stdlib.h>

/* Node structure of sparse matrix */
struct Node
{
      int value;
      int row;
      int column;
      struct Node *next;
};

/* Function to create new node */
void create_new_node(struct Node** start, int non_zero_element,
                                   int row_index, int column_index )
{
      struct Node *temp, *r;
      temp = *start;
      if (temp == NULL)
      {
            /* Create new node */
            temp = (struct Node *) malloc (sizeof(struct Node));
            temp -> value = non_zero_element;
            temp -> row = row_index;
            temp -> column = column_index;
            temp -> next = NULL;
            *start = temp;

      }
      else
      {
            while (temp -> next != NULL)
                  temp = temp -> next;
```

```
            /* Create new node */
            r = (struct Node *) malloc (sizeof(struct Node));
            r -> value = non_zero_element;
            r -> row = row_index;
            r -> column = column_index;
            r -> next = NULL;
            temp->next = r;

        }
}

/* Function to prints contents of linked list */
void PrintList(struct Node* start)
{
      struct Node *temp, *r, *s;
      temp = r = s = start;

      printf("Row No: ");
      while(temp != NULL)
      {
            printf("%d ", temp-> row);
            temp = temp->next;
      }
      printf("\n");
      printf("Col No: ");
      while(r != NULL)
      {
            printf("%d ", r -> column);
            r = r->next;
      }
      printf("\n");
      printf("Value : ");
      while(s != NULL)
      {
            printf("%d ", s -> value);
            s = s -> next;
      }
      printf("\n");
}

/* Main function */
int main()
{
int i, j;
```

```
/* Sample 4x5 sparse matrix */
    int sparseMatric[4][5] =
    {
            {9 , 0 , 0 , 6 , 0 },
            {0 , 0 , 0 , 0 , 7 },
            {0 , 2 , 0 , 0 , 0 },
            {0 , 1 , 0 , 8 , 0 }
    };

    /* Initially empty list */
    struct Node* start = NULL;

    for ( i = 0; i < 4; i++)
            for ( j = 0; j < 5; j++)

                    /* Pass only non-zero Value */
                    if (sparseMatric[i][j] != 0)
                            create_new_node(&start,          sparseMa-
tric[i][j], i, j);

    PrintList(start);
    return 0;
}
/* End of Program */
```

Output

```
Row No: 0 0 1 2 3 3
Col No: 0 3 4 1 1 3
Value : 9 6 7 2 1 8
```

> ***Programming Tips!***
> `create_new_node()` is used to create a new node. `PrintList()` is used to display the contents of linked list.

5.8.6 Sparse Matrix Representation Using Linked List with Python

PyProg-5.7 Sparse matrix representation using linked list

```
"""
Objects of type Node represent all non-zero entries of the
matrix. A Node object  stores the coordinates of the entry, its
value, and has a link to the next non-zero entry to the right
(in the same row) and below (in the same column).
"""

# Defining node of the linked list
class Node:
    __Nodeslots__ = "row", "col", "data", "next"
```

```
    # Constructor init to initialize the values
    def __init__(self, row = 0, col = 0, data = 0, next = None):
        self.row = row
        self.col = col
        self.data = data
        self.next = next

# Convert Sparse Matrix into Linked List
class Sparse:
    # Initialize Class Variables
    def __init__(self):
        self.head = None
        self.temp = None
        self.size = 0

    # Returns the size of the Linked List
    def __len__(self):
        return self.size

    # Checking the Linked List is Empty or not
    def isempty(self):
        return self.size == 0

    # Create Linked List from Sparse Matrix
    def create_node(self, row, col, data):
        # Creating New Node
        newNode = Node(row, col, data, None)

        # Checking the List is empty or not
        if self.isempty():
            self.head = newNode
        else:
            self.temp.next = newNode
        self.temp = newNode

        # Incresing the size
        self.size += 1

    # Display the contents of the Linked List
    def PrintList(self):
        temp = r = s = self.head
        print("Matrix row position:", end=" ")
        while temp != None:
            print(temp.row, end=" ")
            temp = temp.next
        print()
```

```
        print("Matrix column postion:", end = " ")
        while r != None:
            print(r.col, end=" ")
            r = r.next
        print()
        print("Value:", end=" ")
        while s != None:
            print(s.data, end=" ")
            s = s.next
        print()

# Driver code
if __name__ == "__main__":
    # Object Creation
    a = Sparse()

    # Assuming 3x4 Sparse Matrix
    sparseMatrix = [[0, 0, 0, 9],
                    [4, 0, 0, 0],
                    [0, 0, 9, 8]]

    for i in range(3):
        for j in range(4):
            # Creating list for only those elements which are
non-zero
            if sparseMatrix[i][j] != 0:
                a.create_node(i, j, sparseMatrix[i][j])

    # Displaying the sparse matrix using Linked List
    a.PrintList()
## End Program
```

Output

```
Matrix row position: 0 1 2 2
Matrix column postion: 3 0 2 3
Value: 9 4 9 8
```

Programming Tips!

Node and Sparse are two classes created for holding linked list node and sparse matrix respectively. Both classes contain `__init__()` constructor for initialization. `PrintList()` is used to display the list.

5.9 POLYNOMIALS REPRESENTATION USING LINKED LIST

A polynomial p(x) = ($ax^n + bx^{n-1} + ... + jx + k$) is an expression of variable x and $a, b, c ...., k$ which are real numbers. 'n' is a non-negative integer, which is called the degree of the polynomial. An essential characteristic of the polynomial is that each term in the polynomial expression consists of two parts:

- One is the coefficient.
- The other is the exponent.

Example 5.1

Consider the polynomial p(x) = $10x^3 + 26x$. Here, 10 and 26 are coefficients and 3, 1 is its exponential value.

Suppose, the polynomial is $4x^7 + 12x^2 - 15$. This can be represented using a linked list as shown below in Fig. 5.17.

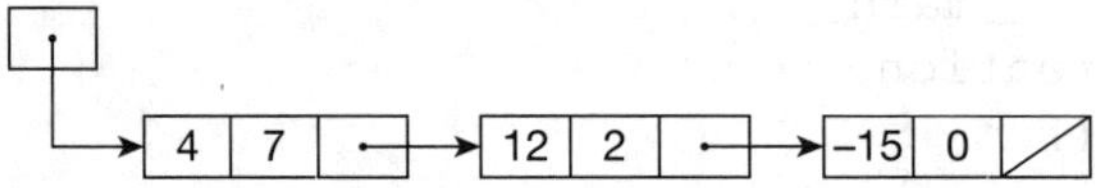

Figure 5.17 Polynomial $4x^7 + 12x^2 - 15$ representation using linked list

> ***Note!***
> A polynomial expression can be represented efficiently using a linked list. A node in the polynomial expression consists of two parts – the coefficient and the exponent.

Adding two polynomials using linked list

Example5.2

Given two polynomial numbers are represented by linked lists. Add these lists (means add the coefficients) which have the same variable powers.

I. **Input**
   1st polynomial number = $5x^2 + 4x + 2$
   2nd polynomial number = $5x + 5$
   Output: $5x^2 + 9x + 7$

II. **Input**
   1st polynomial number = $5x^3 + 4x^2 + 2$
   2nd polynomial number = $5x + 5$
   Output: $5x^3 + 4x^2 + 5x + 7$

5.9.1 Algorithm of Adding Two Polynomials Using Linked List

Algo-5.23 Algorithm to add two polynomials using the linked list

Step 1	For all nodes, we will check for the coefficients of the exponents that have the same value of exponents, and add them to return the final polynomial. So, follow steps 2 and 3.
Step 2	If the value of a node's exponent is greater, copy this node to the result node and head towards the next node.

(Continued)

Step 3	If the values of both nodes' exponents are the same, then add the coefficients. Then copy the added value to the result with the node.
Step 4	Print the resultant node.

5.9.2 Adding Two Polynomials Using Linked List with C

CProg-5.7 Adding two polynomials using linked list

```
#include<stdio.h>
#include<malloc.h>

/* Node structure of a polynomial with power and coefficient */
struct Node
  {
      int cof;
      int pow;
      struct Node *next;
  };

/* Function to create new node */
void create_node(int x, int y, struct Node **temp)
{
      struct Node *r, *z;
      z = *temp;
      if(z == NULL)
      {
           r = (struct Node*)malloc(sizeof(struct Node));
           r -> cof = x;
           r -> pow = y;
           *temp = r;
           r -> next = (struct Node*)malloc(sizeof(struct Node));
           r = r -> next;
           r -> next = NULL;
      }
      else
      {
           r -> cof = x;
           r -> pow = y;
           r -> next = (struct Node*)malloc(sizeof(struct Node));
           r = r -> next;
           r -> next = NULL;
      }
}
```

```
/* Function to Add two polynomial numbers */
void polyadd(struct Node *poly1, struct Node *poly2, struct Node
*poly)
{
  while(poly1->next && poly2->next)
      {
      /* If power of 1st polynomial>2nd,then store 1st as it is
and moves next */
          if(poly1->pow > poly2->pow)
          {
              poly->pow = poly1->pow;
              poly->cof = poly1->cof;
              poly1 = poly1->next;
          }

      /* If power of 2nd polynomial>1st,then store 2nd as it is
& moves next */
          else if(poly1->pow < poly2->pow)
          {
              poly->pow = poly2->pow;
              poly->cof = poly2->cof;
              poly2 = poly2->next;
          }

      /* If power of both polynomial numbers are same then add
their coefficients */
          else
          {
              poly->pow = poly1->pow;
              poly->cof = poly1->cof+poly2->cof;
              poly1 = poly1->next;
              poly2 = poly2->next;
          }

          /* create new node */
          poly->next  =  (struct  Node  *)malloc(sizeof(struct
Node));
          poly = poly->next;
          poly->next = NULL;
      }
  while(poly1->next || poly2->next)
```

```
    {
          if(poly1->next)
          {
                poly->pow = poly1->pow;
                poly->cof = poly1->cof;
                poly1 = poly1->next;
          }
          if(poly2->next)
          {
                poly->pow = poly2->pow;
                poly->cof = poly2->cof;
                poly2 = poly2->next;
          }
          poly->next  =  (struct  Node  *)malloc(sizeof(struct
Node));
          poly = poly->next;
          poly->next = NULL;
    }
}

/* Print Linked list */
void show(struct Node *node)
{
  while(node->next != NULL)
    {
    printf("%dx^%d", node->cof, node->pow);
    node = node->next;
    if(node->next != NULL)
          printf(" + ");
    }
}

/* Main function */
int main()
{
    struct Node *poly1 = NULL, *poly2 = NULL, *poly = NULL;

    /* Create first polynomial 4x^3 + 5x^1 + 6x^0 */
    create_node(4, 3, &poly1);
    create_node(5, 1, &poly1);
    create_node(6, 0, &poly1);

    /* Create second polynomial 7x^1 + 2x^0 */
    create_node(7, 1, &poly2);
    create_node(2, 0, &poly2);
```

```
        printf("\n1st Polynomial: ");
        show(poly1);

        printf("\n2nd Polynomial: ");
        show(poly2);

        poly = (struct Node *)malloc(sizeof(struct Node));

        /* Add two polynomial numbers */
        polyadd(poly1, poly2, poly);

        /* Print resultant List */
        printf("\nResult: ");
        show(poly);

return 0;
}
/* End of program */
```

Output

```
1st Polynomial: 4x^3 + 5x^1 + 6x^0
2nd Polynomial: 7x^1 + 2x^0
Result: 4x^3 + 12x^1 + 8x^0
```

> ***Programming Tips!***
> `create_node()` is used to create a new node. `polyadd()` is used to add two polynomial numbers. `show()` is used for displaying the linked list.

5.9.3 Adding Two Polynomials Using Linked List with Python

PyProg-5.8 Adding two polynomials using linked list

```
# Class definition of a new node
class Node:
   def __init__(self, coefficient = None, exponent = None):
       self.coefficient = coefficient
       self.exponent = exponent
       self.nextval = None
# Class definition of the polynomial
class Polynomial:
   def __init__(self):
       self.headval = None
```

```
    # Function to find out the degree of the polynomial
    def DegreeOfPolynomial(self):
        if self.headval is None:
            return -1
        else:
            return self.headval.exponent

    # Function to print the polynomial
    def printPoly(self):
        expression = ''
        printval = self.headval
        while printval is not None:
         expression = expression+" + "+str(printval.coefficient)+"
x^"+str(printval.exponent)
            printval = printval.nextval
        return expression[3:]

    # Function to insert a node(term) in the polynomial
    def insertNode(self, coefficient, exponent):
        if self.headval is None:
            term = Node(coefficient, exponent)
            self.headval = term
            return term
        else:
            term = Node(coefficient, exponent)
            lastnode = self.headval
            while lastnode.nextval:
                lastnode = lastnode.nextval
            lastnode.nextval = term
            return term
        return None

    # Function to add the polynomials
    def __add__(self, rhs):
        polysum = Polynomial()
        nodeA = self.headval
        nodeB = rhs.headval
        while nodeA is not None and nodeB is not None:
            if nodeA.exponent > nodeB.exponent:
                degree = nodeA.exponent
                coefficient = nodeA.coefficient
                nodeA = nodeA.nextval
            elif nodeA.exponent < nodeB.exponent:
                degree = nodeB.exponent
               coefficient = nodeB.coefficient
                nodeB = nodeB.nextval
            else:
```

```
                degree = nodeB.exponent
                coefficient  =  int(nodeA.coefficient)  +  int(nodeB.
coefficient)
                nodeA = nodeA.nextval
                nodeB = nodeB.nextval
            polysum.insertNode(coefficient, degree)
        return polysum

# Function to find out the correct position for the term to be inserted
    def filter(self, expression):
        terms = expression.split('+')
        for i in range(len(terms)):
            term = terms[i]
            xloc = term.find('x')
            if 1 <= xloc:
                coefficient = term[:xloc]
                exponent = term[xloc + 2:]
            else:
                coefficient = term
                exponent = '0'
            self.insertNode(coefficient, exponent)
        return True

# Take the two polynomials as input and print out their sum
if __name__ == '__main__':
li = Polynomial()
expression1 = input("Enter polynomial as (ax^2+bx^1+c) : ")
li.filter(expression1)
li2 = Polynomial()
expression2 = input("Enter another polynomial as (ax^2+bx^1+c) : ")
li2.filter(expression2)

print("\n")
sum = li + li2
print("Sum"+"\t:"+str(sum.printPoly()))
## End program
```

Output

```
Enter polynomial as (ax^2+bx^1+c) : 3x^2+2x^1+2
Enter another polynomial as (ax^2+bx^1+c) : 3x^2+2x^1+2

Sum :6 x^2 + 4 x^1 + 4 x^0
```

> ***Programming Tips!***
> `DegreeOfPolynomial()` is used to find the degree of the polynomial, `printPoly()` is used to display the polynomial, `insertNode()` is used to insert a node in the polynomial, and `filter()` is used to find the correct position for the term to be inserted.

QUICK RECAP

- ☑ Static data structure array suffers from memory misuse problem. Hence, linear data structure linked list was introduced.
- ☑ A linear collection of data elements (nodes) not stored at contiguous memory locations is called a linked list. Physical placements of elements in the memory do not take place sequentially or in order here. The linked list consists of multiple nodes that contain a data field and a reference (or link) to the next node in the list. The linked list supports dynamic memory allocation.
- ☑ It has a head/start pointer that points to the first node of the linked list. The null pointer indicates the end of the linked list.
- ☑ According to referencing methods, linked lists are of three types: singly linked, circular linked and doubly linked.
- ☑ A singly linked list consists of a sequence of nodes where the head node pointer indicates the first node in the list, and a null pointer reference necessarily indicates the last node of the list.
- ☑ In a circular linked list, the next pointer of the last node points to the first node.
- ☑ Doubly or two-way linked list is a sequence of elements in which every node has a data part and two link parts respectively to its previous element and next element in the sequence.
- ☑ Insertion, deletion, traversing, searching, reversing, and counting number of nodes are the major operations often used to manipulate a linked list. Essential algorithms have been presented for such operations and the corresponding C and Python source codes were given for their practical implementations.
- ☑ Garbage collection is one of the important memory management techniques. It automatically cleans/frees unused memory location, allowing the memory to be used again.
- ☑ Dangling pointer points to the non-existing memory location and it arises when an object is deleted or deallocated without modifying the value of the pointer. The pointer still points to the memory location of the de-allocated memory, even after deletion.
- ☑ In a sparse matrix, the majority of the elements are ZERO. It can be represented efficiently using both array and linked list.
- ☑ A polynomial expression can be represented efficiently using a linked list. Such representation helps programmers to carry out arithmetic operations on multiple polynomials efficiently.

REVIEW QUESTIONS

Multiple Choice Questions (MCQ): Choose the Best Alternative

Easy

1. Which of the following point(s) is/are true about the linked list data structure when it is compared with the array?
   A. Arrays have better cache locality that can make them better in terms of performance.
   B. It is easy to insert and delete elements in the linked list.
   C. Random access is not allowed in a typical implementation of linked lists.
   D. The size of the array has to be pre-decided, linked lists can change their size any time.
   E. All of the above.
2. Which of the following point(s) is/are not true about linked list data structure when it is compared with the array?

A. Arrays have better cache locality that can make them better in terms of performance.
B. It is easy to insert and delete elements in a linked list.
C. Random access is not allowed in a typical implementation of linked lists.
D. Access of elements in the linked list takes less time compared to arrays.

3. Which of the following is not a disadvantage to the usage of an array?
A. Fixed size
B. Chances of wastage of memory space if elements inserted in an array are lesser than the allocated size
C. Insertion based on the position
D. Accessing elements at specified positions.

4. Linked list is considered as an example of ______________ type of memory allocation.
A. dynamic B. static
C. compile time D. heap

5. What differentiates a circular linked list from a normal linked list?
A. You cannot have the 'next' pointer point to null in a circular linked list.
B. It is faster to traverse the circular linked list.
C. You may or may not have the 'next' pointer point to null in a circular linked list.
D. The head node is known in a circular linked list.

Moderate

6. Linked list data structure offers considerable saving in ______________.
A. computational time
B. space utilization
C. space utilization and computational time
D. speed utilization

7. The concatenation of two lists is to be performed in O(1) time. Which of the following implementations of a list should be used?
A. Singly linked list
B. Doubly linked list
C. Circular doubly linked list
D. Array implementation of lists

8. The self-referential pointer concept can be used in defining:
A. Array B. Queue
C. A node of linked list D. All of these.

9. Which of the following is false about a doubly linked list?
A. We can navigate in both the directions.
B. It requires more space than a singly linked list.
C. The insertion and deletion of a node takes a bit longer.
D. Implementing a doubly linked list is easier than a singly linked list.

10. What does the following function do for a given linked list with the first node as the head?

```
void fun1(struct node* head)
{
    if(head == NULL)
        return;
    fun1(head → next);
    printf("%d", head → data);
}
```

A. Prints all nodes of linked lists
B. Prints all nodes of linked list in reverse order
C. Prints alternate nodes of Linked List
D. Prints alternate nodes in reverse order.

Higher-order Thinking Skills (HOTS)

11. How many pointers are involved in insertion of a record in a circularly linked list:
A. No pointer B. 1 pointer
C. 2 pointers D. 3 pointers

12. What is the output of the following function where start points to the first node of the following linked list? 10 → 20 → 30 → 40 → 50 → 60

```
void fun(struct node* start)
{
    if(start == NULL)
    return;
    printf("%d ", start → data);

    if(start → next != NULL )
    fun(start → next → next);
    printf("%d ", start → data);
}
```

A. 10 40 60 60 40 10 B. 10 30 50 50 30 10
C. 10 30 50 10 30 50 D. 10 20 30 50

Hint: fun() prints alternate nodes of the given linked list, first from head to end, and then from end to head. If linked list has an even number of nodes, then it skips the last node.

13. In a doubly linked list, inserting a new node after a specific node requires:
   A. Two pointers exchanges
   B. Four pointers exchanges
   C. One pointers exchanges
   D. No pointers exchanges.
14. Suppose we are trying to insert n elements into an empty singly linked list. If we maintain the linked list to be sorted order, then the worst-case time complexity of code is:
   A. $O(n)$ B. $O(n^2)$
   C. $O(n \log n)$ D. $O(1)$
   Hint: Linked list needs to be maintained in sorted order after each step of iteration of inserting an element into the empty linked list. Each insertion into a sorted linked list will take $\theta(n)$ and hence the total cost for n operations is $\theta(n^2)$.

Short Answer-type Questions

Easy

1. What are the differences between the array and linked list?
2. What is the difference between singly and doubly linked lists?
3. What are the advantages of linked lists?
4. Define a linked list.
5. How does a circular linked list differ from a singly linked list?

Moderate

6. How to represent a linked list node?
7. What do you mean by garbage collection?
8. What are the applications of a linked list?
9. What are the components of a node in a linked list?
10. What is the use of a header node in a linked list?

Higher-Order Thinking Skills (HOTS)

11. Would you prefer to use a singly or a doubly linked list for traversing through a list of elements?
12. What is a dangling pointer?
13. What is a memory leak?
14. Which type of memory allocation is referred to for Linked List? Explain why.
15. What will happen if a free node is not available while inserting a new node in a linked list?

Descriptive-type Questions

Easy

1. Describe different versions of the linked list with examples.
2. Explain the process of garbage collection in computer memory.
3. Write the different operations that can be performed in a linked list.
4. Define and differentiate between circular linked list and doubly linked list.

Moderate

5. What is a sparse matrix? Explain the processes of sparse matrix representation using arrays and linked lists.
6. How are polynomials represented using a linked list? How are two polynomials added using a linked list?
7. Write an algorithm to reverse a singly linked list.
8. Write an algorithm to delete the end node of a singly linked list.
9. Write an algorithm to insert a node at a specific location of a circular linked list.

Higher-Order Thinking Skills (HOTS)

10. Write an algorithm to insert a node at the end of the doubly linked list.
11. Write an algorithm to reverse a doubly linked list.
12. How can we add a node to the beginning of the doubly linked list?
13. Represent the following sparse matrix using array and linked list:

$$\begin{bmatrix} 0 & 0 & 0 & 0 \\ 5 & 0 & 7 & 0 \\ 6 & 0 & 0 & 2 \end{bmatrix}$$

CASE STUDIES

1. Design an algorithm to find the middle of a singly linked list.
2. Design an algorithm for given two sorted linked lists, how can we merge them into a third list in sorted order?

LAB EXERCISES

1. Given a singly linked list of characters, write a C program to check if a linked list is palindrome.

   Example

   x → NULL : Is Palindrome

   y → x → NULL : Not Palindrome

   x → y → x → NULL : Is Palindrome

   z → x → y → x → NULL : Not Palindrome

   x → z → x → y → x → NULL : Not Palindrome

   y → x → z → x → y → x→ NULL : Not Palindrome

   x → y → x → z → x → y → x → NULL : Is Palindrome

2. Write a Python program to reverse a given doubly linked list.

   Example

   Original Linked List

   10
   20
   30
   40

   Reversed Linked List

   40
   30
   20
   10

ANSWER KEYS

Multiple Choice Questions

1. E
2. D
3. D
4. A
5. C
6. C
7. C
8. C
9. D
10. B
11. C
12. B
13. A
14. B

6 Stack

CONTENTS

EXPECTED OUTCOMES OF THIS CHAPTER

After going through this chapter learners will be able

- ☑ To describe the basic concepts of stack along with its associated definitions.
- ☑ To explain the various stack operations.
- ☑ To implement stack using C and Python programs.
- ☑ To understand and use various applications of stack such as arithmetic expression, conversion of infix to postfix, infix to prefix, prefix evaluations and postfix evaluations.
- ☑ To write C and Python programs for various stack applications.

6.1 INTRODUCTION

We come across various real-life stacks of objects in many places. Consider an example of plates or dishes stacked over one another in a restaurant kitchen. The plate which is at the top is the first one to be removed whereas the plate which has been placed at the bottom-most position remains in the stack for the longest duration of time. This type of order followed is Last-In–First-Out (LIFO) or First-In–Last-Out (FILO).

Arrays and linked lists, both allow programmers to insert and delete elements from any place within the list, i.e., from the beginning to the end or even from any middle position. But in computer programming, there may arise situations where insertion or deletion is required only at one end, either at the beginning or at the end of the list. In these situations, the stack will be very helpful.

6.1.1 Definition

A stack is an ordered (linear) list of a similar data type where every time an element is added, it goes on the top, and the only element that can be removed (first-out) is the element that is at the top (last-in) of the stack.

The stack is a linear data structure, and it is an ordered collection of items into which new items may be inserted or deleted at one end, called the top of the stack. Stack follows a particular order in which the operations are performed. The last element to be inserted into the stack will be the first to be removed. So, it simply follows the Last-In–First-Out(LIFO)/First-In–Last-Out (FILO) order. It is also considered an abstract data type in the data structure.

Characteristics of a stack

We can summarize the characteristics of a stack as follows:

> **Note!**
> The stack is a linear data structure and follows the LIFO list.

1. The stack is an ordered list of similar data type.
2. It is one of the important linear data structures.
3. The stack is a LIFO structure, or we can say FILO structure.
4. It is also considered as an abstract data type.
5. `Push` operation is used to insert new elements into the stack and `pop` operation is used to remove an element from the stack.
6. Both insertion and removal are allowed at only one end of the stack called 'top'.
7. The stack is in overflow state when it is completely full and trying to push any data whereas it is in underflow state if the stack is completely empty and trying to pop out data.

6.1.2 Operations

The two basic operations associated with stacks are PUSH and POP. PUSH is the term used to insert an element into a stack. On the other hand, POP is the term used to delete an element from a stack. All insertions and deletions take place at the same end. So the last element added to the stack will be the first element removed from the stack. Stack operations have been shown in Fig. 6.1. When a stack is initiated, the stack base remains fixed while the stack top changes as elements are added and removed. The most accessible element is at the top, and the least accessible element is at the bottom of the stack.

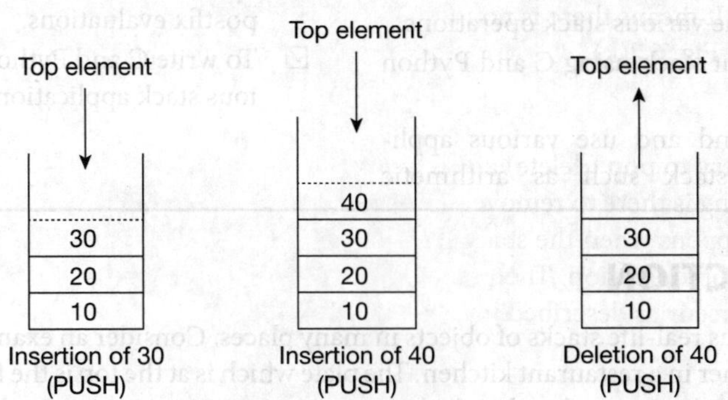

Figure 6.1 Stack operations (PUSH and POP)

PUSH Operation

PUSH an item on the stack operation means to insert a new element at the top of the stack. Only one item can be added by calling a one-time push function/operation.

POP Operation

POP an item from the stack means removing the top item from the stack. Pop operation removes the last element (recently added) from the top of the stack. Only one item can be removed by calling a one-time pop function/operation.

> **Note!**
> Inserting an element into the stack is known as a PUSH operation and deleting an element from the stack is known as POP operation.

6.1.3 Some Basic Terminologies

Top

The top is a pointer that points to the topmost element of the stack. A stack that is initially empty means the initial value of top = –1 or NULL. It returns the top element of the stack. Sometimes it is also called 'peek'. If PUSH operation is performed successfully, then the value of top will be incremented by 1. Let us suppose, if the current value of top is 2, then after insertion of an element (PUSH), the value of top becomes 3 (i.e., top = top + 1). The reverse happens in case of POP operation. If the POP operation is successfully performed, then the value of top will be decremented by 1. If the current value of top is 3, then after the deletion of an element (POP), the value of top becomes 2 (i.e., top = top – 1). Figure 6.2 describes different stack operations (PUSH and POP).

MaxStack/StackSize

MaxStack or StackSize is a variable that indicates a maximum number of elements that can be held by the stack. For example, MaxStack or StackSize is set to 4 to indicate that the stack can contain a maximum of 4 elements. Index Stack[0] through Stack[3].

Empty Stack

Suppose, stack contains a single element (i.e., top = 0) and POP operation is successfully performed on the stack, then the value of stack becomes -1 (i.e. top = -1). If the resulting stack contains no elements, then the stack is called an empty stack as described in Fig. 6.2(g).

Stack is Full

Suppose MaxStack or StackSize value is 4, then we can store a maximum of 4 elements within the stack. In this situation, top = 3 (index stack[0] to stack[3]). It indicates that the top is pointing to the topmost location of the stack. It means there is no more space to insert new items within the stack, and the stack is full as described in Fig. 6.2(k).

Stack Underflow

It happens when we try to pop (delete) an element from the stack when nothing is there to remove (i.e., top = -1). In other words, it happens when the stack is empty, and the user executes a pop operation. Then the 'underflow' error condition will occur as described in Fig. 6.2(h).

> **Note!**
> Top pointer points to the topmost element of the stack. MaxStack variable indicates the maximum number of elements to be held by a stack.

Stack Overflow

It happens when we try to push (insert) one more element onto the stack, but the stack is full currently (i.e., the condition, top = = MaxStack – 1 is true). Then, it is not possible to store more elements within the stack and an 'overflow' error condition will occur. In other words, overflow happens when there is no more room left to store a data element that is pushed as described in Fig. 6.2(l).

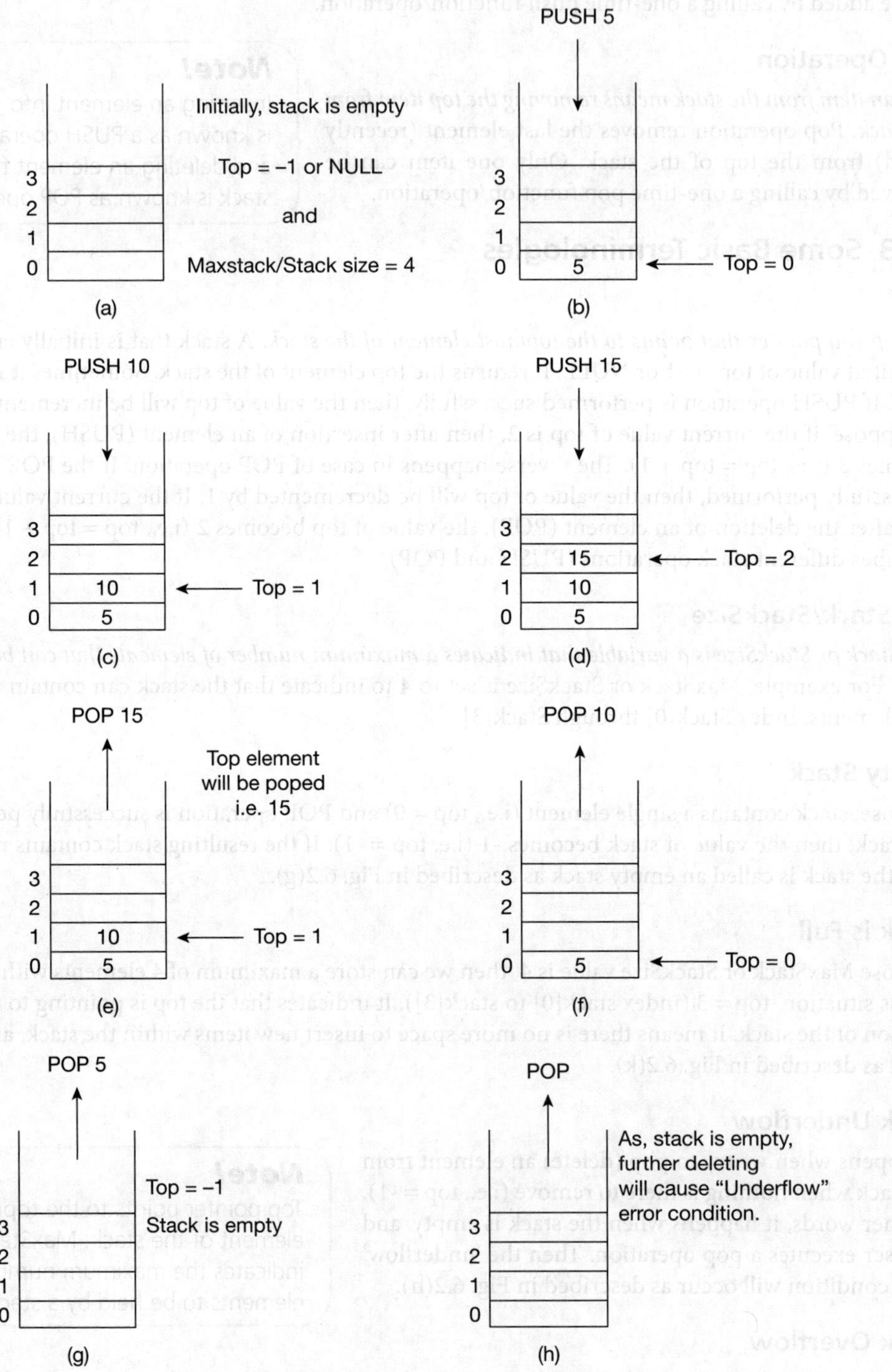

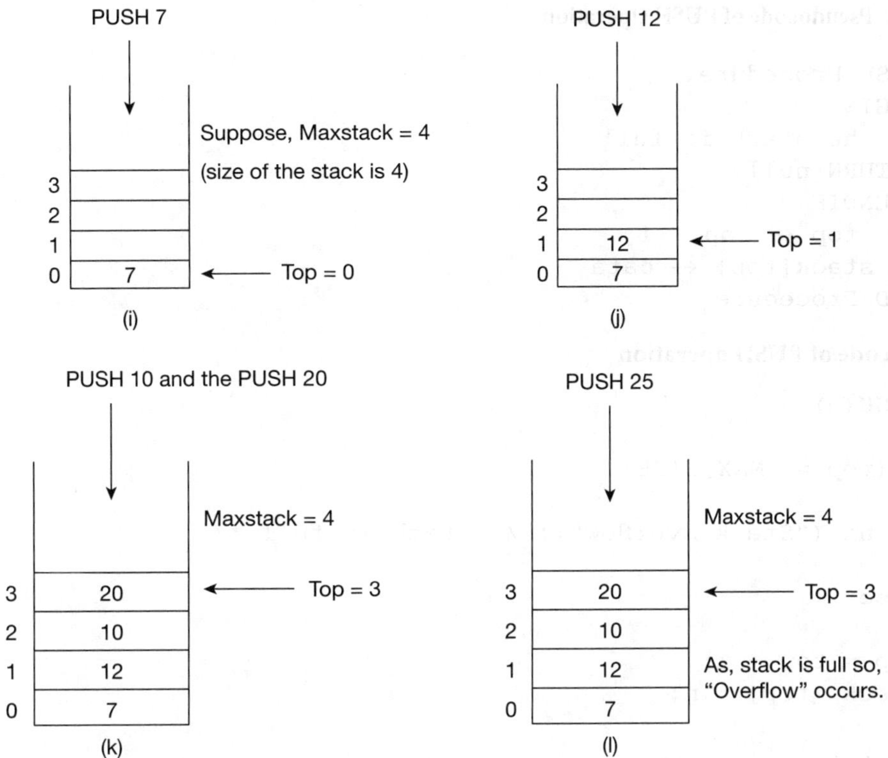

Figure 6.2 Different Stack operations (PUSH and POP)

6.1.4 PUSH and POP Processes

The PUSH and POP operations or processes discussed in Section 6.1.2 are presented here in algorithmic form. These two operations are also implemented using C and Python code besides pseudocodes here.

Push Operation

The process of putting a new data element onto the stack is known as a PUSH operation. PUSH operation involves a series of steps given below as an algorithm.

Algo-6.1 Algorithm of PUSH Operation

Step 1	Check whether the stack is full or not.
Step 2	If the stack is full, produce the 'Overflow' error message, and exit.
Step 3	If the stack is not full, increment the top pointer value point to the next empty space.
Step 4	Add the data element to the stack location, where the top is presently pointing.
Step 5	Return success.

Algo-6.2 Pseudocode of PUSH Operation

```
PUSH Procedure:
BEGIN
IF the stack is full
RETURN null
  ENDIF
    top ← top + 1
   stack[top] ← data
END Procedure
```

C source code of PUSH operation

```
PUSH(n)
{
if(top == MAX_SIZE)
{
print ("Stack Overflow"); /* Stack is full */
}
else
{
top = top + 1;
stack [top] = n;
}
}
/* End push operation */
```

Python source code of PUSH operation

```
def push(stack, item):
      stack.append (item)
      print("pushed to stack " + item)
# End push operation
```

Pop Operation

Removing a topmost element from the stack is known as a pop operation. A pop operation may involve the following steps as an algorithm.

Algo-6.3 Algorithm of POP Operation

Step 1:	Check whether the stack is empty or not.
Step 2:	If the stack is empty, produce the 'Underflow' error message, and exit.
Step 3:	If the stack is not empty, remove the data element at which the top is pointing.
Step 4:	Decrease the value of top by 1.
Step 5:	Return success.

Algo-6.4 Pseudocode of POP Operation

```
POP Procedure:
BEGIN
    IF the stack is empty
        RETURN null
    ENDIF
    data ← stack[top]
    top ← top - 1
    RETURN data
END Procedure
```

C source code of POP operation

```
POP()
{
int n;
if(top == 0) /* Stack is empty */
{
        return NULL;
}
else
{
n = stack [top];
top = top -1;
return n;
}
}
/* End pop operation */
```

Python source code of POP operation

```
def pop(stack):
    if(isEmpty(stack)):
    print("stack empty")
    return str(-maxsize -1) #return minus infinite
    return stack.pop()
##End pop operation
```

> ***Note!***
> Overflow occurs when the stack is full but trying to push element(s). Underflow occurs when the stack is empty but trying to pop element(s).

6.2 DESIGN AND IMPLEMENTATION OF STACK

Since the stack is a linear data structure, it can be implemented by either an array or a linked list. In this section, both array and linked list are used to design and implement the stack. The design of the stack primarily incorporates PUSH and POP operations of elements supplied to the program. The display of stack elements is also to be designed for verifying the elements pushed or popped into the stack. Figure 6.3 presents the PUSH operation for stack design.

The element pushed or inserted first is settled at the bottom of the stack (i.e., 10). Then 20 is pushed and then 30. We can also notice that the stack top is increasing with the insertion of elements into the stack.

On the other hand, the stack top will decrease in case of POP operation as we delete or remove elements from the stack top. Stack top becomes equal to -1 when the stack list is empty. Since array size is limited, we always need to check the top, which should not exceed the maximum size of an array while implementing stack using an array. The following figure presents the POP operation separately for stack design.

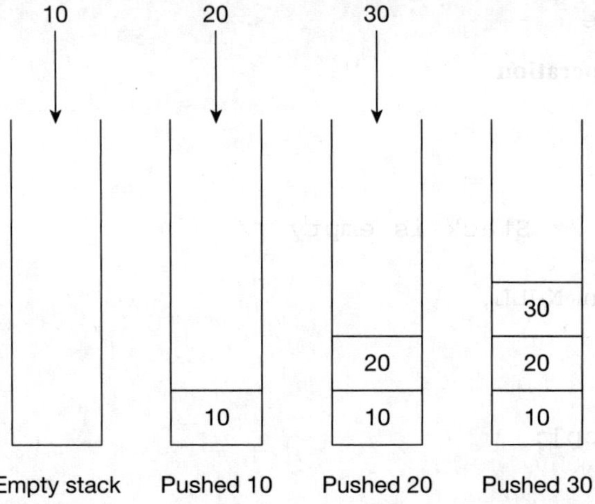

Figure 6.3 PUSH operation of stack implementation

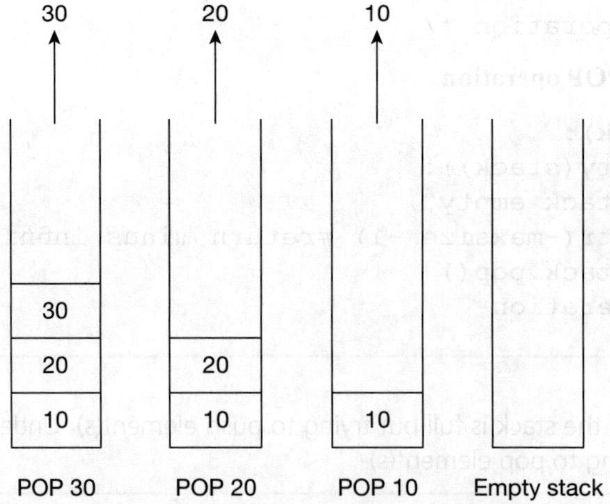

Figure 6.4 Pop operation of stack implementation

Both C and Python programs are given below for the implementation of a stack using array and linked list separately.

> ***Note!***
> Stack can be implemented using both array and linked list data structures.

6.2.1 Stack Implementation Using Array with C

Following is the C program for implementation of the stack (PUSH and POP operations) using an array. The program asks the elements to be pushed (inserted) into the stack or for POP implementation of the elements to be popped (or deleted).

CProg-6.1 Stack implementation using array

```
# include <stdio.h>

int top = -1;
int size = 10;
int stack[10];

/* Function to push the value in stack array */
void push(int value)
  {
if(top == size - 1)
printf("Stack Overflow\n");
    else
       stack[++top] = value;
  }

/* Function to pop the top value in stack array */
void pop()
  {
if(top == -1)
printf("Stack Underflow \n ");
    else
       --top;
  }

/* Function to find peek */
int peek()
  {
if(top == -1)
      {
printf("\nSTACK IS EMPTY");
        return -1;
      }
    else
      return (stack[top]);
  }

/* Function to print the stack array */
void print()
```

```
  {
    int temp = top - 1;
printf("\nTop of stack is: %d \n", peek());
if(temp >- 1);
printf("Other: ");
while(temp >-1)
printf("%d ", stack[temp--]);
    printf("\n");
  }

/* Driver function */
int main()
  {
     int choice, value;
     printf("1.Push\n");
     printf("2.Pop\n");
     printf("3.Display\n");
     printf("4.Quit\n");
     do {
printf("Enter your choice: ");
scanf("%d", &choice);
         switch(choice)
           {
             case 1: printf("Enter value to be pushed: ");
scanf("%d", &value);
                     push(value);
                     break;

             case 2: pop();
                     break;

             case 3: print();
                     break;

             case 4: printf("Exit \n");
                     break;

             default: printf("Invalid Choice \n");
           }
       } while(choice != 4);
     return 0;
  }
/* End of program */
```

Output

```
1.Push
2.Pop
3.Display
4.Quit
Enter your choice: 1
Enter value to be pushed: 15
Enter your choice: 1
Enter value to be pushed: 25
Enter your choice: 1
Enter value to be pushed: 87
Enter your choice: 1
Enter value to be pushed: 59
Enter your choice: 3

Top of stack is: 59
Other: 87 25 15
Enter your choice: 4
Exit
```

> ***Programming Tips!***
> `push()`, `pop()` and `print()` are used to implement the insertion, deletion and display of all stack elements respectively. `peek()` is used to return the top element of the stack.

6.2.2 Stack Implementation Using Array with Python

Following is the Python program for the implementation of the stack (PUSH and POP operations) using an array data type.

PyProg-6.1 **Stack implementation using array**

```
# Class to create a stack
class Stacks:
    # Constructor to initialize the class variables

def __init__(self, size):
        self.size = size
        self.tos = -1   # tos means top of the stack
        self.array = [0] * size

    # Push the element to the stack
    def push(self, value):
        if self.tos == self.size - 1:
            print("Stack is full")
        else:
            self.tos += 1
            self.array[self.tos] = value

    # Pop the element from the stack
    def pop(self):
```

```
        if self.tos == -1:
            print("Stack is empty")
        else:
            self.tos -= 1

    # Traverse the stack elements
    def traverse(self):
        temp = self.tos - 1
        if self.tos == -1:
            print("Stack is empty")
        else:
          print("Top of stack is: " + str(self.array[self.tos]))

            if temp > -1:
                print("Other:", end = " ")

            while temp > -1:
                print(self.array[temp], end = " ")
                temp -= 1
            print()

st = Stacks(4)
for i in range(10, 50, 10):
    st.push(i)      # Pushing 3 elements into the stack

st.traverse()       # Traversing the stack

for i in range(0, 5):
    st.pop()        # Popping elements from the stack
## End Program
```

Output

```
Top of stack is: 40
Other: 30 20 10
Stack is empty
```

> ***Programming Tips!***
>
> `push()`, `pop()` and `traverse()` functions are used to implement the insertion, deletion and display all stack elements respectively. Constructor `__init__()` is used to create and initialize the attributes of the class.

6.2.3 Stack Implementation Using Linked List with C

The major problem with the stack implemented using an array is, it works only for a fixed number of static data values. This means, the amount of data must be specified at the beginning of the implementation itself. Stack implemented using an array is not suitable when we don't know the size of data that we are going to use. A stack data structure can be implemented by using a linked list, which is a dynamic data structure. The stack implemented using the linked list can work for an unlimited number of values depending on memory size. That means a stack implemented using a linked list works for the variable size of data. So, there is no need to fix the size at the beginning of the implementation. The stack implemented using the linked list can organize as many data values as we want.

In linked list implementation of a stack, every new element is inserted as a 'top' element. That means, every newly inserted element is pointed out by 'top'. Whenever we want to remove an element from the stack, simply remove the node which is pointed by 'top' and move 'top' to its previous node in the list. The next field of the first (bottom) element must always be NULL.

Example 6.1

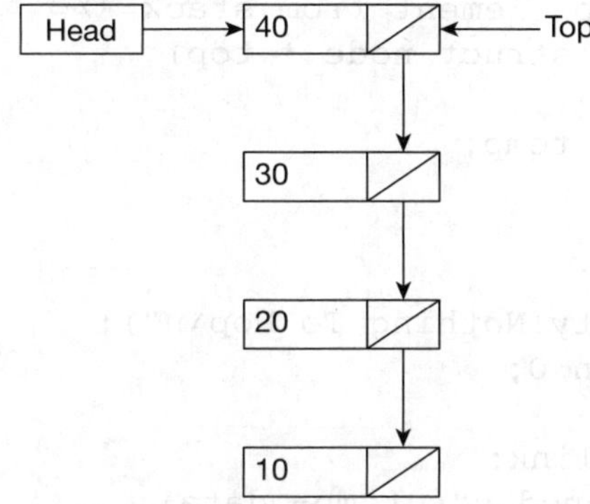

Figure 6.5 Stack implementation using linked list

In the above example, the last inserted node is 40 and the first inserted node is 10. The order of elements inserted is 10, 20, 30, and 40.

Following is the C program for implementation of stack (PUSH and POP operations) using the linked list. The program is designed using the pointer and structure data types of C for implementation of the linked list. Other approaches are similar to the array implementation of a stack.

CProg-6.2 Stack implementation using linked list

```
#include<stdio.h>
#include<malloc.h>

/* Node declaration */
struct node
  {
    int data;
    struct node * link;
  };
void view_stack(struct node *);

/* Function to push element to stack */
struct node * push(struct node * top,int data)
```

```
  {
    struct node * temp;
    temp = (struct node*)malloc(sizeof(struct node));
    temp -> data = data;
    temp -> link = top;
    top = temp;
printf("%d is pushed\n", top -> data);
view_stack(top);
    return top;
  }

/* Function to pop element from stack */
struct node * pop(struct node * top)
  {
    struct node * temp;
    temp = top;
if(top == NULL)
    {
printf("Stack Empty!Nothing To Pop\n");
            return 0;
    }
    top = top -> link;
printf("%d is popped\n", temp->data);
    free(temp);
view_stack(top);
    return top;
  }
/* Function to return top element in a stack */
void peek(struct node * top)
  {
if(top == NULL)
      {
printf("Stack Empty\n");
      }
    else
      {
printf("Top Item = %d", top->data);
      }
  }

/* Function to print stack */
void view_stack(struct node* top)
  {
    struct node* temp = top;
printf("Your Current Stack:\n");
```

```
printf("        \n");
while(temp != NULL)
    {
printf("-------\n|  %d  |\n-------\n", temp->data);
        temp = temp -> link;
    }
  }
/* Driver function */
int main()
{
    struct node *top = NULL;
    top = push(top, 5);
    top = push(top, 6);
    top = push(top, 7);
    top = push(top, 8);
    top = push(top, 9);
    top = pop(top);
    top = pop(top);
    top = pop(top);
    top = pop(top);
    top = pop(top);
}
/* End of Program */
```

Output

```
5 is pushed
Your Current Stack:
-------
|  5  |
-------
6 is pushed
Your Current Stack:
-------
|  6  |
-------
-------
|  5  |
-------
7 is pushed
Your Current Stack:
-------
|  7  |
-------
-------
|  6  |
-------
```

```
-------
|  5  |
-------
8 is pushed
Your Current Stack:
-------
|  8  |
-------
-------
|  7  |
-------
-------
|  6  |
-------
-------
|  5  |
-------
9 is pushed
Your Current Stack:
-------
|  9  |
-------
-------
|  8  |
-------
-------
|  7  |
-------
-------
|  6  |
-------
-------
|  5  |
-------
9 is popped
Your Current Stack:
-------
|  8  |
-------
-------
|  7  |
-------
-------
|  6  |
-------
-------
|  5  |
-------
```

```
8 is popped
Your Current Stack:
-------
|  7  |
-------
-------
|  6  |
-------
-------
|  5  |
-------
7 is popped
Your Current Stack:
-------
|  6  |
-------
-------
|  5  |
-------
6 is popped
Your Current Stack:
-------
|  5  |
-------
5 is popped
Your Current Stack:
```

> ***Programming Tips!***
> `push()` and `pop()` are used to implement the insertion, deletion of stack elements respectively using linked list. `peek()` is used return the top element. `malloc()` is used to create linked list node dynamically.

6.2.4 Stack Implementation Using Linked List with Python

Following is the Python program for implementation of a stack (PUSH and POP operations) using the linked list. The program is designed by defining a class node within which the two operations (or functions), PUSH and POP, are defined.

PyProg-6.2 Implementation using linked list

```
# Class for defining node
class node:
    def __init__(self, value):
        self.data = value
        self.next = None
```

```
# Class for defining Stack
class Stacks:
    # Constructor function
    def __init__(self):
        self.TOS = None

    # PUSH function
    def Push(self, value):
        new_node = node(value)
        new_node.next = self.TOS
        self.TOS = new_node

    # POP function
    def Pop(self):
        if self.TOS == None:
            print("Stack is empty")
        else:
            self.TOS = self.TOS.next

    # Display function for Stack
    def Print_Stack(self):
        if self.TOS == None:
           print("Stack is empty")
        else:
           print("Top of stack is " + str(self.TOS.data))
           if self.TOS.next != None:
              print("Other elements are :", end = " ")
              current = self.TOS.next
              while current != None:
                    print(current.data, end = " ")
                    current = current.next
              print()

# Stack operations
Stack = Stacks()
for i in range(0, 5):
    Stack.Push(i)
Stack.Print_Stack()
for i in range(0, 6):
    Stack.Pop()
Stack.Print_Stack()
## End program
```

Output

```
Top of stack is 4
Other elements are : 3 2 1 0
Stack is empty
Stack is empty
```

Programming Tips!

`push()`, `pop()` and `print_stack()` are used to implement the insertion, deletion and display of stack elements respectively. `__init__()` is the constructor for a class. The self parameter refers to the instance of the object.

6.3 APPLICATIONS OF STACK

Some applications of the stack data structure are presented here. These examples are central to many activities that a computer must do and deserve time with them.

1. **Expression conversion:** An expression can be represented in the prefix, postfix, or infix notation. The stack can be used to convert one form of expression to another. While we use infix expressions for practical purposes, language translators and operating systems have difficulty in executing this format because these include rules of operator precedence and also brackets. Executing instructions with infix expressions requires more iterations than the other two expressions because of these rules. Prefix and postfix expressions are easier to understand and evaluate with minimum time.
2. **Expression evaluation:** Stack can be used to evaluate prefix, postfix, and infix expressions.
3. **Syntax parsing:** Many compilers use a stack for parsing the syntax of expressions, program blocks, etc. before translating into low-level code.
4. **Backtracking (game playing, finding paths, exhaustive searching):** Suppose we want to find a path for solving a maze problem. We need to choose a path and after following it, we may realize that it is wrong. Now we need to go back to the beginning of the path to start a new path. This can be easily done with the help of a stack.
5. **Memory management in run-time environment for nested language features:** Any modern computer environment uses a stack as the primary memory management model for a running program. Whether it is native code (x86, Sun, VAX) or JVM, a stack is at the center of the run-time environment for Java, C++, Ada, FORTRAN, etc.
6. **Functions call**: Stack is used to keep information about the active functions or subroutines in a program.

> ***Note!***
> Applications of the stack include expression or notation conversion, expression evaluation, syntax parsing, backtracking, memory management, and functions call.

6.3.1 Arithmetic Expressions

*An arithmetic expression is also known as a **notation**.* An arithmetic expression can be written in three different but equivalent notations, i.e., without changing the essence or output of an expression. These notations are:

- Infix notation
- Prefix (Polish) notation
- Postfix (Reverse-Polish) notation

Expression Representation

There are three popular methods used for the representation of an expressionas shown in Table 6.1:

Table 6.1 Examples of three arithmetic expressions

Infix	A + B	Operator in between operands.
Prefix	+ AB	Operator before (pre) operands.
Postfix	AB +	Operator after (post) operands.

The following are the reasons why postfix or prefix representations of the expressions are preferred than infix expressions:

- The compiler scans the expression either from left to right or from right to left. Consider the expression: A + B ∗ C + D.
- The compiler first scans the expression to evaluate the expression B ∗ C, then again scans the expression to add A to it. The result is then added to D after another scan.
- The repeated scanning makes it very inefficient. It is better to convert the expression to postfix (or prefix) form before evaluation.

> **Note!**
> Infix, prefix, and postfix are the three types of arithmetic expressions.

Parsing Expressions

As we have discussed, it is not a very efficient idea to design an algorithm or program to parse infix notations. Instead, these infix notations are first converted into either postfix or prefix notations, and then computed to parse any arithmetic expression.We need to take care of both operator precedence and associativity.

Precedence

When operators are in between many different operands, which operator will take the operand first, is decided by the precedence of an operator over others. For example,

A + B ∗ C → A+ (B ∗ C)

As multiplication operation has precedence over addition, B ∗ C will be evaluated first.

Associativity

Associativity describes the rule where operators with the same precedence appear in an expression. For example, in the expression A + B – C, both + and – have the same precedence. So, which part of the expression will be evaluated first, is determined by the associativity of those operators. Here, both + and – are left-associative, so the expression will be evaluated as:

(A + B) – C.

Precedence and associativity determine the order of evaluation of an expression. Table 6.2 gives the operator precedence and associativity rules table (highest to lowest):

> **Note!**
> Left parenthesis '(' and right parenthesis ')' are neither operators nor operands. They act like a separator.

Table 6.2 Operator precedence and associativity

Sr. No.	Operator	Precedence	Associativity
1	Exponentiation ^	Highest	Right Associative
2	Multiplication (∗) and Division (/)	Second Highest	Left Associative
3	Addition (+) and Subtraction (–)	Lowest	Left Associative

6.3.2 Infix-to-Postfix Conversion

As discussed before, infix expressions should be converted either to postfix expressions or to prefix expressions to increase the efficiency of the algorithm by reducing the repetitive tasks to be executed with infix expressions. This section presents the algorithm and corresponding C and Python source code for the said conversion using the stack data structure.

The following is the algorithm for conversion of an infix expression to a postfix expression applying stack.

Algo-6.5 Algorithm of infix-to-postfix conversion

Step 1	Add a ')' write at the end of the infix expression.
Step 2	Push corresponding ')' onto the empty stack.
Step 3	Scan the infix expression from left to right, one by one character. If the scanned character is an operand, store it in an expression array. Else,
3.1	If the precedence of the scanned operator is greater than the precedence of the operator in the stack [or the stack is empty or the stack contains a ')'], push it.
3.2	Else, pop all the operators from the stack, which are greater than or equal to in precedence than that of the scanned operator and store the popped operator in an expression array. After doing that, push the scanned operator to the stack. (If you encounter parenthesis while popping, then stop there and push the scanned operator in the stack).
Step 4	If the scanned character is an '(', push it to the stack.
Step 5	If the scanned character is an ')', pop the characters from the stack one by one and store the pop-out operator in an expression array until a '(' is encountered, and discard both parentheses. Don't store both parentheses either in the stack or in the expression array.
Step 6	Repeat steps 3–6 until the infix expression is scanned totally.
Step 7	Check whether the stack is empty and the scanning of infix expression is totally complete.
Step 8	Print the expression array. This is the postfix expression (our result).
Step 9	End

Step 3 is the most important in the infix-to-postfix conversion algorithm. As mentioned in Step (3.1), if the precedence of the scanned operator is greater than the precedence of the operator in the stack [or the stack is empty, or the stack contains a '('], we have to PUSH it. For example, if operator '^' is a scanned symbol in infix expression, and '+' is already stored in the stack, then '^' will be pushed within the stack. This is because, the scanned symbol is always pushed within the stack, and '^' has higher precedence than '+', so both will stay within the stack.

Real-life Example 1

In real-life example, suppose a very popular cricket star or film star (like Sachin Tendulkar/ Sharukh Khan) suddenly came in front of a common person then he/she will try to stay and look for capturing a selfie and taking an autograph from the super star. So, we can say both will stay in the same place at that same time though we are assuming that a super star has higher popularity (higher precedence) than a common person (lower precedence).

Consider the example to explain the Step 3.2: Operator '+' is the scanned symbol and '^' is already stored in the stack. Then '^' will be pop out from the stack because '^' has a higher precedence and will be stored within expression array. However, '+' will be pushed now because scanned symbol is pushed always within the stack. The same rule is applicable in case of same precedence symbols like '+' and '-', because both have the same precedence.

Real-life Example 2

In real-life example, suppose many common people come running towards a popular cricket star or film star (like Sachin Tendulkar/Sharukh Khan) for a selfie or an autograph, then generally it may be assumed that the super star can stay away and move away from that place to avoid the crowd. So, we cannot say both will stay in the same place (stack) at the same time – the superstar moves from that place and the crowd will stay, though we are assuming that the superstar has higher popularity (higher precedence) than a common person (lower precedence).

Real-life Example 3

In another case, suppose two superstars ('x' and 'y') have ego problems with each other. Suppose they meet at a dinner party, where superstar 'x' arrives first at the party and then superstar 'y' arrives. In that case, superstar 'x' will leave the party ('x' to be stored onto expression array) due to ego problem and superstar 'y' will stay in the party assuming that he/she has the same popularity (same precedence) as compared to superstar 'x' (same precedence 'x' and 'y').

The following example demonstrates the conversion algorithm with the help of an example.

Example 6.2: Convert infix expression A + (B ∗ C - D ^ G) - H to postfix expression.

1. Add a ')' at the end of the infix expression [after 'H'].
   A + (B ∗ C - D ^ G) –H)
2. Push corresponding ')' into the empty stack.

The following Table 6.3 presents the execution of the infix-to-postfix conversion for the infix expression A + (B * C – D ^ G) – H).

Table 6.3: Execution of the infix-to-postfix conversion, A + (B * C - D ^ G) – H)

Move	Current scanned symbol	Stack	Expression array (Postfix)	Comments
1	A	(	A	Scanned symbol 'A' is an operand; store it in an expression array.
2	+	(+	A	Scanned symbol '+' is an operator, and the stack top contains ')'.
3	(	(+ (	A	Scanned symbol '('; push into the stack.

(Continued)

Move	Current scanned symbol	Stack	Expression array (Postfix)	Comments
4	B	(+ (	A B	Scanned symbol 'B' is an operand; store it in the expression array.
5	*	(+ (*	A B	Scanned symbol '*' is an operator, and the stack top contains '('.
6	C	(+ (*	A B C	Scanned symbol 'C' is an operand; store it in an expression array.
7	–	(+ (-	A B C *	Scanned symbol '-' is an operator, and the stack top contains '*' operator. Pop '*' operator from the stack has greater precedence than that of the scanned operator '-'. Store the popped operator '*' in an expression array, and push the scanned operator '-' to the stack. (Remembering RL2)
8	D	(+ (-	A B C * D	Scanned symbol 'D' is an operand; store it in an expression array.
9	^	(+ (- ^	A B C * D	Scanned symbol '^' is an operator, and the stack top contains '-' operator. The precedence of the scanned operator '^' is greater than the precedence of the operator '-' in the stack; both will stay within the stack. (Remembering RL1)
10	G	(+ (- ^	A B C * D G	Scanned symbol 'G' is an operand; store it in an expression array.
11	)	(+	A B C * D G ^ -	Scanned symbol is ')'. Pop elements from the stack, one by one character, and store the popped operators in an expression array until a '(' is encountered. Then discard both the parentheses (don't store both the parentheses either in the stack or in the expression array). So, first, '^' and then '-' will pop out from the stack and be stored into an expression array.
12	-	(-	A B C * D G ^ - +	The scanned symbol '-' is an operator and the stack top contains '+' operator. Pop '+' operator, which has equal precedence like the scanned operator '-' and store the popped '+' operator in an expression array. Push the scanned operator '-' to the stack. (Remembering RL3)
13	H	(-	A B C * D G ^ - + H	Scanned symbol 'H' is an operand; store it in the expression array.
14	)	empty	A B C * D G ^ - + H-	Scanned symbol is ')'. Pop elements from the stack, one by one character and store the popped operators in an expression array until a '(' is encountered. Then discard both the parentheses (don't store both the parentheses, either in the stack or in the expression array). So, '-' will be popped out from the stack and stored into an expression array. The stack is now empty. Print the result which is in the expression array.

The following Table 6.4 presents some more examples of equivalent postfix expressions corresponding to the given infix notations.

Table 6.4 More examples of infix-to-postfix conversions

No.	Infix Notation	Equivalent Postfix Notation
1	(a + b) * c	a b + c *
2	a * (b + c)	a b c + *
3	a / b + c / d	a b / c d / +
4	(a + b) * (c + d)	a b + c d + *
5	((a + b) * c) - d	a b + c * d -
6	A + B * C + D	A B C * + D +
7	A * B + C * D	A B * C D * +
8	A + B + C + D	A B + C + D +

6.3.3 Infix-to-Postfix Conversion with C and Python

The following is a C program for conversion of an infix expression to a postfix expression using stack.

CProg-6.3 Infix-to-postfix conversion

```
#include<stdio.h>
#include<string.h>
#include<stdlib.h>

/* Node declaration */
struct Stack
  {
    int top;
    unsigned capacity;
    int* array;
  };

/* Stack Operations */
struct Stack* createStack(unsigned capacity)
  {
     struct Stack* stack = (struct Stack*) malloc(sizeof(-
struct Stack));
    if (!stack)
    return NULL;
    stack->top = -1;
    stack->capacity = capacity;
  stack->array = (int*) malloc(stack->capacity * sizeof(int));
    if(!stack->array)
```

```
        return NULL;
    return stack;
  }

int isEmpty(struct Stack* stack)
  {
    return stack->top == -1 ;
  }

char peek(struct Stack* stack)
  {
    return stack->array[stack->top];
  }

char pop(struct Stack* stack)
  {
    if(!isEmpty(stack))
        return stack->array[stack->top--];
        return '$';
  }

void push(struct Stack* stack, char op)
  {
    stack->array[++stack->top] = op;
  }

/* A utility function to check if the given character is an
operand */
int isOperand(char ch)
  {
    return (ch>= 'a' &&ch<= 'z') || (ch>= 'A' &&ch<= 'Z');
  }

/* A utility function to return precedence of a given operator
   Higher returned value means higher precedence */
int Prec(char ch)
  {
    switch (ch)
      {
        case '+':
        case '-':
        return 1;
        case '*':
        case '/':
        return 2;
      case '^':
```

```
        return 3;
      }
    return -1;
  }

/* The main function that converts given infix expression to
postfix expression */
int infixToPostfix(char* exp)
  {
    int i, k;

    /* Create a stack of capacity equal to expression size */
    struct Stack* stack = createStack(strlen(exp));
    if(!stack) /* Check if stack was created successfully*/
       return -1 ;
for(i = 0, k = -1; exp[i]; ++i)
      {
        /* If the scanned character is an operand, add it to
output */
        if (isOperand(exp[i]))
        exp[++k] = exp[i];

        /* If the scanned character is an '(', push it to the
stack */
        else if (exp[i] == '(')
push(stack, exp[i]);

        /* If the scanned character is an ')', pop and output
from the stack until an '(' is encountered*/
        else if (exp[i] == ')')
        {
          while(!isEmpty(stack) && peek(stack) != '(')
             exp[++k] = pop(stack);
          if (!isEmpty(stack) && peek(stack) != '(')
             return -1; /* invalid expression */
          else
             pop(stack);
        }
      else /* An operator is encountered */
        {
                  while  (!isEmpty(stack)  &&Prec(exp[i])  <=
Prec(peek(stack)))
             exp[++k] = pop(stack);
push(stack, exp[i]);
        }
     }
```

```
    /* pop all the operators from the stack */
    while (!isEmpty(stack))
        exp[++k] = pop(stack);
    exp[++k] = '\0';
printf( "%s", exp);
  }

/* Driver function */
int main()
  {
    char exp[] = "a+b*(c^d-e)^(f+g*h)-i";
printf("Postfix exp is: ");
infixToPostfix(exp);
    return 0;
  }
/* End of program */
```

Output

```
Postfix exp is: abcd^e-fgh*+^*+i-
```

> ***Programming Tips!***
> `Prec()` is used to return precedence of a given operator for infix-to-postfix conversion.
> `malloc()` is used to create linked list node dynamically.

The following is a Python program for conversion of an infix expression to a postfix expression applying stack.

PyProg-6.3 Infix-to-postfix conversion

```
# Class to convert the expression
class Conversion:
  # Constructor to initialize the class variables
  def __init__(self, capacity):
    self.top = -1
    self.capacity = capacity
    # This array is used a stack
    self.array = []
    # Precedence setting
    self.output = []
    self.precedence = {'+':1, '-':1, '*':2, '/':2, '^':3}

  # check if the stack is empty
  def isEmpty(self):
    return True if self.top == -1 else False
```

```
# Return the value of the top of the stack
  def peek(self):
    return self.array[-1]

  # Pop the element from the stack
  def pop(self):
    if not self.isEmpty():
      self.top -= 1
      return self.array.pop()
    else:
      return "$"

  # Push the element to the stack
  def push(self, op):
    self.top += 1
    self.array.append(op)

  # A utility function to check is the given character
  # is operand
  def isOperand(self, ch):
    return ch.isalpha()

  # Check if the precedence of operator is strictly
  # less than top of stack or not
  def notGreater(self, i):
    try:
      a = self.precedence[i]
      b = self.precedence[self.peek()]
      return True if a <= b else False
    except KeyError:
      return False

  # The function that converts given infix expression
  # to postfix expression
  def infixToPostfix(self, exp):
    # Iterate over the expression for conversion
    for i in exp:
      # If the character is an operand,
      # add it to output
      if self.isOperand(i):
        self.output.append(i)

      # If the character is an '(', push it to stack
      elif i == '(':
        self.push(i)
```

```
    # If the scanned character is an ')', pop and
        # output from the stack until and '(' is found
        elif i == ')':
            while( (not self.isEmpty()) and self.peek() != '('):
                a = self.pop()
                self.output.append(a)
            if (not self.isEmpty() and self.peek() != '('):
                return -1
            else:
                self.pop()

        # An operator is encountered
        else:
            while(not self.isEmpty() and self.notGreater(i)):
                self.output.append(self.pop())
            self.push(i)

    # pop all the operator from the stack
    while not self.isEmpty():
        self.output.append(self.pop())
    print("Postfix exp:","".join(self.output))


# Executing the conversion or driver code
exp = "a+b*(c^d-e)^(f+g*h)-i"
obj = Conversion(len(exp))
obj.infixToPostfix(exp)
## End program
```

Output

```
Postfix exp is: abcd^e-fgh*+^*+i-
```

Programming Tips!

Stack can be used for infix-to-postfix conversion. `__init__()` is the constructor for a class and self parameter refers to the instance of the object. infixToPostfix() is the key function that converts a given infix expression to postfix.

6.3.4 Postfix Evaluation

Like the previous stack example, we will consider the evaluation of an expression that is already in postfix notation. In this case, a stack is again the data structure of choice. However, as you scan the postfix expression, it is the operands that must wait, not the operators as in the conversion algorithm above. Another way to think about the solution is that whenever an operator is seen on the input, the two most recent operands will be used in the evaluation. The following is an algorithm for the evaluation of postfix expression applying stack.

Algo-6.6 Algorithm of postfix evaluation

Step 1	Add a ')' at the end of the postfix expression.
Step 2	Push corresponding '(' into the empty stack.
Step 3	Scan the postfix expression from left to right, one by one character.
Step 4	If scanned element in Step 3 is an operand, push it to the stack.
Step 5	If scanned element in Step 3 is an operator, pop out top two elements from the stack. The top element will be placed at the right side of the operator, and the next-to-top element will be placed at the left side of the operator. Then perform an operation according to the operator symbol.
Step 6	Store the result of Step 5, back to stack.
Step 7	If the scanned character is an ')', pop the result from the stack until a '(' is encountered, and discard both the parentheses. Don't store both the parentheses.
Step 8	Repeat Steps 3-7 until the postfix expression is scanned completely. Scan the expression until all operands are consumed.
Step 9	The pop-out result of Step 7 is the postfix evaluation answer.

The above algorithm is demonstrated with the help of an example below.

Example 6.3: Evaluation of postfix expression "9 3 2 * + 5 –".

1. Add a ')' at the end of the postfix expression 9 3 2 * + 5 –).
2. Push the corresponding ')' into the empty stack.
3. Scan the postfix expression from left to right, one by one character.
4. Scan '9'. It is a number. So push it into the stack. The stack contains '(9'.
5. Scan '3'. It is again a number, and hence push it into the stack. Stack contains '(9 3' now (from bottom to top).
6. Scan '2'. It is again a number, and hence push it into the stack. Stack contains '(9 3 2' now.
7. Scan '*'. It is an operator, and hence pop two operands from the stack. Now, apply the * operator on the operands. Top element '2' will be placed right side of the operator, and next-to-top element, '3' will be placed at the left side of the operator. Now, perform the operation according to the operator symbol, and we will get 6 as result of '3 * 2'. Push the result '6' into the stack. The stack now contains '(9 6'.
8. Scan '+'. It is an operator, and hence pop two operands from the stack. Now apply the + operator on operands. The top element '6' will be placed at the right side of the operator, and next-to-top element '9' will be placed at the left side of the operator. Now, perform the operation according to the operator symbol, and we will get 15 as a result of '9 + 6'. Push the result '15' into the stack. The stack now contains '(15' only.
9. Scan '5'. It is a number, and hence push it into the stack. The stack now contains '(15 5'.
10. Scan '–'. It is an operator, and hence pop two operands from the stack. Now apply the – operator on the operands. The top element '5' will be placed at the right side of the operator, and next-to-top element, '15' will be placed at the left side of the operator. Now, perform the operation according to the operator symbol, and we will get 10 as result of '15 – 5'. Push the result '10' into the stack. The stack now contains '(10' only.

11. Scan character is an ')', and hence pop the result from the stack until a '(' is encountered. A '(' is encountered just left to the '10', discard both the parentheses (don't store both the parentheses). There are no more elements remaining to be scanned, and we need to return the top element '10' from the stack (which is the only element left in the stack).
12. The answer is '10'.

6.3.5 Postfix Evaluation with C and Python

The following is a C program for evaluation of a postfix expression applying stack.

CProg-6.4 Postfix evaluation

```
#include<stdio.h>
#include<string.h>
#include<ctype.h>
#include<stdlib.h>

/* Node declaration */
struct Stack
   {
     int top;
     unsigned capacity;
     int* array;
   };

/* Stack Operations */
struct Stack* createStack( unsigned capacity )
   {
      struct Stack* stack = (struct Stack*) malloc(sizeof(struct
Stack));
     if (!stack) return NULL;
     stack->top = -1;
     stack->capacity = capacity;
     stack->array = (int*) malloc(stack->capacity * sizeof(int));
     if(!stack->array) return NULL;
     return stack;
   }

int isEmpty(struct Stack* stack)
   {
     return stack->top == -1 ;
   }

char peek(struct Stack* stack)
   {
     return stack->array[stack->top];
   }
```

```
char pop(struct Stack* stack)
   {
     if (!isEmpty(stack))
     return stack->array[stack->top--] ;
     return '$';
   }

void push(struct Stack* stack, char op)
   {
    stack->array[++stack->top] = op;
   }


/* The main function that returns a value of a given postfix
expression */
int evaluatePostfix(char* exp)
   {
    /* Create a stack of capacity equal to expression size */
    struct Stack* stack = createStack(strlen(exp));
    int i;

    /* See if the stack was created successfully */
    if (!stack) return -1;

    /* Scan all characters one by one */
    for (i = 0; exp[i]; ++i)
      {
        /* If the scanned character is an operand (number
        here), push it to the stack */
        if (isdigit(exp[i]))
        push(stack, exp[i] - '0');

        /* If the scanned character is an operator, pop two
        elements from stack apply the operator */
        else
         {
            int val1 = pop(stack);
            int val2 = pop(stack);
             switch (exp[i])
              {
                case '+': push(stack, val2 + val1); break;
                case '-': push(stack, val2 - val1); break;
                case '*': push(stack, val2 * val1); break;
                case '/': push(stack, val2/val1); break;
              }
         }
```

```
    }
    return pop(stack);
  }

/* Driver function */
int main()
  {
char exp[] = "58*3-";
    printf ("postfix evaluation: %d", evaluatePostfix(exp));
    return 0;
  }
/* End of program */
```

Output

```
Postfix evaluation: 37
```

> ***Programming Tips!***
> `Prec()` utility function is used to return the precedence of a given operator. `evaluatePostfix()` returns the value of a given postfix expression.

The following is the Python program for evaluation of a postfix expression applying stack.

PyProg-6.4 Postfix evaluation

```
# Class to convert the expression
class post_evaluate:
  # Constructor to initialize the class variables
  def __init__(self, capacity):
    self.top = -1
    self.capacity = capacity
    # This array is used a stack
    self.array = []

  # check if the stack is empty
  def isEmpty(self):
    return True if self.top == -1 else False

  # Return the value of the top of the stack
  def peek(self):
    return self.array[-1]

  # Pop the element from the stack
  def pop(self):
    if not self.isEmpty():
      self.top -= 1
```

```
            return self.array.pop()
        else:
            return "$"

    # Push the element to the stack
    def push(self, op):
        self.top += 1
        self.array.append(op)

    # The main function that converts given infix expression
    # to postfix expression
    def evaluatePostfix(self, exp):
        # Iterate over the expression for conversion
        for i in exp:
            # If the scanned character is an operand
            # (number here) push it to the stack
            if i.isdigit():
                self.push(i)

            # If the scanned character is an operator,
            # pop two elements from stack and apply it.
            else:
                val1 = self.pop()
                val2 = self.pop()
                self.push(str(eval(val2 + i + val1)))
        return int(self.pop())

# Executing the evaluation
exp = "58*3-"
obj = post_evaluate(len(exp))
print("Postfix evaluation: %d"%(obj.evaluatePostfix(exp)))
## End program
```

Output

```
Postfix evaluation: 1
```

> ***Programming Tips!***
> Stack is used here for a purpose. `evaluatePostfix()` is the key function to evaluate postfix expression.

6.3.6 Infix-to-Prefix Conversion

The following is the algorithm for conversion of an infix expression to a prefix expression. To convert an infix expression to postfix expression, we can refer to Section 6.3.2. We use a similar algorithm here, to convert an infix expression to a prefix expression.

Algo-6.7 Algorithm of infix-to-prefix conversion

Step 1	Reverse the infix expression, i.e., A + B * C will become C * B + A. Note that while reversing, each ')' will become ')' and each ')' becomes ')'.
Step 2	Obtain the postfix expression of the modified expression, i.e., CB * A +.
Step 3	Reverse the postfix expression. Hence, the prefix is + A * BC, in our example.

The following Table 6.5 presents some examples of equivalent prefix expressions corresponding to the given infix notations.

Table 6.5: More examples infix-to-prefix conversions

No.	Infix notation	Equivalent prefix notation
1	(a + b) * c	* + a b c
2	a * (b + c)	* a + b c
3	a / b + c / d	+ / a b / c d
4	(a + b) * (c + d)	* + a b + c d
5	((a + b) * c) - d	− * + a b c d
6	A + B * C + D	+ + A * B C D
7	A * B + C * D	+ * A B * C D
8	A + B + C + D	+ + + A B C D

6.3.7 Infix-to-Prefix Conversion with C and Python

The following is a C program for conversion of an infix expression to a prefix expression applying stack.

CProg-6.5 Infix-to-prefix conversion

```
#include<stdio.h>
#include<stdlib.h>
#include<ctype.h>
#include<string.h>
#define SIZE 100

/* Global Variable Declaration */
char stack[SIZE];
int top = -1;

/* Global Function Declaration */
void push(char c);
char pop();
int isoperator(char symbol);
int precedence(char symbol);
void InfixToPrefix(char infix_exp[], char prefix_exp[]);
```

```
/* Deriver function begins */
void main()
  {
     /* Declare infix string and prefix string */
     char infix[SIZE], prefix[SIZE];
printf("\n\n Enter Infix expression : ");
     gets(infix);

     /* Call to convert */
InfixToPrefix(infix, prefix);
printf("\n Prefix Expression: ");

     /* Print prefix expression */
     puts(prefix);
  }

void InfixToPrefix(char infix_exp[], char prefix_exp[])
   {
     int i, j, k, pos, len;
     char item, x, rev[SIZE];

     /* Reverse the infix expression */
     pos=0;
len=strlen(infix_exp);
for(k = len-1; k >= 0; k--)
         {
           rev[pos] = infix_exp[k];
           pos++;
         }
     rev[pos] = '\0';
strcpy(infix_exp, rev);

     /* Make Every " ( " as " ) " and every " ) " as " ( " */
for(i = 0; infix_exp[i] !='\0'; i++)
     {
         if(infix_exp[i] == ')')
infix_exp[i] = '(';
         else if(infix_exp[i] == '(')
infix_exp[i] = ')';
         }

         /*Convert  expression  to  postfix  form.  push  '('  onto
stack */
push('(');
     /* add ')' to infix expression */
```

```
strcat(infix_exp,")");
    i = 0;
    j = 0;
    /* Initialize before loop */
    item=infix_exp[i];
    /* Run loop till the end of the infix expression */
while(item != '\0')
       {
if(item == '(')
         {
             push(item);
         }
        else if( isdigit(item) || isalpha(item))
         {
             /* Add operand symbol to postfix expression */
prefix_exp[j] = item;
             j++;
         }
        else if(isoperator(item) == 1)
         {
              /* pop all higher precedence operator and add
them to postfix expression */
             x = pop();
                while(isoperator(x) == 1 && precedence(x)>=
precedence(item))
               {
prefix_exp[j] = x;
                 j++;
                 x = pop();
               }
              /* push the last pop operator symbol onto the
stack */
             push(x);
            /* push current operator symbol onto the stack */
             push(item);
         }
      /* if current symbol is ')' then pop and keep popping
until '(' encounterd */
        else if(item == ')')
         {
             x = pop();
while(x != '(')
               {
prefix_exp[j] = x;
                j++;
                 x = pop();
```

```
            }
          }
        else
          {
            /* if current symbol is neither operand not '('
nor ')' and nor operator */
printf("\nInvalid infix Expression.\n");
            break;
          }
        i++;
        /* Go to the next symbol of the infix expression */
        item = infix_exp[i];
      } /* End while loop */
if(top > 0)
printf("\n Invalid infix Expression.");
prefix_exp[j] = '\0';

      /* Reverse the prefix expression */
    pos = 0;
len = strlen(prefix_exp);
for(k = len-1; k >= 0; k--)
      {
        rev[pos] = prefix_exp[k];
        pos++;
      }
    rev[pos] ='\0';
strcpy(prefix_exp, rev);
  }

/* Define push operation */
void push(char c)
  {
if(top >= SIZE-1)
printf("\n Stack Overflow.");
    else
      {
        top++;
        stack[top] = c;
      }
  }

/* Define pop operation */
char pop()
  {
    char c;
    c='\0';
```

```
if(top < 0)
printf("\n Stack Underflow.");
    else
     {
        c = stack[top];
        top--;
     }
    return c;
  }

/* Define a function that is used to determine whether any
symbol is an operator or not */
int isoperator(char symbol)
  {
if(symbol == '^' || symbol == '*' || symbol == '/' || symbol
== '+' || symbol == '-')
     return 1;
    else
     return 0;
  }

/* Define a function that is used to assign precedence to
the operator.In this function, we assume that higher integer
value means higher precedence */
int precedence(char symbol)
  {
if(symbol == '^')
return(5);
    else if(symbol == '/')
return(4);
    else if(symbol == '*')
return(3);
    else if(symbol == '+')
return(2);
    else if(symbol == '-')
return(1);
    else
return(0);
  }
/* End of program */
```

Output

```
Enter Infix expression : (a-b/c)*(a/k-l)
Prefix Expression: *-a/bc-/akl
```

Programming Tips!

`isoperator()` is used to determine whether any symbol is an operator or not.
`precedence()` is used to assign precedence to the operator where higher integer value points to higher precedence operator.

The following is a Python program for conversion of an infix expression to a prefix expression applying stack.

PyProg-6.5 Infix-to-prefix conversion

```
# Class to convert the expression
class infix_to_prefix:
   precedence = {'^':5,'*':4,'/':4,'+':3,'-':3,'(':2,')':1}
   # Constructor to initialize the class variables
   def __init__(self):
       self.items = []
       self.size =- 1

   # Push the element to the stack
   def push(self, value):
       self.items.append(value)
       self.size += 1

   # Pop the element to the stack
   def pop(self):
       if self.isempty():
           return 0
       else:
           self.size -= 1
           return self.items.pop()

   # check if the stack is empty
   def isempty(self):
       if(self.size == -1):
           return True
       else:
           return False

   # Return the value of the top of the stack
   def seek(self):
       if self.isempty():
           return False
       else:
           return self.items[self.size]
```

```
# A utility function to check is the given character is operand
def isOperand(self, i):
    if i.isalpha() or i in '1234567890':
        return True
    else:
        return False

# Reverse the stack
def reverse(self, expr):
    rev = ""
    for i in expr:
        if i is '(':
            i = ')'
        elif i is ')':
            i = '('
        rev = i + rev
    return rev

# The main function that converts given infix expression
# to postfix expression
def infixtoprefix(self, expr):
    prefix = ""
    print('prefix expression after every iteration is:')

    # Iterate over the expression for conversion
    for i in expr:
        if(len(expr)%2 == 0):
            print("Incorrect infix expr")
            return False

        # If the character is an operand, add it to output
        elif(self.isOperand(i)):
            prefix += i
        elif(i in '+-*/^'):
            while(len(self.items)and self.precedence[i] < \\
                    self.precedence[self.seek()]):
                prefix += self.pop()
            self.push(i)
        elif i is '(':
            self.push(i)
        elif i is ')':
            o = self.pop()
            while o!='(':
                prefix += o
                o = self.pop()
        print(prefix)
    # End for
```

```
        # Pop all the operator from the stack
        while len(self.items):
            if(self.seek() =='('):
                self.pop()
            else:
                prefix += self.pop()
                print(prefix)
        return prefix

# Executing the conversion or driver code
s = infix_to_prefix()
expr = input('enter the expression ')
rev = ""
rev = s.reverse(expr)
result = s.infixtoprefix(rev)
if (result != False):
    prefix = s.reverse(result)
    print("the prefix expr of :", expr, "is", prefix)
## End program
```

Output

```
enter the expression (a-b/c)*(a/k-l)
prefix expression after every iteration is:

ll
lk
lk
lkalka/-lka/-
lka/-
lka/-c
lka/-c
lka/-cb
lka/-cb/
lka/-cb/a
lka/-cb/a-
lka/-cb/a-*
the prefix expr of : (a-b/c)*(a/k-l) is *-a/bc-/akl
```

> ***Programming Tips!***
> `infixtoprefix()` converts a given infix expression to postfix expression using stack.

6.3.8 Prefix Evaluation

Similar to the postfix evaluation, prefix expressions can be evaluated using stack. This section presents the algorithms and corresponding C and Python source codes for the implementation of prefix evaluation.

Algo-6.8 Algorithm of prefix evaluation

The following is the algorithm for evaluation of a prefix expression applying stack.

Suppose P is an expression written in prefix notation. This algorithm finds the VALUE of prefix expression P.

Step 1	Add '(' at the beginning of P.
Step 2	Push corresponding ')' into the empty stack.
Step 3	Scan P from the right to the left and repeat Step 3 to Step 7 for each symbol of P until sentinel '(' is encountered.
Step 4	If an operand is encountered, push it onto the stack
step 5	If an operator is encountered, then pop two elements from the stack, where A is the topmost element and B is next-to-the-top element.
Step 6	Evaluate B operator A.
Step 7	Push the above result onto the stack.
Step 8	VALUE ← top element on the stack.
Step 9	Exit.

The above algorithm is demonstrated with the help of the following example:

Example 6.4: Evaluation of Prefix expression "+ 9 * 2 6".

1. Add a '(' at the starting of the prefix expression. The expression now is "(+ 9 * 2 6"
2. Push corresponding ')' into the empty stack.
3. Scan the prefix expression from the right to the left, one by one character.
4. Scan '6'. It is a number. So, push it into the stack. The stack now contains ') 6'
5. Scan '2'. It is again a number. So, push it into the stack. The stack now contains ') 6 2' (from bottom to top).
6. Scan '*'. It is an operator, and hence pop two operands from the stack. Now, apply the * operator on the operands. Top element '2' will be placed at the left side of the operator, and next-to-top element '6' will be placed at the right side of the operator. Now, perform the operation according to the operator symbol, and we will get 12 as a result of 6 * 2.Push the result '12' into the stack. The stack now contains ') 12'.
7. Scan '9'. It is a number, and hence push it into the stack. The stack now contains ') 12 9'.
8. Scan '+'. It is an operator, and hence pop two operands from stack. Now, apply the + operator on operands. The top element '9' will be placed at the left side of the operator, and the next-to-top element '12' will be placed at the right side of the operator. Now, perform the operation according to the operator symbol, and we will get 21 as a result of '12 + 9'. Push the result '21' into the stack. The stack now contains ') 21'.
9. Scan character is an '(', and hence pop the result from the stack until a ')' is encountered. A ')' is encountered just after 21, and hence discard both the parentheses (don't store both the parentheses). There are no more elements remaining to be scanned, and hence we need to return the top element '21' from the stack (which is the only element left in the stack).
10. The answer is '21'.

6.3.9 Prefix Evaluation with C and Python

The following is a C program for evaluation of a prefix expression applying stack.

CProg-6.6 Prefix evaluation

```
#include<stdio.h>
#include<string.h>
#include<ctype.h>
#include<stdlib.h>

/* Node declaration */
struct Stack
  {
     int top;
     unsigned capacity;
     int* array;
  };

/* Stack Operations */
struct Stack* createStack( unsigned capacity )
  {
     struct Stack* stack = (struct Stack*) malloc(sizeof(struct Stack));
     if (!stack) return NULL;
     stack->top = -1;
     stack->capacity = capacity;
      stack->array = (int*) malloc(stack->capacity * sizeof(int));
     if (!stack->array) return NULL;
     return stack;
  }

int isEmpty(struct Stack* stack)
  {
     return stack->top == -1 ;
  }

char peek(struct Stack* stack)
  {
     return stack->array[stack->top];
  }

char pop(struct Stack* stack)
  {
     if (!isEmpty(stack))
        return stack->array[stack->top--] ;
     return '$';
  }
```

```
void push(struct Stack* stack, char op)
   {
     stack->array[++stack->top] = op;
   }

/* The function that returns the value of a given postfix
expression*/
int evaluatePostfix(char* exp)
   {
    /* Create a stack of capacity equal to expression size */
     struct Stack* stack = createStack(strlen(exp));
     int i;

     /* See if the stack was created successfully */
     if (!stack) return -1;

     /* Scan all characters one by one */
     for (i = strlen(exp) - 1; i>=0; --i)
      {
          /* If the scanned character is an operand (number
here), push it to the stack */
         if(isdigit(exp[i]))
push(stack, exp[i] - '0');

         /* If the scanned character is an operator, pop two
elements from stack apply the operator */
         else
           {
              int val1 = pop(stack);
              int val2 = pop(stack);
              switch (exp[i])
                {
                  case '+': push(stack, val2 + val1); break;
                  case '-': push(stack, val2 - val1); break;
                  case '*': push(stack, val2 * val1); break;
                  case '/': push(stack, val2/val1); break;
                }
           }
      }
     return pop(stack);
   }

/* Driver function */
int main()
  {
    char exp[] = "+9*26";
```

```
    printf ("prefix evaluation: %d", evaluatePostfix(exp));
    return 0;
  }
/* End of program */
```

Output

```
prefix evaluation: 21
```

Programming Tips!
`evaluatePostfix()` returns the value of a given prefix expression while evaluating prefix expressions.

Following is a Python program for the evaluation of a prefix expression applying stack.

PyProg-6.6 Prefix evaluation

```
# If the character is a digit then it must be an operand
def isOperand(c):
  return c.isdigit();

# The function that converts given infix to postfix expression
def evaluatePrefix(exprsn):
  Stack = [];
  for j in range(len(exprsn) - 1, -1, -1) :
   # Push operand to Stack to convert exprsn[j] to digit subtract
    # '0' from exprsn[j].
    if (isOperand(exprsn[j])) :
      Stack.append(ord(exprsn[j]) - ord('0'));
    else :
      # Operator encountered (pop two elements from the stack)
      o1 = Stack[-1];
      Stack.pop();
      o2 = Stack[-1];
      Stack.pop();

     # Use switch case to operate on o1 and o2 and perform o1Oo2.
      if (exprsn[j] == '+') :
        Stack.append(o1 + o2);
      elif (exprsn[j] == '-') :
        Stack.append(o1 - o2);
      elif (exprsn[j] =='*') :
        Stack.append(o1 * o2);
      elif (exprsn[j] =='/') :
        Stack.append(o1 / o2);
  return Stack[-1];
```

```
# Driver code
if __name__ == "__main__" :
  exprsn = "+9*26";
  print("prefix evaluation", evaluatePrefix(exprsn));
## End program
```

Output

```
prefix evaluation: 21
```

> ***Programming Tips!***
> `evaluatePrefix()` is the key function to evaluate prefix expression.

6.3.10 Short-cut for Infix-to-Prefix and -Postfix Conversions

So far, we have used conventional methods to convert an infix expression to an equivalent prefix or postfix notations. You may have noticed that these methods are lengthy and take a considerable amount of time. You can also expect that there might be some short-cut ways to perform the conversion allowing expressions of any complexity to be correctly transformed.

Step 1: The first technique that we will consider uses the notion of a fully parenthesized expression. Recall that A + B ∗ C can be written as (A + (B ∗ C)) to show explicitly that the multiplication has precedence over the addition. You can see that each parenthesis pair also denotes the beginning and the end of an operand pair with the corresponding operator in the middle.

Step 2: Move all the operators to their corresponding right parenthesis. Look at the right parenthesis in the sub-expression (B ∗ C) above. If we were to move the multiplication symbol to that position and remove the matching left parenthesis, giving us B C ∗, we would, in effect, have converted the sub-expression to a postfix notation.

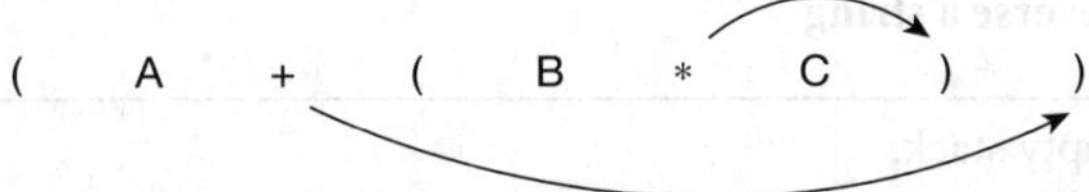

Fig. 6.6: Moving operators to the right for postfix notation

Instead of moving the symbol to the position of the right parenthesis, we may move it to the left and get prefix notation. The position of the parenthesis pair is a clue to the final position of the enclosed operator.

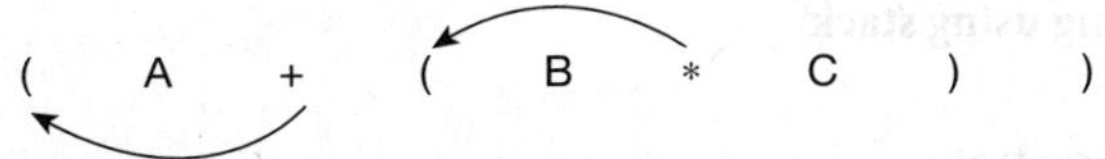

Fig. 6.7: Moving operators to the left for prefix notation

Step 3: Rewrite the expression after removing all left and right parentheses.

Postfix: A B C ∗ +

Prefix: + A ∗ B C

To convert an expression to either prefix or postfix notations, we have to parenthesize the expression fully using the order of operations as per precedence. Then, we move the enclosed operator to the position either to the left or to the right parenthesis depending on whether we want prefix or postfix notation.

Here is a more complex expression: (A + B) ∗ C – (D - E) ∗ (F + G). Figure 6.8 shows the conversion to postfix and prefix notations.

(A + B) ∗ C – (D – E) ∗ (F + G) ⟶ (((A + B) ∗ C) – ((D – E) ∗ (F + G)))

Prefix: – ∗ + A B C ∗ – D E + F G

Postfix: A B + C ∗ D E – F G + ∗ –

Figure 6.8 Converting an expression to prefix and postfix notations

6.3.11 Reversing String Using Stack with C and Python

As a consequence of the LIFO practice, a stack can be applied as a general tool to reverse a data sequence. For example, if the values 1, 2, 3 and 4 are pushed into a stack in that order, they will be popped from the stack in the order 4, 3, 2 and then 1. This idea can be applied in a variety of settings. For example, we might wish to print lines of a file in reverse order to display a data set in decreasing order rather than increasing order. This can be carried out by reading each line and pushing it onto a stack, and then writing the lines in the order they are popped.

Given a string, we can reverse it using stack. For example, 'INDIA' can be converted to 'AIDNI'. The following is a simple algorithm to reverse a string using stack.

Algo-6.9 Algorithm to reverse a string

Step 1	Create an empty stack.
Step 2	One by one, push all characters of the string to the stack.
Step 3	One by one, pop all characters from the stack and put them back to the string.

The following C program can reverse a string supplied to the program using the stack data structure discussed above.

CProg-6.7 Reverse a string using stack

```
#include<stdio.h>
#include<string.h>
#include<stdlib.h>
#include<limits.h>

/* A structure to represent a stack */
struct Stack
```

```
  {
      int top;
      unsigned capacity;
      char* array;
  };

/* Function to create a stack of given capacity. It initializes
the size of the stack as 0 */
struct Stack* createStack(unsigned capacity)
  {
      struct Stack* stack = (struct Stack*) malloc(sizeof(struct
Stack));
      stack->capacity = capacity;
      stack->top = -1;
      stack->array = (char*) malloc(stack->capacity * sizeof(char));
      return stack;
  }

/* Stack is full when the top is equal to the last index */
int isFull(struct Stack* stack)
  {
    return stack->top == stack->capacity - 1;
  }

/* Stack is empty when the top is equal to -1 */
int isEmpty(struct Stack* stack)
  {
    return stack->top == -1;
  }

/* Function to add an item to stack. It increases top by 1 */
void push(struct Stack* stack, char item)
{
     if (isFull(stack))
          return;
     stack->array[++stack->top] = item;
}

/* Function to remove an item from the stack. It decreases top by
1 */
char pop(struct Stack* stack)
  {
      if (isEmpty(stack))
           return;
      return stack->array[stack->top--];
  }
```

```
/* A stack-based function to reverse a string */
void reverse(char str[])
   {
      /* Create a stack of capacity equal to the length of string
*/
      int n = strlen(str);
      struct Stack* stack = createStack(n);

      /* Push all characters of the string to stack */
      int i;
     for(i= 0; i< n; i++)
            push(stack, str[i]);

      /* Pop all characters of string and put them back to str */
      for (i= 0; i< n; i++)
            str[i] = pop(stack);
   }

/* Driver function */
int main()
   {
      char ch[] = "heythere";
      reverse(ch);
     printf("Reversed string: %s", ch);
    return 0;
   }
/* End of program */
```

Output

```
Reversed string: erehtyeh
```

The following Python program can reverse a string supplied to the program applying the stack data structure techniques discussed above.

> ***Programming Tips!***
> `reverse()` is used to reverse a string using stack.

PyProg-6.7 Reverse a string using stack

```
# Function to create empty stack
def createStack():
      stack = []
      return stack

# Function to determine the size of the stack
def size(stack):
      return len(stack)
```

```
# Stack is empty if the size is 0
def isEmpty(stack):
    if size(stack) == 0:
        return true

# Push function of the stack (increases size by 1)
def push(stack, item):
    stack.append(item)

# Pop function of the stack (decreases size by 1)
def pop(stack):
    if isEmpty(stack): return
    return stack.pop()

# A stack based function to reverse a string
def reverse(string):
    n = len(string)

    # Create a empty stack
    stack = createStack()

    # Push all characters of string to stack
    for i in range(0,n,1):
        push(stack,string[i])

    # Making the string empty since all characters are saved
in the stack
    string = ""

    # Pop all characters of string and put them back to string
    for i in range(0,n,1):
        string += pop(stack)
    return string

# Driver code
string = "heythere"
string = reverse(string)
print("Reversed string: " + string)
## End program
```

Output

```
Reversed string: erehtyeh
```

Programming Tips!

`reverse()` is used to reverse a string using stack with Python like the last C Program 6.7.

QUICK RECAP

- ☑ The stack is an ordered list of a similar data type where every time an element is added, it goes on the top, and the only element that can be removed is the element that is also from the top.
- ☑ It is a linear data structure. It follows the LIFO property. It has only one pointer, TOP, that points to the last or topmost element. Insertion and deletion in the stack can only be done from the top.
- ☑ Initially, the stack is empty.
- ☑ Insertion in the stack is known as a PUSH operation. Deletion from the stack is known as POP operation.
- ☑ Before executing PUSH or POP operations, we need to (1) determine whether the stack is empty or not, and (2) check whether the stack is full or not.
- ☑ If the stack is not full, insert a new node at the top of the stack. This operation is termed as PUSH. If the stack is not empty, we can delete the node at its top. This operation is called POP.
- ☑ If the condition, (top = = MaxStack −1) is true and we are trying to push an element, then 'overflow' will occur.
- ☑ If the condition,(top = = −1) is true and we are trying to pop an element, then 'underflow' will occur.
- ☑ We can implement stack using both array and linked list data structures.
- ☑ There are a multitude of applications of the stack, such as expression or notation conversion, expression evaluation, syntax parsing, backtracking, memory management, and functions among which the first two are most important.
- ☑ There are three types of expressions, infix, prefix, and postfix. Executing the instructions with infix expressions requires more iterations than its equivalent prefix or postfix expressions, and hence often we have to convert infix expressions to its other two equivalent forms.
- ☑ Conversions of infix expression to postfix and prefix expressions incorporate stack applications. Evaluation of postfix and prefix expressions also include applications of stack.
- ☑ Both C and Python language can efficiently implement the algorithms of stack data structure related problems.

REVIEW QUESTIONS

Multiple Choice Questions (MCQ): Choose the Best Alternative

Easy

1. ____________ is the process of inserting an element into the stack while it is not full.

A. Create B. Insert
C. Push D. Pop

Hint: Push operation allows users to insert elements into the stack. If the stack is filled completely (stack is full) and we try to perform push operation, stack overflow can happen.

2. When the stack is not empty, we can remove element(s) by ____________ operation.

A. Create B. Push
C. Pop D. Delete

3. Which one of the following data structures is the most suitable to evaluate an arithmetic expression in postfix form?

A. Array B. Stack
C. Queue D. Linked list

4. If you try to remove data from the empty stack, the event is called __________.

A. Overflow
B. Empty collection
C. Garbage collection
D. Underflow

5. Consider a stack of size 5. Which one of the following situations will occur if you perform Push operation (or inserting elements) in this if it already has 5 elements?
A. Heavy B. Crash
C. Underflow D. Overflow

Moderate

6. What will be the output of evaluating the postfix expression 4, 6, 8, *, +, 26, %?
A. 1 B. 2
C. 0 D. 4

7. What will be the prefix expression on conversion of the infix expression: 4 * (5 + 3) / 2 – 7?
A. /*4 + 5 3–2 7
B. -/*+4 5 3 2 7
C. -/*4 + 5 3 2 7
D. None of these.

8. In which of the following situations, the stack should not be used?
A. Allocation of resources like CPU by the operating system
B. Evaluation of a postfix expression
C. Conversion of infix expression to its equivalent postfix expression
D. Recursion.

9. Perform the following operations on a stack of size 6:
push(A); pop(); push(B); push(C); pop(); push(D); pop(); pop(); pop();
Which of the following will occur after these operations?
A. Overflow occurs.
B. Stack operations will be performed smoothly.
C. Underflow occurs.
D. None of these.

10. Suppose 8 + 3 * (2 * 3 – 5) is an infix notation. What will be the result if we convert this infix notation to postfix notation and then evaluate it?
A. 1 B. 22
C. 33 D. 11
Hint: postfix: 8 3 2 3 * 5 - * +

11. The following sequence of operations is performed on a stack:
push(A), push(B), push(C), pop, push(D), pop, push(E), pop, pop, pop,
What will be the sequence of popped out values?
A. A, B, C, D, E B. E, D, C, B, A
C. C, D, E, B, A D. B, C, D, E, A

Higher-order Thinking Skills (HOTS)

12. What will be the maximum number of parentheses that appear on a stack at a time, when the algorithm analyses to determine whether the series of parentheses given by (()(())(())) are balanced?
A. 4 B. 1
C. 2 D. 3
Hint: In the parenthesis balancing method, when the incoming token is a left parenthesis it is pushed into the stack. A right parenthesis makes the pop operation delete the elements in the stack until we get the left parenthesis as the topmost element. Three elements are there in the stack before the right parentheses come. So, the maximum number of elements in the stack at run time is 3.

13. What will be the postfix equivalent of the prefix expression given by * + X Y – W Z?
A. X Y + W Z – * B. X Y W Z + – *
C. X Y W + Z *– D. X Y + – W * D

14. Which of the following applications does not use a stack data structure?
A. A parenthesis balancing program
B. Interchange of data between asynchronous processes
C. Tracking of local variables at run time
D. Compiler syntax analyser.
Hint: Data transfer between the two asynchronous processes uses the queue data structure for synchronization. The rest are all stack applications.

15. Consider the following C code where the stack is implemented using the array.
```
#define size 5
struct stack
  {
    int a[size]
    int top = _________ ;
  }
```
What will be the initial value at which top is initialized?
A. – 1 B. 0
C. 1 D. Garbage

16. An array A[1.......MAXSTACK] is used to implement two stacks, these are grown from opposite ends of the array. There are two pointers T1 and T2 (where T1 < T2) pointing to the topmost elements on each of the stacks. What will be the condition for the stack to be full?
A. (T1 = MAXSTACK/2 –1) and (T2 = MAXSTACK/2 + 1)
B. T1 = T2 – 1
C. T1 + T2 = MAXSTACK
D. (T1 = MAXSTACK/2) or (T2 = MAXSTACK/2 + 1)

Hints:

- When the first stack contains 1 element and the second stack contains 1 element, then T1 = 1 and T2 = MAXSTACK-1, so T1 + T2 = MAXSTACK. Since both stacks are not full, there is no overflow.
- (T1 = MAXSTACK/2) and (T2 = MAXSTACK/2 + 1): This condition is true when both stacks have $n/2$ elements but space is not effectively used; when the first stack has no elements and the second stack has $n - 1$ elements, then it will not detect overflow.
- T1 = T2-1 when this condition is true, it covers all cases when both stacks are full. That is, when first stack is empty and the second stack is full and vice-versa.

17. Compute the postfix equivalent of the following expression:
5 * log(*x* + 1) – *y*/3
A. 5 *x* 1 - log * *y* 3 / +
B. 5 *x* 1 + log * *y* 3 / -
C. 5 *y* 1 + log * *x* 3 / -
D. *x* 1 5 log * *y* 3 / - +
Hints: Step-by-step conversion:
⇒ 5 * (*x* + 1) log – *y*/3 ⇒ 5 * *x* 1 + log – *y* 3 /
⇒ 5 *x* 1 + log * - *y* 3 / ⇒ 5 *x* 1 + log * *y* 3 / -

Short Answer-type Questions

Easy

1. Suppose you are given 10 books arranged one above another. Which data structure is suitable for representation of such an arrangement? Define this data structure and justify your answer.
2. What are the differences between stack and array? Define a stack using C/Python code snip.
3. When does 'overflow' and 'underflow' occur in a stack? Give the conditions with examples.
4. What are the two most fundamental operations in a stack? Write their differences with examples.
5. What is an arithmetic expression? How many types (Infix, Prefix, Postfix) of such expressions are possible? Explain each with examples.
6. What is the difference between Polish and Reverse-Polish notations?
7. What is backtracking in the data structure?

Moderate

8. Distinguish between postfix and prefix expressions. Give examples.
9. Discuss any two applications of the stack. Why would stack be preferable over array for each application? Give reasons.
10. Explain the overflow and underflow error conditions with their remedies.
11. What is the advantage of stack implementation using a linked list over stack implementation using an array?
12. Compare PUSH, POP and PEEK operations in the stack. Give examples to demonstrate which is required where.
13. Which data structure would you prefer to use in data handling during recursion procedures? Give examples.

Higher-Order Thinking Skills (HOTS)

14. Evaluate the postfix expression given by A B + C / D ^ E * with the following values for variables: A = 4, B = 2, C = 4, D = 2, and E = 3. Show the content of the stack, each time, from the expression.
15. Suppose you are given a stack where only PUSH and POP operations are allowed. Explain how to delete an element from the middle position.
Input Stack: [A, B, C, D, E], Output Stack: [A, B, D, E]
16. Assume an array of elements is given. write the steps to sort these array elements using stack. Examples: Input = 6 5 2 1 7 9 8, Output = 1 2 5 6 7 8 9.
17. Given a stack, how can we reverse all the elements of the stack using PUSH and POP operations only?
Hints: First remove all the elements of the stack until it becomes empty. Then insert all the elements in the opposite sequence within the stack.
18. How can we implement two stacks using only one array?

Descriptive-type Questions

Easy

1. Write down the possible applications of the stack data structure in computer programming.
2. Write all the steps of PUSH and POP operations separately for the implementation of a stack data structure.
3. Give the C and/or Python code snips for the implementation of PUSH and POP operations.
4. What are the disadvantages of stack implementation using an array? Explain the process of stack implementations using a linked list for overcoming the above.
5. What do you understand by expression conversion? Give an example for demonstrating the same.

Moderate

6. Write the steps of postfix expression evaluation using stack. Explain the steps with an example.
7. Apply stack data structure for designing the algorithms of prefix notation evaluation.
8. How is stack data structure applied for infix-to-postfix conversion of arithmetic expressions?
9. Write the steps of infix-to-prefix conversion algorithms applying stack data structure.
10. Explain the infix-to-postfix conversion for the expression given by
    A ∗ B + C ∗ D.
11. How can the infix expression given by $(a - b/c) * (a/k - 1)$ be converted to prefix notation using stack?
12. Illustrate the postfix expression evaluation technique using a stack data structure with an example.
13. How to reverse a string using a stack data structure?

Higher-Order Thinking Skills (HOTS)

14. Write the rules associated with arithmetic expressions.
15. Write an algorithm to reverse a number using stack:
    Example: Input: 123 Output: 321
16. What will be the output of the following algorithm for the input string given by 'INDIA'?

```
Declare a Stack
while (at least one character
left to read)
        {
          read a character
          push ()
        }
while (stack is not empty)
        {
          pop ()
          write the character
        }
```

    Hint: The stack data structure follows the LIFO order. When we `pop()` items from the stack, they are popped in reverse order of their insertion (or `push()`).
17. Consider a stack of characters. Suppose the following data A, B, C, D, E, F are to be inserted into the stack. Is it possible to permute the order CBEFDA as output and in the order AEDFBC?
    Hint: Two outputs cannot be generated because B is pushed before C.

CASE STUDIES

1. Convert the following infix expressions into postfix expression (also evaluate it) and prefix expression:
   A. 1 + 2 ∗ 3/ (4 + 5)
   B. 9 ^ 3 – 7 + 2
   C. 5 ∗ 8 – 12 / 3
2. Evaluate the infix expression given by (X ∗ Y – W ∗ Z) / (M - N). Write the operations performed on each iteration to evaluate the expression.
3. Evaluating a prefix expression given by / – ∗ X Y ∗ W Z – M N. Give the operations performed on each iteration to evaluate the expression.

LAB EXERCISES

1. **Checking balanced parentheses:** Write a Python program to check for balanced parentheses in an expression. Given a string expression, write a program to examine whether the pairs and the orders of "{", "}", "(", ")", "[", "]" are correct in expression.
2. Design a C program to determine whether a user input string is a palindrome or not using a stack data structure. You may recall that a palindrome is a sequence of characters/words that reads the same as the sequence in reverse order. Example: 'MADAM' or 'NAYAN'.

ANSWER KEYS

Multiple Choice Questions

1. C	4. D	7. A	10. D	13. A	16. B
2. C	5. D	8. A	11. C	14. B	17. B
3. B	6. C	9. C	12. D	15. A	

7 Queue

CONTENTS

EXPECTED OUTCOMES OF THIS CHAPTER

After going through this chapter learners will be able

- ☑ To understand the abstract data structures queue, deque and priority queue.
- ☑ To compare queue with stack data structure.
- ☑ To implement the queue, deque and priority queue with C and Python.
- ☑ To design and implement a queue as an array and as a linked list.
- ☑ To recognize problem where queues, and dequeues are appropriate data structures.

7.1 INTRODUCTION

A real-world example of a queue can be a single lane at a bank teller counter, where the customer enters first, and gets service (exits) first. Each new customer gets in line at the rear (last). When the teller is ready to help a new customer, the customer at the front of the line is served. Another example of a queue is shown in Fig. 7.1, where the first customer in the line will be served first. The queue at the ticket window of a movie hall ticket counter is also an example of a queue. Whoever comes first, he/she will get the ticket first. Suppose, a computer laboratory has 30 computers networked with a single printer. When students execute their print tasks, these "get in line" with all the other printing tasks that are waiting. The first task is to complete the next job in the queue. If your print job is at the last in the line, you have to wait for all the other tasks of printing ahead of you. We will explore this interesting example in more detail later.

The queue is an abstract data structure, somewhat similar to stacks. Unlike stacks, a queue is open at both its ends. A good example of a queue is any queue of consumers for a resource where the consumer who came first is served first. The difference between stacks and queues is in removing the item. In a stack, we remove the item added most recently, whereas we remove the item added last in a queue.

Figure 7.1 Example of a queue at a counter

7.1.1 Definition

Queue is a collection of elements maintained in a sequence where the addition of elements takes place at one end, called rear (back or tail), and removal of elements takes place from the other end, called front or head. It is a linear structure that follows a particular order in which the operations (addition and removal) are performed. The queue is also an abstract data structure just like a stack. The order of operations is termed as First-In–First-Out (FIFO), which means that the element inserted first will be removed first.

A **circular queue** is also a linear data structure, which follows the same principle of FIFO. But instead of ending the queue at the last position, it again starts from the first position and the queue is not full. Thus, the queue behaves like a circular data structure. The circular queue is discussed in Section 7.2.

Characteristics of a queue

We can summarize the characteristics of a queue as follows:

1. Queue follows the FIFO structure operations.
2. According to the FIFO structure, the element inserted first will be removed first.
3. Queue normally maintains two data pointers, front and rear.

4. The front pointer points to the beginning of the queue element and the rear pointer points to the last element of the queue.
5. In a queue, one end is always used to insert data (Qinsert) and the other end is used to delete data (Qdelete) because the queue is open at both its ends.
6. Qinsert and Qdelete are the two important functions used in a queue.

7.1.2 Operations

The two basic operations associated with a queue are Qinsert (also called enQueue) and Qdelete (also called deQueue). Qinsert is the term used to insert an element into a queue. On the other hand, Qdelete is the term used to delete an element from a queue. Insertions (Qinsert) take place at the rear end only whereas deletion (Qdelete) takes place from the front end only. When a queue is initiated, the value of both the front and rear initializes with –1.

Qinsert Operation

Qinsert operation is used to insert a new element at the last (rear end) of the queue. Qinsert function is defined for such insertion operation. Only one item can be added by calling a one-time Qinsert function. This Qinsert operation is also known as *enQueue* operation in some literature.

Qdelete Operation

Qdelete operation removes an item from the queue. It removes the first element (front pointer) from the queue. Qdelete function is defined for such a deletion operation. Only one item can be removed by calling a one-time Qdelete function. This Qdelete operation is also known as *deQueue* operation in some literature.

> ***Note!***
> Insertion of elements takes place at one end called rear or tail and deletion of elements from the other end called front. Insertion in the queue is also known as Qinsert/enQueue operation and deletion from the queue is also known as Qdelete/deQueue operation.

7.1.3 Some Basic Terminologies

- **Queue[]:** It is an array in which the queue is simulated.
- **Queue Size:** Queue Size is a variable that indicates the maximum number of elements that can be held by the queue. For example, if Queue Size is set to 5, it indicates that the queue can contain a maximum of 5 elements indexed: queue[0] through queue[4]. The maximum number of elements that can be stored in aqueue is defined as Queue Size.
- **Front:** It points to the index where the next deletion will be performed. It also points to the first element of the queue sequence.
- **Rear:** It points to the index after which the next insertion will be performed. It also points to the last element of the queue sequence.
- **Empty Queue:** Suppose a queue contains a single element (i.e., front= =rear≠NULL) and Qdelete operation is performed successfully on that queue, then the value of the queue becomes –1 (i.e., front = -1 && rear = –1). The resulting queue contains no elements, and then the queue is called an empty queue, as shown in Fig. 7.2 (o).

- **Queue is Full:** Suppose the queue size is 5, then we can store maximum 5 (indexed queue[0] to queue[4], like earlier) elements within the queue. In this situation, suppose front = 0 and rear pointer value is 4. It indicates the queue is full. In another scenario, consider a circular queue where front = rear + 1 condition is true; here also say that the queue is full. It means there is no more space to insert new items within the queue and hence the queue is full as shown in Fig. 7.2 (h) and Fig. 7.2 (l).
- **Queue Underflow:** Suppose a queue contains a single element (i.e., front = rear ≠ NULL), and Qdelete operation is performed successfully on the queue. Then the value of front and rear become −1 (i.e., front = −1 && rear = −1). This resultant queue contains no elements and thus it is called an empty queue. In this situation, if you are trying to delete an element from the queue, then "Underflow" will occur. In other words, when the queue is empty and the user executes a delete operation, then "Underflow" error condition will occur as shown in Fig. 7.2 (p).
- **Queue Overflow:** It happens when we try to insert one more element into the queue though the queue is full currently. Consider a queue of size 5 where front = 0 and rear pointer value is 4. It indicates that the queue is full. In another scenario, consider a circular queue where front = rear + 1 condition is true; then also we can say the queue is full. In such cases storing more elements within the queue is not possible, and an "overflow" error condition will occur. In other words, overflow happens when there is no more room left to store a data element for a new insertion within a queue as shown in Fig. 7.2 (i) and 7.2 (m).

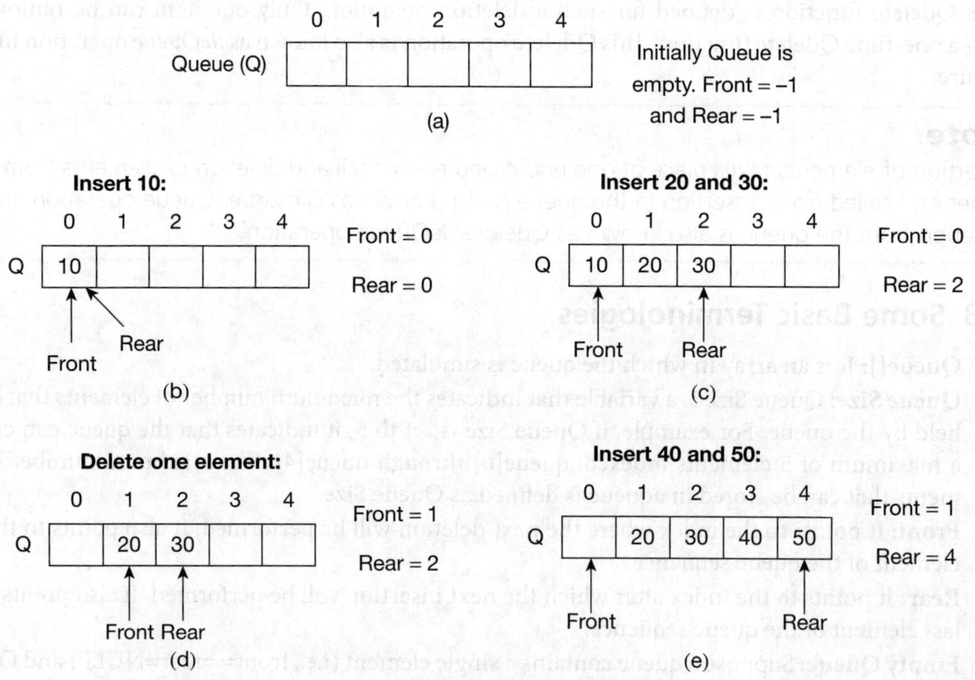

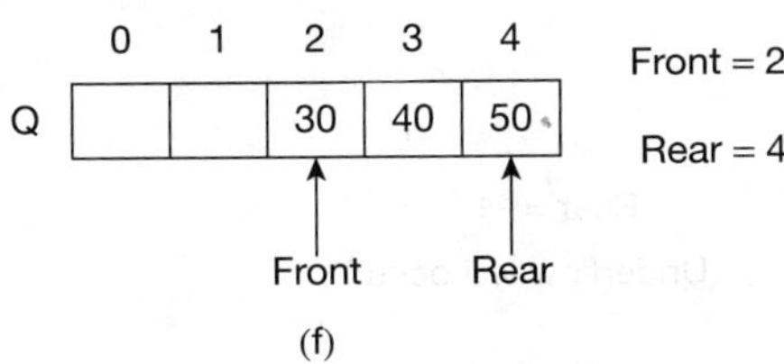
Delete one element:
0 1 2 3 4
Q 30 40 50
Front = 2
Rear = 4
Front Rear
(f)

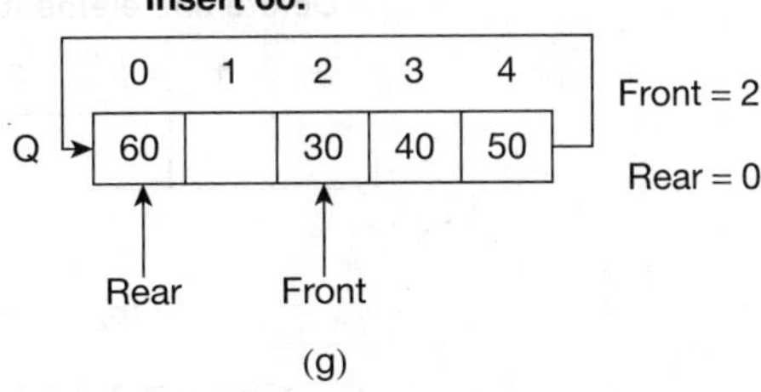
Insert 60:
0 1 2 3 4
Q 60 30 40 50
Front = 2
Rear = 0
Rear Front
(g)

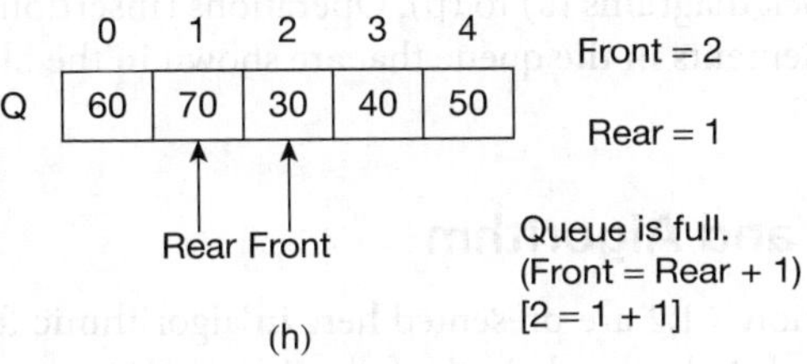
Insert 70:
0 1 2 3 4
Q 60 70 30 40 50
Front = 2
Rear = 1
Rear Front
Queue is full.
(Front = Rear + 1)
[2 = 1 + 1]
(h)

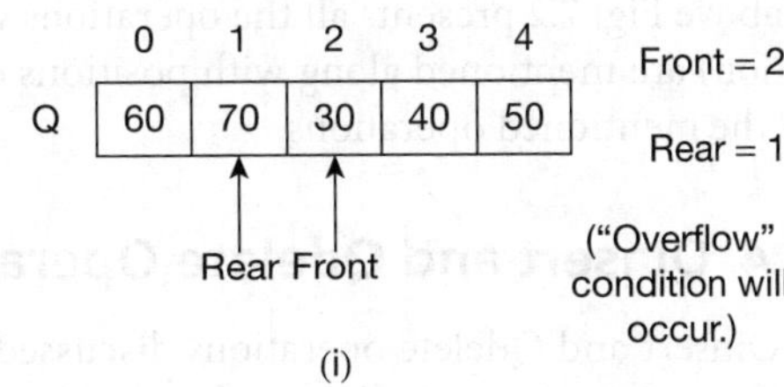
Insert 80:
0 1 2 3 4
Q 60 70 30 40 50
Front = 2
Rear = 1
Rear Front
("Overflow" condition will occur.)
(i)

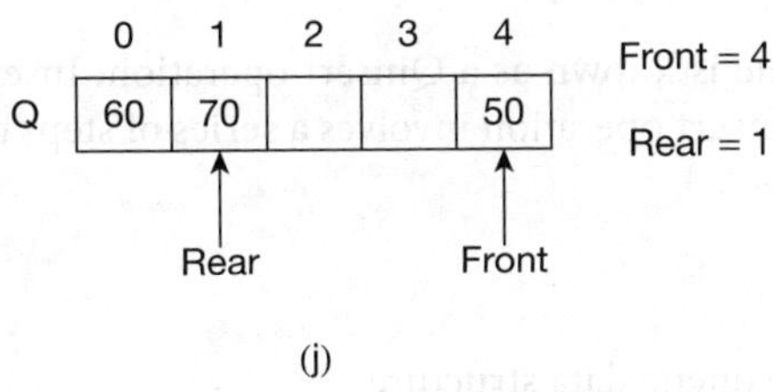
Delete two elements:
0 1 2 3 4
Q 60 70 50
Front = 4
Rear = 1
Rear
Front
(j)

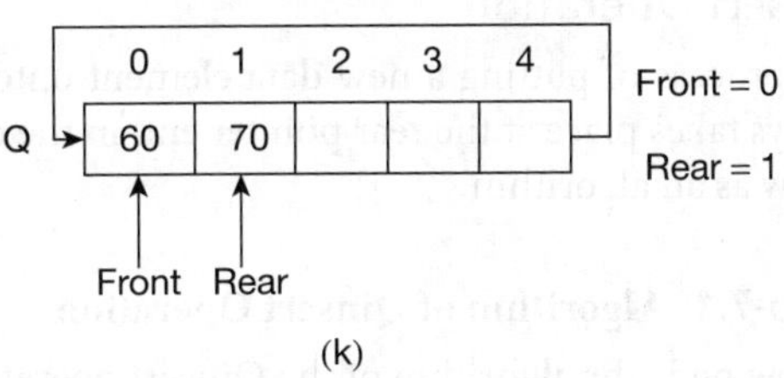
Delete one element:
0 1 2 3 4
Q 60 70
Front = 0
Rear = 1
Front Rear
(k)

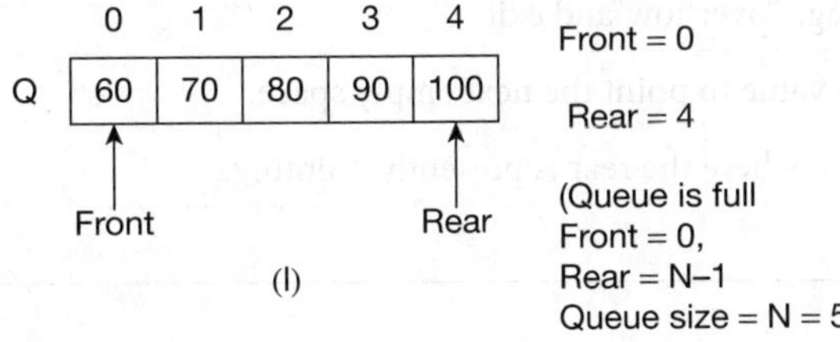
Insert 80,90 and 100:
0 1 2 3 4
Q 60 70 80 90 100
Front = 0
Rear = 4
(Queue is full
Front = 0,
Rear = N–1
Queue size = N = 5)
Front
Rear
(l)

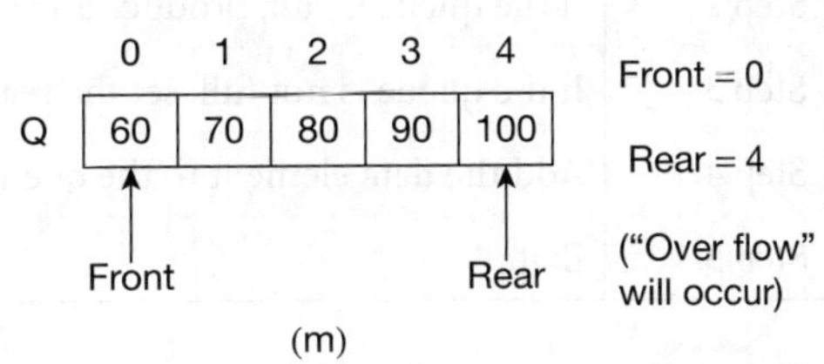
Insert 110:
0 1 2 3 4
Q 60 70 80 90 100
Front = 0
Rear = 4
("Over flow" will occur)
Front
Rear
(m)

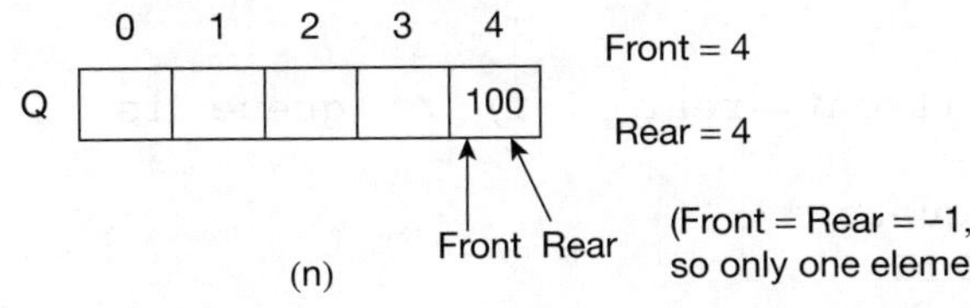
Delete four elements:
0 1 2 3 4
Q 100
Front = 4
Rear = 4
Front Rear
(Front = Rear = –1,
so only one element)
(n)

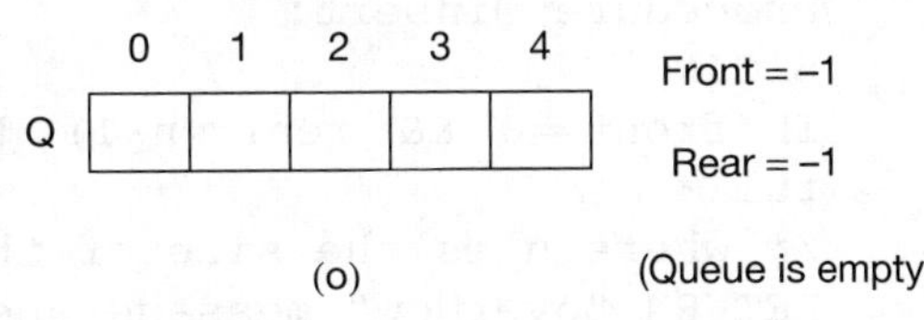
Delete one element:
0 1 2 3 4
Q
Front = –1
Rear = –1
(Queue is empty)
(o)

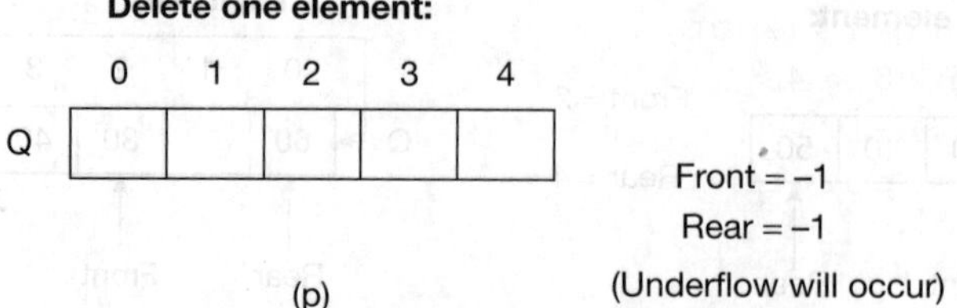

Figure 7.2 Different queue operations

The above Fig. 7.2 presents all the operations with block diagrams (a) to (p). Operations (insertion and deletion) are mentioned along with positions of the elements in the queue that are shown in the blocks after the mentioned operations.

7.1.4 Qinsert and Qdelete Operations and Algorithm

The Qinsert and Qdelete operations discussed in section 7.1.2 are presented here in algorithmic form. These two operations are also implemented using C and Python code in the following sections.

Qinsert Operation

The process of putting a new data element onto the queue is known as a Qinsert operation. Insertion always takes place at the rear pointer end in the queue. Qinsert operation involves a series of steps given below as an algorithm.

Algo-7.1 Algorithm of Qinsert Operation

Following is the algorithm of the Qinsert operation of the queue data structure.

Step	Action
Step 1	Check weather Queue is full or not.
Step 2	If the queue is full, produce an error message "overflow"and exit.
Step 3	If the queue is not full, set the rear pointer value to point the next empty space.
Step 4	Add the data element to the queue location, where the rear is presently pointing.
Step 5	Exit.

Algo-7.2 Pseudocode of Qinsert Operation

```
Procedure Qinsert:
BEGIN
IF(front==0 && rear==n-1) || (front==rear + 1) /* queue is
full*/
/* where n is the size of the queue */
RETURN "overflow" message and EXIT
ENDIF
IF(front==-1 && rear == -1)
```

```
/* If the queue is empty then insert in first position */
SET front=0 and rear=0
ELSE IF(rear==n-1)
/* If rear is pointing the last element, then insert at the
first position */
SET rear=0
ELSE
rear = rear + 1
ENDIF
queue[rear] ← data
ENDProcedure
```

Qdelete Operation

Removing the front element from the queue is known as a Qdelete operation. A Qdelete operation involves the following steps.

Algo-7.3 Algorithm of Qdelete Operation

Following is the algorithm of the Qdelete operation of the queue data structure.

Step 1	Check whether the queue is empty or not.
Step 2	If the queue is empty, produce the "Underflow" message and exit.
Step 3	If the queue is not empty, remove the data element at which the front is pointing.
Step 4	Set the value of the front.
Step 5	Exit.

Algo-7.4 Pseudocode of Qdelete Operation

```
Procedure Qdelete:
BEGIN
IF(front ==-1 && rear ==-1) /* Queue is empty */
RETURN "Underflow" message and EXIT
ENDIF
data ← queue [front]
IF(front == rear) // only one element within the queue
SET front = -1 and rear =-1
   ELSE IF (front == n-1)
/*If front pointing last element then set front pointer at first
position */
SET front =0
   ELSE
front = front -1
   ENDIF
RETURN data
ENDProcedure
```

> **Note!**
> Overflow occurs when a queue is full but we try to insert an element, and underflow occurs when the queue is empty but we try to delete an element.

7.2 DESIGN AND IMPLEMENTATION OF QUEUE

The queue can be designed and implemented either using an array or a linked list since the queue is also a linear data structure. In this section, arrays incorporate Qinsert and Qdelete operations of elements supplied to the program. The display of queue elements is also to be designed for verifying the elements inserted or deleted into the queue. Both C and Python programs are given below for the implementation of the queue using array and linked list separately.

The circular queue has less memory wastage as compared to simple queue. This is because, in a simple queue, while doing insertion after deletion operation, it allocates an extra space at the first, which remains vacant. But in a circular queue, the first position is used as it comes immediately after the last position. A circular queue is also a linear data structure in which the operations are conducted on the basis of FIFO principle. The rear points to the last position, the first position of the queue is empty and it makes a circle. A new item can be inserted at the location from where an item is deleted. Reusability of the memory spaces is the main advantage of this concept. We have implemented a circular queue in the following sections using C and Python languages.

> **Note!**
> Queue can be implemented using array as well as linked list data structures, both.

7.2.1 Queue Implementation Using Array with C

Following is the C program for implementation of the queue (Qinsert and Qdelete operations) using an array data type. The program asks the element to be inserted into the queue or to be deleted.

CProg-7.1 Inserting and deleting an element in circular queue using array

```
/* Circular Queue is based on FIFO principle and the last position
is connected back to the first position to make a circle. */

#include<stdio.h>
int queue[5];
int front = -1, rear = -1, size = 5;
void insert (int value);
void deleteQueue();
void display();

/* Driver function */
int main()
  {
     int choice, value;
printf("1.Insert\n");
printf("2.Delete\n");
printf("3.Display\n");
```

```
    do
      {
printf("Enter choice: ");
scanf("%d", &choice);
         switch(choice)
           {
             case 1:
printf("Enter the value: ");
scanf("%d", &value);
                insert (value);
                break;
             case 2:
deleteQueue();
                break;
             case 3:
display();
                break;
           }
      } while(choice != 3);
    return 0;
  }

/*
Insertion:
1) Check whether queue is Full by ((rear == SIZE-1 && front ==
0) || (rear == front-1)).
2) If it is full then display Queue is full. If the queue is
not full then, check
   if (rear == SIZE - 1 &&front != 0) if it is true then set
rear = 0 and insert element.
*/
/* Inserting the value in the queue */
void insert(int value)
   {
     if ((front == 0 && rear == size - 1)||(rear == (front -
1)%(size - 1)))
      {
printf("\nQueue is full\n");
        return;
      }
    else if (front == -1)
      {
        front = rear = 0;
        queue[rear] = value;
      }
```

```
    else if (rear == size - 1 &&front != 0)
      {
        rear = 0;
        queue[rear] = value;
      }
    else
      {
        rear++;
        queue[rear] = value;
      }
  }

/*
Deletion:
1) Check whether the queue is Empty means check (front==-1).
2) If it is empty then display Queue is empty. If the queue is not
empty then Check if (front==rear)
  if it is true then set front=rear= -1 else check if (front==-
size-1), if it is true then set
   front=0 and return the element.
*/
/* Deleting from queue*/
void deleteQueue()
  {
    if (front == -1)
      {
printf("Queue Underflow\n");
return ;
      }
printf("Element deleted from queue is : %d\n", queue[front]);
if(front == rear)
     {
        front = -1;
        rear = -1;
      }

    else
      {
if(front == size - 1)
           front = 0;
        else
           front = front + 1;
      }
  }
```

```
/* Displaying the queue */
void display()
   {
      int i;
       if(front == -1)
         {
printf("\nQueue is Empty");
          return;
         }
printf("\nCircular Queue elements are: ");
      if (front <= rear)
         {
          for ( i = front; i<= rear; i++)
printf("%d ", queue[i]);
         }
      else
         {
for( i = front; i< size; i++)
printf("%d ", queue[i]);
for( i = 0; i<= rear; i++)
printf("%d ", queue[i]);
         }
   }
/* End of program */
```

Output

```
1.Insert
2.Delete
3.Display
Enter choice: 1
Enter the value: 42
Enter choice: 1
Enter the value: 55
Enter choice: 1
Enter the value: 85
Enter choice: 1
Enter the value: 95
Enter choice: 2
Element deleted from queue is : 42
Enter choice: 3

Circular Queue elements are: 55 85 95
```

Programming Tips!

`insert()`, `deleteQueue()` and `display()` have been used to insert, delete and display elements of the circular queue respectively.

7.2.2 Queue Implementation Using Array with Python

Following is the Python program for the implementation of the queue (Qinsert and Qdelete operations) using an array data type.

PyProg-7.1 Inserting and deleting an element in a circular queue using array

```
# Class to create queue
class CircularQueue():
    # constructor to initialize the class variables
    def __init__(self, size):
        self.size = size

        # initializing queue with none
        self.queue = [None for i in range(size)]
        self.front = self.rear = -1

    def enqueue(self, data):
        # condition if queue is full
        if ((self.rear + 1) % self.size == self.front):
            print(" Queue is Full\n")

        # condition for empty queue
        elif (self.front == -1):
            self.front = 0
            self.rear = 0
            self.queue[self.rear] = data
        else:
            # next position of rear
            self.rear = (self.rear + 1) % self.size
            self.queue[self.rear] = data

    def dequeue(self):
        # codition for empty queue
        if (self.front == -1):
            print ("Queue is Empty\n")

        # condition for only one element
        elif (self.front == self.rear):
            temp=self.queue[self.front]
            self.front = -1
            self.rear = -1
            return temp
        else:
           temp = self.queue[self.front]
           self.front = (self.front + 1) % self.size
           return temp
```

```
    # Function for displaying queue elements
    def display(self):
        # condition for empty queue
        if(self.front == -1):
            print ("Queue is Empty")
        elif(self.rear >= self.front):
          print("Elements in the circular queue are:", end = " ")
            for i in range(self.front, self.rear + 1):
                print(self.queue[i], end = " ")
            print ()
        else:
            print ("Elements in Circular Queue are:", end = " ")
            for i in range(self.front, self.size):
                print(self.queue[i], end = " ")
            for i in range(0, self.rear + 1):
                print(self.queue[i], end = " ")
            print ()
        if((self.rear + 1) % self.size == self.front):
            print("Queue is Full")

# Driver code
ob = CircularQueue(5)
ob.enqueue(14)
ob.enqueue(22)
ob.enqueue(13)
ob.enqueue(-6)
ob.display()
print ("Deleted value = ", ob.dequeue())
print ("Deleted value = ", ob.dequeue())
ob.display()
ob.enqueue(9)
ob.enqueue(20)
ob.enqueue(5)
ob.display()
## End program
```

Output

```
Elements in the circular queue are: 14 22 13 -6
Deleted value =  14
Deleted value =  22
Elements in the circular queue are: 13 -6
Elements in Circular Queue are: 13 -6 9 20 5
Queue is Full
```

> ***Programming Tips!***
> `enqueue()`, `dequeue()` and `display()` have been used to implement the insertion, deletion and display queue element(s) respectively. `__init__()` is the constructor to create an object from the class along with initialization of class attributes.

7.2.3 Queue Implementation Using Linked List with C

The major problem with the queue implementation using an array is that it works only for a fixed number of static data values. This means, the size of the data must be specified at the beginning of the implementation itself. The size of the queue cannot be changed in the runtime of the program. Queue implementation using an array is not suitable when we don't know the size of data that we are going to use in the queue. A queue data structure can be implemented by using the linked list dynamic data structure. Queue implementation using the linked list can work for an unlimited number of values. This means, such implementation works for the variable size of data. So, there is no need to fix the size at the beginning of the implementation. This implementation can organize as many data values as we want.

In linked list implementation of a queue, every new element is inserted at the 'rear' pointer position. Whenever we want to remove an element from the queue, simply we need to remove the node which is pointed by 'front'. We have to move the 'front' to its next node in the list and change the head node contents.

Example 7.1

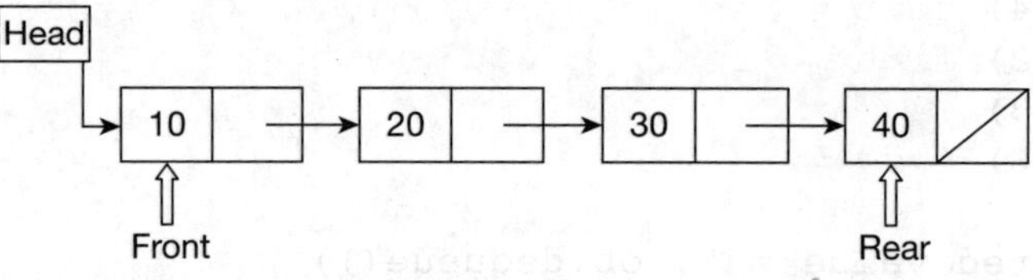

Figure 7.3 Queue implementation using a linked list

In the above example, in Fig. 7.3, the last inserted node is 40 and the first inserted node is 10. The order of elements inserted is 10, 20, 30 and 40. The last inserted node with 40 is pointed by 'rear' and the first inserted node with 10 is pointed by 'front'.

Following is the C program for implementation of the queue (Qinsert and Qdelete operations) using the linked list. The program is designed using the pointer and structure data types of C for the implementation of the linked list. Other approaches are similar to the array implementation of the queue.

CProg-7.2 Inserting and deleting an element in circular queue using linked list

```
#include<stdio.h>
#include<stdlib.h>

/* Defining the linked list node */
typedef struct node
```

```
   {
     int data;
     struct node *next;
   }node;

/* Function to create the circular queue using linked list */
node *createQueue()
   {
     node *rear = NULL, *front = NULL;
printf("How many items you want to create in queue?");
     int n,data;
scanf("%d",&n);
     int i = 0;
while(i< n)
         {
if(i == 0)
       {
printf("Enter the data: ");
scanf("%d",&data);
             node *newNode = (node *)malloc(sizeof(node));
newNode->data = data;
newNode->next = NULL;
             rear = newNode;
             front = rear;
           }
else
       {
printf("Enter the data: ");
scanf("%d",&data);
             node *newNode = (node *)malloc(sizeof(node));
newNode->data = data;
newNode->next = front;
            rear->next = newNode;
             rear = newNode;
           }
         ++i;
       }
     return rear;
   }

/* Displays queue elements */
void display(node *rear, node *front)
  {
     if(!rear)
```

```
        {
printf("\nNOTHING TO DISPLAY\n");
        return;
      }
    node *temp = front;
    if(!rear->next)
        {
printf("%d\n", rear->data);
        return;
      }
if(temp != rear)
        {
printf("%d ", temp->data);
display(rear, temp->next);
      }
      else
        {
printf("%d\n", temp->data);
      }
  }

/* Inserts item in the queue */
void enqueue(node **rear, int data)
  {
    node *newNode = (node *)malloc(sizeof(node));
newNode->data = data;
    if(!(*rear)){
newNode->next=NULL;
    *rear = newNode;
    return;
  }
    node *temp = *rear;
   if(!(*rear)->next)
        {
newNode->next = temp;
      }
      else
        {
newNode->next = temp->next;
      }
    temp->next = newNode;
    *rear = newNode;
  }

/* Delete items from the queue */
int dequeue(node *rear)
```

```
    {
      int data;
      if(!rear)
          {
  printf("\nNO ITEMS IN THE QUEUE\n");
          return 0;
        }
      if(!rear->next)
          {
          data = rear->data;
          free(rear);
          return data;
        }
      node *temp = rear->next;
      data = temp->data;
      rear->next = temp->next;
      free(temp);
      return data;
    }

  /* Driver function */
  int main()
    {
      node *rear = createQueue();
      display(rear,rear->next);
  enqueue(&rear, 99);
      display(rear,rear->next);
      int data = dequeue(rear);
  printf("Delete item is: %d\n",data);
      display(rear,rear->next);
      return 0;
    }
  /* End of program */
```

Output

```
How many items you want to create in queue?3
Enter the data: 52
Enter the data: 41
Enter the data: 56
52 41 56
52 41 56 99
Delete item is: 52
41 56 99
```

Programming Tips!

`enqueue()` and `dequeue()` have been used to implement the insertion and deletion of queue elements respectively using linked list. `malloc()` is used to create linked list nodes dynamically.

7.2.4 Queue Implementation Using Linked List with Python

Following is the Python program for the implementation of a queue (Qinsert and Qdelete operations) using the linked list. The program is designed by defining a class node and two operations (or functions). Qinsert and Qdelete are these functions defined for the purpose.

PyProg-7.2 Inserting and deleting an element in a circular queue using linked list

```
# Structure of a Node
class Node:
  def __init__(self):
    self.data = None
    self.link = None

# Class to create queue
class Queue:
  def __init__(self):
    front = None
    rear = None

# Function to create Circular queue
def enQueue(q, value):
  temp = Node()
  temp.data = value
  if (q.front == None):
    q.front = temp
  else:
    q.rear.link = temp
  q.rear = temp
  q.rear.link = q.front

# Function to delete element from Circular Queue
def deQueue(q):
  if (q.front == None):
    print("Queue is empty")
    return -999999999999

  # If this is the last node to be deleted
  value = None # Value to be dequeued
  if (q.front == q.rear):
    value = q.front.data
    q.front = None
    q.rear = None
  else: # There are more than one nodes
    temp = q.front
    value = temp.data
```

```
    q.front = q.front.link
    q.rear.link= q.front
  return value

# Function displaying the elements of Circular Queue
def displayQueue(q):
  temp = q.front
  print("Elements in Circular Queue are: ",end = " ")
  while (temp.link != q.front):
    print(temp.data, end = " ")
    temp = temp.link
  print(temp.data)

# Driver Code
if __name__ == '__main__':
  # Create a queue and initialize front and rear
  q = Queue()
  q.front = q.rear = None

  # Inserting elements in Circular Queue
  enQueue(q, 14)
  enQueue(q, 22)
  enQueue(q, 6)

  # Display elements present in Circular Queue
  displayQueue(q)

  # Deleting elements from Circular Queue
  print("Deleted value = ", deQueue(q))
  print("Deleted value = ", deQueue(q))

  # Remaining elements in Circular Queue
  displayQueue(q)

  enQueue(q, 9)
  enQueue(q, 20)
  displayQueue(q)
## End program
```

Output

```
Elements in Circular Queue are:  14 22 6
Deleted value =  14
Deleted value =  22
Elements in Circular Queue are:  6
Elements in Circular Queue are:  6 9 20
```

Programming Tips!

`enQueue()`, `deQueue()` and `displayQueue()` have been used to insert, delete and display of queue elements respectively. `__init__()` is the constructor where the self parameter refers to the instance of the object.

7.3 DOUBLE-ENDED QUEUE OR DEQUE

7.3.1 Introduction

Double-ended Queue or deque (pronounced as 'deck') is a comprehensive version of the queue data structure that allows insertion and deletion at both ends but not from any middle positions. Deque can be implemented using both stack and queue operations. Problems where elements need to be removed or added at both ends, can be solved efficiently using deque. We have used the term 'deque' for double-ended queue though literature shows that some authors use the term "dequeue" for the double-ended queue.

Storing a web browser's history is an example of the deque. Newly visited URLs are added to the front of the deque. After some specified number of insertions at the front, the URL at the back of the deque is removed. Undo–Redo actions in software applications also use the deque data structure concept.

7.3.2 Definition

A double-ended queue (or deque) is a data structure in which the insertion and deletion operations are performed at both the ends (front and rear). This means, insertion can take place at both front and rear positions and deletion can take place from both front and rear positions. However, no element can be added or deleted from the middle. Here, the front pointer is called the left pointer and the rear pointer is called the right pointer.

A deque is implemented using either a circular array or a circular doubly linked list. In a deque, two pointers are maintained, Left and Right, which point to either end of the deque. The elements in a deque of *N* elements outspread from the Left end to the Right end, and since it is circular, the *N*-th element of the deque is followed by the first element of the deque. It is also known as a head-tail linked list because elements can be added to or removed from either the front (head) or the back (tail) end. Deque structure and operations are indicated in Fig. 7.4 below.

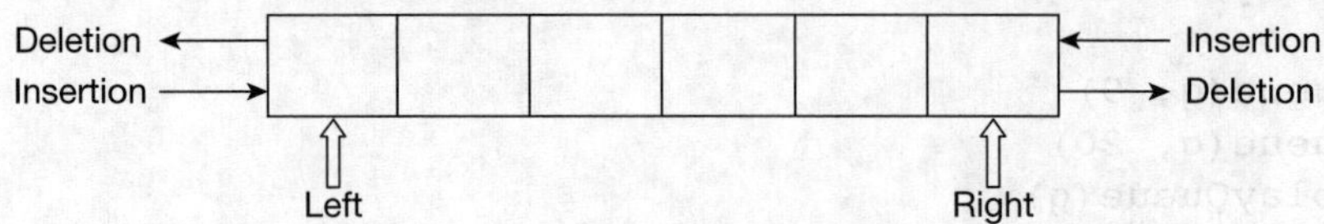

Figure 7.4 Deque structure and operations

Characteristics of a Deque

We can summarize the characteristics of a deque as follows:

1. There can be four basic operations in a deque.
   (a) Insertion at the right pointer end.
   (b) Insertion at the left pointer end.

   (c) Deletion at the left end.
   (d) Deletion at the right end.
2. Queues maintain two data pointers, left and right.
3. The left pointer points to the beginning of the queue element and the right pointer points to the last element of the queue.
4. In a deque, insertion and deletion can take place from both ends but not from any middle position.

The following Fig. 7.5 presents all the deque operations with block diagrams (a) to (p). Operations (insertion and deletion) are mentioned along with positions of the elements in the deque that are shown in the blocks after the mentioned operations.

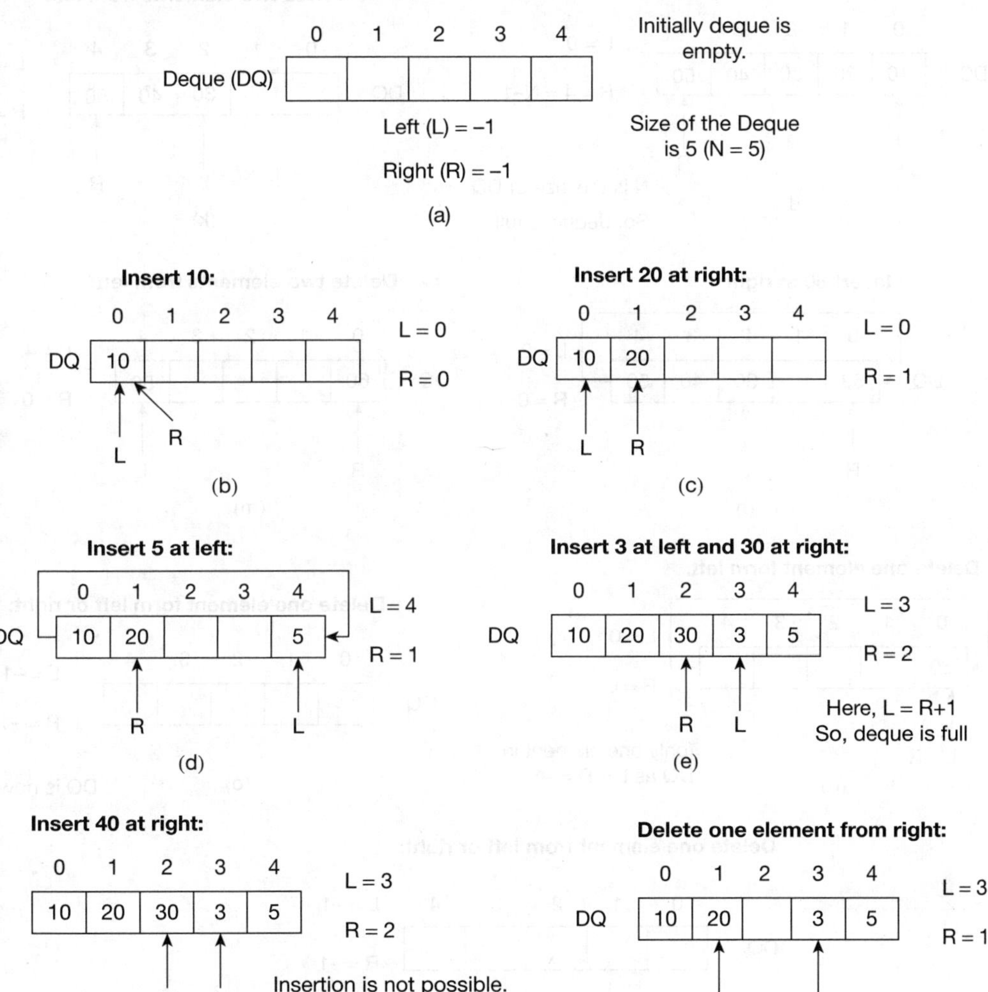

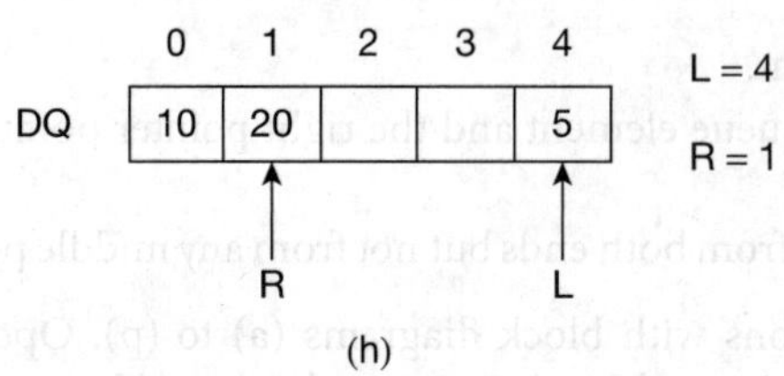

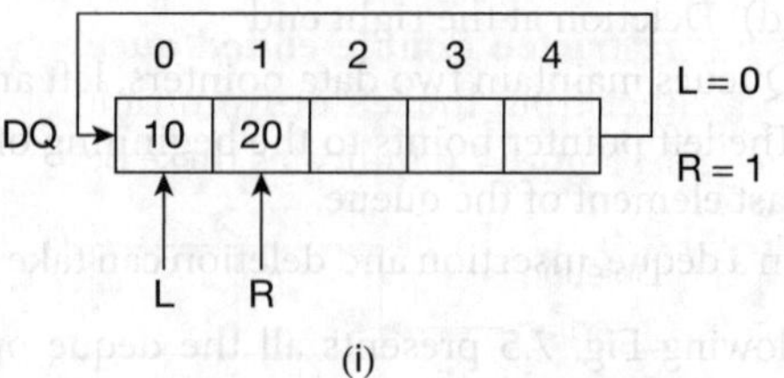

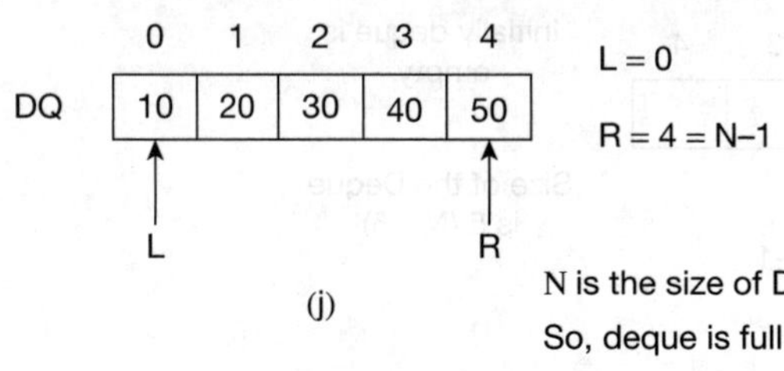

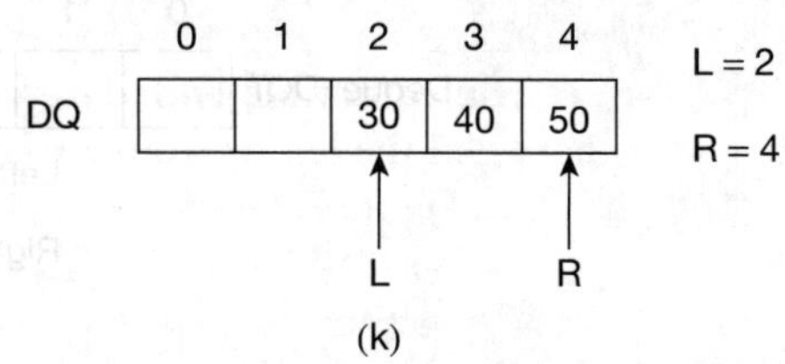

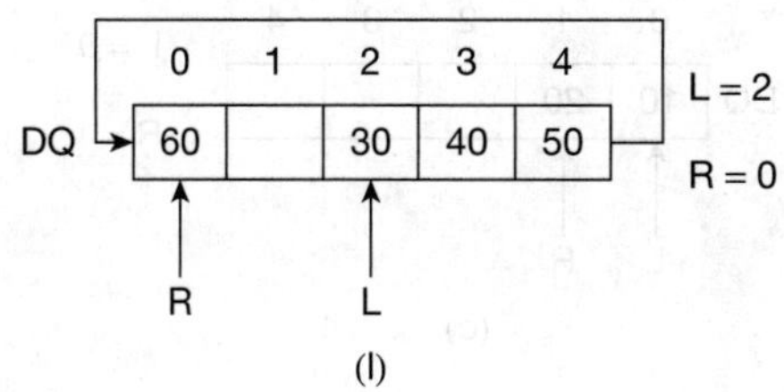

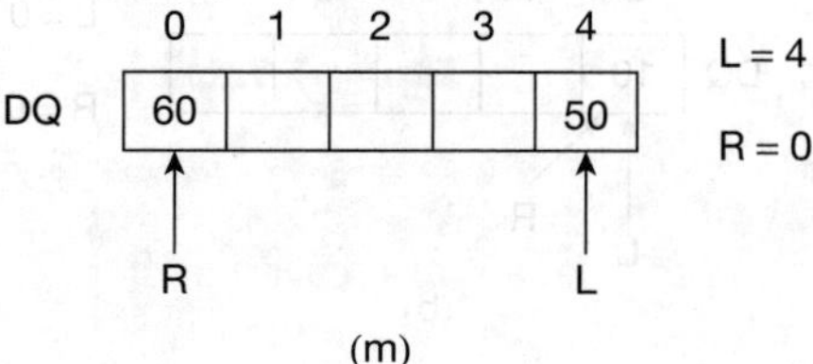

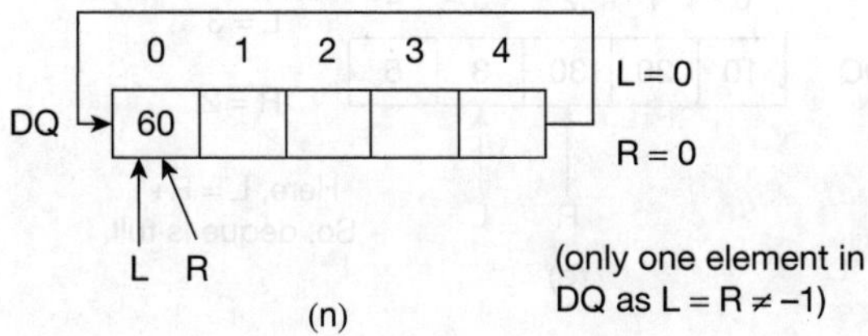

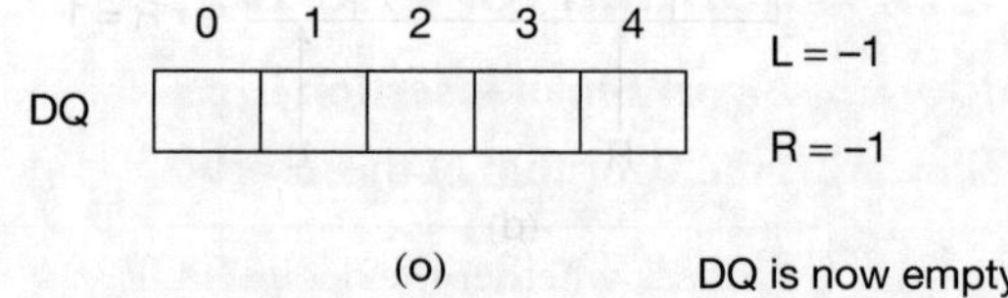

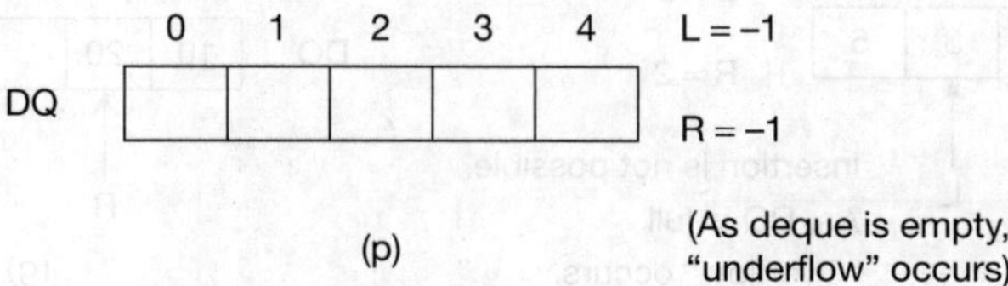

Figure 7.5 Different deque operations.

A double-ended queue can be divided into two extended categories:

1. **Input restricted double-ended queue:** Here, the insertion operation is performed at only one end, either from the left or from right pointer end and deletion operation is performed at both the ends. Figure 7.6 indicates these operations.

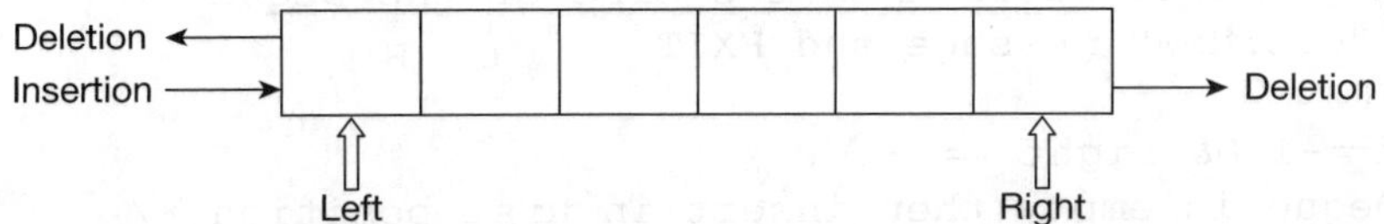

Figure 7.6 Input restricted double-ended queue

2. **Output restricted double-ended queue:** Here, the deletion operation is performed at only one end, either from the left or from the right pointer end and insertion operation is performed at both the ends. Figure 7.7 indicates these operations.

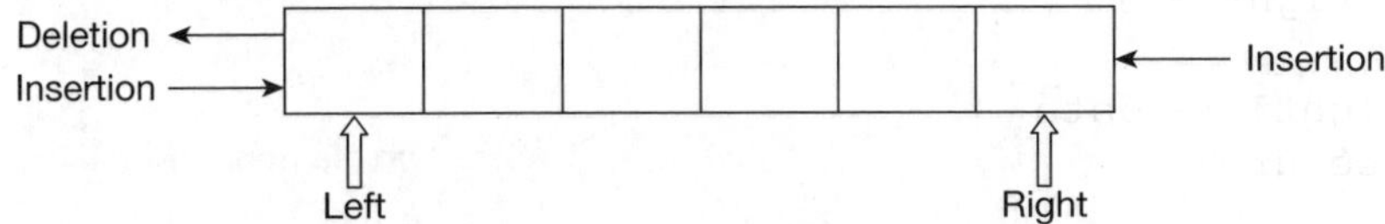

Figure 7.7 Output restricted double-ended queue

> **Note!**
> Double-ended queue is also called deque or dequeue where insertion and deletion operations are performed at both the ends. However, no element can be added or deleted from the middle. The front pointer is called the left pointer and the rear pointer is called the right pointer here.

7.3.3 Algorithm for Insertion and Deletion in Double-ended Queue

Algo-7.5 Algorithm of insertion in a double-ended queue at the right end

Following is the algorithm of the insertion operation of the deque at the right end.

Step 1	Check whether the deque is full or not.
Step 2	If the deque is full, produce an error message “overflow”and exit.
Step 3	If the dequeis not full, set the right pointer value to point to the next empty space.
Step 4	Add the data element to the deque location, where the right is presently pointing.
Step 5	Exit.

Algo-7.6 Pseudocode of insertion in a double-ended queue at the right end

```
Procedure Deque:/* insertion at right */
BEGIN
IF(left==0 && right==n-1) || (left== right + 1)
/* Deque is full where n is the size of the Deque */
RETURN "overflow" message and EXIT
   ENDIF
IF(left==-1 && right == -1)
/* if Deque is empty then insert in first position */
SET left=0 and right=0
   ELSEIF(right==n-1)
/* if right pointing last element then insert at first position
*/
SET right = 0
ELSE
right = right + 1
ENDIF
Deque[right] ← data
END Procedure
```

Algo-7.7 Algorithm of insertion in a double-ended queue at the left end

Following is the algorithm of the insertion operation in the deque at the left end.

Step 1	Check whether Deque is full or not.
Step 2	If the Deque is full, produce an error message "overflow" and exit.
Step 3	If the Deque is not full, set the left pointer value to point the previous empty space.
Step 4	Add the data element to the Deque location, where the left is presently pointing.
Step 5	Exit.

Algo-7.8 Pseudocode of insertion in a double-ended queue at the left end

```
Procedure Deque:/* insertion at left */
BEGIN
IF(left==0 && right==n-1) || (left== right + 1)
/* Deque is full where n is the size of the Deque*/
    RETURN "Overflow" message and EXIT
ENDIF
IF (left==-1 && right == -1)
/* if Dequeis empty then insert in first position */
    SET left=0 and right=0
ELSE IF(left==0)
```

```
/* if left pointing firstelement, then insert at last position */
    SET left = n-1
ELSE
left = left - 1
  ENDIF
Deque[left]← data
END Procedure
```

Algo-7.9 Algorithm of deletion in a double-ended queue at the right end

Removing the right end element from the deque involves the following steps.

Step 1	Check whether the deque is empty or not.
Step 2	If the deque is empty, produce the "Underflow" message and exit.
Step 3	If the deque is not empty, remove the data element at which right is pointing.
Step 4	Set the value of right.
Step 5	Exit.

Algo-7.10 Pseudocode of deletion in a double-ended queue at the right end

```
Procedure Deque:/* Delete from right */
BEGIN
IF(left ==-1 && right ==-1) /*Deque is empty */
RETURN "Underflow" message and EXIT
ENDIF
data ← Deque [right]
IF(left == right) /* only one element within the Deque */
SET left = -1 and right =-1
   ELSEIF (right == 0)
/* if right pointing first element,
then set right pointer at the last position */
SET right = n-1
   ELSE
right = right -1
   ENDIF
RETURN data
END Procedure
```

Algo-7.11 Algorithm of deletion in a double-ended queue at the left end

Removing the left element from the deque involves the following steps.

Step 1	Check whether the deque is empty or not.
Step 2	If the deque is empty, produce the "Underflow" message and exit.

Step 3	If the deque is not empty, remove the data element at which the left is pointing.
Step 4	Set the value of the front.
Step 5	Exit.

Algo-7.12 Pseudocode of deletion in a double-ended queue at the left end

```
Procedure Deque:/* Delete from left */
BEGIN
IF(left ==-1 &&right ==-1) /* Deque is empty */
RETURN "Underflow" message and EXIT
ENDIF
data ← Deque [left]
IF(left == right) /*Only one element within the Deque */
SET left = -1 and right =-1
ELSEIF(left == n-1)
/* if left pointing last element then set left pointer at first
position */
SET left = 0
   ELSE
left = left -1
   ENDIF
RETURN data
END Procedure
```

7.3.4 Implementation of Deque with C

CProg-7.3 Insertion and deletion of an element in the deque

```
#include<stdio.h>
#include<stdlib.h>
/* Defining the linked list node */
struct node
   {
     int info;
     struct node *ptr;
}*front, *rear, *temp, *front1;

int frontelement();
void enque(int data);
void deque();
void empty();
void display();
void create();
void queuesize();
int count = 0;
```

```
/* Driver function */
int main()
  {
     int number;
     int choice;
     int element;
printf( "    Menu   \n»);
printf( "-------------\n»);
printf( " 1 - Enque\n»);
printf( " 2 - Deque\n");
printf( " 3 - Front number\n");
printf( " 4 - Empty\n");
printf( " 5 - Exit\n");
printf( " 6 - Display queue\n");
printf( " 7 - Queue size\n");
printf( "--------------\n");
create();

     while (1)
       {
printf( "--------------\n");
printf(" Enter choice: ");
scanf("\n%d", &choice);
printf( "--------------\n");
         switch (choice)
           {
             case 1:
printf( "--------------\n");
printf(" Enter the number to store in queue: ");
scanf("\n%d", &number);
printf( "--------------\n");
enque(number);
               break;
             case 2:
             deque();
               break;
             case 3:
               element = frontelement();
               if (element != 0)
                {
                   printf("---------------\n");
             printf(" Front number: %d\n", element);
                   printf("---------------\n");
                }
```

```
               else
                {
                  printf("--------------------------------------
-----------------\n");
printf(" No front number in Queue because the queue is EMPTY\n");
                  printf("--------------------------------------
-----------------\n");
                }
               break;
             case 4:
empty();
               break;
             case 5:
               printf("--------------------------------\n");
printf("The program will finish now.\n");
               printf("--------------------------------\n");
exit(0);
             case 6:
display();
               break;
             case 7:
queuesize();
               break;
             default:
         printf("----------------------------------------\n");
printf("Wrong choice, Please enter correct choice: \n");
         printf("----------------------------------------\n");
               break;
          }
       }
     return 0;
   }

/* Create an empty queue */
void create()
   {
     front = rear = NULL;
   }

/* Returns queue size */
void queuesize()
  {
     printf("---------------\n");
printf(" Queue size: ""%d"" numbers in the queue.\n", count);
    printf("---------------\n");
   }
```

```
/* Enqueue operation on the queue */
void enque(int data)
  {
    if (rear == NULL)
      {
        rear = (struct node *)malloc(1*sizeof(struct node));
        rear->ptr = NULL;
        rear->info = data;
        front = rear;
      }
    else
      {
        temp=(struct node *)malloc(1*sizeof(struct node));
        rear->ptr = temp;
        temp->info = data;
        temp->ptr = NULL;
        rear = temp;
      }
    count++;
  }

/* Displaying the queue elements */
void display()
  {
    front1 = front;
if((front1 == NULL) && (rear == NULL))
      {
        printf("---------------\n");
printf(" Queue is empty\n");
       printf("---------------\n");
        return;
      }
   while (front1 != rear)
      {
        printf("---------------\n");
printf(" Displayed queue: ""%d\n", front1->info);
        printf(«---------------\n»);
        front1 = front1->ptr;
      }
if(front1 == rear)
      {
        printf("---------------\n");
printf(" Displayed queue: ""%d\n", front1->info);
        printf("---------------\n");
      }
  }
```

```
/* Dequeue operation on the queue */
void deque()
  {
    front1 = front;
if(front1 == NULL)
    {
  printf("-----------------------------------------------\n");
printf(" Error: Trying to deque number from empty queue!\n");
  printf("-----------------------------------------------\n");
        return;
    }
    else
      if(front1->ptr != NULL)
       {
          front1 = front1->ptr;
          printf(«--------------\n»);
printf(" Dequed number: ""%d\n", front->info);
          printf("---------------\n");
          free(front);
          front = front1;
       }
    else
     {
        printf("---------------\n");
printf("Dequed number: ""%d\n", front->info);;
        printf("---------------\n");
        free(front);
        front = NULL;
        rear = NULL;
    }
   count--;
  }

/* Returns the front element of queue */
int frontelement()
  {
    if ((front != NULL) && (rear != NULL))
      return(front->info);
    else
      return 0;
  }

/* Display if the queue is empty or not */
void empty()
  {
if((front == NULL) && (rear == NULL))
```

```
        {
          printf("-----------------\n");
    printf("Sorry but queue is empty\n");
          printf("-----------------\n");
        }
      else
        {
          printf("-------------------\n");
    printf("Queue is not empty!\n");
          printf("-------------------\n");
        }
    }
    /* End of program */
```

Output

```
    Menu
--------------
 1 - Enque
 2 - Deque
 3 - Front number
 4 - Empty
 5 - Exit
 6 - Display queue
 7 - Queue size
---------------
Enter choice: 1
Enter the number to store in queue: 25
Enter choice: 1
Enter the number to store in queue: 54
Enter choice: 6
Displayed queue: 25
Displayed queue: 54
Enter choice: 3
Front number: 25
Enter choice: 2
Dequed number: 25
Enter choice: 7
Queue size: 1 numbers in the queue.
Enter choice: 5
-----------------------------------
 The program is finished.
-----------------------------------
```

Programming Tips!
Insertion, deletion, display etc. have been used for all deque operations.

7.3.5 Implementation of Deque with Python

PyProg-7.3 Insertion and deletion of an element in the deque

```
# importing collections library for deque operations
import collections

# initializing deque
de = collections.deque([1,2,3])

# To insert element (4) at right end at the end of deque
de.append(4)

# printing modified deque
print("The deque after appending at right is : ")
print(de)

# To insert element (6) at the beginning of deque
de.appendleft(6)

# printing modified deque
print("The deque after appending at left is : ")
print(de)

# To delete element (4) from right end of deque
de.pop()

# Printing modified deque
print("The deque after deleting from right is : ")
print(de)

# To delete element (6) from left end of deque
de.popleft()

# printing modified deque
print("The deque after deleting from left is : ")
print(de)
## End program
```

Output

```
The deque after appending at right is :
deque([1, 2, 3, 4])
The deque after appending at left is :
deque([6, 1, 2, 3, 4])
The deque after deleting from right is :
deque([6, 1, 2, 3])
The deque after deleting from left is :
deque([1, 2, 3])
```

> ***Programming Tips!***
> The deque module is a part of the collection's library in Python. It has the methods for inserting and deleting elements which can be invoked directly with arguments. Collection's library has been imported to declare a deque.

7.4 PRIORITY QUEUE

The priority queue is an abstract data type where each element has a priority assigned to it. It is a variant of the queue data structure in which insertion is performed in the order of arrival and deletion is performed based on the priority. In the priority queue, an element with the highest priority assigned is processed first. If two elements have the same priority, then they are served according to the order they were inserted in the queue.

A priority queue can be of two types:

- **Max-priority queue:** Element with the highest priority is processed first.
- **Min-priority queue:** Element with the lowest priority is processed first.

Example 7.2

Let us say we have an array of 5 elements: {10 (p2), 17 (p3), 11(p2), 15(p1), 12(p3)} and we have to insert all the elements in the max-priority queue. In a max priority queue, elements that have higher priority will be deleted first from the queue. Here, in the above element list, p3 has a higher priority than p1.

First, as the priority queue is empty, 10 will be inserted initially and then 17, 11, 15, 12 respectively, as they arrive. But at the time of deletion, 17 will be deleted first as it has a higher priority. 12 also has the same priority but 17 arrives before 12 (FIFO), and hence 12 will be deleted first because, among {10, 11, 15 and 12}, 12 has higher priority compared to others. Now we have {10, 11, 15} in the queue. Now 10 will be deleted because 10 has priority p2, which arrives before 11; then 11 and 15 will be deleted respectively.

Applications of the priority queue are in CPU scheduling, graph algorithms like Dijkstra's shortest-path algorithm, Prim's minimum spanning tree, and all queue applications where priority is involved.

7.4.1 Implementation of Priority Queue with C

CProg-7.4 Implementing priority queue using linked list

```
#include<stdio.h>
#include<math.h>
#include<stdlib.h>
#define MAX 100 /* Declaring the maximum size of the queue */

void swap(int*, int*);

int main()
   {
      int choice, num, n, a[MAX], data, s;
      void display(int[], int);
      void insert(int[], int, int, int);
```

```
    int del_hi_priori(int[], int, int);
    n = 0; /* Represents number of nodes in the queue */
    int lb = 0; /* Lower bound of the array is initialized to 0 */
while(1)
     {
printf(".....MAIN MENU.....\n");
printf("1.Insert. \n");
printf("2.Delete. \n");
printf("3.Display. \n");
printf("4.Quit. \n");
printf("Enter your choice : ");
scanf("%d", &choice);
        switch(choice)
          {
           case 1: /* choice to accept an element and insert it in
           the queue */
      printf("Enter data to be inserted : ");
      scanf("%d", &data);
      insert(a, n, data, lb);
             n++;
             break;
           case 2:
             s = del_hi_priori(a, n + 1, lb);
      if(s != 0)
      printf("\nThe deleted value is : %d \n", s);
      if(n > 0)
               n--;
             break;
            case 3: /* choice to display the elements of the queue */
             printf("\n");
      display(a, n);
             break;
           case 4: /* choice to exit from the program */
             return 0;
           default:
      printf("Invalid choice. \n");
           }
printf("\n \n");
      }
    return 0;
  }

/* This function inserts an element in the queue */
void insert(int a[], int heapsize, int data, int lb)
```

```
   {
      int i, p;
      int parent(int);
if(heapsize == MAX)
        {
printf("Queue Is Full!! \n");
         return;
        }
i = lb + heapsize;
      a[i] = data;
while(i>lb&& a[p = parent(i)] < a[i])
        {
         swap(&a[p], &a[i]);
i = p;
        }
   }

/* This function deletes an element from the queue */
int del_hi_priori(int a[], int heapsize, int lb)
   {
      int data, i, l, r, max_child, t;
      int left(int);
      int right(int);
if(heapsize == 1)
        {
printf("Queue Is Empty!! \n");
         return 0;
        }
      t = a[lb];
      swap(&a[lb], &a[heapsize - 1]);
i = lb;
heapsize--;
while(1)
        {
if((l = left(i)) >= heapsize)
         break;
if((r = right(i)) >= heapsize)
max_child = l;
         else
max_child = (a[l] > a[r]) ? l : r;
         if(a[i] >= a[max_child])
           break;
        swap(&a[i], &a[max_child]);
i = max_child;
       }
```

```
      return t;
   }

/* Returns parent index */
int parent(int i)
   {
      float p;
      p = ((float) i / 2.0) - 1.0;
      return ceil(p);
   }

/* Returns left child index */
int left(int i)
   {
      return 2 * i + 1;
   }

/* Returns right child index */
int right(int i)
   {
      return 2 * i + 2;
   }

/* This function displays the queue */
void display(int a[], int n)
   {
      int i;
if(n == 0)
        {
printf("Queue Is Empty!! \n");
         return;
        }
for(i = 0; i< n; i++)
printf("%d ", a[i]);
      printf("\n");
   }

/* This function is used to swap two elements */
void swap(int *p, int *q)
   {
      int temp;
      temp = *p;
      *p = *q;
      *q = temp;
   }
/* End of program */
```

Output

```
.....MAIN MENU.....
1.Insert.
2.Delete.
3.Display.
4.Quit.
Enter your choice : 1
Enter data to be inserted : 55
Enter your choice : 1
Enter data to be inserted : 86
Enter your choice : 1
Enter data to be inserted : 49
Enter your choice : 3
86 55 49
Enter your choice : 2
The deleted value is : 86
Enter your choice : 4
---------------------------
```

> ***Programming Tips!***
> `insert()`, `del_hi_prior()` and `display()` have been used to implement the priority queue. Deletion will take place according to the element's priority.

7.4.2 Implementation of Priority Queue with Python

PyProg-7.4 Implementing a priority queue using linked list

```
# Class to create priority queue
class PriorityQueue(object):
  # Constructor to initialize the class variables
  def __init__(self):
    self.queue = []

  def __str__(self):
    return ' '.join([str(i) for i in self.queue])

  # Checking if the queue is empty
  def isEmpty(self):
    return len(self.queue) == []


  # Inserting an element in the queue
  def insert(self, data):
    self.queue.append(data)
```

```
    # Popping an element based on Priority
    def delete(self):
        try:
            max = 0
            for i in range(len(self.queue)):
                if self.queue[i] > self.queue[max]:
                    max = i
            item = self.queue[max]
            del self.queue[max]
            return item
        except IndexError:
            print()
            exit()

# Driver code
if __name__ == '__main__':
    myQueue = PriorityQueue()
    myQueue.insert(12)
    myQueue.insert(1)
    myQueue.insert(14)
    myQueue.insert(7)
    print(myQueue)
    while not myQueue.isEmpty():
        print(myQueue.delete())
## End program
```

Output

```
12 1 14 7
14
12
7
1
```

Programming Tips!

Priority Queue class has been used to create the priority queue. `insert()` and `delete()` are used to implement the operations on priority queue.

Note!

The highest priority element is processed first in a max-priority queue and lowest priority element is processed first in a min-priority queue. If two elements have the same priority, then they are served according to the order in which they were inserted in the queue.

7.5 IMPLEMENT QUEUE USING TWO STACKS WITH THE HELP OF ARRAYS

A queue can also be implemented using two stacks. If we are given a stack with push and pop operations, the task is to implement a queue using instances of stack data structure and operations on them. The following Fig. 7.8 presents this concept diagrammatically. The procedure is given below:

1. Take two stacks – stack1, stack2.
2. push operation will be done on stack1 – like Push 10, 20 and then 30 respectively and then pop() operations will be done on stack1. So, 30 will be popped and will be pushed into stack2, then 20 will be popped out from stack1 and again pushed into stack2. At last, 10 will be popped out and will be pushed into stack2. So, stack1 is now empty. Now stack2 has 30, 20 and 10 respectively.
3. Now, pop operation is called three times from stack2 and 10, 20 and then 30 will pop out respectively. Now, stack2 is empty and we get the elements like a queue sequence.

Example 7.3

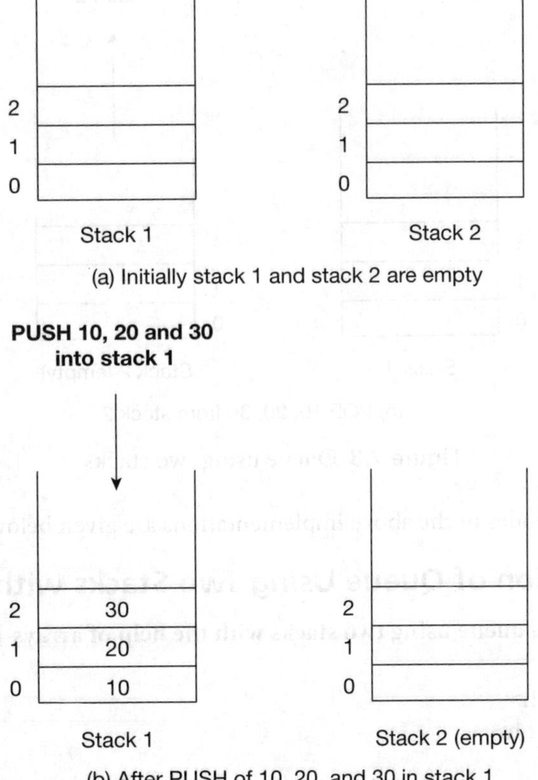

(a) Initially stack 1 and stack 2 are empty

(b) After PUSH of 10, 20, and 30 in stack 1

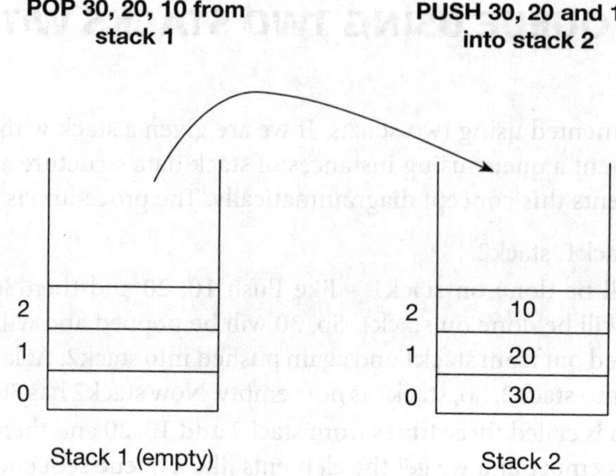

(c) PUSH 30, 20, and 10 into stack 2 from stack 1

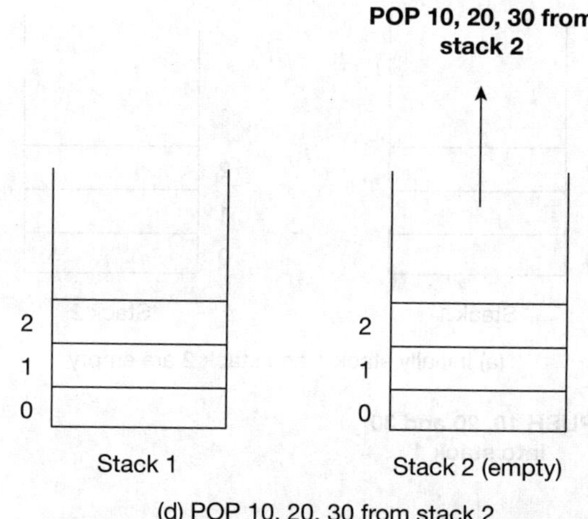

(d) POP 10, 20, 30 from stack 2

Figure 7.8 Queue using two stacks

The C and Python source codes of the above implementations are given below.

7.5.1 Implementation of Queue Using Two Stacks with C

CProg-7.5 Implementing queue using two stacks with the help of arrays

```
#include<stdio.h>
#include<stdlib.h>

/* structure of a stack node */
struct sNode
   {
     int data;
```

```
    struct sNode *next;
  };

/* Function to push an item to stack*/
void push(struct sNode** top_ref, int new_data);

/* Function to pop an item from stack*/
int pop(struct sNode** top_ref);

/* structure of queue having two stacks */
struct queue
  {
    struct sNode *stack1;
    struct sNode *stack2;
  };

/* Function to enqueue an item to queue */
void enQueue(struct queue *q, int x)
  {
    push(&q->stack1, x);
  }

/* Function to dequeue an item from queue */
int deQueue(struct queue *q)
  {
    int x;
    /* If both stacks are empty then error */
    if(q->stack1 == NULL && q->stack2 == NULL)
      {
printf("Q is empty");
getchar();
exit(0);
      }

    /* Move elements from satck1 to stack2 only if stack2 is
    empty */
    if(q->stack2 == NULL)
      {
        while(q->stack1 != NULL)
          {
            x = pop(&q->stack1);
            push(&q->stack2, x);
          }
      }
    x = pop(&q->stack2);
    return x;
  }
```

```
int isEmpty(struct queue *q)
   {
     return (q->stack1 == NULL && q-> stack2 == NULL);
   }

/* Function to push an item to stack*/
void push(struct sNode** top_ref, int new_data)
   {
     /* allocate node */
      struct sNode* new_node = (struct sNode*) malloc(sizeof
(struct sNode));
if(new_node == NULL)
      {
     printf("Stack overflow \n");
getchar();
exit(0);
      }

     /* put in the data */
new_node->data = new_data;

     /* link the old list of the new node */
new_node->next = (*top_ref);

     /* move the head to point to the new node */
     (*top_ref) = new_node;
   }

/* Function to pop an item from stack*/
int pop(struct sNode** top_ref)
   {
     int res;
     struct sNode *top;

    /*If the stack is empty then error */
if(*top_ref == NULL)
      {
printf("Stack overflow \n");
getchar();
exit(0);
      }
     else
      {
         top = *top_ref;
         res = top->data;
        *top_ref = top->next;
```

```
        free(top);
        return res;
      }
   }

/* Driver function to test the above functions */
int main()
   {
        struct  queue  *q  =  (struct  queue*)malloc(sizeof(struct
queue));
    q->stack1 = NULL;
     q->stack2 = NULL;
enQueue(q, 80);
enQueue(q, 100);
enQueue(q, 10);
enQueue(q, 20);
enQueue(q, 30);
     deQueue(q);
enQueue(q, 40);
enQueue(q, 50);
     deQueue(q);
enQueue(q, 60);

     /* Dequeue items */
     while(!isEmpty(q))
printf(«%d\n», deQueue(q));
     return 0;
   }
/* End of program */
```

Output

```
10
20
30
40
50
60
```

> ***Programming Tips!***
> If we are trying to implement a queue using two stacks and push 10, 20, 30 to a stack, we need to call dequeue method 3 times. 10, 20, 30 will be the order of elements to come out if we pop them from the stack. We need to access the elements in reverse order that they exist in the stack.

7.5.2 Implementation of Queue Using Two Stacks with Python

PyProg-7.5 **Implementing a queue using two stacks with the help of arrays**

```
 # Class to create priority queue
 class Queue:
   # Constructor to initialize the class variables
   def __init__(self):
```

```
    self.s1 = []
    self.s2 = []

  def enQueue(self, x):
    # Move all elements from s1 to s2
    while len(self.s1) != 0:
      self.s2.append(self.s1[-1])
      self.s1.pop()

    # Push item into self.s1
    self.s1.append(x)

    # Push everything back to s1
    while len(self.s2) != 0:
      self.s1.append(self.s2[-1])
      self.s2.pop()

  # Dequeue an item from the queue
  def deQueue(self):

    # if first stack is empty
    if len(self.s1) == 0:
      print("Q is Empty")

    # Return top of self.s1
    x = self.s1[-1]
    self.s1.pop()
    return x

# Driver code
if __name__ == '__main__':
  q = Queue()
  q.enQueue(1)
  q.enQueue(2)
  q.enQueue(3)

  print(q.deQueue())
  print(q.deQueue())
  print(q.deQueue())
## End program
```

Output

1
2
3

Programming Tips!

Two instance variables self.s1 and self.s2 have to be used to implement the queue using two stacks. `enQueue()` and `deQueue()` are used for insertion and deletion of elements.

QUICK RECAP

- ☑ The queue is a collection of elements maintained in a sequence where the addition of elements takes place at one end, called rear (or back or tail), and removal of elements takes place from other end, called front or head.
- ☑ It is a linear data structure. It follows the FIFO property. It has two pointers, front and rear, that point to the first and last elements of the queue respectively. Initially, the queue is empty. Insertion and deletion in the queue can only be done from the starting index.
- ☑ Insertion is known as Qinsert and deletion is known as Qdelete. Before executing insertion or deletion operations, we need to (1) determine whether the queue is empty or not, and (2) check whether the queue is full or not. If the queue is not full, insert a new element at the rear of the queue. This operation is termed as Qinsert (or enQueue). If the queue is not empty, we can delete the element at the front pointer end. This operation is called Qdelete (or deQueue).
- ☑ If (front = 0 and rear = queue size −1) OR (front = rear + 1) is true and we are trying to insert an element, then "overflow" will occur. If (front = = −1) is true and we are trying to delete an element, then "underflow" will occur.
- ☑ We can implement a queue using both array and linked list data structures.
- ☑ A double-ended queue is also called deque (or dequeue). In deque, insertion and deletion operations are performed at both the ends (front and rear). However, no element can be added or deleted at the middle. In the deque, the front pointer is called the left pointer and the rear pointer is called the right pointer.
- ☑ In a priority queue, the highest priority element is processed first. If two elements have the same priority, then they are served according to the order in which they were inserted in the queue. In a max-priority queue, the element with the highest priority is processed first whereas in a min-priority queue, the element with the lowest priority is processed first.
- ☑ Both the C and Python language can efficiently implement the algorithms of queue data structure related problems.

REVIEW QUESTIONS

Multiple Choice Questions (MCQ): Choose the Best Alternative

Easy

1. ________ is a linear data structure where elements can be added or removed at either end but not in the middle.

A. Queue B. Tree
C. Stack D. Deque

2. If the elements X, Y, Z and W are placed in a queue and deleted one at a time, what will be the sequence of their removal?

A. XZWY B. WYZX
C. WXYZ D. XYZW

3. What happens if we insert an element into a full queue?

A. Null pointer exception
B. Underflow
C. Overflow
D. Program won't be compiled

4. Priority queue can be implemented using:

A. Array B. Linked List
C. stack D. None of these.

5. Where will a new element be inserted in linked list implementation of a queue?

A. At the head of link list
B. At the last of the link list
C. At the center position in the link list
D. None.

Moderate

6. The deque can be used as:
   A. Stack B. Queue
   C. Both of A and B. D. None of these.
7. A circular queue is implemented using an array of size 5. The array index starts with 0, the front is 3, and the rear is 4. The insertion of the next element takes place at the array index ______.
   A. 0 B. 5
   C. 2 D. 1
8. How to increment the rear end of a circular queue if the array index starts with 0?
   A. rear++ B. (rear+1) % size
   C. (rear % size) + 1 D. rear--
   Hint: Ensures rear takes the values from 0 to size –1.
9. What is the need for a circular queue?
   A. Effective usage of memory
   B. Easier computations
   C. To delete elements based on priority
   D. Implementation of LIFO principle in queues
10. In linked list implementation of a queue, front and rear pointers are tracked. Which of the following pointers will change during an insertion into a non-empty queue?
    A. Only front pointer
    B. Only rear pointer
    C. Both front and rear pointer
    D. No pointer will be changed.
    Hint: Since the queue follows FIFO, a new element is inserted at last.
11. Which of the following conditions is important for a queue to be empty in the linked list implementation?
    A. FRONT is null
    B. FRONT=REAR
    C. FRONT = REAR-1
    D. None of these.
    Hint: The front pointer pointing to the first node of the queue.
12. Which of the following statements is true about the linked list implementation of a queue?
    A. In a push operation, if new nodes are inserted at the beginning, then in pop operation, nodes must be removed from the beginning.
    B. In a push operation, if new nodes are inserted at the beginning of the linked list, then in pop operation, nodes must be removed from the end.
    C. In a push operation, if new nodes are inserted at the end, then in pop operation, nodes must be removed from the end.
    D. In a push operation, if new nodes are inserted at the end, then in pop operation, nodes must be removed from the beginning.

Higher-order Thinking Skills (HOTS)

13. What is the time complexity of inserting a node based on position in a priority queue?
    A. O(nlogn) B. O(logn)
    C. O(n) D. $O(n^2)$
    Hint: In the worst case, we have to traverse the entire list.
14. Let the following circular queue accommodate a maximum of six elements with the following data where the index starts from 0.
    front = 3, rear = 5, queue = _, _, _, L, M, N.
    What will happen after the insertion of X?
    A. front = 2; rear = 5; queue = _, _, L, M, N, X
    B. front = 1; rear = 4; queue = _, L, M, N, X, _
    C. front = 0; rear = 3; queue = L, M, N, X, _, _
    D. front = 3; rear = 0; queue = X, _, _, L, M, N
15. In linked list implementation of queue, if only the front pointer is maintained, which of the following operations takes worst-case linear time?
    A. Insertion
    B. Deletion
    C. To empty a queue
    D. Both insertion and to empty a queue.
    Hint: Since the front pointer is used for deletion, it is the worst casetime for the insertion and empty operations.
16. An array of size MAX_SIZE is used to implement a circular queue. Front, rear, and count are tracked. Suppose front is 0 and the rear is MAX_SIZE - 1. How many elements are present in the queue?
    A. MAX_SIZE – 1 B. MAX_SIZE
    C. Zero D. One
17. Suppose a circular queue of size $(n - 1)$ is represented with an array of n elements. Also assume REAR = FRONT = 0. Which of the following are the conditions to detect whether the queue is full and the queue is empty?
    A. Full: REAR == FRONT, Empty: (REAR+1) mod (n) == FRONT

B. Full: (REAR+1) mod (n) == FRONT, Empty: (FRONT+1) mod (n) == REAR
C. Full: (REAR+1) mod (n) == FRONT, Empty: REAR == FRONT
D. Full: (FRONT+1) mod (n) == REAR, Empty: REAR == FRONT

Hint: When the rear or front is at the index ($n-1$), the next operation will happen at index 0 in a circular queue. We may reserve one empty spot to detect the overflow (queue full) and underflow (queue empty) conditions.

Short Answer-type Questions

Easy

1. What is a queue and where can it be used?
2. What is the difference between queue and deque?
3. What are the differences between stack and queue?
4. What is a priority queue?
5. What is a circular queue?

Moderate

6. Write the characteristics of a queue.
7. What are the applications of the deque?
8. What are the differences between the rear and front nodes in a queue?
9. What are the objectives of enQueue and deQueue functions in the queue?
10. When will overflow and underflow occur in the queue?

Higher-Order Thinking Skills (HOTS)

11. How two stacks can be used for implementing a queue?
12. How can we implement a stack using a single queue?
13. Suppose the top pointer is on a priority queue that has exactly two entries with the same priority. How is the return value of the top selected?
14. How can we reverse the queue elements?
15. Write the rules for operations in a double-ended queue and a priority queue.

Descriptive-type Questions

Easy

1. Write the algorithms of Qinsert and Qdelete of the circular queue.
2. Explain the process of queue implementations using an array.
3. Explain the process of queue implementations using a linked list.
4. Write the algorithms of Qinsert and Qdelete of the double-ended queue
5. Explain the process to implement priority queue using linked lists.

Moderate

6. Briefly explain the applications of the queue data structure.
7. Write the algorithms to insert a node in the deque at the right end.
8. Write the method of inserting a node in the deque at the left end.
9. Write the technique for deleting a node from the deque at the right end.
10. Give the algorithm to delete a node from the deque at the left end.

Higher-Order Thinking Skills (HOTS)

11. Design an algorithm to implement a priority queue using a linked list.
12. In a queue A[0 to $n-1$], assume that SIZE – 1 locations in the array are available for storing the elements (with the other elements used to detect full/empty condition). Write an equation for the number of elements in the queue in terms of rear and front.
13. Implement double-ended queues using linked lists.
14. Write an algorithm to reverse the first n elements of a queue.

CASE STUDIES

1. Suppose a user sends a file to a shared printer for printing and the process is in a queue with other jobs. The user can access and remove the file any time before the printer prints the file. Add a deletion algorithm which expects an integer index as an argument and then deletes the process as well as returns the position (index starts from 0).

2. Consider the series [1, 2, 3, 4, 5, 16, 7, 8, 9, 10]. Divide this series into two parts, [1, 2, 3, 4, 5] and [6, 7, 8, 9, 10]. Design an algorithm to get the output as [1, 6, 2, 7, 3, 8, 4, 9, 5, 10], i.e., combine the two series taking one element from the first and one element from the other part alternately.

LAB EXERCISES

1. Write a C program for reversing a queue.
2. Write a Python program to check if a queue can be sorted into another queue using a stack. Given a queue of first n natural numbers, the task is to check whether the given queue elements can be arranged in increasing order in another queue using a stack. The operations allowed are:
   1. Push and pop elements from the stack
   2. Qdelete from the given queue.
   3. Qinsert in another queue.

   Example: Input: Queue[] = {5, 1, 2, 3, 4},
   Output: Possible

ANSWER KEYS

Multiple Choice Questions

1. D	**4.** B	**7.** A	**10.** B	**13.** C	**16.** B
2. D	**5.** B	**8.** B	**11.** A	**14.** D	**17.** C
3. C	**6.** C	**9.** A	**12.** B	**15.** D	

8 Recursion

CONTENTS

EXPECTED OUTCOMES OF THIS CHAPTER

After going through this chapter learners will be able

- ☑ To learn how to solve computational problems using recursion technique
- ☑ To understand how recursion is implemented by programming languages
- ☑ To understand the differences between recursion and iteration
- ☑ To formulate the following problems using recursion: GCD finding, factorial finding, Fibonacci series finding, Akermann number finding, representation of Pascal's triangle, Tower of Hanoi problem, n-Queens problem, sorting of a stack
- ☑ To explain the concept of dynamic programming and memoization
- ☑ To implement the above problems using C and Python.

8.1 INTRODUCTION

Recursion is a programming technique that allows the programmer to call a function itself. It is the process of repeating a function in a self-similar way. More precisely, recursion is a technique that allows us to break down a problem into one or more sub-problems that are similar to the form of the original problem.

In programming languages, if a program allows you to call a function inside the same function, then it is called a recursive call of the function. In C language, following is the syntax of a recursive function definition:

```
void recursion()
  {
    recursion(); /* function calls itself */
  }

int main()
  {
    recursion();
  }
```

The C programming language supports recursion, i.e., a function can call itself. In the above syntax, 'recursion' function is calling itself. While using recursion, programmers need to be careful to define an exit condition from the function. Otherwise, it will go into an infinite loop. Many learners think that recursion is a technique useful for only a few special problems like computing factorials, Fibonacci series, etc. But, the function implemented using `if-else`, or `while`, or looping statements can also be implemented using recursive functions. This recursive function is much easier to understand compared to its iterative counterpart. There are many differences between iterative function and recursive function, which will be discussed in a later section of this chapter.

8.1.1 Definition

A function that calls itself is known as a recursive function. This function-calling technique is known as recursion. In many cases, a function is invoked by another function. The function executes its code and then returns the control to the calling function. Here, a function can be called by itself, or it may call another function, which in turn, calls the same function inside it. This is known as recursion.

A recursive function must have two properties given below:

1. The function should have certain criteria, called *base criteria,* for which the procedure does not call itself.
2. Each time the procedure calls itself, it must check the base criteria (or condition/case).

> **Note!**
> A function that calls itself is known as a recursive function and such function-calling technique is known as recursion.

Why Do We Use Recursion?

The idea is to represent a bigger problem into small groups of problems (one or more), and add one or more base conditions which will stop the recursion; otherwise, the function will execute infinite times. For example, we can calculate the factorial of a number n if we know the factorial of $(n - 1)$. The base case for this problem would be $n = 0$. We will return 1 when n becomes 0.

In the recursive program, the solution to the base case is provided, and the solution to the bigger problem is expressed in terms of smaller problems.

```
int fact(int n)
 {
    if(n < = 1) // base case
      return 1;
    else
    return n*fact(n-1); // recursive case
 }
```

In the above example, we are calculating factorial n using a C program. Base case is defined by $n <= 1$ while it returns 0. The problem of calculating the factorial of a large number (n) can be solved by converting it to smaller ones and executing these till the base case is reached.

> **Note!**
> A recursive algorithm must have a base case or exit condition.

8.1.2 Classification of Recursion

Recursion can be classified into two categories depending on the function-calling techniques.

1. **Direct recursion**: The function called by itself, is known as a direct recursive function (or recursive function). For example,

```
func1() ◄─┐
{         │
  ......  │
  func1();┘
  ......
}
```

   In the above example, function `func1()` calls itself directly within its body.

2. **Indirect recursion:** When a function calls a different function and this, in turn, calls the original function, it is known as indirect recursion. More than one function is used here. For example,

```
func1()
{
    ......
    func2();
    
}

func2()
{
    ......
    func1();
}
```

In the above example, function `func1()` calls the function `func2()`. Function `func2()` is calling the original function `func1()` within its body. So, `func1()` is calling itself indirectly. This process is called indirect recursion.

Depending upon the *number of recursive calls*, recursion can be divided further into the following three more categories.

1. **Linear recursions:** It performs a single recursive function call. The factorial function is a good example of linear recursion (discussed later in this chapter).
2. **Binary recursions**: Some recursive functions have two recursive calls for each non-base case. Functions with two recursive calls are referred to as binary recursive functions.
3. **Multiple recursions:** It performs many recursive calls.

> ***Note!***
> Depending upon the number of recursive calls, recursion can be divided further into three more categories – linear, binary and multiple recursions.

Depending upon the *nature of recursive call definitions*, recursion can be divided further into two categories.

Tail recursion: The last operation of the function is a recursive call in this recursion. There are no outstanding operations when a function directly returns the result of a recursive call. A single recursive call occurs at the end of the function to implement the tail recursion. No other statements follow the recursive call, and there are no other recursive calls before the call at the end of the function. So, a function is said to be tail-recursive if no operations are pending when the recursive function returns to its caller. Recall the previously discussed example in Section 8.1.1 presenting the factorial of a number.

```
long fact(long n, long m)
 {
  if(n == 0)
     return m;
  else
     return fact(n-1, m*n);
 }
```

To make it tail-recursive, information about pending tasks has to be tracked. Another example of a tail-recursive C function is given below.

```
void tail(int i)
 {
   if(i > 0)
    {
      printf("%d", tail(i-1));
    }
 }
```

Essentially, the tail recursion is a loop. It can be replaced by an iterative algorithm to accomplish the same task. In fact, in most cases, languages supporting loops should use this construct rather than recursion

Non-tail Recursion: There are outstanding operations after the recursive call in this method. When implementing non-tail recursion iteratively, the stack must be explicitly implemented and used. The following example is a non-tail recursive solution for the factorial of a number.

```
int fact(int n)
 {
   if(n == 0)
      return 1;
   else
      return n*fact(n-1);
 }
```

When returning from a recursive call, there is still one pending operation, multiplication. Therefore, the above example code of factorial calculation is a non-tail recursive method.

Tail recursive functions are superior to the non-tail recursive functions. The compiler optimizes tail-recursive functions as there is no task left after the recursive call. It will be easier for the compiler to optimize the code since the recursive call is the last statement, and there is nothing left to do in the current function. Thus, saving the current function's address into the stack is of no use.

> ***Note!***
> Depending upon the nature of recursive call definitions, recursion can be divided into further two categories, tail and non-tail recursions.

8.1.3 Recursion vs. Iteration

A practical way to think of recursive functions is to use iterations where one of the instructions is to repeat the process. This makes it sound very similar to a loop because it repeats the same code. Until now, we have discussed recursion, but both recursion and iteration repeatedly execute the set of instructions. Recursion is required when a statement in a function calls itself repeatedly, whereas iteration is required when a loop repeatedly executes until the condition becomes false. The primary difference between recursion and iteration is that recursion is a process, always applied to a function, and iteration is applied to the set of instructions which programmers want to get repeatedly executed. The following Table 8.1 presents the comparison between recursion and iteration.

Table 8.1 Comparison between recursion and iteration

S. No.	Recursion	Iteration
1.	Function calls itself. Recursion uses a selection structure.	A set of instructions repeatedly executed using a loop structure.
2	Recursion terminates when a base case is recognized. After that, there will be no function call.	Iteration terminates when the termination condition for the loop ceases to be false.
3	Recursion uses more memory than iteration. Recursion is used when code size needs to be small, and time complexity is not an issue.	Iteration uses less memory than recursion. Iteration is used when time complexity needs to be balanced.
4	Recursion makes the source code smaller than that using iteration.	Iteration makes the source code larger than that using recursion.
5	Recursion is usually slower than iteration due to the overhead of maintaining the stack. The time complexity of recursion is exponential in general.	Iteration is usually faster than iteration. The time complexity of iteration is polynomial-logarithmic in general.
6	Recursions have applications in functions.	Iterations have applications in loops.

8.1.4 Relation Between Stack and Recursion

The stack is a LIFO (Last-In–First-Out) data structure as discussed in Chapter 6. Recursion is the technique of solving a problem by calling the same function again and again until some breaking (base) condition occurs where recursion stops. It starts calculating the solution thereon. A function that calls another function must save the temporary state in a stack, so that upon return of the call, the suspended state and any subsequent operations can be resumed. A recursive function is one that calls itself. A typical example is a factorial defined as $1! = 1$; $n! = n^*(n - 1)!$ as discussed in Section 8.1.1. Suppose $n = 5$, it means we are trying to find out the factorial of 5.

If we trace the function fact(5), then

fact(5) = 5 * fact (4)
= 5 * 4 * fact (3)
= 5 * 4 * 3 * fact(2)
= 5 * 4 * 3 * 2 * fact(1)
= 5 * 4 * 3 * 2 * 1
= 120

Stack Representation During the Call

Now in the above example, we have the base condition, either n is 0 or 1 and factorial will be 1. The programmer first calls function F5 (fact(5) here) at the time of execution. F5 calls function 4 (F4) and F5 address will be pushed into the stack. Again, F4 calls function 3 (F3) and it goes on in this way until control reaches the base condition (Fig. 8.1).

The nature of nested function calling and returning is the same as that of a stack. The one that is called at the top level (or the earliest) is returned at the last. The later function is called in the nested hierarchy and the earliest it returns. So, the start/return of a function call turns out analogous to push/pop operations of a stack and thus a stack can be used to mimic this functionality. To calculate the final solution, we need all the numbers in the same order, i.e., last-in–first-out data structure and hence, stack is the best choice.

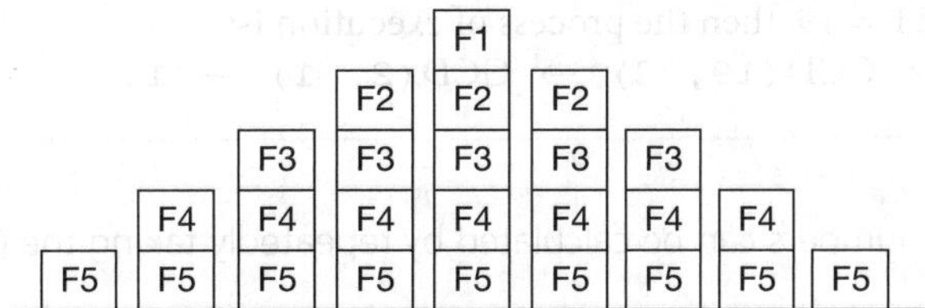

Figure 8.1 Stack representation of recursion call

8.1.5 Applications of Recursive Functions

The applications of recursion are important in the computer science field, especially in computer programming. To make the programmer's task easier and feasible to solve, we break down a problem into smaller sub-problems. This is one of the foundations of artificial intelligence (AI). One important data structure – tree – cannot exist without recursion. Besides using recursion, we may also represent the tree data structure in an iterative way but this will be cumbersome to handle. Many of the well-known sorting algorithms like quick sort and merge sort, (discussed later) use recursion. All the puzzle games (chess, candy crush, etc.) broadly use recursion-based techniques. The uses of recursion are also numerous nowadays because it is the backbone of major sorting and searching algorithms. We will discuss GCD finding, factorial finding, Fibonacci series finding, Akermann number finding, representation of Pascal's triangle, Tower of Hanoi problem, n-Queens problem, and sorting of a stack problem using recursion later in the following sections.

8.2 GCD OF TWO NUMBERS USING RECURSION

In mathematics, the Greatest Common Divisor (GCD)/Highest Common Factor (HCF) is the largest possible integer that divides both of the integers. The condition is that the numbers must be non-zero.

8.2.1 Method of Finding GCD of Two Numbers

Following is the pseudocode to find GCD (or HCF) of two numbers using recursion.

Algo-8.1 Pseudocode for finding GCD of two integers using recursion

```
GCD(a, b) Procedure:
   BEGIN
      IF (a = = 0) THEN
         RETURN b;
      ELSE IF (b = = 0) THEN
         RETURN a;
     ELSE IF (a > b) THEN
        CALL gcd(a % b, b);
      ELSE
         CALL gcd(a, b % a);
      ENDIF
   END
```

Here, we are using the two integer numbers identified by a and b variables. The GCD() function is used to find the GCD of two entered integers using recursion. If the b variable is zero, then the GCD function returns the value of a. If b is not zero, then we are calling GCD function again (recursion) with a new value of b, and the new value a modulo division b (expressed as a%b) is set to b.

Suppose, a = 135, and b = 19, then the process of execution is:
GCD(135, 19) → GCD(19, 2) → GCD(2, 1) → 1.

> **Note!**
> GCD of three or more numbers can be calculated by repeatedly taking the GCDs of pairs of numbers.

8.2.2 GCD of Two Numbers with C and Python

CProg-8.1 Finding the GCD of two integers using recursion

```
#include<stdio.h>
#include<conio.h>

/*GCD function starts*/
int gcd(int a, int b)
{
  if (a == 0)
    return b;
  else if (b == 0)
    return a;
  else if (a > b)
    return gcd(a % b, b);
  else
    return gcd(a, b % a);
} /*GCD function ends*/

/* Driver function */
int main()
{
  int a, b, n;
  printf("Enter the value of a: ");
  scanf("%d", & a);
  printf("Enter the value of b: ");
  scanf("%d", & b);

  /* gcd(a, b) is called and will carry out gcd of a and b */
  printf("GCD of %d and %d is: %d", a, b, gcd(a, b));
}
/* End of program */
```

Output

```
Enter the value of a: 3892
Enter the value of b: 6223
GCD of 3892 and 6223 is: 7
```

Programming Tips!

The `GCD()` is used to find the GCD of two user-entered integers using recursion. If one variable is zero then the function returns the value of another variable. If b is not zero then `GCD()` is called recursively with a new value of 'b' and the new value 'a' modulo division 'b' is set to b.

PyProg-8.1 Finding the GCD of two integers using recursion

```
# GCD function starts
def gcd(a, b):
    # At base case GCD function will be terminate
    if (a == 0):
        return b
    if (b == 0):
        return a
    if (a > b):
        return gcd(a % b, b)
    return gcd(a, b % a)

# Here gcd(a, b) will be call with inputted integer value
a=int(input("Enter First Number: "))
b=int(input("Enter Second Number: "))
print("Gcd Of Given Value Is: ",gcd(a,b))
## end program
```

Output

```
Enter First Number: 10
Enter Second Number: 30
Gcd Of Given Value Is: 10 ""
```

Programming Tips!

`GCD()` is used to find the GCD of two user-entered integers using recursion.

8.3 FACTORIAL OF A NUMBER USING RECURSION

Factorial calculation using recursion was discussed in Sections 8.1.1 and 8.1.4. Recall that $n! = n*(n-1)*(n-2)*...*2*1$, and that $0! = 1$.

This formula may be explained with a function 'factorial' using an example of calculating the factorial of the number 4 below:

factorial(4)
= 4 * factorial(3)
= 4 * 3 * factorial(2)
= 4 * 3 * 2 * factorial(1)
= 4 * 3 * 2 * 1 * factorial(0)
= 4 * 3 * 2 * 1 * 1
= 24

Note!

The base case for the recursive factorial problem would be $n = 0$. It returns 1 when n becomes 0.

8.3.1 Method of Finding the Factorial of a Number

The method of finding the factorial is given with the pseudocode. Following is the pseudocode to find the factorial of a number using recursion.

Algo-8.2 Pseudocode for finding factorial of a number in a recursive way

```
Factorial(n) Procedure:
  BEGIN
    IF n == 0 or 1, THEN
      RETURN 1;
    ELSE
      RETURN n*Call Fact(n-1);
    ENDIF
  END
```

8.3.2 Factorial of a Number with C and Python

CProg-8.2 Finding the factorial of a number using recursion

```
#include<stdio.h>

/* Factorial function starts */
int fact(int n)
  {
    /* Here base condition is 0 or 1 */
    if(n == 1 || n == 0)
      return 1;
    else
      return n * fact(n - 1);
  }

/* Driver function */
int main()
  {
    int n;
     printf("Enter the number for which you want to compute
factorial: ");
    scanf("%d", & n);
    printf("Factorial of %d is: ", n);

      /* Calling the factorial function and print the value
returned */
    printf("%d ", fact(n));
  }
/* End of program */
```

Output

```
Enter the number for which you want to compute factorial: 10
Factorial of 10 is: 3628800
```

> **Programming Tips!**
> `fact()` is used to find the factorial using recursion. If the variable is zero or one then it returns 1, or else it calls `fact()` again by decreasing the value of the variables by one.

PyProg-8.2 Finding the factorial of a number using recursion

```
# Factorial Function Starts
def factorial(n):
    # At base case factorial function will be terminate
    if(n == 0 or n == 1):
        return 1
    else:
        return factorial(n-1)*n

# Here factorial(a,b) will be call with inputted integer value
n = int(input("Enter Number: "))
print("Factorial of",n,"is:",factorial(n))
## end program
```

Output

```
Enter Number: 5
Factorial of 5 is: 120
```

> **Programming Tips!**
> `factorial()` is used to find the factorial using recursion. If the variable is zero or one then it returns 1, or else it calls `factorial()` again by decreasing the value of the variables by one.

8.4 FIBONACCI SERIES USING RECURSION

The Fibonacci number series is defined as follows:

$$f(n) = \begin{cases} 0 & \text{if } n = 0 \\ 1 & \text{if } n = 1 \\ f(n-1) + f(n-2) & \text{otherwise} \end{cases}$$

The series is 0 1 1 2 3 5 8 13 21 ....

Let us consider all the recursive calls for f(5). The following Fig. 8.2 presents all possible recursive calls to `Fib` function.

Figure 8.2 shows the tree-like recursion structure of f(5). It takes a long time since there are many calls. There is a lot of repeated work. For example, f(4) repeats the calculation of f(3).

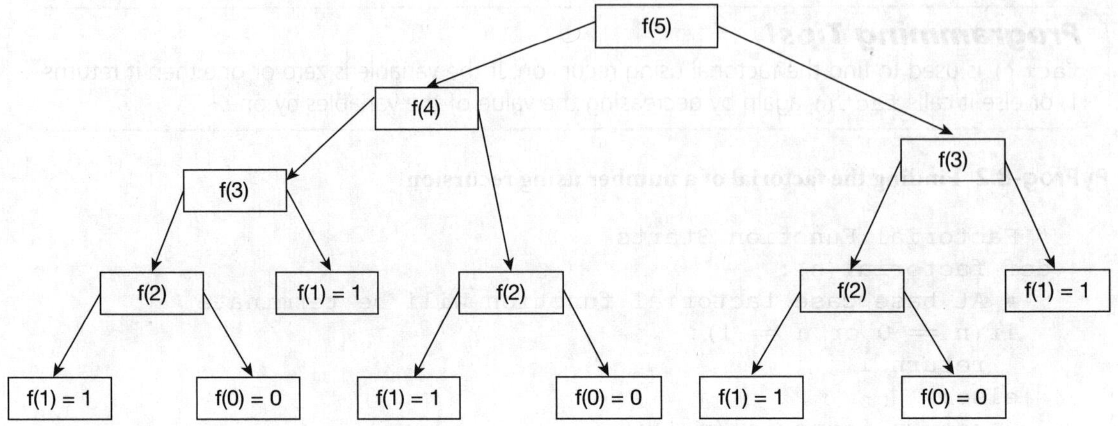

Figure 8.2 Tree structure diagram of Fibonacci series with $n = 5$

8.4.1 Method of Finding Fibonacci Series

The method of finding the Fibonacci numbers is given with the pseudocode. Following is the pseudocode to find the Fibonacci numbers using recursion.

Algo-8.3 Pseudocode for finding Fibonacci series in a recursive way

```
Fibonacci(n) Procedure:
   BEGIN
     IF n <= 1 THEN
        RETURN n
     ELSE
        RETURN call Fibonacci(n-1) + call Fibonacci(n-2)
     ENDIF
   END
```

8.4.2 Fibonacci Series with C and Python

CProg-8.3 Finding Fibonacci series using recursion

```
#include<stdio.h>

/* Defining Fibonacci functions*/
int fibbo(int n)
   {
     if(n == 1)
       return 0;
     else if (n == 2)
       return 1;
     else return fibbo(n - 1) + fibbo(n - 2);
   }
```

```
/*Driver function */
int main()
   {
      int n, i;
      printf("Enter no of terms: ");
      scanf("%d", &n);
      printf("Fibonacci of first %d terms are: ", n);

      /* Calling Fibonacci function and display numbers */
      for(i = 1; i < n + 1; i++)
         {
            printf("%d  ", fibbo(i));
         }
   }
/* End of program */
```

Output

```
Enter no of terms: 10
Fibonacci of first 10 terms are: 0  1  1  2  3  5  8  13  21  34
```

Programming Tips!

fibbo() is used to find the Fibonacci series with recursion. If the variable is one, then it returns 0; or if two, then it returns 1. Else, it calls fibbo() again by decreasing the value by one and by two respectively of the variables and adds the returned values.

PyProg-8.3 Finding Fibonacci series using recursion

```
# Fibonacci function definition
def fibonacci(n):
  # At base case Fibonacci function will be terminate
  if(n == 1):
    return 0
  if(n == 2):
    return 1
  else:
    return int(fibonacci(n-1))+int(fibonacci(n-2))

# Here fibonacci(i) will be called with input integer value
n = int(input("Enter Number: "))
print("Fibonacci of", n, "is:", end = " ")
for i in range(1, n+1):
  print(fibonacci(i), end = " ")
## End program
```

Output

```
Enter Number: 5
Fibonacci of 5 is: 0 1 1 2 3
```

> **Programming Tips!**
> `fibonacci()` is used to find the Fibonacci series with recursion. If the variable is one, then it returns 0; or if two, then it returns 1. Else, it calls `fibonacci()` again by decreasing the value by one and by two respectively of the variables and adds the returned values.

8.5 ACKERMANN FUNCTION USING RECURSION

The Ackermann function is a recursive function defined on non-negative integers. It has two arguments (m, n), each of which can be assigned to any non-negative integer. It can be represented by the following:

$$\text{Ack}(m,n)=\begin{cases} n+1 & \text{if } m=0 \\ \text{Ack}(m-1,1) & \text{if } m>0, \text{ and } n=0 \\ \text{Ack}(m-1,\text{Ack}(m,n-1)) & \text{if } m>0, \text{ and } n>0 \end{cases}$$

German mathematician Wilhelm Friedrich Ackermann introduced this function in the theory of computation. Let $<a_1, \ldots, a_n>$ denote the encoding of $a_1, \ldots, a_n$. Let *f* be an *n*-ary total function. *M* computes the function *f* if for every *n*-tuple $a_1, \ldots, a_n$, M on input $<a_1, \ldots, a_n>$ outputs $y = f(a_1, ..., a_n)$ (may be in binary). In such a case, *f* is called a total computable function.

On the other hand, a function that can be implemented using only `do` loops is called primitive recursive. In contrast, a computable function can be coded using a combination of `for` and `while` loops or `do-while` loops only. Examples of primitive recursive functions include power, GCD etc. *Ackermann function is one of the simplest total computable function that is not primitive recursive.* It provides a counter-example to the belief in the early 1900s that every computable function was also primitive recursive. Following examples show the calculation for finding the Ackermann function in simple initial cases.

Example 8.1 Find Ack(1, 2).

Ack(1, 2)
= Ack(0, Ack(1, 1))
= Ack(0, Ack(0, Ack(1, 0)))
= Ack(0, Ack(0, Ack(0, 1)))
= Ack(0, Ack(0, 2))
= Ack(0, 3)
= 4

Example 8.2 Find Ack (1, 3).

Ack(1, 3)
= Ack(0, Ack(1, 2))
= Ack(0, Ack(0, Ack(1, 1)))
= Ack(0, Ack(0, Ack(0, Ack(1, 0))))
= Ack(0, Ack(0, Ack(0, Ack(0, 1))))

= Ack(0, Ack(0, Ack(0, 2)))
= Ack(0, Ack(0, 3))
= Ack(0, 4)
= 5

Computing the Ackermann function can be represented in terms of an infinite table given in Table 8.2. We place the natural numbers along the top row. To determine a number in the table, take the number immediately to the left, then look up the required number in the previous row, at the position given by the number just taken. If there is no number to its left, simply look at the column headed "1" in the previous row. Here is a small upper-left portion of the table.

Table 8.2 Values of A(m, n)

m \ n	0	1	2	3	4	n
0	1	2	3	4	5	$n+1$
1	2	3	4	5	6	$n+2=$ $2+(n+3)-3$
2	3	5	7	9	11	$2n+3=$ $2(n+3)-3$
3	5	13	29	61	125	$2^{(n+3)}-3$
4	13 = $2^{2^2}-3$	65533 = $2^{2^{2^2}}-3$	$2^{65536}-3$ = $2^{2^{2^{2^2}}}-3$	$2^{2^{65536}}-3$ = $2^{2^{2^{2^{2^2}}}}-3$	$2^{2^{2^{65536}}}-3$ = $2^{2^{2^{2^{2^2}}}}-3$	$\underbrace{2^{2^{\cdot^{\cdot^{2}}}}}_{n+3}-3$

The Ackermann function is used to represent Graham's number by computable recursive formulas. This Graham's number is so large that the observable universe is too small to contain an ordinary digital representation using this number. The Ackermann function can also be used as a benchmark of a compiler's ability to optimize recursion due to its definition in terms of extremely deep recursion.

> ***Note!***
> Ackermann function is one of the simplest total computable functions that is not primitive recursive.

8.5.1 Method of Finding Ackermann Function

Algo-8.4 Pseudocode for finding Ackermann function

```
Ackermann(m, n) Procedure:
  BEGIN
    IF (m == 0) THEN
        Return n+1
    ELSE IF  ((m > 0) and (n = = 0))
        Return acker (m-1, 1)
    ELSE IF ((m > 0) and (n > 0))
       Return acker (m-1, acker (m, n-1))
  END
```

8.5.2 Ackermann Function with C and Python

CProg-8.4 Implementing Ackermann function

```
#include <stdio.h>

/* Ackermann's function */
int acker(int i, int j)
   {
     if(i == 0)
       {
         return j+1;
       }
     else if((i > 0) && (j == 0))
       {
         return acker(i-1, 1);
       }
     else if((i > 0) && (j > 0))
       {
           return acker(i-1, acker(i, j-1));
       }
   }

/* Driver function */
int main()
   {
     int x,m,n;
     printf("\nEnter two arguments ");
     scanf("%d %d", &m, &n);
     x = acker(m, n);
     printf("%d", x);
     return 0;
   }
/* End of program */
```

Output

```
Enter two arguments 3 4
125
Enter two arguments 1 2
4
Desirable values of inputs are m<=3, n<=12 for getting output using a
normal compiler with this program.
```

Programming Tips!
`acker()` is used to find the Ackermann function value with recursion.

PyProg-8.4 Implementing Ackermann function

```
# Definition of Ackermann function
def acker(i, j, s = "% s"):
    print(s % ("acker(% d, % d)" % (i, j)))
    if i == 0:
        return j + 1
    if j == 0:
        return acker(i - 1, 1, s)
    n = acker(i, j - 1, s % ("acker(% d, %% s)" % (i - 1)))
    return acker(i - 1, n, s)

# Calling the Ackermann function with input parameters
print(acker(1, 2))
## End program
```

Output

```
acker( 1,  2)
acker( 0, acker( 1,  1))
acker( 0, acker( 0, acker( 1,  0)))
acker( 0, acker( 0, acker( 0,  1)))
acker( 0, acker( 0,  2))
acker( 0,  3)
4
```

> ***Programming Tips!***
> `acker()` is used to find the Ackermann function value with recursion.

8.6 PASCAL'S TRIANGLE REPRESENTATION USING RECURSION

Pascal's triangle is a numbers pattern where the numbers are arranged in such a way that a triangle is formed. Blaise Pascal, a French mathematician, proposed the idea of Pascal's Triangle in 1653. This triangle has many contributions in mathematics. Binomial expansion and various combination problems can be represented using Pascal's triangle. The structure or representation of this triangle is very simple but it shows many interesting mathematical properties. It can be represented in different ways. Example of a Pascal's triangle with 7 rows are given in Fig. 8.3 below.

```
                  1
               1     1
            1     2     1
         1     3     3     1
      1     4     6     4     1
   1     5    10    10     5     1
1     6    15    20    15     6     1
```

Figure 8.3 Pascal triangle with 7 rows.

Some properties of Pascal's triangle are given below:

1. It starts with 1 on the top row, and then 1's on the two sides of a triangle in the 2nd row. Each subsequent row starts and ends with 1 and a new number is inserted as an interior term by summing the two numbers above it.
2. If we sum each row, then we will get powers of base 2, starting from $2^0 = 1$.
3. The value of a row in Pascal's triangle considered as a decimal value (values larger than 9 carried over) is a power of 11. For example, the 2nd row representing 121 is equal to 11^2, 3rd row representing 1331 is equal to 11^3 and so on.
4. We can find the hidden Fibonacci sequence if we sum the diagonals of the left-justified Pascal triangle.
5. Pascal's triangle determines the coefficients in binomial expansions. For example, coefficients 1, 2, 1 are found in the expansion of $(x + y)^2$, and coefficients 1, 3, 3, 1 are found in the expansion of $(x + y)^3$, and so on.

8.6.1 Method of Solving Pascal's Triangle Representation

We can represent Pascal's triangle using recursion. The recursive technique for representation of Pascal's triangle is given below.

Algo-8.5 Pseudocode for representing Pascal's triangle

```
PascalTriangle(n, k) Procedure:
  BEGIN
     IF (k == 0) OR (k == n):
        r = 1
     ELSE
        r = PascalTriangle(n-1, k-1) + PascalTriangle(n-1, k)
        RETURN r
     ENDIF
  END Procedure

PrintPascal(num)
  BEGIN
     FOR n = 0 to num
         FOR k = 0 to n+1
             PRINT PascalTriangle (n, k)
         ENDFOR k
     ENDFOR n
  END PrintPascal
```

8.6.2 Pascal's Triangle Representation with C and Python

CProg-8.5 Representing Pascal's triangle

```
#include<stdio.h>

long PascalTriangle(int, int); /* Declaration of Pascal's function*/
```

```
/* Driver Code */
int main()
   {
     int n = 0, m = 0, k = 0, s = 0;
     long f;

     /* Taking user input on size of the Pascal's triangle */
    printf ("\nEnter number of rows of the Pascal's triangle: ");
     scanf("%d", &n);

     /* Printing formatted output */
     for(k = 0; n > k; k++) {
        for(s = 0; s < n-k; s++) /* Add spaces before each row */
            printf(" ");
            for(m = 0; k >= m; m++)
              {
                f = PascalTriangle(k, m);
                printf("%ld ", f);
              }
            printf("\n");
    }
   return 0;
}

/* Definition of function for generating elements of Pascal's tri-
angle */
long PascalTriangle(int n, int i)
   {
     if(n == i || i == 0)
         return 1;
     else
        return PascalTriangle(n-1, i) + PascalTriangle(n-1, i-1);
/* Recursive call to function*/
   }
/* End Program */
```

Output

```
Enter number of rows of the Pascal's triangle: 7
          1
         1 1
        1 2 1
       1 3 3 1
      1 4 6 4 1
    1 5 10 10 5 1
   1 6 15 20 15 6 1
```

> ***Programming Tips!***
> `PascalTriangle()` is used to print Pascal's triangle in formatted output with recursion.

PyProg-8.5 Representing Pascal's triangle

```
# Definition of Pascal's triangle function
def PascalTriangle(n, tri=[[1]]):
    if n > len(tri):
        l_row = tri[-1]
        n_row = [x+y for (x, y) in zip([0] + l_row, l_row + [0])]
        return PascalTriangle(n, tri + [n_row])
    return tri

# Driver Codes
# Taking user inter on number of rows of the Pascal's triangle
n = int(input("Enter Number of rows of the Pascal's triangle: "))

# Printing formatted output of Pascal's Triangle
print(*["    ".join(map(str,    line)).center(30)    for    line    in
PascalTriangle(n)], sep ="\n")
# End program
```

Output

```
Enter Number of rows of the Pascal's triangle: 7
              1
             1 1
            1 2 1
           1 3 3 1
          1 4 6 4 1
        1 5 10 10 5 1
       1 6 15 20 15 6 1
```

> ***Programming Tips!***
> `PascalTriangle()` is used to print Pascal's triangle in formatted output with recursion.

8.7 SOLVING THE TOWER OF HANOI PROBLEM USING RECURSION

First, we should understand the Tower of Hanoi (TOH or toh) problem. This is a fun puzzle game where the main aim is to move an entire stack of disks from the source position to the destination position. The Tower of Hanoi puzzle was invented by the French mathematician Edouard Lucas in the year 1883. The following three simple rules should be followed during the game:

1. Only one disk can be moved at a time.
2. Each move consists of taking the upper disk from one of the stacks, and placing it on top of another stack.
3. No larger disk may be placed on top of a smaller disk.

Now, let us try to imagine a real scenario. Suppose we have a stack of three disks. We are trying to move disks from source A (tower) to the destination C (tower) given in Fig. 8.4. We can use B (tower) as a helper to finish this job. Let us go through each of the following steps:

1. Move the top disk from A to C
2. Move the top disk from A to B

3. Move the top disk from C to B
4. Move the top disk from A to C
5. Move the top disk from B to A
6. Move the top disk from B to C
7. Move the top disk from A to C

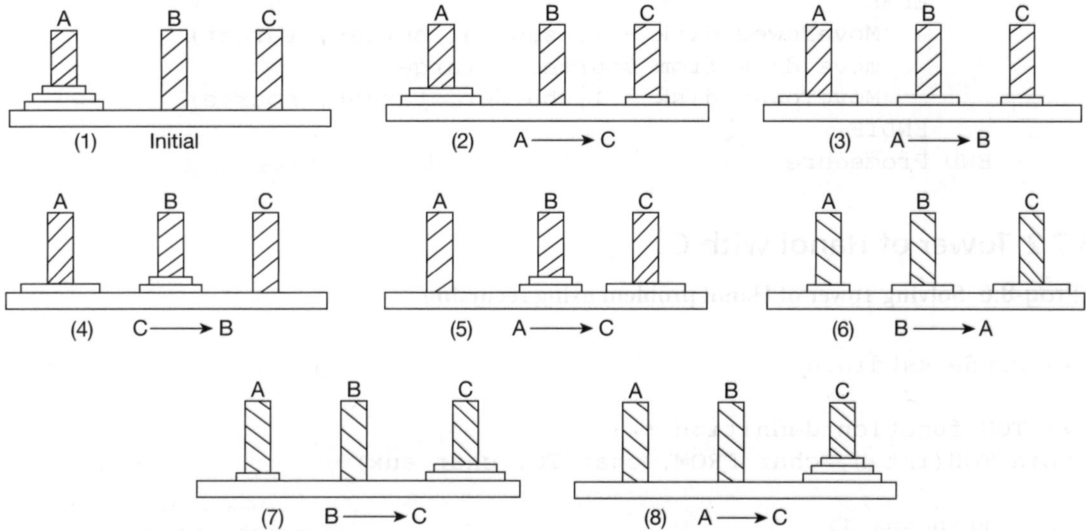

Figure 8.4 Tower of Hanoi solution execution steps

Suppose, we have 4 disks. In that case, we have to follow the steps given below:

- Recursively solve the problem of moving disk 1, 2, and 3 from stack A to stack C.
- Move disk 4 from A to C.
- Recursively solve the problem of moving disk 1, 2 and 3 from stack C to stack B.

The 3-disk puzzle required 7 steps. 4-disk requires 7 + 1 + 7 = 15 steps to be solved. So, we can say that we need $2^N - 1$ steps to move N disks from one stack to another. The number of steps is almost double every time you insert another disk in the stack.

8.7.1 Method of Solving the Tower of Hanoi Problem

To solve the task in a minimum number of steps for a given N number of disks, the following steps are to be followed in the Tower of Hanoi problem:

Step 1:	Move the top $N - 1$ disks to an intermediate stack.
Step 2:	Move the bottom disk to the destination stack.
Step 3:	Move the $N - 1$ disks from the intermediate stack to the destination stack.

The above method can be written with the help of pseudocode using recursion.

Algo-8.6 Pseudocode for the recursive Tower of Hanoi problem

```
MoveTower(disk, source, target, buffer) Procedure:
   BEGIN
       IF disk == 0, THEN
          move the disk from source to target
       ELSE
          MoveTower(disk - 1, source, buffer, target)
          move disk from source to target
          MoveTower(disk - 1, buffer, target, source)
       ENDIF
   END Procedure
```

8.7.2 Tower of Hanoi with C

CProg-8.6 Solving Tower of Hanoi problem using recursion

```
#include <stdio.h>

/* TOH function definition */
void TOH(int n, char FROM, char TO, char aux)
   {
     if(n == 1)
       {
        printf("\n Move disk 1 FROM rod %c TO rod %c\n", FROM, TO);
          return;
       }
     TOH(n - 1, FROM, aux, TO);
    printf("\n Move disk %d FROM rod %c TO rod %c", n, FROM, TO);
     TOH(n - 1, aux, TO, FROM);
   }

/* Driver function */
int main()
   {
     int n;
     printf("Enter number of discs: ");
     scanf("%d", &n);  /* n is number of discs*/
     /* Calling TOH function */
     TOH(n, 'A', 'C', 'B');   /*A, B and C are the name of rod*/
     return 0;
   }
/* End of program */
```

Output

```
Enter number of discs: 4
```

```
Move disk 1 FROM rod A TO rod B

Move disk 2 FROM rod A TO rod C
Move disk 1 FROM rod B TO rod C

Move disk 3 FROM rod A TO rod B
Move disk 1 FROM rod C TO rod A

Move disk 2 FROM rod C TO rod B
Move disk 1 FROM rod A TO rod B

Move disk 4 FROM rod A TO rod C
Move disk 1 FROM rod B TO rod C

Move disk 2 FROM rod B TO rod A
Move disk 1 FROM rod C TO rod A

Move disk 3 FROM rod B TO rod C
Move disk 1 FROM rod A TO rod B

Move disk 2 FROM rod A TO rod C
Move disk 1 FROM rod B TO rod C
```

> ***Programming Tips!***
> `TOH()` is used to solve Tower of Hanoi problem recursively.

8.7.3 Tower of Hanoi with Python

PyProg-8.6 Solving Tower of Hanoi problem using recursion

```
# TOH function definition
def toh(n, From, to, aux):
    if n == 1:
        print("Move disk 1 from rod", From, "to", to)
        return
    toh(n-1, From, aux, to)
    print("Move disk", n, "from rod", From, "to rod", to)
    toh(n-1, aux, to, From)
#toh functionends

# Here fibonacci(i) will be call with inputted integer value
print("Enter Number Of Discs: ", end = " ");
n = int(input()) #n is the number of discs
toh(n,'A', 'C', 'B')
## End program
```

Output

```
Enter Number Of Discs:  4
Move disk 1 from rod A to B
Move disk 2 from rod A to rod C
```

```
Move disk 1 from rod B to C
Move disk 3 from rod A to rod B
Move disk 1 from rod C to A
Move disk 2 from rod C to rod B
Move disk 1 from rod A to B
Move disk 4 from rod A to rod C
Move disk 1 from rod B to C
Move disk 2 from rod B to rod A
Move disk 1 from rod C to A
Move disk 3 from rod B to rod C
Move disk 1 from rod A to B
Move disk 2 from rod A to rod C
Move disk 1 from rod B to C
```

Programming Tips!
`toh()` is used to solve Tower of Hanoi problem recursively.

8.8 SORTING A STACK USING RECURSION

Suppose we are given a stack of elements. It is known that stack data structure follows LIFO (Last-In–First-Out) order. If we consider the stack sorted in ascending order, then the element having maximum value will be stored at the top of the stack. The stored elements may not always be in sorted order. Recursive methods may be used to sort the elements stored in the stack. Here, the problem is to sort the elements using recursion technique, say in descending order for example. In that case, if the input sequence is (50, 30, 20, 40, 10, 15), the expected output is (50, 40, 30, 20, 15, 10).

8.8.1 Method of Sorting a Stack Using Recursion

Algo-8.7 Pseudocode for sorting a stack using recursion

```
StackSort(Stack st) Procedure:
  BEGIN
     IF Stack is not empty THEN
        POP from Stack assign to temporary variable (t)
        StackSort (st)
        InsertStackSort(st, t)
     ENDIF
  END Procedure StackSort

InsertStackSort(Stack st, item) Procedure:
  BEGIN
     IF Stack is empty OR item > top of stack THEN
        PUSH (st, item)
     ELSE
        item = POP (st)
        InsertStackSort (st, item)
        PUSH (st, item)
     ENDIF
  END Procedure InsertStackSort
```

8.8.2 Sorting a Stack Using Recursion with C and Python

CProg-8.7 Sorting a stack using recursion

```
#include <stdio.h>
#include <stdlib.h>

/* Declaration of stack using structure data type */
struct stack
   {
     int data;
     struct stack *next;
   };

/* Initializing stack */
void initialStack(struct stack **st)
   {
     *st = NULL;
   }

/* Checking whether stack is empty or not */
int isEmpty(struct stack *st)
   {
     if(st == NULL)
        return 1;
     return 0;
   }

/* Push operation */
void push(struct stack **st, int x)
   {
     struct stack *p = (struct stack *)malloc(sizeof(*p));
     p->data = x;
     p->next = *st;
     *st = p;
   }

/* Pop operation */
int pop(struct stack **st)
   {
     int x; struct stack *t;
     x = (*st)->data;
     t = *st;
     (*st) = (*st)->next;
     free(t);
     return x;
  }
```

```
/* Returning stack top*/
int top(struct stack *st)
  {
    return (st->data);
  }

/* Pushing elements into the stack in sorted order */
void sortedInsert(struct stack **st, int x)
  {
    int t;
    if(isEmpty(*st) || x > top(*st))
      {
        push(st, x);
      }
    t = pop(st);
    sortedInsert(st, x); /* Recursive Call */
    push(st, t);
  }

/* Sorting all elements of stack */
void sortStack(struct stack **st)
  {
    if(!isEmpty(*st))
      {
        int x = pop(st);
        sortStack(st);
        sortedInsert(st, x);
      }
  }

/* Display all Stack elements */
void printStack(struct stack *st)
  {
    while(st)
      {
        printf("%d ", st->data);
        st = st->next;
      }
    printf("\n");
  }

/* Driver codes */
int main(void)
  {
    int i, n, e; struct stack *top;
```

```
    /* Taking the stack size from the user */
    printf("Enter stack size: ");
    scanf("%d", &n);
    initialStack(&top); /* Initialize the stack */

    /* Taking the stack elements from the user */
    for(i=1; i<=n; i++)
        {
           printf("Enter element [%d]: ", i);
           scanf("%d", &e);
           push(&top, e);
        }

    /* Display stack before sorting operation */
    printf("Before sorting Stack:\n");
    printStack(top);
    printf("\n");

    /* Calling the sort function to start operation */
    sortStack(&top);

    /* Display stack after sorting operation */
   printf("After sorting the stack in descending order:\n");
    printStack(top);
    return 0;
  }
/* End Program */
```

Output

```
Enter Stack size: 5
Enter element [1]: 6
Enter element [2]: 7
Enter element [3]: 9
Enter element [4]: 4
Enter element [5]:7
Before sorting stack:
7 4 9 7 6

After sorting the stack in descending order:
9 7 7 6 4
```

Programming Tips!

`sortStack()` is used to sort the stack in ascending order. `printStack()` is used display the stack elements. `sortedInsert()` is used to push elements into the stack in sorted order.

PyProg-8.7 Sorting a stack using recursion

```
# Recursive function for inserting elements into the stack
def InsertSorted(stack, element):
    if len(stack) == 0 or element > stack[-1]:
        stack.append(element)
        return
    else:
        # pop the element (top)
        t = stack.pop()
        InsertSorted(stack, element)
        # Push back the element again
        stack.append(t)

# Recursive function for sorting stack elements
def StackSort(stack):
    # Check if stack empty or not
    if len(stack) != 0:
        # pop stack elements
        t = stack.pop()
        # Sort remaining elementments
        StackSort(stack)
        # Push back the data elements into sorted stack
        InsertSorted(stack, t)

# Function for displaying the stack elements
def StackPrint(stack):
    for i in stack[::-1]:
        print(i, end = " ")
    print()

# Driver codes
if __name__=='__main__':
    stack = [ ]
    # Taking the stack elements from the user
    n = int(input("Enter number of stack elements: "))
    for i in range(0, n):
        element = int(input())
        stack.append(element)

  # Display stack before sorting operation
    print("\nStack before sorting: ")
    StackPrint(stack)

  # Calling the sort function to start operation
    StackSort(stack)
```

```
    # Display stack after sorting operation
    print("\nStack after sorting: ")
    StackPrint(stack)
# End Program
```

Output

```
Enter number of stack elements: 5
5
6
4
9
8

Stack before sorting:
8 9 4 6 5

Stack after sorting:
9 8 6 5 4
```

> ***Programming Tips!***
> `StackSort()` is used to sort the stack in ascending order. `StackPrint()` is used to display the stack elements. `InsertSorted()` is used to push elements into the stack in sorted order.

8.9 *N*-QUEENS PROBLEM USING RECURSION

Suppose we are given a chess board of n by n ($n \times n$) squares. The problem here is to place n number of chess queens on the board without having any one of them attack the other queens. We may remember that a queen can attack horizontally, vertically, and on both diagonals. So it is a difficult task to place several queens on one board so that they don't attack each other. The 8 queens ($n = 8$) puzzle was originally proposed by the chess player Max Bezzel in 1848 and the first solutions were provided by Franz Nauck in 1850. Nauck also extended the puzzle to a chessboard of arbitrary size with N-queens ($n \times n$) problem.

8.9.1 Method of Solving *N*-Queens Problem

Backtracking: It is a problem-solving scheme by well-organized trial-and-error method. We should make sure that we never try the same logic twice. If the problem is finite, we will eventually try all possibilities. Edsger Dijkstra has shown the power of backtracking in structured programming, and provided a detailed description of the depth-first backtracking algorithm.

Example 8.3 **Two queens ($N = 2$) problem is not solvable.**

Q	Q

Q	
Q	

Q	
	Q

	Q
Q	

Q	Q

Q	
Q	

All six combinations show that the queens can attack each other.
Similarly, the 3-queens problem is also not solvable. The 1-queen problem is solvable since only one square and one queen is there.

Example 8.4 Four queens ($N = 4$) problem is solvable.

Basic idea of solution

1. Start with one queen in the first column, first row.
2. Start with another queen in the second column, first row.
3. Go down with the second queen until we reach an acceptable situation.
4. Advance to the next column, first row and do the same thing.
5. If we cannot find an acceptable situation in one column and reach the bottom of it, then we have to go back to the previous column and move one position down there. This is the backtracking.
6. If we reach an acceptable situation in the last column of the board, then the problem is solved.
7. If you have to backtrack before the first column, then the problem is not solvable.

- 1st Queen Placing

Q	X	X	X
X	X		
X		X	
X			X

- 2nd Queen Placing

Q	X	X	X
X	X	X	
X	Q	X	X
X	X	X	X

The 3rd queen cannot be placed in the 3rd column. So we have to shift the two queens in first two columns one position down

X	X		
Q	X	X	X
X	X	X	
X	Q	X	X

- 3rd Queen Placing

X	X	Q	X
Q	X	X	X
X	X	X	
X	Q	X	X

- 4th Queen Placing

X	X	Q	X
Q	X	X	X
X	X	X	Q
X	Q	X	X

The number of possible ways to solve this problem is often large and difficult to calculate. We may use some thumb rules to get the solution in an easy way. These are given in Table 8.3:

Table 8.3 Examples of N-queens ($N \geq 4$) problem solution

Process	8 Queens	14 queens	15 queens
Divide N by 12. Remember the remainder	$N = 8$ (Remainder 8)	$N = 14$ (Remainder 2)	$N = 15$ (Remainder 3)
Write a list of the even numbers from 2 to n in order.	2, 4, 6, 8	2, 4, 6, 8, 10, 12, 14	2, 4, 6, 8, 10, 12, 14
If the remainder is 3 or 9, move 2 to the end of the list.	Not applicable because remainder 8	Not applicable because remainder 2	4, 6, 8, 10, 12, 14, **2**
Append the odd numbers from 1 to n in order, but if the remainder is 8, switch pairs (i.e., 3, 1, 7, 5, 11, 9, …).	(Remainder 8), so switch the pairs and add numbers 2, 4, 6, 8, **3, 1, 7, 5**	2, 4, 6, 8, 10, 12, 14, 1, 3, 5, 7, 9, 11, 13	4, 6, 8, 10, 12, 14, 2, 1, 3, 5, 7, 9, 11, 13, 15
If the remainder is 2, switch the places of 1 and 3, then move 5 to the end of the list.	Not applicable because remainder is 8	2, 4, 6, 8, 10, 12, 14, **3, 1**, 7, 9, 11, 13, **5**	Not applicable because remainder is 3
If the remainder is 3 or 9, move 1 and 3 to the end of the list.	Not applicable because remainder is 8	Not applicable because remainder is 2	4, 6, 8, 10, 12, 14, 2, 5, 7, 9, 11, 13, 15, **1, 3**
Place the first-column queen in the row with the first number in the list, place the second-column queen in the row with the second number in the list and so on.	2, 4, 6, 8, **3, 1, 7, 5**	2, 4, 6, 8, 10, 12, 14, **3, 1**, 7, 9, 11, 13, **5**	4, 6, 8, 10, 12, 14, 2, 5, 7, 9, 11, 13, 15, **1, 3**

Thus the eight queens puzzle has 92 distinct solutions. The solutions may differ only by symmetry operations (rotations and reflections) of the board, and are counted as one, and hence the puzzle has 12 unique solutions. Similarly 20 queens problem has the following structure.

- 20 queens (remainder 8): 2, 4, 6, 8, 10, 12, 14, 16, 18, 20, 3, 1, 7, 5, 11, 9, 15, 13, 19, 17.

Note!

N-Queens problem can be solved using recursion and backtracking.

Algo-8.8 Pseudocode for the recursive *N*-queens problem

```
SolveNQueen(board, coln) Procedure:
  BEGIN
   IF all columns are filled, THEN
      RETURN true
   ELSE
     FOR each row of the board, do
       IF call isValid(board, i, coln), THEN
         SET queen at place (i, coln) in the board
         IF SolveNQueen(board, coln + 1) = true, THEN
            RETURN  true
         ELSE
            Remove queen from place (i, coln) from board
         ENDIF
       ENDIF
     ENDFOR
     RETURN false
   ENDIF
  END Procedure SolveNQueens

isValid(board, row, coln) Procedure:
  BEGIN
   IF there is a queen at the left of current coln, THEN
      RETURN false
   ENDIF
   IF there is a queen at the left upper diagonal, THEN
      RETURN false
   ENDIF
   IF there is a queen at the left lower diagonal, THEN
      RETURN false
   ELSE
      RETURN  true //otherwise it is valid place
  END Procedure isValid
```

8.9.2 Solving *N*-Queens Problem with C and Python

CProg-8.8 Solving *N*-Queens problem using recursion

```
/* N-Queens Problem Using Backtracking */
#include<stdio.h>
#include<math.h>

int board[20], count;
```

```
/* Main function */
int main()
   {
     int n, i, j;
     void queen(int row, int n);
     printf("-The N Queens Problem Using Backtracking-");
     printf("\n\nEnter the number of Queens: ");
     scanf("%d", &n);
     if(n == 2 || n== 3)
       printf("Problem is not solvable");
     queen(1, n);
     return 0;
   }

/* Function for displaying the solution */
void print(int n)
   {
     int i, j;
     printf("\n\nSolution %d:\n\n", ++count);
     for(i = 1; i <= n; ++i)
     printf("\t%d", i);
     for(i = 1; i <= n; ++i)
       {
         printf("\n\n%d", i);
         for(j = 1; j <= n; ++j) /* For n x n chess board */
           {
             if(board[i] == j)
                printf("\tQ"); /* Queen at i, j position */
             else
                printf("\t-"); /* Empty slot */
           }
       }
   }

/* Funtion to check conflicts if no conflict for desired postion
returns 1 otherwise returns 0 */
int place(int row, int column)
   {
     int i;
     for(i = 1; i <= row - 1; ++i)
       {
         /* Checking column and diagonal conflicts */
         if(board[i] == column)
            return 0;
         else
```

```
            if(abs(board[i] - column) == abs(i - row))
                 return 0;
       }
     return 1; /* No conflicts */
   }

/* Function to check for proper positioning of queen */
void queen(int row, int n)
   {
     int column;
     for(column = 1; column <= n ; ++column)
       {
         if(place(row, column))
           {
             board[row] = column; /* No conflicts so place queen */
             if(row == n)          /* Dead end */
               print(n);         /* Printing the board configuration */
             else                  /* Try queen with next position */
                 queen(row+1, n);
           }
       }
   }
/* End of Program */
```

Output

```
-N Queens Problem Using Backtracking-
Enter number of Queens: 4

Solution 1:

-       1       2       3       4
1       -       Q       -       -
2       -       -       -       Q
3       Q       -       -       -
4       -       -       Q       -

Solution 2:

-       1       2       3       4
1       -       -       Q       -
2       Q       -       -       -
3       -       -       -       Q
4       -       Q       -       -
--------------------------------
Process exited after 3.968 seconds with return value 0
```

Programming Tips!

`place()` is used for checking conflicts. If no conflict is found for desired position then it returns 1, otherwise it returns 0. `queen()` is used to check proper positioning of queen.

PyProg-8.8 Solving *N*-Queens problem using recursion

```
''' Board has dimensions size x size
columns[r] is a number c if a queen is placed at row r and
column c.
columns[r] is out of range if no queen is placed in row r.
Thus after all queens are placed, they will be at positions
(columns[0], 0), (columns[1], 1), ... (columns[size - 1], size
- 1)'''
class QueenChessBoard:
    def __init__(self, size):
        self.size = size
        self.columns = []

    def get_size(self):
        return self.size

    def get_queens_count(self):
        return len(self.columns)

    def place_in_next_row(self, column):
        self.columns.append(column)

    def remove_in_current_row(self):
        return self.columns.pop()

    def is_this_column_safe_in_next_row(self, column):
        row = len(self.columns) # index of next row

        for queen_column in self.columns: # check column
            if column == queen_column:
                return False

       for queen_row, queen_column in enumerate(self.columns):
# check diagonal
            if queen_column - queen_row == column - row:
                return False
```

```
        for queen_row, queen_column in enumerate(self.columns): #
check other diagonal
            if ((self.size - queen_column) - queen_row == (self.
size - column) - row):
                return False
        return True

    def display(self):
        for row in range(self.size):
            for column in range(self.size):
                if column == self.columns[row]:
                    print('Q', end = ' ')
                else:
                    print('.', end = ' ')
            print()
'''Display a chessboard for each possible configuration of placing
n queens on
an n x n chessboard where n = size and print the number of such
configurations.'''
def display_solutions_to_n_queen(size):
    board = QueenChessBoard(size)
    number_of_solutions = display_solutions_helper(board)
    print('Number of solutions:', number_of_solutions)
'''Display a chessboard for each possible configuration of filling
the given board
with queens and return the number of such configurations.'''
def display_solutions_helper(board):
    size = board.get_size()
    if size == board.get_queens_count():# if board is full, print
all solutions
        board.display()
        print()
        return 1
    number_of_solutions = 0
    # place queen in next row
    for column in range(size):
        if board.is_this_column_safe_in_next_row(column):
            board.place_in_next_row(column)
            number_of_solutions += display_solutions_helper(board)
            board.remove_in_current_row()
    return number_of_solutions

# Driver code
n = int(input('Enter n: '))
display_solutions_to_n_queen(n)
# End of Program
```

Output

```
Enter n: 4
. Q . .
. . . Q
Q . . .
. . Q .

. . Q .
Q . . .
. . . Q
. Q . .

Number of solutions: 2

Enter n: 8

Q . . . . . . .
. . . . Q . . .
. . . . . . . Q
. . . . . Q . .
. . Q . . . . .
. . . . . . Q .
. Q . . . . . .
. . . Q . . . .
Number of solutions: 92
One solution out of 92 is printed above.
```

> ***Programming Tips!***
> Chess board is a square matrix. columns[r] is a number c if a queen is placed at row r and column c. columns[r] is out of range if no queen is placed in row r. The queens are at positions (columns[0], 0), (columns[1], 1), ... (columns[size – 1], size – 1) when all queens are placed.

8.10 DYNAMIC PROGRAMMING AND MEMOIZATION

Dynamic programming (DP) is a technique of designing algorithms for solving computational problems using programming languages. It provides an optimal solution to the problem under consideration by combining optimal solutions of each sub-subproblem. Efficient non-recursive solutions are generated using DP to define problems recursively. It was introduced by U.S. mathematician Richard Bellman in 1953 and is typically very useful for optimization problems. DP consists of two sections, namely, a) use of a table to store solutions of sub-problems, and b) use of the solutions of subproblems to solve larger problems. Practical solutions of DP problems involve two actions, memoization and recursion. DP has two approaches given below.

> ***Note!***
> Dynamic programming is an algorithm for solving computational problems by providing optimal solutions to the problem by combining optimal solutions of each sub-subproblem.

8.10.1 Memoization (Top-down)

Memoization is a technique for improving the performance of recursive algorithms. It refers to the optimization technique where we keep a record of (form a memo or memoize) previously computed results. Memoization comes from the word 'memoize'. It is a recursive approach, starting from the larger problem, solving smaller problems as needed. We store the solution when we solve any problem using this approach. Thus we need not compute the same solution twice. Some features of memoization are given below.

- It involves rewriting the recursive algorithm so that the calculated answers to the problems are stored in an array.
- The above solution array, along with the recursion, are used to derive the optimal solution of the problem.
- Recursive calls look up the results in the array instead of recalculating them.
- As mentioned earlier, the results of smaller subproblems are used to solve larger problems.
- Memoization improves the programming performance since partial results are not calculated twice.

Memoization techniques are explained using the Fibonacci series problem in the following section. We should remember the following convenient tricks/steps when we need to design a memoize function:

Step 1: Instantiate an array/table in the outer function's scope.

Step 2: Add a check before the base case in the inner function to see if a given value exists in the array/table, and if so, return it.

Step 3: Store the return value of a recursive call in the array/table with the given input as the key before returning it, else issue recursive calls to solve whatever smaller problems we may need to solve. Obtain the solution to the original problem using the solutions of the samller problems. Store the solution in the solutions array, and return the solution.

Example 8.5

We have already discussed the recursive problem of Fibonacci series, Fibonacci(n). If n is large, then we cannot compute the series in a reasonable amount of time using the previously discussed method. Suppose, we are calculating fibo(5) using the previous recursive method in the following way:

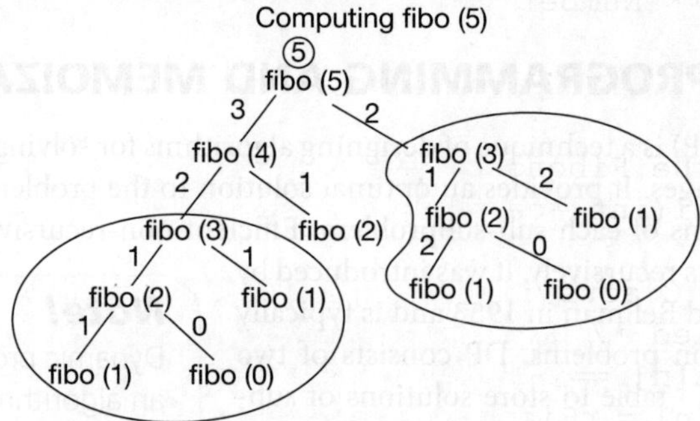

Figure 8.5 Computing Fibonacci (5) series

It has overlapping sub-problems and computational trees growing exponentially as marked in Fig. 8.5. The following Fig. 8.6 shows the design of memoization techniques for solving Fibonacci series problems more efficiently than normal recursive algorithm explained in Section 8.4.

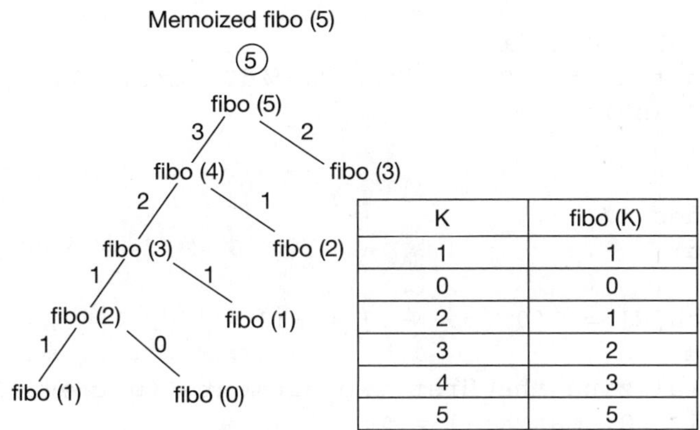

K	fibo (K)
1	1
0	0
2	1
3	2
4	3
5	5

Figure 8.6 Computing Fibonacci (5) series using memoization

Newly computed values are stored in the lookup table assigning keys before starting a recursive definition. Mamoization techniques remember values that have already been computed and stored in the lookup table. The computational tree is linear in this case.

> ***Note!***
> Memoization refers to the top-down optimization technique for improving the performance of recursive algorithms whereas iterative tabulation is a bottom-up approach that solves problems in a sequence.

CProg-8.9 Memoized version of finding Fibonaaci series

```
#include <stdio.h>
#include <stdlib.h>
#define N 20 /* Number of Fibonacci terms required to be dis-
played */
static c = 0;

/* Creating the Fibonacci sequence */
int rFibonacci(int *catch, int n)
   {
    c++;  /* C acts like counter which counts number of times
function called */
     if(catch[n] == -1)
       catch[n] = rFibonacci(catch, n - 1) + r_Fibonacci(catch,
n - 2);
     return catch[n];
   }
```

```
/* Printing the array */
void PrintArray(int *arr, int n)
   {
      int i;
      for(i = 0; i < n; i++)
          printf(i == 0 ? " %d" : ", %d", arr[i]);
      printf(" \n");
   }

/* Driver codes */
int main(void)
   {
      int catch[N] = {[0 ... N-1] = -1};

      /* Initializing the first two elements in the series */
      catch[0] = 0; catch[1] = 1;

      /* Calling Fibonacci function to start operation */
      rFibonacci(catch, N - 1);

      /* Display the Fibonacci series */
      PrintArray(catch, N);
      printf("Total number of times function called = %lu\n", c);
      return 0;
   }
/* End program */
```

Output

```
0, 1, 1, 2, 3, 5, 8, 13, 21, 34, 55, 89, 144, 233, 377, 610, 987,
1597, 2584, 4181
Total number of times function called = 37
```

> ***Programming Tips!***
>
> Variable `c` is used to count the number of times the recursive function is called. `rFibonacci()` is used for creating the Fibonacci sequence where `catch[]` is used to store all elements in the series. `PrintArray()` is used to display the Fibonacci series array.

PyProg-8.9 Memoized version of Fibonacci series

```
# Variable to catch values (using set data type) for memoization
fibonacci_catch = {}

def MemoisedFibonacci(n):
    # If got (memoized) the value, then return
   if n in fibonacci_catch:
        return fibonacci_catch[n]
```

```
    # Calculation of Fibonacci numbers
    if n == 1:
        result = 1
    elif n == 2:
        result = 1
    elif n > 2:
        result = MemoisedFibonacci(n - 1) + MemoisedFibonacci(n - 2)

    # Catch the value and return it
    fibonacci_catch[n] = result

    return result
# End MemoisedFibonacci

# Driver codes
# Displaying fibonacci series
print('Fibonacci series:', end = " ")
for n in range(1, 20):
    print(MemoisedFibonacci(n), end = " ")
# End program
```

Output

```
Fibonacci series: 1 1 2 3 5 8 13 21 34 55 89 144 233 377 610 987 1597
2584 4181
```

Programming Tips!

`MemoisedFibonacci()` is used for calculating Fibonacci series using the memoized method.

8.10.2 Iterative Tabulation (Bottom-up)

This approach solves problems in a sequence (smaller to bigger) using an iterative method. Optimal solutions can be generated with polynomial time complexity, cumulating answers to the top starting from the bottom. The answer to a problem (P) can easily be obtained from answers to smaller sub-problems in this scenario. We can order problems in a sequence (P_0, P_1, P_2, ..., P_K) of reasonable size, so that P_K is our original problem P. The initial problems, P_0 and possibly P_1, P_2, ..., P_R (for some R), become easy to solve (they are base cases).

For $i > R$, each P_i can be easily solved using solutions of P_0, ..., P_{i-1}. If these requirements are met, we can solve the problem P as follows:

- Create the sequence of problems P_0, P_1, P_2, ..., P_K, such that $P_K = P$.
- For $i = 0$ to K, solve P_K and return the solution for P_K.

8.11 SOME SOLVED EXAMPLES OF RECURSION

Example 8.6 **Let x and y be two positive integers and function R recursively defined as:**

$$R(x, y) = \begin{cases} 1; & \text{if } x < y. \\ R(x-y, y); & \text{if } y \leq x. \end{cases}$$

Find $R(1, 3)$ and $R(13, 3)$.

Solution

$R(1, 3) = 1$ since $1 < 3$ (i.e., $x < y$)

$R(13, 3) = R(10, 3) + 1$ since $3 \leq 13$ (i.e., $y \leq x$)

$= [R(7, 3) + 1] + 1 = R(7, 3) + 2$ since $3 \leq 10$ (i.e., $y \leq x$)

$= [R(4, 3) + 1] + 2 = R(4, 3) + 3$ since $3 \leq 7$ (i.e., $y \leq x$)

$= [R(1, 3) + 1] + 3 = R(1, 3) + 4$ since $3 \leq 4$ (i.e., $y \leq x$)

$= 1 + 4$

$= 5$ since $1 < 3$ (i.e., $x < y$)

Hence, $R(1, 3) = 1$ and $R(13, 3) = 5$

Example 8.7 **Calculate $f(7)$ for the recursive sequence $f(a) = 2*f(a - 2) + 3$ which has a base value of $f(3) = 11$.**

Solution

$f(a) = 2 * f(a - 2) + 3$

Here, a = 7.

So, $f(7) = 2 * f(7 - 2) + 3 = 2 * f(5) + 3$

$= 2 * [2 * f(5 - 2) + 3] + 3$

$= 2 * [2 * f(3) + 3] + 3$

$= 2 * [2 * 11 + 3] + 3$ [since $f(3) = 11$]

$= 2 * 25 + 3$

$= 53$

Hence, $f(7) = 53$.

Example 8.8 **The recursive sequence $f(a) = 2 * f(a - 1) + 3$ and $f(4) = 2$, Find f(6).**

Solution

$f(a) = 2 * f(a - 1) + 3$

Here, a = 6.

So, $f(6) = 2 * f(6 - 1) + 3$

$= 2 * f(5) + 3$

$= 2 * [2 * f(5 - 1) + 3] + 3$

$= 2 * [2 * f(4) + 3] + 3$

$= 2 * [2 * f(4) + 3] + 3$

$= 2 * [2 * 2 + 3] + 3$ [since f(4) = 2]

$= 2 * 7 + 3$

$= 17$

Hence, $f(6) = 17$.

QUICK RECAP

- ☑ A function that calls itself is known as a recursive function. This function-calling technique is known as recursion. A recursive algorithm must have a base case, or exit condition.
- ☑ The function which is called by itself is known as a direct recursive function. When a function calls a different function, and this in turn calls the original function, it is known as indirect recursion.
- ☑ Depending upon the number of recursive calls, recursion can be divided further into three more categories, namely linear, binary, and multiple recursions.
- ☑ Depending upon the nature of recursive call definitions, recursion can be divided into further two categories, tail and non-tail recursions. The last operation of a function is a recursive call in tail recursions. There are outstanding operations after the recursive call in non-tail recursions.
- ☑ The primary difference between recursion and iteration is that recursion is a process, always applied to a function and iteration is applied to a set of instructions which programmers want to execute repeatedly.
- ☑ We can calculate the GCD of two integers, factorial of a number, Fibonacci numbers, create Pascal's triangle, solve Tower of Hanoi problem, and sort stack using recursive methods efficiently.
- ☑ We can solve the *N*-Queens problem (place *n* number of chess queens on an $n \times n$ board without having any one of them attack the other queens) using recursion and backtracking.
- ☑ Dynamic programming is an algorithm design technique for solving computational problems using programming languages by providing optimal solutions to the problem by combining the optimal solutions of each sub-subproblem.
- ☑ Memoization refers to the top-down optimization technique for improving the performance of recursive algorithms where we record (or form a memo – memoize) previously computed results. Iterative tabulation is a bottom-up approach that solves problems in a sequence (smaller to bigger) using an iterative method.

REVIEW QUESTIONS

Multiple Choice Questions (MCQ): Choose the Best Alternative

Easy

1. A function called by itself, is known as:

A. Itself function. B. Recursive function.
C. Main function. D. All of them.

2. Which data structure is mostly used to perform recursion?

A. Tree B. Queue
C. Linked List D. Stack

Hint: Stack data structure is used to perform recursion. Recursion uses the system stack for storing the return addresses of the function calls.

3. In recursion, the condition for which the function will stop calling itself is called ________.

A. base case
B. worst case
C. best case
D. There is no such condition.

Hint: For recursion to end at some point, there always has to be a condition for which the function will not call itself. This condition is known as the base case.

4. Iteration uses a repetition structure whereas recursion uses ________.

A. sorting structure
B. controlling structure
C. selection structure
D. All of them.

5. Which of the following is correct with respect to recursive and non-recursive implementation of a problem in general?
   A. Time and space complexities, both are better in non-recursive implementation than recursive implementation.
   B. Time and space complexities, both are better in recursive implementation than non-recursive implementation.
   C. Space complexity is better in recursive implementation whereas time complexity is better in the non-recursive implementation.
   D. Time complexity is better in recursive implementation whereas space complexity is better in the non-recursive implementation.

   Hint: Generally non-recursive implementation is better in both time and space. Recursive implementation often creates the worst scenario. Thus, recursive cases do not always ensure the best case.
6. The stack is useful for implementing ______.
   A. radix search B. breadth-first search
   C. recursion D. None of these.

Moderate

7. Which of the following problems cannot be solved using recursion?
   A. GCD of two numbers.
   B. Problems without a base case.
   C. Factorial of a number.
   D. Fibonacci number.

   Hint: Problems without base case leads to infinite recursion calls.
8. What happens if the base condition is not defined in recursion?
   A. Stack overflow B. Stack underflow
   C. Both A and B. D. None of these.

   Hint: The recursion will run indefinitely until stack overflow when the base condition is not defined in recursion.
9. What will be the output of the following code?

```
int c = 0;
void rec(int n)
  {
      if(n == 0)
      return;
      c++;
      rec(n/10);
  }
int main()
  {
      rec(123456789);
      printf("%d",c);
      return 0;
  }
```

   A. 123456789 B. 9
   C. 987654321 D. 10

   Hint: The program prints the number of digits in the number 123456789, which is 9.
10. What is the base case for the following code?

```
void rec(int n)
  {
      if(n == 0)
      return;
      printf("%d", n);
      rec(n-1);
  }
int main()
  {
      rec(10);
      return 0;
  }
```

   A. return B. printf("%d ", n)
   C. if(n== 0) D. recur(n–1)

   Hint: For the base case, the recursive function is not called. So, "if(n== 0)" is the base case.
11. Solution of a problem depends on ______ in recursive methods.
   A. greater instances of the same problem
   B. greater instances of a different problem
   C. lesser instances of different problems
   D. lesser instances of the same problem
12. Which of the following methods can be used to solve *n*-queens problem?
   A. Iterative improvement
   B. Backtracking
   C. Divide-and-conquer
   D. Greedy algorithm
13. In dynamic programming, the technique of storing the previously calculated values is called ______.
   A. Memoization
   B. Saving value property
   C. Storing value property
   D. Mapping

Higher-order Thinking Skills (HOTS)

14. What will be the output of *f*(3, 8)?

```
int f(int m, int n)
{
    if(n == 0)
        return 0;
    if(n == 1)
        return 1;
    return m + f(m, n-1);
}
```

A. 21 B. 22
C. 24 D. 42

15. Predict the output of following program:

```
#include <stdio.h>
int f(int n)
{
  if(n <= 1)
      return 1;
  if(n%2 == 0)
      return f(n/2);
  return f(n/2) + f(n/2+1);
}

int main()
{
  printf("%d", f(11));
  return 0;
}
```

A. Stack overflow B. 5
C. 4 D. 3

Hint: On successive recursion f(11) will be decomposed into
f(5) + f(6) → f(2) + f(3) + f(3) → f(1) + 2 * [f(1) + f(2)] → 1 + 2 * [1 + f(1)] → 1 + 2 * (1 + 1) → 5.

16. What will be the output of *f*(12)?

```
void f(int n)
{
  if(n = = 0)
    return;
  printf("%d", n%2);
  f(n/2);
}
```

A. 1100 B. 0011
C. 1001 D. 1000

17. What does the following function do?

```
int f(unsigned int n)
{
    if (n = =  0 || n = = 1)
        return n;
    if (n%3 ! =  0)
        return 0;
    return f(n/3);
}
```

A. It returns 1 when n is a multiple of 3, otherwise returns 0.

B. It returns 1 when n is a power of 3, otherwise returns 0.

C. It returns 0 when n is a multiple of 3, otherwise returns 1.

D. It returns 0 when n is a power of 3, otherwise returns 1.

18. How many fundamental solutions are there for the 3-queen problem on a 3 * 3 matrix?

A. 10
B. 9
C. 0
D. 3

Hint: There are zero solutions to the 3-queen puzzle for 3 * 3 chess boards. Hence there are no fundamental solutions.

19. Consider the following recursive C function that takes two arguments:

```
unsigned int f(unsigned int n, unsigned int m)
{
    if(n > 0)  return (n%m + f(n/m, m));
    else return 0;
}
```

What is the return value of the function f when it is called as f(425, 10) ?

A. 425
B. 12
C. 11
D. 10

Hint: f(425, 10) returns sum of decimal digits (because radix/base is r = 10). Sum of digits for 425 is 4 + 2 + 5 = 11.

20. Consider the same recursive function that takes two arguments:

```
unsigned int f(unsigned int n,
unsigned int m)
  {
     if (n  > 0)   return (n%m +
f(n/m, m));
     else return 0;
  }
```

What will be the return value of the f() when it is called as *f*(513, 2)?

A. 2 B. 513
C. 9 D. 256

Hint: f(513, 2) returns 1 + f(256, 2). Then f(256, 2)) will be called again where 256 is divisible by 2 and in this way, it continues up to the last call f(1, 2). The last call f(1, 2) returns 1. So, the value returned by f(513, 2) will be 1 + 0 + 0.... + 0 + 1 = 2. Note that the function f(n, 2) returns the sum of bits in the number n.

Short Answer-type Questions

Easy

1. What do you mean by recursion?
2. What are the differences between recursion and iteration?
3. Write the various applications of recursion.
4. State the base condition of factorial recursive function.
5. What is the difference between direct and indirect recursion?

Moderate

6. What is Ackermann's function?
7. What do you mean by dynamic programming?
8. How recursion relates to stack data structure?
9. What is the base condition in recursion?
10. Distinguish between tail and non-tail recursion.
11. State the three rules of Tower of Hanoi problem.

Higher-Order Thinking Skills (HOTS)

12. Mention a few disadvantages of recursion.
13. "Every recursive function can be implemented using an iterative procedure" – Justify the statement.
14. How can we distinguish a tail recursion from others?
15. Define exponential recursion.
16. Why is the base condition required in recursions?

Descriptive-type Questions

Easy

1. Describe the different types of categories of recursions with examples.
2. Write an algorithm to reverse a stack using recursion.
3. Write a recursive algorithm for the solution of *n*-queens problem where $n = 8$.
4. What is the difference between dynamic programming and memoization?
5. Write a recursive algorithm for the Tower of Hanoi problem.

Moderate

6. Write an algorithm to find the LCM of two numbers using recursion.
7. Write an algorithm to generate *n* terms of Fibonacci series using recursion.
8. Write an algorithm to find the power of a number using recursion.
9. Design an algorithm to find the sum of natural numbers using recursion.
10. Write a program using C or Python to generate a random number sequence using recursion.

Higher-Order Thinking Skills (HOTS)

11. Find out and explain the complexity of the recurrence $T(n) = 2T(n - 1) - 2^n$
12. Write a recursive function to reverse a string.
13. Design an algorithm to find the sum of digits of a positive integer using recursion.
14. Predict the output of the following function and also discuss the function call flow using a diagram when $n = 4$.

```
void f(int n)
  {
     if(n > 0)
     {
        f(--n);
        printf("%d\n", n);
        f(--n);
     }
  }
```

CASE STUDIES

1. Design an algorithm to find the *n*th root of a number.
2. Study the following recursive function. Explain the tasks of the recursive function `func` and analyze recursive calls using a suitable diagram.

```
int func(int a[], int s)
  {
    if (s == 0)
      return 0;
    else if(a[s - 1] % 2 == 1)
      return func(a, s - 1) + a[
s - 1];
    else
      return func(a, s - 1);
  }
```

LAB EXERCISES

1. Write a Python program to find whether a string is a palindrome or not using recursion.
   Examples:
   a. Input → India; Output → String is not a palindrome!
   b. Input → Madam; Output → String is a palindrome!
2. Write a C program to sort a stack using recursion:
   Input → Stack elements before sorting: −50 40 −30 20 10
   Output → Stack elements after sorting: 40 20 10 −30 −50

ANSWER KEYS

Multiple Choice Questions

1. B	**4.** C	**7.** B	**10.** C	**13.** A	**16.** B	**19.** C
2. D	**5.** A	**8.** A	**11.** D	**14.** B	**17.** B	**20.** A
3. A	**6.** C	**9.** B	**12.** B	**15.** B	**18.** C	

9 Trees

CONTENTS

EXPECTED OUTCOMES OF THIS CHAPTER

After going through this chapter learners will be able

- ☑ To understand binary tree data structures and represent it using array and linked list.
- ☑ To demonstrate different binary tree traversal algorithms and implement the traversal techniques using C and Python.
- ☑ To understand the underlying organization of binary search trees (BST) and implement the basic operations on BST.
- ☑ To visualize the AVL or height balanced trees and explore rotation techniques for balancing the height of the search trees.
- ☑ To demonstrate the concept and creation of B trees and B+ trees besides distinguishing these trees.

9.1 INTRODUCTION

We have explained the linear data structures like array, linked list, stack, and queue in the previous chapters. All data structures related problems are not always linear. *A tree is a non-linear data structure* through which we can solve many real-world problems. In this structure, each element is called a node. It is structured hierarchically, in which each node can store data value and address of other next-level nodes. Here, nodes are connected by edges. Tree is also a very popular non-linear data structure widely used in many applications. Tree organization is used in every file and directory within a file system. The tree is also used to implement searching operations fast and efficiently.

9.1.1 Definition of Tree

A tree is defined as a finite set of elements (nodes connected by edges) in such a way that:

- *A specially designated node at the top of the tree is called root node;*
- *The remaining elements (nodes) are partitioned into a collection of subtrees T_1, T_2,..., T_n.*

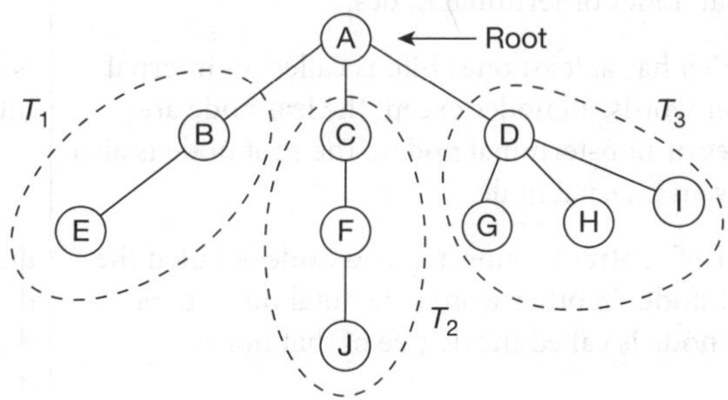

Figure 9.1 Structure of a tree

Figure 9.1 demonstrates a sample tree structure (*T*) where node 'A' is the root of the tree and contains three subtrees T_1, T_2, and T_3, which are organized in a hierarchical structure. This structure may continue recursively.

> ***Note!***
> A tree is a non-linear data structure where each element is called a node that is structured hierarchically.

9.1.2 Basic Terminologies

There are many terms associated with trees. Figure 9.1 presents the concepts associated with these terminologies and Table 9.1 presents the definitions with examples.

Table 9.1 Basic tree terminologies definitions with examples

Terms	Description	Example (Figure 9.1)
Node (vertex)	Each data element of a tree is called a *vertex*. It is also known as a node. It specifies the links (edge) to other nodes.	A, B, C, D are known as vertices or nodes.
Edge (Links)	An *edge* is a connection between two nodes. It is also known as links.	The link between nodes A and B is represented as a link or edge.
Root	It is the first node of a tree. The root is also the top node of a tree.	Node A is the root node.
Parent/ Predecessor node	A node which is having further sub-branches is called the parent node of those sub-branches. If a particular node is positioned previous to some other node, then that particular previous node is called the predecessor of the other node.	Node D is a parent as well as the predecessor node of G, H and I.
Child/ Successor node	The nodes which have a link from its parent node are called child nodes or successor nodes. In a tree, any parent node can have many child nodes.	Nodes G, H, and I are children of nodes D.
Sibling	Child nodes belonging to the same parent are called siblings.	Nodes G, H, and I are siblings because they all have the same parent node D.
Leaf	The node which does not have a child is called a leaf node. So, a leaf node has zero children. The leaf nodes are also called external nodes or terminal nodes.	Nodes E, J, G, H, and I are leaf nodes.
Internal node	The node which has at least one child is called an internal node. In other words, all nodes except the leaf node are internal nodes or non-terminal nodes. The root node is also considered as an internal node.	Nodes A, B, C, D, and F are internal nodes.
Degree	Total number of subtrees connected to a node is called the *degree* of that node. In other words, the total number of children of a node is called the degree of that node.	degree(A) = 3, degree(B) = 1, degree(C) = 1, degree(D) = 3, degree(F) = 1.
Level	The level is the rank of the hierarchy. The root node is always considered at level 0 and the children of the root node are at level 1 and so on. If a particular node is at level 'L', then its child nodes are at level 'L+1' and its parent node should be at level 'L–1' level. The level count starts with 0 (root) and is incremented by one at each step.	Node A (root node) is at level 0. B, C and D are at level 1. E, F, G, H and I are at level 2. Node J is at level 3.

(Continued)

Terms	Description	Example (Figure 9.1)
Depth or Height of a Tree	The maximum number of nodes that is possible in a path starting from the root node to a leaf node is called the height or depth of that tree. The total number of edges (links) from the root node to the leaf node through the longest path is called the height or depth. So, $h = l_{max} + 1$, where 'h' is the height of a tree, and 'l_{max}' is the maximum level of the tree.	The height or depth of the tree is denoted by h and $h = 3 + 1 = 4$ (because root at level 0 and the maximum level number is 3).
Path	The sequence of nodes and links from one node to another node is called a path between those two nodes. The length of a path is the total number of nodes in that path.	The path between nodes A to G is A–D–G (length = 3).

Forest: *A set of disjoint trees is called a forest.* In other words, a forest is a collection of acyclic graphs that are not connected. Figure 9.2 presents the forest pictorially. Social networking sites (such as Facebook, LinkedIn, Twitter, etc.) use tree data structure for their data representation. When adding two people as friends, you are creating a forest of two people.

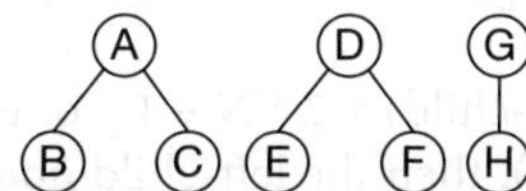

Figure 9.2 Example of a forest

9.1.3 Definition of Binary Tree

As explained above, a tree can have nodes having any number of children. *A binary tree is a special type of tree in which every node can have a maximum of two children.* In other words, a tree in which every node can have a maximum of two children is called a binary tree. One child is known as a left child (placed left pictorially) and the other is known as the right child (placed right pictorially). Figure 9.3 shows an example of a binary tree.

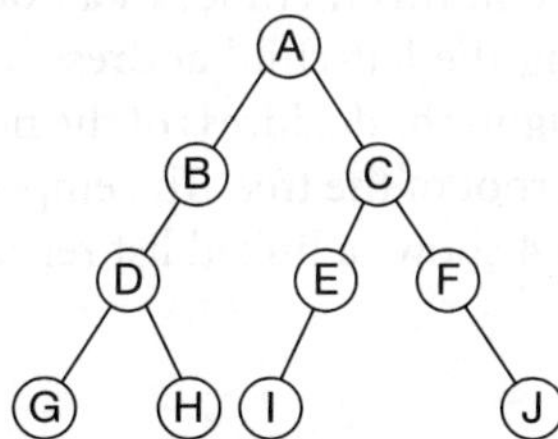

Figure 9.3 Example of a binary tree

> ***Note!***
> A binary tree is a special type of tree in which every node can have a maximum of two children.

9.1.4 Binary Tree Representation

A binary tree structure is represented using two conceptual structures.

1. Array representation or sequential representation
2. Linked list representation.

Array Representation of Binary Tree

In this type of representation, a binary tree can be represented using a one-dimensional (1D) array. Consider the Fig. 9.3 example of a binary tree. It can be represented using the array below.

	A[0]	A[1]	A[2]	A[3]	A[4]	A[5]	A[6]	A[7]	A[8]	A[9]	A[10]	A[11]	A[12]	A[13]	A[14]
Given list A	A	B	C	D	-	E	F	G	H	-	-	I	-	-	J

Figure 9.4 Example of array representation of a binary tree

This method is easy to understand and implement. The following steps are to be followed to implement a binary tree using arrays:

Take a binary tree and allocate numbers to its nodes from left to right. The root (A) is stored in A[0]. Then the left child (B) and right child (C) are stored in A[1] and A[2] respectively in the next level. Then again, the left child of B is stored at A[3] and so on. Suppose, we have a partial (or incomplete) binary tree and node *i* is absent. We have to put some value that represents 'no data' in the *i*-th position of the array. Three simple formulae allow us to go from the index of the parent to the index of its children and vice-versa.

If index(parent) = N, then index(left-child) = $2 * N + 1$. For example, suppose in Fig. 9.3, the parent node index is $N = 2$ (here A[2] stores C), then the left-child node index will be $2 * 2 + 1 = 5$ (i.e. here, node E will be stored in A[5]).

If index(parent) = N, then index(right-child) = $2 * N + 2$. For example, suppose in Fig. 9.3, parent node index is $N = 2$ (here A[2] stores C), then the right-child node index will be $2 * 2 + 2 = 6$ (here, node F will be stored in A[6]).

If index(child) = N, index(parent) = $(N - 1)/2$ (integer division with truncation). For example, suppose in Fig. 9.3, parent node index is $N = 5$ (here A[5] stores E), then parent node (C) index will be $(5 - 1)/2 = 2$ (i.e. here, A[2] stores C).

Linked list representation of a binary tree

We use double-linked pointers to represent a binary tree in this method. In a double-linked list, every node consists of three fields. The first field is for storing the left-child address, the second field is for storing actual data and the third node is for storing the right-child address of the node. The head node of the linked list contains the address of the first node, i.e., root of the tree. The empty tree simply contains NULL at the head pointer, not an empty node. Figure 9.4 shows a linked list representation of a binary tree given in Fig. 9.3.

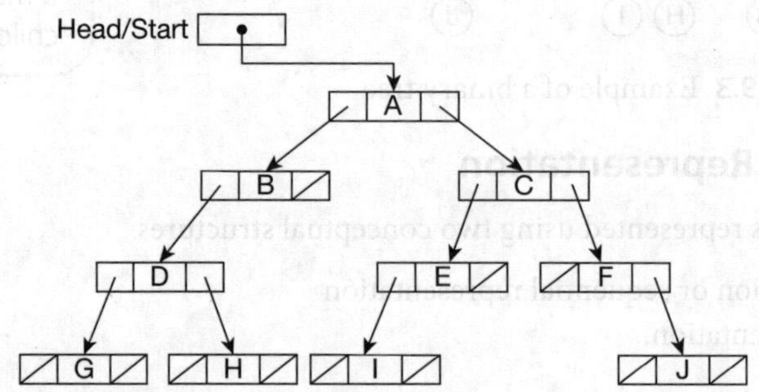

Figure 9.4 Example of linked list representation of a binary tree

9.2 CHARACTERISTICS OF BINARY TREES

There are many types of binary trees. Here, the different concepts associated with the binary tree are presented with definitions and examples.

9.2.1 Binary Tree Types with Example

Types	Description	Example
Full binary tree	If a binary tree contains the maximum possible number of nodes at all levels, then it is called a full binary tree. All leaf nodes are present and at the same level (last level) here.	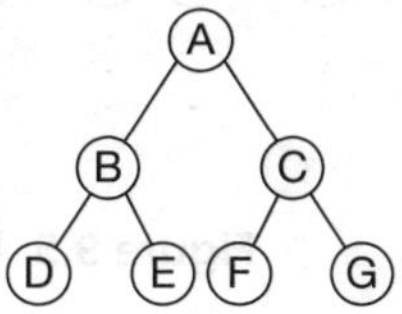
Complete binary tree	A binary tree is complete if all levels have the maximum number of possible nodes, except possibly the last level. All nodes should be present as far left as possible at the last level.	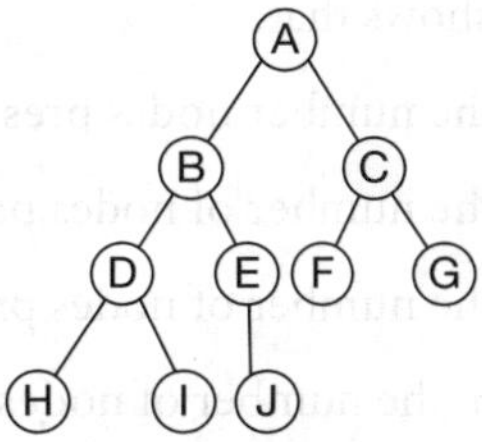
Extended binary tree (2-tree)	In this binary tree, each node has either two children or zero (no) children. The node which has no children is called an external node and the node which has two children is called an internal node.	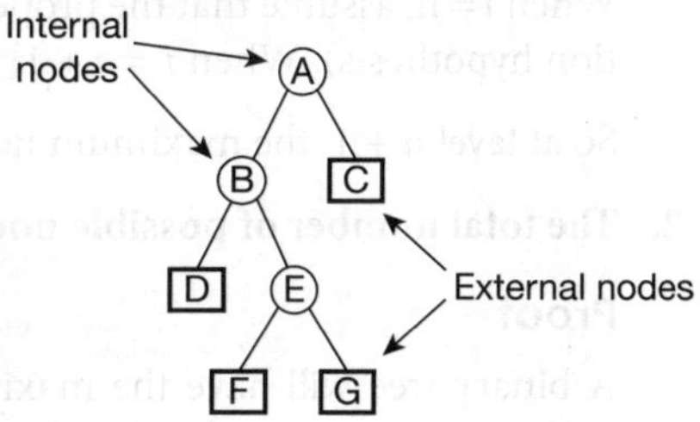 Internal nodes External nodes
Heap trees	A heap is a complete binary tree where the root-node key is compared with its children and arranged accordingly. Nodes are arranged based on their values in a heap. Two types of heap are possible: 1. **Max-heap:** Every parent node contains greater than or equal value to its child nodes. 2. **Min-heap:** Every parent node contains a smaller value than its child nodes.	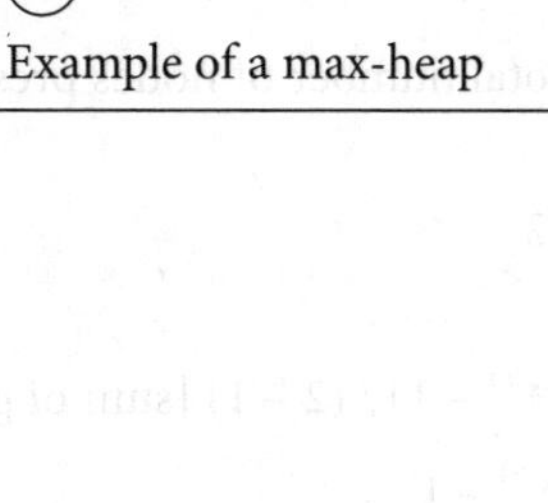 Example of a max-heap

9.2.2 Properties of Binary Trees

1. **Maximum number of nodes at level *i* is 2^i.**

Proof

We will prove this property by the method of induction.

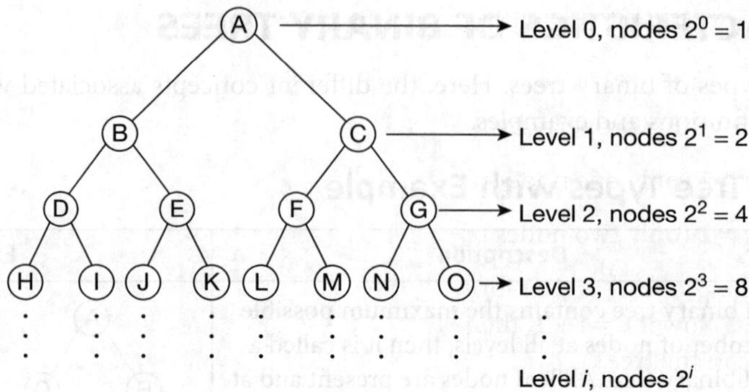

Figure 9.5 Level-wise representation of a binary tree

Figure 9.5 shows that:

At level 0, the number nodes present is $2^0 = 1$;

At level 1, the number of nodes present is $2^1 = 2$;

At level 2, the number of nodes present is $2^2 = 4$ and so on.

So, at level i, the number of nodes present is 2^i.

When $i = n$, assume that the property is true for n-th level, so at level n there are 2^n nodes (induction hypothesis). When $i = n + 1$, the maximum number of children of a particular node is 2.

So at level $n + 1$, the maximum number of nodes can be $2 * 2^n = 2^{n+1}$; hence it is proved.

2. **The total number of possible nodes is $2^h - 1$, where h is the height of the tree.**

Proof

A binary tree will have the maximum number of nodes only if there is maximum number of nodes present at each level.

Figure 9.5 shows:

At level 0, the number of nodes present is $2^0 = 1$;

At level 1, the number of nodes present is $2^1 = 2$;

At level 2, the number of nodes present is $2^2 = 4$, and so on.

So, at level i, the number of nodes present is $= 2^i$.

So, the total number of nodes present in that binary tree is,

$$n = \sum_{i=0}^{l_{\max}} 2^i$$

$= (2^{l_{\max}+1} - 1) / (2 - 1)$ [sum of geometric series]

$= 2^{l_{\max}+1} - 1$

$= 2^h - 1$ [as $h = l_{\max} + 1$, where h is the height of a tree and $l_{\max}$ is the maximum level of the tree according to the definition of leaf]

3. **A non-empty binary tree with n nodes has exactly $n - 1$ edges.**

Proof

We will prove this property by the method of induction.

Assume $n = 1$ (only one node (root) present), so the number of edges is 0.

Assume $n = 2$ (only two nodes present), so the number of edges is 1.

Assume the property is true for $n = i$ (induction hypothesis). In that case, there are $(i - 1)$ edges for i nodes. Now if $n = i + 1$, then one more node is inserted in the tree and that also includes one extra edge in the tree.

So, the total number of edges is $(i - 1) + 1 = i$, and the property is proved.

4. **If n_0 be the total number of leaf nodes and n_2 be the total number of nodes having two children in a binary tree, then prove that $n_0 = n_2 + 1$.**

Proof

Suppose, total number of nodes with one child is n_1

So, total number of nodes in a binary tree is $N = n_0 + n_1 + n_2$

So, total number of edges $E = n_0 * 0 + n_1 * 1 + n_2 * 2$

So, $n_1 * 1 + 2 * n_2 = (n_0 + n_1 + n_2) - 1$ (since $E = N - 1$ according to Property 3)

$\Rightarrow n_2 = n_0 - 1$

$\Rightarrow n_0 = n_2 + 1$ [Proved]

5. **In an extended binary tree (2-tree):**
Total number of external nodes (E) = Total number of internal nodes (I) + 1.

Proof

A node which has zero children is called an external node (denoted by E) and a node which has two children is called an internal node (denoted by I).

So, the total number of nodes in an extended binary tree (2-tree) is $N = E + I$.

So, total number of edges = $E * 0 + I * 2$.

So, $E * 0 + 2 * I = N - 1$ (Since number of edges = $N - 1$ according to property 3)

$\Rightarrow 2 * I = E + I - 1$ [Since $N = E + I$]

$\Rightarrow E = I + 1$ [Proved].

6. **In an extended binary tree (2-tree): External path length (L_E) = Internal path length (L_I) + 2 * n, where, n is the total number of internal nodes.**

External path length (L_E): It is the sum of all path lengths summed over each path (summation of all edges) from the root to an external node.

Internal path length (L_I): It is the sum of all path lengths summed over each path (summation of all edges) from the root to an internal node.

Proof (by the method of induction)

Suppose an extended binary tree (T) has n number of internal nodes.

Base case: $n = 1$, $L_I = 0$, $L_E = 2 = L_I + 2n$.

Assumption: $L_E = L_I + 2n$ holds for $0 < n < k$ where k is a positive integer.

Induction: When $n = k > 1$, partition the tree into three parts, the root, the left subtree L, and the right subtree R. Assume L has k_l internal nodes, and R has k_r internal nodes, then $k = k_l + k_r + 1$ (the root).

Since each node (internal and external) in L and R has one more length of the height in T, and the number of external nodes is 1 plus the number of internal nodes for the binary tree,

$L_I = [L_I(L) + k_l] + [L_I(R) + k_r]$, where the first term is for L and the last term is for R.
$L_E = [L_E(L) + k_l + 1] + [L_E(R) + k_r + 1]$, where the first term is for L and the last term is for R.

Thus, $L_E = L_E(L) + L_E(R) + k + 1$, since $k = k_l + k_r + 1$;

$= L_I(L) + 2k_l + L_I(R) + 2k_r + k + 1$;

$= [L_I(L) + k_l + L_I(R) + k_r] + k_l + k_r + k + 1$;

$= L_I + k_l + k_r + k + 1$, since $L_I = [L_I(L) + k_l] + [L_I(R) + k_r]$;

$= L_I + 2k$, since $k = k_l + k_r + 1$;

$= L_I + 2n$,

So, $L_E = L_I + 2n$ also holds good for $n = k > 1$.

Hence the property is proved by the method of induction.

9.2.3 Expression Tree

A binary expression tree is a particular form of an extended binary tree (or 2-tree). It is used to represent expressions. Operands are stored in leaves (or in external nodes) of the binary expression tree and operators are stored in non-leaf nodes (or in internal nodes). An expression tree does not contain any parenthesis. It may not be unique for expression but it must produce correct results.

We have to convert an infix expression into a postfix expression as discussed in Chapter 5 on the stack. Then we have to generate its corresponding expression tree for a resultant postfix expression and then compute the value of the expression. Following are the steps (or algorithm) to construct an expression tree from a given postfix expression:

1. Create a stack.
2. Read the given postfix symbol, one at a time, and repeat Steps 3 to 9.
3. If the symbol is an operand, then create a single-node expression tree with the operand and push the root pointer of the generated tree into the stack.
4. If the symbol is an operator, then pop out pointers to the two trees (T1 and T2) from the stack.
5. Create a new tree with the operator as the root. Left-child and right-child point to trees T2 and T1, respectively.
6. Push the root pointer of this new tree back into the stack.
7. The stack will contain a single tree; return it as the final expression tree.

Example 9.1: Conversion of expression $(a - b) + (c * d)$ into an expression tree.

$(a - b) + (c * d)$

⇓ Infix to postfix conversion

$ab - cd * +$

Figure 9.6(a) Converting $(a - b) + (c * d)$ into an expression tree

(a) First, the infix expression $(a - b) + (c * d)$ is converted into a postfix expression $ab - cd * +$.

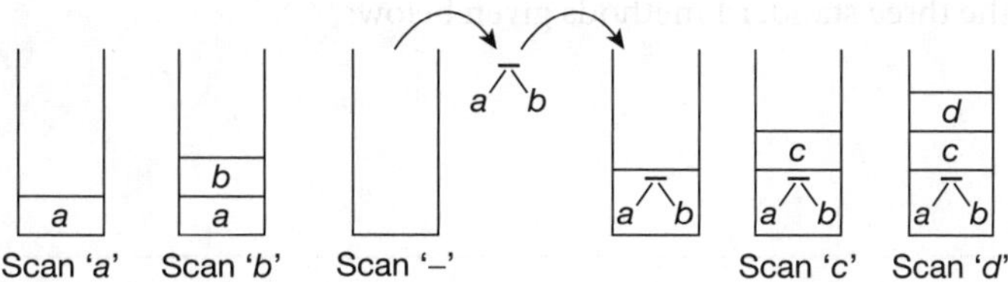

Figure 9.6(b) Converting $(a - b) + (c * d)$ into an expression tree

(b) Scan the elements from the postfix expression, one by one. First, take the operands *a* and *b*. Then push these two operands into a stack. Next take the symbol '–', which is an operator. Then pop out the top two elements *b* and *a* from the stack. Create a new tree with the operator '–' as the root. Left-child and right-child are *a* and *b* respectively. Push the new tree back into the stack. Then the next two symbols *c* and *d* (operands) are pushed into the stack.

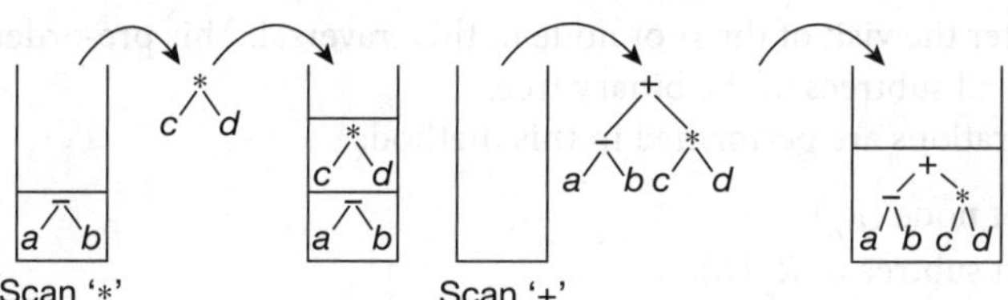

Figure 9.6(c) Converting $(a - b) + (c * d)$ into an expression tree

(c) The next symbol '*' is an operator. We have to pop out the top two elements *d* and *c* from the stack then. We have to create a new tree with the operator '*' as the root. Left-child and right-child are *c* and *d* respectively. Push the new tree back into the stack.
The next symbol '+' is an operator. Now, we have to pop out the top two elements (subtrees) from the stack. A new tree is to be created with the operator '+' as the root. The top subtree will be the right child of the operator '+' and the next-to-top subtree will be the left-child of the operator '+' respectively. Now, the new tree is to be pushed back into the stack.

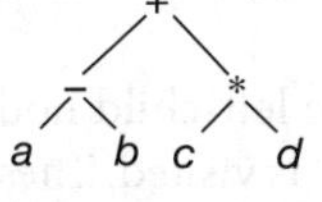

Final expression tree

Figure 9.6(d) Converting $(a - b) + (c * d)$ into an expression tree

Now, the expression is complete and hence we can pop out from the final expression tree as shown in Fig. 9.6.

> **Note!**
> A binary expression tree is a particular form of a 2-tree used to represent expressions.

9.3 BINARY TREE TRAVERSAL ALGORITHMS

Binary tree traversal is the process of visiting all elements of the tree only once. Binary tree traversal can be performed using the three standard methods given below:

- Preorder
- Inorder
- Postorder

> **Note!**
> Binary tree traversal is the process of visiting all elements of the tree only once using three standard methods, namely preorder, inorder and postorder traversal.

9.3.1 Preorder Traversal

The root node is visited before the left-child and right-child nodes in the preorder traversal. 'Pre' means 'before'. So, the root node will be placed before the left and right node. Left node and right node are visited sequentially after the visit of the root node in this traversal. This pre-order traversal is applicable for every root node of all subtrees of the binary tree.

The following operations are performed in this method:

(a) Process the root node (R_o).
(b) Traverse the left subtree of R_o (L).
(c) Traverse the right subtree of R_o (R).

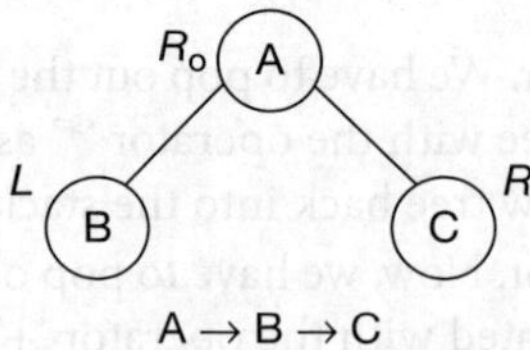

Figure 9.7 Preorder traversal of $R_o - L - R$

The preorder traversal of A – B – C ($R_o - L - R$) is presented in Fig. 9.7.

First, the root node A is visited. Then the left-child node B is visited. In the end, the right-child node C is visited. These are presented using arrows in the above Fig. 9.7.

> **Note!**
> The root node is visited before the left- and right-child in the preorder.

9.3.2 Algorithm of Preorder Traversal

Algo-9.1 Pseudocode for preorder traversal of a binary tree by recursive way

```
Preorder (node PTR)
   BEGIN
      IF (PTR ≠ NULL)
         PRINT (data (PTR))
         Preorder (left (PTR))
         Preorder (right (PTR))
     ENDIF
   END
```

We can implement the preorder traversal in a non-recursive way. The stack data structure is used here to store the elements since we are not using recursion.

Algo-9.2 Algorithm for preorder traversal of a binary tree by non-recursive way

Step 1	Create an empty stack S.
Step 2	Initialize PTR as root.
Step 3	Print the PTR and if PTR.right ≠ NULL then push it to S and set PTR = PTR.left and continue till PTR.left = = NULL.
Step 4	If PTR = = NULL and S is empty then 'Exit'.
Step 5	Else if PTR = = NULL then pop the top node from the S and set it as PTR = popped_node, and go to Step 3.

Example (Non-recursive)

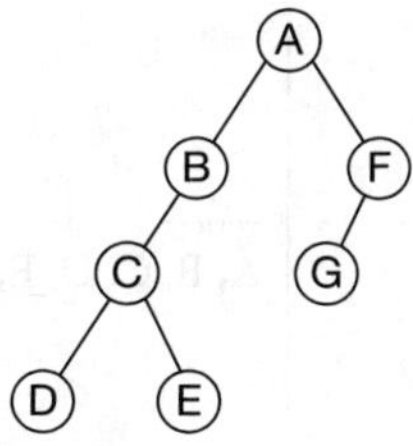

Figure 9.8 Binary tree for preorder traversal

Consider the binary tree shown in Fig. 9.8 for applying a non-recursive preorder traversal algorithm. We have to find out the preorder sequence using the non-recursive method.

Actions	Node scanned	Process/Print	Stack (S)
We have to process the root A of the tree, and then check for the right child; F is the present right child. So, we have to push F into a stack (S), and set the root to the left child B.	A	A	Stack (S) F | | | | | 0 1 2 3 4 5
We have to process B next, and then check for the right child. No right child is present here. So, we have to set the root to the left child C.	B	A, B	Stack (S) F | | | | | 0 1 2 3 4 5
We have to process C next, and then check for the right child. E is the right child present here. So, we have to push E into the stack, and set the root to the left child D.	C	A, B, C	Stack (S) F | E | | | | 0 1 2 3 4 5
We have to process D next, and then check for the right child. No right child is present here. So, we have to check for the left child. No left child is present here. So, we have to pop from the stack, and set the pop-out node E as root.	D	A, B, C, D	Stack (S) F | | | | | 0 1 2 3 4 5
We have to process E next, and then check for the right child. No child (right and left) is present here. So, we have to pop from the stack, and set the pop-out node F as root.	E	A, B, C, D, E	Stack (S) | | | | | 0 1 2 3 4 5
We have to process F next and then check for the right child. No child (left or right) is present here. So, we have to set the root to the left child G.	F	A, B, C, D, E, F	Stack (S) | | | | | 0 1 2 3 4 5
We have to process G next and then check for the right child. No child (left or right) is present here. The stack is now empty. So, the process is completed.	G	A, B, C, D, E, F, G (Final preorder traversal sequence)	Stack (S) | | | | | 0 1 2 3 4 5

9.3.3 Preorder Traversal (Non-recursive and Recursive) with C

CProg-9.1 C source code for non-recursive and recursive preorder traversal of a binary tree

```
#include<stdio.h>
#include<conio.h>
#include<stdlib.h>

/* Node Declaration */
typedef struct binary_tree
 {
 int data, flag;
 struct binary_tree *left, *right;
 } node;

/*Node creation*/
node *create(node *r, int x)
 {
 if(r == NULL)
  {
  r = (node *)malloc(sizeof(node));
  r->data = x;
  r->left = r->right = NULL;
  }
 else
  {
  if(r->data <= x)
   r->right = create(r->right, x);
  else
   r->left = create(r->left, x);
  }
 return r;
 }

/* Recursive function of preorder traversal*/
void preOrder(node *r)
 {
 if(r != NULL)
  {
  printf("%d\t", r->data);
  preOrder(r->left);
  preOrder(r->right);
  }
 }
```

```
/* Non-Recursive function of preOrder traversal*/
void nonPreOrder(node *r)
 {
 int top = 0;
 node *s[20], *pt = r;
 s[0]=NULL;
 while(pt != NULL)
  {
  printf("%d\t", pt->data);
  if(pt->right != NULL)
   s[++top] = pt->right;
  if(pt->left != NULL)
   pt = pt->left;
  else
   pt = s[top--];
  }
 }

/* Driver code */
void main()
{
 int x;
 char ch = 'Y';
 node *head = NULL;

 /* Taking input from user */
 while(toupper(ch) == 'Y')
 {
  printf("Enter the value to insert:");
  scanf("%d", &x);
  head = create(head, x);
  printf("Do you want to continue (y/n):");
  fflush(stdin);
  ch = getchar();
 }

 printf("\nPreorder recursive:\n");
 preOrder(head);
 printf("\nPreorder non-recursive:\n");
 nonPreOrder(head);
 getch();
}
/* End of program */
```

Output

```
Enter the value to insert:1
Do you want to continue(y/n):y
Enter the value to insert:2
Do you want to continue(y/n):y
Enter the value to insert:3
Do you want to continue(y/n):y
Enter the value to insert:4
Do you want to continue(y/n):y
Enter the value to insert:5
Do you want to continue(y/n):n
Preorder recursive:
1       2       3       4       5
Preorder non-recursive:
1       2       3       4       5
```

Programming Tips!
A binary tree node is created using `create()`. A node is created dynamically using `malloc()`. `preOrder()` is used recursively for preorder traversal. `nonPreOrder()` is used for preorder traversal non-recursively.

9.3.4 Preorder Traversal (Non-recursive) with Python

PyProg-9.1 Non-recursive preorder traversal of a binary tree

```
# Class to create tree node
class Node:
    # Constructor to create a new node
    def __init__(self, data):
        self.data = data
        self.left = None
        self.right = None

# An iterative process to print preorder traversal of BT
def iterativePreorder(root):
    # Base case
    if root is None:
        return

    # Create an empty stack and push root to it
    nodeStack = []
    nodeStack.append(root)

    # Pop all items one by one. Do following for every popped item
    # a) print it, b) push its right child, c) push its left child
    # Note that right child is pushed first so that left is processed
     first
```

```
    while(len(nodeStack) > 0):
        # Pop the top item from stack and print it
        node = nodeStack.pop()
        print(node.data),

        # Push right and left children of the popped node to stack
        if node.right is not None:
            nodeStack.append(node.right)
        if node.left is not None:
            nodeStack.append(node.left)

# Driver program to test above function
root = Node(10)
root.left = Node(8)
root.right = Node(2)
root.left.left = Node(3)
root.left.right = Node(5)
root.right.left = Node(2)
iterativePreorder(root)
## End program
```

Output

```
10
8
3
5
2
2
```

> ***Programming Tips!***
> `iterativePreorder()` is used for implementing an iterative process to print a preorder traversal sequence of a binary tree.

9.3.5 Inorder Traversal

The left node is visited before the root node and right child nodes in the inorder traversal. 'In' means 'in-between'. So, the root node will be placed in between the left and right nodes. In this traversal, the left node is visited first, then its root node. The right node is visited after the left and root node. This inorder traversal is applicable for every root node of all subtrees in the tree.

The following operations are performed in this method:

(a) Traverse the left subtree of R_o (L).
(b) Process the root node (R_o).
(c) Traverse the right subtree of R_o (R).

Preorder traversal of B – A – C ($L - R_o - R$) is presented below in Fig. 9.9.

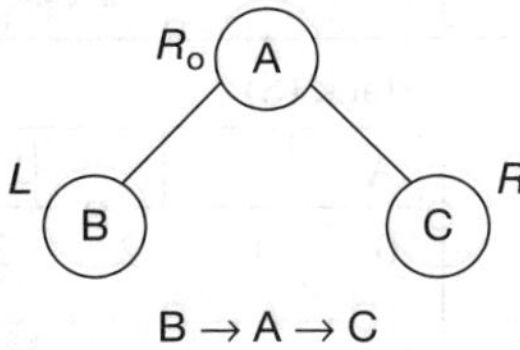

Figure 9.9 Inorder traversal of $L - R_o - R$

> **Note!**
> The left node is visited before the root node and right child, both in inorder.

First, the left child node B is visited. Then the root node A is visited. At the end, the right child node C is visited. These are presented using arrows in the above Figure 9.9.

9.3.6 Algorithms of Inorder Traversal

Algo-9.3 Pseudocode for inorder traversal of a binary tree by recursive way

```
Inorder (node PTR) Procedure:
   BEGIN
      IF (PTR ≠ NULL)
         Inorder (left (PTR))
         PRINT (data (PTR))
         Inorder (right (PTR))
     ENDIF
   END
```

We can implement the inorder traversal in a non-recursive way. The stack data structure is used here like preorder traversal to store the elements since we are not using recursion.

Algo-9.4 Algorithm for inorder traversal of a binary tree by non-recursive way

Step 1	Create an empty stack S.
Step 2	Initialize the root node as PTR.
Step 3	Push the PTR to S and set PTR = PTR.left until PTR is NULL
Step 4	If PTR is NULL and S is not empty then 4.1: Pop the top item from S; 4.2: Print the popped item, set PTR = popped_item.right; 4.3: Go to step 3;
Step 5	If PTR is NULL and S is empty then exit.

Example 9.2

Let us consider the binary tree shown in Fig. 9.8 and apply a non-recursive inorder traversal algorithm to find out the inorder sequence.

Actions	Node scanned	Process/ Print	Stack (S)
We have to set the root A of the tree, and then push the root node A into the stack (S). Then we have to set the root to the left child B.	A		Stack (S) | A | | | | | | 0 1 2 3 4 5
We have to push node B into the stack. Then, we have to set the root to the left child C.	B		Stack (S) | A | B | | | | | 0 1 2 3 4 5
We have to push node B into the stack. Then, we have to set the root to the left child D.	C		Stack (S) | A | B | C | | | | 0 1 2 3 4 5
We have to push node D into the stack. Then, we have to check for the left child of D.	D		Stack (S) | A | B | C | D | | | 0 1 2 3 4 5
No left child of node D is present. So, pop the top element from the stack and process/print D.		D	Stack (S) | A | B | C | | | | 0 1 2 3 4 5
We have to check for the right child of D. No right child of node D is present. So, we have to pop the top element C from the stack, and process/print C.		D, C	Stack (S) | A | B | | | | | 0 1 2 3 4 5
We have to check for the right child of C. Right child of node C is present here. So, we have to push E into the stack. Then, we have to check for the left child of E.	E	D, C	Stack (S) | A | B | E | | | | 0 1 2 3 4 5
No left child of node E is present. So, we have to pop the top element from stack, and process/print E.		D, C, E	Stack (S) | A | B | | | | | 0 1 2 3 4 5
We have to check for the right child of E. No right child of node E is present here. So, we have to pop the top element B from the stack, and process/print B.		D, C, E, B	Stack (S) | A | | | | | | 0 1 2 3 4 5

(Continued)

Actions	Node scanned	Process/ Print	Stack (S)
We have to check for the right child of B. No right child of node B is present here. So, pop the top element A from the stack, and process/print A.		D, C, E, B, A	Stack (S) [, , , , ,] 0 1 2 3 4 5
We have to check for the right child of A. The right child of node F is present here. So, we have to push F into the stack. Then we have to check for the left child of F.	F	D, C, E, B, A	Stack (S) [F, , , , ,] 0 1 2 3 4 5
The left child of F is present here. So, we have to push node G into the stack. Then, we have to check for the left child of G.	G	D, C, E, B, A	Stack (S) [F, G, , , ,] 0 1 2 3 4 5
No left child of node G is present here. So, we have to pop the top element from the stack, and process/print G.		D, C, E, B, A, G	Stack (S) [F, , , , ,] 0 1 2 3 4 5
We have to check for the right child of G. No right child of node G is present here. So, we have to pop the top element F from the stack, and process/print 'F'.		D, C, E, B, A, G, F	Stack (S) [, , , , ,] 0 1 2 3 4 5
We have to check for the right child of F. No right child of node F is present here. So, we have to pop a node from the stack, but the stack is empty. It indicates that the process is completed.		D, C, E, B, A, G, F **(Final inorder traversal sequence)**	Stack (S) [, , , , ,] 0 1 2 3 4 5

9.3.7 Inorder Traversal (Non-recursive and Recursive) with C

CProg-9.2 C source code for non-recursive and recursive inorder traversal of a binary tree

```
#include<stdio.h>
#include<conio.h>
#include<stdlib.h>

/* Node Declaration*/
typedef struct binary_tree
```

```
{
int data, flag;
struct binary_tree *left, *right;
} node;

/* Node creation */
node * create(node *r, int x)
 {
 if(r == NULL)
  {
  r = (node *)malloc(sizeof(node));
  r->data = x;
  r->left = r->right = NULL;
  }
 else
  {
  if(r->data <= x)
   r->right = create(r->right, x);
  else
   r->left = create(r->left, x);
  }
 return r;
 }

/* Recursive function of inorder traversal */
void inOrder(node *r)
 {
 if(r != NULL)
  {
  inOrder(r->left);
  printf("%d\t", r->data);
  inOrder(r->right);
  }
 }

/* Non-recursive function of inorder traversal*/
void nonInOrder(node *r)
 {
 int top = 0;
 node *s[20], *pt = r;
 s[0] = NULL;
 while(pt != NULL)
  {
  s[++top] = pt;
  pt = pt->left;
  }
```

```
 pt = s[top--];
 while(pt != NULL)
  {
  printf("%d\t", pt->data);
  if(pt->right != NULL)
   {
   pt = pt->right;
   while(pt != NULL)
    {
    s[++top] = pt;
    pt = pt->left;
    }
   }
   pt = s[top--];
  }
 }

/* Driver Code */
void main()
{
 int x;
 char ch = 'Y';
 node *head = NULL;

 /* Taking input from user */
 while(toupper(ch) == 'Y')
 {
  printf("Enter the item to insert:");
  scanf("%d", &x);
  head = create(head, x);
  printf("Do you want to continue(y/n):");
  fflush(stdin);
  ch = getchar();
 }

 /* Displaying output */
 printf("\nInorder recursive\n");
 inOrder(head);
 printf("\nInorder non-recursive:\n");
 nonInOrder(head);
 getch();
}
/* End of program */
```

Output

```
Enter the item to insert:5
```

```
Do you want to continue(y/n):y
Enter the item to insert:4
Do you want to continue(y/n):y
Enter the item to insert:3
Do you want to continue(y/n):y
Enter the item to insert:2
Do you want to continue(y/n):y
Enter the item to insert:1
Do you want to continue(y/n):n

Inorder recursive:
1       2       3       4       5
Inorder non-recursive:
1       2       3       4       5
```

Programming Tips!

A binary tree node is created using `create()`. A node is created dynamically using `malloc()`. `inOrder()` is used for inorder traversal recursively. `nonInOrder()` is used for inorder traversal non-recursively.

9.3.8 Inorder Traversal (Non-recursive) with Python

PyProg-9.2 Non-recursive inorder traversal of a binary tree

```
# Class to create tree node
class Node:
    # Constructor to create a new node
    def __init__(self, data):
        self.data = data
        self.left = None
        self.right = None

# Definition of iterative function for inorder tree traversal
def inOrder(root):
    # Set current to root of binary tree
    current = root
    stack = [] # initialize stack
    done = 0
    while True:
        # Reach the left most Node of the current Node
        if current is not None:
            # Place pointer to a tree node on the stack
            # before traversing the node's left subtree
            stack.append(current)
            current = current.left
```

```
        # BackTrack from the empty subtree and visit the Node
at the top of the stack;
        # however, if the stack is empty you are done
        elif(stack):
            current = stack.pop()
            print(current.data, end = " ")
            # We have visited the node and its left
            # subtree. Now, it's right subtree's turn
            current = current.right
        else:
            break
    print()

# Driver program to test above function
""" Constructed binary tree is
            1
          /   \
         2     3
       /   \
      4     5   """

root = Node(1)
root.left = Node(2)
root.right = Node(3)
root.left.left = Node(4)
root.left.right = Node(5)

# Executing Inorder traversal
inOrder(root)
## end program
```

Output

```
4 2 5 1 3
```

> ***Programming Tips!***
> `inOrder()` is used for implementing an iterative process to print an inorder traversal sequence of a binary tree.

9.3.9 Postorder Traversal

The sequence of visiting the nodes in postorder traversal is left node, right node, and then root node. 'Post' means 'after'. So, the root node will be placed after the left and right nodes in the sequence of traversal. This postorder traversal is applicable for every root node of all subtrees in the binary tree.

In Fig. 9.10, first we visit the left node 'B', then visit the right node 'C', then visit the root node 'A' of the binary tree.

The following operations are performed in this method:

(a) Traverse the left subtree of R_o (L).
(b) Traverse the right subtree of R_o (R).
(c) Process the root node (R_o).

Postorder traversal of B – C – A ($L – R – R_o$) is presented below in Fig. 9.10.

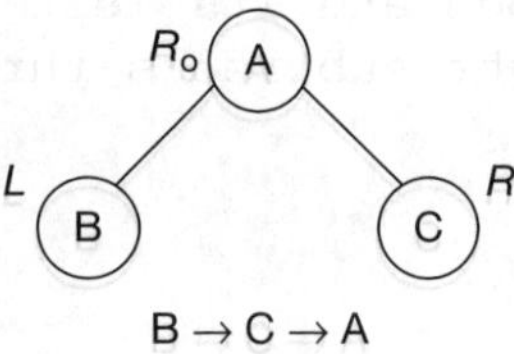

Figure 9.10 Postorder traversal of L – R – R_o

> **Note!**
> The sequence of visiting the nodes in postorder traversal is left, right, and then root respectively.

First, the left child node B is visited. Then, the right node C is visited. At the end, the root node A is visited. These are presented using arrows in the above Fig. 9.10.

9.3.10 Algorithm of Postorder Traversal

Algo-9.5 Pseudocode for postorder traversal of a binary tree by recursive way

```
Postorder(node PTR) Procedure:
   BEGIN
      IF (PTR ≠ NULL)
         Postorder (left (PTR))
         Postorder (right (PTR))
         PRINT (data (PTR))
     ENDIF
   END
```

We can implement the postorder traversal in a non-recursive way. The stack data structure is used here since we are not using recursion.

Algo-9.6 Algorithm for postorder traversal of a binary tree by non-recursive way

Step 1	Create an empty stack S.
Step 2	Initialize the root node as PTR.
Step 3	Push PTR into the stack and check the right child. If PTR.right ≠ NULL, then push it to S with a negative sign along with set PTR = PTR.left and continue till PTR = NULL.
Step 4	If PTR = = NULL and S is empty, then 'Exit'.
Step 5	Else if PTR = = NULL, then pop the top node from S and **print** till a negative node is got. If negative node then remove negative sign and set PTR = Stop and then go to Step 3.

Example 9.3

Consider the binary tree shown in Fig. 9.8 for applying a non-recursive postorder traversal algorithm. We have to find out the postorder sequence.

Actions	Node scanned	Process/ Print	Stack (S)
We have to set the root A of the tree, and then push the root node A into a stack (S). Then we have to check for the right child. F is the right child present here. So, we have to push '–F' (with the negative symbol) into the stack, and set the root to the left child B.	A		Stack (S) A | –F | | | | 0 1 2 3 4 5
We have to push node B into the stack, and then check for the right child. No right child of B is present here, So we have to set the root to the left child C.	B		Stack (S) A | –F | B | | | 0 1 2 3 4 5
We have to push the root node C into the stack, and then check for the right child. E is the right child present here. So we have to push '–E' (with the negative symbol) into the stack, and set the root to the left child D.	C		Stack (S) A | –F | B | C | –E | 0 1 2 3 4 5
We have to push the node D into the stack and check for the right child. No right child of D is present.	D		Stack (S) A | –F | B | C | –E | D 0 1 2 3 4 5
We have to check for the left child. D has no left child. So we have to pop D, and process/ print D.		D	Stack (S) A | –F | B | C | –E | 0 1 2 3 4 5
We have to pop '–E' next from the stack. E is a negative node ('–'). We have to set 'E' (removing the negative symbol), and push it back to the stack. We have to set E as the root.	E	D	Stack (S) A | –F | B | C | E | 0 1 2 3 4 5
We have to check for the right child of E. No right of E is present here. We have to check the left child of E. E has no left child. So, we have to pop the elements from the stack, one by one, and process/print E, C, B sequentially until we get a negative symbol node (i.e., '–F').		D, E, C, B	Stack (S) A | –F | | | | 0 1 2 3 4 5

(*Continued*)

Actions	Node scanned	Process/ Print	Stack (S)
We have to pop '–F'; F is a negative node ('–'). Since F is a negative node, we have to push it back again into the stack for removing negative symbols. We have to set the root as F.	F	D, E, C, B	Stack (S) [A, F, , , ,] (indices 0 1 2 3 4 5)
We have to check for the right child of F. No right of F is present. So, we have to check the left child of F, and set the root to the left child G of F. We have to push node G into the stack.	G	D, E, C, B	Stack (S) [A, F, G, , ,] (indices 0 1 2 3 4 5)
We have to check for the right child. No right child of G is present. We have to check for the left child of G. G has no left child. So, we have to pop the elements from the stack, one by one, and process/print G, F, A until the stack is empty. It indicates that the process is completed.		D, E, C, B, G, F, A **(Final Postorder traversal sequence)**	Stack (S) [, , , , ,] (indices 0 1 2 3 4 5)

9.3.11 Postorder Traversal (Non-recursive and Recursive) with C

CProg-9.3 C source code for non-recursive and recursive postorder traversal of a binary tree

```
#include<stdio.h>
#include<conio.h>
#include<stdlib.h>

/* Node Declaration */
typedef struct binary_tree
 {
   int data, flag;
   struct binary_tree *left, *right;
 } node;

/* Node creation */
node *create(node *r, int x)
 {
 if(r == NULL)
  {
  r = (node *)malloc(sizeof(node));
  r->data = x;
  r->left = r->right = NULL;
 }
```

```
 else
  {
  if(r->data <= x)
   r->right = create(r->right, x);
  else
   r->left = create(r->left, x);
  }
 return r;
 }

/* Recursive function of postorder traversal*/
void postOrder(node *r)
 {
 if(r != NULL)
  {
  postOrder(r->left);
  postOrder(r->right);
  printf("%d\t", r->data);
  }
 }

/* Non-Recursive function of postorder traversal*/
void nonPostOrder(node *root)
 {
 node *stack[100];
 int top = -1;
 node *temp = root;
 while(temp != NULL)
  {
  while(temp != NULL)
   {
   top++;
   stack[top] = temp;
   temp = temp->left;
   }
  label:temp = stack[top];
  top--;
  if(temp->flag==1)
   {
   printf("%d\t", temp->data);
   break;
   }
  else
   {
  temp->flag=1;
```

```
      top++;
      stack[top] = temp;
      temp=temp->right;
      }
    }
   if(top >= 0)
    goto label;
  }

/* Driver code */
void main()
{
 int x;
 char ch = 'Y';
 node *head = NULL;

 /* Taking inputs from users */
 while(toupper(ch) == 'Y')
 {
  printf("Enter the value to insert:");
  scanf("%d", &x);
  head = create(head, x);
  printf("Do you want to continue (y/n):");
  fflush(stdin);
  ch = getchar();
 }

 /* Displaying the output */
 printf("\nPostorder recursive:\n");
 postOrder(head);
 printf("\nPostorder non-recursive:\n");
 nonPostOrder(head);
 getch();
}
/* End of program */
```

Output

```
Enter the value to insert:1
Do you want to continue (y/n):y
Enter the value to insert:2
Do you want to continue (y/n):y
Enter the value to insert:3
Do you want to continue (y/n):y
Enter the value to insert:4
Do you want to continue (y/n):y
Enter the value to insert:5
Do you want to continue (y/n):n
```

```
Postorder recursive:
5       4       3       2       1
Postorder non-recursive:
5       4       3       2       1
```

Programming Tips!

`create()` is used to create a binary tree node. A node is created dynamically using `malloc()`. `postOrder()` is used for postorder traversal recursively. `nonPostOrder()` is used for postorder traversal non-recursively.

9.3.12 Postorder Traversal (Non-recursive) with Python

PyProg-9.3 Non-recursive postorder traversal of a binary tree

```
# Stores the answer
ans = []

# Class definition of a binary tree node
class Node:
    # Constructor to create a new node
    def __init__(self, data):
        self.data = data
        self.left = None
        self.right = None

def peek(stack):
    if len(stack) > 0:
        return stack[-1]
    return None

# Definition of iterative postorder traversal function
def postOrderIterative(root):
    # Check for empty tree
    if root is None:
        return
    stack = []
    while(True):
        while (root):
            # Push root's right child and then root to stack
            if root.right is not None:
                stack.append(root.right)
            stack.append(root)

            # Set root as root's left child
            root = root.left
```

```
        # Pop an item from stack and set it as root
        root = stack.pop()

        # If the popped item has a right child and the right child
          is not processed yet,
        # then make sure right child is processed before root
        if (root.right is not None and peek(stack) == root.right):
            stack.pop() # Remove right child from stack
            stack.append(root) # Push root back to stack
            root = root.right # Change root so that the right child
            is processed next

        # Else print root's data and set root as None
        else:
            ans.append(root.data)
            root = None

        if (len(stack) <= 0):
                break
# Driver code
root = Node(1)
root.left = Node(2)
root.right = Node(3)
root.left.left = Node(4)
root.left.right = Node(5)
root.right.left = Node(6)
root.right.right = Node(7)

print("Post Order traversal of binary tree is")
postOrderIterative(root)
print(ans)
## End program
```

Output

```
Post Order traversal of binary tree is
[4, 5, 2, 6, 7, 3, 1]
```

> ***Programming Tips!***
> `postOrderIterative()` is used for an iterative process to print a postorder traversal sequence of a binary tree.

9.4 CONSTRUCTION OF A BINARY TREE USING TREE TRAVERSAL

It is not possible to construct a unique binary tree from a single traversal. A unique binary tree can be constructed when inorder and preorder traversal are given, or when the inorder and postorder traversal are given. At least two traversals are essential, out of which one traversal sequence should be inorder. A binary tree cannot be unique if only preorder and postorder traversals are given.

9.4.1 Using Inorder and Preorder Sequence

Process

1. The first element in the preorder sequence will be the root of the tree.
2. Now, we have to search the root element in the inorder sequence. All nodes which are at the left side of the root, belong to the left subtree; and those at the right side of the root, belong to the right subtree.
3. Now, the problem reduces to the formation of subtrees and the same procedure can be applied repeatedly (it may be noted that in left and right subtrees, the first element in the preorder sequence is the root node of that subtree).

Example 9.4

Consider the following preorder and inorder traversals of a binary tree to show the different steps to create a binary tree.

- **Preorder: 10, 5, 22, 6, 17, 12, 15;**
- **Inorder: 22, 5, 6, 10, 12, 17, 15;**

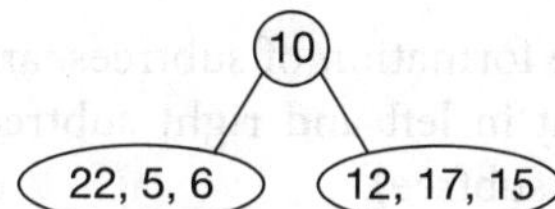

Figure 9.11 (a) Example of a binary tree construction

Here, 10 is the first element in the preorder sequence. So, 10 is the root of the tree. Now we have to search the root element 10 in the inorder sequence. All nodes which are at the left side (22, 5, 6) of the root belong to the left subtree, and those at the right side (12, 17, 15) of root belong to the right subtree as described in the Fig. 9.11 (a).

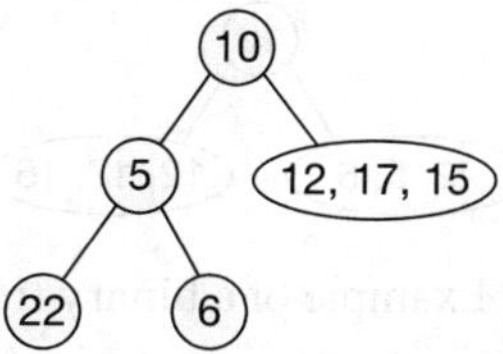

Figure 9.11 (b) Example of a binary tree construction

Now, 5 is the next element in the preorder sequence. Here, 5 belongs to the left subtree. So, 5 is the root of the subtree in which 5 belongs. If 5 is the root of the left subtree, then 22 is the left child, and 6 is the right child of 5 from the inorder sequence as described in Fig. 9.11 (b). So, all elements in the left subtree become a single list. It indicates that the left subtree has been completed.

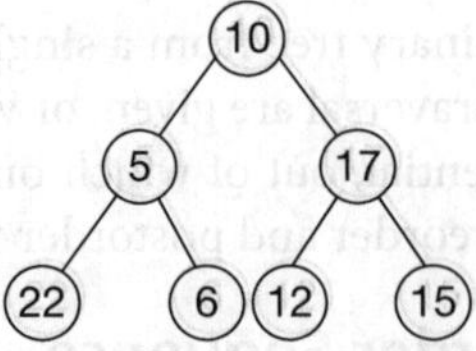

Figure 9.11 (c) Example of a binary tree construction

Now, 17 is the next element in the preorder sequence after 22 and 6. Here, 17 belongs to the right subtree. So, 17 is the root of the subtree in which 17 belongs. If 17 is the root of the right subtree, then 12 is the left child, and 15 is the right child of 17 from the inorder sequence as described in Fig. 9.11(c). So, all elements in the right subtree become a single list. It indicates that the right-subtree has been completed, and Fig. 9.11 (c) shows the final binary tree.

> ***Note!***
> The first element of the preorder traversal sequence is the root of the tree.

9.4.2 Using Inorder and Postorder Sequence

Process

1. The last element in the postorder sequence will be the root of the tree.
2. Now, we have to search the root element in the inorder sequence. All nodes which are at the left side of the root belong to the left subtree; and those at the right side of the root belong to the right subtree.
3. Now, the problem reduces to the formation of subtrees, and the same procedure can be applied repeatedly (it may be noted that in left and right subtrees, the last element in the postorder sequence is the root node of that subtree).

Example 9.5

Consider the following postorder and inorder traversals of a binary tree to show different steps to create the binary tree.

- **Postorder: 22, 6, 5, 12, 15, 17, 10;**
- **Inorder: 22, 5, 6, 10, 12, 17, 15;**

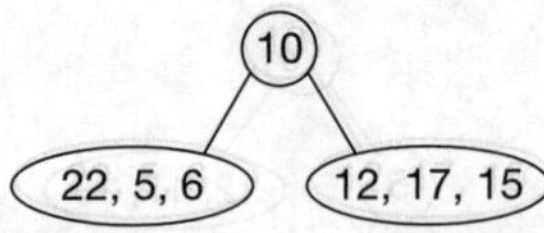

Figure 9.11 (d) Example of a binary tree construction

Here, 10 is the last element in the postorder sequence. So, 10 is the root of the tree. Now, we have to search the root element 10 in an inorder sequence. All nodes which are at the left side (22, 5, 6) of the root belong to the left subtree, and those at the right side (12, 17, 15) of the root belong to the right subtree as shown in the Fig. 9.11(d).

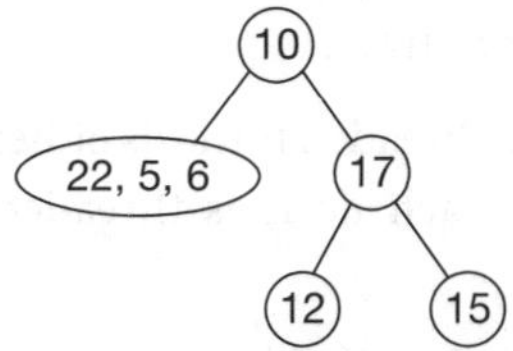

Figure 9.11 (e) Example of a binary tree construction

Now, 17 is the next element in the postorder sequence. Here, 17 belongs to the right subtree. So, 17 is the root of the subtree in which 17 belongs. If 17 is the root of the right subtree, then 12 is the left child and 15 is the right child of 17 from the inorder sequence as shown in Fig. 9.11(e). So, all elements in the right subtree become a single list. It indicates that the right subtree has been completed.

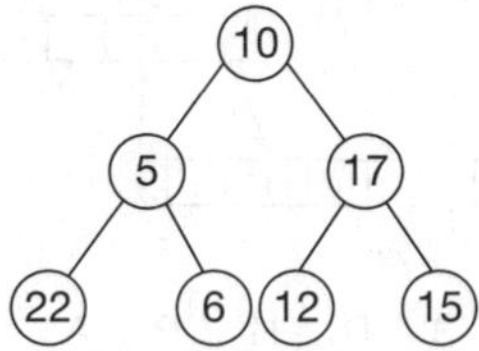

Figure 9.11(f) Example of a binary tree construction

Now, 5 is the next element in the postorder sequence after 12 and 15 from the right side. Here, 5 belongs to the left subtree. So, 5 is the root of the subtree in which 5 belongs. If 5 is the root of the left subtree, then 22 is the left child, and 6 is the right child of 5 from the inorder sequence as shown in Fig. 9.11(f). So, all elements in the left subtree become a single list. It indicates that the left subtree has been completed, and Fig. 9.11(f) shows the final binary tree.

> ***Note!***
> The last element of the postorder traversal sequence is the root of the tree.

9.5 THREADED BINARY TREE

A binary tree can be represented using a linked list as shown in Fig. 9.4. If the link part of the node does not have a child, it is filled with a NULL pointer. So almost half of the links are filled with NULL pointers. If there are $2N$ numbers of links, then $N + 1$ number of links are generally filled with NULL in this linked list representation of the binary tree. This NULL pointer does not play any role except indicating that there is no link (no child). So, it is a waste of memory. Also, we may recall that backtracking is not possible in a singly linked list as it was considered as one of the main drawbacks, in Chapter 4.

A J Perlis and C Thornton proposed a new binary tree called 'Threaded Binary Tree', which makes use of the NULL pointers. If we store any predecessor node address in place of the NULL pointer, then we can traverse back. Thus, it will be an effective utilization of memory, and such representation is called a threaded binary tree where NULL pointers are replaced by the address of other nodes in the tree. These extra references are called threads.

A binary tree is converted to a threaded binary tree by making all leaf nodes to a single child node's link pointer that would normally be a null pointer. If we replace the NULL (if it exists) pointer by the inorder predecessor address, then we can backtrack the nodes in this tree. It thus becomes possible to discover the parent of a node from a threaded binary tree without explicit use of parent pointers. If there is no inorder predecessor or inorder successor, then it points to the root node.

There are two types of threaded binary trees:

1. **One-way threading:** Each node is threaded towards either the left or right the inorder predecessor.
2. **Two-way or double threading:** Each node is threaded towards both (left and right) inorder predecessors.

The following Fig. 9.12 shows a two-way threaded binary tree of the example tree presented in Fig. 9.4.

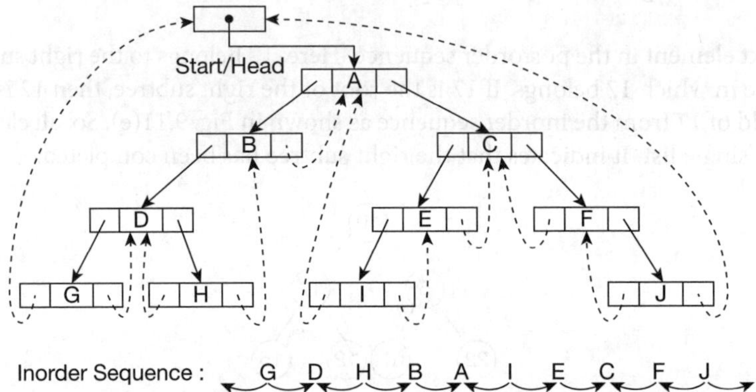

Figure 9.12 Two-way threaded binary tree for the example presented in Fig. 9.4

> ***Note!***
> A binary tree is converted to a threaded binary tree to overcome the back traversing disadvantage.

9.6 BINARY SEARCH TREE (BST)

A Binary Search Tree (BST) is a binary tree in which every node contains only smaller values in its left subtree, and greater values (or equal) in its right subtree. Data in the nodes are ordered in a particular way in this tree. In other words, starting at any given root node, any node of its left subtrees must all be less than the data in the given root node, and the data in any node of its right subtrees must be greater than or equal to the data in the given root node. The BST is sometimes called an ordered or sorted binary tree. An example of BST is shown in Fig. 9.13. In this tree, the left subtrees of every node contain nodes with smaller values, and the right subtrees of every node contain larger values.

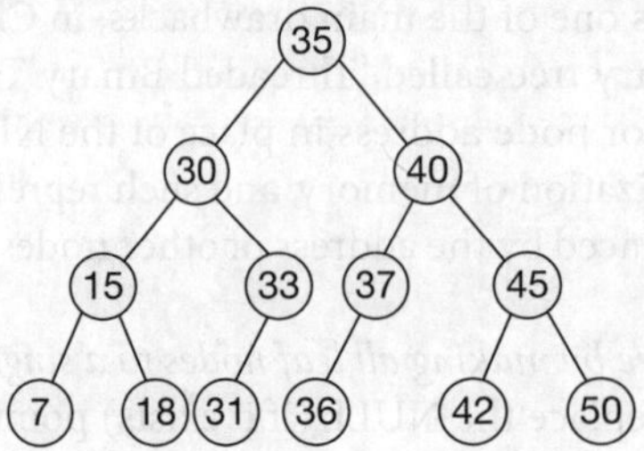

Figure 9.13 Example of a BST

> ***Note!***
> BST is often used for the alphabetical ordering of strings based on their ASCII value.

Properties of Binary Search Trees

The main property of binary search trees is that it remains ordered. It provides quicker search than many other data structures. The properties of binary search trees are as follows:

- The left subtree of a node contains only nodes with keys less than the root node's key.
- The right subtree of a node contains only nodes with keys greater than or equal to the root node's key.
- Each left and right subtree must also be a binary search tree.
- Each node can have a maximum of two successor nodes.
- A binary tree has a time complexity of O(n) for search operation, O(1) for insertion operation, O(n) for deletion operation. We mostly use binary search trees to increase the efficiency of search operations.

> ***Note!***
> The inorder traversal sequence of a BST produces an ascending order sequence.

Advantages of Binary Search Trees

The major advantages of binary search trees are as follows:

- The shape of the binary search tree depends totally on the order of node insertions, and it can be different if the insertion sequence is different.
- If nodes in the binary search tree are huge in number, then execution time for binary search trees may increase.
- If a binary search tree becomes left-skewed or right-skewed, then the searching advantages of that tree will be lost (discussed in detail in AVL tree).

> ***Note!***
> A BST is a binary tree in which every node contains only smaller values in its left subtree, and greater values (or equal) in its right subtree.

9.6.1 Operations on Binary Search Tree

The following operations (search, insertion, and deletion) are often performed on a binary search tree.

Searching within a BST

A BST arranges its nodes in a sorted manner. The most important application of BST is in searching, as explained above.

Algo-9.7 Algorithm for searching within a binary search tree

Step 1	Read the search element.
Step 2	Compare the search element (or key) with the value of the root node.
Step 3	If both are equal then display "searching is successful" and exit.
Step 4	If the search element is smaller than root, then continue the search process in the left subtree.
Step 5	If the search element is greater than root, then continue the search process in the right subtree.
Step 6	Repeat Steps 2 to 5 until searching is successful, or until the search element is compared with the leaf node.
Step 7	If we reach the leaf node, and if it is still missing the searched element, then display "Unsuccessful searching", or "Key is not found in the tree", and exit.

In a binary search tree, the search operation is performed with O(log *n*) time complexity since there are fewer comparison steps as opposed to a binary tree. It is just like binary searching which will be explained in Chapter 12.

Insertion Operation in BST

In a binary search tree, the insertion operation is performed with the time complexity of O(log *n*). A new node is always inserted as a leaf node in a BST. Following is the algorithm of inserting a node in BST.

Algo-9.8 Algorithm for inserting binary search trees

Step 1	Create a NewNode with a specific value, and set both its left and right links to NULL.
Step 2	Check whether the tree is empty. If the tree is empty, then set NewNode as root.
Step 3	If the tree is not empty, then check whether the value of NewNode is smaller or greater than the root node.
Step 4	If NewNode is smaller than the node, then it moves to its left child. If NewNode is greater than or equal to the node, then move to its right child.
Step 5	Repeat the above Step 4 until we reach the leaf node (i.e., links = NULL).
Step 6	After reaching the leaf node, insert the NewNode as a left child if the NewNode is smaller or equal to that leaf node, or else insert it as the right child.

Example 9.6

Let us create a binary search tree from the following given sequence of elements:

35, 40, 37, 30, 45, 50, 15, 18, 42

The first element is 35. As the tree is empty, we have to insert 35 as the root of the tree.

Insert 35 (35)

Now we have to insert the next element 40 and hence we compare 40 with the root 35. Since 40 > 35, we insert 40 as the right child of 35.

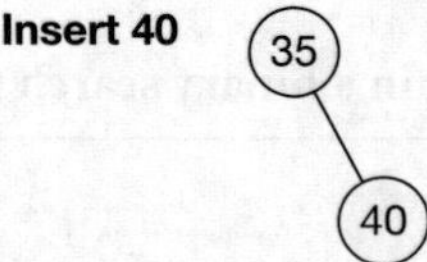

Next, we have to insert the next element 37, and hence we compare 37 with the root node 35. Since 37 > 35, we move towards the right subtree. Then, we compare 35 with 40. Since 37 < 40, we insert 37 as the left child of 40.

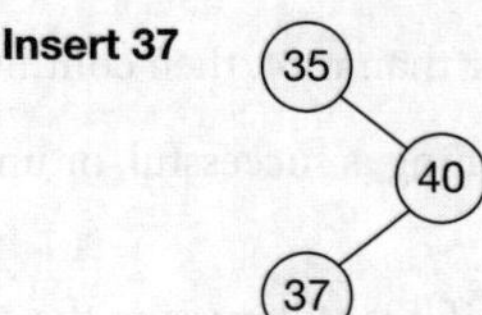

Then, we have to insert the next element 30, and hence we compare 30 with the root node 35. Since 30 < 35, we insert 30 as the left child of 35.

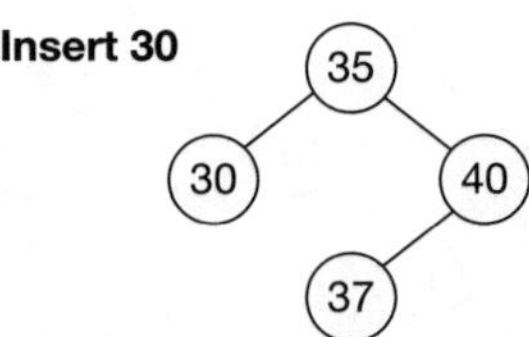

Now, we have to insert the next element 45, and hence we compare 45 with the root node 35. Since 45 > 35, we move towards the right subtree. Then, we compare 45 with 40. Since 45 > 40, we insert 45 as the right child of 40.

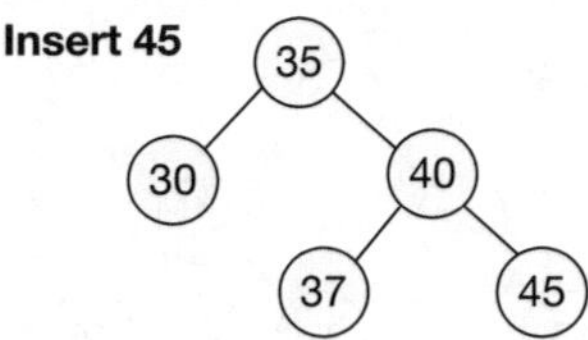

Now, we have to insert the next element 50, and hence we compare 50 with the root node 35. Since 50 > 35, we move towards the right subtrees. Then, we compare 50 with 40. Since 50 > 40, we move towards the right subtrees. Next, we have to compare 50 with 45. Since 50 > 45, we insert 50 as the right child of 45.

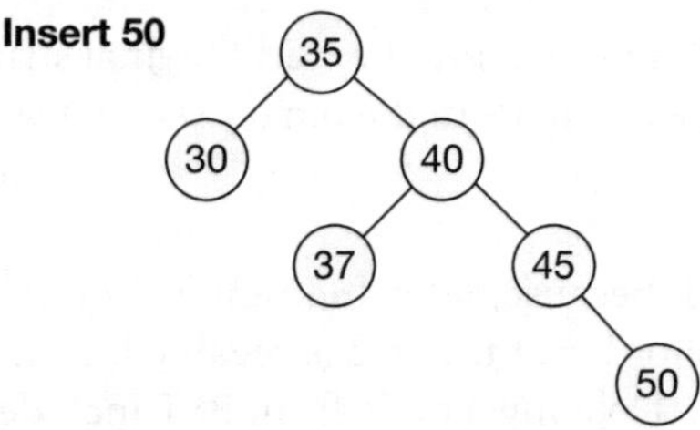

Now, we have to insert the next element 15, and hence we compare 15 with the root node 35. Since 15 < 35, we move towards the left subtrees. Then, we compare 15 with 30. Since 15 < 30, we insert 15 as the left child of 30.

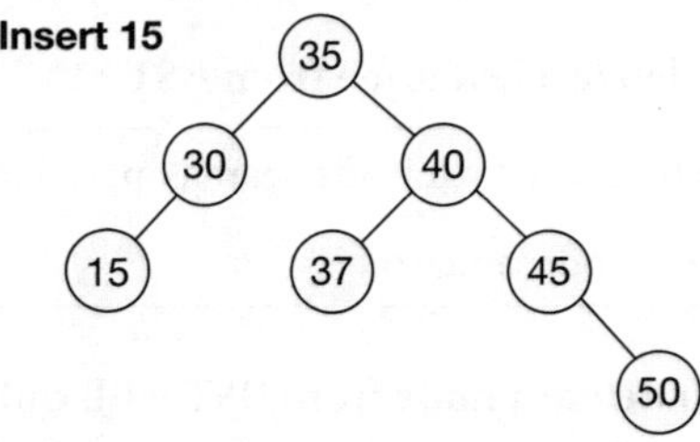

Now, we have to insert the next element 18, and hence we compare 18 with the root node 35. Since 18 < 35, we move towards the left subtrees. Then, we compare 18 with 30. Since 18 < 30, we move towards the left subtrees. Then, we compare 18 with 15. Since 18 > 15, we insert 18 as the right child of 15.

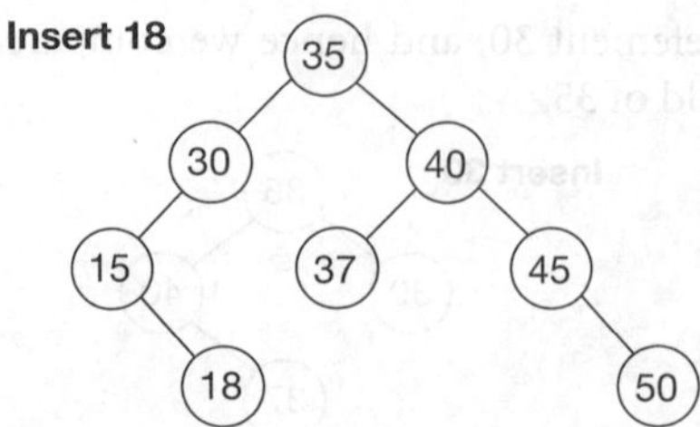

Now, we have to insert the next element 42, and hence we compare 42 with the root node 35. Since 42 > 35, we move towards the right subtree. Then, we compare 42 with 40. Since 42 > 40, we move towards the right subtree. Then, we compare 42 with 45. Since 42 < 45, we insert 42 as the left child of 45.

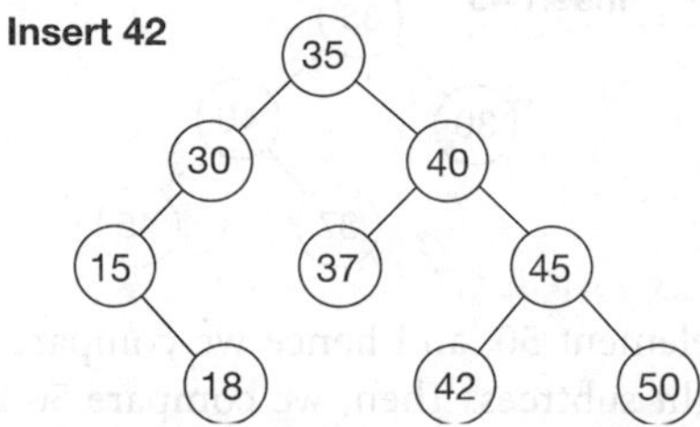

Figure 9.14 Final BST after inserting 35, 40, 37, 30, 45, 50, 15, 18, 42

Since there are no more elements left to insert in the tree, the final structure of the tree will be as shown in Fig. 9.14, formed by inserting the elements in the binary search tree.

Deletion Operation in BST

Deletion is very important in BST because, after the removal of an element, the other elements are shuffled in such a manner that the order of the tree is regained. Deletion operation is performed with O(log n) time complexity in a BST. Deleting a node from BST includes the following three cases:

- Case 1: Deleting a leaf node (a node with no children).
- Case 2: Deleting a node with only one child.
- Case 3: Deleting a node with two children exactly.

Algo-9.9 Case 1 – Algorithm to delete a leaf node from BST

Step 1	Find the node which is to be deleted using the search operation.
Step 2	Delete the node as it is a leaf node, and exit.

Algo-9.10 Case 2 – Algorithm to delete a node from BST with only one child

Step 1	Find the node which is to be deleted using the search operation.
Step 2	If it has only one child, then we have to create a link between its parent node (or predecessor node) and its child node (or successor node).
Step 3	Delete the node as it has only a single child, and exit.

Algo-9.11 Case 3 – Algorithm to delete a node from BST with exactly two children

Step 1	Find the node which is to be deleted (target node) using the search operation.
Step 2	If the node has two children, then find the successor node from the inorder traversal sequence of BST.
Step 3	Delete the target node and replace the node with successor node from the inorder traversal sequence of BST.
Step 4	Check whether the successor node is under Case 1 (no child) or Case 2 (only one child).
Step 5	If it comes to Case 1 (no child), then delete using Case 1 procedure, and exit.
Step 6	If it comes to Case 2 (single child), then delete using Case 2 procedure, and exit.

Example 9.7

Case 1: Let us consider deleting leaf node 18 from the BST in Fig. 9.14
18 has no child, and hence it is considered in Case 1. 18 is simply deleted, and now it appears that node 15 has no child (i.e., 15 becomes leaf node).

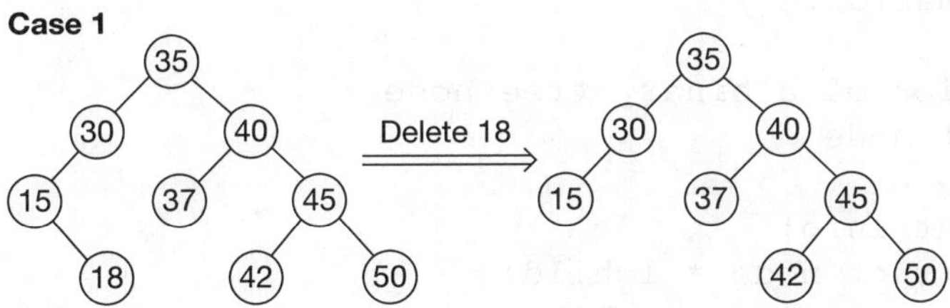

Figure 9.15 Deleting a leaf node 18 in Fig. 9.14

Case 2: Let us consider deleting node 15 with only one child from the BST in Fig. 9.14
15 has only one child 18, and hence it is considered in Case 2. 15 is deleted, and the parent node of 15 (i.e., 30) is linked to the child node 18 of 15. It appears that 18 has no child, and hence the process is stopped. 15 is deleted, and 18 takes its position.

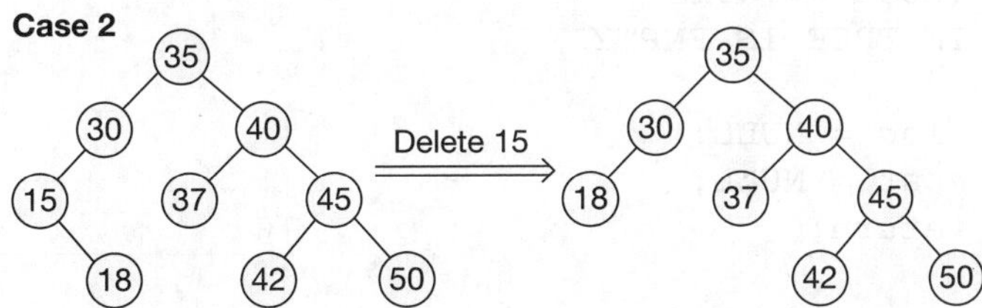

Figure 9.16 Deleting node 15 with only one child from the BST in Fig. 9.14

Case 3: Let us consider deleting node 40 with two children from the BST in Fig. 9.14
40 has two children 37 and 45, and hence it is considered in case 3. Now we have to find out the inorder traversal sequence (15, 18, 30, 35, 37, 40, 42, 45, 50) of the BST. Here, 42 is the successor node of 40 in the inorder sequence. So, 40 is deleted and replaced by 42. Now, consider 42 for the next deletion

operation. Here, 42 has no child, and hence it is considered as Case 1 because 42 is deleted from its original position.

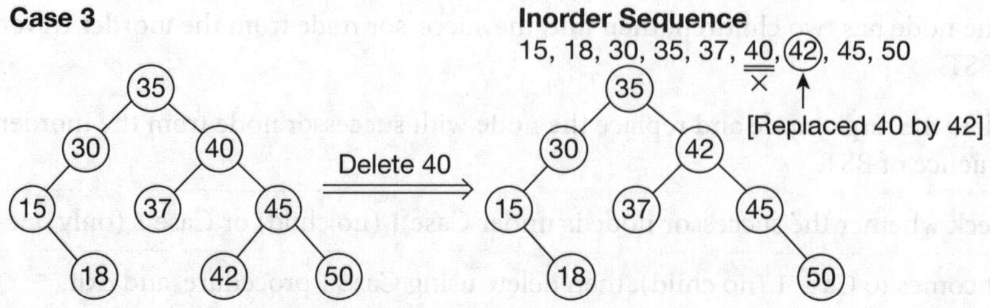

Figure 9.17 Deleting Node 40 with two children from the BST in Fig. 9.14

9.6.2 Operations on BST with C

CProg-9.4 Creation, insertion and deletion of a node in BST

```
#include<stdio.h>
#include<malloc.h>

/* Definition of a binary tree node */
    struct node
      {
        int info;
        struct node * lchild;
        struct node * rchild;
      }* root;

/* Search function */
void find(int item, struct node ** par, struct node ** loc)
      {
       struct node * ptr, * ptrsave;
       if (root == NULL)
       /* IF TREE IS EMPTY */
        {
         * loc = NULL;
         * par = NULL;
          return;
        }
       if (item == root -> info)
        /* ROOT ELEMENT */
        {
         * loc = root;
         * par = NULL;
          return;
        }
```

```
    /* INITIALIZE PTR */
    if (item < root -> info)
        ptr = root -> lchild;
    else
        ptr = root -> rchild;
    ptrsave = root;

    while (ptr != NULL)
      {
        if (item == ptr -> info)
         {
            * loc = ptr;
            * par = ptrsave;
            return;
         }
        ptrsave = ptr;
        if (item < ptr -> info)
            ptr = ptr -> lchild;
        else
            ptr = ptr -> rchild;
      }

    * loc = NULL;
    * par = ptrsave;
}

/* Insert function */
void insert(int item)
  {
    struct node * tmp, * parent, * location;
    find(item, & parent, & location);
    if (location != NULL) {
        printf("Item present IN list ");
        return;
    }
    tmp = (struct node * ) malloc(sizeof(struct node));
    tmp -> info = item;
    tmp -> lchild = NULL;
    tmp -> rchild = NULL;

    if (parent == NULL)
        root = tmp;
    else
    if (item < parent -> info)
      parent -> lchild = tmp;
    else
```

```
      parent -> rchild = tmp;
  } /* End of insert */

void case_a(struct node * par, struct node * loc)
  {
    if (par == NULL) /* Item to be deleted is root node */
        root = NULL;
    else
    if (loc == par -> lchild)
        par -> lchild = NULL;
    else
        par -> rchild = NULL;
  } /* END OF CASE A */

void case_b(struct node * par, struct node * loc)
  {
    struct node * child;

    /* INITIALIZE CHILD */
    if (loc -> lchild != NULL)
        /* ITEM DELETED HAVING LCHILD */
        child = loc -> lchild;
    else /* ITEM DELETED HAVING RCHILD */
        child = loc -> rchild;

    if (par == NULL) /* ITEM DELETED HAVING ROOT NODE */ root =
    child;
    else
    if (loc == par -> lchild) /* item is lchild of its parent */
        par -> lchild = child;
    else /* Item is rchild of its parent */
        par -> rchild = child;
  } /* END OF CASE B */

void case_c(struct node * par, struct node * loc)
  {
    struct node * ptr, * ptrsave, * suc, * parsuc;
    ptrsave = loc;
    ptr = loc -> rchild;
    while (ptr -> lchild != NULL)
    {
        ptrsave = ptr;
        ptr = ptr -> lchild;
    }
    suc = ptr;
    parsuc = ptrsave;
```

```
    if (suc -> lchild == NULL && suc -> rchild == NULL)
        case_a(parsuc, suc);
    else
        case_b(parsuc, suc);

    if (par == NULL)
        root = suc;
    else
    if (loc == par -> lchild)
        par -> lchild = suc;
    else
        par -> rchild = suc;

    suc -> lchild = loc -> lchild;
    suc -> rchild = loc -> rchild;
  } /* END OF CASE C */

/* Delete function */
int del(int item)
  {
    struct node * parent, * location;
    if (root == NULL)
    {
      printf("Tree empty");
      return 0;
    }

    find(item, & parent, & location);
    if (location == NULL)
     {
        printf("Item not present in tree");
        return 0;
    }

    if (location -> lchild == NULL && location -> rchild == NULL)
        case_a(parent, location);
    if (location -> lchild != NULL && location -> rchild == NULL)
        case_b(parent, location);
    if (location -> lchild == NULL && location -> rchild != NULL)
        case_b(parent, location);
    if (location -> lchild != NULL && location -> rchild != NULL)
        case_c(parent, location);
    free(location);
  } /* End of del */
```

```
/* Preorder traversal function */
int preorder(struct node * ptr)
  {
    if (root == NULL)
    {
        printf("Tree is empty");
        return 0;
    }
    if (ptr != NULL)
    {
        printf("%d  ", ptr -> info);
        preorder(ptr -> lchild);
        preorder(ptr -> rchild);
    }
  } /* End of preorder() */

/* Driver function */
int main()
  {
    int choice,
    num;
    root = NULL;
    while (1) {
        printf("\n");
        printf("1.Insert\n");
        printf("2.Delete\n");
        printf("3.Preorder Traversal\n");
        printf("Enter your choice : ");
        scanf("%d", & choice);

        switch (choice)
        {
        case 1:
            printf("Enter the number to be inserted : ");
            scanf("%d", & num);
            insert(num);
            break;
        case 2:
            printf("Enter the number to be deleted : ");
            scanf("%d", & num);
            del(num);
            break;
        case 3:
            preorder(root);
            break;
```

```
        case 7:
            break;
        default:
            printf("Wrong choice\n");
        } /* END SWITCH */
    } /* END WHILE */
  }
/* End of program */
```

Output

```
1.Insert
2.Delete
3.Preorder Traversal
Enter your choice : 1
Enter the number to be inserted : 10
1.Insert
2.Delete
3.Preorder Traversal
Enter your choice : 1
Enter the number to be inserted : 20
1.Insert
2.Delete
3.Preorder Traversal
Enter your choice : 1
Enter the number to be inserted : 1
1.Insert
2.Delete
3.Preorder Traversal
Enter your choice : 3
10  1  20
1.Insert
2.Delete
3.Preorder Traversal
Enter your choice : 2
Enter the number to be deleted : 10
1.Insert
2.Delete
3.Preorder Traversal
Enter your choice : 3
20  1
1.Insert
2.Delete
3.Preorder Traversal
Enter your choice :
```

Programming Tips!

`case_a()` is used for deleting a leaf node (a node with no children) from BST. `case_b()` is used for deleting a node with only one child. `case_c()` is used for deleting a node with exactly two children.

9.6.3 Operations on BST with Python

PyProg-9.4 Creation, insertion and deletion of a node in BST

```
# Class definition of a binary tree node
class node:
    # Constructor to create a new node
    def __init__(self, data):
        self.data = data
        self.left = None
        self.right = None

# Class definition of a binary tree node
class BinarySearchTree:
    # Constructor to create a new node
    def __init__(self):
        self.head = None

    # Insert definition of new node
    def Insert(self, value):
        temp = node(value)
        if(self.head == None):
            self.head = temp
        else:
            current = self.head
            while current != None:
                if value < current.data:
                    if current.left != None:
                        current = current.left
                    else:
                        current.left = temp
                        return
                else:
                    if current.right != None:
                        current = current.right
                    else:
                        current.right = temp
                        return

    # Search function for tree node
    def Search(self, value):
        current = self.head
        while current != None:
            if value < current.data:
                current = current.left
            elif value > current.data:
                current = current.right
```

```
            else:
                print("Element " + str(value) + " Found")
                return
        print("Element " + str(value) + " not Found")

    # Function for minimum value
    def Min_Value(self, head):
        while head.left != None:
            head = head.left
        return head.data

    # Function for deleting key
    def Delete_Key(self, head, value):
        if head == None:
            return head

        if value < head.data:
            head.left = self.Delete_Key(head.left, value)
        elif value > head.data:
            head.right = self.Delete_Key(head.right, value)
        else:
            if head.right == None:
                return head.left
            elif head.left == None:
                return head.right

            head.data = self.Min_Value(head.right)
            head.right = self.Delete_Key(head.right, head.data)

        return head

    def Delete(self, value):
        self.head = self.Delete_Key(self.head, value)

# Driver code
BST = BinarySearchTree()

BST.Insert(5)
BST.Insert(7)
BST.Insert(9)
BST.Insert(8)
BST.Insert(6)
BST.Insert(4)
```

```
BST.Search(9)
BST.Search(2)

BST.Delete(7)
BST.Delete(5)
BST.Delete(4)

BST.Search(9)
BST.Search(2)
BST.Search(5)
BST.Search(6)
## End program
```

Output

```
Element 9 Found
Element 2 not Found
Element 9 Found
Element 2 not Found
Element 5 not Found
Element 6 Found
```

> ***Programming Tips!***
> `insert()` is used for inserting a node in the BST. `search()` is used for searching a particular node in the BST.

9.7 AVL TREE OR HEIGHT-BALANCED TREE

Consider the binary search trees presented in Fig. 9.18. We can observe that both are BST, but these turn out to be left-skewed (Fig. 9.18 a), and right-skewed (Fig. 9.18 b) respectively.

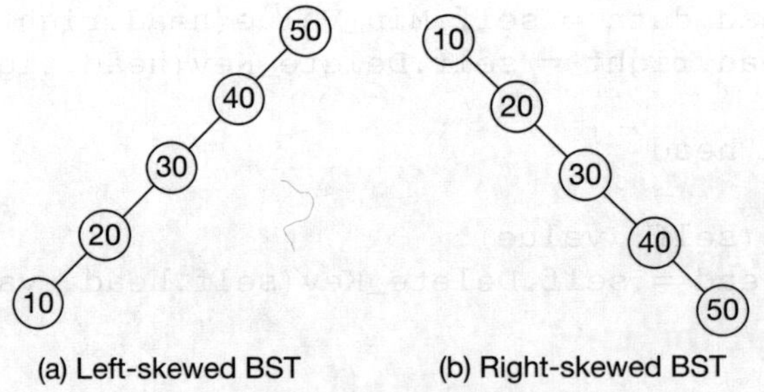

Figure 9.18 Skewed BST

If a BST becomes a skewed tree, then searching advantages may be lost. The disadvantage of a skewed binary tree is that worst-case time complexity becomes O(n) for searching. So, it is very important to maintain balance within a BST. Our goal here is to keep the height of a binary search tree O(log n). The AVL tree or height-balanced tree is named after G M Adelson (A), Velsky (V), and E M Landis (L), who proposed this concept in 1962.

> ***Note!***
> If a BST becomes a skewed tree, then searching advantages may be lost. The AVL tree (height-balanced tree) concept was introduced to overcome this loss.

9.7.1 Definition of AVL Tree

An AVL tree is also a binary search tree, but it is balanced. *A binary search tree is said to be balanced if the difference between the heights of the left and right subtrees of every node is -1 or 0 or +1, and every subtree is an AVL tree. It is also called a height-balanced binary search tree.*

Each node is associated with a balance factor in the AVL tree. The heights of the left and right subtrees differ at most by 1 at any node in the tree. The balance factor of a node is the difference between the heights of the left and right subtrees of that node. The balance factor of a node is calculated as:

$$\text{Balance factor} = \text{Height (Left subtree)} - \text{Height (Right subtree)}$$

In an AVL tree, every node maintains extra information known as balance factor. The balance factor of every node is −1 or 0 or +1 in an AVL tree. Here, the left height is considered as positive (+), and right height considered as negative (−). The balance factor −1 of a node indicates that we are considering a particular node as root, and the right subtree has one more level than the left subtree. Similarly, a balance factor +1 of a node indicates that we are considering a particular node as root, and the left subtree has one more level than the right subtree. If a node has balance factor 0, it indicates that we are considering a particular node as root, and the left subtree has the same number of levels as of the right subtree. We should also note that all AVL trees are BST but every BST need not be an AVL tree. The following Fig. 9.19 presents one example of BST but non-AVL tree (a) and AVL tree (b). In Fig. 9.19(a), Node 20 has balance factor +2. So, this is not an AVL tree, but it is a binary search tree. Whereas each node has balance factor −1, 0, or +1 in Fig. 9.19(b), and hence this is an AVL tree.

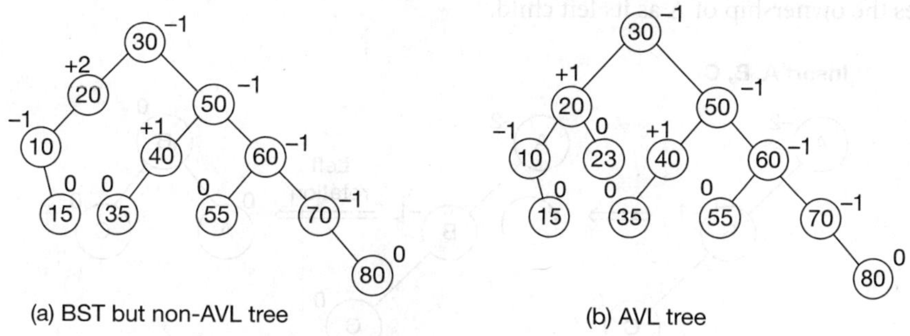

Figure 9.19 Examples of AVL and non-AVL tree

9.7.2 Rotational Techniques for AVL Tree

In the AVL tree, after insertion and deletion operations, we need to check the balance factor of each node in the binary search tree. If each node satisfies the balance factor condition (i.e., −1, 0, +1), then we can proceed further; otherwise, we must balance the tree. Whenever the tree becomes unbalanced due to any operation, we have to use rotation operations to make the BST balanced. Rotation operations are used to make the tree balanced.

Rotation is the process of moving nodes either to left or to right to make the binary search tree balanced. There are four rotations and they are classified into two types. These are presented in Fig. 9.20.

> **Note!**
> Rotation techniques are used to balance the height of a BST.

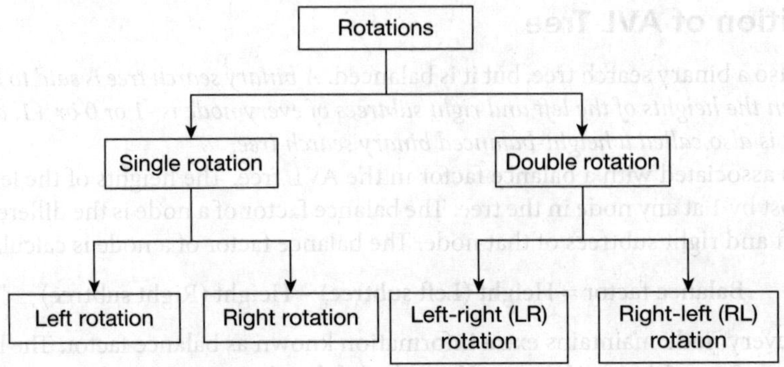

Figure 9.20 Classification of AVL tree rotations

Single Left Rotation (LL Rotation)

If there is an unbalance in the right child of the right subtree, then we have to perform a left rotation. Figure 9.21 shows that node A has a balance factor –2. This indicates that it is unbalanced due to the right child of the right subtree. So, a single left rotation is required to make the tree balanced. This is done in the following steps:

1. B becomes the new root.
2. A takes ownership of B's left child as its right child, but in this case it is NULL.
3. B takes the ownership of A as its left child.

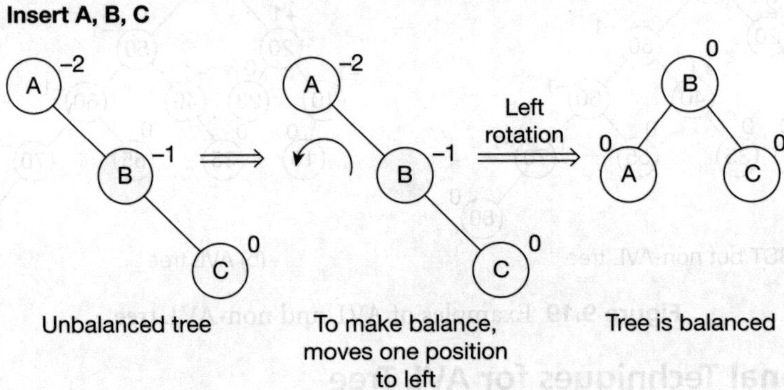

Figure 9.21 Single left rotation

Single Right Rotation (RR Rotation)

If there is an unbalance in the left child of the left subtree, then we have to perform a right rotation. Figure 9.22 shows that node C has a balance factor +2. This indicates that it is unbalanced due to the left child of the left subtree. So, a single right rotation is required to make the tree balanced. This is done using the following steps:

1. B becomes the new root.
2. C takes ownership of B's right child as its right child but in this case it is NULL.
3. B takes ownership of C as its right child.

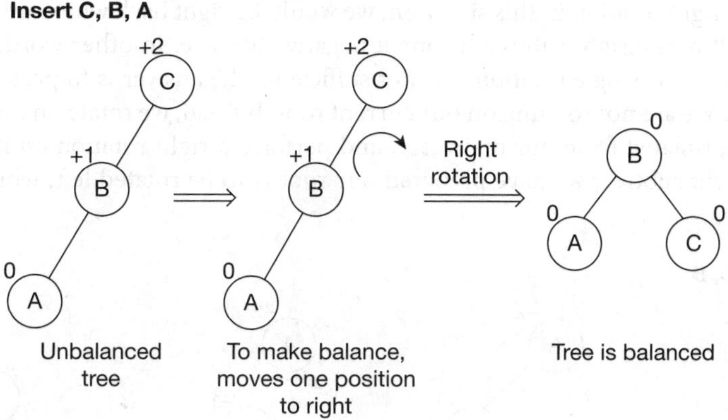

Figure 9.22 Single right rotation

Left-Right Rotation (LR): (Double rotations)

If there is an unbalance in the right child of the left subtree, then we have to perform a right-left rotation. Figure 9.23 shows that node C has a balance factor +2, C is unbalanced due to node B, and B is the right child of the subtree. This indicates that it is unbalanced due to the right child of the left subtree. So, double right rotations are required to make the tree balanced.

If we do a single right rotation in this situation, we would be right back to where we started. The reason is that this is a result of the left subtree having a positive balance. In other words, because the left subtree is right-heavy, our single rotation is not sufficient. The answer is to perform a left rotation on the left subtree. However, we do not rotate on our current root. We rotate on our left child. Think of our left subtree, isolated from our main tree, and perform a left rotation on it. After performing a rotation on our left subtree, we have to prepare our root C to be rotated right, which is similar to the actions in Figure 9.22.

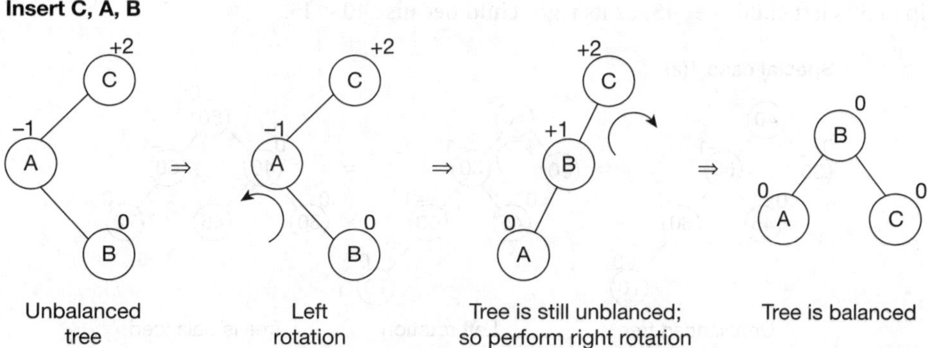

Figure 9.23 Left-right rotation

Right-Left Rotation (RL): (Double rotations)

If there is an unbalance in the left child of the right subtree, then we have to perform a left-right rotation. Figure 9.24 shows that node A has balance factor −2, A is unbalanced due to node B, and B is the left child of the subtree. This indicates that it is unbalanced due to the left child of the right subtree. So, double right rotations are required to make the tree balanced.

If we do a single right rotation in this situation, we would be right back where we started. The reason is that this is a result of the right subtree having a negative balance. In other words, because the right subtree was left-heavy, our single rotation was not sufficient. The answer is to perform a right rotation on the right subtree. We are not rotating on our current root. Instead, we rotate on our right child. Think of our right subtree, isolated from our main tree, and perform a right rotation on it. After performing a rotation on our right subtree, we have prepared our root A to be rotated left, which is similar to the actions in Fig. 9.21.

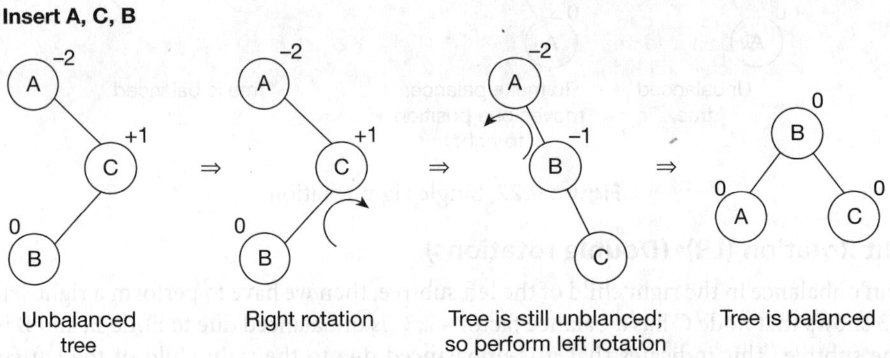

Figure 9.24 Right-Left Rotation

Special cases

We can consider two special cases here and these are also classified into two types.

Special case – 1(a): Right high-unbalanced tree rotation

Figure 9.25 (a) shows that node 40 has a balance factor –2. 40 is unbalanced due to node 70, and node 70 is the direct right child of the subtree. This indicates that the tree is unbalanced due to the right child of the right subtree. So, a single left rotation is required to make the tree balanced in this case. 40 takes ownership of 50's left child (i.e., 45) as its right child because 40 < 45.

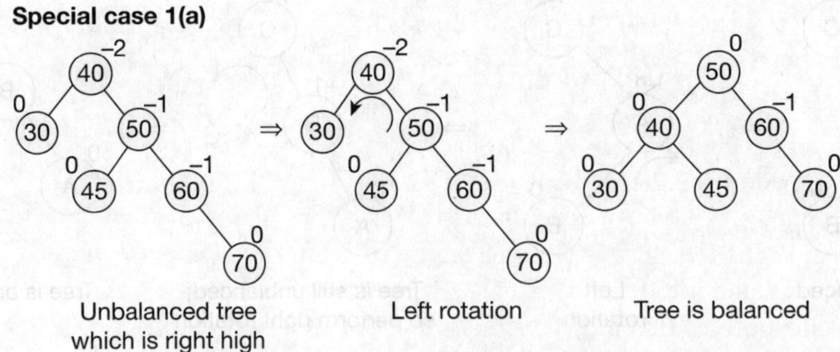

Figure 9.25 (a) Rotation of right high-unbalanced tree

Special case – 1 (b): Left high-unbalanced tree rotation

Figure 9.25 (b) shows that node 40 has balance factor +2, 40 is unbalanced due to node 10 and 10 is the direct left child of the subtree. This indicates that the tree is unbalanced due to the left child of the left subtree. So, a single right rotation is required to make the tree balanced in this case. 40 takes ownership of 30's right child (i.e., 35) as its left child because 40 > 35.

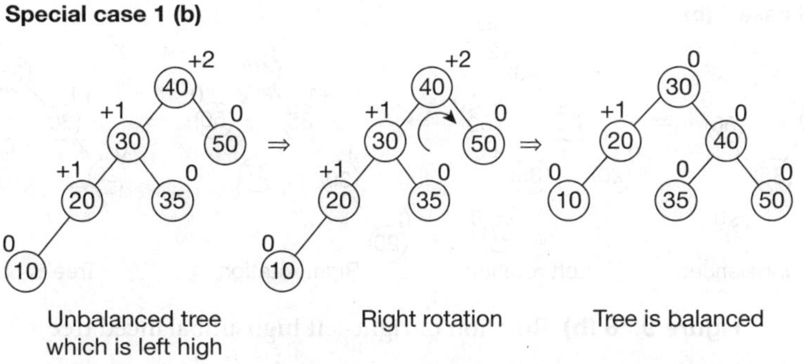

Special case 1 (b)

Figure 9.25 (b) Rotation of left high-unbalanced tree

Special case – 2(a): Left-right high-unbalanced tree rotation

Figure 9.26 (a) shows that node 40 has a balance factor −2, 40 is unbalanced due to node 42, and 42 is the left child of the right subtree. This indicates that the tree is unbalanced due to the left child of the right subtree. So, double right rotations are required to make the tree balanced. If we do a single right rotation in this situation, we would be right back where we started. The reason is that this is a result of the right subtree having a negative balance. In other words, our single rotation is not sufficient because the right subtree is left-heavy. The answer is to perform a right rotation on the right subtree. We are not rotating on our current root. Instead, we rotate on our right child. Think of our right subtree, isolated from our main tree, and perform a right rotation on it. After performing a rotation on our right subtree, we have to prepare our root 40 to be rotated left. Now, 45 will be the root, and 40 takes ownership of 42 as the right child.

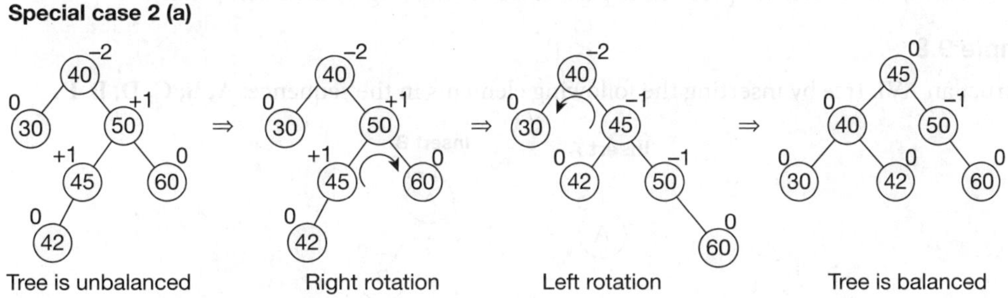

Special case 2 (a)

Figure 9.26 (a) Rotation of left-right high-unbalanced tree

Special case – 2(b): Right-left high unbalanced tree rotation

Figure 9.26 (b) shows that node 40 has a balance factor +2. 40 is unbalanced due to node 37, and 37 is the right child of the left subtree. This indicates that the tree is unbalanced due to the right child of the left subtree. So, double right rotations are required to make the tree balanced. If we do a single right rotation in this situation, we would be right back where we started. The reason is that this is a result of the left subtree having a positive balance. In other words, because the left subtree is right-heavy, our single rotation is not sufficient. The answer is to perform a left rotation on the left subtree. We do not rotate on our current root, but rotate on our left child. We have to think of our right subtree, isolated from our main tree, and perform a left rotation on it. After performing a rotation on our left subtree, we have to prepare our root 40 to be rotated right. Now 35 will be the root and 40 takes ownership of 37 as a left child.

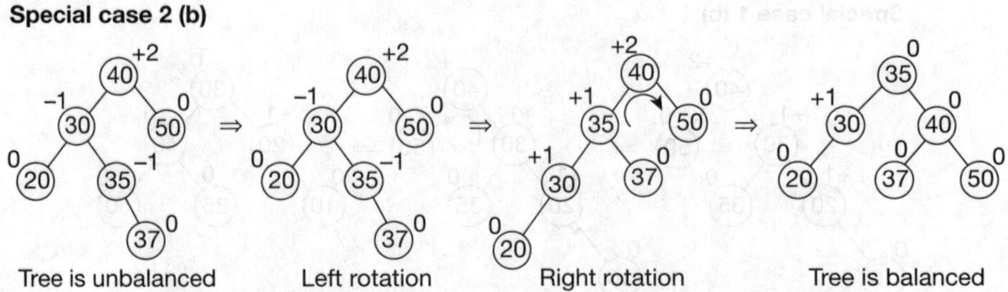

Figure 9.26 (b) Rotation of right-left high-unbalanced tree

9.7.3 Creation of AVL Tree

A new node is always inserted as a leaf node in the AVL tree. The following steps are to be implemented for the creation of a newly inserted node into the AVL tree.

Algo-9.12 Algorithm for creation of AVL tree

Step 1	Perform standard BST insert operation first.
Step 2	After insertion, check the balance factor of each of the nodes of the BST.
Step 3	If the balance factor of every node is −1 or 0 or +1, then the tree is balanced, go to Step 1.
Step 4	If the balance factor of any node is other than −1 or 0 or +1, then the tree is unbalanced and we need to perform a suitable rotation operation to make it balanced, and then go to Step 1.

In an AVL tree, the insertion operation is performed with O(log n) time complexity.

Example 9.8

Construct an AVL tree by inserting the following elements in the sequence: **A, B, C, D, E, F**.

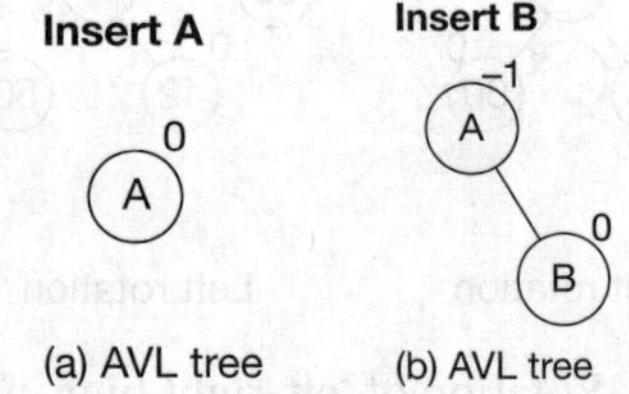

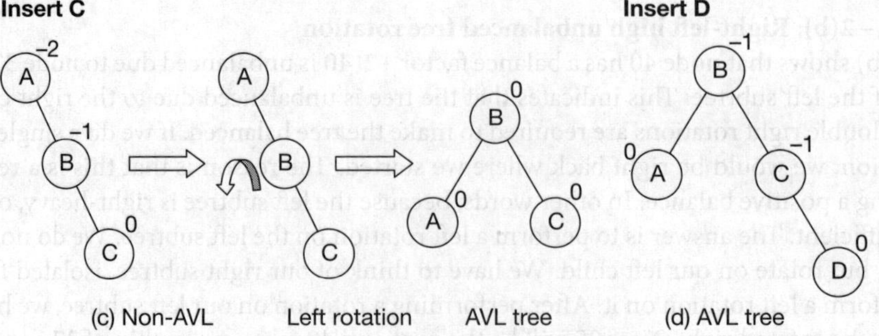

Figure 9.27 Construct of an AVL tree with elements A, B, C, D, E, F (*Continued*)

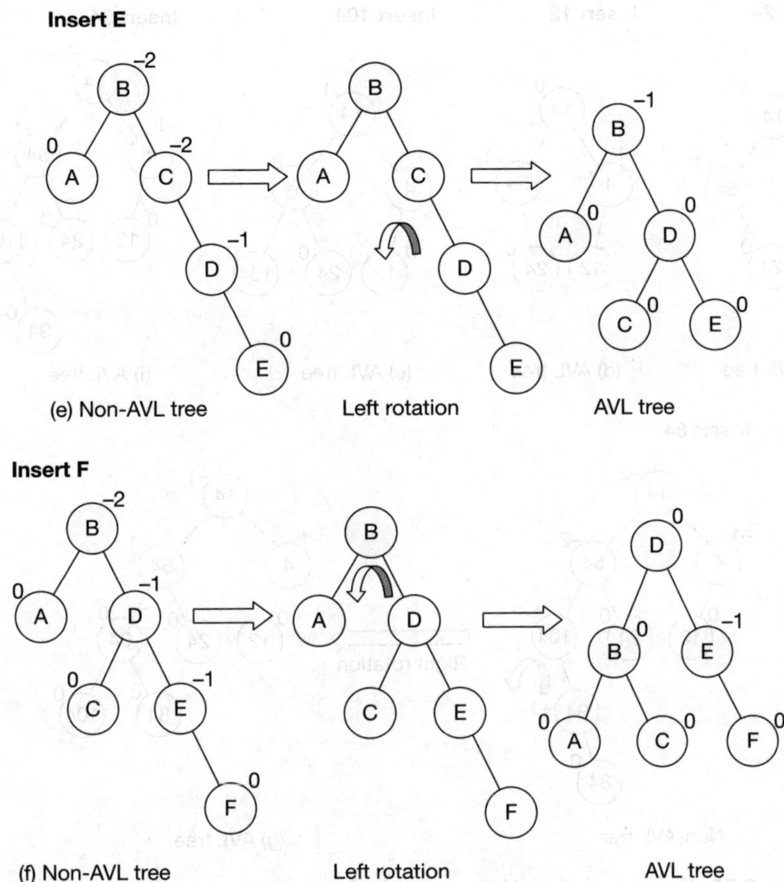

Figure 9.27 Construct of an AVL tree with elements A, B, C, D, E, F

Example 9.9

Construct an AVL tree by inserting the following elements in the sequence: 54, 4, 14, 24, 12, 104, 94, 84.

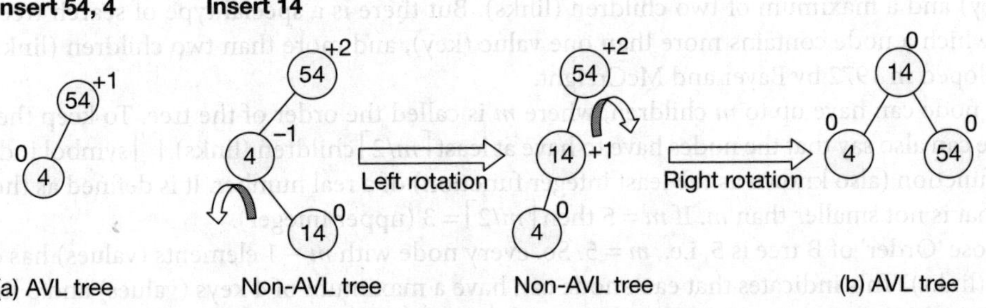

Figure 9.28 Construct of an AVL tree with elements 54, 4, 14, 24, 12, 104, 94, 84 (*Continued*)

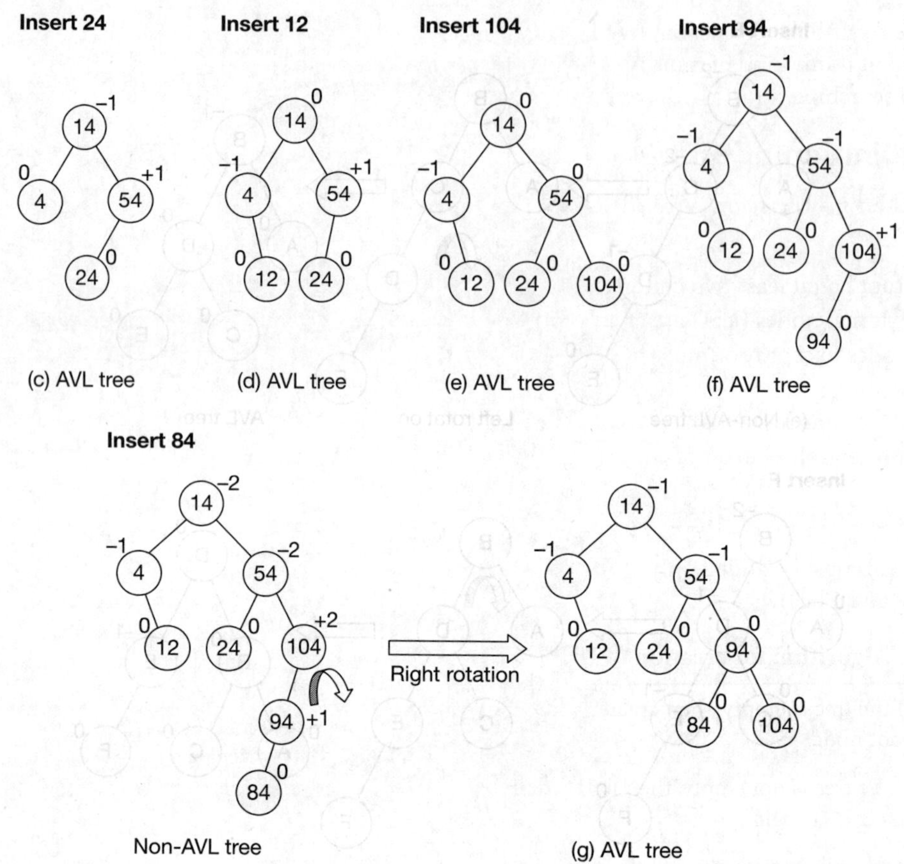

Figure 9.28 Construct of an AVL tree with elements 54, 4, 14, 24, 12, 104, 94, 84

9.8 B TREE (BALANCED TREE)

A 'B tree' is different from a general binary tree. The 'B' stands for 'balanced' in the B tree. Each node in a B tree may have more than 2 children. In general, every node (of the binary tree) contains only one value (key) and a maximum of two children (links). But there is a special type of search tree, called B Tree, in which a node contains more than one value (key), and more than two children (links). B Tree was developed in 1972 by Bayer and McCreight.

Each node can have up to m children, where m is called the order of the tree. To keep the tree balanced, we can also say that the nodes have to have at least $\lceil m/2 \rceil$ children (links). $\lceil\ \rceil$ symbol indicates the 'ceiling' function (also known as the least integer function) of a real number. It is defined as the smallest integer that is not smaller than m. If $m = 5$ then $\lceil m/2 \rceil = 3$ (upper integer).

Suppose 'Order' of B tree is 5, i.e., $m = 5$. So, every node with $m - 1$ elements (values) has exactly m children (links). This indicates that each node can have a maximum of 4 keys (values) and 5 links (children) part including root. Each node has minimum $\lceil m/2 \rfloor$ children (links) except the root node. If $m = 5$ then $\lceil m/2 \rceil = 3$. So, every node with minimum 2 elements (values) and 3 children (links) part except root. Consider any node with $m - 1$ elements, for example. Then $p_1 < p_2 < \ldots < p_{m-1}$ since the elements are ordered where $p_{i,}$ is the i-th element of the tree for $1 \leq i \leq m - 1$.

B tree is a self-balanced search tree in which every node contains multiple keys and has more than two children. It is one kind of multi-way search tree or *m*-way search tree. We can find its use in external sorting and searching.

9.8.1 Definition of B Tree

A 'B tree' is an *m-way search tree* if the B tree is not empty. A 'B tree' of order *m* has the following properties:

- The root has at least two children (links).
- All external nodes (leaf) are at the same level.
- All nodes except root must have at least $\lceil m/2 \rceil$ children (links) and a maximum of *m* children (links).
- The root node has a maximum of *m* children (links) and minimum 2 children (links).
- All the key values in a node must be in ascending order/descending order.

9.8.2 Creation of B Tree

A new element must be added only at the leaf node in a B Tree. The steps for insertion of a new element in B tree are given below:

Algo-9.13 Algorithm for creation of B tree

Step 1	If the tree is empty, then create a new node with a new key-value and insert it into the tree as a root node.
Step 2	If the tree is not empty, then find a suitable leaf node to which the new key value can be added using BST logic.
Step 3	If the number of values of that leaf node is less than the order of the tree, then insert a new key value to that leaf node in ascending order of key values within the node.
Step 4	If the leaf node is already full (is equal to the order of the B tree), split that leaf node by sending the middle value to its parent node. Repeat the same until the sending value is fixed into a node.
Step 5	If the splitting is performed at the root node, then the middle value becomes the new root node for the tree and the height of the tree is increased by one.

Example 9.10

Consider a sequence of numbers:
55, 61, 60, 56, 65, 58, 62, 67, 64, 59, 73, 63, 72, 78, 57, 66, 68, 74, 75, 70
as a growth of a B Tree of order 5 into an initial empty tree.

> **Note!**
> Every node contains values (keys) and links in a B-tree.

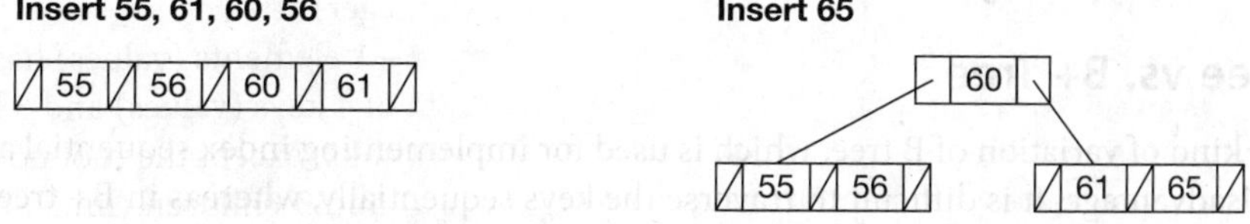

Figure 9.29 Example for the creation of a B tree (*Continued*)

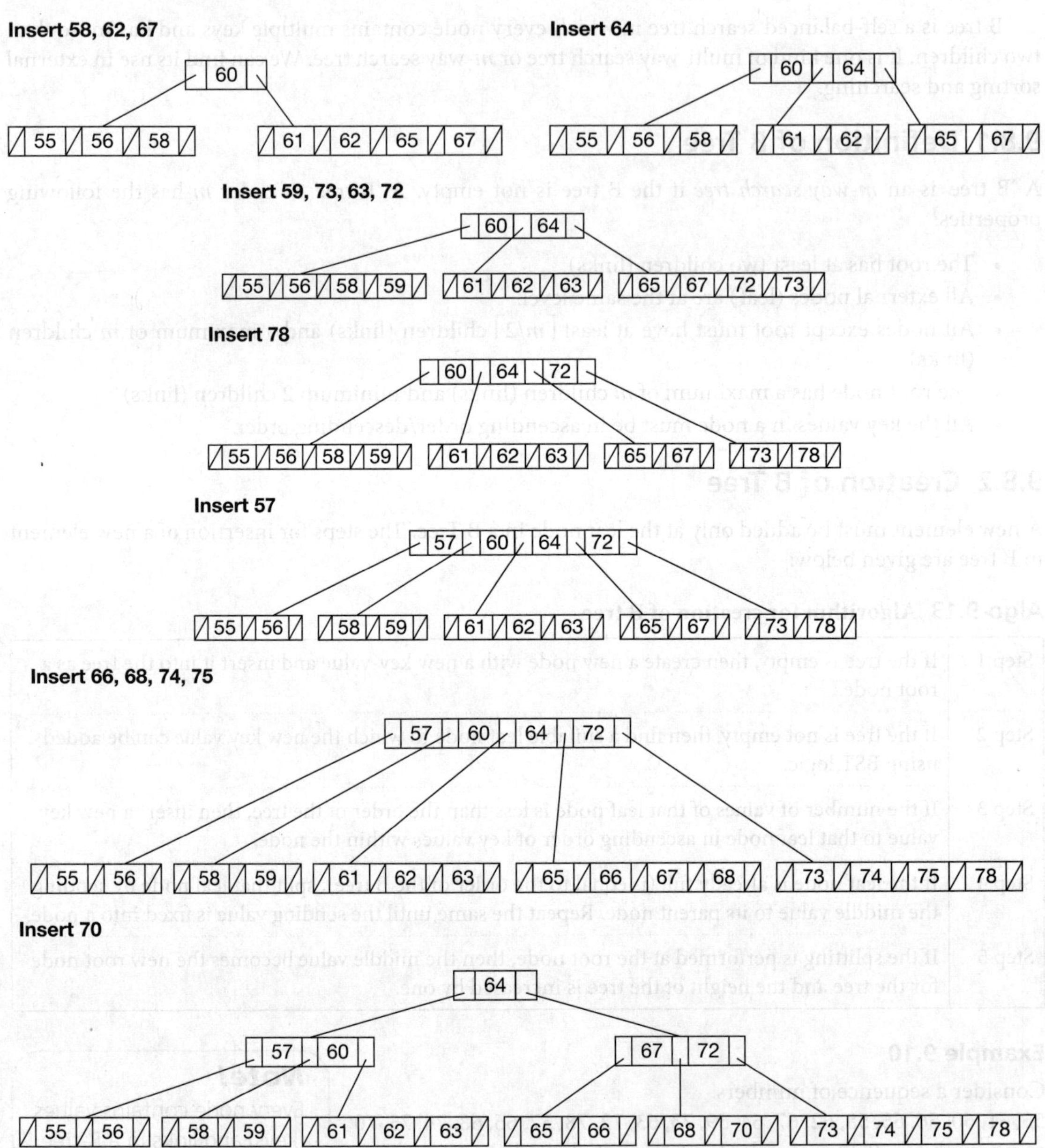

Figure 9.29 Example for the creation of a B tree

9.8.3 B Tree vs. B+ Tree

B+ tree is one kind of variation of B tree, which is used for implementing index sequential access of files. B tree has a disadvantage. It is difficult to traverse the keys sequentially, whereas in B+ tree all elements are maintained in leaves, and elements are replicated in non-leaf nodes. The major difference between B tree and B+ tree is that the internal nodes of the B+ tree are used only for storing key values that help in searching. All leaf (external) nodes are sequentially connected through a linked list. Figure 9.30 shows an example of a B+ tree.

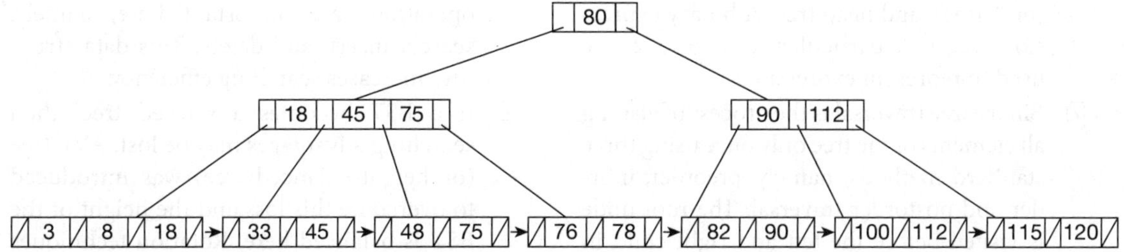

Figure 9.30 Example of B+ tree

The differences between the B tree and B+ tree are presented in Table 9.2.

> ***Note!***
> B+ tree is a kind of variation of B tree where all elements are maintained in leaves, and elements are replicated in non-leaf nodes.

Table 9.2 Difference between B tree and B+ Tree

B Tree	B+ Tree
Data is stored in internal nodes as well as in leaf nodes.	Data is stored in leaf nodes only.
Internal nodes and leaf nodes have the same structure.	Internal nodes and leaf nodes have a different structure.
Number of children per node is less.	Number of children per node is more.
Deletion is a complex operation.	Data can be directly deleted from the leaf nodes, and hence it is easy.
Leaf nodes cannot be linked together.	Leaf nodes can be linked together to form a linked list.
No redundant search keys are present.	Redundant search keys may be present.
Searching is slower since data is stored in internal as well as leaf nodes.	Searching is faster since the data is stored in the leaf nodes only.
It is used for indexing.	It is used for storing table structures.

QUICK RECAP

- ☑ A tree is a non-linear data structure through which we can solve many real-world problems. Each element is called a node and is structured hierarchically. Each node can store the data value and address of next-level nodes connected by edges.
- ☑ A binary tree is a special type of tree in which every node can have a maximum of two children. Array and linked list, both can separately be used to represent a binary tree. It has categories like a full binary tree, complete binary tree, extended binary tree

(or 2-tree), and heap tree. A binary expression tree is a particular form of a 2-tree used to represent expressions.

☑ Binary tree traversal is the process of visiting all elements of the tree only once using three standard methods, namely, preorder, inorder and postorder traversal. The root node is visited before the left and right child in the preorder. The left node is visited before the root node and right child in inorder. The sequence of visiting the nodes in postorder traversal is left, right, and then root.

☑ A binary tree can be constructed using tree traversal using inorder–preorder sequence and inorder–postorder sequence.

☑ A binary tree is converted to a threaded binary tree by making all leaf nodes to a single child node's link pointer, which would normally be a null pointer.

☑ A Binary Search Tree (BST) is a binary tree in which every node contains only smaller values in its left subtree, and greater values (or equal) in its right subtree. Three operations are important here, namely, search, insert, and delete. This data structure increases searching efficiency.

☑ If a BST becomes a skewed tree, then searching advantages may be lost. AVL tree (or height-balanced tree) was introduced to overcome this loss and the height of the BST is balanced here. Rotation techniques are used to balance the height of a BST.

☑ A 'B tree' (or balanced tree) is different from a general binary tree in that each node of the B tree may have more than 2 children. In general, every node (of a binary tree) contains only one value (key) and a maximum of two children (links). But the B-tree node contains more than one value (key), and more than two children (links).

☑ B+ tree is one kind of variation of B tree. All elements maintained in leaves and elements are replicated in non-leaf nodes in the B+ tree. The major difference between B tree and B+ tree is that the internal nodes of the B+ tree are used only for storing key-values that help in searching.

REVIEW QUESTIONS

Multiple Choice Questions (MCQ): Choose the Best Alternative

Easy

1. In a height-balanced tree or AVL tree, the height difference of two subtrees will be maximum ___________ for each node.
   A. 0 B. 1
   C. 2 D. 3
2. A 'B tree' has the following properties:
   A. All leaves are on the same level
   B. An ordered tree
   C. Balanced
   D. All of these.
3. Which of the following is required for converting an infix expression to its equivalent postfix expression?
   A. An operand stack
   B. An operator stack
   C. An operand stack and operator stack
   D. An operator queue.
4. Which one of the following is required to reconstruct a unique binary tree?
   A. Both preorder and postorder sequences
   B. Only preorder sequence
   C. Both Inorder and postorder sequences
   D. Only postorder sequence.
5. Which of the following structures is used for efficient access of data residing in disk memory?
   A. B Tree B. AVL Tree
   C. Binary tree D. None of these.

Moderate

6. The inorder and postorder traversal of a binary tree are DBEAFC and DEBFCA respectively. What will be the total number of nodes in the left subtree of the given tree?
   A. 4 B. 1
   C. 5 D. None of these.

7. The maximum possible height of an AVL tree with 7 nodes is ______.
A. 1 B. 4
C. 5 D. 3
8. The prefix expression for the infix expression $x * (y - z) / w + m$ is ______.
A. $/ * x - yz + wm$ B. $+ /* - xyzwm$
C. $+/* x - yzwm$ D. None of these.
9. If we sort the values of each node in ascending order in a BST, then which of the following traversal should we use?
A. Preorder B. Inorder
C. Postorder D. All of these.
10. The depth of a complete binary tree with n nodes is ______.
A. $\log(n + 1) - 1$ B. $\log(n)$
C. $\log(n - 1) + 1$ D. $\log(n) + 1$
11. If the inorder and preorder traversal of a binary tree are D, B, F, E, G, H, A, C and A, B, D, E, F, G, H, C respectively, then, the postorder traversal of that tree is ____________.
A. D, F, G, A, B, C, H, E
B. F, H, D, G, E, B, C, A
C. C, G, H, F, E, D, B, A
D. D, F, H, G, E, B, C, A
12. The minimum height of a binary tree of n nodes is ______.
A. n B. $n/2$
C. $n/2 - 2$ D. $\log_2(n + 1)$
13. A binary tree has m leaf nodes. The number of nodes of degree 2 in this binary tree is ____.
A. $\log m$ B. $m + 1$
C. m D. None of these.

Higher-Order Thinking Skills (HOTS)

14. The number of nodes possible in a full binary tree of height h, is ______.
A. $2^{h+1} - 1$ B. $2^h - 1$
C. $2^{h+1} - 2$ D. $2^h - 2$
15. If we represent a binary tree using array method and if the index number of a child node is 4, then the index number of its present node is _____.
A. 2 B. 1
C. 4 D. 5
16. How many possible BSTs can we form with 3 different nodes?
A. 7 B. 5
C. 3 D. 1
17. Suppose, preorder traversal of a BST is 14, 9, 11, 10, 19, 17, 15, 18. What will be the postorder traversal of this tree?
A. 9, 10, 11, 14, 15, 17, 18, 19
B. 10, 11, 9, 15, 18, 17, 19, 14
C. 19, 18, 17, 15, 14, 11, 10, 9
D. 18, 15, 17, 19, 10, 11, 9, 14

Hint: Here, in this given sequence, the first element of preorder traversal is always root. We first construct the root and then find the index of the first element, which is greater than root. Let the index be 'k'. The values between root and 'k' will be part of the left subtree, and the values between 'k+1' and '$n - 1$' will be part of the right subtree. Divide the given preorder at index 'k' and recur for left and right subtrees. For example, in {14, 9, 11, 10, 19, 17, 15, 18}, 14 is the first element, so we make it root. Now we have to look for the first element greater than 14 and find 19. So, {19, 17, 15, 18} will be the right subtree. We recursively follow the above steps for the left subtree {9, 11, 10} and right subtree {19, 17, 15, 18} and get the complete tree.

In postorder (left-right-root) root (i.e., 14) is always at the last and hence we have to choose between options B and D. Then, the next right subtree root will be 19 which will be just previous to the last number. So, option B is the correct answer.

18. Consider the array representation of a binary tree, which is also a min-heap containing 511 elements. What is the minimum number of comparisons required to find the maximum in the heap?
A. 510 B. 511
C. 256 D. 255

Hint: There are ceil(n/2) leaf nodes in a min-heap with n elements. So, there will be ceil(511/2) = ceil(255.5) = 256 elements as external nodes. To find the maximum of n elements, we need $(n - 1)$ comparisons. Compare the first two, select the maximum and compare with the next one, again select the maximum and compare with the next one and so on. So, we need 255 (= 256 – 1) minimum number of comparisons to find the maximum in the given heap. Hence, option D is correct.

19. Which one of the following statements are correct about the B+ tree data structure used for creating an index of a relational database table?

I. B+ Tree is a height-balanced tree.
II. Key values in each node are kept in sorted order.
III. Non-leaf nodes have pointers to data records.
IV. Each leaf node has a pointer to the next leaf node.

A. I, II B. I, III, IV
C. I, II, IV D. I, II, III, IV

Hint: B+ tree is a height balanced search tree, where key values in each node are kept in sorted order. All leaf nodes are at the same level and connected to the next leaf node. So, option C is correct.

20. The number of possible min-heaps containing each value from {A, B, C, D, E, F, G} exactly once is ____________.

A. 70 B. 80
C. 87 D. 99

20. Hint: Set the minimum element (i.e., A) as root. Now the remaining six elements {B, C, D, E, F, G} and left subtree will include three elements, and each left subtree combination can be permuted in 2! ways. So total ways to design min-heap with seven-elements = $^6C_3$ * 2! * 2! = 20 * 2 * 2 = 80. So, option B is correct.

Short Answer-type Questions

Easy

1. What do you mean by a tree and how is it different from a binary tree?
2. What is a heap? Write the characteristics of a tree to term it as head.
3. What are the differences between the binary search tree and AVL tree?
4. Define: AVL tree and B tree.
5. What is the difference between a complete binary tree and a fully binary tree?
6. Mention three different types of tree traversal methods and explain them with an example.
7. Mention a few advantages of the binary search tree.

Moderate

8. Justify the statement: "Linked list representation of a binary tree is more advantageous than array representation".
9. Which data structure is more advantageous – a B tree or a B+ tree?
10. Define a forest.
11. Why is threading important?
12. Write a function in C or Python to count the number of children of a node.
13. Insert following numbers to form a complete binary tree:
    5, 7, 8, 3, 2, 16, 13, 9, 1
14. Justify the statement: "All AVL trees are BST but all BSTs are not AVL trees".

Higher-Order Thinking Skills (HOTS)

15. Prove that the number of external nodes (E) is one more than the number of internal nodes (I) of an extended binary tree $E = I + 1$.
16. If n_0 be the total number of leaf nodes and n_2 be the total number of nodes having two children in a binary tree, then prove that $n_0 = n_2 + 1$.
17. Create an expression tree using the following expression: $a - b * c + d - f$.
18. Create a binary search tree with the following sequence:
    97, 12, 47, 43, 56, 26, 56, 7, 3, 8, 55.
19. Write a C function to find the degree of a binary tree.
20. Write a Python function to count the number of nodes in a binary tree.

Descriptive-type Questions

Easy

1. Create a binary tree from the following inorder and postorder traversals sequence:
   Postorder: 80, 40, 90, 50, 20, 100, 60, 110, 120, 70, 30, 10.
   Inorder: 80, 40, 20, 90, 50, 10, 60, 100, 30, 110, 70, 120.
2. Create a binary tree from the following inorder and preorder traversals sequence:
   Preorder: A, B, D, G, H, E, I, C, F, J, K.
   Inorder: G, D, H, B, E, I, A, C, J, F, K.
3. Design a non-recursive algorithm for the inorder traversal of a binary tree.
4. Prove that for any non-empty binary tree T, if n_0 be the number of leaves and n_2 be the number of nodes of degree 2, then $n_0 = n_2 + 1$.
5. Why are the following three trees important in data structure?
   a. Threaded binary tree
   b. AVL tree
   c. B tree

Moderate

6. Design an algorithm to delete a node from a binary search tree.
7. Write an algorithm to insert a node into a binary search tree.
8. Create an AVL tree with the following sequence: 10, 20, 30, 40, 50, 60.
9. Create a B tree of order 3 with the following sequence:
   90, 28, 8, 9, 16, 2, 3, 15, 10, 21, 73, 80, 19.
10. Write all tree traversal algorithms in a non-recursive way.
11. Write an algorithm to count the number of nodes in a binary tree.
12. Write an algorithm to display all elements of a BST in ascending order.

Higher-Order Thinking Skills (HOTS)

13. Insert the following keys in the order given to build them into an AVL tree:
    a z b y c x d w e v (Clearly mention rotations and balanced factors).
14. Design an algorithm to search a particular value in a BST.
15. Design an algorithm to insert a node into a B+ tree.
16. Design an algorithm to check whether a node is the left child or the right child of a binary tree.
17. Design three different recursive functions to find preorder, inorder and postorder traversal of a binary tree.

CASE STUDIES

1. Suppose two numbers n_1 and n_2 are given in a BST. Design an algorithm to find all the elements of the BST in the range n_1 and n_2 and also try to analyze the time complexity.
2. Design a procedure for converting a list of elements of a singly linked list sorted in ascending order into a height-balanced BST.
3. Design an algorithm which will check whether a given binary tree is a BST or not.
4. Suppose we have a proper binary tree with root R. What does the following algorithm do? Also explain how it works.

```
Algorithm:
TT(R):
if(not r): return 1
else:
      a = TT(r.left_child)
      b = TT(r.right_child)
      return a + b
```

Hint: It computes the number of leaves in the tree.

5. Designing a procedure to insert an element into an AVL tree. The procedure should also check whether any height imbalance is occurring after each insertion. Design appropriate rotation functions when the BST is imbalanced.

LAB EXERCISES

1. Write a Python program to create and count the number of nodes in a binary tree.
2. Write a menu-driven recursive C program to display the elements of a binary tree in preorder, inorder and postorder traversal.

ANSWER KEYS

Multiple Choice Questions

1. B	**4.** C	**7.** D	**10.** A	**13.** D	**16.** B	**19.** C
2. D	**5.** A	**8.** C	**11.** D	**14.** B	**17.** B	**20.** B
3. B	**6.** D	**9.** B	**12.** D	**15.** B	**18.** D	

10 Graphs

CONTENTS

EXPECTED OUTCOMES OF THIS CHAPTER

After going through this chapter learners will be able

- ☑ To explain the basic terminologies of graph.
- ☑ To understand how to implement a graph ADT.
- ☑ To implement algorithms to traverse (BFS and DFS) a graph.
- ☑ To describe minimum spanning tree algorithms.
- ☑ To explain the Dijkstra's algorithm for shortest-path evaluation.
- ☑ To explain the grid path problem using examples.
- ☑ To illustrate the longest common subsequence finding problem.

10.1 INTRODUCTION

The previous chapters of this book covered different data structures like array, linked list, stack, queue, and trees. Another very important data structure called graph is explored here. Graph is an abstract data structure. In this chapter, we will also learn about how the graph is represented in computer memory and study a few algorithms that use graphs to solve some real-life problems.

Graph is the representation of a set of items where some pairs of items are connected by links. A problem can often be represented as a graph for finding the solution to the problem using the graph data structure. It offers many state-of-the-art applications in computer science and engineering. For example, graphs are used to represent the network which includes paths in a city, telephone network, travel applications, gaming, and many more. Graph is also very much used in social networking sites like Facebook, Twitter, LinkedIn, etc.

10.1.1 Definition

Graph is a collection of vertices (or nodes) and edges (or arcs) in which vertices are connected with edges. It is a non-linear data structure.

Mathematically, a graph G is represented as $G = (V, E)$*, where V is the set of vertices given by* $V = \{v_1, v_2, v_3, \ldots, v_n\}$ *and E is set of edges given by* $E = \{e_1, e_2, e_3, \ldots, e_n\}$.

10.1.2 Basic Terminologies

There are many terms associated with graphs. Figure 10.1 represents the concepts associated with these terminologies, and Table 10.1 presents the descriptions with examples.

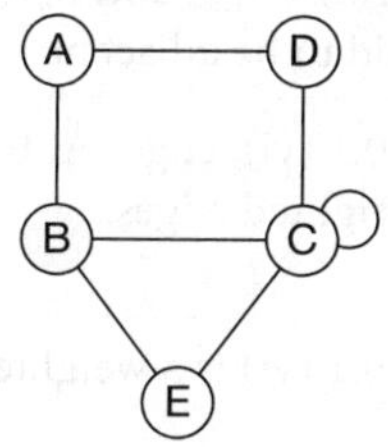

Fig. (i) Undirected graph

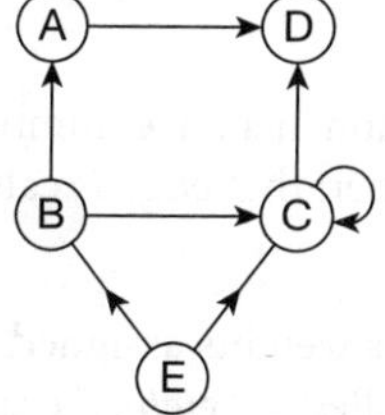

Fig. (ii) Directed graph

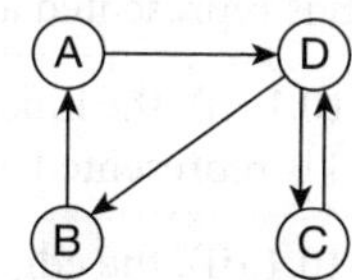

Fig. (iii) Directed graph

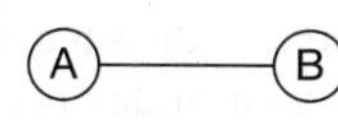

Fig. (iv) Undirected graph with pendant vertices

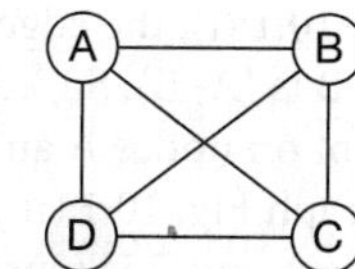

Fig. (v) Complete graph

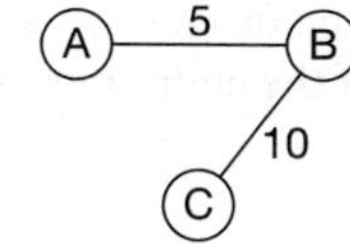

Fig.(vi) Weighted graph

Figure 10.1 Diagrammatic representation of different graphs

Table 10.1 Graph terminologies with examples

Key terms	Description	Example
Vertex	Each data element of a graph is called *vertex*. It is also known as a node.	In Fig. 10.1 (i) and 10.1 (ii), A, B, C, D, and E are vertices or nodes.
Edge	An *edge* is a linking between two vertices. It is also known as an *arc*. Edges are two types. • **Undirected Edge:** An *undirected edge* is a bidirectional edge. In Fig. 10.1 (i), all the edges are undirected. An edge between vertices A and B, i.e., (A, B) is equal to the edge (B, A). • **Directed Edge:** A *directed edge* is a unidirectional edge. In Fig. 10.1 (ii), all the edges are directed. There is a direction on the edge between vertices B and A. So edge (B, A) is valid but edge (A, B) is not valid.	In Fig. 10.1 (i), the link between vertices A and B is represented as (A, B). In Fig. 10.1 (i), there are 7 edges (i.e., (A, B), (A, C), (A, D), (B, D), (B, E), (C, D), (C, C), (D, E)). In Fig. 10.1 (ii), the link between vertices A and B is represented as (B, A). There are 7 edges (i.e., (B, A), (A, D), (C, D), (B, C), (E, B), (C, E), (C, C) in this figure.
Undirected graph	A graph with all undirected edges only is said to be an *undirected graph.*	Fig. 10.1 (i).
Directed graph	A graph with all directed edges only is said to be a *directed graph*. It is also called a *digraph*.	Fig. 10.1 (ii).
Adjacency node	Vertices A and B are said to be *adjacent* if there is an edge between them.	If there is an edge between vertices [Fig. 10.1 (i)] A and B, then both A and B are said to be adjacent.
Weighted edge	If there is a non-negative number assigned to an edge, then that edge is called a *weighted edge.*	Fig. 10.1 (vi), edge (A, B), and edge (B, C) are weighted edges.
Weighted graph	If a graph has weights assigned to all of its edges, it is called a *weighted graph.*	Fig. 10.1 (vi) is a weighted graph.
Predecessor node	If (B, A) represents a directed edge from B to A, then B is a *predecessor node* of A.	In Fig. 10.1 (ii), the link between vertices A and B is represented as (B, A).
Successor node	If (B, A) represents a directed edge from B to A then A is a *successor* node of B.	In Fig. 10.1 (ii), the link between vertices A and B is represented as (B, A).
Origin and Destination	If an edge is directed, its first endpoint is said to be its *origin*, and the other endpoint is said to be the *destination* of that edge.	In Fig. 10.1 (ii), the edge between vertices A and B is represented as (B, A). So, B is the origin and A is the destination.
Incidence	Edge is said to be *incident* on a vertex if the vertex is one of the endpoints of that edge.	In Fig. 10.1 (i), the edge between vertices A and B is (A, B). So, edge (A, B) is incident on nodes A and B. In digraph Fig. 10.1 (ii), the edge between vertices A and B is represented as (B, A). So, edge (B, A) is incident from vertex B and is incident to vertex A.

(*Continued*)

Key terms	Description	Example
Outgoing edge	A directed edge is said to be an *outgoing edge* from its source vertex.	In digraph Fig. 10.1 (ii), (B, A) is the outgoing edge from its source vertex B.
Incoming edge	A directed edge is said to be an *incoming edge* on its destination vertex.	In digraph Fig. 10.1 (ii), (B, A) is the incoming edge on its destination vertex A.
Degree	The total number of edges connected to a vertex is said to be the *degree* of that vertex or node.	In Fig. 10.1 (i), degree(A) = 2, degree(B) = 3, degree(C) = 3 + 2 = 5, degree(D) = 2, degree(E) = 2.
Pendant vertex	A vertex with degree one is called a *pendant vertex.*	In Fig. 10.1 (iv), A and B both are pendant vertices.
Self-loop	If an edge has its two endpoints the same, it is called a *self-loop*.	In Fig. 10.1 (i) and 10.1 (ii), C is the self-loop. In an undirected graph, self-loop is counted twice whereas in directed graph self-loop is counted one in indegree and one in outdegree.
Indegree	The total number of incoming edges connected to a vertex is said to be *indegree* of that vertex.	In Fig. 10.1 (ii), indegree(A) = 1, indegree(B) = 1, indegree(C) = 2 + 1 = 3, indegree(D)= 2, indegree(E) = 0.
Outdegree	The total number of outgoing edges connected to a vertex is said to be *outdegree* of that vertex.	In Fig. 10.1 (ii), outdegree(A) = 1, outdegree(B) = 1, outdegree(C) = 1 + 1 = 2, outdegree(D) = 0, outdegree(E) = 2.
Sink	A vertex that has no outgoing edges but has incoming edges is called a *sink*. The outdegree of a sink vertex is zero.	In Fig. 10.1 (ii), vertex D is a sink.
Source	A vertex that has no incoming edges but has outgoing edges is called a *source*. The indegree of a sink vertex is zero.	In Fig. 10.1 (ii), vertex E is a source vertex.
Path and length	A *path* is a sequence of vertices and edges that starts at a vertex and ends at another vertex where each edge is incident to its predecessor and successor vertex. The total number of edges on a path is called its *length*.	In Fig. 10.1 (ii), the path between vertices E and D is either E-B-A-D (length = 4) or E-C-D (length = 3).
Cycle	A path that starts and ends at the same vertex is called a *cycle.*	In Fig. 10.1 (iii), path B-A-D-B has formed a cycle.
Parallel edges or multiple edges	If there are two undirected edges with same end vertices and two directed edges with the same origin and destination, such edges are called *parallel edges* or multiple edges.	In Fig. 10.1 (iii), (C, D) and (D, C) are parallel edges or multiple edges.

(*Continued*)

Key terms	Description	Example
Multi-graph	A graph having parallel edges is known as a *multi-graph.*	The graph in Fig. 10.1 (iii) is an example of a multi-graph.
Connected graph	An undirected graph in which there is a path between each pair of nodes is called a *connected graph.*	The graph in Fig. 10.1 (i) is an example of a connected graph.
Complete graph	An undirected graph in which there is a direct edge between each pair of nodes is called a *complete graph.* The total number of edges in a complete graph will be $n(n-1)/2$, where n is the total number of vertices or nodes.	The graph in Fig. 10.1 (v) is an example of a complete graph.
Order	The *order* of a graph is the number of vertices contained by the graph.	Order of the graph in Fig. 10.1 (i) is 5. The order of the graph in Fig. 10.1 (ii) is also 5.

***Property 1:* In an undirected graph, the number of edges = sum of the degrees of all vertices / 2**

In an undirected graph, the summation of all degrees of all the vertices of a graph is equal to twice the number of edges. Each edge counts twice, once for its initial vertex, and second for its terminal vertex. This is also called the **Handshaking Theorem.**

Suppose, $G = (V, E)$ be an undirected graph.

Then, $2E = \sum\text{deg}(V)$, i.e., sum of degrees of all vertices = 2 * number of edges

Or, we can write, the number of edges = sum of degrees of all vertices / 2.

***Property 2:* An undirected graph has an even number of vertices of odd degree.**

Suppose, v_1 and v_2 $(V = v_1 + v_2)$ are the sets of vertices of even and odd degrees respectively.

As per handshaking theorem (Property 1), $2E = \sum\text{deg}(V)$. So, $2E = \sum\text{deg}(v_1) + \sum\text{deg}(v_2)$.

We know that the sum of degrees of vertices with even degree is even. Then, $2E$ is also even, which means that the sum of degrees of vertices with odd degrees must be even. So, the number of vertices with odd degrees is even.

> **Note!**
> Graph is a collection of vertices (nodes) and edges (arcs) are links where vertices are connected with edges.

10.2 REPRESENTATION OF GRAPH

In this section, we discuss about representing a graph in computer memory. We only focus on capturing details related to the different vertices and edges while representing the graph. There are several ways to represent a graph in the computer memory, but the following three are the most commonly used methods:

1. Adjacency matrix
2. Incidence matrix
3. Adjacency list

> **Note!**
> Adjacency matrix, incidence matrix, and adjacency list are the most important ways to represent a graph in the computer memory.

10.2.1 Adjacency Matrix

The adjacency matrix is a sequential representation. In this representation, the graph is represented using a matrix of size equal to the total number of vertices by the total number of vertices. That means, a graph with 5 vertices is represented using a matrix of size 5 × 5 (See Fig. 10.2). In the matrix, both rows and columns represent vertices. The full matrix is filled with either 1 or 0. Here, 1 represents that there is an edge from row vertex to column vertex, and 0 represents that there is no edge from the row vertex to the column vertex.

To construct a $n \times n$ adjacency matrix $A = [a_{i,j}]_{n \times n}$,
$a_{i,j} = 1$, if there is any edge from a vertex i to vertex j;
$a_{i,j} = 0$, otherwise.

Example 10.1

The following Fig. 10.2 shows the representations of undirected and directed graphs using adjacency matrices.

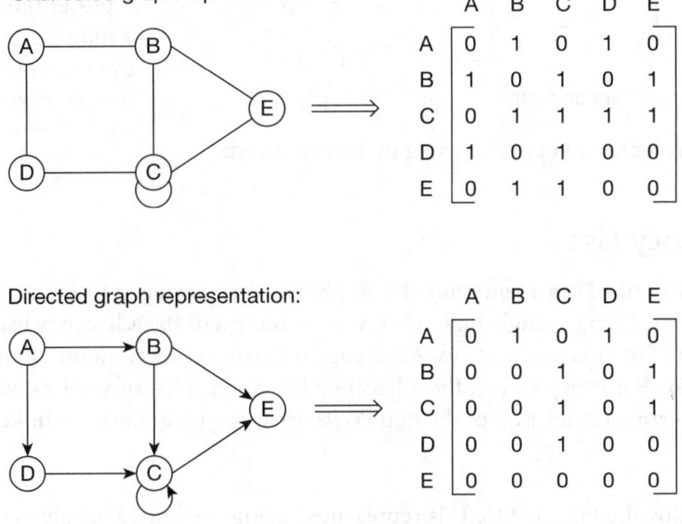

	A	B	C	D	E
A	0	1	0	1	0
B	1	0	1	0	1
C	0	1	1	1	1
D	1	0	1	0	0
E	0	1	1	0	0

	A	B	C	D	E
A	0	1	0	1	0
B	0	0	1	0	1
C	0	0	1	0	1
D	0	0	1	0	0
E	0	0	0	0	0

Figure 10.2 Representation of graph using adjacency matrix

Suppose, a graph with 100 vertices contains only 1 edge. Though it has only one edge, we still have to take a 100 × 100 matrix with lots of zeros in the adjacency matrix. So, representation with an adjacency matrix is easier to implement, but if the matrix becomes a sparse matrix (as discussed in Chapter 5 on the linked list), there will be lots of wastage of memory to store a huge number of zeros. It takes a lot of space and time to visit all the neighbors of a vertex. It also becomes inefficient for graphs that have a large number of vertices.

> **Note!**
> Adjacency matrix uses sequential representation of graph with a square matrix of size equal to the total number of vertices.

10.2.2 Incidence Matrix

In this representation, the graph can be represented using a matrix depending on the total number of vertices by the total number of edges. If a graph has 4 vertices and 5 edges (Fig. 10.3), then it can be represented using a matrix of order 4 × 5. In this matrix, say $A = [a_{i,j}]_{m \times n}$, rows represent vertices, and columns represent edges. The value of the matrix will be either 0 or 1 or −1, where,

$a_{i,j} = 0$ if edge j is not connected to that row vertex i;
$a_{i,j} = 1$ if edge j is connected as outgoing edge to row vertex i;
$a_{i,j} = -1$ if edge j is connected as incoming edge to row vertex i.

Example 10.2

Following is an example of the graph (left) that is represented using the incidence matrix (right):

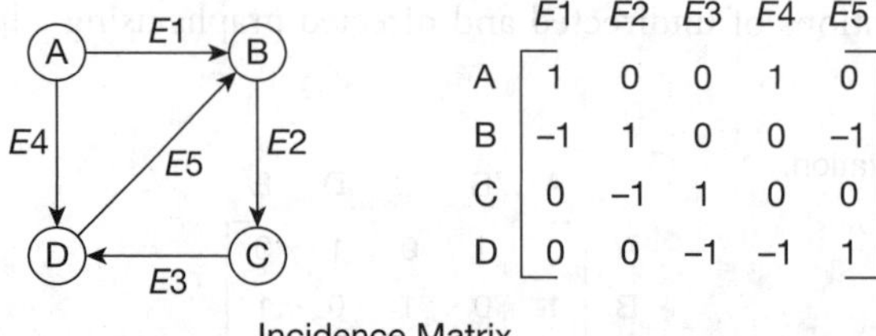

	E1	E2	E3	E4	E5
A	1	0	0	1	0
B	−1	1	0	0	−1
C	0	−1	1	0	0
D	0	0	−1	−1	1

Note!
Incidence matrix representation of graph uses a matrix size depending on the total number of vertices by the total number of edges.

Figure 10.3 Representation of graph using incidence matrix

10.2.3 Adjacency List

The adjacency list is a linked representation of a graph. For each vertex in the graph, we maintain the list of its neighbor's vertex. Using a singly linked list, we can represent the adjacency list. Every vertex of the graph contains a list of its adjacent vertices. Adjacency list requires less amount of memory compared to the adjacency matrix. For every vertex, the adjacency list stores a list of vertices, which are adjacent to the current one. Insertion or deletion of the node is very easy as we are using a linked list data structure.

Example 10.3

The graph in the following Fig. 10.4 (left) is represented using the linked list given on the right side.

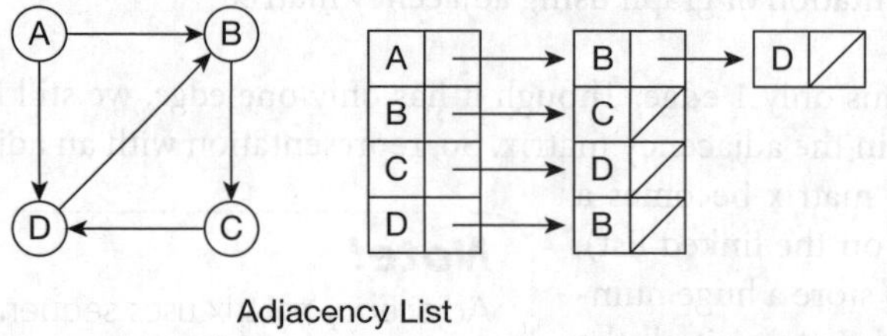

Note!
Adjacency list uses a linked representation of graph maintaining the list of its neighbor's vertex for each vertex.

Figure 10.4 Representation of graph using adjacency list

10.3 APPLICATIONS OF GRAPH

Since graph data structure is a very efficient abstraction, it can be used to solve many real-world problems. These are a few important applications of graphs data structure:

- Social networks like Facebook, Twitter, LinkedIn, etc.
- Biological networks
- Neural networks
- Blockchain technology
- Network traffic
- Transportation network

10.3.1 Social Network

Social connections such as who communicates with whom, who knows whom, who influences whom or other relationships can be represented using graphs that help us to understand these social structures. Social networking applications incorporate these graphs for modeling their system workflows. An example is the Facebook graph of who follows whom. These can be used to determine how information flows, how communities develop, how topics become hot, or even who might be a good match for whom. All social, professional, and research networking applications use such graphs. Figure 10.5 presents the social network system diagrammatically using graphs.

Figure 10.5 Example of a social network graph

10.3.2 Biological Network

Protein–protein interaction network studies molecular pathways or chains of molecular interactions in a cellular process in biology. Vertices represent proteins, and edges represent interactions between them that carry out some biological function in the cell. Humans have over 120K proteins with millions of interactions among them. Figure 10.6 shows typical protein interactions diagrammatically using graphs.

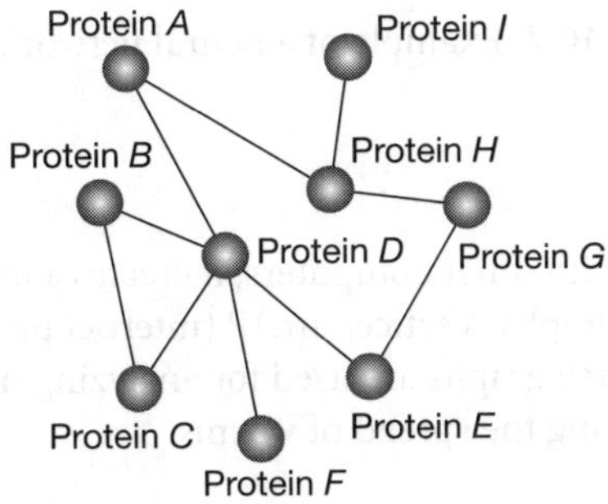

Figure 10.6 Example of a biological (protein–protein interaction) network graph

10.3.3 Neural Network

The human brain has about 10^{11} neurons and close to 10^{15} synapses. Vertices represent neurons and edges represent the synapses between them. Neural networks are used to understand how our brain works, and how connections change when our brains learn something. Figure 10.7 shows a neural network graph.

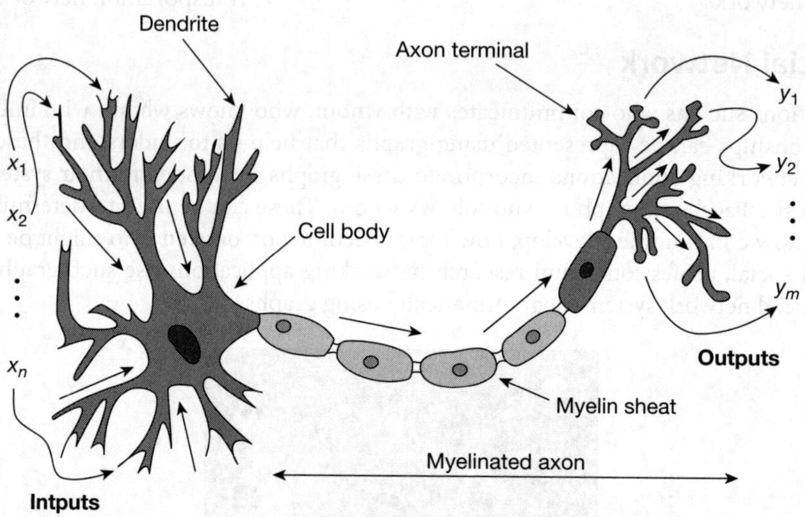

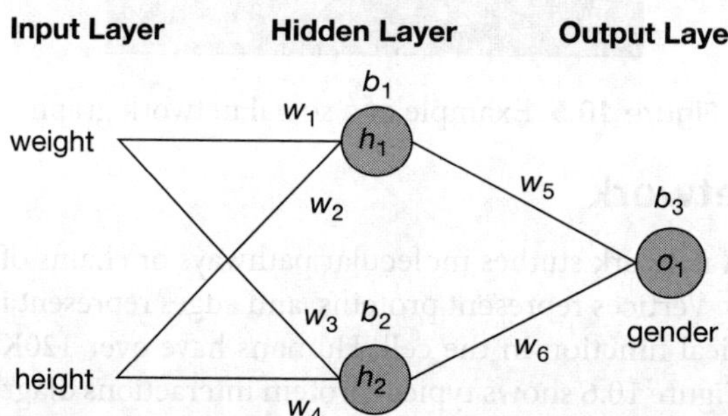

Figure 10.7 Example of a neural network graph

10.3.4 Network Traffic

When a computer communicates with other computers, it creates a mesh of networks (Fig. 10.8). Such a network can be represented using graphs. Vertices are IP (internet protocol) addresses and edges are the packets that flow between them. Such graphs are used for analyzing network security, tracking criminal or non-criminal activity, and studying the spread of worms.

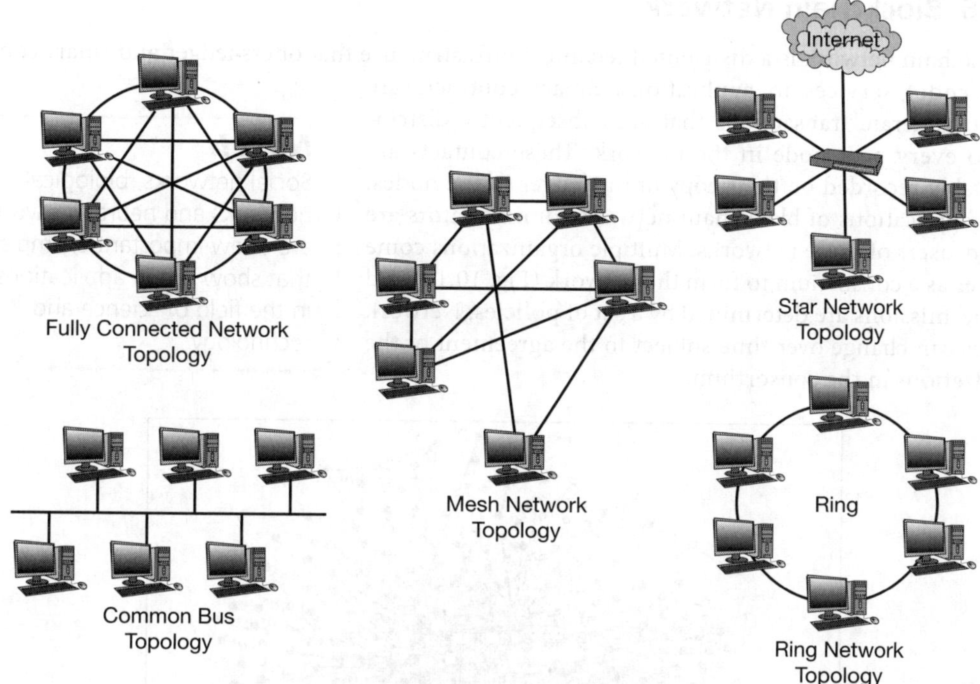

Figure 10.8 Example of a computer network graph

10.3.5 Transportation Network

Roads used for transportation networks can be represented using graphs (Fig. 10.9). Vertices are the crossing or intersections of roads and edges are the road segments between them in road networks. In public transportation networks, vertices are stops and edges are the links between them. These networks are used by many map programs like Google maps, Bing maps, etc., to find the best routes between locations. They are also used to study traffic light timings, traffic patterns, and many aspects of transportation.

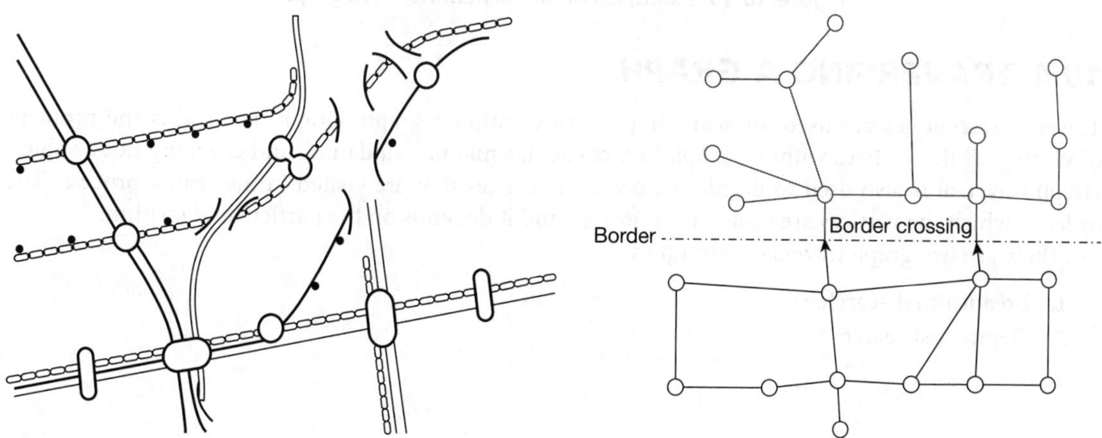

Figure 10.9 Example of a transportation network graph

10.3.6 Blockchain Network

A blockchain network is a distributed technical infrastructure that offers ledger and smart contract (chain-code) services to applications. Smart contracts are used to generate transactions that are subsequently distributed to every peer node in the network. These contacts are immutably recorded on their copy of the ledger in the nodes. Client applications of blockchain network administrators are the end-users of these networks. Multiple organizations come together as a consortium to form the network (Fig. 10.10) and their permissions are determined by a set of policies. Network policies can change over time subject to the agreement of the organizations in the consortium.

> **Note!**
> Social networks, biological networks and neural networks are a few important examples that show graph applications in the field of science and technology.

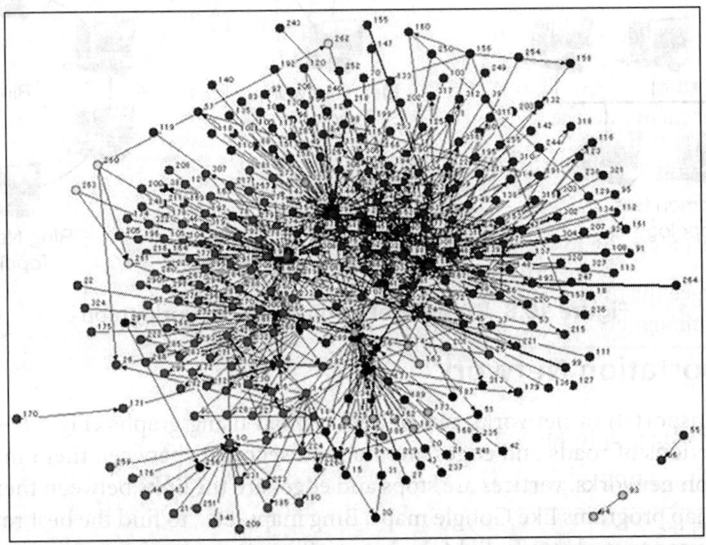

Figure 10.10 Examples of blockchain network graphs

10.4 TRAVERSING A GRAPH

Traversal techniques are used for searching a vertex within a graph. Graph traversal is the problem of visiting all the vertices within a graph in a particular manner, updating, and checking node values. Graph traversal is also used to decide the order of vertices that are visited in the search process. The order in which the vertices are visited is important and it depends on the particular algorithm.

There are two graph traversal techniques:

1. Breadth-first search.
2. Depth-first search.

10.4.1 Breadth-first Search (BFS)

A breadth-first search (BFS) explores the nodes nearest to the root before exploring other nodes further away. BFS uses a queue data structure for this exploration or search process. When a dead-end occurs in any iteration, it gets the next vertex to start a search again. This graph traversal is called BFS since it traverses a graph in a breadth-ward motion.

First, the BFS technique visits the adjacent unvisited vertex, marks the visited vertex besides inserting it in a queue, and prints it. The vertex is removed from the queue if no adjacent vertex is found. The process is repeatedly carried out until the queue is empty.

The following algorithm presents the BFS technique systematically:

Algo-10.1 Algorithm of breadth-first search (BFS) for graph traversal

Step 1	Define a queue Q where size (Q) = m, the total number of vertices in the graph.
Step 2	Choose any vertex as a starting point for traversal. Visit that vertex and insert it into the Q.
Step 3	Visit all the non-visited vertices that are adjacent to the current vertex in front of the Q and insert them into the Q.
Step 4	When no new vertex is there to be visited from the vertex in front of the Q, then delete that vertex.
Step 5	Repeat Steps 3 and 4 until Q becomes empty.
Step 6	Produce the final spanning tree by removing unused edges from the graph when the Q becomes empty.

Example 10.4

Consider the following graphs given in Table 10.2 to perform BFS traversal.

Table 10.2 Example of BFS of graph traversal

Actions	Graphs	Queue (Q)
The original graph to be traversed.	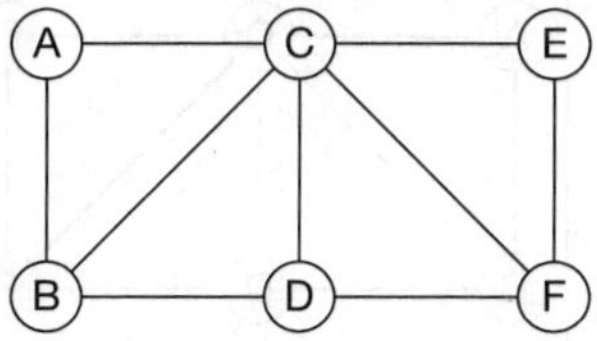 A, C, E, B, D, F	Queue (Q) [, , , , ,] 0 1 2 3 4 5
Select the vertex A as a starting point (Visit A), and insert A into the queue.	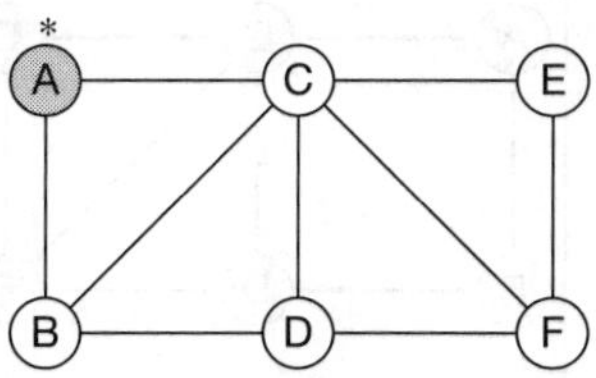 * A, C, E, B, D, F	Queue (Q) [A, , , , ,] 0 1 2 3 4 5

(Continued)

Actions	Graphs	Queue (Q)
Visit all the adjacent vertices of A (in front of the queue), which are unvisited (B, C). Insert the newly visited vertices B, C into the queue, and delete A from the queue as A is in the front of this queue.	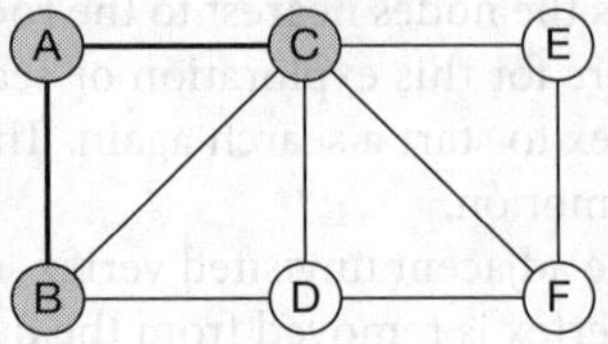	Queue (Q) [, B, C, , ,] 0 1 2 3 4 5
Visit all the adjacent vertices of B (in front of the queue), which are still unvisited (D). Insert the newly visited vertex D into the queue and delete B from the queue as B is in the front of the queue.	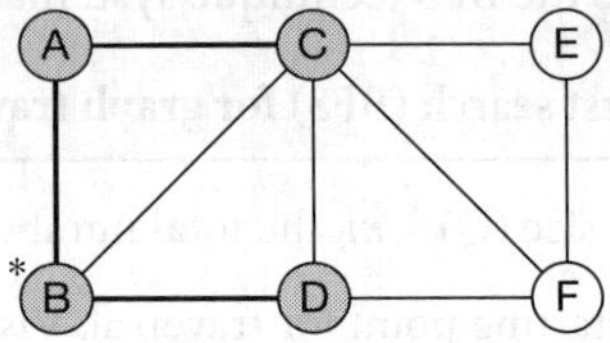	Queue (Q) [, , C, D, ,] 0 1 2 3 4 5
Visit all the adjacent vertices of C (in front of the queue), which are still unvisited (E, F). Insert the newly visited vertices E, F into the queue, and delete C from the queue as C is in the front of this queue.	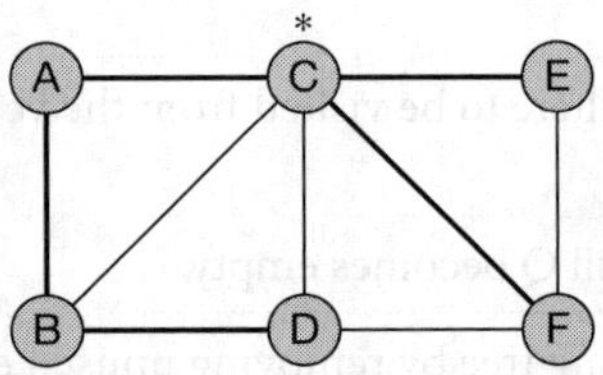	Queue (Q) [, , , D, E, F] 0 1 2 3 4 5
Visit all the adjacent vertices of D (in front of the queue), which are still unvisited (there is no unvisited vertex). So, delete D from the queue as D is in the front of this queue.	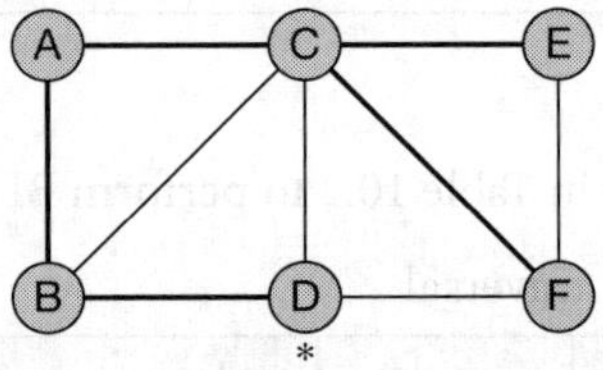	Queue (Q) [, , , , E, F] 0 1 2 3 4 5
Visit all the adjacent vertices of E (in front of the queue), which are still unvisited (there is no unvisited vertex). So, delete E from the queue as E is in the front of this queue.	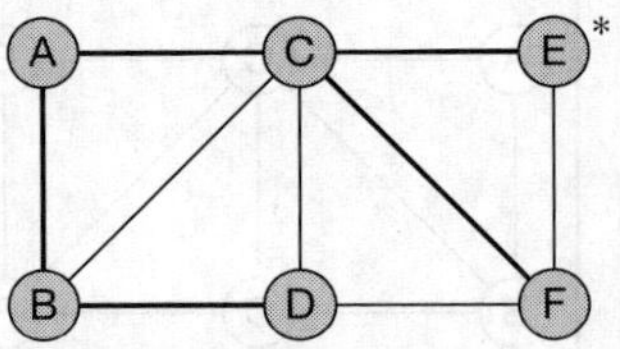	Queue (Q) [, , , , , F] 0 1 2 3 4 5
Visit all the adjacent vertices of F (in front of the queue), which are still unvisited (there is no unvisited vertex). So, delete F from the queue as F is in the front of the queue. Now the queue is empty, so stop the BFS process.	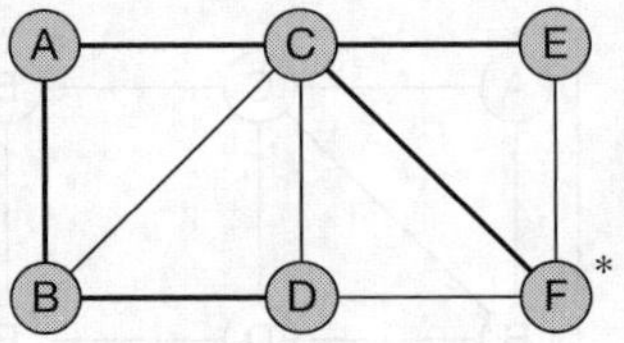	Queue (Q) [, , , , ,] 0 1 2 3 4 5

(Continued)

Actions	Graphs	Queue (Q)
Final result/output of BFS.	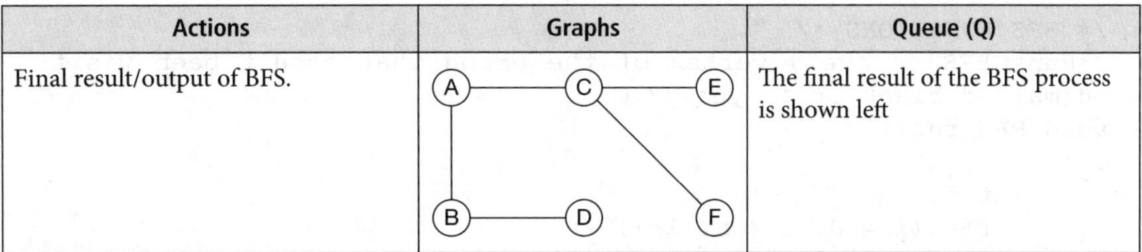	The final result of the BFS process is shown left

> ***Note!***
> BFS explores the nodes nearest the root before exploring other nodes further away, and uses a queue for the search process.

When we use the adjacency list, then the time complexity of BFS will be O($V + E$), where V is the number of vertices, and E is the number of edges in the graph.

10.4.2 BFS Graph Traversal with C and Python

CProg-10.1 Implementation of BFS graph traversal

```
/*BFS on graphs using adjacency matrix; Uses 1-based on indexing
for vertices */
#include<stdio.h>
#include<stdlib.h>
#define MAX 1000

/* Initiation of data structures */
int queue[MAX]; /* the queue array */
int graph[MAX][MAX]; /* the graph 2-D array*/
int state[MAX];
/* Array that stores 1 for visited nodes(black), 0 for unvisited
nodes(white) */

int n; /* Number of vertices in the graph */

/* Queue pointers: */
int front = -1;
int rear = -1;

/* Function declarations */
int dequeue(int n);
int front1();
int enqueue(int e);
int isempty();
void graph_initiator();
void BFS(int node);
```

```
/* BFS FUNCTIONS */
/*Runs BFS on every vertex of the graph that hasn't been visit-
ed(marked black or 1) yet */
void BFS_run()
  {
     int i;
       for (i = 0; i < n; i++)
     /* initializing state of each vertex as 0(white) */
     state[i] = 0;
     int v;
     for(i = 0; i < n; i++)
       {
        if (state[i] != 1)
           BFS(i);
       }
   }

/* BFS first enqueues each unvisited vertex to the queue, marks it
as visited and stores its value in val. Then it dequeues the ver-
tex at the front of the queue itself from the queue. For the row
of val in the adjacency matrix, every column that is marked 1 has
an edge from the val vertex to that vertex. Hence they form the
neighbors of val. Check if the neighbors have already been vis-
ited or not. If not, then it enqueues the neighbor and marks it as
visited. Else, it moves on to the next neighbor. */
void BFS(int node)
   {
     int i;
       enqueue(node);
     state[node] = 1;
     while(!isempty())
       {
         int val = front1();
           printf("%d ",val + 1);
           dequeue(n);
           for(i = 0; i < n; i++)
             {
             if(graph[val][i] == 1)
               /* Checks for existence of edge between two nodes */
                 {
                   if(state[graph[val][i]] != 1)
                     /* Checks for neighbours of node to perform
BFS on */
                       {
                         enqueue(graph[val][i]);
                         state[graph[val][i]] = 1;
                       }
```

```
                }
            else
                continue;
        }
    }
}

/* FUNCTIONS FOR QUEUE */
/* Function to enqueue, i.e., insert new element at the rear of
the queue array, adds 1 to the rear pointer after each insertion.
Handles isempty case by setting front = 0 */
int enqueue(int e)
  {
    if(front == -1)
    front = 0;
    rear = rear + 1;
    queue[rear] = e ;
  }

/* Function to delete elements from the front of the queue and
return them. Returns queue underflow while trying to dequeue from
an empty queue */
int dequeue(int n)
  {
    int elmnt;
    if(front == -1 || front > rear)
      {
        printf("Queue Underflow\n");
          exit(1);
      }
    elmnt = queue[front];
    front += 1;
    return elmnt;
  }

/* Returns the element at front of the queue */
int front1()
  {
    if(isempty() )
        {
        printf( "Empty queue!!\n" );
        }
    else
          return queue[front];
  }
```

```
/* Returns 1 if queue is empty, else 0 */
int isempty()
  {
     if (front == -1 || front > rear)
       return 1;
     else
          return 0;
  }
void matrix_initiator(int origin, int destin)
  {
     /* assigns vertices and edges */
     graph[origin - 1][ destin - 1] = 1;
  }

/* Function to initiate the graph from edges input by user */
void graph_initiator()
  {
     int i,j;
       n = 4;
     int e = 6;
     for(i = 0; i < n; i++) /* Initialize whole graph matrix with
0s */
       {
         for (j = 0; j < n; j++)
            graph[i][j] = 0;
       }
     matrix_initiator(1, 2);
     matrix_initiator(1, 3);
     matrix_initiator(2, 3);
     matrix_initiator(3, 4);
     matrix_initiator(3, 1);
     matrix_initiator(4, 4);
}

/* Driver function */
int main()
  {
     graph_initiator();
     BFS_run();
     printf("\n");
  }
/* End of program */
```

Output

```
BFS of the graph :
```

Output

```
1 2 3 4
```

> ***Programming Tips!***
> enqueue() is used to insert a new element at the rear of the queue array. It adds 1 to the rear pointer after each insertion. isempty() case is got by setting front = 0.

> ***Programming Tips!***
> dequeue() is used to delete elements from the front and return them. It returns underflow while trying to dequeue from an empty queue. graph_initiator() is used to initiate the graph from edge inputs.

PyProg-10.1 Implementation of BFS graph traversal

```
# Importing collections
from collections import deque

# Class definition of a graph
class Graph:
   # Constructor to create a new node
   def __init__(self, num_vertices):
       self.num_vertices = num_vertices
       self.adj_list = [[] for _ in range(num_vertices)]

   def addEdge(self, source, destination):
       self.adj_list[source].append(destination)

   # Function for breadth-first-search
   def bfs(self, start):
       visited = [False] * self.num_vertices
       l=[]
       queue_vertex = deque([])
       visited[start] = True
       queue_vertex.append(start)
       while len(queue_vertex) != 0:
           current = queue_vertex.popleft()
           l.append(current)
```

```
                for vertex in self.adj_list[current]:
                    if (not visited[vertex]):
                        visited[vertex] = True
                        queue_vertex.append(vertex)
            return l

# Driver function
def main():
    # Create a graph with vertices and nodes
    # Creating nodes
    nodes = int(input("Enter the number of nodes: "))
    graph = Graph(nodes)
    # Create edges
    edges = int(input("Enter the number of edges: "))
    print("Enter the edges separated by space: ")
    for i in range(edges):
        u, v = map(int,input().split(" "))
        graph.addEdge(u, v)

    print("Breadth First Traversal is:",end=' ')
    print(*graph.bfs(0),sep=' ')

if __name__ == '__main__':
    main()
## end program
```

Output

```
Enter the number of nodes: 8
Enter the number of edges: 14
Enter the edges separated by space:
0 1
0 2
1 2
1 4
2 0
2 3
3 3
3 6
4 0
4 5
5 6
5 7
6 2
7 3
Breadth First Traversal is: 0 1 2 4 3 5 6 7
```

Programming Tips!
Constructor __init__() is used to create and initialize the attributes of the class. addEdge() is used for edge append, and bfs() is used for BFS traversal using queue.

10.4.3 Depth-first Search (DFS)

Depth-first search (DFS) is used for traversing a finite graph. This method is called DFS because it traverses the depth of any particular path before exploring its breadth. The depth-first search algorithm is very similar to the standard algorithm for traversing the binary tree. It uses a stack data structure. It traverses a graph in a depth-ward motion, and gets the next vertex to start a search when a dead-end occurs in any iteration.

DFS first visits the adjacent unvisited vertex, and marks it as visited vertex. Then it prints the visited vertex, and pushes it in a stack. If no adjacent vertex is found, we have to pop up a vertex from the stack. These are repeated until the stack is empty. The following algorithm presents the DFS technique systematically:

Algo-10.2 Algorithm of depth-first search (DFS) for graph traversal

Step 1	Define a stack S where size(S) = m, the total number of vertices in the graph.
Step 2	Choose any vertex as a starting point for traversal. Visit that vertex, and push it on to S.
Step 3	Visit any one of the non-visited adjacent vertices that are at the top of S, and push it on to S.
Step 4	Repeat Step 3 until there is no new vertex to be visited, which is at the top of S.
Step 5	Use backtracking and pop one vertex from the stack when there is no new vertex to visit.
Step 6	Repeat Steps 3, 4, and 5 until S becomes empty.
Step 7	Produce the final tree by removing unused edges from the graph when S becomes empty.

Example 10.5

Consider the following graphs given in Table 10.3 to perform DFS traversal.

Table 10.3 Example of DFS of graph traversal

Actions	Graphs	Stack (S)
The original graph to be traversed	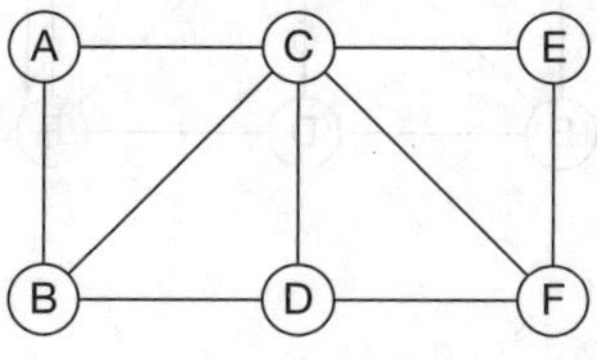 A, C, E, B, D, F	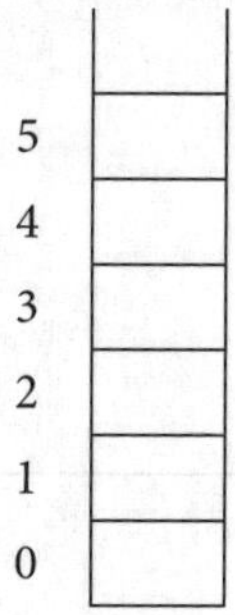 5 4 3 2 1 0

(Continued)

Actions	Graphs	Stack (S)
Choose vertex A as the starting point (visit A). Push A into the stack.	A C E B D F	5 4 3 2 1 0 A
Visit any adjacent vertex of A, which is unvisited. Push the newly visited vertex C into the stack.	A C E B D F	5 4 3 2 1 C 0 A
Visit any adjacent vertex of C, which is still unvisited. Push the newly visited vertex E into the stack.	A C E B D F	5 4 3 2 E 1 C 0 A
Visit any adjacent vertex of E, which is still unvisited. Push the newly visited vertex F into the stack.	A C E B D F	5 4 3 F 2 E 1 C 0 A

(Continued)

Actions	Graphs	Stack (S)
Visit any adjacent vertex of F, which is still unvisited. Push the newly visited vertex D into the stack.		5 4 D 3 F 2 E 1 C 0 A
Visit any adjacent vertex of D which is still unvisited. Push the newly visited vertex B into the stack.		5 B 4 D 3 F 2 E 1 C 0 A
Now, there is no unvisited vertex from B; so pop element one by one and print till the stack is empty. If the stack is empty, then stop the DFS process.		The final result of the DFS process is shown on the left

When we use the adjacency list, then the time complexity of DFS will be $O(V + E)$, where V is the number of vertices and E is the number of edges in the graph.

Note!

DFS is used to traverse the depth of any particular path before exploring its breadth. DFS uses a stack for this exploration process.

10.4.4 DFS Graph Traversal with C and Python

CProg-10.2 Implementation of DFS graph traversal

```
#include <stdio.h>
#include <stdlib.h>

/* Structure for each vertex in graph */
struct node
   {
     int data;
     struct node* next;
   };

/* Function to add node at the end of given root */
struct node* insert(struct node *root, int d)
   {
      struct node *newPtr = (struct node*)malloc(sizeof(struct
node));
     newPtr->data = d;
     newPtr->next = NULL;
     root->next = newPtr;
     return newPtr;
   }

/* Function to perform DFS */
void explore(int node, int vis[], struct node start[])
   {
     printf("%d ", node);
     vis[node] = 1;
     struct node *ptr = start[node].next;
     for(;ptr != NULL; ptr = ptr->next)
         {
           if(vis[ptr->data] == 0)
             {
               explore(ptr->data, vis, start);
             }
         }
   }

/* Driver function */
int main()
   {
     int no_of_vertices = 7, i, vis[8];
     struct node start[8];
     for(i = 1; i <= no_of_vertices; i++)
```

```
    {
      start[i].data = i;
      start[i].next = NULL;
      vis[i] = 0;
    }

  /*
  Creates the following graph :
              1
            /   \
           2     3
          / \   / \
         4   5 6   7
  */
  struct node *cur;
  cur = insert(&start[1], 2);
  insert(cur,3);
  cur = insert(&start[2], 4);
  insert(cur,5);
  cur = insert(&start[3], 6);
  insert(cur,7);

 /* The loop takes care of non connected graph also */
  printf("DFS of the graph : \n");
  for(i = 1; i <= 7; i++)
    {
      if(vis[i] == 0)
          explore(i, vis, start);
    }
  return 0;
 }
/* End of program */
```

Output

```
DFS of the graph :
1 2 4 5 3 6 7
```

Programming Tips!

insert() is used to add a node at the end of given root. explore() is used for performing DFS traversal.

PyProg-10.2 Implementation of DFS graph traversal

```
# Class definition of a graph
class graph:
 # Constructor to create a new node
 def __init__(self, num_vertices):
   self.num_vertices = num_vertices
   self.adj_list = [[] for _ in range(num_vertices)]

 def add_edge(self, source, destination):
   self.adj_list[source].append(destination)

 # Function for depth-first-search
 def dfs(self, start):
   visited = [False] * self.num_vertices
   stack_vertex = []
   visited[start] = True
   stack_vertex.append(start)
   while len(stack_vertex) != 0:
     current = stack_vertex.pop()
     print(current,end=' '),
     for vertex in self.adj_list[current]:
       if (not visited[vertex]):
         visited[vertex] = True
         stack_vertex.append(vertex)

# Create a graph with 8 vertices
graph = graph(8)

# Create arcs
graph.add_edge(0, 1)
graph.add_edge(0, 2)
graph.add_edge(1, 2)
graph.add_edge(1, 4)
graph.add_edge(2, 0)
graph.add_edge(2, 3)
graph.add_edge(3, 3)
graph.add_edge(3, 6)
graph.add_edge(4, 0)
graph.add_edge(4, 5)
graph.add_edge(5, 6)
graph.add_edge(5, 7)
graph.add_edge(6, 2)
graph.add_edge(7, 3)
```

```
print("Depth First Traversal is:")
graph.dfs(0)
print("")
## end program
```

Output

```
Depth First Traversal is: 0 2 3 6 1 4 5 7
```

Programming Tips!

Constructor __init__() is used to create and initialize the attributes of the class. add_edge() is used for edge appending and dfs() is used for DFS traversal using stack.

10.4.5 BFS vs. DFS

The following table presents the comparison between BFS and DFS techniques:

Table 10.4 Comparison between BFS and DFS

BFS	DFS
BFS is a vertex-based algorithm.	DFS is an edge-based algorithm.
Queue is used to store the nodes.	Stack is used to store the nodes.
Structure of the constructed tree is wide and short.	Structure of the constructed tree is narrow and long.
Traversing is done by first exploring the oldest unvisited vertex.	Traversing is done by first exploring the vertices along the edge.
Time complexity of BFS is $O(V + E)$, we use an adjacency list.	Time complexity of DFS is also $O(V + E)$, we use an adjacency list.

10.5 SPANNING TREE

A *spanning tree* is a subgraph that includes all vertices of the original graph without any cycles. A spanning tree of a graph G is a set of $|V|-1$ edges that connect all vertices of the graph, where $|V|$ is the cardinality of V.

Thus, a spanning tree for G is a graph, $T = (V', E')$ with the following properties:

- $V' = V$.
- T should be connected and T is without any cycle.
- If we start a breadth-first search at any vertex of the graph, and the graph is connected, then $n - 1$ edges are used to get to the unvisited vertices defining the *breadth-first spanning tree.*

Note!

A spanning tree is a subgraph including all vertices of the original graph, without any cycles.

10.5.1 Minimum Spanning Tree (MST)

If we accumulate the weights of all the edges in a spanning tree, it gives us the cost of that tree. Spanning trees are not unique and there can be many. When the cost of the spanning tree is minimum among all the spanning trees, it is called the *minimum spanning tree* (MST). There can also be several minimum spanning trees as MSTs are not generally unique. However, they do become unique if the weights of all the edges are pairwise distinct. An MST is also an undirected, connected and weighted graph. There are many techniques for creating MST for a weighted graph. Two basic algorithms for creating MST are discussed in this chapter. They are Prim's Algorithm and Kruskal's Algorithm.

> ***Note!***
> MST is a spanning tree where the cost of the spanning tree is minimum among all the spanning trees.

10.5.2 Prim's Algorithm

Prim's algorithm finds a minimum spanning tree for a connected weighted graph. It finds a subset of the edges that form a tree, which includes every vertex and minimizes the total weight of all the edges in the tree. The Prim's algorithm grows a single tree and adds a light edge in each iteration.

Algo-10.3 Prim's Algorithm for finding minimum spanning tree

Step 1	Initialize a tree with a single vertex selected arbitrarily from the graph.
Step 2	Grow the tree by one edge from the edges that connect the tree to vertices not yet in the tree. Find the minimum-weight edge, and transfer it to the tree
Step 3	Repeat Step 2 until all vertices are in the tree.

Example 10.6

Suppose G is a connected graph as shown in the first row of Table 10.5. V is the set of all vertices. Choose any element, set $S = \{v_1\}$ (take as the root of the spanning tree.); initially MST = {NULL}.

First, we have to find the lightest edge such that one endpoint is in S, and the other is in $(V - S)$. Add this edge to MST and its (other) endpoint to S. This is to be repeated till $(V - S)$ = NULL, where we need to stop as we get the output (minimum) spanning tree (S, MST).

Table 10.5 Example of finding MST using Prim's Algorithm

Graphs	Explanation
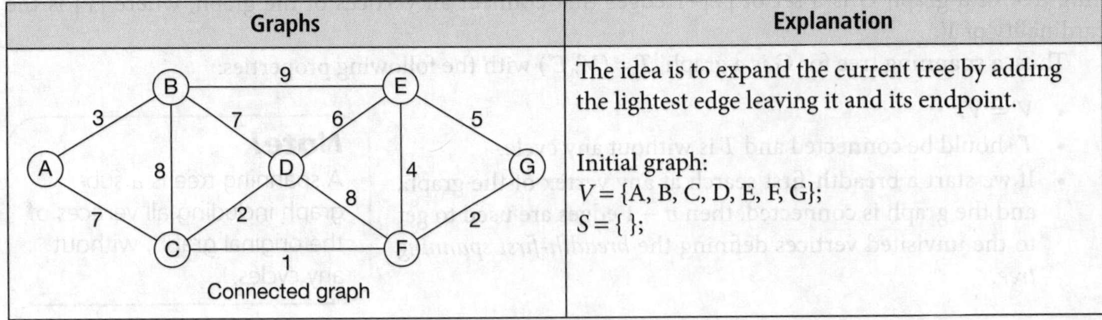 Connected graph	The idea is to expand the current tree by adding the lightest edge leaving it and its endpoint. Initial graph: $V = \{A, B, C, D, E, F, G\}$; $S = \{\}$;

(Continued)

Graphs	Explanation
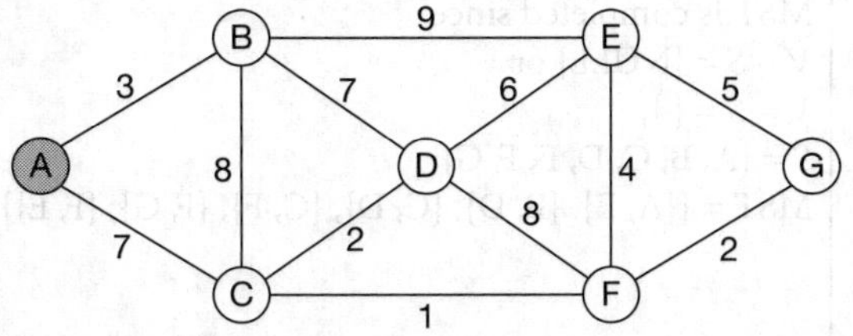	S = {A}, assume A is the starting vertex or root and the lightest edge. = {A, B} with weight 3. S = {A}; $V - S$ = {B, C, D, E, F, G}; MST = {NULL}
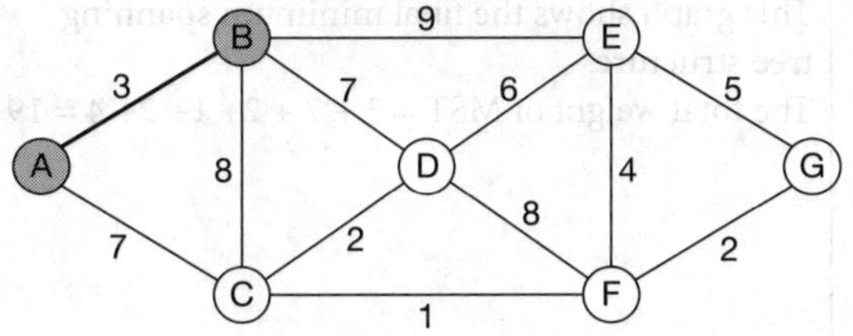	The lightest edge = {B, D} and {A, C} (both weight 7; any edge can be chosen). We are taking edge {B, D}. S = {A, B}; $V - S$ = {C, D, E, F, G}; MST = {{A, B}}.
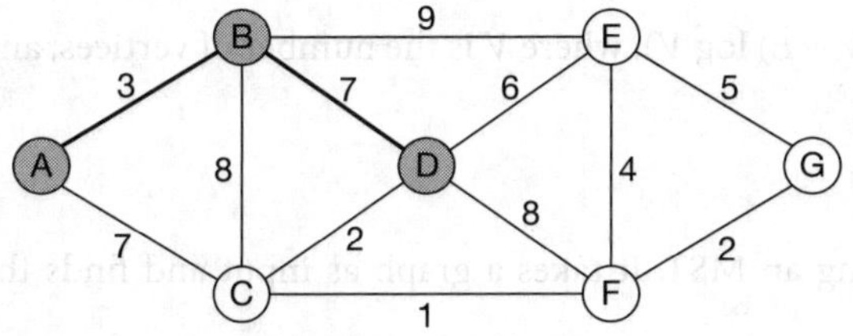	The lightest edge = {D, C} with weight 2. S = {A, B, D}; $V - S$ = {C, E, F, G}; MST = { {A, B}. {B, D} }.
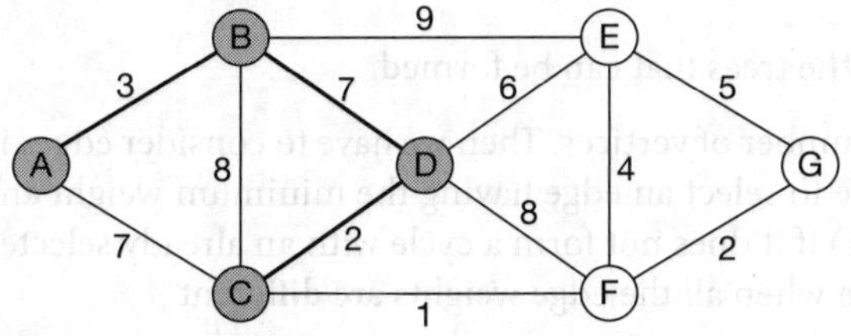	The lightest edge = {C, F} with weight 1. S = {A, B, C, D}; $V - S$ = {E, F, G}; MST = { {A, B}, {B, D}, {C, D} }.
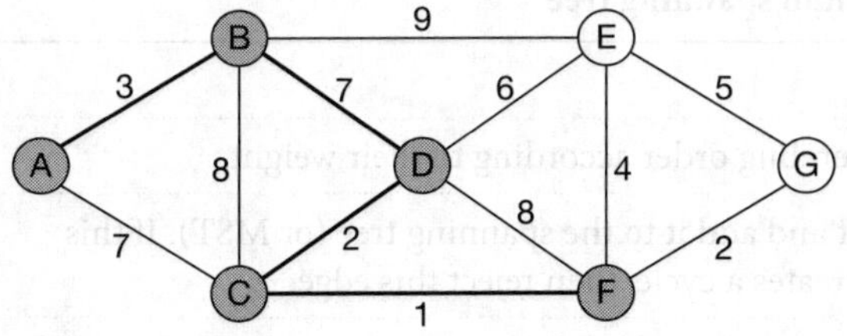	The lightest edge = {F, G} with weight 2. S = {A, B, C, D, F}; $V - S$ = {E, G}; MST = { {A, B}. {B, D}, {C, D}, {C, F} }.
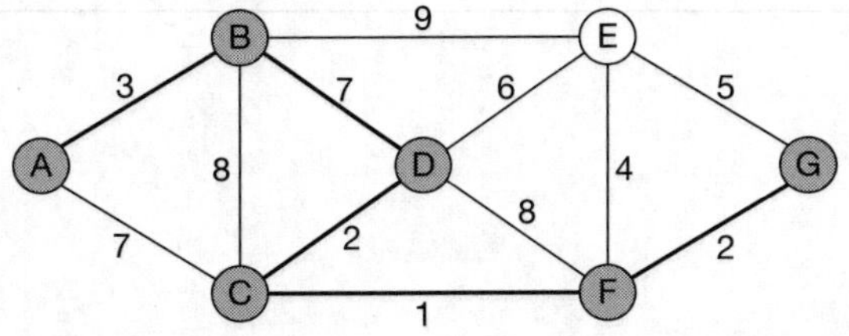	The lightest edge = {F, E} with weight 4. S = {A, B, C, D, F, G}; $V - S$ = {E}; A = {{A, B}. {B, D}, {C, D}, {C, F}, {F, G}}

(Continued)

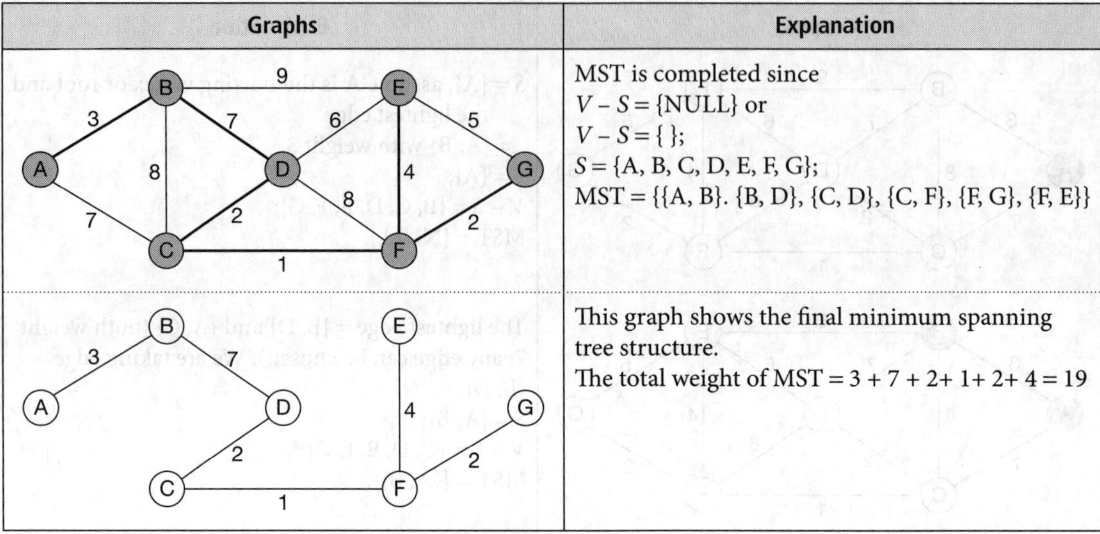

Graphs	Explanation
	MST is completed since $V - S = \{NULL\}$ or $V - S = \{\}$; $S = \{A, B, C, D, E, F, G\}$; MST = {{A, B}. {B, D}, {C, D}, {C, F}, {F, G}, {F, E}}
	This graph shows the final minimum spanning tree structure. The total weight of MST = 3 + 7 + 2+ 1+ 2+ 4 = 19

The time complexity of the Prim's Algorithm is $O((V + E) \log V)$, where V is the number of vertices, and E is the number of edges of the graph.

10.5.3 Kruskal's Algorithm

Kruskal's algorithm is also an algorithm for creating an MST. It takes a graph as input and finds the subset of edges which:

- form a tree including all vertices;
- has the minimum sum of weights among all the trees that can be formed.

We have to start with a forest (a set of trees) with *n* number of vertices. Then we have to consider edges in ascending order of weight (cost). After that, we have to select an edge having the minimum weight and add it to the MST (initialized or under construction) if it does not form a cycle with an already selected edge. A minimum-weighted spanning tree is unique when all the edge weights are different.

Algo-10.4 Kruskal's Algorithm for finding a minimum spanning tree

Step 1	Initialize the MST.
Step 2	Sort all edges of the input graph in ascending order according to their weight.
Step 3	Take the edge having minimum weight and add it to the spanning tree (or MST). If this addition of edge to the spanning tree creates a cycle, then reject this edge.
Step 4	Continue adding edges until all vertices are reached.

Example 10.7

Table 10.6 Example of finding MST using Kruskal's Algorithm

Graphs	Explanation
	Initially all 11 edges are in the heap and each vertex is isolated. MST = {{A}, {B}, {C}, {D}, {E}, {F}, {G}}
	Then after the next 2 minimum edges, A–3–D and C–3–E are chosen as shown. MST = {{A, D}, {B}, {C, E}, {F}, {G}}
	Then D–4–F is chosen. MST = {{A, D, F}, {B}, {C, E}, {G}}
	Then B–5–E is chosen. MST = {{A, D, F}, {C, E, B}, {G}}

(Continued)

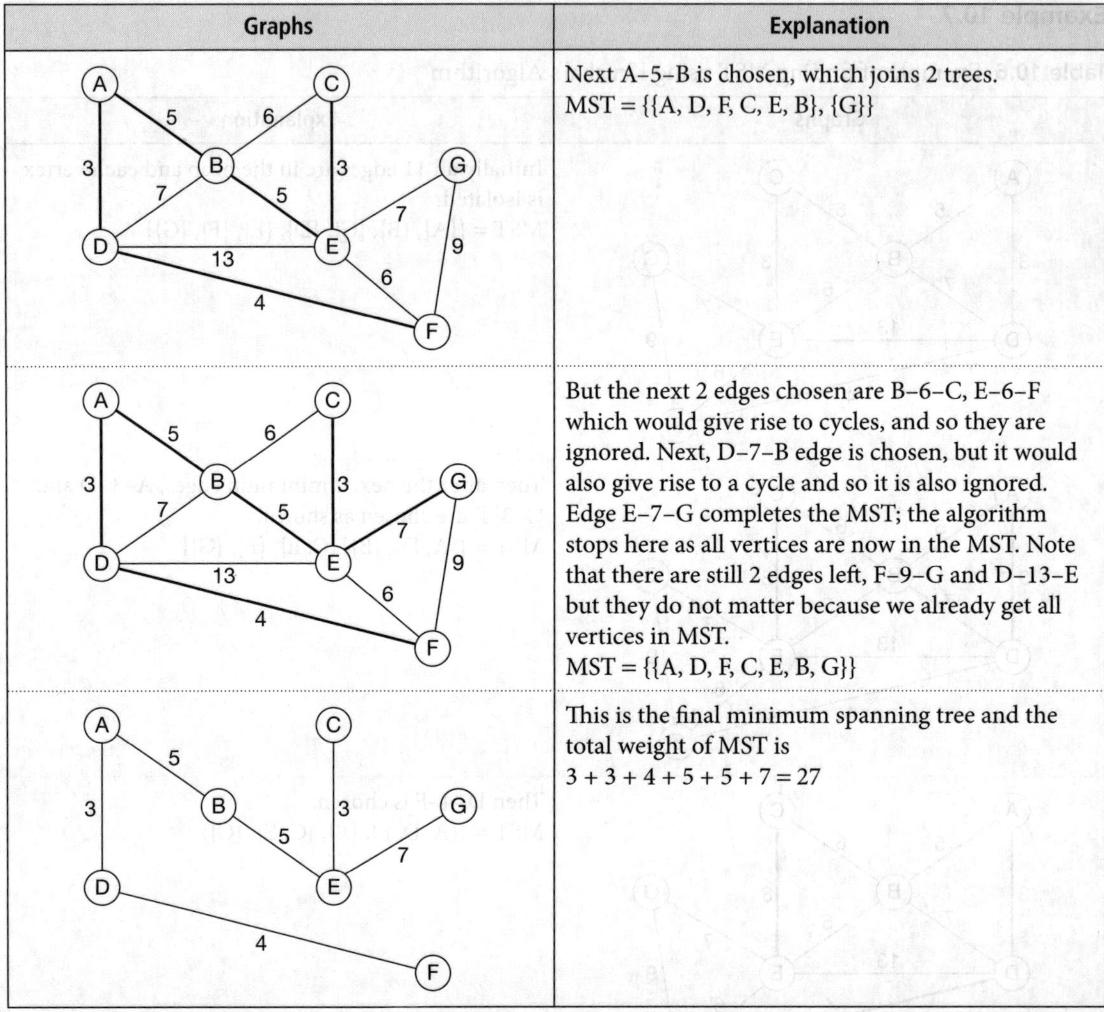

Graphs	Explanation
	Next A–5–B is chosen, which joins 2 trees. MST = {{A, D, F, C, E, B}, {G}}
	But the next 2 edges chosen are B–6–C, E–6–F which would give rise to cycles, and so they are ignored. Next, D–7–B edge is chosen, but it would also give rise to a cycle and so it is also ignored. Edge E–7–G completes the MST; the algorithm stops here as all vertices are now in the MST. Note that there are still 2 edges left, F–9–G and D–13–E but they do not matter because we already get all vertices in MST. MST = {{A, D, F, C, E, B, G}}
	This is the final minimum spanning tree and the total weight of MST is 3 + 3 + 4 + 5 + 5 + 7 = 27

In Kruskal's algorithm, the overall time complexity of the algorithm will be O(*E*. log *V*).

10.6 DIJKSTRA'S ALGORITHM FOR SHORTEST-PATH EVALUATION

The shortest-path problem is formulated to find the shortest length (or least number of edges) between two vertices (a path) such that the sum of the weights of its constituent edges is minimized. This is similar to the problem of finding the shortest-path (with minimum distance) between two crossings on a road map. The vertices of the graph correspond to the road crossings, and edges correspond to the road segments between the crossings. The weights of edges correspond to the length of the road segments. The MST problem is to find a set of edges so that there is a path between each node. The shortest-path problem is to identify the set of edges connecting all nodes such that the sum of the edge lengths from the root to each node is minimized.

Dijkstra's algorithm is built to solve the problem of finding the shortest-path from a source node to a destination node within a graph. It is also known as a single-source shortest-path problem since one can find the shortest-paths from a given source to all points in a graph at the same time. The graph with all paths from one node to all the other nodes must be a spanning tree, and it must include all nodes. There will be no cycle since it would define more than one path from one source node to one destination node. The following algorithm by Dijkstra presents the method of shortest-path evaluation between two nodes of a graph.

> ***Note!***
> Dijkstra's algorithm is used to solve the problem of finding the shortest-pathshortest-path from a source node to a destination node within a graph based on MST.

Algo-10.5 Dijkstra's algorithm for shortest-path evaluation

Step 1	Initially, select the root node to form the set *S*1. Assign a path length 0 to this node. Keep all other nodes in the set *S*2.
Step 2	Compute the lengths of the paths to all nodes directly reachable from *S*1 through a node in *S*1. Select the node in *S*2 with the smallest path length. Let the edge connecting this node with *S*1 be (i, j). Add this edge to the shortest-path tree. Add node j to the set *S*1 and delete it from the set *S*2.
Step 3	Finish if the set *S*1 includes all the nodes, stop with the shortest-path tree. Otherwise, repeat Step 2.

The distance from u to v, denoted by $\delta(u,v)$, is the length of the minimum-length path if there is a path from u to v; otherwise, it is denoted by ∞ (infinity). Dijkstra's algorithm operates by maintaining a subset of vertices $S \subseteq V$, where true distance $d[v] = \delta(s,v)$. Initially $S = \emptyset$, the empty set; and we set $d[s] = 0$ and $d[v] = \infty$ for all other vertices v, then select vertices one by one from $V - S$ and add to S.

So, V = Set of vertices;

$d[V]$ = Distance between source and vertex concerned;

Pred[V] = The predecessor pointer (Pred[] is for determining the shortest-path from vertex set V);

Adj[S] = When processing a vertex u, the algorithm will examine all vertices $v \in$ Adj[u]. For each vertex $v \in$ Adj[u], a new path from s to v is found. If the new path from s to v is shorter than $d[v]$, then update $d[v]$ to the length of this new path.

Color[V] = The set S can be implemented using an array of vertex colors. Initially all vertices are white, and we set color[v] = black to indicate that $v \in$ S.

Priority queue: We store the vertices of $V - S$ in a priority queue, where the key value of each vertex v is $d[v]$. Extract the item with the minimum key value in the priority queue.

Example 10.8

Table 10.7 Example of Dijkstra's algorithm for shortest-path evaluation

Graphs	Explanation
Graph: S→B (7), S→A (2), B→C (1), A↔B (3, 2), A→C (8), C↔D (4, 5), A→D (5)	Input graph for shortest-path evaluation.
d: S=0, A=∝, B=∝, C=∝, D=∝	V: S A B C D; d[v]: 0 ∝ ∝ ∝ ∝; pred[v]: – – – – –; color[v]: W W W W W. Priority queue: V: S A B C D; d[v]: 0 ∝ ∝ ∝ ∝. Adj [S] = {A, B}, work on A and B, then update table.
d: S=0 (S shaded), A=2, B=7, C=∝, D=∝	V: S A B C D; d[v]: 0 2 7 ∝ ∝; pred[v]: – S S – –; color[v]: B W W W W. Priority queue: V: A B C D; d[v]: 2 7 ∝ ∝. After Step 1, A has the minimum key/weight in the priority queue. As Adj [A] = {B, C, D}, work on B, C, D and update information.
d: S=0, A=2 (shaded), B=5, C=10, D=7	V: S A B C D; d[v]: 0 2 5 10 7; pred[v]: – S A A A; color[v]: B B W W W. Priority queue: V: B C D; d[v]: 5 10 7. After Step 2, B has the minimum key in the priority queue. As Adj [B] = {A, C}, work on A, C and update information.
d: S=0, A=2, B=5 (shaded), C=6, D=7	V: S A B C D; d[v]: 0 2 5 6 7; pred[v]: – S A B A; color[v]: B B B W W. Priority queue: V: C D; d[v]: 6 7. After Step 3, C has the minimum key in the priority queue. As Adj [C] = {D}, work on D and update information.

(Continued)

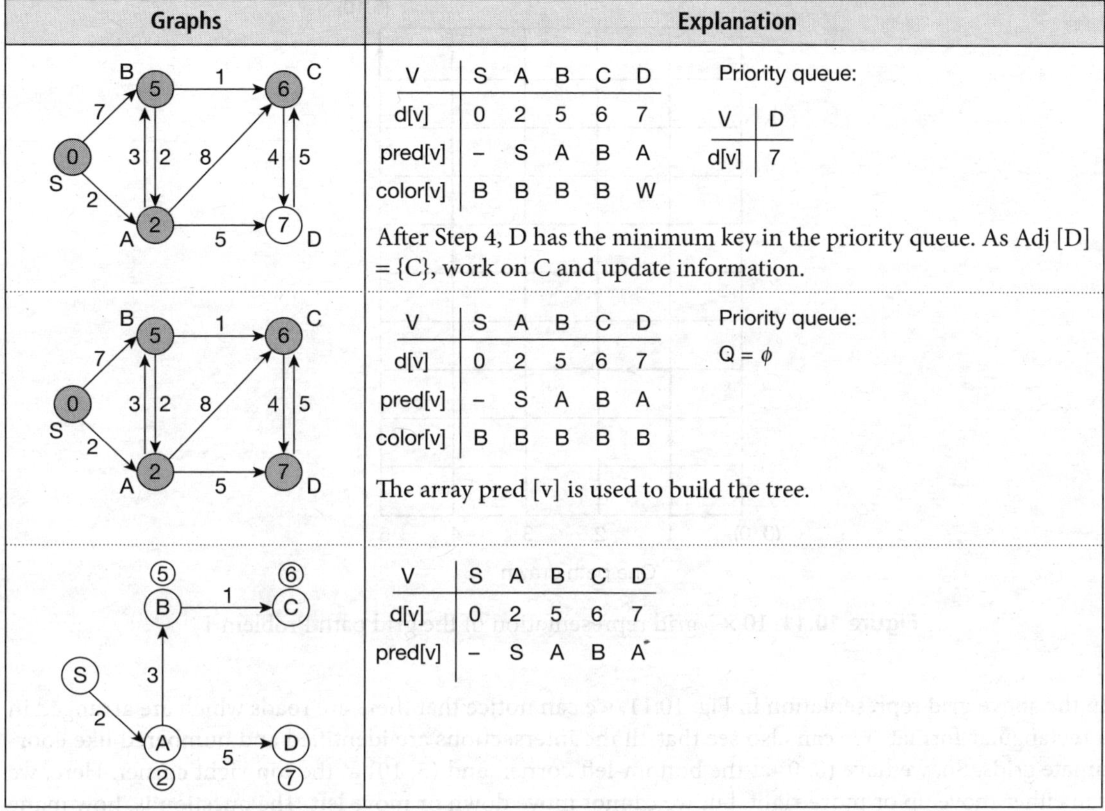

Graphs	Explanation
	Priority queue: V: D; d[v]: 7

V	S	A	B	C	D
d[v]	0	2	5	6	7
pred[v]	–	S	A	B	A
color[v]	B	B	B	B	W

After Step 4, D has the minimum key in the priority queue. As Adj [D] = {C}, work on C and update information.

Priority queue: Q = ϕ

V	S	A	B	C	D
d[v]	0	2	5	6	7
pred[v]	–	S	A	B	A
color[v]	B	B	B	B	B

The array pred [v] is used to build the tree.

V	S	A	B	C	D
d[v]	0	2	5	6	7
pred[v]	–	S	A	B	A

The time complexity of Dijkstra's algorithm using the priority queue will be O(E Log V).

10.7 GRID PATH PROBLEM

Computational thinking is the process one goes through while dividing a bigger problem into several smaller pieces. Once the smaller pieces are well understood, the entire problem is well understood. It is more manageable to understand the overall assembly of the problem. Grid path problem is a computational thinking problem because it can be broken into smaller pieces, and the smaller pieces give more awareness about how we will get results.

First, we will solve a simple combination problem called the grid path problem. Counting the number of paths from one corner of a general $M \times N$ grid to the other. We must start at the bottom left corner and we must finish at the top right corner. We are only allowed to move one step up and one step to the right (moving down or left is not allowed).

Problem 1: How many paths exist, which extend from the bottom-left square to the top-right square in a 10×5 grid (10 rows and 5 columns)?

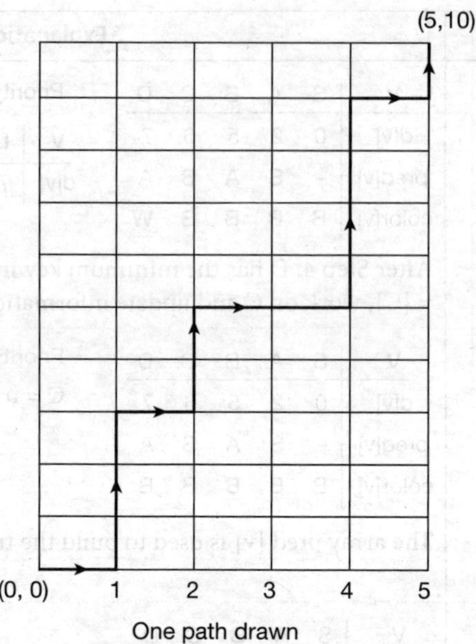

Figure 10.11 10 × 5 grid representation of the grid path Problem 1

In the above grid representation in Fig. 10.11, we can notice that there are roads which are arranged in a rectangular format. We can also see that all the intersections are identified and numbered like coordinate grids. So, we have (0, 0) at the bottom-left corner, and (5, 10) at the top-right corner. Here, we can either move up or move right, but we cannot move down or move left. The question is, how many ways (paths) are there to go from the bottom-left corner to the top-right corner. We have to count the number of grid paths here. So, a grid path problem is one which follows the above rule of only going up or right.

The path must consist of 15 (10 rows + 5 columns) moves, ten of which should be up, and five of which should be right. In fact, the order of the moves does not matter as long as there are a total of 15 moves, five of which are right. By using combinations, we can find the total number of ways to select a right move from the collection of 15 moves (five right, ten up) = ${}^{15}C_5$ = 3003. Therefore, 3003 unique paths are there.

We may use the up moves in place of the right moves. Let us start at the beginning, and approach this problem in a different way. From the bottom-left corner, there are exactly two moves we can take. We can either move right or move up. Therefore, there is only one unique path that will take us from the bottom-left square to the square on its right. Likewise, there is only one path that extends from the square at the bottom-left corner to the square directly above it. We denote this by placing a 1 in these squares (see Fig. 10.12). Consider the square in the second row and second column. There are two unique paths that start in the bottom-left square and end there. We denote this by placing a 2 in this square. Continue calculating the number of unique paths that lead to each square in the grid. If we observe it carefully, we can notice an emerging pattern.

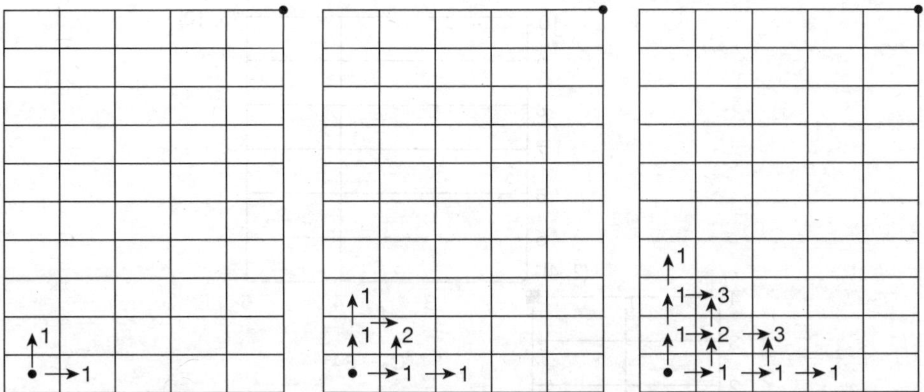

Figure 10.12 Movement of paths from origin to destination in the grid

It appears that the numbers in the grid are emerging like a Pascal's triangle. This observation will allow us to fill the squares in the grid with ease. For example, we will find 6 in the third row and third column. To get 6, we add 3 + 3, the number in the square below, and the number in the square to the left.

Problem 2: Consider the 10 × 5 grid in the Fig. 10.13 with a missing crossing (highlighted). How many unique paths can be drawn from the bottom-left square to the top-right square avoiding the missing crossing?

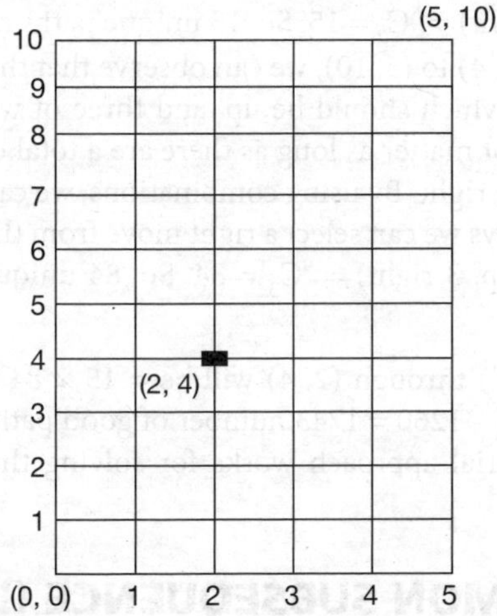

Figure 10.13 10 × 5 grid with crossing (2, 4) marked according to Problem 2

We can use a combinatorial argument in order to block a path. We must have to go to (2, 4) and then to (5, 10). If we can only count how many paths go from (0, 0) to (2, 4), and then how many paths go from (2, 4) to (5, 10), these are all the bad paths. So, we can count these bad paths, and subtract them from the good paths to get the desired count of paths in the problem. The above problem of reaching (5, 10) from (0, 0) through (2, 4) is divided into two subproblems: (a) from (0, 0) to (2, 4), and (b) from (2, 4) to (5, 10) as shown in the Fig. 10.14.

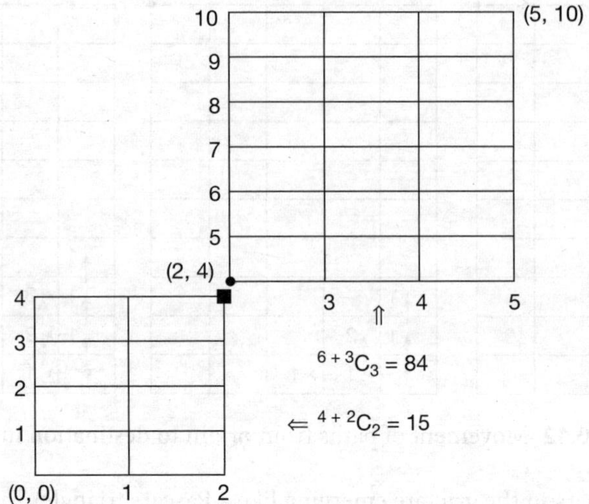

Figure 10.14 Dividing the 10 × 5 grid into 2 sub-grids

(a) To count the paths from (0, 0) to (2, 4), we can observe that the path must consist of 6 (4 rows + 2 columns) moves, four of which should be up, and two of which should be right. In fact, the order of the moves does not matter as long as there are a total of 6 moves, two of which are right. By using combinations, we can find the total number of ways to select a right move from the collection of 6 moves (4 up, 2 right) = $^6C_2$ = 15. So, 15 unique paths are there.

(b) To count the paths from (2, 4) to (5, 10), we can observe that the path must consist of 9 (6 rows + 3 columns) moves, six of which should be up, and three of which should be right. In fact, the order of the moves does not matter as long as there are a total of 9 moves, three of which are right. By using combinations, we can find the total number of ways we can select a right move from the collection of 9 moves (6 up, 3 right) = $^9C_3$ = 84. So, 84 unique paths are there.

Hence, the number of paths (bad) through (2, 4) will be = 15 × 84 = 1260. Similarly, there will be 3003 – 1260 = 1743 number of good paths avoiding (2, 4). So, a combinatorial approach works for solving this problem.

> ***Note!***
> Grid path problem is a computational problem as it can be broken into smaller pieces. It gives more awareness about getting results.

10.8 LONGEST COMMON SUBSEQUENCE (LCS)

A string sequence has a vital role in algorithm design technique. For example, if any user searches a text within a file, then the result depends upon the presence of the string to be searched. Here, we will illustrate a common method that tests the similarity between two strings. This concept is not substring analysis but it is a subsequence analysis. Similarity testing of LCS is used in DNA sequence. Compressing genome resequencing data and authenticating users within their mobile phone through in-air signatures are two common applications of LCS.

10.8.1 Method of Finding LCS

Suppose a subsequence of characters $x_0, x_1, x_2, \ldots, x_{n-1}$ is a string of the form $x_{i1}, x_{i2}, \ldots, x_{ik}$. For example, if the string is "ABCDEFGHIJK", and the subsequence is "ACEGJIK", then it is true. If subsequence is "DFGHK", then also it is true, but "DAGH" is not subsequence.

Problem 1: Given two strings X and Y, the longest common subsequence (LCS) problem is to find the longest subsequence common to both X and Y.

For example, ABCDEFG and XZACKDFWGH have ACDFG as the longest common subsequence. There are many methods to solve this problem, but a dynamic-programming approach (discussed in Chapter 8) to the LCS problem is the best suitable method. Define $L[i, j]$ to be the length of the LCS of $X[0..i]$ and $Y[0..j]$. Allow for -1 as an index, and $L[-1, k] = 0$ and $L[k, -1] = 0$, to indicate that the null part of X or Y has no match with the other. Then we can define $L[i, j]$ in the general case as follows:

1. If $x_i = y_j$, then $L[i, j] = L[i-1, j-1] + 1$ (We can add this match.)
2. If $x_i \neq y_j$, then $L[i, j] = \max\{L[i-1, j], L[i, j-1]\}$ (We have no match here.)

Let us understand LCS with an example.

If S_1 = {B, C, D, A, A, C, D} and S_2 = {A, C, D, B, A, C}, then common subsequences are {B, C}, {C, D, A, C}, {D, A, C}, {A, A, C}, {A, C}, {C, D} and so on. Among these subsequences, {C, D, A, C} is the longest common subsequence.

Let us take two subsequences X and Y. 1st Sequence: X: A C A D B, 2nd sequence Y: C B D A. The following steps are used for finding the longest common subsequence.

Step 1: Create a table of dimension $n + 1 \times m + 1$ where n and m are the lengths of X and Y respectively. The first row and the first column are filled with zeros.

(L)	–1	C	B	D	A
–1	0	0	0	0	0
A	0				
C	0				
A	0				
D	0				
B	0				

Step 2: Fill each cell of the table using the following logic.

a. If the character corresponding to the current row and current column are matching, then fill the current cell by adding one to the diagonal element. Point an arrow to the diagonal cell.
b. Else, take the maximum value from the previous column and previous row element for filling the current cell. Point an arrow to the cell with maximum value. If they are equal, point to any of them.

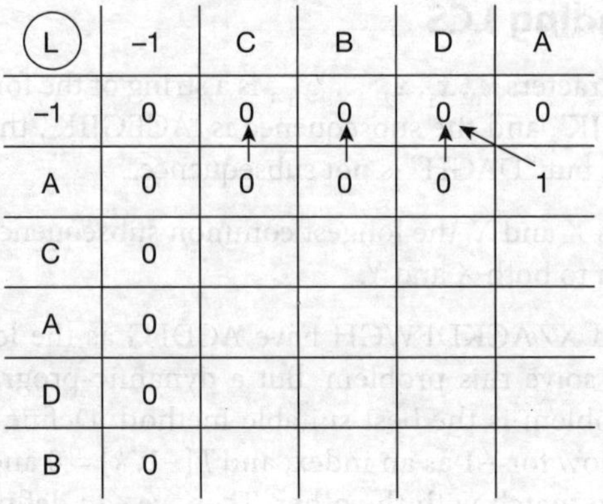

L	–1	C	B	D	A
–1	0	0	0	0	0
A	0	0	0	0	1
C	0				
A	0				
D	0				
B	0				

Step 3: Repeat Step 2 until the table is filled.

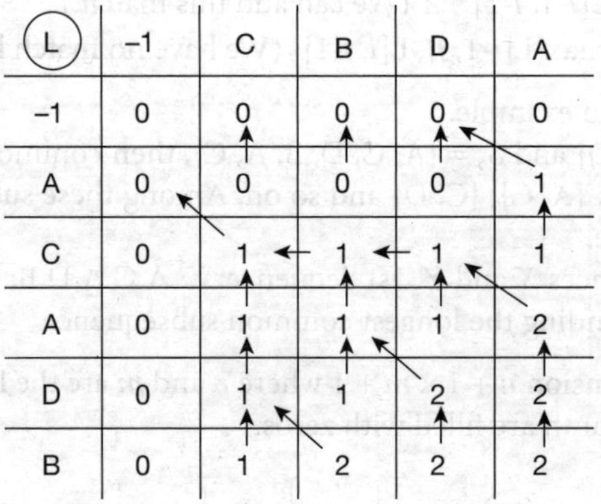

L	–1	C	B	D	A
–1	0	0	0	0	0
A	0	0	0	0	1
C	0	1	1	1	1
A	0	1	1	1	2
D	0	1	1	2	2
B	0	1	2	2	2

Step 4: The value in the last row and the last column is the length of the longest common subsequence.

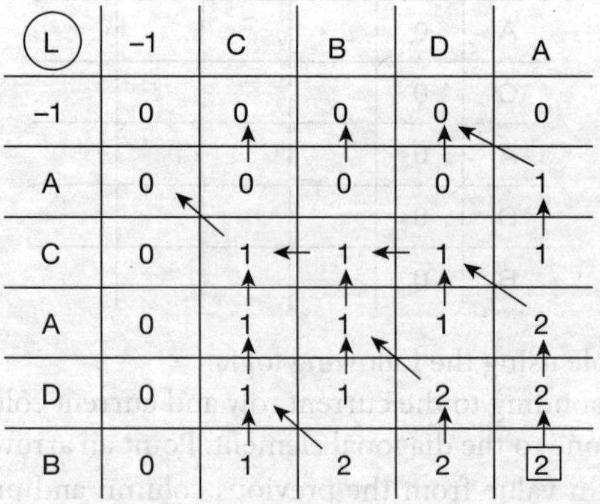

L	–1	C	B	D	A
–1	0	0	0	0	0
A	0	0	0	0	1
C	0	1	1	1	1
A	0	1	1	1	2
D	0	1	1	2	2
B	0	1	2	2	2

Step 5: In order to find the longest common subsequence, start from the last element and follow the direction of the arrow. The elements corresponding to diagonal arrow symbols form the longest common subsequence.

L	–1	C	B	D	A
–1	0	0	0	0	0
A	0	0	0	0	1
C	0	1	1	1	1
A	0	1	1	1	2
D	0	1	1	2	2
B	0	1	2	2	2

Thus, the longest common subsequence is CA.

L	–1	C	B	D	A
–1	0	0	0	0	0
A	0	0	0	0	1
C	0	1	1	1	1
A	0	1	1	1	2
D	0	1	1	2	2
B	0	1	2	2	2

> ***Note!***
> Longest common subsequence analysis is a common method used to test the similarity between two strings.

Algo-10.6 Pseudocode for finding LCS

```
LCSFunc()
   X ← Sequence1, Y ← Sequence2
   Initialize LCS ← length(X) x length(Y)
   X.label = X, Y.label = Y, LCS[0][] = 0, LCS[][0] = 0
   Compare X[i] and Y[j] starting from LCS[1][1]
       IF X[i] == Y[j]
           LCS[i][j] = 1 + LCS[i-1, j-1]
           Point an arrow to LCS[i][j]
       ELSE
           LCS[i][j] = max(LCS[i-1][j], LCS[i][j-1])
          Point an arrow to max(LCS[i-1][j], LCS[i][j-1])
       ENDIF
END LCSFunc
```

10.8.2 Finding LCS with C and Python

CProg-10.3 Implementation of finding LCS

```
#include <stdio.h>
#include <string.h>

int i, j, m, n, LCSTable[20][20];
char X[20] = "ACADB", Y[20] = "CBDA", b[20][20];

void lcsFunc()
   {
    m = strlen(X);
    n = strlen(Y);

    /* Filling 0's in the matrix */
     for(i = 0; i <= m; i++)
        LCSTable[i][0] = 0;
    for(i = 0; i <= n; i++)
         LCSTable[0][i] = 0;

     /* Building the matrix in bottom-up way */
     for(i = 1; i <= m; i++)
         for(j = 1; j <= n; j++)
             {
             if(X[i - 1] == Y[j - 1])
                 {
                 LCSTable[i][j] = LCSTable[i - 1][j - 1] + 1;
                 }
               else if (LCSTable[i - 1][j] >= LCSTable[i][j - 1])
                 {
                 LCSTable[i][j] = LCSTable[i - 1][j];
                 }
                else
                 {
                 LCSTable[i][j] = LCSTable[i][j - 1];
                 }
           }
           int index = LCSTable[m][n];
           char lcsFunc[index + 1];
           lcsFunc[index] = '\0';
           int i = m, j = n;
           while(i > 0 && j > 0)
```

```
            {
              if(X[i - 1] == Y[j - 1])
                  {
                  lcsFunc[index - 1] = X[i - 1];
                  i--;
                  j--;
                  index--;
                }
              else if(LCSTable[i - 1][j] > LCSTable[i][j - 1])
                 i--;
              else
                 j--;
            }

        /* Printing the sub sequences */
        printf("X : %s \nY : %s \n", X, Y);
        printf("LCS: %s", lcsFunc);
     }

/* Driver code */
int main()
     {
        lcsFunc();
        printf("\n");
     }

/* End Program */
```

Output

```
X : ACADB
Y : CBDA
LCS: CB
```

> ***Programming Tips!***
> lcsFunc() is used for filling 0's in the matrix, building the matrix in bottom-up way and for printing the subsequences.

PyProg-10.3 Implementation of finding LCS

```
# Function to find lcs
def lcsFunc(X, Y, m, n):
    LL = [[0 for x in range(n+1)] for x in range(m+1)]

    # Building the matrix in bottom-up way
    for i in range(m+1):
        for j in range(n+1):
            if i == 0 or j == 0:
                LL[i][j] = 0
            elif X[i-1] == Y[j-1]:
                LL[i][j] = LL[i-1][j-1] + 1
```

```
            else:
                LL[i][j] = max(LL[i-1][j], LL[i][j-1])
    index = LL[m][n]
    lcsFunc = [""] * (index+1)
    lcsFunc[index] = ""
    i = m
    j = n
    while i > 0 and j > 0:
        if X[i-1] == Y[j-1]:
            lcsFunc[index-1] = X[i-1]
            i -= 1
            j -= 1
            index -= 1
        elif LL[i-1][j] > LL[i][j-1]:
            i -= 1
        else:
           j -= 1

    # Printing the sub sequences
    print("X : " + X + "\nY : " + Y)
    print("LCS: " + "".join(lcsFunc))

# Driver code
X = "ACADB"
Y = "CBDA"
m = len(X)
n = len(Y)
lcsFunc(X, Y, m, n)
# End Program
```

Output

```
X : ACADB
Y : CBDA
LCS : CB
```

> ***Programming Tips!***
> lcsFunc() is used for building the matrix in bottom-up way, and then printing the subsequences.

QUICK RECAP

- ☑ **Graph** is the pictorial representation of a set of items where some pairs of items are connected by links. A problem can often be represented as a graph for finding the solution to the problem using the non-linear abstract data structure. It offers many real-life and state-of-the-art applications.
- ☑ The graph is a collection of **vertices** (nodes) and **edges** (arcs) in which vertices are connected with edges. There are several ways to represent a graph in the computer memory, among which adjacency matrix, incidence matrix, and adjacency list are most important.

☑ **The adjacency matrix** is a sequential representation where the graph is represented using a square matrix of size equal to the total number of vertices. In the **incidence matrix**, the graph can be represented using a matrix of size depending on the total number of vertices by the total number of edges. **The adjacency list** is a linked representation of a graph where we maintain the list of its neighbor's vertex for each vertex in the graph.

☑ There are a huge number of **applications** of graphs that exist in the field of computer science and information technology, among which social networks, biological networks, neural networks are a few important ones that can be mentioned.

☑ Traversal techniques are used for searching a vertex within a graph. The **BFS** explores the nodes nearest the root before exploring other nodes further away. BFS uses a queue data structure for this exploration or search process. **DFS** is used to traverse the depth of any particular path before exploring its breadth.

☑ A spanning tree is a subgraph that includes all vertices of the original graph without any cycles. If we accumulate the weights of all the edges in a spanning tree, it gives us the cost of that tree. The **minimum spanning tree** (MST) is a spanning tree where the cost of the spanning tree is minimum among all the spanning trees.

☑ Two basic algorithms for creating MST are Prim's Algorithm and Kruskal's Algorithm. Dijkstra's algorithm is built to solve the problem of finding the **shortest path** from a source node to a destination node within a graph, based on MST.

☑ **Grid path** problem is a computational thinking problem because it can be broken into smaller pieces, and the smaller pieces give more awareness of how we will get the results.

☑ **Longest common subsequence** analysis method is used to illustrate a common method that tests the similarity between two strings.

REVIEW QUESTIONS

Multiple Choice Questions (MCQ): Choose the Best Alternative

Easy

1. A path in a graph is:
   A. A closed walk with no vertex repetition
   B. An open walk with no edge repetition
   C. An open walk with no vertex repetition
   D. A closed walk with no edge repetition.
2. The target of the BFS traversal is:
   A. To scan all edges before moving to the other vertex
   B. Same as backtracking
   C. To scan adjacent unvisited vertex as soon as possible.
   D. None of these.
3. ________ data structure is used for BFS traversal.
   A. Queue B. Stack
   C. Both stack and queue. D. None of these.
4. The adjacency matrix of an undirected graph:
   A. Identity B. Symmetric
   C. Asymmetric D. None of these.
5. Which data structure is generally used to implement DFS?
   A. Stack B. Queue
   C. Both A and B. D. None of these.

Moderate

6. A vertex of in-degree zero in a directed graph is called:
   A. Articulation point B. Sink
   C. Root vertex D. Isolated vertex.

7. The removal of a vertex in which a graph become disconnected is known as:
   A. Pendant vertex
   B. Articulation point/Cut-vertex
   C. Bridge
   D. Colored vertex
8. Any connected graph with n vertices must have at least ______.
   A. $n + 1$ edges B. n edges
   C. $n - 1$ edges D. $n/2$ edges
9. A graph where all vertices have same degree is called:
   A. Complete graph
   B. Multi graph
   C. Simple graph
   D Regular graph
10. A complete directed graph of 5 nodes has ______ number of edges.
    A. 5 B. 10
    C. 20 D. 25

    Hint: (n * (n – 1)) / 2 = 5 * (5 – 1) / 2 = 20 / 2 = 10

Higher-Order Thinking Skills (HOTS)

11. What is the maximum number of edges present in a simple directed graph with 7 vertices if there exists no cycles or parallel edges in the graph?
    A. 6 B. 7
    C. 8 D. 21
12. In a k-node undirected graph without self-loop, the maximum number of edges possible is:
    A. k^2
    B. $k * (k - 1)/2$
    C. $k - 2$
    D. $(k + 1)(k - 1)/2$
13. In a graph where V is the number of vertices and E is the number of edges, $V = \{v_1, v_2, \ldots, v_{100}\}$; $E = \{(v_i, v_j) \mid 1 \le v_i, v_j \text{ is } |i - j|\}$. What is the weight of the minimum spanning tree of the graph?
    A. 100 B. 99
    C. 01 D. 98

    Hint: There are 100 vertices (v_1 to v_{100}). Edges present in this graph $E = \{(v_i, v_j) \mid 1 \le (v_1, v_2), (v_1, v_3), \ldots, (v_{99}, v_{100})$, i.e., 1 for each edge in the graph. There are 99 edges possible in a minimum spanning tree of 100-vertices graph, since $v(v-1)$ edges are possible in the minimum spanning tree with v vertices. The weight of minimum spanning tree of the graph is 99*1 = 99 where each edge is assigned a weight 1.
14. BFS is applied on a binary tree. Root is the starting vertex. There is a vertex K at a distance five from the root. If K is the N-th vertex in this BFS traversal, then the maximum possible value of N is ______.
    A. 63 B. 31
    C. 64 D. 32

    Hint: Distance is 5 from the root. So the height of the tree is 5.
    Max number of nodes = $2^{(h+1)} - 1 = 2^6 - 1 = 63$.
    So, the last node is 63.
15. Consider an undirected graph with n vertices and 50 edges. Each vertex has degree at least 4. Then the maximum possible value of n will be:
    A. 20 B. 17
    C. 24 D. 25

    Hint: As we know, in every finite undirected graph, the number of vertices with odd degree is always even. Let v be the number of vertices in the graph. So, 4 * v <= 2 * 50 [Sum of degree of all vertices <= 2 * no. of edges]. Therefore, v <= 25 and hence option D is correct.

Short Answer-type Questions

Easy

1. Define a graph.
2. What do you mean by minimum spanning tree?
3. How can we represent an adjacency matrix?
4. How can we represent an adjacency list?
5. Define "degree of a graph".

Moderate

6. How can we represent a graph in computer memory?
7. What do you understand by traversal of the graph?
8. Prove that: "An undirected graph has an even number of vertices of odd degree."
9. What will be the maximum degree of a node in an N-nodes graph?
10. What is the maximum number of edges in an undirected simple graph with k vertices where self-loops are not allowed?

Higher-Order Thinking Skills (HOTS)

11. Justify the statement: "In an undirected graph, the number of edges = (1/2) × Sum of degrees of all vertices."
12. Can we construct a tree of *n* vertices that has P_i subgraphs for *i* = 2, 3, 4, ... , *n*? Is the tree unique if constructed?
13. Prove that the maximum number of edges in a simple graph with *n* nodes is {*n* * (*n* – 1)} / 2.
14. A graph has 8 vertices, each having degree 2, is isomorphic – Justify.

Descriptive-type Questions

Easy

1. Write the algorithms of Prim's minimum spanning tree.
2. Explain the Kruskal algorithm with an example.
3. Give the algorithm of depth-first search in a graph.
4. Explain the breadth-first search in a graph with an example.
5. What are the differences between DFS and BFS?

Moderate

6. Find the result of BFS and DFS traversals from the following graph with 3 as the starting node.

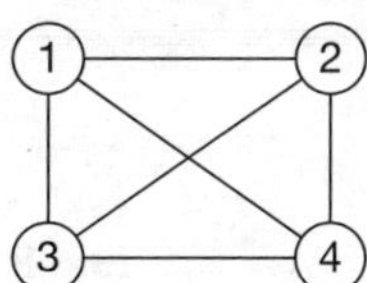

7. Consider a connected graph G of order *n*. Find the maximum number of cut-vertices G can hold. Explain with an example
8. Write an algorithm that counts the number of connected components of a graph, which is represented as an adjacent matrix within the memory.
9. Write a procedure to detect a cycle in an undirected graph.
10. Suppose, we have two graphs G_1 and G_2. How can we check whether they are isomorphic graphs or not? Explain the procedure.

Higher-Order Thinking Skills (HOTS)

15. Consider the 5 × 4 grid below. How many paths that start in the top left square, can you draw to the missing square, and end in the bottom right square?

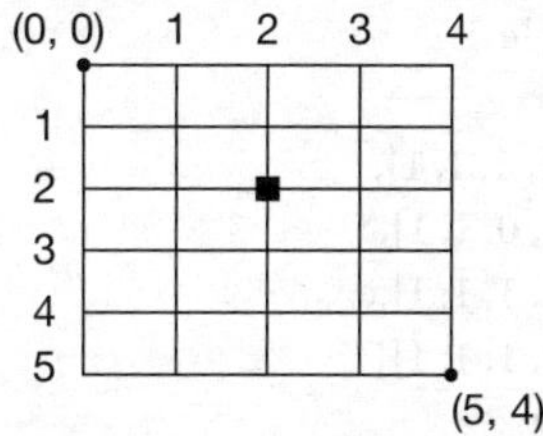

16. Using Dijkstra's shortest-path algorithm, find out the least-cost path to all other nodes 1 through 6 from the following graph:

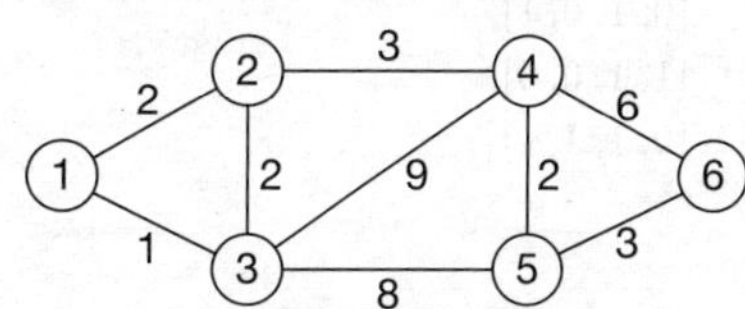

17. Find the minimum spanning tree of the following graph using Kruskal's and Prim's algorithm.

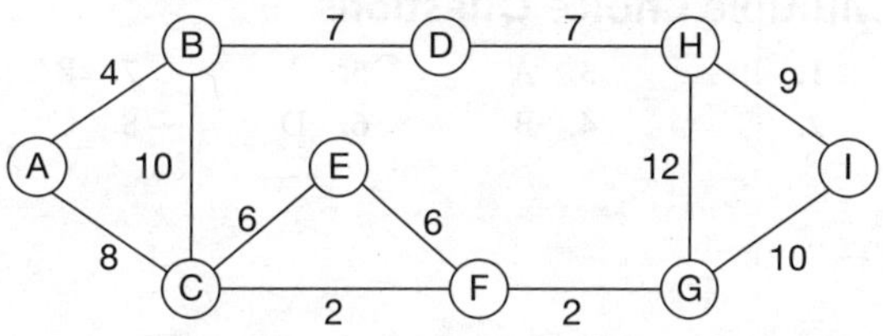

18. Find the longest common subsequence from the given sequence of characters:
A = (W, X, Y, Z, X, Y, Z, Y, Z, Z); B = (X, Y, Z, Y, Z).

CASE STUDIES

1. Design an algorithm to find the degree of a node in a graph.
2. Design an algorithm to find a list of vertices in a graph, that have a self-loop.

LAB EXERCISES

1. Given a graph, count the number of triangles in it. The graph can be directed or undirected.

   Example:

   Input:

   [[1, 1, 1, 1],
   [1, 0, 1, 1],
   [1, 1, 1, 1],
   [0, 1, 1, 1]]

   Output:

   The number of triangles in undirected graph: 3

   Input:

   [[0, 1, 1, 0],
   [0, 1, 0, 1],
   [1, 1, 0, 0],
   [0, 1, 1, 1]]

   Output:

   The number of triangles in directed graph: 1
2. Write a C Program to demonstrate adjacency list representation of graphs.

   Example:

   Adjacency list of vertex 0
   head → 1-→ 1-→ 2
   Adjacency list of vertex 1
   head → 4 → 0 → 2 → 0 → 1 → 1
   Adjacency list of vertex 2
   head → 1→ 3 → 0
   Adjacency list of vertex 3
   head → 2
   Adjacency list of vertex 4
   head → 1

ANSWER KEYS

Multiple Choice Questions

1. B **2.** C **3.** A **4.** B **5.** A **6.** D **7.** B **8.** C **9.** D **10.** B **11.** A **12.** B **13.** B **14.** A **15.** C

11 Sorting

CONTENTS

EXPECTED OUTCOMES OF THIS CHAPTER

After going through this chapter learners will be able

- ☑ To understand the popular sorting techniques with practical examples.
- ☑ To explain the sorting algorithms, namely, bubble sort, insertion sort, selection sort, quick sort, merge sort, heap sort and radix sort.
- ☑ To implement these sorting techniques using C and Python.
- ☑ To analyse the complexity of the sorting techniques.

11.1 INTRODUCTION

Sorting means defining the arrangement of an unordered set of data elements and arranging them in ascending or descending order. We will arrange data that are stored in an array. Let A be an array of *n* elements given by $A_1, A_2, A_3, \ldots, A_n$. Sorting means arranging all the data elements of the array A either in ascending or descending order. The following statements represent the different orders of elements.

$A_1 < A_2 < A_3 < \ldots < A_n$ Increasing order (Ascending)

$A_1 > A_2 > A_3 > \ldots > A_n$ Decreasing order (Descending)

$A_1 \leq A_2 \leq A_3 \leq \ldots \leq A_n$ Non-decreasing order

$A_1 \geq A_2 \geq A_3 \geq \ldots \geq A_n$ Non-increasing order

In this chapter, we will present the seven most popular sorting techniques along with the C and Python source codes for implementing them.

11.1.1 Definition

Sorting is the process of arranging a list of elements in a particular order (ascending or descending) or arranging unarranged data elements. It is the storage of data in sorted order. It arranges the data in a sequence that makes data searching easier.

There are a variety of sorting techniques that can be used to sort a given set of data elements. The kind of sorting technique to be used for a particular sorting situation depends on two factors:

- Size of the input data set.
- Algorithm efficiency or execution time of the program.

> ***Note!***
> Sorting is the process of arranging a list of elements in a particular order (ascending or descending).

11.1.2 Classification of Sorting Techniques

Sorting can be classified into two categories:

Internal Sorting

In this type, sorting is performed on the primary or main memory. This sorting technique is implemented on a small size of data. All the data can be loaded into primary memory while the sorting process is executed. It is used when the input data size is small. Bubble sort, insertion sort and quick sort are examples of internal sorting.

External Sorting

In this type, sorting is performed in secondary memory. In most cases, the processes require such large amounts of memory that no computer's RAM can handle it. So, access to additional external memory is required for effective sorting operations. *The process of accessing a task for sorting data from external storage (hard disk, network file server, disk drive, etc.) is known as external sorting.* Many important sorting applications involve the processing of very large files. Large files may not fit into the primary memory of any computer. These also involve a large amount of processing external to the CPU. Merge sort is an example of external sorting.

> **Note!**
> Internal sorting is performed in the primary memory whereas external sorting is performed in secondary memory.

11.1.3 Stable vs. Unstable Sorting Algorithm

A sorting algorithm is said to be stable if it maintains the relative order of numbers when the same number occurs more than once. For example, if our input set is (10, 10, 20, 30), then if we don't change the order of the first two tens, our algorithm is called stable. But if we swap them, it becomes unstable though the overall result or sorting order remains the same. Examples of stable algorithms are merge sort, insertion sort and bubble sort.

On the other hand, the algorithm in which the order of elements with the same key value is not maintained in the sorted order in intermediate steps is known as an unstable sorting algorithm. Examples of unstable algorithms are quick sort, heap sort and selection sort.

> **Note!**
> A sorting algorithm is said to be stable if it maintains the relative order of numbers when the same number occurs more than once.

11.2 BUBBLE SORT

Bubble sort is a simple sorting algorithm. It is also known as the *exchange sort. This sorting technique arranges data by iterating over the list several times. In each iteration, the larger value bubbles up and is placed at the end of the list.* This algorithm uses multiple passes. Each pair of adjacent elements is compared and the elements are swapped if they are not in expected order. For example, when data is to be sorted in ascending order, if the first data item is greater than the second data, then the two items are swapped (interchanged), otherwise no swapping is done. Next, the items in the second data and third data are compared. If the second one is greater than the third, then they are swapped; otherwise there is no change. This process continues for each consecutive pair of data items until all data are sorted.

Example 11.1

Consider the following list of elements denoted by A (indexed from 0 to 4 and identified by A[0] to A[4]) that are to be arranged or sorted in **ascending** order.

	A[0]	A[1]	A[2]	A[3]	A[4]
Given list A	23	76	47	82	15

The technique of sorting is explained stepwise below:

Pass 1

Array Elements	Actions
A[0] A[1] A[2] A[3] A[4] 23 76 47 82 15	23 < 76 (i.e., the value of A[0] is compared with the value of A[1], and found in ascending order). ⇒ Values are **not** to be **swapped.** (Comparison 1)
A[0] A[1] A[2] A[3] A[4] 23 76 ⇄ 47 82 15	76 > 47 (i.e., the value of A[1] is compared with the value of A[2], and found not in ascending order). ⇒ Values are to be **swapped.** (Comparison 2)
A[0] A[1] A[2] A[3] A[4] 23 47 76 82 15	76 < 82 (i.e., the value of A[2] is compared with the value of A[3], and found in ascending order). ⇒ Values are **not** to be **swapped.** (Comparison 3)
A[0] A[1] A[2] A[3] A[4] 23 47 76 82 ⇄ 15	82 > 15 (i.e., the value of A[3] is compared with the value of A[4], and found not in ascending order). ⇒ Values are to be **swapped.** (Comparison 4)
A[0] A[1] A[2] A[3] A[4] 23 47 76 15 82	After pass 1, the largest value 82 has bubbled up, and is placed at the end of the list in A[4]. But the array is still not sorted.

Pass 2

Array Elements	Actions
A[0] A[1] A[2] A[3] A[4] 23 47 76 15 82	23< 47 (i.e., the value of A[0] is compared with the value of A[1], and found in ascending order). ⇒ Values are **not** to be **swapped.** (Comparison 1)
A[0] A[1] A[2] A[3] A[4] 23 47 76 15 82	47 < 76 (i.e., the value of A[1] is compared with the value of A[2], and found in ascending order). ⇒ Values are **not** to be **swapped.** (Comparison 2)
A[0] A[1] A[2] A[3] A[4] 23 47 76 ⇄ 15 82	76 > 15 (i.e., the value of A[2] is compared with the value of A[3], and found not in ascending order). ⇒ Values are to be **swapped.** (Comparison 3)
A[0] A[1] A[2] A[3] A[4] 23 47 15 76 82	After Pass 2, the next largest value 76 has bubbled up, and is placed in the list in A[3]. But the array is still not sorted.

Pass 3

Array Elements	Actions
A[0] A[1] A[2] A[3] A[4] 23 47 15 76 82	23 < 47 (i.e., the value of A[0] is compared with the value of A[1], and found in ascending order). ⇒ Values are **not** to be **swapped**. (Comparison 1)
A[0] A[1] A[2] A[3] A[4] 23 47 ⇄ 15 76 82	47 > 15 (i.e., the value of A[1] is compared with the value of A[2], and found not in ascending order). ⇒ Values are to be **swapped**. (Comparison 2)
A[0] A[1] A[2] A[3] A[4] 23 15 47 76 82	After Pass 3, the next largest value 47 has bubbled up, and is placed in the list in A[2]. But the array is still not sorted.

Pass 4

Array Elements	Actions
A[0] A[1] A[2] A[3] A[4] 23 ⇄ 15 47 76 82	23 > 15 (i.e., the value of A[0] is compared with the value of A[1], and found not in ascending order) ⇒ Values are to be **swapped**. (Comparison 1)
A[0] A[1] A[2] A[3] A[4] 15 23 47 76 82	After Pass 4, the next largest value 23 has bubbled up, and is placed in the list in A[1]. Also, 15 is placed in its proper place in A[0]. Now, the **array is sorted in ascending order.**

The **advantage** of bubble sort is that it is a very simple and easy method to sort a list of elements. On the other hand, the disadvantage of bubble sort is that it is slow to sort a list of elements.

> ***Note!***
> The larger value bubbles up after each pass and is placed at the proper position in the list.

11.2.1 Bubble Sort Algorithm

The bubble sort algorithm is presented below with the help of pseudocode for better understanding.

Algo-11.1 Pseudocode of bubble sorting

```
BubbleSort(array)
  FOR i ← 0 to array.count - 1
      FOR j ← 0 to array.count - i - 1
          IF array[j] > array[j+1] THEN
            SWAP array[j] and array[j+1]
          END IF
      END FOR(j)
  END FOR(i)
END BubbleSort
```

11.2.2 Bubble Sort with C

CProg-11.1 Bubble sort

```
#include<stdio.h>

/*Function for bubble sort */
void Bubble_Sort(int array[], int size)
 {
   int i, j, temp, flag;
   for( i = 0; i < size - 1; i++)
   {
       flag = 0;
       for( j = 0; j < size - i - 1; j++)
       {
           // Do swapping
           if (array[j] > array[j + 1])
           {
               temp = array[j];
               array[j] = array[j + 1];
               array[j + 1] = temp;
               flag++;
           }
       }
       if(!flag)
           break;

   }

 }

/* Function to print elements of the array */
void Print_Array(int array[], int size)
 {
   int i;
   printf("Sorted array: ");
   for(i = 0; i < size; i++)
      printf("%d ", array[i]);
    printf("\n");
  }

/* Driver Function */
void main()
 {
   int n, i;
   int array[20];
   printf("Enter the number of elements in your array: ");
   scanf("%d", &n);
```

```
    printf("Enter your array: ");
    for (i = 0; i < n; i++)
        scanf("%d", &array[i]);
    Bubble_Sort(array, n);
    Print_Array(array, n);
    //return 0;
  }
/* End of the program */
```

Output

```
Enter the number of elements in your array: 5
Enter your array: 52 48 23 2 79
Sorted array: 2 23 48 52 79
```

> ***Programming Tips!***
> `Bubble_Sort()` is used to sort data. Two data arrays `array[j]` and `array[j+1]` are swapped with the help of the temp variable. `Print_Array()` is used to print array elements after sorting.

11.2.3 Bubble Sort with Python

PyProg-11.1 **Bubble sort**

```
# Function for bubble sort
def Bubble_Sort(list):
    for i in range(0, len(list) - 1):
        for j in range(0, len(list) - i - 1):
            # swapping
            if list[j] > list[j + 1]:
                list[j], list[j + 1] = list[j + 1], list[j]

# Function to print list
def Print_list(list):
    for i in range(0, len(list)):
        print(list[i], end = " ")
    print()

# Input data elements using list
list = [2, 4, 3, 1, 6, 8, 4]
# Call sort function
Bubble_Sort(list)
# Display the sorted list
Print_list(list)
## end program
```

Output

```
1 2 3 4 4 6 8
```

Programming Tips!

`Bubble_Sort` function is used to sort data. `Print_list()` is used to print array elements after sorting.

11.2.4 Complexity Analysis

The complexity of the bubble (or exchange) sort algorithm is based on the number of comparisons required within the given set of elements. Here, we assume n is the size of the list.

Best Case, Average Case, and Worst Case

In our bubble sort example, initially, the total number of elements is $n = 5$. It is clearly shown that in pass 1, we require four comparisons, i.e., we can say, $(n - 1)$ comparisons are required in the first pass. In pass 2, there are three comparisons, i.e., we can say that $(n - 2)$ comparisons are required in the second pass. In pass 3, there are two comparisons, i.e., we can say that $(n - 3)$ comparisons are required in the third pass. In pass 4, we have just 1 comparison, i.e., we can say that $(n - 4)$ comparisons are required in the fourth pass.

So, the total number of comparisons required in our example is: $4 + 3 + 2 + 1 = 10$, in all four passes.

The total number of comparisons required (in general)
$= (n - 1) + (n - 2) + (n - 3) + ... + 3 + 2 + 1$
$= n * (n - 1)/2 = (n^2/2) - (n/2) \in O(n^2)$

Hence, the time complexity of bubble sort is $O(n^2)$.

In all three cases (i.e., best, average, and worst) of bubble sort, we have to compare $n(n - 1)/2$ numbers to see whether the array is reverse sorted or not. So, we can say that bubble sort complexity in the best case, average case, and worst case is $O(n^2)$.

Note!

The complexity of bubble sort is $O(n^2)$ in all three cases (best, average, and worst).

11.2.5 Optimized or Modified Bubble Sort Algorithm

We can decrease the complexity of bubble sort by introducing a flag variable to identify whether the list is already sorted. To optimize this algorithm, we have to use the flag variable to check whether elements are getting swapped inside the inner `for` loop in the first pass. If no swapping takes place after the first pass, it means the array has already been sorted and we can jump out of the `for` loop, instead of executing all the passes.

Let us consider an array with values {10, 20, 30, 40, 50}. After the first pass, the flag variable value remains the same. Hence, we can easily understand that the input array is already sorted. So, best case complexity becomes $O(n)$ in optimized or modified bubble sorting because we require only $(n - 1)$ number of comparisons in the first pass.

Note!

No swapping in first-pass is indicated by a flag in bubble sort. Thus, it exempts all other iterations and hence reduces complexity.

Algo-11.2 Pseudocode of optimized or modified bubble sort

```
ModifiedBubbleSort(array)
  flag = false
  FOR i ← 0 to array.count - 1
      FOR j ← 0 to array.count - i - 1
          IF array[j] > array[j+1] THEN
             SWAP array[j] and array[j+1]
             flag = true
             IF flag is true
                Break
             END IF
          END IF
      END FOR(j)
  END FOR(i)
END ModifiedBubbleSort
```

11.3 INSERTION SORT

Insertion sort is a simple sorting algorithm that sorts the list by shifting elements one by one, similar to how most people arrange a poker card. Start with the first card in your hand then pick the next card and insert it into its proper position. Repeat the previous step for all cards until all the cards are placed in an ordered sequence. Here, we pick data and insert it in the correct position and that is why it is called insertion sort. It is a stable sorting technique and does not change the order of equal elements.

Example 11.2

Let the following list A be given in an unsorted array. Suppose, the element to be sorted in an ascending order using the insertion sorting technique.

	A[0]	A[1]	A[2]	A[3]	A[4]
Given list A	23	76	47	82	15

The technique of insertion sorting is explained stepwise below for this example:

Pass 1

Array elements	Actions
A[0] A[1] A[2] A[3] A[4] 23 76 47 82 15 ↑ (A[1])	Start with second element A[1] (i.e., 76) and compare with A[0] (i.e., 23). 76 > 23, so they are in order, and hence **no insertion** is required.

Pass 2

Array elements	Actions
A[0] A[1] A[2] A[3] A[4] 23 | 76 | 47 | 82 | 15	Start with third element A[2] (i.e., 47) and compare with A[1] (i.e., 76). 47 < 76, so they are not in order. Hence, 47 is to be inserted in the correct position before A[2] (i.e., either A[1] or A[0] position). Then, we continue comparing. Now, A[2] (i.e., 47) is compared with A[0] (i.e., 23) 47 > 23, so they are in order.
A[0] A[1] A[2] A[3] A[4] 23 | 47 | 76 | 82 | 15	So, 47 (i.e., initial position A[2]) is to be **inserted** after 23 in A[1] position as all values up to A[0] are checked already. We have to **shift** the value of A[1] to the next (i.e., in A[2]) to get the position for insertion. We have to stop pass 2 since A[2] has been inserted into its correct position. Note that all positions up to A[2] are in sorted order after pass 2.

Pass 3

Array elements	Actions
A[0] A[1] A[2] A[3] A[4] 23 | 47 | 76 | **82** | 15	Start with fourth element A[3] (i.e., 82) and compare with A[2] (i.e., 76). 82 > 76, so they are in order, and hence no insertion is required and the pass is stopped here.

Pass 4

Array elements	Actions
A[0] A[1] A[2] A[3] A[4] 23 | 47 | 76 | 82 | **15**	Start with fifth element A[4] (i.e., 15) and first compare with A[3] (i.e., 82); 15 < 82, so they are not in order and we have to compare A[4] with A[2] (i.e., 76); 15 <76, so they are not in order and we have to compare A[4] with A[1] (i.e., 47); 15 < 47, so they are not in order and we have to compare A[4] with A[0] (i.e., 23); 15 < 23, they are not in order and we have finished all elements. We have to insert 15 (i.e., A[4]) in A[0] position and shift 23, 47, 76, 82 to the right side by one room, to the position A[1], A[2], A[3] and A[4] respectively.
A[0] A[1] A[2] A[3] A[4] 15 | 23 | 47 | 76 | 82	The array is now sorted in ascending order and we have reached the last element (i.e., A[4]), so the process is stopped.

The **advantage** of insertion sort is that it is also a very simple and efficient method for a small data set. It is a stable method in the sense that it does not change the relative order of elements with the same values. On the other hand, the disadvantage of insertion sort is that it repeatedly scans the list of elements and hence it takes more time. The insertion sort does not deal well with a big list of elements.

> ***Note!***
> Insertion sort is a stable sorting technique that arranges a list by inserting the elements in appropriate positions by shifting subsequent elements, one by one.

11.3.1 Insertion Sort Algorithm

The insertion sort algorithm is presented below with the help of pseudocode for better understanding.

Algo-11.3 Pseudocode of insertion sort

```
InsertionSort(array)
  unsorted ← 1
  WHILE unsorted < array.count
        hold ← array[unsorted]
        i ← unsorted - 1
        WHILE i ≥ 0 and hold < array[i]
              array[i + 1] ← array[i]
              i ← i- 1
        END WHILE
        array[i + 1] ← hold
        unsorted ← unsorted + 1
  END WHILE
END InsertionSort
```

11.3.2 Insertion Sort with C

CProg-11.2 Insertion sort

```
#include<stdio.h>

/* Function for insertion sort */
void Insertion_Sort(int array[], int size)
  {
    int temp, j, i;
    for(i = 1; i< size; i++)
      {
        temp = array[i];
        j = i - 1;
        /* Do swapping */
        while(j >= 0 && array[j] > temp)
         {
            array[j + 1] = array[j];
            j--;
         }
```

```
            array[j + 1] = temp;
        }
    }

/* Function to print elements of the array */
void Print_Array(int array[], int size)
    {
        int i;
            printf("\nSorted array = ");
        for( i = 0; i < size; i++)
            printf("%d ", array[i]);

        printf("\n");
    }

/* Driver Function */
int main()
    {
        int i, num = 6;
        printf("Enter how many numbers do you want to sort: ");
        scanf("%d", &num);
        int array[num];
        printf("Input array = ");
        for (i = 0; i < num; i++)
            {
                scanf("%d", &array[i]);
            }
        Insertion_Sort(array, num);
        Print_Array(array, num);
        return 0;
    }
/* End of program */
```

Output

```
Enter how many numbers do you want to sort: 5
Input array = 55 36 54 75 92

Sorted array = 36 54 55 75 92
```

Programming Tips!

`Insertion_Sort()` is used to sort data. `Print_Array()` is used to print array elements after sorting.

11.3.3 Insertion Sort with Python

PyProg-11.2 **Insertion sort**

```
# Function for insertion sort
def Insertion_Sort(myList):
    for i in range(1, len(myList)):
        temp = myList[i]
        j = i - 1
        while j >= 0 and myList[j] > temp:
            myList[j + 1] = myList[j]
            j -= 1
        myList[j + 1] = temp

# function to print myList
def Print_myList(myList):
    for i in range(0, len(myList)):
        print(myList[i], end = " ")
    print()

# Input data elements using List
myList = [1, 6, 3, 3, 5, 2]

# Call sort function
Insertion_Sort(myList)
# Display the sorted myList
Print_myList(myList)
## end program
```

Output

```
1, 2, 3, 3, 5, 6
```

> ***Programming Tips!***
> `Insertion_Sort()` is used to sort data and `Print_myList()` is used to print array elements after sorting.

11.3.4 Complexity Analysis

Best Case

In the best case, the input array is already in sorted order, i.e., A[0] < A[1] < . . . < A[n – 1], (example, A = {10, 20, 30, 40}). Only one comparison is required in each stage i ($i = 1, 2, 3, \ldots, n - 1$) to sort an already sorted array with n number of elements.

Total number of comparisons = $1 + 1 + \ldots + 1 = n - 1 \in O(n)$.

So, the best-case complexity of insertion sort is $O(n)$.

Average Case and Worst Case

Total number of required comparisons in the average case = 1 + 2 + 3 + ... + $(n-1) = (n(n-1))/2$.

So, the average case complexity of insertion sort is $O(n^2)$.

In the worst case, the inputs array contains n distinct items in reverse order, i.e., A[0] > A[1] > . . . > A[n – 1];. Example, A = {40, 30, 20, 10}.

i comparisons and i moves are required in each stage i, where $i = 1, \ldots, n-1$.

Total number of required comparisons in the worst case
$= 1 + 2 + \ldots + n - 1.$
$= n * (n-1)/2 \in O(n^2)$.

So, the worst-case complexity of insertion sort is $O(n^2)$, which is the same in the average case.

> **Note!**
> The best-case complexity of insertion sort is $O(n)$ and the worst-case complexity of insertion sort is $O(n^2)$, which is the average case.

11.4 SELECTION SORT

The selection sort algorithm is used to arrange a list (or array) of elements in either ascending or descending order. It is based on the maximum and minimum values of the list of elements. In ascending order arrangement, at first, we have to check the minimum value in the list, and place it at the first position (i.e., A[0]) of the list. Next, we have to find the second minimum element in the list and place this value in the second position (i.e., A[1]) and so on. This procedure is repeated until the entire list is sorted.

Example 11.3

Let the following array A be given in an unsorted array. Suppose the elements are to be sorted in an ascending order using the selection sort technique.

	A[0]	A[1]	A[2]	A[3]	A[4]
Given list A	23	76	47	82	15

The technique of selection sort is explained stepwise below:

Pass 1

Array elements	Actions
A[0] A[1] A[2] A[3] A[4] 23 76 47 82 **15** ↑ (A[4])	Starting from the second element 76 (i.e., A[1]), we have to search for the smallest element among the rest, which is 15.
A[0] A[1] A[2] A[3] A[4] **15** 76 47 82 **23**	Now, compare 15 (i.e., A[4]) with the first element 23 (i.e., A[0]). 23 > 15, so 23 and 15 values are swapped.

Pass 2

Array elements	Actions
A[0] A[1] A[2] A[3] A[4] 15 | 76 | 47 | 82 | **23** ↑ (A[4])	Now, start from the third element 47 (i.e., A[2]) and we have to search for the smallest element among the rest, which is 23.
A[0] A[1] A[2] A[3] A[4] 15 | **23** | 47 | 82 | **76**	Now, compare 23 (i.e., A[4]) with the second element 76 (i.e., A[1]). 76 > 23, so 76 and 23 are swapped.

Pass 3

Array elements	Actions
A[0] A[1] A[2] A[3] A[4] 15 | 23 | 47 | 82 | **76** ↑ (A[4])	Now, start from the fourth element 82 (i.e., A[3]) and we have to search for the smallest element among the rest, which is 76.
A[0] A[1] A[2] A[3] A[4] 15 | 23 | **47** | 82 | **76**	Now, compare 76 (i.e., A[4]) with the third element 47 (i.e., A[2]). 47 < 76, so 47 and 76 are not swapped. The order remains the same.

Pass 4

Array elements	Actions
A[0] A[1] A[2] A[3] A[4] 15 | 23 | **47** | 82 | **76** ↑ (A[4])	Now, start from the fifth element 76 (i.e., A[4]) and we have to search for the smallest element among the rest, which is 76 only.
A[0] A[1] A[2] A[3] A[4] 15 | 23 | 47 | **76** | **82**	Now, compare 76 (i.e., A[4]) with the fourth element 82 (i.e., A[3]). 82 < 76, so 76 and 82 are swapped. **The array is now sorted and arranged in ascending order.**

The advantage of selection sort is that it is also a very simple method to sort elements. On the other hand, the disadvantage of selection sort is that it is a time consuming or slow process.

> ***Note!***
> In the selection sort (in ascending order), first we check the minimum value in the list and place it in the proper position in each pass.

11.4.1 Selection Sort Algorithm

The selection sort algorithm is presented below with the help of the pseudocode.

Algo-11.4 Pseudocode of selection sort

```
SelectionSort(array)
  FOR i = 1 to n - 1
      min = i (/* set current element as minimum */)
      FOR j = i+1 to n
         IF array[j] < array[min] THEN (/*check the element
to be minimum */)
            min = j
         END IF
      END FOR(j)
      IF indexmin ≠ i THEN
       /* swap the minimum element with the current element */
         SWAP array[min] and array[i]
      END IF
  END FOR(i)
END SelectionSort
```

11.4.2 Selection Sort with C

CProg-11.3 Selection sort

```
#include<stdio.h>

/* Function for selection sort */
void Selection_Sort(int array[], int size)
  {
    int min_index, temp, i, j;

    for(i = 0; i < size - 1; i++)
      {
        min_index = i;
        for(j = i + 1; j < size; j++)
            if(array[j] < array[min_index])
                min_index = j;
        temp = array[i];
        array[i] = array[min_index];
        array[min_index] = temp;
      }
  }
```

```
/* Function to print elements of the array */
void Print_Array(int array[], int size)
  {
    int i;
    printf("Sorted array: ");
    for(i = 0; i < size; i++)
        printf("%d ", array[i]);
    printf("\n");
  }

/* Driver function */
int main()
  {
    int i,num;
    printf("Enter the number of elements: ");
    scanf("%d", &num);
    int array[num];
    printf("\nEnter the array ");
    for( i = 0; i < num; i++)
    {
        scanf("%d", &array[i]);
    }
    Selection_Sort(array, num);
    printf("\n Sorted array: ");
    Print_Array(array, num);
    return 0;
  }
/* End of program */
```

Output

```
Enter the number of elements: 5
Enter the array: 57 58 90 58 32
Sorted array: 32 57 58 58 90
```

Programming Tips!

`Selection_Sort()` is used to sort data. `min_index` variable is used to store the minimum value array position. `Print_Array()` is used to print sorted array elements.

11.4.3 Selection Sort with Python

PyProg-11.3 Selection sort

```
# Function for selection sort
def Selection_Sort(array):
    for i in range(0, len(array) - 1):
        min_index = i
```

```
        for j in range(i + 1, len(array)):
            if array[j] < array[min_index]:
                min_index = j
        array[i], array[min_index] = array[min_index], array[i]

# Function to print list
def Print_list(array):
    print("Sorted list: ")
    for i in range(0, len(array)):
        print(array[i], end = " ")
    print()

# Input data elements using list
num = int(input("Enter the number of elements to sort: "))
print("Enter the elements")
array = []
for i in range(0, num):
    array.append(int(input()))

# Call sort function
Selection_Sort(array)
# Display the sorted list
Print_list(array)
## end program
```

Output

```
Enter the number of elements to sort: 5
Enter the elements
9
1
2
8
2
Sorted list:
1 2 2 8 9
```

> ***Programming Tips!***
> `Selection_Sort()` is used to sort data. `min_index` variable is used to store the minimum value array position. `Print_list()` is used to print array elements after sorting.

11.4.4 Complexity Analysis

In all three cases (best, average, and worst), selection sort is not difficult to analyze compared to other sorting algorithms, since none of the loops depend on the data in the array. Selecting the minimum element requires scanning all n elements, which takes $(n - 1)$ comparisons, and then swapping it into the first position. Finding the next minimum element requires scanning the remaining $(n - 1)$ number of elements, and so on.

So, total number of comparisons $= (n - 1) + (n - 2) + ... + 2 + 1$
$= n * (n - 1) / 2 \in O(n^2)$.

In all three cases of selection sort, we have to conduct $n * (n - 1)/2$ number of comparisons, whether the array is reversely sorted or not. So, we can say that the complexity of selection sort in the best case, average case, and worst case is $O(n^2)$.

Note!
The complexity of selection sort in all three (best, average, and worst) cases is $O(n^2)$.

11.5 QUICK SORT

The name 'quick sort' indicates the sorting of a list of elements very quickly. Quick sort is a very fast data sorting technique. This algorithm was invented by C A R Hoare. It is constructed using the 'divide-and-conquer' strategy. This sorting is also known as partition-exchange sort. The quick sort algorithm attempts to divide the list of elements into two parts and then apply quick sort in each part recursively. The partition of the list is performed based on an element called the *pivot*. Here, the pivot element is one of the elements in the list. There are many ways to choose the pivot element in the quick sort. Following are some of the ways by which a pivot element is selected:

- Choose the first element as a pivot.
- Choose the last element as a pivot.
- Median of the array as a pivot.
- A random element as a pivot.

We will choose the first element as the pivot in this chapter. Using quick sort logic, the pivot element will be placed at its final sorted position. The elements list is divided into two partitions. All the elements to the left of the pivot are less than the pivot, and all elements to the right of the pivot are greater than or equal to the pivot. The elements to the left and right may not be sorted. Again, we will pick sub-arrays (elements on the left side of the pivot, and the elements on the right side of the pivot) and partition them by choosing a pivot (in the sub-arrays) again using the same logic. This process continues until the full array is sorted.

Example 11.4

Let the following list A be given in a sorted array. Suppose the elements are to be sorted in an ascending order using a quick sorting technique, and the first element '15' of the list is chosen as a pivot.

	A[0]	A[1]	A[2]	A[3]	A[4]	A[5]	A[6]	A[7]
Given list A	15	13	18	1	14	16	2	17

The technique of quick sorting is explained stepwise below:

Pass 1

Array elements	Actions
A[0] A[1] A[2] A[3] A[4] A[5] A[6] A[7] 15 | 13 | 18 | 1 | 14 | 16 | 2 | 17 Pivot (A[0]), Left (A[1]), Right (A[7])	The pivot is A[0] (i.e., 15), initially the left pointer points A[1], and the right pointer points A[7]. So, left (pointer) = 1 and right (pointer) = 7, pivot = 15. Now, start comparing A[1] with the pivot. If A[left] > pivot, then stop comparing left pointers; otherwise increase the left pointer to the next index (i.e., left ++). Start comparing A[right] with pivot. If A[right] < pivot then stop the right pointer; otherwise decrease the right pointer to the previous index (i.e., right −−). Repeat the same until left >= right. If both left and right pointers are stopped but left < right, then swap A[left] with A[right] and continue the process. If left >= right, then swap pivot position with A[right].
A[0] A[1] A[2] A[3] A[4] A[5] A[6] A[7] 15 | 13 | 18 | 1 | 14 | 16 | 2 | 17 Pivot (A[0]), Left (A[2]), Right (A[6])	A[1] (i.e., 13) < pivot, so increment left by one; A[2] (i.e., 18) > pivot, so stop left pointer movement with left = 2. A[7] (i.e., 17) > pivot, so decrement the right pointer by one; A[6] (i.e., 2) < pivot, so stop right pointer movement with right = 6.
A[0] A[1] A[2] A[3] A[4] A[5] A[6] A[7] 15 | 13 | 2 | 1 | 14 | 16 | 18 | 17 Pivot (A[0]), Left (A[2]), Right (A[6])	Now, left < right, so swap A[left] (i.e., 18) and A[right] (i.e., 2).
A[0] A[1] A[2] A[3] A[4] A[5] A[6] A[7] 15 | 13 | 2 | 1 | 14 | 16 | 18 | 17 Pivot (A[0]), Right (A[4]), Left (A[5])	A[2] (i.e., 2) < pivot, so increment left by one; A[3] (i.e., 1) < pivot, so increment left by one; A[4] (i.e., 14) < pivot, so increment left by one; A[5] (i.e., 16) > pivot, so stop left pointer movement with left = 5. A[6] (i.e., 18) > pivot, so decrement the right pointer by one; A[5] (i.e., 16) > pivot, so decrement the right pointer by one; A[4] (i.e., 14) < pivot, so stop right pointer movement with right = 4.

Array elements	Actions
A[0] A[1] A[2] A[3] A[4] A[5] A[6] A[7] 14 13 2 1 **15** 16 18 17 Pivot (A[4])	Now, left > right (i.e., 5 > 4), and both pointers crossed each other. So, swap pivot (i.e., 15) with A[right]) (i.e., A[4] or 14). Note that pivot element 15 takes its appropriate position since all numbers left to 15 are smaller than 15, and all numbers right to 15 are greater than 15. But the array is not sorted yet.

Pass 2

Array elements	Actions
A[0] A[1] A[2] A[3] A[4] A[5] A[6] A[7] 14 13 2 1 **15** 16 18 17 Pivot (A[0]) Left (A[1]) Right (A[3]) Pivot (A[5]) Left (A[6]) Right (A[7])	In the left sub-list (A[0] to A[3]), the pivot is 14. There are no numbers greater than the pivot. So, left will keep on incrementing and will stop at 1 (i.e., {A[3]). As A[3] (i.e., 1) < pivot, right will stop at A[3] (same position). Now left = right = 3, so we swap pivot with A[right] (i.e., 14 is swapped with 1).
A[0] A[1] A[2] A[3] A[4] A[5] A[6] A[7] 1 13 2 **14** **15** 16 18 17 Pivot (A[5]) Left (A[6]) Right (A[7])	In the right sub-list (A[5] to A[7]), the pivot is 16. A[left] (i.e., A[2] or 18) > pivot, so, stop left pointer movement with left = 6. A[right] (i.e., 17) > pivot, so right will keep on decrementing, and will stop at A[5] (i.e., pivot) with right = 5. left > right, so we swap pivot with the right pointer (i.e., 16 is swapped with 16 - itself).
A[0] A[1] A[2] A[3] A[4] A[5] A[6] A[7] 1 13 2 **14** **15** **16** 18 17	**Repeat this recursive process on both left, and right sub-lists until all numbers are sorted.**
A[0] A[1] A[2] A[3] A[4] A[5] A[6] A[7] **1** **2** **13** **14** **15** **16** **17** **18**	**Now, we get the final sorted list, which is in ascending order.**

The advantage of quick sort is that it is the fastest method on the average and best cases among all sorting methods as shown later in the complexity analysis section. On the other hand, it is a slow process if the initial array is in reverse order (i.e., in the worst case).

> ***Note!***
> Quick (or partition-exchange) sort divides the list into two parts and then applies a quick sort in each part recursively.

11.5.1 Quick Sort Algorithm

The quick sort algorithm is presented below with the help of the pseudocode for a better understanding of the algorithm.

Algo-11.5 Pseudocode of quick sort

```
QuickSort(array[], p, r)
   IF  (p < r)
      q = partition (array, p, r)
      quicksort (array, p, q-1)
      quicksort (array, q+1, r)
   END IF
END QuickSort

partition(array[], p, r)
   pivot = array[p]; i = p; j = r;
   WHILE(TRUE)
      WHILE (array[i] < pivot and array[i] ≠ pivot) i++
         WHILE (array[j] > pivot and array[j] ≠ pivot) j--
            IF (i < j) THEN
            temp = array[i]; array[i] = array[j]; array[j] = temp;
            ELSE
               RETURN j
            END IF
         END WHILE(j)
      END WHILE(i)
   END WHILE(TRUE)
END partition
```

11.5.2 Quick Sort with C

CProg-11.4 Quick sort

```
#include<stdio.h>

/*Swapping the values in the array */
void swap(int *a,int *b)
   {
     int temp= *a;
     *a = *b;
     *b = temp;
   }

/* Partition the array by pivot point */
int partition (int arr[], int low, int high)
```

```
  {
    /* Taking the last value of array as the pivot */
    int pivot = arr[high];
      int j;
    int i = (low - 1);
    for (j = low; j <= high - 1; j++)
      {
        if (arr[j] <= pivot)
          {
            i++;
            swap(&arr[i], &arr[j]);
          }
      }
    swap(&arr[i + 1], &arr[high]);
    return (i + 1);
  }

/* Quick sort function */
void quickSort(int arr[], int low, int high)
  {
    if (low < high)
      {
        /* Partitioning the array */
        int pi = partition(arr, low, high);
        quickSort(arr, low, pi - 1);
        quickSort(arr, pi + 1, high);
      }
  }

/* Driver function*/
int main()
  {
    int t;
    //Testcase
    printf("Enter number of times you want to sort: ");
    scanf("%d", &t);

    while(t--)
      {
        int n, i;
        printf("Enter the Size of the Array: ");
        scanf("%d", &n);
        int arr[n];
        printf("Enter Array:\n");
        for(i = 0; i < n; i++)
```

```
        scanf("%d", &arr[i]);
      quickSort(arr, 0, n-1) ;
      printf("Sorted Array:\n");
      for(i = 0; i < n; i++)
          printf("%d ", arr[i]);
      printf("\n");
    }
  return 0;
}
/* End of program */
```

Output

```
Enter number of times you want to sort: 1
Enter the Size of the Array: 5
Enter Array:
23 55 42 65 55
Sorted Array:
23 42 55 55 65
```

> ***Programming Tips!***
> `quickSort()` is used recursively to sort data partition arrays. `partition()` is used for partitioning the array by pivot point. `swap()` is used to swap the array values.

11.5.3 Quick Sort with Python

PyProg-11.4 **Quick sort**

```
# Conquer
def Partition(list, left, right):
    pivot = list[left]
    index = right
    for j in range(right, left - 1, -1):
        if list[j] > pivot:
            list[index], list[j] = list[j], list[index]
            index -= 1
    list[index], list[left] = list[left], list[index]
    return index

# Divide list into halves
def Quick(list, left, right):
    if left < right:
        pivot = Partition(list, left, right)
        Quick(list, left, pivot - 1)
        Quick(list, pivot + 1, right)

# Calling divide function
def Quick_Sort(list):
    Quick(list, 0, len(list) - 1)
```

```
# Function to print list
def Print_list(list):
    for i in range(0, len(list)):
        print(list[i], end=" ")
    print()

# Input data elements using list
list = [2, 4, 3, 1, 6, 8, 4]
# Call sort function
Quick_Sort(list)
# Display the sorted list
Print_list(list)
## end program
```

Output

```
1 2 3 4 4 6 8
```

> ***Programming Tips!***
> `quick()` is used to divide the list into halves recursively. `partition()` makes the partition of the array by pivot point. `Print_list()` is used to print the list.

11.5.4 Complexity Analysis

Best and Average Case

Assume that the list size is n and hence $n = 2^m$ where m is the number of subdivisions of the list.

So, $m = \log_2 n$ (taking log on both sides).

The pivot is placed in the middle of the list or sub-list in the appropriate position. So, maximum $(n - 1)$ comparisons are required in the first pass to place the pivot. Then the list will be divided into two sub-lists with size $n/2$ approximately. For each of these sub-lists, there will be $n/2$ comparisons approximately. Similarly, the sub-lists will be divided with sizes $n/4$, $n/8$, … etc. in subsequent passes.

So, total number of comparisons $= n + 2 * (n/2) + 4 * (n/4) + 8 * (n/8) + \dots + n * (n/n)$
$= n + n + n + n + \dots + n$ (m terms) [because the full list is subdivided into m terms)
$= n * m$ [as we know, $m = \log_2 n$]
$= (n * \log_2 n) \in O(n * \log_2 n)$

So, the complexity of quick sort is $O(n * \log_2 n)$ in the best and average cases.

Worst Case

Suppose the list is to be sorted in reverse order. That means, the target is to sort a list in ascending order, given the list is in descending order. Here, partitioning leads to an unbalanced sub-division since the pivot is placed in the right (there are no elements on the right side of the pivot) and all the elements are less than the pivot. So, the original list is split into sub-lists of sizes 1 to $n - 1$ in subsequent passes.

So, the total number of comparisons $= (n - 1) + (n - 2) + (n - 3) + \dots + 3 + 2 + 1$
$= n * (n - 1)/2 \in O(n^2)$.

So, the complexity of quick sort is $O(n^2)$ in the worst case where sub-lists are found to be unbalanced after placing the pivot in each pass.

> **Note!**
> Complexity of quick sort is $O(n \log_2 n)$ for best or average cases and $O(n^2)$ for the worst case.

11.6 MERGE SORT

Merge sort is another sorting technique which is also based on the 'divide-and-conquer' rule, like the quick sort, and is used to sort a given set of elements recursively. The basic concept of merge sort is dividing the problem (or list) into several smaller sub-problems (or sub-lists) of approximately equal size, and sorting them separately. This principle of merge sort is presented below in Fig. 11.1.

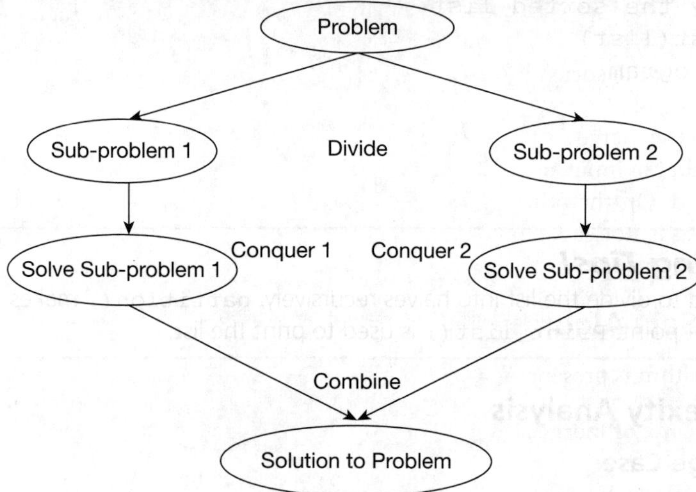

Figure 11.1 Principle (divide-and-conquer) of merge sort

Recursively continue this procedure until the list is sorted. Various sorted sub-lists are merged to form a sorted parent list after getting the sorted sub-lists, i.e., this process goes on recursively till the desired sorted list is arrived at.

Example 11.5

Let the input list be [44, 89, 6, 2, 67, 48, 18, 30]. These elements of the list are to be sorted in ascending order. We first compare the elements for each sub-list, and then combine them into the total list in a sorted manner. Following this principle, the given input list is divided into four sub-lists, namely, (44, 89), (6, 2), (67, 48), and (18, 30). In pass one, 44 and 89 are in sorted order. Next, we compare 6 and 2, and in the target list we put 2 first, followed by 6. We then change the order of 48 and 67 whereas 18 and 30 are in order. In the next pass 2 of the combining phases, we compare lists of two data values, and merge them into a list of data values from pass 1 placing all in sorted order. It appears as a reverse tree structure given in Fig. 11.2 below:

Input list: 44, 89, 6, 2, 67, 48, 18, 30.

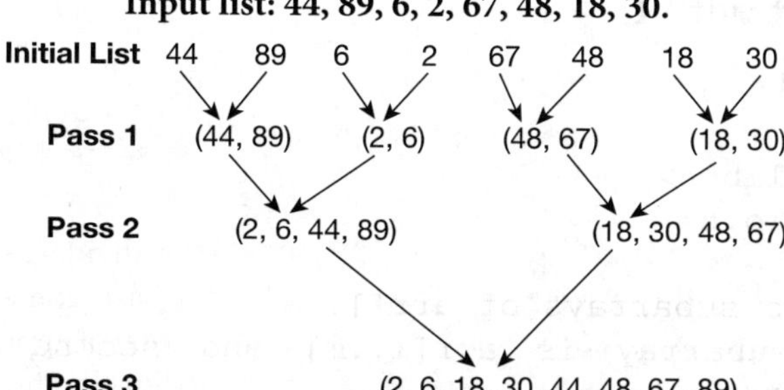

Figure 11.2 Example of merge sort

After the final merging, the sorted list is found in ascending order as 2, 6, 18, 30, 44, 48, 67, 89.

The advantage of the merge sort is that it is suitable for an extremely large number of input elements. It is also a fast and stable sorting method. On the other hand, implementation of this type of sorting is not easy, and it requires additional storage during merging operations.

> ***Note!***
> Merge sort divides the list into several smaller sub-lists of approximately equal size and sorts them separately. These sorted sub-lists are merged to form a sorted parent list.

11.6.1 Merge Sort Algorithm

The merge sort algorithm is presented below with the help of the pseudocode for better understanding.

Algo-11.6 Pseudocode of merge sort

```
MergeSort(array)
  IF array.count = 1 THEN (/* already sorted */)
    RETURN array
  END IF
  m ← array.count/2
  left ← array(m)
  right ← array(array.count - m)
  FOR i ← 0 to left.count-1
    left[i] ← array[i]
  END FOR
  FOR i ← 0 to right.Count-1
    right[i] ← array[i]
  END FOR
  left ← MergeSort(left)
  right ← MergeSort(right)
END MergeSort
```

11.6.2 Merge Sort with C

CProg-11.5 Merge sort

```
#include<stdlib.h>
#include<stdio.h>

/* Merges two subarrays of arr[].
   First subarray is arr[l..m] and second subarray is
arr[m+1..r] */
void merge(int arr[], int l, int m, int r)
  {
  int i, j, k;
  int n1 = m - l + 1;
  int n2 = r - m;

  /* Create temp arrays */
  int L[n1], R[n2];

  /* Copy data to temp arrays L[] and R[] */
  for (i = 0; i < n1; i++)
    L[i] = arr[l + i];
  for (j = 0; j < n2; j++)
    R[j] = arr[m + 1+ j];

  /* Merge the temp arrays back into arr[l..r]*/
  i = 0; // Initial index of first subarray
  j = 0; // Initial index of second subarray
  k = l; // Initial index of merged subarray
  while (i < n1 && j < n2)
    {
    if (L[i] <= R[j])
      {
      arr[k] = L[i];
      i++;
      }
    else
      {
      arr[k] = R[j];
      j++;
      }
    k++;
    }
```

```
  /* Copy the remaining elements of L[], if there
  are any */
  while (i < n1)
    {
      arr[k] = L[i];
      i++;
      k++;
    }

  /* Copy the remaining elements of R[], if there
  are any */
  while (j < n2)
    {
      arr[k] = R[j];
      j++;
      k++;
    }
  }

/* l is for left index and r is the right index of the sub-array
of arr to be sorted */
void mergeSort(int arr[], int l, int r)
  {
  if (l < r)
    {
     /* Same as (l+r)/2, but avoids overflow for large l and h */
     int m = l+(r-l)/2;
     /* Sort first and second halves */
     mergeSort(arr, l, m);
     mergeSort(arr, m+1, r);
     merge(arr, l, m, r);
    }
  }

/* Function to print an array */
void printArray(int A[], int size)
  {
  int i;
  for (i=0; i < size; i++)
    printf("%d ", A[i]);
  printf("\n");
  }
```

```
/* Driver program to test above functions */
int main()
  {
  int arr[] = {12, 11, 13, 5, 6, 7};
  int arr_size = sizeof(arr)/sizeof(arr[0]);

  printf("Given array is \n");
  printArray(arr, arr_size);

  mergeSort(arr, 0, arr_size - 1);

  printf("\nSorted array is \n");
  printArray(arr, arr_size);
  return 0;
   }
/* End of program */
```

Output

```
Given array is
12 11 13 5 6 7
Sorted array is
5 6 7 11 12 13
```

> ***Programming Tips!***
>
> Two sub-arrays are merged using `merge()` where first sub-array is `arr[l..m]` and second sub-array is `arr[m+1..r]`. `mergeSort()` is a recursive function where the `l` variable is for the left index and `r` is the right index of the sub-array of the array to be sorted. `printArray()` is used to print the sorted array.

11.6.3 Merge Sort with Python

PyProg-11.5 **Merge sort (2-way)**

```
# Conquer
def conquer_merge(list, left, right, mid):
    #temp = [None] * len(list)
    i = left
    j = mid + 1
    k = left
    while i <= mid and j <= right:
        if list[i] <= list[j]:
            temp[k] = list[i]
            i += 1
        else:
```

```
            temp[k] = list[j]
            j += 1
        k += 1
    while i <= mid:
        temp[k] = list[i]
        i += 1
        k += 1
    while j <= right:
        temp[k] = list[j]
        j += 1
        k += 1
    while left <= right:
        list[left] = temp[left]
        left += 1

# Divide list into halves
def divide(list, left, right):
    if left < right:
        mid = left + (right - left) / 2
        mid = int(mid)
        divide(list, left, mid)
        divide(list, mid + 1, right)
        conquer_merge(list, left, right, mid)

# Function for merge sort
def Merge_Sort(list):
    global temp
    temp = [0] * len(list)
    divide(list, 0, len(list) - 1)
    del temp

# Function to print list
def Print_list(list):
    for i in range(0, len(list)):
        print(list[i], end=" ")
    print()

# Driver code
list = [2, 4, 3, 1, 6, 8, 4]
Merge_Sort(list)
Print_list(list)
## End of Program
```

Output

```
1 2 3 4 4 6 8
```

> ***Programming Tips!***
> `divide()` is used to divide lists into halves. `conquer_merge()` is used to merges two subarrays. `Merge_Sort()` is used to sort an array using merge sort technique. `Print_list()` is used to print the sorted array.

11.6.4 Complexity Analysis

Assume that the list has n elements. Merge sort technique is divided into two sub-sections. The first section keeps dividing the list until n different sub-lists of one element each are generated, and the second section keeps inserting pairs of sub-lists until the main list with n elements is generated.

We know that the size of the list (i.e., n) is a power of 2.
So, $n = 2^m$, where m is the number of subdivisions of the list.
$\Rightarrow m = \log_2 n$ (taking log on both sides).

So, the number of steps required for dividing the list is $\log_2 n$, and the number of steps required for merging the lists is also $\log_2 n$. So, the total number of steps $= 2 \log_2 n$.

So, the total number of comparisons $= n * 2 \log_2 n$ (since n elements are compared in each step).
$= 2\, n \log_2 n \in O(n \log_2 n)$

In all three cases (i.e., best, average, and worst) of merge sort, we have to conduct the same number of comparisons, whether the given list is reverse-sorted or not. So, the complexity of the merge sort is $O(n \log_2 n)$ in all three cases.

> ***Note!***
> The complexity of merge sort is $O(n \log_2 n)$ in all three cases.

11.7 HEAP SORT

Heap sort is an improvement of selection sort. It divides the input list into sorted and unsorted regions. The unsorted regions are shrunk iteratively by extracting the largest element and putting it into the sorted region. Instead of a linear time scan of an unsorted region like selection sort, heap sort maintains the unsorted region in a heap to find the largest element more quickly in each step.

A heap is a tree-based data structure, where the root-node key is compared with its children and arranged accordingly. Nodes are arranged based on their values in a heap as discussed in Chapter 9.

The following are two types of the heap:

- **Max-heap:** It is a complete binary tree in which every parent node contains greater or equal value than its child nodes.
- **Min-heap:** It is also a complete binary tree in which every parent node contains a smaller value than its child nodes.

> ***Note!***
> Heap is a complete binary tree.

Heap sort is based on a binary tree. It is a fast and widely used data sorting technique. This algorithm is divided into two basic parts. It first creates a heap from the given list of elements, and then applies the heap to sort the list.

If we delete the root element one by one from the heap tree and store it in a list then finally, we will get all elements in order within the array. We use the max-heap to arrange all elements in descending order, and min-heap to arrange all elements in ascending order in this algorithm.

We are using max-heap to arrange a list of elements in descending order. Following are the steps of insertion operation in a max-heap:

Step 1	Insert a new node as the last (rightmost) leaf node (left to right) at the last level.
Step 2	Compare the new node value with its parent node.
Step 3	If the new node value is greater than its parent, then swap both of them.
Step 4	Repeat Step 2 and Step 3 until the new node value is less than its parent node, or until the new node reaches the root.

> ***Note!***
> Max-heap is used to arrange all elements in descending order and Min-heap is used to arrange all elements in ascending order.

Example 11.6

Suppose we want to create a heap from the following list of elements:

80, 90, 10, 20, 25, 70, 50, 22

Consider the above max-heap operation method. Insert a new node with a value 80.

Insert 80

Insert the first node (new node) with the value 80 as root.

Insert 90

Insert the next new node with value 90 as the last leaf at the next level from left to right. That means the new node 90 is added as a left child of the node of 80. Now, compare 90 with its parent node 80. Since 90 > 80, we have to interchange 90 and 80 as shown in Fig. 11.3 below.

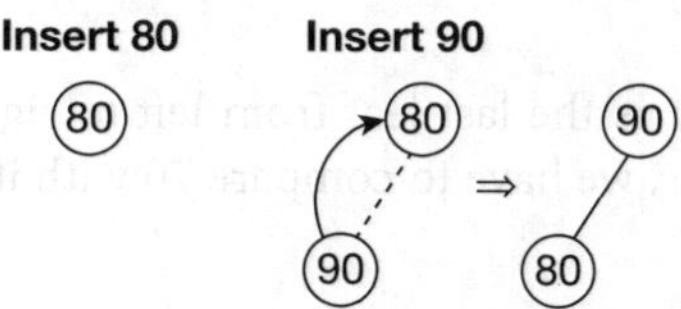

Figure 11.3 Insertion of the root node 80 (left) and insertion of a node 90 (middle and right)

Insert 10

Insert a new node next with value 10 as the last leaf from left to right. That means the new node 10 is added as the right child of node 90. Now, compare 10 with its parent node 90. Since 10 < 90, we don't interchange 10 and 90 (Fig. 11.4).

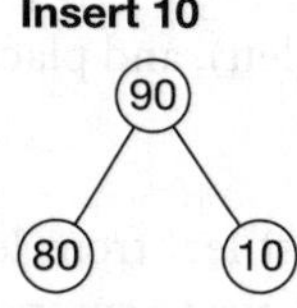

Figure 11.4 Insertion of 10

Insert 20

Insert a new node next with value 20 as the last leaf at the next level from left to right. That means the new node 20 is added as a left child node of 80. Now, compare 20 with its parent node 80. Since 20 < 80, we don't interchange 80 with 20 (Fig. 11.5).

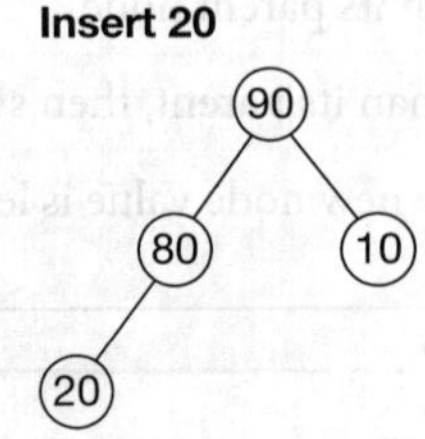

Figure 11.5 Insertion of 20

Insert 25

Insert new node next with value 25 as the last leaf from left to right. That means the new node 25 is added as a right child node of 80. Now, we have to compare 25 with its parent node 80. Since 25 < 80, we don't interchange 25 with 80 as shown in Fig. 11.6.

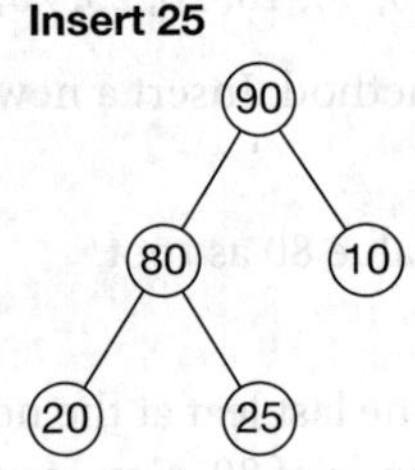

Figure 11.6 Insertion of 25

Insert 70

Insert new node next with value 70 as the last leaf from left to right. That means the new node 70 is added as a left child of node 10. Now, we have to compare 70 with its parent node 10. Since 70 > 10, we have to interchange 70 and 10.

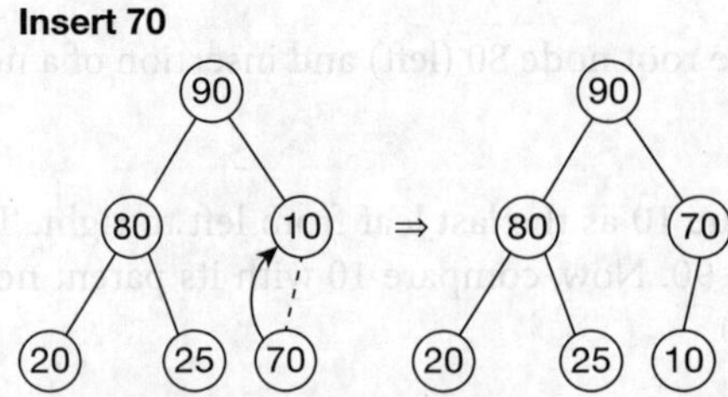

Figure 11.7 Insertion of 70 (left), and placing 70 appropriately (right)

Insert 50

Insert new node next with value 50 as the last leaf from left to right. That means the new node 50 is added as the right child of node 70. Now, we have to compare 50 with its parent node 70. Since 50 < 70, we don't need to interchange.

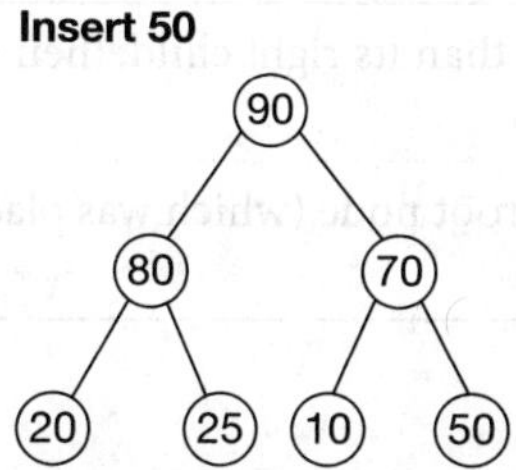

Figure 11.8 Insertion of 50

Insert 22

Insert new node next with value 22 as the last leaf at the next level from left to right. That means the new node 22 is added as a left child node of 20. Now, compare 22 with its parent node 20. Since 22 > 20, we have to interchange 22 and 20 as shown in Fig. 11.9 below.

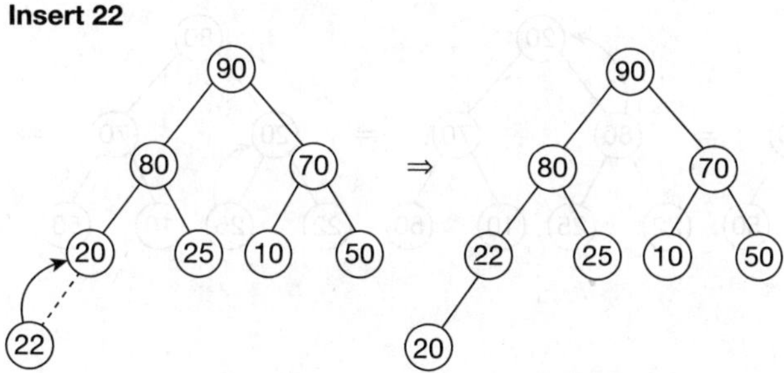

Figure 11.9 Insertion of 22

Deletion Operation in the Max-heap

If we delete the root element one by one from the heap tree and store it in a list (or array), then finally we will get all elements in order within the list. We use the max-heap technique to arrange all elements in descending order, and min-heap to arrange all elements in ascending order in this heap sorting algorithm. In the present context, we are using a max-heap that will provide the final sorted array in descending order.

We use the following steps to delete the root node from a max-heap tree structure.

Step 1	Delete the root node, and store it in an array; now place (or move) last node (rightmost node of the last level) in max-heap root position.
Step 2	Now, compare the root value with its left child value.
Step 3	If the root value is smaller than its left child, then compare the left child with its right sibling; else go to step 5.
Step 4	If the left child value is greater than its right sibling, then swap the root with the left child, otherwise swap the root with its right child.
Step 5	If the root value is greater than its left child, then compare the root value with its right child value.

Step 6	If the root value is smaller than its right child, then swap root with the right child, otherwise stop the process.
Step 7	Repeat the same until the root node (which was placed at the root in step 1) fixes at its exact position.

Example 11.7

Delete 90 (root node)

Consider the above max-heap. Delete root node (90) from the max-heap, and store the deleted root node (90) in the array (or list) A. Now, move the last node (rightmost node of the last level) 20 to the max-heap root position. Now, 80 and 70 are children of 20. Since 80 > 20 as well as 70, 80 and 20 will be interchanged. Now, 22 and 25 are children of 20. Since 25 > 20 as well as 22, 25 and 20 will be interchanged as shown in Fig. 11.10.

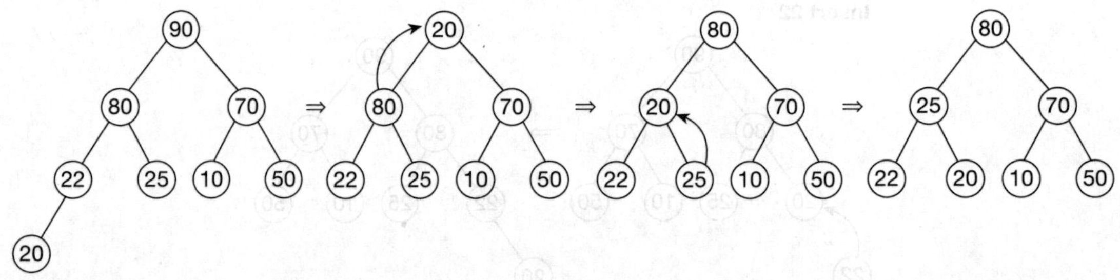

Figure 11.10 Deletion of root node 90.

	A[0]	A[1]	A[2]	A[3]	A[4]	A[5]	A[6]	A[7]
Given list A	90							

Delete 80 (root node)

Now, delete root node (80) from the max-heap, and store the deleted root node (80) in the array A. Then, move the last node (rightmost node of the last level) 50 to the max-heap root position. Now, 25 and 70 are children of 50. Since 70 > 50, 70 and 50 will be interchanged. Now, 10 is a child of 50. Since 10 < 50, we don't interchange 10 and 50 (Fig. 11.11).

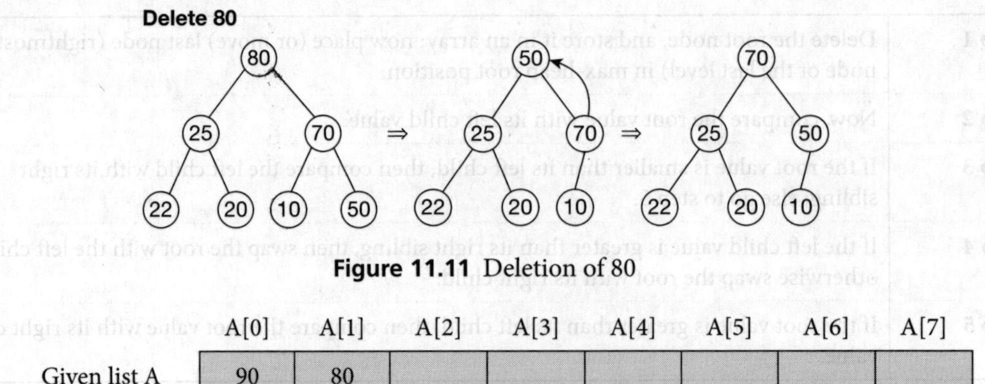

Figure 11.11 Deletion of 80

	A[0]	A[1]	A[2]	A[3]	A[4]	A[5]	A[6]	A[7]
Given list A	90	80						

Delete 70 (root node)

Delete root node (70) from the max-heap, and store the deleted root node (70) in the array A. Now, we have to move the last node (rightmost node of the last level) 10 to the max-heap root position. Now, 25 and 50 are children of 10. Since 50 > 10, as well as 25, 50 and 10 will be interchanged. Now, 50 is the root of the tree (Fig. 11.12).

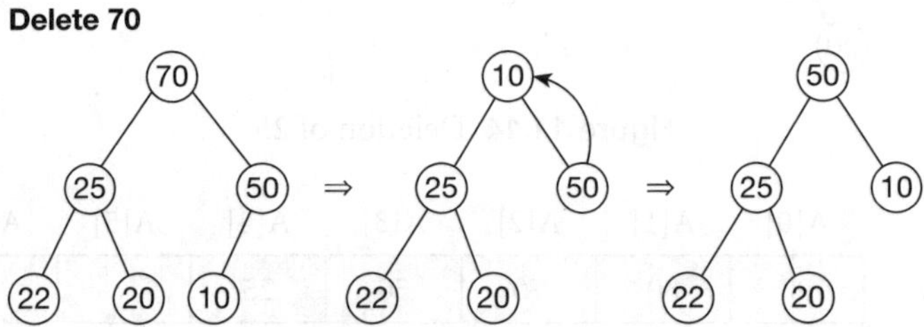

Figure 11.12 Deletion of 70

	A[0]	A[1]	A[2]	A[3]	A[4]	A[5]	A[6]	A[7]
Given list A	90	80	70					

Delete 50 (root node)

Delete root node (50) from the max-heap and store the deleted root node (50) in the array A. Now we have to move the last node (rightmost node of the last level) 20 to max-heap root position. Now, 25 and 10 are children of 20. Since 25 > 20, 25 and 20 will be interchanged. Now, 22 is a child of 20. Since 22 > 20, 22 and 20 will be interchanged (Fig. 11.13).

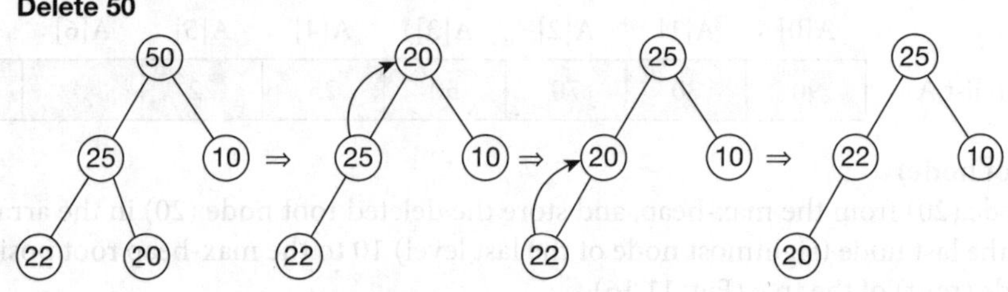

Figure 11.13 Delete 50

	A[0]	A[1]	A[2]	A[3]	A[4]	A[5]	A[6]	A[7]
Given list A	90	80	70	50				

Delete 25 (root node)

Delete root node (25) from the max-heap, and store the deleted root node (25) in the array A. Now, we have to move the last node (rightmost node of the last level) 20 to the max-heap root position. Now, 22 and 10 are children of 20. Since 22 > 20 as well as 10, 22 and 20 will be interchanged. Now, 22 is the root of the tree (Fig. 11.14).

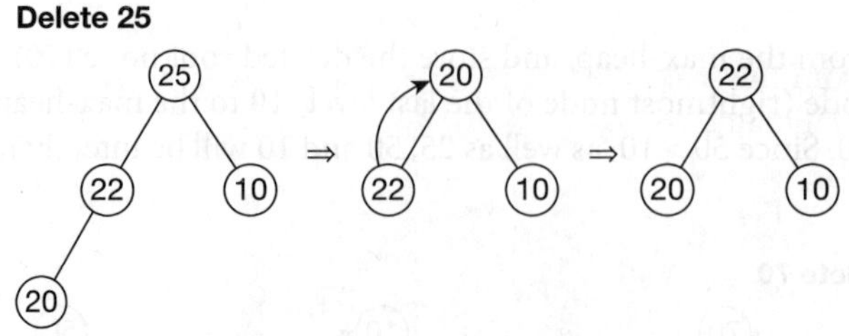

Figure 11.14 Deletion of 25

	A[0]	A[1]	A[2]	A[3]	A[4]	A[5]	A[6]	A[7]
Given list A	90	80	70	50	25			

Delete 22 (root node)

Delete root node (22) from the max-heap, and store the deleted root node (22) in the array A. Now, we have to move the last node (rightmost node of the last level) 10 to the max-heap root position. Now, 20 is a child of 10. Since 20 > 10, 20 and 10 will be interchanged. Now, 20 is the root of the tree (Fig. 11.15).

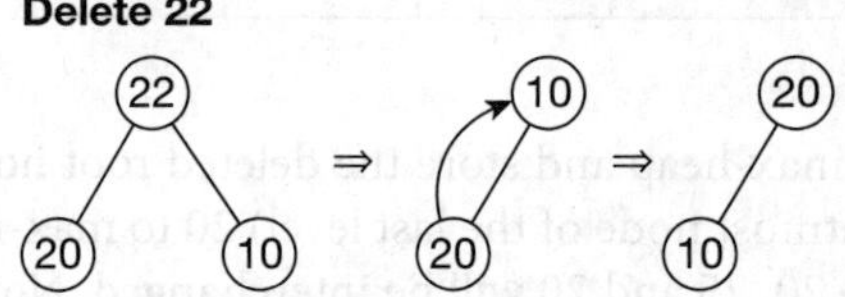

Figure 11.15 Deletion of 22

	A[0]	A[1]	A[2]	A[3]	A[4]	A[5]	A[6]	A[7]
Given list A	90	80	70	50	25	22		

Delete 20 (root node)

Delete root node (20) from the max-heap, and store the deleted root node (20) in the array A. Now, we have to move the last node (rightmost node of the last level) 10 to the max-heap root position. Now, 10 is the only node (root) of the tree (Fig. 11.16).

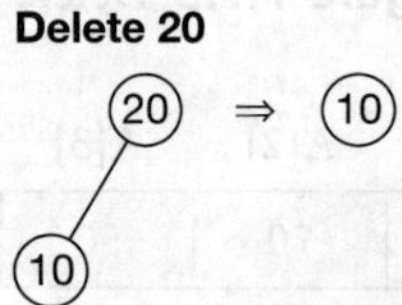

Figure 11.16 Deletion of 20

	A[0]	A[1]	A[2]	A[3]	A[4]	A[5]	A[6]	A[7]
Given list A	90	80	70	50	25	22	20	

Delete 10 (root node)

Delete root node (10) from the max-heap, and store the deleted root node 10 in the array A. Now, the tree is empty (Fig. 11.17). Finally, array A is sorted in descending order using heap sort.

Delete 10

(10) ⇒ Tree is empty

Figure 11.17 Delete 10

	A[0]	A[1]	A[2]	A[3]	A[4]	A[5]	A[6]	A[7]
Given list A	90	80	70	50	25	22	20	10

The **advantage** of the heap sort is that it is very fast and widely used for sorting. On the other hand, heap sort is not a stable sort and requires a constant space for sorting a list.

> ***Note!***
> If we delete the root element one by one from the heap tree, and store it in a list, then we get all elements in order finally.

11.7.1 Heap Sort Algorithm

The heap sort algorithm is presented below with the help of the pseudocode for better understanding.

Algo-11.7 Pseudocode of heap sort

```
HeapSort(array)
  BuildHeap(array)
  FOR i ← length(array) down to 2
    SWAP array[1] and array[i]
    heapsize ← heapsize - 1
    Heapify(array, 1)
  END FOR
END HeapSort

BuildHeap(array)
  heapsize ← length(array)
  FOR i ← floor(length/2) down to 1
  Heapify(array, i)
END BuildHeap

Heapify(array, i)
  le ← left(i)
  ri ← right(i)
  IF (le ≤ heapsize) and (array[le]>array[i]) THEN
    max ← le
  ELSE
    max ← i
 END IF
```

```
    IF (ri ≤ heapsize) and (array[ri] > array[max]) THEN
      max ← ri
    END IF
    IF (max ≠ i)
      SWAP array[i] <-> array[max]
      Heapify(array, max)
    END IF
  END Heapify
```

11.7.2 Heap Sort with C

CProg-11.6 Heap sort

```
#include<stdio.h>

/*Conquer places the newly added element to its right posi-
tion while building a heap*/
void Heapify(int array[], int root, int size)
  {
    int left = 2 * root + 1, largest;
    int right = left + 1, temp;

    if(left < size && array[left] > array[root])
        largest = left;
    else
        largest = root;

    if(right < size && array[right] > array[largest])
        largest = right;

    if(largest != root)
      {
        temp = array[root];
        array[root] = array[largest];
        array[largest] = temp;
        Heapify(array, largest, size);
      }
  }

/* Divide array into halves and call for heapify */
void Build_Heap(int array[], int size)
  {
    int i;
      for( i = (size - 1) / 2; i >= 0; i--)
        Heapify(array, i, size);
  }
```

```
/* Heap sort function definition */
void Heap_Sort(int array[], int size)
  {
    Build_Heap(array, size);
    int temp, i;

    for(i = size - 1; i > 0; i--)
      {
        temp = array[0];
        array[0] = array[i];
        array[i] = temp;
        Heapify(array, 0, i);
      }
  }

/* Function to print elements of the array */
void Print_Array(int array[], int size)
  {
    int i;
      for( i = 0; i < size; i++)
        printf("%d ", array[i]);

    printf("\n");
  }

/* Driver function */
int main()
  {
    int n, i;
    printf("Enter the number of elements in your array: ");
    scanf("%d", &n);
    int array[n];
    printf("Enter your array: ");
    for (i = 0; i < n; i++)
        scanf("%d", &array[i]);
    Heap_Sort(array, n);
    printf("Sorted array is: ");
    Print_Array(array, n);
    return 0;
  }
/* End of program */
```

Output

```
Enter the number of elements in your array: 5
Enter your array: 85 74 12 32 12
Sorted array is: 12 12 32 74 85
```

> ***Programming Tips!***
> `Heap_Sort()` is used for sorting a heap. `Heapify()` is used to conquer the places for newly added elements to the right position while building a heap. `Build_Heap()` is used to divide the array into halves and call `Heapify()`. `Print_Array()` is used to print the sorted array.

11.7.3 Heap Sort with Python

PyProg-11.6 Heap sort

```
# To heapify subtree rooted at index i, n is size of heap
def heapify(arr, n, i):
    largest = i  # Initialize largest as root
    l = 2 * i + 1  # left = 2*i + 1
    r = 2 * i + 2  # right = 2*i + 2

     # See if left child of root exists and is greater than
root
    if l < n and arr[i] < arr[l]:
        largest = l

    # See if right child of root exists and is greater than
root
    if r < n and arr[largest] < arr[r]:
        largest = r

    # Change root, if needed
    if largest != i:
        arr[i], arr[largest] = arr[largest], arr[i]  # swap
        # Heapify the root.
        heapify(arr, n, largest)

# The main function to sort an array of given size
def heapSort(arr):
    n = len(arr)

    # Build a maxheap.
    for i in range(n, -1, -1):
        heapify(arr, n, i)

    # One by one extract elements
    for i in range(n-1, 0, -1):
        arr[i], arr[0] = arr[0], arr[i]  # swap
        heapify(arr, i, 0)
```

```
# Input data elements using list
arr = [12, 11, 13, 5, 6, 7]
# Call sort function
heapSort(arr)

# Display the sorted list
n = len(arr)
print("Sorted array is:")
for i in range(n):
    print("%d" % arr[i]),
## end program
```

Output

```
Sorted array is:
5
6
7
11
12
13
```

> ***Programming Tips!***
> `heapsort()` is used for sorting heap. `Heapify()` is used to find the subtree rooted at index `i`. Here, `n` is the size of the heap.

11.7.4 Complexity Analysis

Assume that the list has n elements. Heap sort is a tree-based sorting technique that is divided into two sub-units. The first unit keeps inserting in the binary tree until all n elements are inserted in the binary tree (i.e., creating a heap), and the second unit keeps deleting elements until the tree is empty (i.e., deleting the heap).

We know that the size of the list (i.e., n) is a power of 2.
So, $n = 2^m$, where m is the number of sub-divisions of the list.
$\Rightarrow m = \log_2 n$ (taking log on both sides),

So, the number of steps required for inserting the list is $\log_2 n$, and the number of steps required for deleting the list is also $\log_2 n$.

The total number of required steps $= 2 \log_2 n$.
The total number of comparisons
$= n * 2 \log_2 n$ (since n elements are compared in each step).
$= 2n \log_2 n \in O(n \log_2 n)$.

In all three cases (i.e., best, average, and worst) in heap sort, we have to conduct the same number of comparisons, whether the given list is reverse-sorted or not. So, the complexity of heap sort is $O(n \log_2 n)$ in all three cases.

> ***Note!***
> The complexity of heap sort is $O(n \log_2 n)$ in all three cases.

11.8 RADIX SORT

Radix sort (or bucket sort) is a method that can be used to sort a list of numbers by its base or radix. If we want to sort a list of English words, where the radix or base is 26, then 26 buckets are used to sort the words. To sort an array of single-digit decimal numbers (where the radix or base is 10), we need 10 buckets and can be numbered as 0, 1, 2, 3, 4, 5, 6, 7, 8, and 9. Sorting is performed from the least significant digit (LSD) to the most significant digit. Radix sort algorithm requires the number of passes to be equal to the number of digits present in the largest number among the list of numbers. For example, if the largest number is a 3-digit number, then that list is sorted with 3 passes.

Example 11.8

Consider the following list:

	A[0]	A[1]	A[2]	A[3]	A[4]	A[5]	A[6]
Given list A	70	901	100	12	140	66	23

Step 1

Define ten queues each represented by a bucket, for digits 0 to 9 (Fig. 11.18).

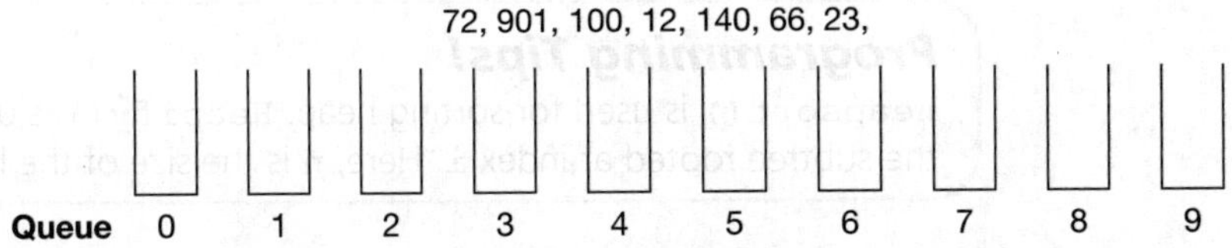

Figure 11.18 Representation of Step 1 of radix sort

Step 2

Insert all numbers of the list into a respective queue based on the LSD (based on the unit place) of each number (Fig. 11.19).

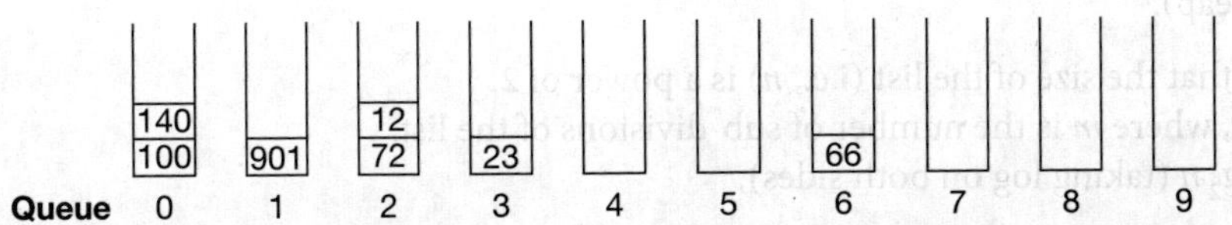

Figure 11.19 Representation of Step 2 of radix sort

Grouping all numbers from queue 0 to queue 9 in the order as they have been inserted, we get 100, 140, 901, 72, 12, 23, 66. This list is considered as input in the next step.

Step 3

Insert all numbers of the input list (i.e., 100, 140, 901, 72, 12, 23, 66) into a respective queue based on the tens-place digit (2nd digit from the right side or 2nd LSD) of each number (Fig. 11.20).

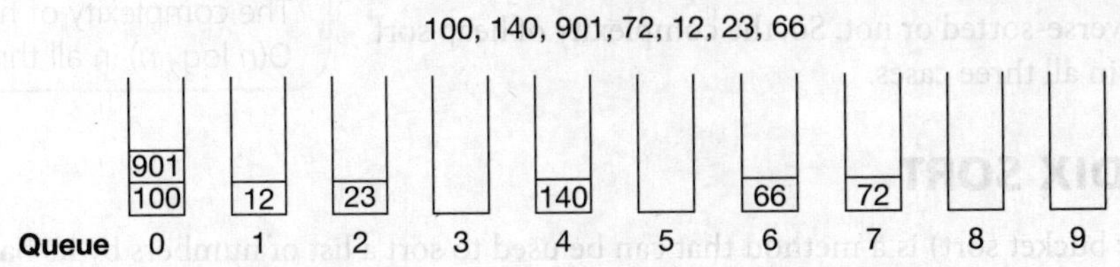

Figure 11.20 Representation of Step 3 of radix sort

Grouping all numbers from queue 0 to queue 9 in the order as they have been inserted, we get 100, 901, 12, 23, 140, 66, 72. This list is considered as input in the next step.

Step 4

Insert all the numbers of the input list (i.e., 100, 901, 12, 23, 140, 66, 72) into respective queues based on the hundredths place digit (3rd digit from the right side or 3rd LSD) of each number (Fig. 11.21).

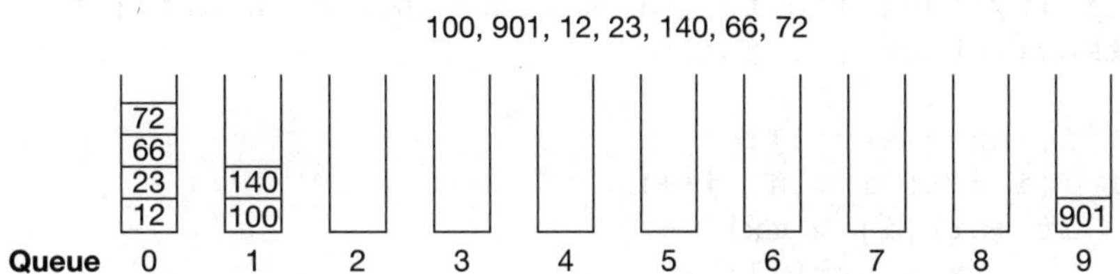

Figure 11.21 Representation of Step 4 of radix sort

Grouping all numbers from queue 0 to queue 9 in the order as they have been inserted, we get 12, 23, 66, 72, 100, 140, 901. This list is considered as input in the next step.

Finally, the list is sorted using the radix sort technique and appears as follows.

	A[0]	A[1]	A[2]	A[3]	A[4]	A[5]	A[6]
Given list A	12	23	66	72	100	140	901

The advantage of radix sort is that it is fast when the input list is less in number. On the other hand, radix sort depends on the number of digits or letters, and it is much less flexible than other sorts.

> ***Note!***
> In radix (or bucket) sort, the number of passes is equal to the number of digits present in the largest element.

11.8.1 Radix Sort Algorithm

The radix sort algorithm is presented below with the help of the pseudocode for a better understanding of the algorithm.

Algo-11.8 Pseudocode of radix sort

```
RadixSort(array, maxkeysize)
  /* maxkeysize ≥ 0 and represents the largest key size in
the array*/
  queues ← Queue[10]
  indexofkey ← 1
  FOR i ← 0 to maxkeysize - 1
    FOReach item in array
     queues [getqueueIndex (item, indexofkey)].enqueue(item)
    END FOReach
    array ← collapsequeues(queues)
    clearqueues(queues)
    indexofkey ← indexofkey + 10
  END FOR
END RadixSort
```

11.8.2 Radix Sort with C

CProg-11.7 Radix sort

```
#include<stdio.h>

/* A utility function to get maximum value in arr[] */
int getMax(int arr[], int n)
  {
    int i, mx = arr[0];
    for ( i = 1; i < n; i++)
        if (arr[i] > mx)
           mx = arr[i];
    return mx;
  }

/* A function to do counting sort of arr[] according to the
digit represented by exp*/
void countSort(int arr[], int n, int exp)
  {
    int output[n]; // output array
    int i, count[10] = {0};

    /* Store count of occurrences in count[] */
    for (i = 0; i < n; i++)
        count[ (arr[i]/exp)%10 ]++;
    /* Change count[i] so that count[i] now contains actual
position of this
       digit in output[] */
    for (i = 1; i < 10; i++)
        count[i] += count[i - 1];

    /* Build the output array */
    for (i = n - 1; i >= 0; i--)
    {
        output[count[ (arr[i]/exp)%10 ] - 1] = arr[i];
        count[ (arr[i]/exp)%10 ]--;
    }

   /* Copy the output array to arr[], so that arr[] now contains
sorted numbers
       according to current digit */
    for (i = 0; i < n; i++)
        arr[i] = output[i];
  }
```

```
/* The main function to that sorts arr[] of size n using Radix
Sort */
void radixsort(int arr[], int n)
  {
    int exp;
      /* Find the maximum number to know the number of digits
*/
    int m = getMax(arr, n);

    /* Do counting sort for every digit. Note that instead of
passing digit number,
          exp is passed. exp is 10^i where i is the current
digit number */
    for (exp = 1; m/exp > 0; exp *= 10)
        countSort(arr, n, exp);
  }

/* A utility function to print an array */
void print(int arr[], int n)
  {
    int i;
      for ( i = 0; i < n; i++)
        printf("%d  ", arr[i]);
  }

/* Driver function */
int main()
  {
    int arr[] = {170, 45, 75, 90, 802, 24, 2, 66};
    int n = sizeof(arr)/sizeof(arr[0]);
    printf("Array before sorting: \n");
    print(arr, n);
    radixsort(arr, n);
    printf("\nSorted array is: \n");
    print(arr, n);
    return 0;
  }
/* End of program */
```

Output

```
Array before sorting:
170  45  75  90  802  24  2  66
Sorted array is:
2  24  45  66  75  90  170  802
```

> ***Programming Tips!***
> `getMax()` is used to get the maximum value of the array. `countSort()` is used to do counting sort of the array according to the digit. The `radixsort()` is used to sort an array of size *n* using radix sort technique. `print()` is used to print the sorted array.

11.8.3 Radix Sort with Python

PyProg-11.7 Radix sort

```
# A function to do counting sort of arr[] according to the digit
represented by exp.
def countingSort(arr, exp1):
    n = len(arr)
    # The output array elements that will have sorted arr
    output = [0] * (n)
    # initialize count array as 0
    count = [0] * (10)
    # Store count of occurrences in count[]
    for i in range(0, n):
        index = (arr[i]/exp1)
        count[int((index) % 10)] += 1
    # Change count[i] so that count[i] now contains actual
    # position of this digit in output array
    for i in range(1, 10):
        count[i] += count[i-1]
    # Build the output array
    i = n-1
    while i >= 0:
        index = (arr[i]/exp1)
        output[count[int((index) % 10)] - 1] = arr[i]
        count[int((index) % 10)] -= 1
        i -= 1
   # Copying the output array to arr[], so that arr now contains
sorted numbers
    i = 0
    for i in range(0, len(arr)):
        arr[i] = output[i]

# Function to execute Radix Sort
def radixSort(arr):
    # Find the maximum number to know number of digits
    max1 = max(arr)
    # Do counting sort for every digit. Note that instead of
passing digit number,
    # exp is passed. exp is 10^I, where i is current digit number
```

```
        exp = 1
        while max1/exp > 0:
            countingSort(arr, exp)
            exp *= 10

    # Input data elements using list
    arr = [170, 45, 75, 90, 802, 24, 2, 66]
    # Call sort function
    radixSort(arr)

    # Display the sorted list
    for i in range(len(arr)):
        print(arr[i]),
    ## End program
```

Output

```
2
24
45
66
75
90
170
802
```

> ***Programming Tips!***
> `countingSort()` is used to do counting sort of the array according to the digits. `radixSort()` is used to execute radix sort.

11.8.4 Complexity Analysis

Radix sort is dependent on the following three things:

- The number of digits in the largest element (d).
- Radix or base (example, $r = 10$ for decimal digits, $r = 26$ for English letters and $r = 2$ for binary numbers).
- The number of elements in the array (n).

Suppose that radix sort requires several passes. In passes, each element is compared with the bucket elements. So, the total number of comparisons required by radix sort, $f(n) \le r * d * n$.

Average Case

It is very hard to define the time complexity in this case because it will depend on the choice of the radix r and also on the number of digits in the largest element (i.e., the number of passes). The loop (outer) is traversed for each digit (m times) and the inner loop is traversed (n times) for each element. So, the sorting method requires the time complexity of $O(m * n)$ approximately. The m is approximated by $\log_2 n$, and hence $O(m * n)$ approximates to $O(n \log_2 n)$

Best Case

Here, the array is already sorted. So, the loop (outer) is traversed for each digit (*m* times), and the inner loop is traversed (*n* times) for each element. So, the sorting method requires the time complexity of $O(m * n)$ approximately. The *m* is approximated by $\log_2 n$, and hence $O(m * n)$ approximates to $O(n \log_2 n)$.

Worst Case

Here, the array is sorted in reverse order. Suppose that the number of digits (*d*) in the largest element is equal to the number (*n*) of elements in the array.

So, the total number of comparisons (or passes) $= (n - 1) + (n - 2) + (n - 3) + ... + 3 + 2 + 1$
$= n * (n - 1)/2 \in O(n^2)$.

So, the worst-case complexity of radix sort is $O(n^2)$.

> **Note!**
> The complexity of radix sort is $O(n \log_2 n)$ in best and average cases, and $O(n^2)$ in the worst case.

11.9 COMPARISON OF TIME COMPLEXITY OF SORTING METHODS

The comparison of sorting methods is often performed using their time complexities. Table 11.1 provides the time complexities of all the sorting methods discussed in this chapter assuming that there are *n* elements in the list to be sorted.

Table 11.1 Complexity of all sorting algorithms

Sorting method	Best case	Average case	Worst case
Bubble sort	$O(n^2)$	$O(n^2)$	$O(n^2)$
Insertion sort	$O(n)$	$O(n^2)$	$O(n^2)$
Selection sort	$O(n^2)$	$O(n^2)$	$O(n^2)$
Quick sort	$O(n \log_2 n)$	$O(n \log_2 n)$	$O(n^2)$
Heap sort	$O(n \log_2 n)$	$O(n \log_2 n)$	$O(n \log_2 n)$
Merge sort	$O(n \log_2 n)$	$O(n \log_2 n)$	$O(n \log_2 n)$
Radix sort	$O(n \log_2 n)$	$O(n \log_2 n)$	$O(n^2)$

QUICK RECAP

☑ **Sorting** is the process of arranging a list of elements in a particular order (ascending or descending). It arranges the data in a sequence that makes searching easier.

☑ **Internal** sorting is performed on the primary memory whereas **external** sorting is performed in secondary memory. A sorting algorithm is said to be **stable** if it maintains the relative order of numbers, in case the same number occurs more than once.

- ☑ **Bubble** sort (or exchange sort) is the simplest sorting technique where each pair of adjacent elements is compared, and the elements are swapped if they are not in expected order in an iterative manner. The larger value bubbles up and is placed at the end of the list. The complexity of bubble sort is O(n^2) in all three cases (best, average, and worst).
- ☑ An **optimized bubble** sort uses a flag variable to check whether the elements are getting swapped inside the inner `for` loop in the first pass. No swapping in first-pass indicated by a flag can exempt all other iterations and hence, it reduces complexity.
- ☑ **Insertion** sort is a stable sorting technique that arranges a list by inserting the elements in appropriate positions by shifting subsequent elements, one by one. The best-case complexity of insertion sort is O(n) and the worst-case complexity of insertion sort is O(n^2), which is the same in the average case.
- ☑ In the **selection** sort (in ascending order) technique, first, we check the minimum value in the list and place it in the first position. Next, we find the second minimum and place this value in the second position, and so on until the entire list is sorted. While arranging in descending order, the maximum value is placed in the first position initially, and so on. The complexity of selection sort in the best case, average case, and worst case is O(n^2).
- ☑ **Quick** (or partition-exchange) sort divides the list into two parts, and then applies a quick sort in each part recursively (conquer). The pivot element divides the list and is placed at its final sorted position. The same process is recursively executed for the left and right sub-lists. The complexity of quick sort is O($n \log_2 n$) for best and average cases, and O(n^2) for the worst case.
- ☑ **Merge** sort divides the list into several smaller sub-lists of approximately equal size and sorts them separately. These sorted sub-lists are merged to form a sorted parent list. The complexity of merge sort is O($n \log_2 n$) in all three cases.
- ☑ The binary tree-based **heap** sort method first creates a heap from the given list, and the root-node key is compared with its children and arranged accordingly. If we delete the root elements one by one from the heap tree and store them in a list, then finally we get all elements in order. The complexity of heap sort is O($n \log_2 n$) in all three cases.
- ☑ **Radix** (or bucket sort) is performed using 10 buckets (or queues 0 to 9, for example, in decimal number sorting), and placing the elements in each pass based on LSD to MSD. The elements from the bucket are then grouped recursively. The number of passes is equal to the number of digits present in the largest element. The complexity of radix sort is O($n \log_2 n$) in best and average cases, and O(n^2) in the worst case.

REVIEW QUESTIONS

Multiple Choice Questions (MCQ): Choose the Best Alternative

Easy

1. While shorting elements is an array, merge sort uses:
   A. Backtracking approach.
   B. Heuristic search.
   C. Divide-and-conquer strategy.
   D. Greedy approach.
2. Time complexity of selection sort with n elements is ______.
   A. O($n \log n$)
   B. O($\log n$)
   C. O(n^2)
   D. O(1)

3. Complexity of insertion sort in the best case is ______.
   A. $O(n^2)$ B. $O(n \log_2 n)$
   C. $O(n^3)$ D. $O(n)$
4. The average case time complexity of merge sort is ______.
   A. $O(n \log n)$ B. $O(n^2)$
   C. $O(n^2 \log n)$ D. $O(n \log n^2)$
5. Which of the following is not a stable sorting algorithm?
   A. Selection sort B. Insertion sort
   C. Bubble sort D. Merge sort

Moderate

6. Sorting algorithm stability is important for:
   A. Sorting records based on multiple keys
   B. Worst-case performance of sorting algorithm
   C. Sorting alphanumeric keys as they are likely to be the same.
   D. None of these.
7. If the given array is already almost sorted, which of the following is the fastest sorting algorithm?
   A. Merge sort B. Quick sort
   C. Insertion sort D. Bubble sort
8. Among the following time complexities, which one of the following indicates the best time complexity for an algorithm?
   A. $O(n)$ B. $O(n^2)$
   C. $O(\log_2 n)$ D. $O(n \log_2 n)$
9. For the time complexities, which of the following sorting procedures is the slowest?
   A. Merge sort
   B. Bubble sort
   C. Quick sort
   D. Heap sort
10. How many swaps are needed to sort numbers 18, 122, 17, 19, 131, 119, 15, 113 in ascending order when we use the bubble sort method?
    A. 12 B. 14
    C. 13 D. 11
11. What is an internal sorting algorithm?
    A. Algorithm that is considered in place
    B. Algorithm that uses main memory during the sort
    C. Algorithm that involves swapping
    D. Algorithm that uses tape or disk during the sort.
12. Suppose the given array is {30, 40, 50, 21, 11}. The number of iterations required in bubble sort and selection sort respectively are:
    A. 4 and 5 B. 5 and 4
    C. 2 and 4 D. 2 and 5
    Hint: Since the input array is not sorted, bubble sort takes 5 iterations and selection sort takes 4 (i.e., n – 1) iterations.

Higher-Order Thinking Skills (HOTS)

13. An algorithm required a minimum of 100 sec to sort 1000 numbers using a quick sort method. The minimum time required to sort 100 numbers will approximately be:
    A. 50.2 sec B. 11.2 sec
    C. 6.7 sec D. 72.7 sec
    Hint: 100 * 100 / 1000 * log 100 / log 1000 = 20/3 or approx. 6.7 seconds
14. Which one of the following is the recommended method to choose a pivot element?
    A. Median-of-three partitioning method.
    B. Choosing the last element as the pivot.
    C. Choosing the first element as the pivot.
    D. Choosing a random element as the pivot.
    Hint: Choosing the median-of-three partitioning element is the recommended method to choose the pivot element since it is very unlikely that a median-of-three partitioning method's pivot would consistently provide a poor partition.
15. Which of the following is the concept that inspires the heap sort algorithm?
    A. Binary tree B. Fibonacci heap
    C. Priority queue D. FIFO
    Hint: Heap sort is based on the algorithm of the priority queue and it gives the best sorting time.
16. For merging two sorted lists of sizes m and n into a sorted list of size $m + n$, we require comparisons of ______.
    A. $O(n)$ B. $O(m)$
    C. $O(m + n)$ D. $O(\log m + \log n)$
17. Suppose that the pivot element is chosen uniformly at random in an array of 20 unique elements that are to be sorted using quick sort. What will be the probability of the pivot element to be placed in the worst possible location in the first pass of partitioning?
    A. 0.08 B. 0.1
    C. 0.01 D. 0.001

Hint: Pivot element is chosen uniformly at random. So, there are only 2 worst-case positions of the pivot element, either first or last. Therefore, required probability = 2/20 = 0.1.

18. Suppose that a merge sort program, in the worst-case design, takes 1 minute for an input size of 64. What will be the maximum input size closely approximated by the program if 12 minutes are allocated?

A. 1024 B. 512

C. 256 D. 128

Hint: Worst-case time complexity of merge sort $= \Theta(n \log n)$, where n is the input size.

According to the given problem, $p * 64 * (\log 64) = 60$, where p is constant.

$\Rightarrow p * 64 * 6 = 60, = p = 60/(64 * 6) = 5/32$

Now, when 12 minutes is allocated, we have to find the input size n.

Therefore, $(5/32) * n * \log n = 12*60$,

$\Rightarrow n \log n = 12 * 60 * 32/5 = = 4608 = 512 * 9 = 512 * \log 512$

$\Rightarrow n = 512$.

Short Answer-type Questions

Easy

1. Why do we need sorting techniques in a data structure?

2. What is stable sorting? Give an example.

3. Distinguish between internal and external sorting.

4. How can we calculate average/best-case complexity of quick sort?

5. Write the basic concept of the merge sort.

6. Differentiate between max- and min-heap.

Moderate

7. Explain – "Best-case insertion sort is better than bubble sort".

8. How is insertion sort different from bubble sort?

9. Why is radix sort known as bucket sort?

10. How can we improve the bubble sort algorithm?

11. Compare the efficiencies of different sorting algorithms using big-O notation.

Higher-Order Thinking Skills (HOTS)

12. Suppose that we are given an array of n integers in the range of $[0 \text{ to } n^2 - 1]$. How can we sort the array in $O(n)$ time?

13. Which sorting method is better to sort elements within a linked list? Justify your answer.

14. In a binary tree, is it possible to print its elements in sorted order in $O(n)$ time by using Inorder tree traversal?

Descriptive-type Questions

Easy

1. Write an algorithm to explain bubble sort.

2. Explain the algorithm for insertion sort and give a suitable example.

3. Explain the algorithm for quick sort (or partition exchange sort) and give a suitable example.

4. Explain the algorithm for merge sort and give a suitable example.

5. What is a heap? Write an algorithm to explain a heap sort.

Moderate

6. Demonstrate the selection sort results for each pass for the following initial array of elements: 20 16 30 57 23 9 14 28 12.

7. Demonstrate the radix sort results for each pass for a few arrays of elements.

8. Explain the time complexities of bubble sort, insertion sort, selection sort, quick sort, merge sort, heap sort, and radix sort separately.

9. Write the advantages and disadvantages of bubble sort, insertion sort, selection sort, quick sort, merge sort, heap sort, and radix sort.

Higher-Order Thinking Skills (HOTS)

10. Design an algorithm for checking the presence of repeated elements in an array of n numbers where some numbers are repetitive. We can use temporary variables.

11. Is it possible to sort an array of n numbers, each of which is less than 1000, in linear time?

12. Design an algorithm that finds the number that appears the maximum number of times within an array.

CASE STUDIES

1. Design an algorithm to modify a quick sort procedure where quick sort calls the insertion sort method to sort any sub-list whose size is less than 50 items. Compare the performance of this modified algorithm with the original one, using different data sets.
2. Design an algorithm to find the missing elements in an array [0,…, $n - 1$] of unique elements, where the range of the array known by [low, high] is given.
   Examples: Input: arr[] = {4, 7, 10, 11}, [low = 4, high = 11], Output: 5, 6, 8, 9.

LAB EXERCISES

1. Write a C program to sort strings in the dictionary order.
   Examples:

Input	**Output**
Enter 5 words:	In the lexicographical order:
india	atanu
chandan	biyas
atanu	chandan
biyas	india
riju	riju

2. Given an array consisting of 0s, 1s, and 2s, write a function that sorts the given array. The functions should put all 0s first, then all 1s and all 2s in the last.

ANSWER KEYS

Multiple Choice Questions

1. C	5. A	9. B	13. C	16. C
2. C	6. B	10. B	14. A	17. B
3. D	7. C	11. B	15. C	18. B
4. A	8. C	12. B	15. C	

12 Searching

CONTENTS

EXPECTED OUTCOMES OF THIS CHAPTER

After going through this chapter learners will be able

- ☑ To understand the search techniques.
- ☑ To explain linear, binary and interpolation search techniques.
- ☑ To implement the searching techniques using C and Python.
- ☑ To analyze the complexity of the searching techniques.

12.1 INTRODUCTION

Searching methods are developed to find an element in a given list (or array, or set) of numbers. If the element is found present in the list, then searching is said to be successful; otherwise, it is considered unsuccessful. The search operation returns the location or memory address of the element. The general response times of searching techniques have partly to do with the size and speed of the memory access for storage by the processor. The fastest access is achieved using internal or primary memory. Searching can be done from external storage also.

12.1.1 Definition

Searching is the process of finding elements in a given list. It is the operation of finding a given value position from a list of values. It decides whether a search key is present in the data or not. Any search is said to be successful or unsuccessful depending upon whether the element that is being searched is found or not.

> **Note!**
> Searching is the process of finding elements in a given list.

12.1.2 Classification of Searching

Searching can be classified into two categories:

1. *Internal search:* Searching is performed in the primary memory in this case. This searching technique is implemented on a small size of data. All data can be loaded into primary memory while the searching process is executed. Linear or sequential search, binary search and interpolation search are examples of internal search.
2. *External search:* Searching is performed in the secondary memory in this case. In most cases, the processes require such large amounts of memory that no computer's RAM can handle. So, access to additional external memory is needed for effective search operations. The process of accessing a task or sorting data from external storage (such as hard disk, network file server, disk drive, etc.) is known as external searching. B-tree structure discussed in Chapter 9 can be used for an external search.

> **Note!**
> Internal searching is performed in primary memory and external searching is performed in secondary memory.

12.2 LINEAR SEARCH

This technique is also known as a *sequential search*. The linear search method finds a given element in a list of elements. It takes O(n) time complexity where n is the total number of elements present in the list. A linear search starts comparing the search element with the first element in the list. If both elements are matched, then the result is a successful search; otherwise the search element is compared with the next element in the list. Repeat this process until searching is successful or if the list is ended and the target element still not found in the list. It is the simplest searching algorithm. The linear search algorithm is applied when no information is given about the list and the given list is unsorted or the elements are unordered.

Example 12.1

Consider the following list of elements denoted by A (indexed from 0 to 5 and identified by A[0] to A[5]) and the element to be searched is 13.

	A[0]	A[1]	A[2]	A[3]	A[4]	A[5]
Given list A	11	27	24	15	13	17

The technique of searching is explained stepwise below:

Step 1	Search element 13 is compared with the first element A[0], i.e., 11. These are not equal. So we have to move to the next element.
Step 2	Search element 13 is then compared with the second element A[1], i.e., 27. These are not equal again. So we have to move to the next element again.
Step 3	Search element 13 is then compared with the third element A[2], i.e., 24. These are not equal again. So we have to move to the next element again.
Step 4	Search element 13 is then compared with the fourth element A[3], i.e., 15. These are not equal again. So we have to move to the next element again.
Step 5	Search element 13 is then compared with the fifth element A[4], i.e., 13. Both are equal and hence we have to stop comparing further and print the index value 4 where our target element is found. This is successful searching.

12.2.1 Linear Search Algorithm

> ***Note!***
> The linear search is preferably applied when the given array is unsorted.

Linear search is implemented using the following algorithm:

Algo-12.1 Algorithm of linear search

Step 1	Read the search element.
Step 2	Compare the search element with the first element of the list.
Step 3	If both are equal, then display "element is found" and return the list index value.
Step 4	If both are not equal, then compare the search element with the next element of the list.
Step 5	Repeat Steps 3 and 4 until the search element is compared with the last element of the list.
Step 6	If the last element of the list also is not matched, then display "element is not found" and return.

12.2.2 Linear Search with C

CProg-12.1 C source code of linear search

```
#include<stdio.h>

/* Function to linear search item elt in given array a[]. If the
element is present then return its location, otherwise return
-1 */
int search(int a[], int size, int elt)
```

```
    {
        int i, flag = -1;
        for(i = 0; i < size; i++)
            if(a[i] == elt)
              {
                flag = i+1;
                break;
              }
        return flag;       //Return position
    }
/* Driver function */
int main()
    {
        int num, i;
        printf("Enter the number of elements: ");
        scanf("%d", &num);
        int arr[num];
        printf("Enter the list of elements: ");
        for(i = 0; i < num; i++)
        {
            scanf("%d", &arr[i]);
          }
        int pos;
        int desired;
        printf("Enter the element to be searched: ");
        scanf("%d", &desired);
        pos = search(arr, num, desired);
        if(pos != -1)
           printf("The number found at %d\n", pos);
        else
           printf("The number not found\n");
    }
/* End of program */
```

Output

```
Enter the number of elements: 3
Enter the list of elements: 5 4 7
Enter the element to be searched: 4
The number found at 2
```

Programming Tips!

`search()` is used here for linear search of an item in a given array. If the element is present, then its location returned; otherwise –1 is returned.

12.2.3 Linear Search with Python

PyProg-12.1 Python source code of linear search

```
# Function for linear search
def linearSearch(list, desired):
    for i in range(0, len(list)):
        # return position if found
        if(list[i] == desired):
            return i
    return -1

num = int(input("Enter number of elements: "))

print("Enter the elements: ")
list = []
for i in range(0, num):
    list.append(int(input()))

# Enter search element
desired = int(input("Enter the elements to search: "))

# Call search function and display result
if(linearSearch(list, desired) != -1):
    print("Found")
else:
    print("Number not found")
## end program
```

Output

```
Enter number of elements: 5
Enter the elements:
5
8
9
7
6
Enter the elements to search: 7
Found
```

> ***Programming Tips!***
> `linearSearch()` is used here for linear search of an item in a given array. If the element is present, then its location is returned; otherwise −1 is returned.

12.2.4 Complexity Analysis of Linear Search

The complexity of linear search algorithm is based on the number of comparisons required within the given set of elements. Here, we assume n is the size of the list.

Best case

The element being searched may be found in the first position. In this case, the search terminates in success with just one comparison. So, in the best case, the linear search algorithm takes O(1) operation.

Worst case

In this case, the element being searched may be present in the last position or not present in the array. If the search terminates in success with n comparisons or if the search terminates in failure with n comparisons, the linear search algorithm takes $O(n)$ operations in the worst case.

Average case

In this case, we assume that the element is there in the list and it can be present at any position. So, the number of comparisons can be any of the numbers 1, 2, 3, 4, …, n; and each number occurs with probability $p = 1/n$. So, in the average case, the linear search algorithm takes $O(n)$ operations.

> **Note!**
> The complexity of the linear search is O(1) in the best case and O(n) in both worst and average cases.

12.3 BINARY SEARCH

The binary search algorithm has a prerequisite. It is only used with a sorted list of elements, either in ascending order or in descending order. This means that the binary search is used only with an array of elements that are already arranged in an order. Binary searching technique cannot be used for an array of elements in random order. We start comparing the search element with the middle element of the array. If both are equal, then the result is "successful"; otherwise, we have to check whether the search element is smaller or larger than the middle element. If the search element is smaller, then we have to repeat the above-mentioned procedure for the left sub-list of the middle element. If the search element is larger, then we have to repeat the same process for the right sub-list of the middle element. We have to repeat this until we find the search element in the list or until the left/right sub-list is of only one element. If that element does not equal the search element, then the result is "unsuccessful search".

Example 12.2

Let the following list A be given in a sorted linear array of size N. Suppose element 30 has to be searched in it using the binary search algorithm.

	A[0]	A[1]	A[2]	A[3]	A[4]	A[5]	A[6]
Given list A	10	20	30	40	50	60	70

Step 1

Initially, begin = 0 and end = 6. Ascending array index starts with A[0] and ends with A[6]. Compute the location of the middle element as:

mid = $\lfloor$(begin + end) / 2$\rfloor$ = $\lfloor$(0 + 6) / 2 = 3$\rfloor$ [$\lfloor\ \rfloor$ indicates floor (greatest integer less than or equal) of the real number.]

Here, A [mid] = A[3] = 40 $\neq$ 30 and begin < end.

> **Note!**
> When N is even, the mid-point is at $N/2$ (two halves are of different sizes). We take floor of (begin + end)/2 as mid.

Step 2

Since A[mid] = 40 > 30, we take end = mid – 1 = 3 – 1 = 2 but begin remains unchanged.

Compute middle element again as:

mid = $\lfloor$(begin + end) / 2$\rfloor$ = $\lfloor$(0 + 2) / 2 $\rfloor$ = 1

So, A[mid] = A[1] = 20 $\neq$ 30 and begin < end.

Step 3

Since A[mid] = 20 < 30, so begin = mid + 1 = 1 + 1 = 2 but end remains unchanged.

Compute middle element again as:

Mid = $\lfloor$(begin + end) / 2$\rfloor$ = $\lfloor$(2 + 2) / 2$\rfloor$ = 2

Now, A[mid] = A[2] = 30 which is equal to the element being searched.

So, search successfully terminates and index 2 is returned.

> ***Note!***
> The binary search has a prerequisite – it is used only with a sorted list of elements.

12.3.1 Binary Search Algorithm

Let A be a sorted array of size *n*, and ITEM be the given element to be searched. The variables begin, end, and middle denote the beginning, end, and the middle elements of the array respectively. The binary search algorithm is used to find the 'position' of the ITEM in the array A. If the ITEM is not found in the array, then the position will return NULL.

Algo-12.2 Algorithm of binary search

Step 1	Set begin = 0; end = n −1.
Step 2	Repeat step 2(a) to 2(d) while begin < end and ITEM ≠ A[middle].
Step 2a	middle = $\lfloor$(begin + end)/2$\rfloor$.
Step 2b	If ITEM = = A[middle], then position = mid, return position and exit.
Step 2c	If ITEM < A[middle] then end = middle – 1.
Step 2d	Otherwise begin = middle + 1.
Step 3	position = NULL.
Step 4	return position and exit.

12.3.2 Binary Search with C

CProg-12.2 C source code of binary search

```
#include <stdio.h>

/* A recursive binary search function returns the location of
search item x
in the given array arr[l..r] if it is present, otherwise -1 */
int binarySearch(int arr[], int l, int r, int x)
```

```
    {
      if(r >= l)
        {
          int mid = l + (r - l) / 2;

        /* Checking whether the element is present at the middle
itself */
          if(arr[mid] == x)
            return mid;

          /* If the element is smaller than mid, it can only be
present in left
            sub-array */
          if(arr[mid] > x)
            return binarySearch(arr, l, mid - 1, x);

        /* Else the element can only be present in right sub-ar-
ray */
          return binarySearch(arr, mid + 1, r, x);
        }
      /* If the element is not present in the array */
      return -1;
    }

/* Driver function */
int main(void)
    {
      int arr[] = {2, 3, 4, 10, 40};
      int n = sizeof(arr) / sizeof(arr[0]);
      int x;
      printf("Enter the element to be search: ");
      scanf("%d",&x);
      int result = binarySearch(arr, 0, n - 1, x);
      (result == -1) ? printf("Element is not present in array")
        : printf("Element is present at index: %d", result);
      return 0;
    }
/* End of program */
```

Output

```
Enter the element to be search: 4
Element is present at index: 2
```

> ***Note!***
> A recursive `binarySearch()` returns the location of search item x in the given array if it is present; otherwise –1 is returned.

12.3.3 Binary Search with Python

PyProg-12.2 Python source code of binary search

```
# Returns index of x in arr if present, else -1
# Function for binary search
def binarySearch(arr, l, r, x):
    # Check base case
    if r >= l:
        mid = l + (r - l) // 2
        # If element is present at the middle itself
        if arr[mid] == x:
            return mid
        # If element is smaller than mid, then it
        # can only be present in left subarray
        elif arr[mid] > x:
            return binarySearch(arr, l, mid-1, x)
        # Else the element can only be present
        # in right subarray
        else:
            return binarySearch(arr, mid + 1, r, x)
    else:
        # Element is not present in the array
        return -1

# Driver Code
# Input array for searching
arr = [2, 3, 4, 10, 40]
# Element to search
x = 10

# Call binary search function and display result
result = binarySearch(arr, 0, len(arr)-1, x)
if result != -1:
    print("Element is present at index: % d" % result)
else:
    print("Element is not present in array")
## end program
```

Output

```
Element is present at index: 3
```

Programming Tips!

A recursive `binarySearch()` returns the location of search item x in the given array if it is present; otherwise –1 is returned.

12.3.4 Complexity Analysis of Binary Search

Best case

The best case occurs in the binary search algorithm when the element to be searched is present in the middle of the array. In that case, only one comparison is required to perform the search operation. So, the complexity of a binary search is O(1) in the best case.

Average case and worst case

In each recursive call, the search gets reduced to half of the array. So, for n elements in the array, $\log_2(n)$ iterations or recursive calls are required. Let us say the iterations of binary search terminate after p time repetitions. In the above example, in Section 12.3, it terminates after 3 iterations, so here $p = 3$. After each iteration, the array is divided into two halves. The size of the array at any iteration is n. After Step 1, the length of the array A = n. After Step 2, the length of the array A = $n/2$. After Step 3, length of array A = $(n/2)/2 = n/(2)^2$. Therefore, after step p, the length of the array A = $n/(2)^p$.

After p divisions, the length of the array A becomes 1. Therefore, length of the array, $n/(2)^p = 1$ and hence $n = 2^p$. Applying log function on both sides, we get,

$$\log_2(n) = \log_2(2^p),$$
$$\Rightarrow \log_2(n) = p\log_2(2),$$
$$\Rightarrow p = \log_2(n), \text{ as we know, } (\log_a(a) = 1).$$

So, the time complexity of the binary search is $O(\log_2(n))$ for both the cases (average and worst) where n is the size of the search array. We have to carry on our search operation more than once (i.e., $p > 1$) for successful search in both the cases. So, the same complexity analysis is applicable in both average and worst cases.

> **Note!**
> The complexity of the binary search is O(1) in the best case and $O(\log_2(n))$ in both worst and average cases.

Table 12.1 Difference between linear search and binary search

Linear search	Binary search
The sorted list is not a prerequisite for linear search	The sorted list is a prerequisite for binary search
It can be used in linked list implementation	It cannot be used in linked list implementation.
The average number of comparisons is very high.	The average number of comparisons is relatively less.

12.4 INTERPOLATION SEARCH

Interpolation search is very similar to the binary search algorithm, except the formula to calculate the mid position. An interpolation search is an improvement over the binary search for scenarios where the values in a sorted array are uniformly distributed. Binary search works by checking the middle element, whereas an interpolation search may go to different locations according to the value of the key being searched. For example, if the value of the key is close to the last element, the interpolation search is likely to start searching toward the end side. It is considered as an improvement of the binary search technique and requires no auxiliary (extra) space to carry out the search. The calculation of the middle position is complicated in the interpolation search compared to the binary search algorithm. It increases the execution time. If the items within the search array are uniformly distributed, then only interpolation search will provide better performance.

Let us assume, A is the array of data elements, low is the lowest index of the list, high is the highest index of the list, A[*n*] is the value stored at the *n*th index in the list, and X is a target element to be searched. Then the calculation of the middle position of interpolation search will be based on the following formulae:

middle = low + (high - low)*((X – a[low]) / (a[high] – a[low]))

Example 12.3

Search for the key X = 20 in the following array using interpolation search.

int[] a = {0,2, 4, 6, 8, 10, 12, 14, 16, 18, 20, 22, 24, 26, 28, 30}

The calculation of middle is given by:

middle = low + (high – low) * ((X – A[low]) / (A[high] – A[low]))

So, middle = 0 + Ceiling[(15 – 0) * ((20 – 0) / (30 – 0))] = 0 + 10 = 10,v

a[middle] = a[10] = 20, which is equal to X.

So, X is found at index 10.

> **Note!**
> Interpolation search is similar to binary search, except the formula to calculate the mid position.

12.4.1 Interpolation Search Algorithm

The interpolation search algorithm is given below with the help of the following pseudocode.

Algo-12.3 Pseudocode of interpolation search

```
InterpolationSearch(A,X)
BEGIN
   SET low ← 0, SET mid ← -1, SET high ← N-1.

   WHILE X does not match the target
      IF low equals to high or A[low] equals to A[high]
         stop: unsuccessful search, target not found
      ENDIF

     middle = low + Ceiling[(high - low)*((X - a[low])/(a[high]
- a[low]))]

      IF A[mid] = X
         stop: Successful search, Target found
      ELSE
         IF A[mid] < X
            Set low ← mid+1
         ELSE IF A[mid] > X
            SET high ← mid-1
         ENDIF
      ENDIF
   ENDWHILE
END
```

12.4.2 Interpolation Search with C

CProg-12.3 C source code of interpolation search

```
#include<stdio.h>
#define MAX 200

/* Interpolation search function */
int interpolationSearch(int a[], int bottom, int top, int item)
   {
     int mid;
     while (bottom <= top)
         {
            mid = bottom + (top - bottom)*((item-a[bottom])/
(a[top]-a[bottom]));
         if (item == a[mid])
            return mid + 1;
         if (item < a[mid])
            top = mid - 1;
         else
            bottom = mid + 1;
         }
     return -1;
   } /* End of interpolationSearch() */

/* Driver function */
int main()
   {
     int arr[MAX];
     int i, num;
     int item, pos;
     printf("\nEnter total elements (num < %d): ", MAX);
     scanf("%d", &num);
     printf("Enter %d Elements in ascending order:\n", num);
     for (i = 0; i < num; i++)
        scanf("%d", &arr[i]);
     printf("\nSearch For: ");
     scanf("%d", &item);
     pos = interpolationSearch(&arr[0], 0, num - 1, item);
     if (pos == -1)
        printf("\nElement %d not found\n", item);
     else
       printf("\nElement %d found at position %d\n", item, pos);
     return 0;
}
/* End of program */
```

Output

```
Enter total elements (num < 200): 5
Enter 5 Elements in ascending order:
5 8 89 96 105

Search For: 96

Element 96 found at position 4
```

Programming Tips!

A `interpolationSearch()` returns the location of a search item in the given array if it is present; otherwise, –1 is returned.

12.4.3 Interpolation Search with Python

PyProg-12.3 Python source code of interpolation search

```
# If x is present in arr[0..n-1], then returns index of it, else
returns -1
# Function for interpolation search
def interpolationSearch(arr, n, x):
    # Find indexes of two corners
    lo = 0
    hi = (n - 1)

    # Since array is sorted, an element present
    # in array must be in range defined by corner
    while lo <= hi and x >= arr[lo] and x <= arr[hi]:
        if lo == hi:
            if arr[lo] == x:
                return lo
            return -1

        # Probing the position with keeping uniform distribution
in mind.
        pos = lo + int(((float(hi - lo)/(arr[hi] - arr[lo])) *
(x- arr[lo])))

        # Condition of target found
        if arr[pos] == x:
            return pos

        # If x is larger, x is in upper part
        if arr[pos] < x:
            lo = pos + 1

        # If x is smaller, x is in lower part
        else:
            hi = pos - 1
    return -1
```

```
# Driver Code
# Array of items in which search will be conducted
arr = [10, 12, 13, 16, 18, 19, 20, 21, 22, 23, 24, 33, 35, 42, 47]
n = len(arr)

# Element to be searched
x = 18

# Call interpolation search function
index = interpolationSearch(arr, n, x)

# Display result
if index != -1:
    print("Element found at index", index)
else:
    print("Element not found")
## end program
```

Output

```
Element found at index 4
```

> ***Programming Tips!***
> `interpolationSearch()` returns the location of the search index in the given array if it is present; otherwise, –1 is returned.

12.4.4 Complexity Analysis of Interpolation Search

Best/Average case

Interpolation search is a modified algorithm of binary search, reducing complexity. If the items are uniformly distributed, the average case time complexity is $O(\log_2(\log_2(n)))$. This will occur when the elements of the array are uniformly distributed over their interval like, [13, 15, 18, 20, 23, 25]. We get the search result in just one step in both the best and average cases. So, the complexity analysis will be the same in both these situations.

Worst case

The worst-case complexity of interpolation search is $O(n)$ which will occur when the elements are not fairly uniformly distributed over their interval like, [13, 15, 18, 20, 23, 100].

The following Table 12.2 presents the best-case, average-case and worst-case complexities of all three searching methods as discussed in this chapter.

> ***Note!***
> The complexity of interpolation search is $O(\log2(\log2(n)))$ in the best and average cases both but $O(n)$ in the worst case.

Table 12.2 Comparison of complexities of searching algorithms

Searching method	Best case	Average case	Worst case
Linear search	O(1)	$O(n)$	$O(n)$
Binary search	O(1)	$O(\log_2(n))$	$O(\log_2(n))$
Interpolation search	$O(\log_2(\log_2(n)))$	$O(\log_2(\log_2(n)))$	$O(n)$

QUICK RECAP

- ☑ Searching is the process of finding elements in a given list. It decides whether a search key is present in the data or not. It also finds the position of the element within a list of values.
- ☑ Searching is of two types, internal and external. Internal searching is performed on primary memory and external searching is performed on secondary memory. Linear or sequential search, binary search, and interpolation search are examples of internal search.
- ☑ Linear search is applied when the given array is unsorted. It starts comparing search elements with the first element. If both elements are matched then the result is a successful search, otherwise the search element is compared with the next element. Repeat this process until searching is successful or if the list is ended and still the target element is not found in the list.
- ☑ The complexity of the linear search is O(1) in the best case, and $O(n)$ in both worst and average cases.
- ☑ The binary search has a prerequisite – it is used only with a sorted (ascending or descending) list of elements. It starts comparing the search element with the middle element of the array. If both are equal, then the result is 'successful'; otherwise, we have to check whether the search element is smaller or larger than the middle element. If the search element is smaller, then we have to repeat the procedure for the left sub-list of the middle element. If the search element is larger, then we have to repeat the same process for the right sub-list of the middle element. We have to repeat these until we find the search element in the list or until the left/right sub-list is of only one element. If that element does not equal the search key, then the result is 'unsuccessful search'.
- ☑ The complexity of the binary search is O(1) in the best case and $O(\log_2(n))$ in worst and average cases both.
- ☑ Interpolation search is similar to binary search, except the formula to calculate the mid position. The calculation of middle position of interpolation search will be based on the following formula:

  middle = low + (high – low)*((X – a[low]) / (a[high] – a[low]))
- ☑ The complexity of interpolation search is $O(\log_2(\log_2(n)))$ in best and average cases both, but O(n) in worst case.

REVIEW QUESTIONS

Multiple Choice Questions (MCQ): Choose the Best Alternative

Easy

1. Which of the following searching methods cannot be used in linked lists?
   A. Binary search B. Linear search
   C. Both A and B D. None of these.
2. What will be the time complexity of binary search technique?
   A. O(*n*) B. O(log *n*)
   C. O(*n*/2) D. O(*n* log *n*)
3. The prerequisite condition of the binary search technique is:
   A. Unsorted array
   B. Ascending order array
   C. Descending order array
   D. Sorted array
4. Finding whether an element is present in a list or not is called ____________.
   A. Sorting B. Storing
   C. Searching D. None
5. Binary search can be applied on the sorted ____________.
   A. pointers B. array or list
   C. arguments D. queues
6. Which of the following is the necessary condition(s) for interpolation search?
   A. Give list should be sorted
   B. The values of the give list should be uniformly distributed
   C. None of these.
   D. Both of these.

   Hint: Desired conditions for interpolation search are both A and B. The list should be sorted and values should be uniformly distributed.
7. Which of the following searching techniques is used with a sorted list of elements, of which interpolation search is a variation?
   A. Linear search B. Binary search
   C. None of these. D. Both of these.

   Hint: Interpolation search is a variation of binary search which gives the best result when the values of the list are uniformly distributed.
8. Which of the following is used to calculate the position in interpolation search?

   Assume, *s* = Element to search, Arr[] = Input array, low = Leftmost index of Arr[], high = Rightmost index of Arr[].
   A. *s* + ((*s* – Arr[low]) * (high – low)) / (Arr[high] – Arr[low])
   B. ((*s* – Arr[low]) * (high – low)) / (Arr[high] – Arr[low])
   C. high + ((*s* – Arr[low]) * (high – low)) / (Arr[high] – Arr[low])
   D. low + ((*s* – Arr[low]) * (high – low)) / (Arr[high] – Arr[low])

Moderate

9. What is the best-case complexity of a linear search?
   A. O(1) B. O(*n*.log(*n*))
   C. O(log(*n*)) D. O(*n*)

   Hint: The target element is at the first element of the array, hence O(1).
10. Binary search technique uses ____.
    A. Heuristic search
    B. Divide-and-reduce strategy
    C. Divide-and-conquer strategy
    D. Both B and C
11. Which of the following is not an application of binary search?
    A. Debugging
    B. Union of intervals
    C. To find the lower bound in an ordered sequence
    D. To search in an unordered list

    Hint: In the binary search, the elements in the list should be sorted. Hence, binary search in the unordered list is not an application.
12. Which of the following is a disadvantage of a linear search?
    A. Greater time complexities compared to other searching algorithms
    B. Requires more space
    C. Not easy to implement
    D. Not easy to understand

    Hint: The complexity of linear search is O(*n*), which is much greater than binary search complexity (O(log(*n*))). Linear search is easier to implement and understand than other searching techniques.

13. What is the worst-case complexity of binary search using recursion?
    A. O(n.log(n)) B. O(n)
    C. O(log(n)) D. O(n^2)
    Hint: Using the divide-and-conquer master theorem.

Higher-order Thinking Skills (HOTS)

14. Consider the following C function given below. The array list contains at least one element (n) and the array is sorted in ascending order.

```
int PA(int *list, int y, int n)
  {
    int a, b, c;
    a = 0;
    b = n-1;
    do
      {
        c = (a+b)/2;
        if (y <= list[c])
             b = c-1;
        if (list[c] <= y)
             a = c+1;
      }
    while (a <= b);
    if (list[c] == y)
        return(c);
    else
        return -1;
  }
```

Which one of the following statements is true for function PA?
    A. It will run into an infinite loop when y is not in the list.
    B. It will always find the maximum element in the list.
    C. It will return −1 even when y is present in the list.
    D. It is an implementation of binary search.
15. The average number of key comparisons done in a successful sequential search in a list of length n is:
    A. $(n + 1)/2$ B. $(n - 1)/2$
    C. $n/2$ D. $\log n$
16. Given an array arr = {15, 16, 78, 79, 89} and key = 79. Find the number of iterations until the element is found.
    A. 2 B. 1
    C. 3 D. 4
    Hint: Iteration 1: mid = 78; Iteration 2 : mid = 79;
17. In an interpolation search, the updated values of high and low in the list will be given by one option from the following, when the element being searched is lower than the value at the calculated index where position = current position.
    A. high = position – 1, low remains unchanged
    B. low = position + 1, high = high – 1
    C. low = position + 1, high = position – 1
    D. low = position + 1, high remains unchanged
18. Find the fastest search method when the input list has uniformly distributed values that are not sorted.
    A. Linear search
    B. Binary search
    C. Interpolation search
    D. None of these
    Hint: Linear search is the searching method which can be applied to lists which are not sorted and time complexity this method is O(n) in the worst case.

Short Answer-type Questions

Easy

1. 'Finding whether an element is present in a list or not'. - Explain the above statement with an example.
2. What are the differences between linear search and binary search?
3. Which Python operator is used to search an element from a list of elements?

Moderate

4. What are the prerequisites of binary searching?
5. Compare the binary search and the interpolation search.
6. How can we calculate the average- and worst-case complexity of binary search?
7. Give some examples of computer applications where searching is most important.

Higher-Order Thinking Skills (HOTS)

8. Suppose an unsorted list is given. First sort the list and search for a particular element in the list. Design an algorithm and analyze the time complexity of this problem.
9. When and why interpolation search performs better than binary search?
10. What is the auxiliary space requirement for interpolation search?

Descriptive-type Questions

Easy

1. Write the algorithms of linear searching.
2. Explain the binary searching method with an example.
3. Illustrate the interpolation searching algorithm. Give an example to demonstrate the method.

Moderate

4. Compare linear search, binary search and interpolation search.
5. Compare the complexities of linear, binary and interpolation searching.
6. Explain the role of searching techniques in computer science, especially in information retrieval.

Higher-Order Thinking Skills (HOTS)

7. Given an array of n numbers, write an algorithm for checking whether there are any duplicate elements present.
8. Suppose a sorted array of n elements is given where duplicate elements may be there. Write a function to find the number of occurrences of a number (frequency of the elements).
9. Suppose an array of n numbers is given. Write an algorithm to check which element appears the maximum number of times in the array.

CASE STUDIES

1. Suppose an array of positive integers is given. All integers occur in the array an even number of times, except one, which occurs an odd number of times. Design an algorithm to find that number which is present an odd number of times and also analyze the time complexity of your algorithm.
   Example: Input = [10, 20, 30, 20, 30, 10, 30], Output = 30.
2. Suppose, an array where all elements of the array are in range 1 to n, and also all elements occur only once except three numbers which occur twice. Design an algorithm to find the two repeating numbers.
   For example, if the array is 2, 1, 3, 5, 2, 3, 4, the array size is 7 and n = 5. This input has n + 2 = 7 elements with all elements occurring once except 2 and 3 which occur twice. So the output should be 2, 3.

LAB EXERCISES

1. Write a C program that removes all duplicate elements from an array.
   Example:
   Enter array size: 5
   Enter 5 array elements: 10
   20
   10
   3
   10
   Original array is: 10 20 10 3 10
   New array is: 10 20 3
2. Write a Python program to search the frequency of the elements in a list.
   Original List: [10, 100, 10, 100, 20, 100, 20, 20, 400, 400, 150, 150, 25]
   Frequency of the elements in the list: Counter({100: 3, 20: 3, 10: 2, 400: 2, 150: 2, 25: 1})

ANSWER KEYS

Multiple Choice Questions

1. A	**4.** C	**7.** B	**10.** C	**13.** C	**16.** A
2. B	**5.** B	**8.** D	**11.** D	**14.** D	**17.** A
3. D	**6.** D	**9.** A	**12.** A	**15.** A	**18.** A

13 Hashing

CONTENTS

EXPECTED OUTCOMES OF THIS CHAPTER

After going through this chapter learners will be able

- ☑ To understand the concepts associated with hashing
- ☑ To explain popular hashing methods
- ☑ To introduce the different collision resolution techniques that occur during hashing
- ☑ To implement the different collision resolution techniques using C and Python.
- ☑ To analyse the hashing techniques using load factor
- ☑ To explain the concept of rehashing.

13.1 INTRODUCTION

Suppose we have 100 different books on computer science. We have to arrange these books on a bookshelf in such a way that searching the books will be efficient and convenient. What can we do if we have at most 100 entries with integer keys, but the keys are in the range 0 to 1,000,000,000? We still want to insert, delete, find in O(1) time, but do not want to use 1,000,000,000 memory cells to store only 100 entries. Here, hashing comes into play in an important role.

Hashing is a useful searching technique. Search techniques have been discussed in Chapter 12. Linear or sequential search requires O(n) comparisons to search for an element within a list. When the data size is large, we need a huge number of comparisons that are not desirable at all. On the other hand, binary search requires a much lesser number of comparisons, compared to linear search. $O(\log_2 n)$ average comparisons are required to search for an element from a sorted data set in binary search. In hashing, each data element is assigned a key (hash) or id. It involves less number of comparisons using keys, and searching can be performed in constant time O(1).

13.1.1 Definition

Hashing is the method of indexing and retrieving data to afford a faster way of finding the element using a hash key. In this approach, the time required to search for an element does not depend on the total number of elements. Using hashing data structure, a target element is searched for with constant time complexity. Hashing is an effective way to reduce the number of comparisons to search for an element in a data structure.

> **Note!**
> Hashing is a searching process with constant time O(1) to find an element from a list.

13.1.2 Hash Table and Hash Function

The hash table is an array of m elements (indexed 0 to $m - 1$). It is just an array that maps a key into the data structure with the help of a hash function such that insertion, deletion, and search operations are performed with constant time complexity O(1). The idea is to discover the location of a key by simply examining the keys. For this, we need to design a hash function.

We use a hash table to store the data for the purpose explained above. The hash key value is used while inserting the data values into the hash table. The hash table stores the location of the key k with index $H(k)$. The hash key value is used to map with an index in the hash table. Thus, *the hash key is generated for all the data using the function called hash function.* So, every element in the hash table is supported by the hash key value generated using the hash function. Hence, a hash function is a function $H(k)$ that transforms a key into an address. The hash function must be consistent across its domain. It is a function that takes data (i.e., key) as input and converts a hash value (integer) as output, which maps the data to a particular index (in between 0 to $m - 1$) in the hash table. The main idea behind any hash function is to find a one-to-one correspondence between the key value and index in the hash table where the key value will be placed. Figure 13.1 shows the above mapping or correspondence between the key set (K) and index set (I), where H denotes the mapping function from K to I.

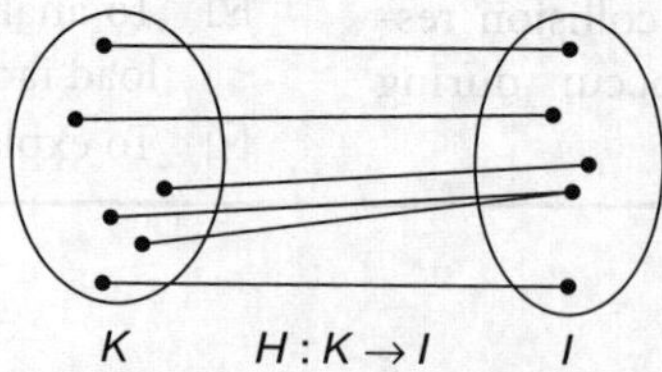

Figure 13.1 Mapping between hash key (K) and index set (I) for hashing

A hash function can be expressed as $H: K \rightarrow I$, where H is a hash function, K is a set of keys, and I is an index (or a set of memory address). A hash function has the following important basic requirements:

- To design a good hashing function, the function H should be very simple, straightforward, and quick to compute.

- The function H should attain an even distribution of keys that occur across the range of indices. It should provide a uniform distribution across the hash table, and should not result in clustering.
- *Collisions occur when pairs of elements are mapped to the same hash value.* Such incidents should be avoided. Irrespective of how good a hash function is, collisions occur. Therefore, to maintain the performance of a hash table, it is important to manage collisions through various collision resolution techniques, which will be discussed in the following sections.

Figure 13.2 describes the basic concept of hashing and hash tables.

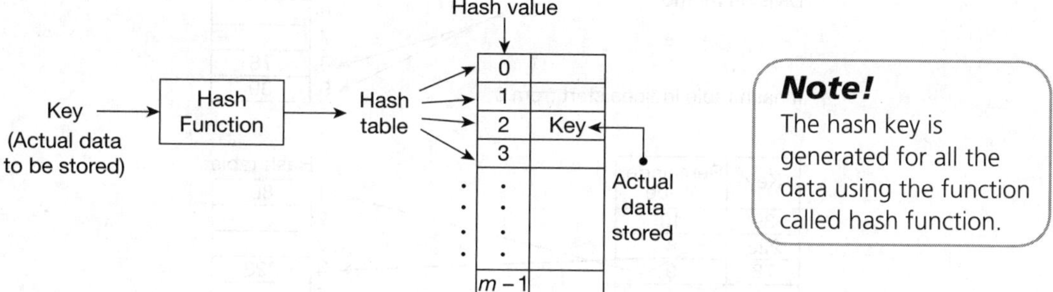

Figure 13.2 Basic concept of hashing and hash table

13.2 POPULAR HASHING METHODS

The following are some popular hash functions which are commonly applied in various applications.

13.2.1 Division Method

This method is the simplest of all the methods of hashing. A key k is to be divided by m (a prime number, or a number without small divisors or hash table size) and then the remainder is to be used as a memory index to store the key. It is obtained by using the modulo operator. First, we have to convert the key to an integer, then divide it by the size of the index range, and take the remainder as the result. We are trying to divide by memory size (hash table size), otherwise many memory locations will be wasted or empty. The number m is usually chosen as a prime number or a number without small divisors since this usually minimizes the number of collisions. The form of $H(k)$ is given below:

$$H(k)=\begin{cases} k \,\%\, m; & \text{if indices start from 0} \\ (k \,\%\, m)+1; & \text{if indices start from 1} \end{cases}$$

Example 13.1

Consider a hash table with 10 slots and keys 39, 223, 78, and 80.

$H(39) = 39 \bmod 10 = 9$, if indices start from 0.
$H(39) = 39 \bmod 10 = 9 + 1 = 10$, if indices start from 1.

$H(223) = 223 \bmod 10 = 3$, if indices start from 0.
$H(223) = 223 \bmod 10 = 3 + 1 = 4$, if indices start from 1.

$H(78) = 78 \bmod 10 = 8$, if indices start from 0.
$H(78) = 78 \bmod 10 = 8 + 1 = 9$, if indices start from 1.

$H(80) = 80 \bmod 10 = 0$, if indices start from 0.
$H(80) = 80 \bmod 10 = 0 + 1 = 1$, if indices start from 1.

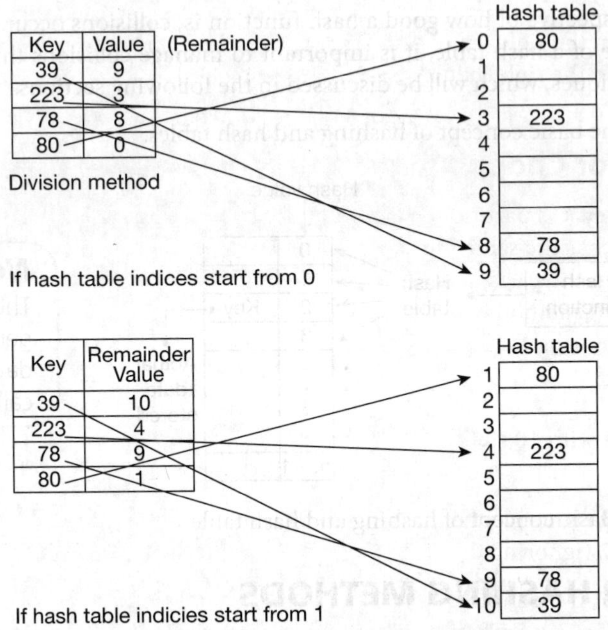

Figure 13.3 Hash table for division method for indices starts from 0 and 1

13.2.2 Mid-square Method

This mid-square-based hash function has been used in many applications. The key k is squared, and then some particular digits from the middle of the k^2 (for example 3rd or 4th digits from right-hand side [i.e., from the least significant bit or LSB] of the number) are extracted to get memory location.

$$H(k) = \text{some digits of } (k^2)$$

where k^2 is obtained by selecting an appropriate number of digits from the middle of the square of the key value k. This method is criticized as it is time consuming. However, it provides better results when uniform distribution of the keys over the hash table is considered.

Example 13.2

Consider a hash table with 10 slots and keys 39, 223, 78 and 80. Here, we are taking the 3rd digits from the right-hand side (i.e., from LSB) of the square number of each key.

$H(39)$ = 3rd digit from the right-hand side after squaring 39 ($39^2 = 1521$) = 5, if the indices start from 0.
$H(39)$ = 3rd digit from the right-hand side after squaring 39 ($39^2 = 1521$) = 5 + 1 = 6, if the indices start from 1.

$H(223)$ = 3rd digit from the right-hand side after squaring 223 ($223^2 = 49729$) = 7, if the indices start from 0.
$H(223)$ = 3rd digit from the right-hand side after squaring 223 ($223^2 = 49729$) = 7 + 1 = 8, if the indices start from 1.

$H(78)$ = 3rd digit from the right-hand side after squaring 78 ($78^2 = 6084$) = 0, if the indices start from 0.
$H(78)$ = 3rd digit from the right-hand side after squaring 78 ($78^2 = 6084$) = 0 + 1 = 1, if the indices start from 1.

$H(80)$ = 3rd digit from the right-hand side after squaring 80 ($80^2 = 6400$) = 4, if the indices start from 0.
$H(80)$ = 3rd digit from the right-hand side after squaring 80 ($80^2 = 6400$) = 4 + 1 = 5, if the indices start from 1.

13.2.3 Folding or Chopping Method

In this method, the key k is partitioned into several subparts $k_1, k_2, k_3, \ldots, k_n$, where each part, except possibly the last part, has the same number of digits as the required address. The key is partitioned into several parts, and then the parts are added together. There are many variations of this method. One of them is the fold shifting method where the even number parts are reversed before the addition. The parts are added together ignoring the last carry as given by $H(k) = k_1 + k_2 + k_3 + \ldots + k_n$.

Example 13.3

Consider a hash table with 10 slots and keys 39, 223, 78 and 80. Here, we are partitioning the key with size one digit.

$H(39) = 3 + 9 = 12 = 2$ (ignoring the carry '1'), if the indices start from 0.
$H(39) = 3 + 9 = 12 = 2$ (ignoring the carry '1') = 2 + 1 = 3, if the indices start from 1.

$H(223) = 2 + 2 + 3 = 7$, if the indices start from 0.
$H(223) = 2 + 2 + 3 = 7 = 7 + 1 = 8$, if the indices start from 1.

$H(78) = 7 + 8 = 15 = 5$ (ignoring the carry '1'), if the indices start from 0.
$H(78) = 7 + 8 = 15 = 5$ (ignoring the carry '1') = 5 + 1 = 6, if the indices start from 1.

$H(80) = 8 + 0 = 8$, if the indices start from 0.
$H(80) = 8 + 0 = 8 = 8 + 1 = 9$, if the indices start from 1.

13.3 COLLISION RESOLUTION TECHNIQUES

If the two keys, k_1 and k_2, take the same memory position in the hash table for some hash function, then it is called a collision. The situation of collision occurs when more than one key maps to the same location of hashes. In this situation, two or more elements are qualified to be mapped to the same location in the hash table. Suppose we have a class of 24 students, and if we ask all students about their date of birth, then the probability that two students have the same date will be calculated as follows:

There are 365 days in a year if it is not a leap year. Suppose, one student marks a date in a particular calendar, then the probability of the second student having a different birthday now is 364/365. This way, the probability that the third student has a different birthday from the previous two students is 363/365. If we continue on the same lines, then the probability of the nth student having a different birthday is $(365 - n + 1)/365$. So, we can get the probability that n students all have a different birthday is:

$$(364/365) \times (363/365) \times (362/365) \times \ldots \times ((365 - n + 1)/365)).$$

This probability is near 0.5 when $n \geq 24$. So, almost fifty percent chances are there for a collision of birthdays. Here, 365 is the size of the hash table, and there are 24 elements to be mapped. We have 50% chances for the collision. So, the collision cannot be avoided. There are two important methods to resolve collisions in the hashing technique. Figure 13.4 shows that collision resolution techniques can be divided into two groups.

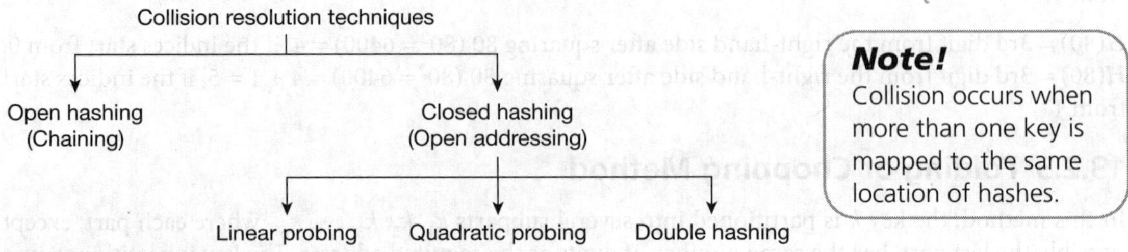

Figure 13.4 Different collision resolution techniques

> **Note!**
> Collision occurs when more than one key is mapped to the same location of hashes.

13.3.1 Closed Hashing or Open Addressing

The simplest method to resolve a collision is closed hashing. In this method, the hash table is considered as circular so that when the last location is reached, the search proceeds to the first location of the table. This is why the method is called a closed hashing. The search process will continue until any one of the following cases occurs:

1. The key value is found.
2. When the collision occurs, use a systematic procedure to store elements in a free location of the hash table until an unoccupied location is encountered.
3. It continues until the index reaches the location where the search was started.

> **Note!**
> Closed hashing or open addressing is considered as circular when the last location is reached, the search proceeds to the first location of the table.

Linear Probing

Suppose, two keys k_1 and k_2 are trying to occupy the same location (L) in the hash table. Now to solve this collision, search memory location for an empty place like $L + 1, L + 2, \ldots, L + i$. If any location is available, then we have to store the key in the first available location.

Example 13.4

Consider a hash table with 7 slots and keys are 22, 18, 32, 23, 16 and 15. Table indices start from 0 and the collision resolution technique is linear probing, and we are using division methods.

Initially, the hash table is empty.

$H(22) = 22 \bmod 7 = 1$

$H(18) = 18 \bmod 7 = 4$

$H(32) = 32 \bmod 7 = 4$ (Collision occurs – 32 is placed next empty position)

$H(23) = 23 \bmod 7 = 2$

$H(16) = 16 \bmod 7 = 2$ (Collision occurs – 16 is placed next empty position)

$H(15) = 15 \bmod 7 = 1$ (Collision occurs – 15 is placed next empty position)

All steps are described in the following Fig. 13.5.

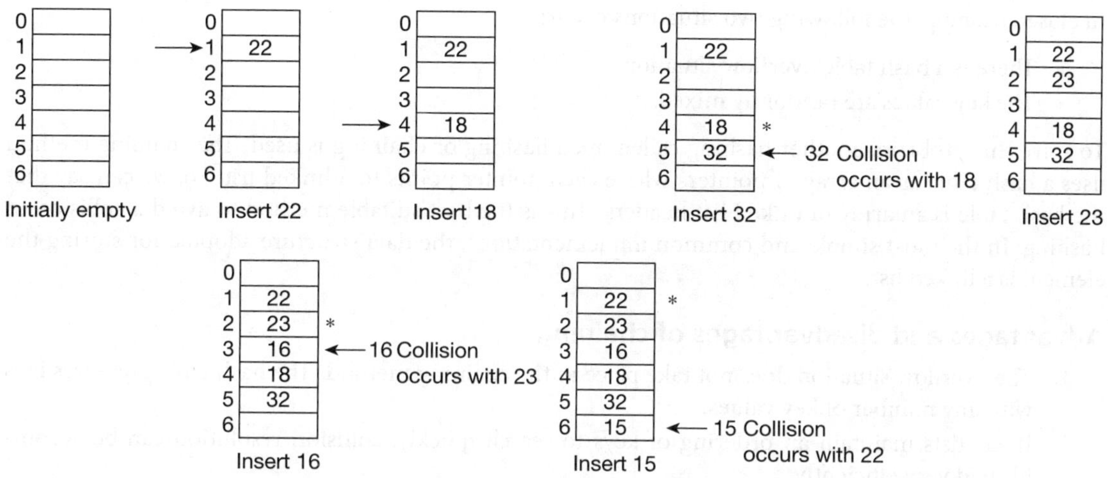

Figure 13.5 Example of linear probing with the division method

Quadratic Probing

A *probe* is defined as an access to a table location. As clusters increase in length, the average number of probes needed for insert and search operations also increase. This is especially evident for unsuccessful search, since they will only terminate at an empty location (at the end of the cluster). With the increase of cluster length, the run-times for insert along with search operations will increase and will approach O(*N*). When half of the hash table is filled, there is a tendency towards clustering. The key values are clustered in large groups and hence sequential search becomes slower and slower.

When the collision resolution methods are applied, the keys are placed in a clustered way since the next empty slots to the coincident location are positioned. Quadratic probing is a collision resolution method that eliminates the above clustering problem of linear probing. For quadratic probing, the next location after L will be $L + 1^2$, $L + 2^2$, ..., $L + i^2$, for $i = 1, 2, 3, \ldots$. We have to store the key in the first available position. As half of the hash table is filled, there is a tendency towards clustering. The key values are clustered in large groups and as a result, sequential search becomes slower and slower.

Double Hashing

When two hash functions are used to avoid clustering, then it is called double hashing. It uses the idea of applying a second hash function to the key when a collision occurs. Double hashing function can be defined as,

$$\text{Double\_Hash (key)} = (\text{Hash1(key)} + i * \text{Hash2(key)})\ \%\ \text{Hash\_Table\_Size}$$

$$\text{Hash1(key)} = \text{key}\ \%\ \text{Hash\_Table\_Size}$$

$$\text{Hash2(key)} = \text{PRIME} - (\text{key}\ \%\ \text{PRIME})$$

where Hash1() and Hash2() are two hash functions, Hash_Table_Size is the size of the hash table and PRIME is a prime number smaller than the Hash_Table_Size. We should repeat the above hash calculation by increasing *i* when collision occurs.

13.3.2 Open Hashing or Chaining

In closed hashing, the following two situations occur:

- There is a hash table overflow situation.
- The key values are randomly mixed.

To solve this problem, another hashing called open hashing or chaining is used. The chaining method uses a hash table as an array of pointers where each pointer points to a linked list. So, we can say that the hash table is an array of linked list headers. This is the best suitable method to avoid a collision in hashing. In the most simple and common implementations, the data structure adopted for storing the element is a linked list.

Advantages and disadvantages of chaining

1. The overflow situation does not take place in the chaining method. The hash table preserves lists with any number of key values.
2. If the lists maintain an ordering of keys to search quickly, collision resolution can be accomplished very efficiently.
3. Insertion and deletion are quick and straightforward tasks in chaining. Deletion takes place in the same way as the deletion of a node in a singly linked list.
4. Chaining uses dynamic memory management strategy, and hence it is best suitable in applications having several key values varying drastically.
5. Extra storage space is required to be allocated for maintaining the linked list in chaining.

> **Note!**
> In open hashing or chaining, a hash table is an array of pointers where each pointer points to a linked list.

Example 13.5

Consider a hash table with 7 slots with keys 22, 18, 32, 23, 16 and 15. The table indices start from 0, and the collision resolution technique is chaining. We are using the division method here.

Initially, the hash table is empty.

$H(22) = 22 \bmod 7 = 1$ (List header number)

$H(18) = 18 \bmod 7 = 4$ (List header number)

$H(32) = 32 \bmod 7 = 4$ (List header number)

$H(23) = 23 \bmod 7 = 2$ (List header number)

$H(16) = 16 \bmod 7 = 2$ (List header number)

$H(15) = 15 \bmod 7 = 1$ (List header number)

Figure 13.6 presents the above allocations through linked lists.

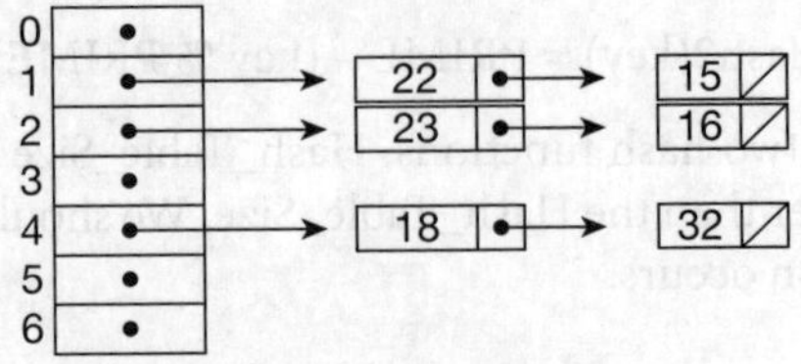

Figure 13.6 Example of chaining

13.3.3 Closed vs. Open Hashing

Closed hashing incorporates three ways of collision resolutions, among which linear and quadratic probing suffers from clustering problems. Double hashing has been introduced to take care of this problem. Both linear and quadratic probing are very simple to compute, and efficient with respect to cache performances. Double hashing requires more computations, and it has less cache performance compared to linear and quadratic probing methods. A comparison between closed and open hashing is given in Table 13.1 below:

Table 13.1 Differences between open and closed hashing

Closed hashing (or Open addressing)	Open hashing (or Chaining)
Closed hashing requires more computation.	Open hashing is simpler to implement.
The table may become full in closed hashing.	Hash tables never fill up in open hashing. We can always add more elements to the chain.
Closed hashing requires extra efforts to avoid clustering (or load factor).	Open hashing is less sensitive to the hash function (or load factors).
Closed hashing is used when the number of keys and frequency are known.	Open hashing is often used when it is unknown, how many and how frequently keys may be inserted or deleted.
Closed hashing offers better cache performance since everything is stored in the same table.	Cache performance of open hashing is not good since keys are stored using a linked list.
A slot can be used even if the input does not map to it in closed hashing.	The memory space becomes wasted since some parts of the hash table are never used in open hashing.
No linking takes place in closed hashing.	Open hashing uses extra space for links.

13.4 IMPLEMENTATIONS OF COLLISION RESOLUTION TECHNIQUES

The following subsections present the implementations of collision resolution techniques with C and Python. Closed hashing or open addressing techniques are implemented using C and Python source codes. On the other hand, the implementation of open hashing or chaining is nothing but an application of linked list programs discussed in Chapter 4 and not given here.

13.4.1 Linear Probing with C

CProg-13.1 Implementation of linear probing for collision resolution

```
#include<stdio.h>
#include<stdlib.h>
#define MAX 10
```

```
int a[MAX];
void linear_probing(int, int[]);
void linear_probing_search(int key, int a[MAX]);
void display(int a[MAX]);

/* Driver function */
int main()
   {
     int i, key, ch ;
     for(i = 0; i < MAX; i++)
     a[i] = '\0';
     do{
         printf("\n\n Program for insertion/searching keys with
linear probing ");
         printf("\n 1. Insert keys ");
         printf("\n 2. Search key ");
         printf("\n 3. Display keys ");
         printf("\n 4. Exit ");
         printf("\n Enter your choice: ");
         scanf("%d",&ch);
         switch(ch)
            {
               case 1: do{
                    printf("\n Enter key value [type -1 for
stop]: ");
                   scanf("%d", &key);
                   if(key != -1)
                        linear_probing(key, a);
                   }while(key != -1);
                   display(a);
                   break;
              case 2: printf("\n Enter search key value: ");
                   scanf("%d", &key);
                   linear_probing_search(key, a);
                   break;
               case 3: display(a);
                       break;
               default: exit(1);
            }
        } while(ch != 4);
   }

/* Function linear_probing find a location for key and insert it */
void linear_probing(int key, int a[MAX])
```

```
    {
      int loc;
      loc = key % MAX;
      while(a[loc] !='\0')
         loc = ++loc % MAX;
      a[loc] = key;
    }

/* Function linear_probing_search find a location for a key
*/
void linear_probing_search(int key, int a[MAX])
    {
      int loc;
      loc = key % MAX;
      while((a[loc] != key) && (a[loc] != '\0'))
          loc =++ loc%MAX;
      if (a[loc] != '\0')
            printf("\n Searching is successful at index %d",
loc);
      else
          printf("\n Searching is unsuccessful ");
    }

/* Function for displaying results */
void display(int a[MAX])
    {
      int i;
      printf("\n List of keys ('0' indicate that the location
is empty): \n");
      for (i = 1; i < MAX; i++)
        printf(" %d ", a[i]);
    }
/* End of program */
```

Output

```
Program for insertion/searching keys with linear probing
1. Insert keys
2. Search key
3. Display keys
4. Exit
Enter your choice: 1
Enter key value [type -1 for stop]: 3
Enter key value [type -1 for stop]: 2
Enter key value [type -1 for stop]: 4
```

```
Enter key value [type -1 for stop]: -1
List of keys ('0' indicate that the location is empty):
0  2  3  4  0  0  0  0  0
Enter your choice: 2
Enter search key value: 4
Searching is successful at index: 4
Enter your choice: 4
```

> **Programming Tips!**
> `linear_probing()` finds a location for a key and then inserts it. `linear_probing_search()` finds a location for a key.

13.4.2 Linear Probing with Python

PyProg-13.1 Implementation of linear probing for collision resolution

```
# Importing sys package
import sys

# Initialization
size = int(input("Enter the Hash Table size: "))
modfn = 10
newlist = [None for x in range(size)]
print(newlist)

# Function for insertion
def insert(listname, key):
   pos = key%modfn

   while(pos <= len(listname)):

           if listname[pos] != None:
               pos = pos+1

               if pos == key%modfn:
                   print("Cannot insert!!!Hash table full")
                   break
               elif pos >= len(listname):
                   pos = 0
           else:
               listname[pos] = key
               break
   return listname

# Function for display
def display(listname):
   for i in range(len(listname)):
       print(i, end = " ")
       print(listname[i])
```

```
# Function for search element
def search(listname, key):
   pos = key%modfn
   flag = 0
   while(pos < len(listname)):

           if listname[pos] == key:
               print("Successfully found", key, " at ", pos)
               flag = 1
               break
           else:
               pos = pos+1
   if flag == 0:
       print("Element ", key , " not found")

#Driver program
while(1):
   print(" 1-> Insert\n 2-> Display\n 3-> Searching\n 4-> Exit\n")
   choice=int(input("Enter your Choice: "))

   if choice == 1:
       ele = int(input("Enter key element to insert: \n"))
       insert(newlist, ele)

   elif choice == 2:
       display(newlist)

   elif choice == 3:
       ele = int(input("Enter key element to search: \n"))
       search(newlist, ele)

   else:
       sys.exit()
## end program
```

Output

```
Enter the Hash Table size: 5
[None, None, None, None, None]
1-> Insert
2-> Display
3-> Searching
4-> Exit

Enter your Choice: 1
Enter key element to insert:
3
```

```
1-> Insert
2-> Display
3-> Searching
4-> Exit

Enter your Choice: 1
Enter key element to insert:
2
1-> Insert
2-> Display
3-> Searching
4-> Exit

Enter your Choice: 1
Enter key element to insert:
4
1-> Insert
2-> Display
3-> Searching
4-> Exit

Enter your Choice: 2
0 None
1 None
2 2
3 3
4 4
1-> Insert
2-> Display
3-> Searching
4-> Exit

Enter your Choice: 3
Enter key element to search:
2
Successfully found 2  at  2
1-> Insert
2-> Display
3-> Searching
4-> Exit

Enter your Choice: 4
```

Programming Tips!

`insert()` adds a key into the hash table and `search()` finds a location for a key within a hash table.

13.4.3 Quadratic Probing with C

CProg-13.2 Implementation of quadratic probing for collision resolution

```
#include<stdio.h>
#include<stdlib.h>
#define MAX 10

int a[MAX];
void quardratic_probing(int, int[]);
void quardratic_probing_search(int key, int a[MAX]);
void display(int a[MAX]);

/* Driver function */
int main()
   {
     int i, key, ch ;
     for(i = 0; i < MAX; i++)
     a[i] = '\0';
     do{
         printf("\n\n Program for insertion/searching keys
with quadratic probing ");
         printf("\n 1. Insert keys ");
         printf("\n 2. Search key ");
         printf("\n 3. Display keys ");
         printf("\n 4. Exit ");
         printf("\n Enter your choice ");
         scanf("%d", &ch);
         switch(ch)
           {
            case 1:
               do {
                    printf("\n Enter key value [type -1 for
stop] ");
                    scanf("%d", &key);
                    if(key != -1)
                         quardratic_probing(key, a);
                 }while(key != -1);
              display(a);
              break;
            case 2:
              printf("\n Enter search key value ");
              scanf("%d", &key);
              quardratic_probing_search(key, a);
              break;
```

```
                case 3:
                    display(a);
                    break;
                    default:
                    exit(1);
                }
            }while(ch != 4);
        return 0;
    }

void quardratic_probing(int key, int a[MAX])
    {
        int loc, i = 1;
        loc = key % MAX;
        while (a[loc] !='\0')
          {
            loc = (key % MAX + i*i) % MAX;
            i++;
          }
        a[loc] = key;
    }

/* Find a location for a key  */
void quardratic_probing_search(int key, int a[MAX])
    {
        int loc;
        loc = key % MAX;
        while((a[loc] != key) && (a[loc] !=-1))
           loc = ++loc % MAX;
        if(a[loc] != '\0')
         printf("\n Searching is successful at index %d", loc);
        else
           printf("\n Searching is unsuccessful ");
    }

void display(int a[MAX])
    {
        int i;
        printf("\n List of keys ('0' indicate that the location
is empty): \n");
        for(i = 0; i < MAX; i++)
            printf(" %d ", a[i]);
    }
/* End of program */
```

Output

```
Program for insertion/searching keys with quadratic probing
1. Insert keys
2. Search key
3. Display keys
4. Exit
Enter your choice: 1
Enter key value [type -1 for stop]: 3
Enter key value [type -1 for stop]: 4
Enter key value [type -1 for stop]: 5
Enter key value [type -1 for stop]: -1
List of keys ('0' indicate that the location is empty):
0  0  0  3  4  5  0  0  0  0
Enter your choice: 2
Enter search key value: 3
Searching is successful at index: 3
Enter your choice: 4
```

Programming Tips!

`quardratic_probing()` inserts a key into the hash table. `quardratic_probing_search()` finds the location for a key within a hash table.

13.4.4 Quadratic Probing with Python

PyProg-13.2 Implementation of quadratic probing for collision resolution

```
# Importing sys package
import sys

# Initialization
size = int(input("Enter the Hash Table size: "))
modfn = 10
newlist = [None for x in range(size)]
print(newlist)

# Function for insertion
def insert(listname, key):
   pos = key%modfn
   i = 0
   while(pos <= len(listname)):
           if listname[pos] != None:
               pos = (key % modfn + i*i) % modfn
               i += 1
               if pos == key%modfn:
```

```
                    print("Cannot insert!!!Hash table full")
                    break
                elif pos >= len(listname):
                    pos = 0
            else:
                listname[pos] = key
                break
    return listname

# Function for display
def display(listname):
    for i in range(len(listname)):
        print(i, end = " ")
        print(listname[i])

# Function for search element
def search(listname, key):
    pos = key%modfn
    flag = 0
    while(pos<len(listname)):
            if listname[pos] == key:
                print("Successfully found", key, " at ", pos)
                flag = 1
                break
            else:
                pos = pos + 1
    if flag == 0:
        print("Element ", key, " not found")

#Driver codes
while(1):
    print(" 1-> Insert\n 2-> Display\n 3-> Searching\n 4->
Exit\n")
    choice = int(input("Enter your Choice: "))
    if choice == 1:
        ele=int(input("Enter key element to insert: \n"))
        insert(newlist, ele)
    elif choice == 2:
        display(newlist)
    elif choice == 3:
        ele=int(input("Enter key element to search: \n"))
        search(newlist,ele)
    else:
        sys.exit()
## end program
```

Output

```
Enter the Hash Table size: 5
[None, None, None, None, None]
1-> Insert
2-> Display
3-> Searching
4-> Exit
Enter your Choice: 1
Enter key element to insert: 3
Enter your Choice: 1
Enter key element to insert: 2
Enter the Hash Table size: 5
[None, None, None, None, None]
Enter your Choice: 1
Enter key element to insert: 1
Enter your Choice: 1
Enter key element to insert: 3
Enter your Choice: 2
0 None
1 1
2 2
3 3
4 None
Enter your Choice: 4
```

Programming Tips!

`insert()` adds a key into the hash table and `search()` finds a location for a key within a hash table using quadratic probing method.

13.4.5 Double Hashing with C

CProg-13.3 Implementation of double hashing for collision resolution

```
#include<stdio.h>
#include<stdlib.h>
#define MAX 10

int a[MAX];
void double_hashing(int , int[]);
void double_hashing_search(int key, int a[MAX]);
void display(int a[MAX]);

/* Driver function */
int main()
   {
     int i, key, ch;
     for(i = 0; i < MAX; i++)
     a[i] = '\0';
     do{
```

```
        printf("\n Program for searching keys with double hashing
");
        printf("\n 1. Insert keys ");
        printf("\n 2. Search key ");
        printf("\n 3. Display keys ");
        printf("\n 4. Exit ");
        printf("\n Enter your choice: ");
        scanf("%d", &ch);
        switch(ch)
          {
           case 1:
                do{
                 printf("\nEnter key value [Enter -1 for Exit]: ");
                    scanf("%d", &key);
                    if (key != -1)
                       double_hashing(key, a);
                  }while(key != -1);
                break;
           case 2:
                printf("\n Enter search key value: ");
                scanf("%d", &key);
                double_hashing_search(key, a);
                break;
           case 3:
                display(a);
                  break;
           default: exit(1);
          }
      }while(ch != 4);
  }

/* Find the location for a key and insert it */
void double_hashing(int key, int a[MAX])
  {
     int loc, i = 0;
     loc = key % MAX;
     while (a[loc] !='\0')
     loc = (loc + ++i*(key % (MAX -1))) % MAX;
     a[loc] = key;
     display(a);
  }

/* Find the location for a key */
void double_hashing_search(int key, int a[MAX])
  {
     int loc, i = 0;
     loc = key % MAX;
```

```
    while((a[loc] != key) && (a[loc] !='\0'))
        loc = (loc + ++i*(key % (MAX -1))) % MAX;
    if (a[loc] != '\0')
       printf("\n Searching is successful at index %d",loc);
    else
        printf("\n Search is unsuccessful ");
  }

void display(int a[MAX])
  {
    int i;
     printf("\n List of keys, 0 indicate that the location
is empty \n");
    for (i = 0; i < MAX; i++)
    printf(" %d ", a[i]);
  }
/* End of program */
```

Output

```
Program for searching keys with double hashing
1. Insert keys
2. Search key
3. Display keys
4. Exit
Enter your choice: 1
Enter key value [Enter -1 for Exit]: 5
List of keys, 0 indicate that the location is empty
0  0  0  0  0  5  0  0  0  0
Enter key value [Enter -1 for Exit]: 3
List of keys, 0 indicate that the location is empty
0  0  0  3  0  5  0  0  0  0
Enter key value [Enter -1 for Exit]: 4
List of keys, 0 indicate that the location is empty
0  0  0  3  4  5  0  0  0  0
Enter key value [Enter -1 for Exit]: -1
Enter your choice: 2
Enter search key value: 3
Searching is successful at index 3
Enter your choice: 3
List of keys, 0 indicate that the location is empty
0  0  0  3  4  5  0  0  0  0
Enter your choice: 4
exit status 1
```

Programming Tips!

`double_hashing()` inserts a key into the hash table and `double_hashing_search()` finds a location for a key within a hash table using double hashing.

13.4.6 Double Hashing with Python

PyProg-13.3 Implementation of double hashing for collision resolution

```
# Importing sys package
import sys

# Initialization
size = int(input("Enter the Hash Table size: "))
modfn = 10
newlist = [None for x in range(size)]
print(newlist)

# Function for insertion
def insert(listname, key):
    pos = key%modfn
    i = 0
    while(pos <= len(listname)):
            if listname[pos] != None:
                pos = (pos + ++i*(key % (modfn -1))) % modfn
                i += 1
                if pos == key%modfn:
                    print("Cannot insert!!!Hash table full")
                    break
                elif pos >= len(listname):
                    pos = 0
            else:
                listname[pos] = key
                break
    return listname

# Function for display
def display(listname):
    for i in range(len(listname)):
        print(i,end=" ")
        print(listname[i])


def search(listname,key):
    pos = key%modfn
    flag = 0
    while(pos < len(listname)):
            if listname[pos] == key:
                print("Successfully found", key, " at ", pos)
                flag = 1
                break
```

```
            else:
                pos = pos + 1
    if flag == 0:
        print("Element ", key , " not found")

#Driver program
while(1):
    print(" 1-> Insert\n 2-> Display\n 3-> Searching\n 4->
Exit\n")
    choice = int(input("Enter your Choice: "))
    if choice == 1:
        ele = int(input("Enter key element to insert: \n"))
        insert(newlist, ele)
    elif choice == 2:
        display(newlist)
    elif choice == 3:
        ele = int(input("Enter key element to search: \n"))
        search(newlist, ele)
    else:
        sys.exit()
## end program
```

Output

```
Enter the Hash Table size: 5
[None, None, None, None, None]
1-> Insert
2-> Display
3-> Searching
4-> Exit
Enter your Choice: 1
Enter key element to insert: 3
Enter your Choice: 1
Enter key element to insert: 4
Enter your Choice: 1
Enter key element to insert: 2
Enter your Choice: 2
0 None
1 None
2 2
3 3
4 4
Enter your Choice: 3
Enter key element to search:
3
Successfully found 3  at  3
Enter your Choice: 4
```

Programming Tips!

`insert()` adds a key into the hash table and `search()` finds a location for a key within a hash table using double hashing method.

13.5 ANALYSIS OF HASHING TECHNIQUES AND LOAD FACTOR

The capacity of the hash table is equal to the size of the array holding the data for hashing operation. *The load factor is the number of keys stored in the hash table divided by the capacity of the hash table.* The table size should be chosen so that the load factor is less than 1. According to the definition,

Load factor (α) = The number of keys stored in the table / Capacity of the table.

If you have a table that has 500 locations, and 250 of them are filled, the table has a load factor of 250 / 500 = 0.5.

If Load factor (α) = Constant, then the time complexity of insert, search and delete operations are all O(1). $\alpha = 0$ indicates an empty table. $\alpha = 0.5$ means the table is half-full. Similarly, $\alpha = 1$ indicates that the hash table is full. For closed hashing, α can never exceed 1 but in open chaining, there is no bar on the value of α.

> **Note!**
> The load factor is the number of keys stored in the hash table divided by the capacity of the hash table.

For linear probing, as α approaches 1, the number of collisions increases. The probability of a collision increases as the load factor increases. For open addressing, the load factor should not exceed 0.5. The threshold of a *hash table* is the product of the current capacity of the hash table and load factor.

So, Threshold = (Current capacity) * (Load factor).

For example, if the hash table is created with initial capacity of 16 and load factor of 0.75, then threshold will be: Threshold = 16 * 0.75 = 12.

> **Note!**
> The table size should be chosen so that the load factor is less than 1.

13.6 REHASHING TECHNIQUE

Rehashing means hashing again after the first attempt. If, at any stage, the hash table becomes full or overflow occurs, then it will be difficult to find a free slot for the new key. In this situation, a new hash table is created. This new hash table is double in length than the existing one. Now, the previous hash table is scanned, and each key is calculated again for a new table index. These calculated keys are then stored into the created hash table.

When the load factor increases to more than its predefined value (default value of load factor is 0.75), the complexity increases. To overcome this, the size of the array is doubled and all the values are hashed again, and stored in the new double-sized array to maintain a low load factor and low complexity. This might not give the required time complexity of O(1). So, rehashing must be done when increasing the size of the array to reduce the load factor and time complexity.

> **Note!**
> Rehashing means hashing again after the first attempt.

QUICK RECAP

- ☑ Hashing is an effective way to reduce the number of comparisons to search an element in a data structure. Hashing is a searching technique that takes constant time O(1) to find an element from a list.
- ☑ A hash table is an array of m elements (indexed 0 to $m - 1$) that maps a key into the data structure with the help of a hash function such that insertion, deletion and search operations are performed with constant time complexity O(1).
- ☑ The idea is to discover the location of a key by simply examining the key. For this, we need to design a hash function. Thus, the

hash key is generated for all the data using the function called hash function.

☑ There are three popular hashing methods. In the division method, a key k is to be divided by m (a prime number or hash table size) and then the remainder is to be used as a memory index to store the key. It is obtained by using the modulo operator.

☑ In the mid-square method, the key k is squared, and then some particular digits from the middle of the k^2 are extracted to get memory location.

☑ In the chopping or folding method, the key k is partitioned into several subparts $k_1, k_2, k_3, \ldots, k_n$, where each part, except possibly the last part, has the same number of digits as the required address. The key is partitioned into several parts, and then the parts are added together to get the memory location.

☑ If the two keys, k_1 and k_2, take the same memory position in the hash table for some hash function then it is called a collision. The situation of collision occurs when more than one key maps to the same location of hashes.

☑ Closed hashing and open hashing are the two ways for collision resolutions. In closed hashing, the hash table is considered as circular so that when the last location is reached, the search proceeds to the first location of the table. Open hashing is carried out in three ways: linear probing, quadratic probing, and double hashing.

☑ C and Python, both can efficiently implement the above three methods for collision resolution.

☑ Open hashing or chaining occurs either when a hash table is overflowed, or the key values are randomly mixed. It uses a hash table as an array of pointers where each pointer points to a linked list.

☑ The load factor is the number of keys stored in the hash table divided by the capacity of the hash table. The table size should be chosen so that the load factor is less than 1.

☑ Rehashing means hashing again after the first attempt. If, at any stage, the hash table becomes full or overflow occurs, then it will be difficult to find a free slot for the new key. In this situation, a new hash table is created, which is known as rehashing.

REVIEW QUESTIONS

Multiple Choice Questions (MCQ): Choose the Best Alternative

Easy

1. Which of the following techniques is a hash function?

   A. Open addressing B. Quadratic probing
   C. Chaining D. Closed addressing

2. The ratio of the number of items in a hash table to the table size, is called the ______.

   A. load factor. B. balance factor.
   B. item factor. D. All of these.

3. What is a hash function?

   A. A function has allocated memory to keys.
   B. A function that creates an array.
   C. A function that computes the location of the key in the array.
   D. A function that computes the location of the values in the array.

   Hint: In a hash table, there are fewer array positions than the keys, so the position of the key in the array has to be computed; this is done using the hash function.

4. What is the search complexity of direct addressing?

   A. O(n) B. O(log(n))
   C. O(1) D. O(n.log(n))

   Hint: Since every key has a unique array position, searching takes constant time.

5. Which of the following terms is not related to hashing?

   A. Probing B. Collision
   C. Load factor D. Balance

Moderate

6. Which of the following is not a requirement of a good hashing function?

A. Avoid collision

B. Make faster retrieval

C. Reduce the storage space

D. None of these.

7. The linear probing technique for collision resolution can lead to ________.

A. overflow

B. primary clustering

C. secondary clustering

D. efficiency storage utilization

8. If several elements are competing for the same bucket in the hash table, it is called ________.

A. Collision B. Diffusion

C. Replication D. Duplication

Hint: If several elements are in the same bucket, then a collision will occur among the elements. The collision is reduced by adding elements to a linked list and the head address of the linked list is placed in the hash table.

9. Which of the following is not a technique to avoid a collision?

A. Make the hash function appear random.

B. Use the chaining method.

C. Use uniform hashing.

D. Increasing hash table size.

Hint: On increasing hash table size, space complexity will increase as we need to reallocate the memory size of the hash table for every collision. It is not the best technique to avoid a collision. We can avoid collisions by making the hash function random, using chaining method and uniform hashing.

10. An advantage of chained hash table (external hashing) over the open addressing scheme is:

A. Worst case complexity of search operations is less.

B. Space used is less.

C. Deletion is easier.

D. None of the above.

Hint: In open addressing, we may not sometimes be able to delete the element though it is present if an empty place comes in between while searching for that element; whereas an external hashing scheme is free from these limitations. So, option C is the correct answer.

Higher-order Thinking Skills (HOTS)

11. Consider a hash table H with 20 slots that can store 1000 elements. The load factor α for H is ________.

A. 100 B. 0.05

C. 50 D. 0.5

Hint: Load factor = (No. of elements) / (No. of table slots) = 1000 / 20 = 50.

12. A hash function h defined by $h(\text{key})$ = key mod 7, with linear probing, is used to insert the keys 51, 52, 72, 48, 84, 32, 56 into a table indexed from 0 to 6. What will be the location of the key 32?

A. 3 B. 4

C. 5 D. 6

Hint: keys 51, 52, 72, 48, 84, 32, 56

$H(\text{key}) = \text{key mod } 7$

$H(51) = 51 \text{ mod } 7 = 2$

$H(52) = 52 \text{ mod } 7 = 3$

$H(72) = 72 \text{ mod } 7 = 2$

but 2 is already filled 51, linear probing is applied but 3 is also filled.

So, 72 will occupy 4.

$H(48) = 48 \text{ mod } 7 = 6$

$H(84) = 84 \text{ mod } 7 = 0$

$H(32) = 32 \text{ mod } 7 = 4$ but 4 is occupied by 72 so, it will occupy 5.

$H(56) = 56 \text{ mod } 7 = 0$. 0 is also occupied, so it will occupy 1.

So, Option C is correct.

13. If h is a hashing function and it is used to hash n keys into a table of size m where $n \le m$, what is the expected number of collisions involving a particular key x?

A. Less than n.

B. Less than 1.

C. Less than m.

D. Less than $n/2$.

14. A double hashing scheme considers the following two hash functions:

$h1(k) = k \text{ mod } 20$

$h2(k) = 1+(k \text{ mod } 15)$

Assume that the table size is 21. Then the address returned by probe 1 in the probe sequence (assume that the probe sequence begins at probe 0) for key value $k = 85$ is ________.

A. 16 B. 15

C. 17 D. 21

Hint: Table size = 21, key value k = 85, probe i = 1 (probe 1 in the probe sequence). According to double hashing formula, $(H1(k) + i * H1(k))$ mod (table size),

Now, $H1(k) = k \bmod 20 = 85 \bmod 20 = 5$, and $H2(k) = 1+(k \bmod 15) = 1+(85 \bmod 15) = 11$.

Address returned by probe 1 (Using to double hashing)

$= (H1(k) + i * H2(k)) \bmod (\text{table size}) = (5 + 11) \bmod 21 = 16 \bmod 21 = 16$.

15. Consider a hash table with 50 slots. Collisions are resolved using chaining. Assuming simple uniform hashing, what is the probability that the first 7 slots are unfilled after the first 3 insertions?

A. $(7 \times 7 \times 7)/50^3$.

B. $(43 \times 43 \times 43)/50^3$.

C. $(49 \times 48 \times 47)/50^3$.

D. $(50 \times 49 \times 48)/(3! \times 50^3)$

Hint: Probability that the first 7 slots are unfilled after the first 3 insertions

= (Probability of 1st element not entering in any of the first 7 slots) * (Probability that the second item does not go in any of the first 7 slots) * (Probability that the third item does not go in any of the first 7 slots)

$= (43/50) * (43/50) * (43/50)$

$= (43 \times 43 \times 43)/50^3$.

Short Answer-type Questions

Easy

1. What is a hash key?
2. What is a hash function?
3. What do you mean by a hash table?
4. What do you understand by quadratic probing and double hashing?
5. What are the differences between linear probing and quadratic probing?

Moderate

6. How is mid-square hashing different from division-based hashing methods?
7. How can we calculate the keys in rehashing?
8. How can we calculate the load factor?
9. If we compare open hashing and closed hashing, which of these is more advantageous?
10. Consider a hash table with 10 slots and keys 19, 23, 78 and 80. If indices start from 0, then what will be the value of $H(19)$, $H(23)$, $H(78)$, and $H(80)$?

Higher-Order Thinking Skills (HOTS)

11. "The table size should be chosen in such a way, so that the load factor is less than 1" – Explain and justify the statement.
12. "Hashing is a searching technique that takes constant time O(1) to find an element from a list" – Justify.
13. Suppose we have a class of 24 students and we ask all the students for their date of birth. Calculate the probability that two students have the same date.
14. Suppose the hash functions on integers are keys uniformly distributed over 10 buckets numbered 0 to 9 for i ranging from 0 to 100. Then what will be the hash function?
15. Mention a few problems criteria where hash tables are not suitable.

Descriptive-type Questions

Easy

1. State the principles of the hash table and draw a suitable diagram of the hash table.
2. Discuss the different types of collision resolution techniques with suitable diagrams.
3. Compare the division method, mid-square method and folding method.
4. Discuss briefly about rehashing technique.
5. What are the characteristics of a good hash function? Explain briefly.

Moderate

6. What is the load factor? Analyze the different types of collision resolution techniques with the help of load factor.
7. What is the advantage of hashing over linear and binary searching?
8. Explain the different popular hashing methods.
9. Consider a hash table with 7 slots and keys as 9, 23, 8 and 8. Find the hash table using the chopping or folding method.
10. Explain how chaining works.

Higher-Order Thinking Skills (HOTS)

11. Suppose you are given two arrays of unordered numbers. Explain the procedure to check whether both the arrays have the same set of numbers or not
12. Design an algorithm to implement collision resolution techniques and discuss the time complexities of the function.
13. Explain the different applications of hashing and explain why hashing is required for these applications.
14. Design an algorithm for implementation of the hash table with linear probing.

CASE STUDIES

1. Suppose we have an array of 52 elements. Out of them, 25 elements are unique, 12 elements are repeated 2 times and one element is repeated 3 times. Design an algorithm to find the element that is repeated 3 times in O(1) and analyze the time complexity.
2. Consider an array of n numbers. Design an algorithm to display all pairs of numbers whose sum is any specific integer using a hash table and analyze the time complexity of the algorithm.

LAB EXERCISES

1. Write a C program for division method and linear probing for the hashing.
2. Write a Python program to implement the chaining technique in hashing.

ANSWER KEYS

Multiple Choice Questions

1. B	**4.** C	**7.** B	**10.** C	**13.** C
2. A	**5.** D	**8.** A	**11.** C	**14.** A
3. C	**6.** C	**9.** D	**12.** B	**15.** B

14 File Organization

CONTENTS

EXPECTED OUTCOMES OF THIS CHAPTER

After going through this chapter learners will be able

- ☑ To understand how files and records can be placed on disks
- ☑ To explain the effective ways in which records can be organized into files
- ☑ To differentiate among different file types commonly used for file organization
- ☑ To explain the data structures to support file operations
- ☑ To implement simple file operations like read, write and append with C and Python.

14.1 INTRODUCTION

A file is a sequence of records and file organization refers to the physical structuring of records existing in a file. File organization controls the ways by which records are stored and accessed.

A file could be defined as a contiguous set of words or bytes. It is considered as a collection of data. Users can store different forms of information within a file. For example, source codes, images, texts documents, etc., are the data to be stored. Files are of different types depending on the information stored in a file and therefore each file has its own structure. It is the job of the operating system to map this sequence of files into physical memory. The part of an operating system that maps various files into the physical memory is called file organization and management system. Different file access methods are available, by which the information in the file can be accessed.

We consider storage, organization and accessing (or retrieval) of data while processing information using a computing device. The knowledge of data structure will help us to carry out all these data processing operations. Data structures deal with data in main memory whereas file structures deal with data in secondary storage devices that are stored in a file.

14.1.1 Definition

File organization is a method of arranging the records in a file when the file is stored on a disk. It refers to the way data is stored in a file. A relation is also typically stored as a file of records. A file is organized logically as a sequence of records whereas records are mapped onto disk blocks. Files are provided as a basic construct in operating systems; so we can assume the existence of a primary file system. Blocks are of a fixed size determined by the operating system whereas record sizes may vary. We may consider the retrieval of employee records in alphabetical order of name, for example. A good file organization sorts the file by employee name. But, if we want to retrieve all employees whose marks are in a certain range, a file ordered by employee name would not be a good file organization.

> **Note!**
> A file is a sequence of records stored as a contiguous set of words or bytes.

14.1.2 Advantages of File Organization

The following are the advantages of file organization:

- File organization helps quick retrieval of records.
- The records can be of different sizes but users can still access an organized file.
- File organization allows ease of file creation and maintenance.
- It offers efficient means of storing and information retrieval.
- In a few file organizations, the sorting makes it easy to access records.
- In a few file organizations, records are stored randomly but accessed directly.

> **Note!**
> File organization is a method of arranging the records in a file when the file is stored on a disk. It helps quick and efficient retrieval of records having different sizes.

14.2 CLASSIFICATION OF FILE ORGANIZATIONS

File organization incorporates various methods. Each method has pros and cons based on access or assortment. During file organization, the programmer decides the best-suited file organization method according to the requirements. Different types of file organizations are important because it determines the methods of access, efficiency, flexibility and storage devices to use.

There are six types of files according to the file organizations used for structuring the files. They are serial, sequential, direct or random access, indexed-sequential access, heap, and hash. These are explained below.

14.2.1 Serial Files

This type of file organization was used in early days of computer systems (1950–1960). The records were arranged one by one. If the user wanted to add a new record, it was included at the end of the file. Files were stored in magnetic tapes. In serial files, if the size of the file increases then the time required to access data increases. This happens because this file organization follows a linear searching style. It is useful in secondary files. A book without page numbers is an example of this structure. Here, searching will be difficult due to the absence of page numbers.

> **Note!**
> Serial files store the records arranged one by one.

14.2.2 Sequential Access Files

In this method, the information record is processed in order, one by one, in the file. This is the most common mode of accessing the files. For example, text editors usually access files in this fashion. There is no key value in this file organization. One gap is left so that new records can be added to maintain the order. These files were also stored in magnetic tapes. When the size of the file increases, the time required to access the data increases. This is because there is no key. The sequential access method is used in master files. An example of this is arranging cards in sequential order (A 2 3 4 5 6 7 8 9 10 J Q K).

> **Note!**
> Information record in the sequential access file is processed, one by one, in order.

14.2.3 Direct- or Random-Access Files

A random-access data file enables us to read or write information anywhere in the file. It is also known as a direct-access file. In this method of record access, the file is viewed as a numbered sequence of blocks. The file allows arbitrary blocks to be read or written. There are no restrictions on the order of reading and writing for a direct access file. There are key values in a direct access file. CD-like disk devices use this type of file organization. Searching within this direct file is quite faster. It has a more complex structure compared to the last two file organizations.

> **Note!**
> A random- or direct-access data file enables us to read or write information anywhere in the file.

14.2.4 Indexed Sequential Access Files

Indexed sequential access file combines both sequential file and direct access file organization. This was invented by IBM. In an indexed sequential access file, records are stored randomly on a direct access device such as an external disk, by a primary key. This file has multiple alphanumeric keys according to which the records are ordered. The data can either be accessed sequentially or randomly using an index. The index is stored in a file and read into the memory when the file is opened. Searching is fast here since the index is searched first, and then the key is searched. This file organization is used in the banking system. For example, consider a book where topics are the keys and each topic has an index page number. Every topic is found in a particular page number.

> **Note!**
> Indexed sequential access file combines both sequential file and direct-access file organization.

14.2.5 Heap Files

It is the simplest and most basic type of file organization. It works with data blocks. In this method, a particular record is inserted at the end row. When the data block is full, the new record is stored in another block. This new data may not be the next data block. It can be stored in any data block in the memory. The heap file is also known as an unordered file. It is a very good method of file organization for bulk insertions. This method is inefficient for large record-based files because it takes more time to search and modify the records. Let us suppose five records A1, A3, A4, A5, and A6 are in a heap and now we want to insert a new record A2 in the heap after A1. If there is no space between A1 and A3, then it may be inserted in any of the selected space between the consecutive memory blocks by the operating system.

> **Note!**
> The heap file is the simplest and most basic type of file organization and it works with data blocks.

14.2.6 Hash Files

This file organization uses the calculation of hash function on the fields of records. The hash function determines the location of the memory block where the records are to be placed. The memory address, identified by generating the hash key, is used to insert the record. In the same way, when a new record has to be retrieved, the address is generated using the hash key. The same process is applied in the case of delete and update operations. Searching and sorting the entire file is not required in this file organization.

> **Note!**
> Hash file organization uses the calculation of hash function on fields of the records.

14.3 FILE OPERATIONS

When a file is used, information is read and accessed using computer memory. There are several operations that can be performed on the information of the file. The following eight operations can be performed when working on or accessing a file:

14.3.1 Create

This operation *creates a file in the memory*. It is the first operation to deal with a file. Two steps are necessary for creating a file:

- The required space has to be allocated.
- The new file entry is to be made in the directory.

The new file entry records the file name in the directory and location in the file system.

14.3.2 Write

This operation is written within a file. It requires a system call with the name and information to be written into the file. It consists of the following three steps:

- The system searches the directory structure to locate the desired file.
- The system controls the writing pointer that keeps track of writing location in the file.
- The system updates the writing pointer each time a file write operation occurs.

14.3.3 Read

This operation reads data from a file. It consists of the following four steps:

- The system calls the files specifying its name and block to read from it.
- The system searches the directory for the desired file.
- The system controls the reading pointer that keeps track of the reading location in the file.
- The system updates the reading pointer each time a file read operation occurs.

14.3.4 Execute

The `execute` operation loads and executes the instructions or code stored within a file. EXE files and BATCH files are such example of files which the system executes to perform certain tasks.

14.3.5 Append

The `append` operation is used to augment or append in an existing file. The information to be appended is added at the end of a file generally, during the append operation.

14.3.6 Delete

The `delete` operation frees the memory space or locations that were allocated for the file. For this purpose, first, the directory structure is searched. Then after getting the desired file, the memory locations previously allocated for the file while creating it, is made available for further use.

14.3.7 Open

Before working with a file, the file needs to be opened. While opening the file, the files are loaded into the primary memory and a pointer is set up, which points to the first character in it. The file open command returns NULL if it is unable to open the file. The files are brought to the primary memory so that the CPU can directly access the available information stored inside the file. The files are normally opened in three modes: read, write and append.

14.3.8 Close

The files are closed after executing all the instructions therein or after the opened files are modified. Many operating systems close the files after their operations, by default. The closing operation frees the primary memory allocated for the file operations and makes it accessible to other programs. Files are also closed for security reasons.

14.4 IMPORTANCE OF FILE ORGANIZATION

File organization is a very important issue for structuring and organizing the data in a file. The benefits or importance of the data are realized while executing the various file operations. Some of the major advantages of file organization are given below:

- It contains an optimal selection of records, i.e., records can be selected as fast as possible.
- File organization is crucial to perform insert, delete or update transactions on the records quickly and easily.
- Duplicate records cannot be induced as a result of insert, update or delete due to the effectiveness of file organizations.
- Records can be stored more efficiently by file organization, thus minimizing storage cost.

14.5 FILE READ–WRITE–APPEND OPERATIONS WITH C AND PYTHON

14.5.1 Writing Data in a File with C

CProg-14.1 Writing data in a text file

```
#include <stdio.h>
#include <stdlib.h>

int main()
{
 int n;
 FILE *fp;  /* Declaring a file pointer */

 /* Creating a file in default folder in write mode */
 fp = fopen("dsprogram.txt", "w");

 if(fp == NULL)
  {
   printf("cannot create a file");
   exit(1);
  }

 printf("Enter a number: ");
 scanf("%d", &n); /* Reading an integer from the console */

 /* Writing the integer to a file */
 fprintf(fp, "%d", n);
 fclose(fp); /* Closing the file */
 return 0;
}
/* End program */
```

Output

```
Enter a number:
5
Content of 'dsprogram.txt' will be
5
```

> ***Programming Tips!***
> fp is a file pointer. A file named "dsprogram.txt" is created in the default folder in `write` mode.

14.5.2 Reading Data in a File with C

CProg-14.2 Reading data in a text file

```
#include <stdio.h>
#include <stdlib.h>
```

```
int main()
{
 int n;
 FILE *fp; /* Declaring a file pointer */

 if((fp = fopen("dsprogram.txt", "r")) == NULL)
  {
   printf("cannot open file");
   /* If the file pointer returns NULL then terminated the program */
   exit(1);
  }

 /* Reading from a file */
 fscanf(fp,"%d", &n);

 printf("Value of n = %d", n);
 fclose(fp); /* Closing the file */
 return 0;
}
/* End program */
```

Output

```
Value of n = 5
```

Programming Tips!

fp is a file pointer. A file named "dsprogram.txt" is created in the default folder in `read` mode.

14.5.3 Appending Data in a File with C

CProg-14.3 Appending data in a text file

```
#include <stdio.h>
#include <stdlib.h>

/* Function for reading a file character by character and print on
the console */
void readFile(FILE * fPtr);

int main()
{
  FILE *fPtr; /* File pointer to hold reference of input file */
  char filePath[80];
  char dataToAppend[500];
```

```
  /* Input file path */
  printf("Enter file path: ");
  scanf("%s", filePath);

  /* Opening all files in append mode. */
  fPtr = fopen(filePath, "a");
  /* Returns NULL if unable to open file in given mode*/

  if (fPtr == NULL)    /* Check inability to open file and hence
exit */
  {
    printf("\nUnable to open '%s' file.\n", filePath);
  printf("Check whether file exists and you have write privilege\n");
    // exit();
  }

  /* Taking input data to append */
  printf("\nEnter data to append: ");
  fflush(stdin);          /* To clear extra white space characters
in stdin */
  fgets(dataToAppend, 1000, stdin);

  /* Appending data to file */
  fputs(dataToAppend, fPtr);

  /* Reopening file in read mode to print file contents */
  fPtr = freopen(filePath, "r", fPtr);

  /* Printing file contents after appending the string */
  printf("\nSuccessfully appended data to file. \n");
  printf("Changed file contents:\n\n");
  readFile(fPtr);

  /* Closing file. */
  fclose(fPtr);

  return 0;
} /* end main */

/* Function definition for reading a file character by character and
prints on console */
void readFile(FILE * fPtr)
{
  char ch;
  do
```

```
    {
      ch = fgetc(fPtr);
      putchar(ch);
    } while (ch != EOF);
  }
  /* End program */
```

Output

```
Enter file path: C:\MyData\Append.txt
Enter data to append: Data Structure and Algorithm with C and Python.
Successfully appended data to file.
Changed file contents:
I love programming.
Programming with files is fun.
Data Structure and Algorithm with C and Python.
```

> ***Programming Tips!***
> readFile() is used for reading a file, character by character, and printing on the console. fPtr is a file pointer. A file in the default folder is created in `append` mode.

14.5.4 Writing Data in a File with Python

PyProg-14.1 Writing data in a text file

```
filename = 'myTextFile.txt'
with open(filename, 'w') as f:
     f.write("Data Structure & Algorithm with C and Python")
## end code
```

Output

```
The content of 'myTextFile.txt' will be
Data Structure & Algorithm with C and Python
```

> ***Programming Tips!***
> We have opened a file named "myTextFile.txt". `open()` is used to open a file and return a file object.

14.5.5 Reading Data in a File with Python

PyProg-14.2 Reading data in a text file

```
filename = 'myTextFile.txt'
with open(filename) as  f_obj:
     contents = f_obj.read()
print(contents)
## end program
```

Output

```
The content of 'myTextFile.txt' will be displayed
Data Structure & Algorithm with C and Python
```

> ***Programming Tips!***
> We have opened a file named "myTextFile.txt" in write mode. `open()` is used to open a file and return a file object.

14.5.6 Appending Data in a File with Python

PyProg-14.3 Appending data in a text file

```
filename = "myTextFile.txt"

with open(filename, 'a') as f:
    f.write("Data Structure & Algorithm with C and Python \n")
    f.write("Theory and Practical for University and GATE
Examinations.\n")
## End program
```

Output

```
Running 2 times the above code we will get content of myTextFile.txt:
Data Structure & Algorithm with C and Python.
Theory and Practical for University and GATE Examinations.
Data Structure & Algorithm with C and Python.
Theory and Practical for University and GATE Examinations.
```

> ***Programming Tips!***
> A file named "myTextFile.txt" in opened in append mode. `open()` is used to open a file and return a file object.

14.6 FILE ORGANIZATION AND OPERATING SYSTEM

One of the main purposes of the file structuring or organizing is to make it understandable to the operating system concerned. The following issues are to be remembered while organizing a file for the above purpose:

- A text file is a sequence of characters (or strings) organized into lines.
- A file has a defined and fixed structure primarily according to its type, with respect to its purpose.
- A source file is a sequence of procedures and functions to be executed by the operating system or other system software.
- An object file is a sequence of bytes understandable by the machine. It is organized into blocks.
- The operating system contains the code to support file structures that are defined within the system only.
- MS-DOS and UNIX operating systems support a minimum number of file structures.

QUICK RECAP

- ☑ A file is a sequence of records stored as a contiguous set of words or bytes. Users can store different forms of information within a file. File organization is a method of arranging the records in a file when the file is stored on a disk.
- ☑ File organization helps quick and efficient retrieval of records having different sizes. It allows ease of file creation and maintenance. The records may be stored randomly but accessed directly. Sorting makes it easy to access records.
- ☑ During file organization, the programmer decides the best-suited file organization method according to the requirements. There are six types of file organizations used for structured files. These are serial, sequential, direct (or random) access, indexed-sequential access, heap, and hash.
- ☑ Serial files store the records arranged one by one. Information in the sequential-access file is processed, one by one record, in order. A random- or direct-access data file enables us to read or write information anywhere in the file. Indexed sequential-access file combines both sequential file and direct-access file organization. The heap file is the simplest and most basic type of file organization. It works with data blocks. Hash file organization uses the calculation of hash function on fields of the records. The hash function determines the location of the memory block where the records are to be placed.
- ☑ Eight major operations are normally used during a file organization. The `create` operation generates a file in the memory. The `read` operation reads data from a file. The `write` operation writes within a file. The `execute` operation loads the instruction with a file and executes those instructions. The `append` operation augments or appends the information at the end of a file. The `delete` operation makes the allocated memory locations free to be reused by other programs. The `open` operation loads the file into the main memory to be accessed by the CPU. The allocated primary memory for the file operations is made free to become accessible by other programs by the `close` operation.
- ☑ File organization is very important for structuring the data within a file. An organized file contains an optimal selection of records on which insert, delete or update transactions can be performed quickly and easily. Duplicate records cannot be induced as a result of these operations. Efficient and optimal costing of storage can be provided.
- ☑ C and Python, both offer in-built functions for file organizations by which developers can efficiently manage the files within the system.

REVIEW QUESTIONS

Multiple Choice Questions (MCQ): Choose the Best Alternative

Easy

1. Files are logically partitioned into storage units of fixed-length known as ____.

   A. Sectors B. Blocks
   C. Tracks D. Segments

2. A ________ is the basic element of data where an individual field contains a single value, such as an employee's last name, a data or the value of the sensor reading.

   A. Record B. Field
   C. File D. Database

3. Directories, pricing tables, schedules, and name lists are examples of ________.

   A. indexed files
   B. direct files
   C. sequential files
   D. indexed sequential files

4. ________ are typically used in batch applications and are generally optimum for such applications if they involve the processing of all the records.
   A. Direct files
   B. Indexed files
   C. Sequential files
   D. Indexed sequential files
5. A ________ is a collection of related fields that can be treated as a unit by an application program.
   A. file B. field
   C. record D. database

Moderate

6. How can variable-length records arise in a file?
   A. Record types that allow variable lengths for one or more fields
   B. Storage of multiple record types in a file
   C. Record types that allow repeating fields, such as arrays or multi-sets
   D. All of the mentioned.
   Hint: Variable-length records arise in a system in several ways. These include storage of multiple record types in a file, record types that allow variable lengths for one or more fields and record types that allow repeating fields, such as arrays or multi-sets.
7. Which of the following is true about file header?
   A. It generally contains the address of the first record in it.
   B. It is allocated at the beginning of the file.
   C. It has information about the file.
   D. All of the mentioned.
   Hint: A file header is a certain number of bytes allocated at the beginning of the file. It contains a variety of information about the file and it can be used to point to the first record by storing the address of the first record in it.
8. The ________ greatly reduces the time required to access a single record, without sacrificing the sequential nature of the file.
   A. indexed file
   B. pile
   C. sequential file
   D. indexed sequential file
9. In ________ file organization, a fixed format is used for records where all records are of the same length, consisting of the same number of fixed-length fields in a particular order.
   A. sequential B. indexed sequential
   C. indexed D. pile

Higher-Order Thinking Skills (HOTS)

10. An alternative to organize the sequential file physically is a ________.
    A. stack B. queue
    C. list D. linked list
11. Which of the following file organization is preferred for secondary key processing?
    A. Sequential file
    B. Inverted file organization
    C. Index sequential file
    D. Indexed file

Short Answer-type Questions

Easy

1. What is a file? How is it different from data?
2. What do you mean by file organization?
3. What are the differences between the indexed sequential file and the sequential file?
4. What are the advantages and disadvantages of an indexed sequential file organization?
5. Differentiate between serial and sequential files.
6. Write the steps of creating a file.
7. Write the name of basic file operations.
8. Write the process of reading a file operation.

Moderate

9. What is a random-access file? Is it different from a direct file?
10. What is the purpose of hash files?
11. Give the purpose and example of executing file operations.
12. Why are pointers used for file storage in C?
13. Why is closing necessary after opening a file?

Higher-Order Thinking Skills (HOTS)

14. What is the difference between `write` and `append` file operations?
15. Why do we need to `open` and `close` a file operation?
16. What happens if a file is not found while trying to `read` or `write` on it?

Descriptive-type Questions

Easy

1. Describe all structured file organizations.
2. What are the advantages of file organization?
3. Explain the classification of files for data structure.
4. Explain the different types of file organization.

Moderate

5. Write an algorithm to insert a record within a sequential file.
6. Write an algorithm to delete a record within a sequential file.
7. Distinguish between the file organizations in C and Python.
8. How to take care of I/O errors during file operation using Python?

Higher-Order Thinking Skills (HOTS)

9. Discuss the role of an operating system in file organization.
10. Explain the importance of file organization in data structure.
11. Differentiate between the heap file and the hash file.
12. How is file organization different from databases?

CASE STUDIES

1. Compare and present the differences between file organization techniques in C and Python languages in a tabular form. Mention the names of the built-in functions/modules offered by these languages. Is it possible to identify the file or directories from user input string on a file/directory?
2. Consider the following cases and identify the appropriate method(s)/technique(s) and data structure(s):
   a. Alternative ways to physically organize sequential files
   b. Secondary key processing
   c. File that reduces the access time of a single record without sacrificing sequential structure
   d. Collection of related fields treated as a unit by an application program
   e. File used for batch application processing of records
   f. File to store directories, tables, and name lists
   g. Storage units of fixed length into which files are logically partitioned.
3. Execute the following Python codes for exploring the file system of a folder (myFolder):

```
import os
for (dirpath, dirnames, filenames) in os.walk('myFolder/'):
    for f in filenames:
        print('File :', os.path.join(dirpath, f))
    for d in dirnames:
        print('Folder :', os.path.join(dirpath, d))
```

Output

```
File : myFolder/Ex17.xlsx
File : myFolder/scan_0003.pdf
File : myFolder/WhatsApp Image.jpeg
Folder : myFolder/Communications
File : myFolder/Communications\@Comm 2019.docx
```

LAB EXERCISES

1. Write programs in C to copy the whole content of a text/csv file to another text/csv file with a different name.
2. Write a program in Python to count the number of lines, words and characters in a text file.
3. Develop a Python program to read a csv file in a file. Count the number of values stored in that file. Check whether a given value is stored in the file or not.

ANSWER KEYS

Multiple Choice Questions

1. B
2. B
3. B
4. C
5. C
6. D
7. D
8. D
9. A
10. D
11. B

Index